Public Relations

Public Relations
The Profession and the Practice

Fourth Edition

Otis Baskin
Pepperdine University

∎

Craig Aronoff
Kennesaw State College

∎

Dan Lattimore
The University of Memphis

Boston, Massachusetts   Burr Ridge, Illinios   Dubuque, Iowa
Madison, Wisconsin   New York, New York   San Francisco, California   St. Louis, Missouri

McGraw·Hill

A Division of The **McGraw·Hill** *Companies*

Book Team

Executive Publisher *Edgar J. Laube*
Project Editor *Kassi Radomski*
Publishing Services Coordinator *Peggy Selle*
Proofreading Coordinator *Carrie Barker*
Art Editor *Rita L. Hingtgen*
Permissions Coordinator *Gail Wheatley*
Production Manager *Beth Kundert*
Production/Imaging and Media Development Manager *Linda Meehan Avenarius*
Production/Costing Manager *Sherry Padden*
Visuals/Design Freelance Specialist *Mary L. Christianson*
Marketing Manager *Amy Halloran*
Copywriter *Jennifer Smith*

Basal Text *10/12 Times Roman*
Display Type *Geneva*
Typesetting System *Macintosh™ QuarkXPress™*
Paper Stock *50# Restore Cote*
Production Services *Impressions Book and Journal Services, Inc.*

Executive Vice President and General Manager *Bob McLaughlin*
Vice President, Business Manager *Russ Domeyer*
Vice President of Production and New Media Development *Victoria Putman*
National Sales Manager *Phil Rudder*
National Telesales Director *John Finn*

A Times Mirror Company

The credits section for this book begins on page 497 and is considered an extension of the copyright page.

Cover design by Cunningham & Welch Design Group, Inc., Madison, WI

Cover image © David Tillinghast/The Image Bank

Photo research by Shirley Lanners

Copyedited by Jean Tucker; Proofread by Denise Kieler

Library of Congress Catalog Card Number: 96–83186

ISBN 0–697–20122–8

Printed in the United States of America by Times Mirror Higher Education Group, Inc., 2460 Kerper Boulevard, Dubuque, IA 52001

10 9 8 7 6 5

CONTENTS

PART II
Public Relations: The Process

15 Public Affairs: Relations with Government *343*

PART IV
Public Relations: The Practice

16 Public Relations in Not-for-Profit Organizations *366*

17 Public Relations in Government *392*

PREFACE

P ublic relations is an emerging profession. In a complex global society, business, government, nonprofit, and other organizations must have people who
can communicate the needs of the organization to its various constituents and, at
the same time, communicate the concerns of those publics back to the organization. In this environment of rapid social change, every organization must evolve
or die. Public relations practitioners must possess the communications expertise
and social sensitivity necessary to help organizations adapt to their changing
environments.

Because public relations is now a critical dimension of management, practitioners are no longer mere technicians who shape and transmit messages from
organizations to their publics. All managers now recognize that they themselves
practice public relations, and they also see that public relations practitioners
should be part of the management mainstream.

To this broadened role, the public relations practitioner must bring all of the
traditional skills of the craft. The ability to understand public opinion, to plan
public relations programs, to create effective messages in all media for all organizational publics, and to evaluate public relations effectiveness remain crucial
areas of talent, skill, and knowledge. Public relations as it is practiced today, however, demands much more. A full understanding of all communication processes
and a close acquaintance with the methods of management are critical to the successful practice of public relations. Thorough knowledge of the environment of
the organization in which the practitioner works is a prerequisite to public relations effectiveness.

The spirit of innovation that characterized the first editions of our text continues in this fourth edition. The book deals with public relations in the overall
context of organizational communications. It stresses the practitioner's role in organizational and societal communication systems. It comes to grips with challenges to the profession from within organizations and from organizations' surrounding environments. It views public relations from the perspective of overall
organizational decision making, examining how public relations affects and is

affected by decisions that are made. It does these things within the context of a constantly changing environment, facing issues of rapid technological change in communication, increasing societal diversity, and expanding global markets.

The fourth edition benefits from the tremendous feedback we received on our earlier efforts. It also benefits from insight gained through the addition of a new coauthor, Dan Lattimore, APR. Professor Lattimore brings years of professional experience and public relations teaching to the book. He has been involved actively with the Public Relations Society of America, including serving as the 1996 chair of the Educator Section. He is also vice-president of the Accrediting Council on Education in Journalism and Mass Communication.

The fourth edition has kept the organization of the earlier versions but contains completely rewritten chapters on theory and ethics. Although technological changes, diversity issues, and global concerns are addressed throughout the book, new sections on each of these issues have been added to chapter 18, on corporate public relations.

We have tried to maintain the easy-to-read, personal style throughout the text. In doing this we have added new examples and mini-cases, while keeping some of the classic cases. Public relations spotlights are included to give you special insight into particular issues or concerns. We have kept the integrating case study in chapters 6 through 9. Still present in a chapter on public relations careers is a strong emphasis on preparing to get a job in public relations.

Our goals in writing this edition remained quite ambitious. We feel we have probed the deepest issues of public relations for a profession whose time has come. Part I describes the current situation, historical roots, and future issues of *the profession.* Part II examines the core issues of *the process* that underlies public relations, and Part III focuses on *the publics* that are the objects of these efforts. Finally, Part IV summarizes *the practice* of public relations in its various environments.

We believe that our work here truly reflects the progression of public relations as a discipline and an emerging profession. This book, like the profession it describes, is fundamentally eclectic, drawing its major theories, research, and principles from journalism, psychology, speech communication, and management. This eclecticism is, of course, due to the graduate training, research, and teaching experience of the authors in each of these disciplines, but it also reflects the needs of students who will be practicing public relations in diverse environments.

We have attempted to give public relations students and practitioners the tools and knowledge they need in ways that reflect the reality of the public relations world. Moreover, we have consistently attempted to provide that information in a direct, interesting, and highly readable form. We have resisted the temptation to include extraneous information that might be helpful but that also would overwhelm the undergraduate student. In short, we have tried to make *Public Relations: The Profession and the Practice* the public relations textbook most able to move ahead with the profession into the 21st century.

Acknowledgments

Our thanks are due to many people: colleagues with whom we have worked in public relations, leading practitioners with whom we have spent hours in rewarding conversation, students and fellow teachers on whom we have tested concepts contained in this book. They are too numerous to name, but all have our gratitude.

We owe a particular debt of gratitude to our public relations mentors, including Alan Scott and Scott Cutlip. Gene Donner, Darrel Alexander, Nick Del Calzo, and Guy Brown are public relations practitioners who have influenced our careers and our insight into the profession. Thanks to Professor Rick Fischer, APR, of the University of Memphis, who authored the material that constitutes the new chapter on public relations theories.

The following professors reviewed our manuscript and helped us make it as useful as possible to students and teachers:

Thomas Bivins
University of Oregon

Jamie M. Byrne
Millersville University

Jeffrey L. Courtright
Miami University (Ohio)

Roberta L. Crisson
Kutztown University

Benita Dilley
University of Colorado at Denver

John A Kaufman
California State Polytechnic University-Pomona

Brad L. Rawlins
James Madison University

Donald Rybacki
Northern Michigan University

Joseph V. Trahan, III
University of Tennessee at Chattanooga

We are deeply appreciative to those who distilled from their professional and teaching experience the cases that appear after each chapter. Our thanks to:

James Anderson
University of Florida

E. W. Brody
University of Memphis

Mary Cawley
Kennesaw State College

Mark Dvorak
Atlanta United Way

Fred Kiesner
Loyola Marymount University

Donald B. McCammond, APR
Public Relations Society of America

Lynne Sallot
University of Georgia

Walt Seifert
Ohio State University

Nancy Somerick
University of Akron

Dulcie Straughan
University of North Carolina at Chapel Hill

Robert Taylor
University of Wisconsin at Madison

Joe Truhan III
University of Tennessee, Chattanooga

James VanLeuven
Colorado State University

Our love and thanks go to our wives, Maryan, Kathy, and Bonnie, who have suffered with us through this and many collaborations. Our appreciation goes to our universities and departments for support, services, and resources. Finally, we give our sincere thanks to the professionals at Brown & Benchmark Publishers, particularly our editor, Kassi Radomski, who worked so hard and long with us.

Otis W. Baskin, Ph.D., *Pepperdine University*
Craig E. Aronoff, Ph.D., *Kennesaw State College*
Dan Lattimore, Ph.D., *University of Memphis*

PART I

Public Relations
The Profession

This book deals with public relations—its process, its publics, the kinds of organizations in which it is practiced, and the critical issues that confront it. *Public Relations: The Profession and the Practice* takes a practical approach, drawing on the experiences of many practitioners and executives. It also incorporates the theoretical perspectives of researchers and scholars from various disciplines, including communications, business, and psychology. It is intended to provide students with a thorough understanding of public relations and a basis for successful practice today and in the future.

Part I covers fundamentals of public relations practice. Chapter 1 gives a working definition of public relations, reviewing and refining the definitions of previous studies. Chapter 2 describes the history of public relations, providing a useful perspective on the field. Chapter 3 deals with communications and systems theory, and chapter 4 discusses the most important application of public relations—its contribution to organizational decision making. Finally, chapter 5 looks at the ethical and professional responsibilities of public relations practitioners in our society.

CHAPTER 1

The Nature of Public Relations

Preview

Public relations is a management function that helps define organizational objectives and philosophy. Public relations practitioners communicate with all relevant internal and external publics in the effort to create consistency between organizational goals and societal expectations.

Public relations practitioners develop, execute, and evaluate organizational programs. Their goal is to promote the exchange of influence and understanding among an organization's constituent parts and publics.

Public sentiment is everything. With public sentiment, nothing can fail; without it, nothing can succeed.

—Abraham Lincoln

I t began in Seattle when a TV station informed the local Pepsi franchise bottler that an 82-year-old Tacoma man had found a hypodermic needle in a can of Diet Pepsi. The report was broadcast that evening on the local news. It would be the nation's top story for the next 96 hours. Within hours, another syringe turned up in another locality. Soon news reports from different parts of the country also had people finding needles in Pepsi cans.[1] More than 50 allegations were made in 23 states.[2]

Pepsi-Cola set up a crisis management team at its corporate headquarters in Somers, New York. The team was led by Craig Weatherup, Pepsi-Cola president and CEO. Rebecca Madeira, Pepsi's vice-president for public affairs, directed the team's actions and coordinated the communications so the company could speak with one voice.

First, the Pepsi crisis team had to determine the source of the problem. The crisis response plan had these key points:

Put public safety first.   Assess the problem through the public's eyes. Be clear that their needs and concerns come first.

Find it. Fix it.   Work around the clock with regulatory officials to investigate every aspect of the plant operation to identify and, if possible, correct the problem.

Communicate quickly and frequently. Using tools and timetables reporters use.

Take responsibility for solving the crisis.   Don't point fingers, assign blame, or pass the buck. Make your team accountable for a swift and sound resolution to the problem.[3]

Pepsi-Cola Company utilized timely Video News Releases to assure millions of TV viewers that the Pepsi canning process could not be tampered with.

Once Pepsi had gathered its facts and felt secure that this was not a manufacturing problem, Pepsi took the offensive. President Weatherup said repeatedly through the media that "a can is the most tamper-proof packaging in food supply. We are 99.99 percent certain that this didn't happen in Pepsi plants."[4]

The crisis team decided to use **Video News Releases (VNR)** to show consumers that it was extremely difficult to tamper with Pepsi's canning process. High-tech, high-speed equipment was shown filling cans. Each can is turned upside down, cleaned with a powerful jet of air or water, inverted, filled, and closed—all in less than one second! Video footage of the canning process was beamed by satellite to TV stations across the country. Within 48 hours, the first Video News Release was seen around the world by 296 million viewers, three times the number that watched the Super Bowl that year.

The company used the video to combat the visual images of the syringe that had been shown repeatedly on network television since the first instance in Seattle. Pepsi created three more VNRs within three days. By the end of the week, the president had appeared on a dozen network TV news shows and talk shows and Pepsi spokespersons had conducted more than 2,000 interviews with newspaper, magazine, TV, and radio reporters. The strategy was to reassure the public that what was happening was really a hoax. The real turning point came with the third video. It showed an in-store surveillance camera filming a shopper slipping a syringe into an open Diet Pepsi can while the cashier's back was turned. Pepsi could not release the tape, though, until the next day when an arrest was made. From the time that VNR ran—the same day that FOA Commissioner David Kessler officially denounced the crisis at a national press conference—viewers were overwhelmingly supportive of Pepsi. According to the company's own follow-up evaluation, Pepsi's response worked. Sales for the key July 4 period were not affected adversely, which was quite important.

This case illustrates many of the public relations principles you will examine throughout this book. For instance, the case shows the public relations process—research or fact-finding, action planning, communication, and evaluation. You can see in the Pepsi hoax many of the tasks a public relations person has to do, from counseling management to relating to the media to doing research.

What Is Public Relations?

Attempts to define the public relations discipline are frequently conflicting and generally diverse. Some definitions list the kinds of organizations that use public relations (all kinds); some dwell on the media used for public relations communications (all media); and still others focus on the publics, or target audiences, with which public relations communicates (all publics). Many authorities give exhaustive lists of what public relations is *not,* while a few even claim that "public relations" as such no longer exists, preferring another name for the process. Indeed, in major corporations, the term *corporate communications* has replaced public relations as the most common name for departments having that responsibility.[5]

A Working Definition

Public relations is difficult to sum up in a brief statement. The very nature of the profession and its constant adaptation to the needs of society make it at best a moving target for definition.

Public relations is practiced in organizations that range in type from giant, multinational oil companies to small, human service agencies. A public relations manager for a private university may devote most of his or her efforts to fundraising and student recruitment. The public relations staff of a large corporation may be responsible for the firm's relationships with customers, suppliers, investors, employees, and even foreign governments.

Public relations practitioners are individuals who help others establish and maintain effective relationships with third parties. Their work is usually performed in organizational environments like those already mentioned, even if they are not employees of that organization. Some public relations practitioners are independent counselors, some work for public relations firms, and still others are directly employed by individual organizations.

For the purposes of this book—and to establish a broad, realistic, and accurate description of the public relations function—we offer the following working definition:

> Public relations is a management function that helps achieve organizational objectives, define philosophy, and facilitate organizational change. Public relations practitioners communicate with all relevant internal and external publics to develop positive relationships and to create consistency between organizational goals and societal expectations. Public relations practitioners develop, execute, and evaluate organizational programs that promote the exchange of influence and understanding among an organization's constituent parts and publics.

Not all people who say they practice public relations do everything implied by this definition. Some interpret their jobs even more broadly, but for now and for the foreseeable future, this description captures the essential aspects of public relations practice. Chapter 2 demonstrates that this definition is valid for much of the past as well.

We have divided the chapters in this book into four parts: the profession, the process, the publics, and the practice. Figure 1.1 illustrates the progression of the book and the relationship between the various sections.

An Overview of Public Relations

The profession sets the historical foundations of the field in a context that will help explain the origins and reasons for much current practice. Likewise, the theoretical foundations are presented in the context of relevant application. The pivotal role of public relations in organizational decision making further defines its management function along with its ethical and social responsibilities. These elements fit together to describe a professional climate that feeds every aspect of the process.

The process begins and ends with research. Although public relations began as a reactive force, it has become proactive through its ability to predict trends and respond to needs before they become emergencies. As a management function, public relations gathers information, makes plans, implements action, and evaluates results.

The publics are the targets of public relations action and the source of feedback for evaluation. Any identifiable group can be considered a public; however, most are encompassed by the following: media, employees, consumers, the

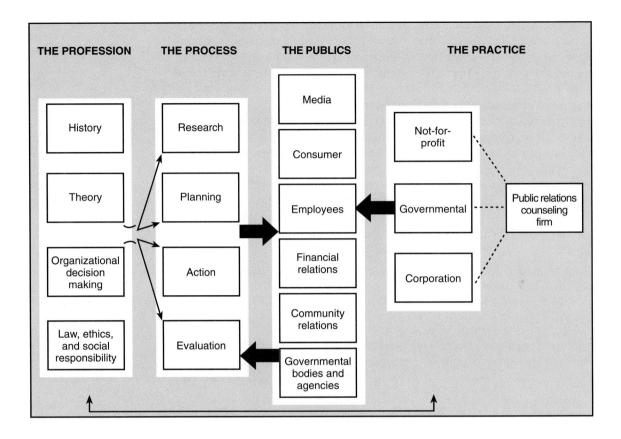

| THE PROFESSION | THE PROCESS | THE PUBLICS | THE PRACTICE |

Figure 1.1 A conceptual schema for studying public relations

financial community, and government. These are the target audiences of public relations practice.

The practice of public relations is molded to a great extent by the publics it responds to and the types of organizations it serves. The ever-increasing and changing varieties of public relations practice all fall into one of the categories discussed in part IV.

In this first chapter, we will explain some of the ways to define public relations—as a management function, as communication, and as a means of influencing public opinion. We will also define the specific tasks performed by public relations practitioners. Finally, we will look at the field from a systems view.

Public Relations as a Management Function

To begin with, it is necessary to recognize that public relations is a management function. Although it may support or facilitate production or sales, public relations is not merely an adjunct of personnel, marketing, or advertising. Ideally, public relations helps an organization establish its philosophy, achieve its objectives, adapt to a changing environment, and successfully compete in today's markets.

The managerial responsibilities associated with the public relations function are both general and specific. Some public relations duties are shared by all managers. For example, all managers spend much of their time communicating with various external or internal publics. All managers, indeed virtually all employees, represent their organizations to some public. Public relations also contributes to general management. Recent research into the job responsibilities of senior production managers found that public relations is one of "the most demanding aspects of their jobs. It is the part of their jobs for which they feel least prepared and qualified."[6]

Other public relations functions are the particular responsibility of public relations specialists. Editors of internal publications and managers of government, consumer, media, and financial relations, for example, tend to be public relations professionals trained specifically for their areas of expertise.

Public relations can make important contributions to forming an organization's ideas about itself—what it should do and what society wants and expects from it. Charles Steinberg describes this aspect of public relations as the "structuring of company philosophy and carrying out of that philosophy in practice so that what the institution says is not at variance with what it does."[7]

Defining Objectives, Philosophies, and Policies

Many public relations authorities make the point that as a profession, public relations is obligated to advise management in the development of sound policies that are in the best interests of the public as well as the company.[8] Of course, public relations practitioners rarely have final authority in setting objectives, policies, or philosophy within their organizations, but in most modern organizational structures, they are important members of policy-making groups. The participation of Rebecca Madeira, vice-president of public affairs, in Pepsi's crisis management team during the Pepsi hoax is just one example.

The role of public relations is critically important, especially in crisis situations, for two reasons. First, because public relations monitors public opinion, practitioners can represent the public interest and predict public reaction to institutional decisions. Second, public relations communicates organizational decisions to the public. Thus, the commitment and understanding gained from helping to make those decisions are tremendous assets.

All managers are concerned with adapting their organizations to changing environments, but public relations managers play a particularly important role in this area. Indeed, facilitating organizational change has become a frequently mentioned part of public relations definitions.

Helping Organizations Change

Robert Dilenschneider, former Hill & Knowlton CEO and now president of the Dilenschneider Group, cites six key factors that suggest why business needs more and better public relations than ever before:

technology—forcing companies to communicate instantly around the globe

increased oversight by government

trade—forcing business to deal with foreign governments and cultures

mergers and acquisitions

third-world countries trying to attract investment

tourism—the world's second largest industry[9]

Again, public relations managers do not make all the decisions that lead to change within organizations, but because they constantly monitor and interact with the organizational environment, they often possess information that suggests a need for change or indicates the direction change should take. Public relations practitioners can discover a problem when it is still manageable, thus avoiding unnecessary crises. Indeed, Scott Cutlip, the leading public relations historian, feels that "the public relations practitioner's most important responsibility is to interpret the public opinion climate to management."[10]

Rex Harlow's historical review of public relations definitions indicates that emphasis on change has grown steadily since the 1940s, when *PR News* suggested this definition: "Public relations is the activities of a corporation . . . building and maintaining sound and productive relations . . . so as to adapt itself to the environment."[11]

By the 1970s, leaders in public relations were describing their profession in terms that reflected the turbulence of society. David Finn, chairman of Ruder and Finn, Inc., one of the world's leading public relations firms, suggested that public relations practitioners try "to prevent the crisis from getting out of hand . . . to help clients conduct their business in a way that is responsive to the new demands made by concerned scientists, environmentalists, consumerists, minority leaders, underprivileged segments of the community, the young generation."[12]

These definitions make an important point about the fundamental nature of public relations—it reflects the needs of the society in which it is practiced. While the 1980s in some ways were calmer than the 1960s and the 1970s, the rise of mergers and acquisitions in the United States and worldwide have brought to the forefront a whole new level of societal concern. In the 1990s, we are dealing with the issues of an appropriately educated workforce, continuing transformation of the workplace by new technology, and the increasing demand for information.[13] Through it all, public relations continues to help harmonize organizations with their environments and promote positive organizational change. The process of defining goals and facilitating change is discussed further in chapter 4.

Public Relations as Communication

Some definitions emphasize the communication function of public relations. All managers are involved in and responsible for communication, but public relations managers have additional, more specific responsibilities in this area. *Communication* applies to the definition of the public relations role in at least four specific ways. It refers to *skills* possessed by public relations practitioners, to *tasks* performed, to *systems* established, and to *operations* of established systems.

Skills

Many authors point out that public relations practitioners need to be excellent writers and speakers. Some call for expertise in graphics or audiovisual communication as well. Public relations authority Allen Center, calling public relations practitioners "technicians in communication," adds to the list a "knack for persuasion."[14] As we approach the 21st century, the practitioner now must also be able to communicate effectively in cyberspace. Practitioners are certainly more than technicians. The ability to write and speak effectively is still a basic prerequisite; however, they also must be able to conduct research, formulate plans, and evaluate results.

Tasks

Many commentators on public relations point out the tasks and goals of communication. In his book *The Nature of Public Relations,* John Marston defines the process as "planned, persuasive communication designed to influence significant publics."[15] The early work of public relations scholars Gene Harlan and Alan Scott also stressed a task orientation: "skilled communication of ideas to various publics with the object of producing desired results."[16] Production of a media release, an annual report, an employee magazine, or an electronic newspaper might be among the tasks of public relations practitioners. Other tasks include the creation and management of campaigns to achieve awareness of an issue or change opinions about a subject.

Systems

Rather than stressing individual skills or tasks, some public relations writers have advocated the establishment of systems for ongoing communications. For example, Frank Jefkins describes "a system of communications to create goodwill,"[17] and Rex Harlow emphasizes "establishment and maintenance of mutual lines of communication."[18] The systematic methods of gathering information, the relationships established with editors and publishers, and the creation of community or consumer groups to provide insights and perspectives are examples of ongoing communication systems.

Systems Operations

Several observers concentrate on how such systems should be used once established. Most who carry the definitions to this extent hold that public relations is responsible for maintaining systematic two-way communication. The nature of communication is treated more extensively in chapter 3, and specific problems in communicating to external and internal audiences are covered in chapters 10 and 11.

Public Relations as a Means of Influencing Public Opinion

As we have already mentioned, exerting influence on public opinion is often considered a part of the public relations mission. How public relations should deal with public opinion, however, is a matter of considerable debate. The opinions of scholars in the field range from simple plans to complex prescriptions for pumping up corporate prestige and establishing mutual understanding between management and its publics.

Public relations practitioners often keep three major persuasion objectives in mind when they are developing their stategies:

1. maintain favorable opinion;

2. create opinion where none exists, or where it is latent;

3. neutralize hostile opinion.

First, an organization should not neglect to take positive steps to keep its *favorable* publics "on its side." That's one reason so much effort in public relations is spent on improving employee and community relations. Employees must maintain a good opinion of the organization if external public relations efforts are to succeed. Similarly, the community an organization is part of must also be favorable if the organization is to continue to do business successfully.

Second, public relations practitioners often have the opportunity to create opinion where none exists. Many times stakeholders simply don't know about the issue they must be persuaded to take action on. It might be as simple as making the community aware of a new theatrical season at the local community playhouse. The objective may be to sell season tickets to the community theater. Communicating the shows, moderate ticket prices, and that the shows are appropriate for the family may increase season ticket sales. Creating positive opinion could come, in this case, because the audience, unaware of the upcoming season, had no opinion of it. Latent opinion might also be present. Perhaps it has been several years since some of the audience had been to the theater. Making them aware of the season may create the positive latent opinion about going to the community theater.

Third, psychologists often suggest that when a segment of the audience holds a hostile opinion about an organization, the best a practitioner may be able to do is to neutralize that hostile opinion. If, for example, a company wants to build a gas refinery on a rural site near a historical and recreational area, the residents may have strong hostile opinions about those plans. This happened to Phillips Petroleum when it decided to put a gas plant near Independence, Texas. It took considerable effort (positive action, not just rhetoric) on Phillips's part to neutralize the hostile opinion. Although Phillips didn't convince its opponents to favor the plant site, it did lessen the opposition by taking enough positive action and communicating that action to opponents. Phillips could then convince those who were favorable or had no opinion that the well would be mutually beneficial to Phillips and the community.[19]

Perhaps the most basic way that public relations influences public opinion is by enhancing an organization's prestige. Harlow and Jefkins touch on this aspect of public relations in another simple and widely quoted conception of public relations: "good performance publicly appreciated."[20] Indeed, effective public relations depends on the effective performance of the organization being represented. Another theme holds that it is the task of public relations to supply accurate information concerning subjects of value to the public. Most news releases seek to achieve this goal. When Dayton-Hudson, the big retailing concern, opens stores in a new city, it makes major contributions to local charities—then issues news releases to let local customers know of the role Dayton-Hudson plays when it comes to town. Beyond dispassionately dispensing information, public relations should be an active process of interpreting the organization to its publics. This interpretation leads directly to a definition of public relations that stresses pursuit of public understanding and acceptance of the organization.

Thus far, our attempts to define how public relations influences public opinion have dealt with informing, promoting, understanding, and interpreting, but affecting public opinion also implies conscious efforts to exert influence. *Effective influence or persuasion inevitably rests on an understanding of those to whom the effort is directed.* The price of influence is being influenced. Not surprisingly, certain writers suggest that communication must not flow in only one direction. Edward Stan called it a "planned effort to influence opinion through acceptable performance and two-way communication."[21] Once the recognition of two-way communication has been established, public relations can be defined in literal terms, that is, in terms of *relations with publics.*

A **public** is a group of people who share a common problem or goal and recognize their common interest. A term often used by practitioners to refine the concept of public to mean those with a vested interest or "stake" in an organization is **stakeholder.** The cumulative experience of public relations practitioners suggests that public opinion is an ornery beast, nearly impossible to push or prod. It will move, however, if you understand its needs and cater to them. Some practitioners believe that rather than seeking to engineer, control, or convince the public, public relations is a means of seeking common ground. It is the linking pin in a relationship that looks past short-term goals and interests toward the kind of long-term success that requires positive public opinion. Author and practitioner Charles S. Steinberg's 1958 definition of public relations exemplifies this viewpoint:

Establishing Relations with Publics

> Public relations is that specific operating philosophy by which management sets up policies designed to serve both in the company's and the public's interest . . . [the] long-range, carefully nurtured effort to develop and maintain a strong, resilient and positive consensus from all of the publics upon whom the activities of the institution impinge.[22]

While certain aggressive organizations still seek to create their own public opinion climates, most perceive public opinion as a significant environment that needs constant attention and active response. A primary aim of public relations, rather than attempting to manipulate various publics, is to sensitize the organization to public images and expectations. Public relations staffs effectively link institutions and help organizations harmonize their behavior with the expectations of various external and internal publics.

Many thoughtful observers of the contemporary world maintain that adaptability is an organization's greatest asset. For example, in 1985, when sales of the "new Coke" went flat, the Coca-Cola Company proved itself an effective organization by reacting rapidly to the negative response and bringing back the old formula, newly labeled "Coca-Cola Classic." With regard to public relations, this view suggests that emphasis should be placed on gathering and interpreting information from the organization's relevant publics and disseminating it to management. Thus, the traditional direction of public relations information flow is reversed. This idea is closely related to the general function of facilitating organizational change.

Interpreting Public Opinion

Such an approach to public relations suggests that some of the most important messages communicated by public relations practitioners are aimed neither at the media, nor at customers and the general public, nor even at employees. The most important messages, rather, are developed with management in mind and deal with fundamental aspects of organizational direction, decision making, and coordination. With this perspective, public relations is established as an integral part of organizational management. Although public relations definitions stressing interpretation of public opinion vary, opinion research and management consultation are the most commonly mentioned activities. Alan Scott sums it up best by emphasizing "the sensitive interpretation of the human scene to management . . . evaluating and interpreting public opinion, public issues and the public demands."[23] Further discussion of the nature of public opinion and the public relations issues involved in it can be found in chapter 6.

Exercising Social Responsibility

Whenever the potential for influencing public opinion exists, the issue of social responsibility becomes significant. During the past 30 years, social responsibility has become a major concern in American society. Many thoughtful observers feel that institutions should assume responsibility for the consequences of their actions. Within the context of public relations, according to Donald Wright, this implies that "public relations people . . . should act at all times with the best interests of society in mind."[24]

Rex Harlow makes much of the social responsibility theme, maintaining that the public relations practitioner "defines and emphasizes the responsibility of management to serve the public interest."[25] In addition, he says, the practitioner suggests ways the organization can adjust its behavior to meet social, political, and economic responsibilities and the needs created by shifting human standards and attitudes. Moreover, the practitioner tries to help the organization demonstrate a keen sense of social responsibility with profit responsibility. The logical extreme of this position, which suggests that public relations be defined as representing the public and attempting to influence management, has been argued. Some even claim that public relations gives the public "a voice at policy-making tables."[26]

Although the exercise of social responsibility should not be mistaken for the sum total of the practice, it remains vitally important as a public relations ideal. Social responsibility is increasingly perceived as an integral aspect of the public relations function, as we discuss more extensively in chapter 5.

The Nature of Public Relations Work

One of the best ways to define public relations is to describe what its practitioners do. The Public Relations Society of America (PRSA) formally adopted one such description (see public relations spotlight 1.1.).

Practitioners of public relations apply their skills and knowledge in many different ways. The *Occupational Outlook Handbook* suggests that public relations specialists are responsible for maintaining positive relationships with the press, employees, community, consumers, investors, regulatory agencies, contributors, constituents, and a number of other publics. They can be involved in activities as diverse as sales promotion, political campaigning, interest group representation, fund-raising, and employee recruitment.[27]

The Duties of the Profession

Public relations practitioners are basically responsible for assimilating and communicating information between an organization and its environment. Public relations employees span the boundaries of an organization. They attempt to relate

Public Relations Spotlight 1.1

Public relations helps our complex, pluralistic society to reach decisions and function more effectively by contributing to mutual understanding among groups and institutions. It serves to bring the public and public policies into harmony.

Public relations serves a wide variety of institutions in society such as businesses, trade unions, government agencies, voluntary associations, foundations, hospitals and educational and religious institutions. To achieve their goals, these institutions must develop effective relationships with many different audiences or publics such as employees, members, customers, local communities, shareholders and other institutions, and with society at large.

Public relations practitioners must consider many audience groups when developing public relations strategies.

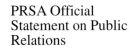

The managements of institutions need to understand the attitudes and values of their publics in order to achieve institutional goals. The goals themselves are shaped by the external environment. The public relations practitioner acts as a counselor to management, and as a mediator, helping to translate private aims into reasonable, publicly acceptable policy and action.

As a management function, public relations encompasses the following:

- Anticipating, analyzing and interpreting public opinion, attitudes and issues which might impact, for good or ill, the operations and plans of the organization.
- Counseling management at all levels in the organization with regard to policy decisions, courses of action and communication, taking into account their public ramifications and the organization's social or citizenship responsibilities.

- Researching, conducting and evaluating, on a continuing basis, programs of action and communication to achieve informed public understanding necessary to the success of an organization's aims. These may include marketing, financial, fund-raising, employee, community or government relations and other programs.
- Planning and implementing the organization's efforts to influence or change public policy.
- Setting objectives, planning, budgeting, recruiting and training staff, developing facilities—in short, *managing* the resources needed to perform all of the above.
- Examples of the knowledge that may be required in the professional practice of public relations include communication arts, psychology, social psychology, sociology, political science, economics and the principles of management and ethics. Technical knowledge and skills are required for opinion research, public issues analysis, media relations, direct mail, institutional advertising, publications, film/video productions, special events, speeches and presentations.

In helping to define and implement policy, the public relations practitioner utilizes a variety of professional communication skills and plays an integrative role both within the organization and between the organization and the external environment.

Source: "Public Relations: An Overview" (New York: PRSA Foundation, 1991): 4–5. *Statement formally adopted by PRSA Assembly, November 6, 1982.*

---

to the needs and interests of its publics, informing them about the organization's impact on their lives and thus building positive relationships.

As they perform these services, public relations practitioners must maintain effective relationships with the media representatives who publish or broadcast information about the organization and its publics. Public relations departments are frequently the source of information for special reports and news and feature articles for television, radio, newspapers, and magazines.

Public relations messages do not always advertise the organization or its services and products directly. Instead, releases may be designed to aid consumers or some other public, and only indirectly contribute to a positive image for the organization. Information about health, nutrition, energy, and the environment may be researched and communicated because the organization recognizes an obligation to respond to its publics in a socially responsible way.

Public relations duties may also include arranging for company representatives to have direct contact with various publics. Speakers' bureaus, which arrange for members of the organization to speak to civic and social groups on topics of current interest, frequently come under the umbrella of public relations. In addition to arranging such events, public relations specialists may write speeches for members of the organization or even serve as representatives themselves. Other common public relations activities include editing in-house publications, producing and distributing films, slides, and other audiovisual programs, and managing fund-raising campaigns and community activities. Spotlight 1.2 suggests the duties or elements of public relations. Public relations practitioners may work either in

Public Relations Spotlight 1.2

Elements of Public
Relations

- **Counseling.** Providing advice to the management of an organization concerning policies, relationships and communications; in effect, "what to do."
- **Research.** Determining attitudes and behaviors of publics and their causes in order to plan, implement and measure activities to influence or change the attitudes and behavior.
- **Media Relations.** Relating with communications media in seeking publicity or responding to their interest in an organization.
- **Publicity.** Disseminating planned messages through selected media without payment to further an organization's interest.
- **Employee/Member Relations.** Responding to concerns and informing and motivating an organization's employees or members, its retirees and their families.
- **Community Relations.** Continuing, planned and active participation with and within a community to maintain and enhance its environment to the benefit of both an organization and the community.
- **Public Affairs.** Developing effective involvement in public policy, and helping an organization adapt to public expectations; also, term used by military services and some government agencies to describe their public relations activities.
- **Government Affairs.** Relating directly with legislatures and regulatory agencies on behalf of an organization, usually as a central element of a public affairs program; often called "lobbying."
- **Issues Management.** Identifying and addressing issues of public concern in which an organization is, or should be, concerned.
- **Financial Relations.** Creating and maintaining investor confidence and building positive relationships with the financial community; also, sometimes known as Investor Relations or Shareholder Relations.
- **Industry Relations.** Relating with other firms in the industry of an organization and with trade associations.
- **Development/Fund Raising.** Demonstrating the need for and encouraging an organization's members, friends, supporters and others to voluntarily contribute to support it.
- **Minority Relations/Multicultural Affairs.** Relating with individuals and groups in minorities.
- **Special Events and Public Participation.** Stimulating an interest in a person, product or organization by means of a focused "happening," also, activities designed to enable an organization to listen to and interact with publics.
- **Marketing Communications.** Combination of activities designed to sell a product, service or idea, including advertising, collateral materials, publicity, promotion, packaging, point-of-sale display, trade shows and special events.

Source: "Public Relations: An Overview," 3–4.

departments found in business organizations, nonprofit organizations, government, or in public relations counseling firms or agencies. The department work is examined in part IV, the practice section, including chapters 16, 17, and 18. Many of these departments are small, with more than half of practitioners working in departments with four or fewer public relations professionals.[28]

Public Relations Counseling Firms

Many organizations find it useful to contract for the services of a **counseling firm.** Chester Burger names six reasons for hiring outside consultants:

1. Management has not previously conducted a formal public relations program and lacks experience in organizing one.

2. Headquarters may be located away from New York City, the communications and financial center of the nation.

3. A wide range of up-to-date contacts is maintained by an agency.

4. An outside agency can provide services of experienced executives who would be unwilling to move to other cities or whose salaries could not be afforded by a single firm.

5. An organization with its own PR department may be in need of highly specialized services that it cannot afford on a permanent basis.

6. Crucial matters of overall outside policy dictate a need for the independent judgment of an outsider.[29]

Basically, an organization may decide to retain the services of a counseling firm because of special needs that it cannot meet internally. In addition to supplementing their own talent, organizations frequently employ outside public relations consultants to provide a third-party opinion. "We tell our clients not only how to say things but what to say," notes Michael Rowan, vice-president for survey research at Hill & Knowlton.[30]

The principal advantages of an in-house public relations staff—familiarity with issues, loyalty, team membership—may also be important drawbacks in some decision-making situations. Like all managers, public relations executives may be too close to a situation to maintain an objective point of view. Public relations consultants can often bring a startlingly fresh approach to the problems and programs of an organization. They are called on to assess the effectiveness of various programs and to help plan public relations strategies. PR firms are now offering other services as well—rehearsals for hostile news conferences, advice on lobbying, strategic counsel on new product marketing and takeover defenses, and arrangement of corporate sales meetings.

With the mergers and acquisitions of the 1980s and early 1990s, public relations counseling firms have changed drastically. Many smaller firms were bought by larger firms who were themselves acquired by other major organizations, advertising agencies, and others. In addition to changes in the structure of counseling firms, the practice of public relations also changed. The most important changes affecting the function of public relations counseling firms, according to Robert Dilenschneider, are "globalization and specialization."[31] Most major public relations organizations now have branches and affiliates worldwide, and an increasing number of practitioners now specialize in communicating with one of the numerous publics whose opinion a client might want to influence. Most major public relations firms have responded to these changes by dividing their businesses by discipline. In this way, they have experts in the specific public relations needs of any client who might call asking for help. Table 1.1 lists the top 10 public relations firms in 1994 billings.

In a survey of business executives that asked them what were the most valuable skills they wanted from a public relations firm the following were included in order of preference:

1. Communication strategies that support business objectives.

2. Maximum input/results for investment.

3. Responsiveness.

4. Understanding of our industry and of the particular problems we face.[32]

The implication for public relations agencies of the future is that agencies must be more knowledgeable about a client's business and the problems of that particular business or industry. In other words, there will be more specialization among public relations firms in terms of industries served as well as services and skills offered. The agency must also be in harmony with the concerns of top management, embrace and create better ways to measure results and the value of public relations, and enlarge its scope to become global.[33]

While smaller agencies may become more specialized—for instance, an agency may serve only high-tech companies—larger agencies can simply reorganize their firms around either specialties or practice areas. The globalization of public relations, made possible by rapid advances in communication technology, has made organization of firms by geographic region much less necessary. Top officers of public relations firms say that agency management now emphasizes

TABLE 1.1 Top 10 Public Relations Agencies in Billings

	Agency	1994 Net Fees	No. of Employees
1.	Burson-Marsteller Ltd. (A)	$192,999,000	1,700
2.	Shandwick PLC	160,100,000	1,813
3.	Hill & Knowlton (A)	139,300,000	1,227
4.	Communications Int'l Group (A)	111,720,434	1,183
5.	Daniel J. Edelman Inc.	74,908,804	819
6.	Fleishman-Hillard	73,898,000	775
7.	Ketchum Public Relations (A)	55,405,000	467
8.	Ogilvy Adams & Rinehart (A)	31,300,000	411
9.	Robinson/Lake/Sawyer/Miller (A)	37,800,000	250
10.	Rowland Worldwide Inc. (A)	35,000,000	301

(A) means ad agency–related
Source: O'Dwyer's *PR Services Report,* vol. 10, no. 1 (January 1996): 27.

practice areas and interdisciplinary cooperation. "Office and staff managers are a vanishing breed," according to these top agency officials in a recent *Public Relations Journal* survey.[34]

The interviews with the heads of major public relations firms also suggested a different structure or organization for the future. Work groups are emphasized with practitioners working in teams on projects and problem-solving tasks. There is more attention now paid to teamwork, continuing professional education, and quality control. For example, Burson-Marsteller has restructured itself based on "practice rather than geography." CEO Thomas D. Bell said, "In the future, we will be increasingly organized around the disciplines and industry sectors which are the most important to our clients."[35]

The consensus of the firms surveyed is that the "hottest" practice areas in the next five years will be dealing with corporate change, finance, and issues management. Health care, public affairs, and technology will also be emphasized in the immediate future.[36]

Despite the trend toward less reliance upon geographical distribution of public relations firms, jobs in counseling firms still tend to be concentrated in the larger cities because of access to government, media, corporate, union, and trade association headquarters. This has changed to some degree and is likely to change more as technology makes global communications even easier. Still, more than half of the approximately 2,000 public relations counseling firms are located in New York, Los Angeles, Chicago, and Washington, D.C.

Public Relations Professionals at Work

Public relations departments range in size from more than 400 members in large corporations to one or two individuals in small organizations. Large corporations frequently have an officer at the vice-presidential level who is in charge of the public relations function and helps develop overall policy as a member of top management. Large organizations also typically include various other public relations managers at both corporate and division levels, and they may employ a number of public relations specialists such as writers, researchers, and representatives to the media. In a small organization, however, one individual may handle all these responsibilities. Public relations counseling firms may contain specialists in a particular area, such as merger or takeover campaigns, or generalists who advise management on a wide range of matters.

This great diversity in the duties of public relations practitioners is illustrated by the list of public relations functions published by PRSA in a booklet entitled, *Careers in Public Relations.*

1. *Programming.* This involves analyzing problems and opportunities, defining goals and the publics (or groups of people whose support or understanding is needed), and recommending and planning activities. It may include budgeting and assignment of responsibilities to the appropriate people, including non–public relations personnel. For example, an organization's president or executive director is often a key figure in public relations activities.

2. *Relationships.*   Successful public relations people develop skill in gathering information from management, from colleagues in their organizations, and from external sources. Continually evaluating what they learn, they formulate recommendations and gain approval for them from their managements. Many public relations activities require working with, and sometimes through, other organizational units such as personnel, legal, and marketing staffs.

   The practitioner who learns to be persuasive with others will be most effective. But in all their relationships—including people in industry groups, regulatory agencies, governmental and educational institutions, and the public in general—public relations personnel are at work on behalf of their organizations.

3. *Writing and Editing.*   Since the public relations worker is often trying to reach large groups of people, an important tool is the printed word. Examples of its use are found in reports, news releases, booklets, speeches, film scripts, trade magazine articles, product information, and technical material, employee publications, newsletters, shareholder reports, and other management communications directed to both organization personnel and external groups. A sound, clear style of writing that communicates effectively is a must for public relations work.

4. *Information.*   Establishing systems for the dissemination of material to appropriate newspaper, broadcast, general and trade publication editors, and communicating with them to enlist their interest in publishing an organization's news and features are normal public relations activities. This requires knowledge of how newspapers and other media operate, the areas of specialization of publications, and the interests of individual editors. (Competition is keen for the attention of editors and broadcasters who have a limited amount of space and time at their disposal.)

   As one public relations practitioner puts it, "You have to get to the right editor of the right publication with the right story at the right time." Although ideas are accepted on the basis of newsworthiness and other readership values, an ability to develop relationships of mutual respect and cooperation with the news media can be useful to both the practitioner and the news people.

5. *Production.*   Various publications, special reports, films, and multimedia programs are important ways of communicating. The public relations practitioner need not be an expert in art, layout, typography, and photography, but background knowledge of the techniques of preparation is needed for intelligent planning and supervision of their use.

6. *Special Events.*   News conferences, convention exhibits and special showings, new facility and anniversary celebrations, contests and award programs, tours and special meetings are only a few of the special events used to gain attention and acceptance of groups of people. They involve

Events like Coretta King's leading the march to commemorate the 30th anniversary of the civil rights march from Selma to Montgomery, Alabama, create photo and story opportunities for media. The sponsor's name (SCLC in this case) should be visible in the photos of the event.

careful planning and coordination, attention to detail, preparation of special booklets, publicity, and reports.

7. *Speaking.* Public relations work often requires skill in face-to-face communication—finding appropriate platforms, the preparation of speeches for others, and the delivery of speeches. The person who can effectively address individuals and groups will enjoy an advantage over those whose facility of expression is limited to writing.

8. *Research and Evaluation.* An important activity undertaken by a public relations practitioner is fact-gathering. As previously indicated, this can be highly personal, through interviews, review of library materials, and informal conversations. It can also involve the use of survey techniques and firms specializing in designing and conducting opinion research.

    After a program is completed, the public relations practitioner studies its results and evaluates the program's planning, implementation, and effectiveness. More and more managers expect research and evaluation from their public relations advisers or staffs.

The Changing Nature of the Profession

The changing nature of public relations work is illustrated in table 1.2, which lists the rank order of PR employers' emphasis on knowledge/skill areas. It should be noted that customer and client relations and decision making and problem solving are both managerial functions. They do not depend only on hands-on skills that enable individuals to complete a piece of work from start to finish but instead emphasize the ability of the practitioner to accomplish his or her job through the cooperation of other people.

TABLE 1.2 Rank Order of PR Employers' Emphasis on Knowledge/Skill Area

Very Important

1. Customer/client relations	2. Decision making/problem solving

Moderately Important to Very Important

3. Copywriting/proofreading	9. Writing collateral pieces
4. Writing print advertising copy	10. Graphic design of print advertising
5. Writing news releases	11. Budgeting
6. Project management	12. Writing direct mail pieces
7. Account sales/service	13. Media relations
Coordination of creative efforts	14. Writing corporate publications
8. Graphic design of print advertising	

Moderately Important

15. Graphic design of direct mail pieces	24. Research
16. Photographic design/direction	25. Management counsel regarding organizational
17. Speech writing	decisions
18. Writing broadcast advertising	26. Community relations
19. Graphic design of corporate publications	27. Writing promotional and training films/videos
20. Special events planning and coordination	28. Trafficking
21. Writing slide shows/filmstrips	29. Graphic design of promotional films/videos
22. Employee/labor relations	30. Photographic shooting skills
23. Graphic design of slide shows/film strips	

Moderately Unimportant to Moderately Important

31. Graphic design of broadcast advertising	35. Stockholder relations
32. Trade shows and exhibits	36. School relations
33. Convention and meeting planning	37. Graphic design of news releases
34. Governmental relations	38. Fundraising and development

Source: Gay Wakefield and Laura Perkins Cottone, "Knowledge and Skills Required by Public Relations Employers," *Public Relations Review* (Fall 1987).

A Systems View of Public Relations

We began this discussion by defining public relations as a management function. Since then, we have discussed various other definitions, each dealing with a particular aspect of the practice of public relations and helping us to better understand this rapidly expanding, multifaceted field. In preparing to read the remainder of this book, think back to where this discussion began—management. The managerial context is required to understand public relations most completely.

One of the most widely accepted views of management can be found within the concept of systems theory. This view describes organizations in our society as systems with permeable boundaries. Two-way communication flows between organizations and their environments. Systems of this type are called open systems; you will read about them further in chapter 9. Open systems are composed of various subsystems that give them their identity and purpose, such as the production of goods or a service. The management subsystem is at the center of each organizational system.

Figure 1.2 Public relations
as an organizational
subsystem

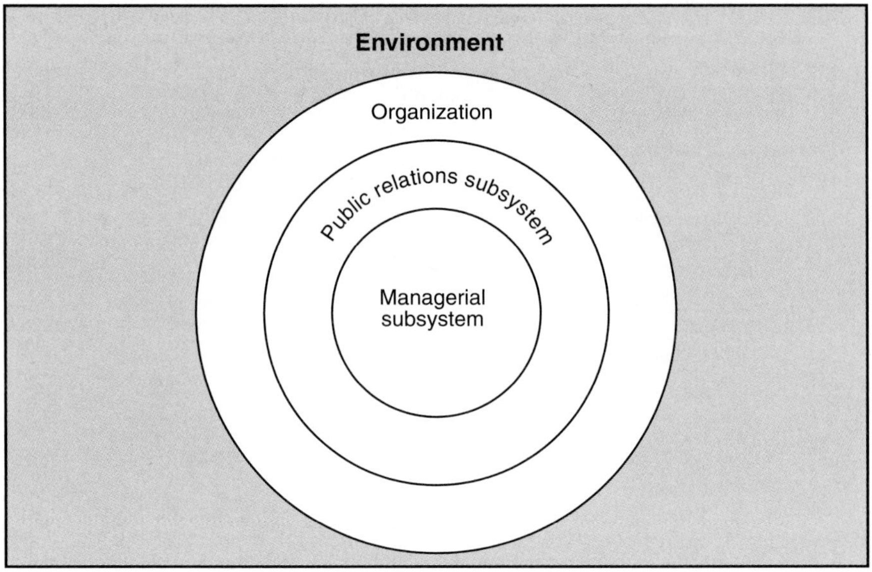

Open systems, with their permeable boundaries, must constantly respond to
and interact with their environment. This interaction makes public relations a part
of every manager's job, as figure 1.2 shows. The earlier example of Pepsi-Cola's
crisis group formed during the hoax also illustrates this point. *Public relations be-*
comes the central subsystem through which management responds to and at-
tempts to influence an organization's environment.

Systems theory also provides an excellent vehicle to describe public relations. Figure 1.3 presents public relations as a system within society, bounded by
the environment to which it must respond. At the center of this system is a four-
step process that is its core: research, planning, action, and evaluation. Surrounding this core are successive rings of permeable boundaries. Inputs from the environment penetrate through these boundaries and become throughputs when the
process of public relations occurs. After the public relations process has responded, outputs are directed back through the boundaries to the environment.

For example, when the Houston Independent School District was faced with an
outside group's discovery that lead-based paint had been used to refinish student desks
(input), officials checked the facts and formulated a response strategy (throughput).
Once the strategy of repainting the desks over the Thanksgiving and Christmas holidays was set, it was announced to the news media and parents (output).

This system illustrates that public relations responds to certain elements of
the general environment we have previously defined as publics. While these are
most frequently the media, consumers, employees, the financial community, and
governmental bodies, any definable group can be classified as a public. These

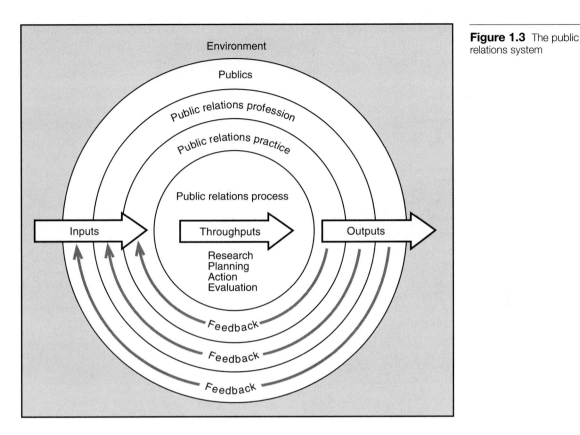

Figure 1.3 The public relations system

publics are serviced by a profession that has a distinct history, an expanding body of knowledge, and a governing code of ethics.

Summary

Although many useful definitions of public relations are available from a variety of sources, the concept of public relations as a management function encompasses most aspects. The duties of public relations practitioners go far beyond the skills of communicating, because effective communication requires planning and implementing organizational objectives. The public relations practitioner, like his or her counterparts in other functional areas of the organization, must be adept at influencing policy decisions and developing strategies to implement them. The perspective of this book is broad enough to consider all aspects of public relations practice—from the fundamental skills necessary to obtain a first job to the decision-making ability needed to direct the public relations actions of a large corporation.

"Doing" Public Relations

By Nancy M. Somerick
School of Communication
University of Akron

Case Study

Y ou have applied for a public relations position with a $10.2 million savings and loan association, a conservative financial institution that has been in existence for over 50 years. The organization has never employed a public relations person before. Now that its assets have risen above $10 million, however, the president of the institution feels it is time to hire someone to "do the PR."

During an interview, the president admits he is not sure what public relations is, but he is fairly sure he wants the person he hires to plan promotions and stage events that will attract new customers, write stories that will get free space and time in the local media, and start an employee publication. The president also states that he is open to suggestions about the position and asks you to explain how you would establish a professional, effective public relations program if you were hired.

Questions

1. Do the responsibilities outlined by the president indicate that he understands how the public relations function can be utilized most effectively? Use the overview given in this chapter to list and discuss some areas of public relations the president has not mentioned that could benefit his company.

2. What would you tell the president about your plans for establishing an effective public relations program for the financial institution? Briefly discuss how the eight functions from *Careers in Public Relations* listed in this chapter could be a part of your response to the president. Relate your plans to the definition of public relations at the beginning of the chapter.

Notes

1. "The Pepsi Hoax: What Went Right?" (Case study prepared by Pepsi-Cola Public Affairs, Somers, N.Y., 1993).

2. Ray Stitle, Delta Beverage, in a speech for the Memphis Chapter of PRSA, 13 September 1995.

3. Ibid.

4. Ibid.

5. "Corporate Communication Most Popular Name Used," *Communication World* (September 1983): 2.

6. Howard Feldman, unpublished dissertation, 6.22–6.25.

7. Charles S. Steinberg, *The Creation of Consent: Public Relations in Practice* (New York: Hastings House, 1975), 19.

8. Frank Vogel, "Sounds of Silence," from "International Economics and U.S. Public Relations," the Fifth Arthur W. Page Lecture, *Public Relations Journal* (December 1986): 35–37.

9. Craig Mellow, "Remaking PR's Image," *Across the Board* (July/August 1989): 33–39.

10. Scott M. Cutlip quoted in Susan Fry Bovet, "Interpret Public Opinion for

Top Management," *Public Relations Journal* (October 1995): 8.

11. Rex F. Harlow, "Public Relations Definitions Through the Years," *Public Relations Review* (Spring 1977): 56.

12. Ibid., 61.

13. K. Richmond Temple, "Is Public Relations Ready for the 1990s?" *Public Relations Quarterly* (Winter 1989–90): 4–6.

14. Allen H. Center, "What About the State of the Art?" *Public Relations Journal* (January 1976): 30–31.

15. John Marston, *The Nature of Public Relations* (New York: McGraw-Hill, 1963).

16. Gene Harlan and Alan Scott, *Contemporary Public Relations: Principles and Cases* (New York: Prentice-Hall, 1955), 3.

17. Frank Jefkins, *Public Relations in World Marketing* (London: Crosby, Lockwood and Son, 1966), 4.

18. Harlow, "Public Relations Definitions," 56.

19. Bill Adams, "The Quarry Qualms," Phillips Petroleum Company case study.

20. See Harlow, "Public Relations Definitions," 56; Irwin Ross, *The Image Merchants* (New York: Doubleday, 1958), 16; and Raymond Simon, *Perspectives in Public Relations* (Norman, Okla.: University of Oklahoma Press, 1966), 63.

21. Edward Stan, *What You Should Know About Public Relations* (New York: Oceana Publications, 1968), 1.

22. Charles S. Steinberg, *The Mass Communicators: Public Relations, Public Opinion and Mass Media* (New York: Harper, 1958), 16, 198.

23. Alan W. Scott, "Does PR Need Redefinition?" *Public Relations Journal* (July 1970): 23–24.

24. Donald K. Wright, "Professionalism and Social Responsibility in Public Relations," *Public Relations Review* (Fall 1979): 23.

25. Harlow, "Building a Definition," 36.

26. Ibid., 35.

27. U.S. Department of Labor, Bureau of Labor Statistics, Bulletin 1978, *Occupational Outlook Handbook,* 1980 ed., 476–478.

28. Christopher Beyer, "Salary Survey," *Public Relations Journal* (June 1986): 28.

29. Chester Burger, *Primer of Public Relations Counseling* (Counselors Section of the Public Relations Society of America, 1972), 81.

30. Alyse Lynn Booth, "Who Are We?" *Public Relations Journal* (June 1985): 15.

31. Ibid., 34.

32. Susan Thomas, "PR Agency of the Future," *The Business Journal* (June 1994) on Nexis: 90.

33. Ibid.

34. "A Blueprint for the Future," *Public Relations Journal* (October 1995): 23.

35. Ibid., 23, 28–29.

36. Ibid., 28.

CHAPTER 2

The History of Public Relations

Preview

Public relations is an outgrowth of three factors: the recognition of the power of public opinion, continuous competition among institutions for public support, and the development of media through which the public can readily be reached.

Historically, public relations has gone through three overlapping stages: manipulation, information, and mutual influence and understanding. Their development was sequential, but all three still exist. Public relations has generally moved from using any available means to achieve desired public opinion toward informing the public and providing information and counsel to management.

The future of public relations can be better predicted and prepared for if trends in its history are identified and understood.

Vox populi, vox Dei. (The voice of the people is the voice of God.)

—Ancient Roman proverb

P
ublic opinion has always been a force in human events. Leaders have courted the sentiments of the people to sustain their power and gain support for their actions. Only those rulers believed to be gods, or chosen by gods, could afford to ignore public attitudes—and even they usually took pains to assure their subjects that their faith was well placed. Many despots, believing they held absolute power and were thus immune to public opinion, later lost their heads.

Public opinion is a force that has been reckoned with in all civilizations. Artifacts of what can be construed as public relations materials survive from ancient India, Mesopotamia, Greece, and Rome. The Crusades, the exploits of Lady Godiva, the actions of Martin Luther, and the adventures of the Conquistadores seeking El Dorado have all been explained as examples of ancient public relations activities. The creation in the 17th century of the Congregatio de Propaganda (the congregation for propagating the faith) by the Roman Catholic Church is often pointed to as a keystone in the development of public relations. The action brought us the term *propaganda* but was not a significant development in a church that exists to propagate the faith.

Because public opinion has been a powerful and important factor throughout human history, it is easy to claim that public relations has similarly ancient antecedents. Such a pedigree might be attractive to the public relations historian, but it would be erroneous. Sporadic examples of what might be considered public relations can be traced to earliest recorded history. Nonetheless, the widespread practice of public relations as a necessary and respected organizational function is a fairly recent development.

Modern-day public relations is a product of the recognition that public opinion is powerful, the establishment of strong constituent relationships, and competition among institutions for public support. The United States was and is the perfect crucible in which to mold public relations. With its republican government, its democratic sensibilities, its free markets, its various systems of checks and balances, and its independent population forever voting with ballots and dollars while increasing their levels of affluence and education, public relations was in truth "made in America."

American Antecedents to Public Relations

Occasional examples of public relations–like activities were identifiable in the early days of the American colonies. For example, Harvard College initiated the first systematic U.S. fund-raising campaign in 1641. The campaign was supported by the first fund-raising brochure, entitled *New England's First Fruits*. In 1758, King's College (now Columbia University) issued the first press release—to announce graduation exercises.

Public relations prospers under adverse circumstances—when power is threatened or when public support is needed. Public relations has prospered most in times of extreme pressure or crisis. Such were the circumstances preceding the American Revolution, when Samuel Adams initiated what can be called a public relations campaign. Adams was to the communication dimension of the Revolution what George Washington was to the military dimension. He recognized the value of using symbols that were easily identifiable and aroused emotions.

The Boston Tea Party was staged by Adams in 1773 to influence public opinion.

Adams used slogans that are still remembered, like "Taxation without representation is tyranny." Because he got his side of the story to a receptive public first, shots fired into a group of rowdies became known as "the Boston Massacre." Adams directed a sustained-saturation public relations campaign using all available media. He staged the Boston Tea Party to influence public opinion. In the Sons of Liberty and Committees of Correspondence, he maintained mechanisms to implement the actions made possible by his public relations campaign.[1]

Public Relations in a Young Nation

In the infancy of the United States, public relations was practiced primarily in the political sphere. The publication and dissemination of the *Federalist Papers,* leading to the ratification of the U.S. Constitution, has been called "history's finest public relations job."[2]

During the 1820s and 1830s, the vote was granted to a larger portion of the population. Expanding public education increased literacy. The mass medium of the penny press was developing. The campaign that brought Andrew Jackson to the White House was the first to appeal directly to the public rather than to the land-owning elite. Amos Kendall, a member of the famous "kitchen cabinet," served as the candidate's pollster, counselor, ghostwriter, and publicist. Although he did not hold the title, Kendall effectively served as the first presidential press secretary and congressional liaison. Jackson, who did not express himself terribly well, used Kendall as a specialist to convey his ideas to Congress and the American people.

Jackson's foes were forced to adopt similar tactics in the effort to gain public favor. In March 1831, the Bank of the United States, locked in a life-or-death struggle with President Jackson, decided "to cause to be prepared and circulated such documents and papers as may communicate to the people information in regard to the nature and operations of the bank."[3] Jackson and Kendall, however, prevailed.

With the majority of Americans living on farms or in small communities, communication was primarily person-to-person and face-to-face during the 19th century. There was limited need for public relations intermediaries. Still, the various potentials and applications of public relations began to be explored.

"Manifest Destiny" and America's settlement of her western frontier were driven by publicity. From Daniel Boone to Davy Crockett to Buffalo Bill, skillful and sometimes exaggerated promotion was the way to move easterners to the West. Even Jesse James got in the act when he issued a news release about one of his particularly daring train robberies.

Business became aware of publicity's virtues. When Burlington Railroad initiated its 1858 publicity campaign, Charles Russell Lowell stated, "We must blow as loud a trumpet as the merits of our position warrants."[4] Political agents gained increasing sophistication as Tammany Hall, New York City's famous political machine, used interviewing to obtain information in the late 1850s.

More dramatic were campaigns related to the issues of the day—movements for the abolition of slavery, women's rights, and prohibition. Demonstrations and endorsements by public figures and the press were used to promote these and other causes.

Still, through the better part of the 19th century, public relations remained a rudimentary adjunct to political activities. The vigorous expansion of American business was tremendously popular and faced few challenges. In its early days, big business played its cards close to the vest—the less the public knew, the better. By the latter part of the century, however, business had overplayed its hand.

Propaganda almanac for the Temperance Crusade of 1875

Institutions in Conflict

The 1880s saw government's first major steps into the marketplace. Markets and the size of business organizations grew rapidly. Simultaneously, dramatic shifts occurred in public attitudes toward business and in the roles played by several institutions. Workers began to organize themselves into unions, and they perceived their interests in many cases as directly opposed to those of business owners. Business was at once highly successful and increasingly besieged.

By this era, big institutions removed from people's day-to-day interactions were emerging. In an increasingly diverse society, consensus was breaking down, with a rise in the incidence of conflict and confrontation.

Not surprisingly, the term *public relations* came into use at this time; its earliest appearance was probably in Dorman B. Eaton's 1882 address to the graduating class of the Yale Law School. The concept, as noted, was not new, but the coining of the term suggested a new level of importance and consciousness. As historian Marc Bloch has commented, "The advent of a name is a great event even when the object named is not new, for the act of naming signifies conscious awareness."[5]

The Industrial
Revolution

The Industrial Revolution hit America with full force during the last quarter of the
19th century. The nation's population doubled as immigrants rushed to the land of
opportunity. New products and new patterns of life rapidly emerged. The enforced
rhythm of the factory, the stress of urban life, and the vast distinction between the
bosses and the workers were new and not always pleasant realities of American life.

According to historian Merle Curti:

> Corporations gradually began to realize the importance of combating hostility and
> courting public favor. The expert in the field of public relations was an inevitable
> phenomenon in view of the need for the services he could provide.[6]

By 1883, American Telephone and Telegraph (AT&T) leader Theodore Vail
expressed concern about the company's relationship with the public and the public's conflicts with the company. In 1888, the Mutual Life Insurance Company
employed Charles J. Smith to manage a "species of literary bureau" in response to
similar concerns.

In 1889, George Westinghouse, founder of the industrial giant that still
bears his name, saw the light. He established the first corporate public relations
department and hired E. H. Heinrichs, a Pittsburgh newspaperman, to run it. Hein-
rich's immediate task was to direct a fierce struggle with Thomas Alva Edison
over whether the nation would be wired for alternating or direct electric current.

Edison was a formidable adversary. Forest McDonald describes the battle
this way:

> Edison General Electric attempted to prevent the development of alternating current
> by unscrupulous political action and by even less savory promotional tactics. . . .
> The promotional activity was a series of spectacular stunts aimed at dramatizing the
> deadliness of high voltage alternating current, the most sensational being the
> development and promotion of the electric chair.[7]

Ultimately, Westinghouse won. Consequently, we use alternating current
today. Seeing his success, other businesses followed Westinghouse's example.
Just as the era brought changes to business, politics was forced to adapt to new realities. The hard-fought 1896 Bryan-McKinley presidential race was the first to
use modern methods of political campaigning.

The massive social and economic changes of the late 19th century and the
resulting pressures on business forced the most dramatic change in the attitudes of
businessmen. A philosophy of pure competition gave way to different concerns.
Social and economic benefits had to be considered when weighing alternative reasons. As the 20th century began, public relations practitioners concentrated increasingly on this aspect of corporate legitimacy.

Public Relations: Three Stages of Development

The development of public relations in the United States can be divided into three
stages. To some degree, their progression was sequential, but all have existed simultaneously, and still do so today. Moreover, while the intellectual and theoretical bases of all three stages evolved rapidly during the first quarter of this century,
in practice, the most advanced stage has only recently gone beyond the point of
novelty. The three stages are as follows:

1. *Manipulation.*   Public relations is assumed to use whatever means are available to achieve desired public opinion and action. Traditionally, practitioners of this type of public relations have been called **press agents.**

2. *Information.*   Public relations is regarded as a conduit for information flowing from organizations to the public so that the public will understand, sympathize with, and patronize the organization. Practitioners of this form of public relations are called **publicity agents.**

3. *Mutual influence and understanding.*   In this most recent stage, public relations accepts the responsibilities of Stage 2, but also provides information and counsel to management on the nature and realities of public opinion and methods by which the organization can establish policy, make decisions, and take action in light of public opinion. Practitioners who follow this approach are called **public relations counselors.** Not everyone who assumes this title, however, deserves it.

Manipulation was the technique of 19th-century press agents who served political campaigns and carnival shows more than mainstream business. The frequently quoted remark "There's a sucker born every minute" exemplifies the manipulative approach.

Stage 1: Manipulation

In their efforts to promote land sales in the American West or attract attention for politicians, early publicists did not hesitate to embellish the truth. Press agents made exaggeration into a high art. The myth of Davy Crockett was a creation of the political enemies of Andrew Jackson. Matthew St. Clair Clarke, Crockett's press agent, was attempting to lure the frontier vote away from Jackson.[8]

Old-time press agents played upon the credulity of the public. Exaggeration, distortion, and deception were their stock-in-trade. They became masters of the publicity stunt or what later came to be known as the "pseudo event," a planned happening that occurs for the purpose of being reported.

P. T. Barnum   Phineas T. Barnum has always been considered the master of press agentry—a promoter with endless imagination in a calling in which imagination is the main ingredient. Barnum promoted the midget General Tom Thumb; Jenny Lind, the "Swedish Nightingale"; Jumbo the elephant; and Joice Heath, a 161-year-old woman (an autopsy report after her death put her age at 70 to 80). Barnum used publicity to make money, pure and simple.

Nearly a century after his death, the Ringling Brothers, Barnum and Bailey Circus still uses Barnum's technique with virtually no alteration. In the 1985–86 season, the circus claimed to exhibit a living example of the mythical unicorn. Informed opinion said that the horn had been grafted to the head of a young goat. The Society for the Prevention of Cruelty to Animals protested and picketed, but people bought tickets to see the creature—circus revenues rose 22 percent that year.[9] Barnum's spirit must have smiled from that three-ring circus in the sky.

When P. T. Barnum died, the *London Times* fondly called him a "harmless deceiver." As long as press agentry is used to promote circuses, entertainment, and professional sports, its negative potential is limited. Its use in business and politics, however, is more threatening.

In the quest to gain media and public attention, press agentry becomes increasingly outrageous, exploitive, and manipulative. Moreover, the manipulative attempt to gain the attention of the public through the media has an even darker side.

The Downside of Press Agentry In 1878, French socialist Paul Brousse described what he called "the propaganda of the deed." The term refers to a provocative act committed to draw attention toward an idea or grievance in order to get publicity.

For European anarchists in the late 19th and early 20th centuries, propaganda of the deed meant bombing, murder, and assassination. During those days, fear gripped the people of Paris because they knew they might be victims of a bomb exploded in the effort to gain attention. Although these techniques were used less often after the start of World War I, they have been revived since the 1960s and used quite broadly throughout the world during recent decades. Violent forms of **propaganda of the deed** today are known as terrorism.

Violent efforts to attract attention must be differentiated from illegal but nonviolent efforts. Exemplified by the philosophies and activities of Gandhi and Martin Luther King, Jr., these acts also are akin to the tactics of press agentry.

The tools of press agentry, and any of the means and methods of public relations, are available to all—true or false, right or wrong, good or evil. The success of press agents in attracting attention and public response, coupled with their blatantly manipulative aims, inevitably arouse hostility from the press and the public. Press agentry gives public relations an odor that persists to this day.

Stage 2: Information   By the early 1900s, business was forced to submit to more and more governmental regulations and encountered increasingly hostile criticism from the press. Because of the social forces that gathered against business at the turn of the 20th century, public relations became a specialized function broadly accepted in major corporations. Corporations rapidly recognized that deception, manipulation, and self-serving half-truths were inappropriate responses to challenges raised by media and government. Edward L. Bernays, public relations pioneer, first teacher of public relations at the college level, and author of the first book on the subject, explained the emergence of the public relations function in this way:

> The first recognition of distinct functions of the public relations counsel arose, perhaps, in the early years of this century from the insurance scandals coincident with the muckraking of corporate finance in the popular magazines. The interests attacked suddenly realized that they were completely out of touch with the public they were professing to serve, and required expert advice to show them how they could understand the public and interpret themselves to it.[10]

Publicity Bureaus Former journalists began to find it possible to make a living in the public relations business. In 1900, George V. S. Michaelis established the Publicity Bureau in Boston. His job, as he saw it, was to gather factual information about his clients for distribution to newspapers. By 1906, his major clients were the nation's railroads. The railroads engaged the Publicity Bureau to head off

Edward L. Bernays, a pioneer in public relations education

adverse regulations being promoted by Theodore Roosevelt. The agency used fact-finding publicity and personal contact to push its clients' position, but kept secret its connection with the railroad. Publicity Bureau staff increased dramatically, with offices set up in New York, Chicago, St. Louis, Topeka, and Washington, D.C. and with agents in California, South Dakota, and elsewhere.

President Roosevelt, who saw the presidency as "a bully pulpit," proved to be more than a match for the Publicity Bureau. The first president to make extensive use of press conferences and interviews, Roosevelt was said to rule the country from the newspapers' front pages. The passage of the Hepburn Act extended government control over the railroad industry and represented a clear victory for the Roosevelt Administration.

Other early publicity offices were established by William Wolf Smith in Washington, D.C., in 1902; Hamilton Wright, San Francisco, 1908; Pendleton Dudley, New York's Wall Street district, 1909; Rex Harlow, Oklahoma City, 1912; and Fred Lewis and William Seabrook, Atlanta, 1912.

Ivy Lee   The father of public relations, however, and the man who nurtured the fledgling profession, was Ivy Ledbetter Lee, son of a Georgia preacher. Lee was a reporter who saw better prospects in the publicity arena. After working in New York's 1903 mayoral campaign and for the Democratic National Committee, Lee joined George Parker, another newspaper veteran, to form the nation's third publicity agency in 1904.

Two years later, coal operators George F. Baer and Associates hired the partnership to represent their interests during a strike in the anthracite mines. John Mitchell, leader of the labor forces, was quite open and conversant with the press, which treated him and his cause with considerable sympathy. The tight-lipped Baer would not even talk to the president of the United States.

Lee took the assignment and persuaded Baer to open up. Then he promptly issued a "Declaration of Principles" to all newspaper city editors. The sentiments expressed in this document clearly indicated that public relations had entered its second stage.

As Eric Goldman observes, "The public was no longer to be ignored, in the traditional manner of business, nor fooled, in the continuing manner of the press agent."[11] Lee declared that the public was to be informed. The declaration read:

> This is not a secret press bureau. All our work is done in the open. We aim to supply news. This is not an advertising agency; if you think any of our matter ought properly to go to your business office, do not use it. Our matter is accurate. Further details on any subject treated will be supplied promptly, and any editor will be assisted most cheerfully in verifying directly any statement of fact. . . . In brief, our plan is, frankly and openly, on behalf of business concerns and public institutions, to supply to the press and public of the United States prompt and accurate information concerning subjects which it is of value and interest to the public to know about.[12]

From his actions and effectiveness in dealing with the coal strike, Lee clearly was not just a press agent coveting publicity. Indeed, he had a sophisticated grasp of the fundamental nature, problems, and opportunities of conflict.

Lee realized that a corporation could not hope to influence the public unless its publicity was supported by good works. Performance determines publicity. To achieve necessary and positive consistency between words and actions, Lee urged his clients in business and industry to align their senses and their policies with the public interest.

Railroads   As previously indicated, railroads were among the early users of public relations consultants. In 1906, the Pennsylvania Railroad retained Lee as publicity counselor. Beginning in 1897, the term *public relations* was frequently used in railroad trade publications. Indeed, publications of the day maintained that as early as 1893, railroads had begun "to research and study the social condition of its public."[13] Lee's activities for the Pennsylvania included publicizing employee benefits and railroad safety. He also emphasized the large numbers of people who owned the railroad's stock (not mentioning that a very few people held the vast majority of stock). He urged executives to accept public exposure and to cooperate fully with community projects. Most controversially, Lee released complete, factual information about accidents. Traditionally, such news had been suppressed.

The railroad industry was convinced of the value of public relations. By 1909, an industry leader called on all major companies to create a

> Vice President in charge of public relations, a man . . . of mature years and judgment, skilled in railway affairs and human affairs as well, and carrying enough weight in the councils of his company so that his suggestions would be apt to be carried out.[14]

Such an adviser, it was held, could reveal and eliminate the unpopularity of the railroad industry by evaluating and improving customer service.

In a similar vein, a 1912 article stressed that "real publicity" goes beyond appointment of a special agent to court journalists. "It should be inground in the entire staff from top to bottom. . . ."[15] An early textbook entitled *Railroad Administration* included a chapter devoted to "Public Relations of a Railroad."[16] J. Hampton Baumgartner was hired in 1910 to handle publicity for the Baltimore and Ohio Railroad. In 1913, he told the Virginia Press Association that railroads had endeavored to establish closer relations with the public, chiefly through the press and with its cooperation.

Despite their early adoption of public relations techniques, the railroads were notably unsuccessful in lobbying their cause before government bodies. Over 2,000 laws affecting railroads were passed by Congress and the various state legislatures in the period between 1908 and 1913.

Not-for-Profit Organizations Not-for-profit organizations—including colleges, churches, charitable causes, and health and welfare agencies—began to use publicity extensively during this era. In 1899, Anson Phelps Stokes converted Yale University's office of secretary into an effective alumni and public relations office. Harvard President Charles W. Eliot, who spoke as early as 1869 on the need to influence public opinion toward advancement of learning, was among the Publicity Bureau's first clients in 1900. The University of Pennsylvania and the University of Wisconsin set up publicity bureaus in 1904. By 1917, the Association of American College News Bureaus was formed.

In 1905, the Washington, D.C., YMCA sought $350,000 for a new building. For the first time, a full-time publicist was engaged in a fund-raising drive. By 1908, the Red Cross and the National Tuberculosis Association were making extensive use of publicity agents. The New York Orphan Asylum was paying a publicity man $75 per month.

Churches and church groups were quick to recognize the value of an organized publicity effort. New York City's Trinity Episcopal Church was one of Pendleton Dudley's first clients in 1909. The Seventh-Day Adventist Church established its publicity office in 1912. George Parker, Ivy Lee's old partner, was appointed to handle publicity for the Protestant Episcopal Church in 1913.

Business Publicity and public relations were making their greatest strides in business. In 1907, AT&T's Theodore N. Vail hired James Drummond Ellsworth for that corporation's public relations. Ellsworth promoted efficient operation and consideration of customers' needs, a systematic method for answering complaints, and acceptance of governmental regulation as the price for operating a privately owned natural monopoly.

Samuel Insull, an associate of George Westinghouse, rose to head the Chicago Edison Company, an electric utility. In 1903, he began to publish *The Electric City,* a magazine aimed at gaining the understanding and goodwill of the community. He pioneered films for public relations purposes in 1909. In 1912, he introduced bill stuffers, messages to customers in their monthly statements.

Among the greatest of industrial publicity users was Henry Ford. One commentator suggests "He may have been an even greater publicist than mechanic." The Ford Company pioneered use of several public relations tools. The employee periodical *Ford Times* was begun in 1908 and continues today. In 1914, a corporate film department was established. Ford surveyed 1,000 customers to gain insights into their attitudes and concerns.

The company set up demonstrations for the media, including car races and speed records. Ford sought publicity at every opportunity. Presenting himself as the price-reducing champion of the common man, he was totally accessible to the press and quotable on any subject. *Ford* became a household word.

Business leaders were convinced of the legitimacy and importance of publicity and public relations. In the 1911 AT&T annual report, corporation president Theodore Vail advocated a policy of absolute truthfulness, even in treating unfavorable information:

> In all times, in all lands, public opinion has had control at the last word—public opinion is but the concert of individual opinion, and is as much subject to change or to education.

Another business leader who spoke out on public relations was U.S. Steel Board Chairman Elbert H. Gary. In 1909, he maintained, "I believe thoroughly in publicity. . . . The surest and wisest of all regulations is public opinion."[17] B. C. Forbes wrote of Gary,

> "Perhaps his greatest achievement was his leading of [U.S. Steel] out of the old ways of secrecy into the path of 'pitiless publicity.' All America owes him a profound debt for this. When Judge Gary began his great work, everybody considered business a private matter, and the public had a right to look in upon it only when some crime was alleged. Today, business in general is in the open; and the more everybody knows about it the more everybody concerned is pleased. Hats off to Judge Gary for this."[18]

World War I   The greatest public relations effort in history, up to its time, was the one mounted in support of the United States effort in World War I. The military had utilized publicity for several years; the Marine Corps established a publicity bureau in Chicago in 1907. Never before had such a massive, multifaceted, coordinated program been mounted. Moreover, though often used by big business in a defensive fashion, public relations took the offensive when it came to war.

Woodrow Wilson set up a Committee on Public Information in 1917. Newspaperman George Creel was asked to run it. With a staff of journalists, scholars, artists, and others skilled at manipulating words and symbols, Creel mobilized the home front. Before the war, the Red Cross had 486,194 members in 372 chapters and $200,000 in funds. At the war's end, the organization's numbers were 20 million members in 3,864 chapters and $400 million raised. On May 1, 1917, there were 350,000 holders of U.S. bonds. Six months later 10 million held bonds.

Creel did not just work out of a central office; he decentralized the organization and the effort. Every industry had a special group of publicity workers tending to their particular contributions to the war effort. Political scientist Harold D. Lasswell was involved in the Creel organization. Looking back to assess the situation, Lasswell concluded, "Propaganda is one of the most powerful instrumentalities in the modern world."[19]

Indeed, this commitee was a crucial point in pushing public relations to its next level. Many publicists trained in the war effort set out to make careers for themselves when the war ended. Impressed with their results, organizations were eager to use their services. In 1919, the Knights of Columbus, a Catholic organization, set up a publicity bureau. Two years later, the American Association of Engineers held its first national conference on public information and published its proceedings as a book called *Publicity Methods for Engineers.* Also in 1921, Sears, Roebuck and Company retained Hayes, Loeb and Company to counter a movement by thousands of local merchants fighting mail-order competition. In 1922, a National Publicity Council for Welfare Services was set up. Public relations was becoming more sophisticated. Edward Bernays used market research, social surveys, and public opinion polls in efforts to, as he called it, "engineer public consent."

Still, the ends to be served by public relations and its practitioners were not always noble by any means. Between 1920 and 1923, for example, Edward Y. Clark and Bessie Tyler increased the membership of the Ku Klux Klan, a group that thrives on notions of bigotry and white supremacy, from a few thousand to some 3 million members.

World War I U.S. Liberty Bond poster encouraging support for the war effort

Stage 3: Mutual Influence and Understanding

To dedicated and thoughtful public relations professionals in the decade following 1910, it became increasingly obvious that organizations communicate with the public not only by words released through the press, but also by their policies and actions. Consequently, public relations professionals sought to advise business executives in such matters, attempting to gain a place in the heart of business organization—the decision-making and operational aspects. Ivy Lee was again in the vanguard, recognizing that good words had to be supported by good deeds. Lee sought to elevate his own status to that of "brain trust" for his clients.

N. W. Ayer & Son published a booklet in 1912 recommending that business executives discuss with their advertising agents "if conditions in the business are in harmony with an advertising program." Like Lee, Ayer wanted business executives to understand that a successful publicity campaign involved their companies' basic policies as much as their procedures for telling the public about goods or services.[20] These basic policies included both external and internal concerns. Following this theme, it was perhaps not surprising that George Michaelis, who had founded the Publicity Bureau in Boston, advised Westinghouse in 1914 to pay more attention to internal "human relations."[21]

A protracted and violent strike against Colorado Fuel and Iron Company gave Ivy Lee the opportunity to become a consultant on the internal workings of a business. John D. Rockefeller, Jr., the company's principal stockholder, employed Lee in 1914 after savage criticism for his handling of the strike. Lee publicized management's position in the strike (without revealing himself as the source of the information). He also persuaded Rockefeller to visit the stricken area. The man who was perceived as a reclusive tycoon talked with the miners, ate in their dining halls, and danced with their wives. Beyond these traditional actions, however, Lee strongly recommended to management that they improve their communication with workers and establish mechanisms to redress workers' grievances.[22] Thus, Lee became an adviser to Rockefeller not only in relation to dealings with the press and the public but also in relation to the actual operation of the business. His emphasis on counseling management to take postive action marked a major shift in public relations theory and practice. Lee served Rockefeller until his own death in 1934.

Inward Focus   In addition to its outward focus, public relations was gaining an inward focus. This had several results. Employees became recognized as a significant public and an appropriately important audience for public relations efforts. In this regard, Lee persuaded client American Tobacco Company to introduce profit sharing for its employees.

By 1925, more than half of all major manufacturing companies were publishing employee magazines.[23] Textbooks stressed the integration of public relations with general business activities. Samuel Kennedy maintained that from the viewpoint of companies, it was of little importance which person had immediate responsibility for directing publicity and giving out news. What mattered was that the policies of the organization be guided by executives aware of political considerations.[24]

By the 1920s, the vanguard of public relations practitioners considered themselves responsible not only for informing the press and the public, but also for educating management about public opinion. They saw themselves as advising managerial decisions and actions in terms of public response. Only rarely, however, were public relations persons actually allowed to play such roles.

A new understanding of publicity was developing, based on recognition of its tremendous potentials and its very real limitations. Bernard J. Mullaney, who served Samuel Insull's efforts to establish utilities as privately owned natural monopolies, concluded in 1924:

> Honest and intelligent publicity efforts are a most important part of a public relations program . . . but not the whole program; and not even a part of it, as 'publicity' is commonly understood. . . . Publicity that seeks to 'put over' something is unsound; in the long run it defeats itself.

Arthur W. Page   The third stage in the development of public relations was established at American Telephone & Telegraph during the career of Arthur W. Page. A successful businessman, public servant, writer, and editor, Page was approached with an offer to become vice president of AT&T, succeeding the pioneer public relations specialist James D. Ellsworth. Page agreed to accept the position only on the condition that he would not be restricted to publicity in the traditional sense. He demanded and received a voice in company policy and insisted that the company's performance be the determinant of its public reputation. Page practiced the Stage 2 informative approach to public relations. He maintained that:

> all business in a democratic country begins with public permission and exists by public approval. If that be true, it follows that business should be cheerfully willing to tell the public what its policies are, what it is doing, and what it hopes to do. This seems practically a duty.[25]

Arthur Wilson Page, AT&T's
public relations pioneer

Under Page's leadership, however, the company recognized that winning public confidence required not merely ad hoc attempts to answer criticism. Rather, a continuous and planned program of positive public relations was needed, using institutional advertising, the usual stream of information flowing through press releases, and other methods. Bypassing the conventional print media, the company went directly to the public, establishing, for instance, a film program to be shown to schools and civic groups.

AT&T sought to maintain direct contact with as many of its clients as possible. The company made a total commitment to customer service. Moreover, deposits were broadly distributed among banks; legal business was given to attorneys throughout the country; and contracts for supplies and insurance were made with many local agencies. AT&T paid fees for employees to join outside organizations, knowing that through their presence the company would be constantly represented in many forums. Finally, the company sought to have as many people as possible own its stock. Today, AT&T and the successor companies that were created by divestiture in 1984 are the most widely held of all securities.

What truly set Page apart and established him as a pioneer was his insistence that the publicity department act as an interpreter of the public to the company, drawing on a systematic and accurate diagnosis of public opinion. Page wanted data, not hunches. Under his direction, the AT&T publicity department (as it was still called) kept close check on company policies, assessing their impact on the public. Thus, Page caused the company "to act all the time from the public point of view, even when that seems in conflict with the operating point of view."[26]

In 1931, General Motors followed AT&T's lead. The automobile giant set up an internal department under Paul Garrett to ascertain public attitudes and execute a program to bring the company fully into public approval. Garrett was told to put the interests of the public first. (See spotlight 2.1 for a brief biographical sketch of leading public relations pioneers.)

Public Relations Pioneers

Public Relations Spotlight 2.1

Samuel Adams. Most active prior to and during the American Revolution, Adams organized the Sons of Liberty, used the liberty tree symbol, minted slogans like "Taxation Without Representation Is Tyranny," staged the Boston Tea Party, named the Boston Massacre, and mounted a sustained propaganda campaign.

Amos Kendall. During the 1820s and 1830s, Kendall served candidate and President Andrew Jackson as public relations counselor, pollster, and speechwriter. He spearheaded the successful campaign against the Bank of the United States.

Matthew St. Clair Clarke. As publicist for the Bank of the United States in the 1830s, Clarke saturated the press with releases, reports, and pamphlets in the most extensive, albeit unsuccessful, public relations campaign to that date. In an effort to develop a politician to oppose Andrew Jackson, he created the myths surrounding the historical figure Davy Crockett.

P. T. Barnum. A consummate showman during the middle and late 1800s, Barnum originated many methods for attracting public attention. He didn't let truth interfere with his publicity and press agentry techniques. While he contributed positively to our understanding of the power of publicity, his lack of honesty led to a legacy of mistrust of publicity efforts that exists sometimes even today.

George Michaelis. Organizer of the nation's first publicity firm, the Publicity Bureau of Boston in 1900, Michaelis used fact-finding publicity and personal contact to saturate the nation's press.

Ivy Lee. Often called the father of modern public relations, Lee believed the public should be informed. He recognized that good words had to be supported by positive actions on the part of individuals and organizations. His emphasis on public relations as a management function put public relations on the right track with corporate America. His career spanned 31 years from its beginning in 1903 until his death in 1934.

George Creel. As head of the Committee on Public Information during World War I, Creel used public relations techniques to sell Liberty Bonds, build the Red Cross, and promote food conservation and other war-related activities. In so doing, he proved the power of public relations and trained a host of the 20th century's most influential practitioners.

Edward Bernays. An intellectual leader in the field, Bernays coined the phrase "public relations counsel," wrote *Crystallizing Public Opinion* (the first book on public relations), and taught the first college-level public relations course at New York University in 1923. Bernays emphasized the social science contribution to public relations and was a leading advocate for public relations professionalism through practitioner licensing or credentialing. He remained an active counselor, writer, and speaker until his death in 1995 at age 103.

Arthur Page. When offered a vice-presidency at AT&T, Page insisted he have a voice in shaping corporate policy. He maintained that business in a democratic country depends on public permission and approval.

John Hill. Along with Don Knowlton, John Hill opened a public relations agency in Cleveland, Ohio, in 1927. When John Hill moved to New York a few years later to open Hill & Knowlton of New York, Knowlton was not part of the agency. The New York–based agency, though, continued to bear both their names. It became the largest public relations agency in the world and continues to rank in the top three depending on the year. John Hill had major steel and tobacco accounts in his counseling career. He died in 1977 at age 86. His agency was sold to J. Walter Thompson in 1980 for $28 million. In 1987, it was sold to the English-based WPP Group for $585 million.

Doris Fleishman Bernays. Wife of Edward Bernays, Doris Fleishman Bernays was his counselor partner from their marriage in 1922 until retirement in 1962. She counseled corporations, government agencies, and presidents along with her husband. She struggled for equality, not with her husband, but with the attitudes of American business that often paid less attention to the advice given by a woman public relations practitioner.

Carl Byoir. Carl Byoir was another member of George Creel's Committee on Public Information in World War I. As a 28-year-old he was appointed associate chairman of the committee. After the war he founded Carl Byoir and Associates in 1930 to promote tourism in Cuba. He was known for his use of third-party campaigns, use of newspaper advertising as a public relations tool, and development of lobbying in legislative battles for clients such as A&P, Libby-Owens-Ford, and Eastern Railroads. He died in 1957 but his firm lived on to become at various times the largest in the world. It was sold in 1978 to Foote, Cone and Belding, an advertising agency leading the way for other advertising agencies to purchase most of the major public relations agencies.

Rex Harlow. Harlow was a leading public relations educator and researcher. He began teaching a public relations course at Stanford in 1939 and may have been the first full-time professor in public relations. He founded the American Council on Public Relations also in 1939. The council eventually merged with the National Association of Public Relations Councils to form the Public Relations Society of America in 1947. In 1944 Harlow founded the *Public Relations Journal* and in 1952 founded *Social Science Reporter.* He died in 1993 at age 100.

The 1930s to the Present

Two major forces influenced the development of public relations in the United States during the 1930s: (1) the Depression and (2) the threatening military situation in Europe.

The Depression

The impact of the Depression on public relations was twofold. First, the economic conditions of the day were viewed widely as a failure by business to maintain prosperity due to speculative excess. Rocked by the criticism and legislative reforms of the New Deal, public relations changed from occasional defensive efforts to positive continuous programs. Stage 3 public relations was reinforced because depressed economic circumstances called for compassionate and responsive business actions and policies. Persuasion and publicity could be effective only when they were coupled with responsible performance. (See mini-case 2.1 for an example of how Carl Byoir used public relations techniques to raise money nationally to help polio victims and to find a cure for the crippling disease.)

The nation's diminished economic capacities created increased societal needs with reduced societal means. The need for active and informed constituencies became very clear when welfare, education, defense, other governmental goals, business, and labor fought for limited resources and the support of an awakened public.

Mini-Case 2.1

Carl Byoir and FDR

Franklin Roosevelt became ill with polio in 1921 while vacationing, a few months after his defeat as vice-president on the James Cox Democratic ticket in the 1920 elections. Roosevelt narrowly escaped death from the polio and would fight the crippling effects of the disease for the rest of his life.

In 1926, Roosevelt bought a run-down spa in Warm Springs, Georgia, from friend and philanthropist, George Peabody. The spa—with 1,200 acres, hotel, and cottages—was in poor shape, but the curative powers of the hot, mineral springs held promise for many polio victims.

When Roosevelt was elected governor of New York in 1928, he realized he wouldn't have time to oversee the rehabilitation effort at Warm Springs. Roosevelt asked his law partner, Basil O'Conner, to lead the effort. O'Conner formed the Warm Springs Foundation to raise money for the refurbishing of the health resort. However, the stock market crash in 1929 made fund-raising difficult.

When Roosevelt became president in 1932, the foundation was nearly bankrupt. However, one of the foundation fund-raisers, Keith Morgan, hired a public relations counselor, Carl Byoir, to do the job. Byoir had founded his own public relations agency in 1930 to promote tourism in Cuba. Byoir's fundraising idea for the Warm Springs Foundation was to create a special event to raise the money. That event turned out to be birthday balls around the country to celebrate President Roosevelt's birthday on January 30, 1934.

Byoir sent letters to newspaper editors around the country asking them to nominate a birthday ball director for their area. If an editor didn't respond, he went to either the Democratic Party chairman in the area or to the Roosevelt-appointed postmaster to ask them to do the ball. Media were besieged with information about the balls. Nationally syndicated columnist and broadcaster Walter Winchell presented an appeal that was so good it would be used for years for both birthday balls and for March of Dimes. Radio personalities tried to outdo each other in promoting the balls. In the end 6,000 balls were held in 3,600 communities and more than $1 million was raised for the foundation.

The next two years the event was changed to split the proceeds 70 percent to the local communities and 30 percent to a newly created national polio research commission.

Carl Byoir led the first three birthday balls. He left after the third because he became disillusioned with President Roosevelt when FDR "packed" the Supreme Court in 1937.

But, out of Byoir's effort not only came the birthday balls, but also the March of Dimes, the National Foundation for Infantile Paralysis, and finally victory over polio. Carl Byoir had elevated fund-raising to a new level through his public relations efforts and had given new insight into techniques that public relations practitioners continue to use today.

Source: Scott M. Cutlip, *The Unseen Power* (Hillsdale, N.J.: Lawrence Erlbaum Associates, 1994), 553–563.

The deteriorating military and political situation in Europe caused the military to move massively into public relations in the 1930s. In 1935, Chief of Staff General Douglas MacArthur appointed Major Alexander Surles to head a public relations branch. His orders: "The dual job of getting before the public the War Department's anxiety over things to come in Europe and helping newsmen pry stories out of the War Department."[27]

World War II

Each branch of the service built its own public relations apparatus. The Army Air Corps, under former information officer General H. H. "Hap" Arnold, promoted air power. The Army's efforts employed 3,000 military and civilian personnel.

The greatest application of public relations techniques in the 1930s occurred not in the United States, however, but in Germany. In the hands of the Nazis, propaganda demonstrated its effectiveness, but became a dirty word.

In June 1942, with America fully engaged in worldwide struggle, the Office of War Information (OWI) was established. Similar to Creel's effort in World War I, a massive public relations effort was mounted to rally the home front. Elmer Davis directed the program. The goals of the Office of War Information included selling war bonds, rationing food, clothing, and gasoline, planting victory gardens, and recruiting military personnel. Other issues promoted were factory productivity and efficiency.

Several important communication agencies still active today trace their beginnings to OWI. These include the United States Information Agency (USIA), the Voice of America, and the Advertising Council.

Following the war, public relations gained increased respectability, acceptance, and professionalism. In 1947, Boston University established the first school of public relations. Two years later, one hundred colleges and universities offered classes in the subject.

The PostWar Era

Earl Newsom was perhaps the model public relations professional of the immediate post–World War II era. Hired by Standard Oil in 1945, Newsom was best known for helping young Henry Ford II become a public figure known for responsible business management. Newsom was a public relations counselor in the purest sense. He wrote no news releases. He held no press conferences. He simply advised business leaders at the highest levels. His laws of public opinion are still appropriate today.

In 1954, the Public Relations Society of America developed the first code of ethics for the profession. The society set up a grievance board for code enforcement in 1962 and a program of voluntary accreditation in 1964.

In the late 1960s and the 1970s, public relations seemed to be enjoying a renaissance of sorts. Corporations again felt themselves beset by adverse circumstances. Some have compared the 1970s with the muckraking era and maintain that public relations was more concerned with helping corporations avoid destructive attacks than with attempting to gain positive attention. "The public relations man now is far less of an ingenious producer of marvelous editorial gifts for his clients," said David Finn in 1977, "and far more of an experienced counselor in relating to potential or actual media attacks."[28]

During this period, new emphasis was placed on public relations functions other than marketing. Business/government relations became increasingly important as the federal government entered a new era of regulation. Environmentalism, consumerism, equal opportunity, urban problems, and nuclear power became issues confronting many organizations and demanding managed responses. The Vietnam War created special problems at home and abroad. Dow Chemical was picketed on college campuses, while overseas, branches of the Bank of America were frequently bombed. Sit-ins and marches were nonviolent events staged to influence public discussion and discourse. But radical young people in the United States and elsewhere also used riots and bombings as propaganda of the deed.

Public relations had to increase its sophistication in a hurry. New tools and processes were developed. These included issues management, audience analysis, environmental scanning, and strategic planning. Indeed, with the importance of business's traditional technological and economic criteria increasingly challenged on social and political grounds, corporations expanded public relations staffs, budgets, and programs and elevated the function to a higher status in the organizational hierarchy.[29]

All managers and virtually all employees developed a strong public relations dimension in their work. Chief executives assumed more and more public relations responsibility. At companies like McGraw-Edison (where public relations convinced top management to abandon the use of the chemical PCB in electrical capacitors) public relations has reached the third stage of development. In return, the results-oriented approach of top management demands from public relations demonstrable achievements similar to those expected of all other corporate functions.

The Present

Since the 1930s, the theory and practice of public relations has centered around variations on the three themes or stages previously discussed. More and more, public relations is continuous rather than episodic, positive rather than defensive. It is now accepted as a legitimate function within virtually all institutions and organizations.

Other trends are less clear. The argument over the professionalism of public relations practitioners continues. While the practice of public relations often calls for sophisticated technical skills and capabilities, public relations within organizations is frequently practiced, if not directed, by managers with training in other fields. Public relations practitioners as a group are more professionally ethical today than in the early years when the residue of press agentry still tainted the practice, but instances of laundering press releases through subsidized agencies, manipulating statistics, doing selective reporting, and staging events still occur. Perhaps for this reason, the term public relations is still misused to indicate a coverup or distortion of truth.

William A. Durbin, former chairman of Hill & Knowlton Public Relations, said:

> The PR function is about to cross the threshold from a primarily communications function to a management function participating systematically in the formation of policy and the decision-making process itself.[30]

Durbin sees the profession at the same threshold seen by Michaelis, Lee, and Bernays—the threshold that was crossed more than half a century ago by Arthur W. Page. His perception illustrates how things change and remain the same.

By the 1980s, over 60 percent of the workforce were information workers. The precise role public relations will play in post-industrial America is impossible to predict. Societal complexity and interdependence are greater than ever before. International competition and concerns about productivity and the quality of life have reemphasized traditional economic concerns as well. More information and voices compete for resources, attention, acceptance, approval, and support.

Society, however, exists through consensus, which seems ever harder to find. Public relations must not only assist those seeking attention, but also help nurture consensus and promote adaptation to changing environments. That public relations in all its stages will prosper for some years to come is a safe bet.

The Future of Public Relations

The future is always difficult to gauge, but by identifying and describing historical trends, one can make good guesses. We will summarize public relations history and try to fathom its future by identifying and describing 10 trends that appear to influence the direction of the practice today.

Public relations is moving

From	*To*
Manipulation	Adaptation
External counselor	Internal team member
Marketing	Management
Program	Process
Craftsperson	Manager
Items	Issues
Output	Input
Firefighter	Fire preventer
Illegitimacy	Legitimacy
U.S. profession	Global profession

Let's look at each of these trends.

From Manipulation to Adaptation

We begin with the consideration of this trend because it encompasses the entire past century of public relations evolution and because changes in this area are prerequisites for the development of other trends we will discuss. Public relations was born as a manipulative art. Its intent was to achieve specific results in terms of customer response, election outcomes, media coverage, or public attitudes. Public relations' purpose was to communicate in such ways as to assure the compliance of relevant publics' behavior and attitudes with an individual or organization's plans. The means, methods, and media of communication were determined by what it took to get the job done and little else. Stunts, sensationalism, and embellished and highly selective truth were hallmarks of the trade.

The blatantly manipulative aims of public relations in the past aroused the hostility of press and public. Residual effects of that early hostility still linger.

Moreover, in a more subtle and serious way, mistrust of manipulative techniques caused those who employed public relations practitioners to consciously limit their internal influence. Until public relations practitioners moved beyond manipulation, their practice was restricted to specific tasks. They were the errand boys (and sometimes prostitutes) their journalistic colleagues accused them of being.

As practitioners began to establish trust and credibility, the manipulative phase became history. Only then could public relations begin to make gains in stature and responsibility within organizations.

As the 20th century progressed, it became apparent that organizations achieved success not just by seeking compliance to their plans from outside entities, but by responding and adapting effectively to environmental demands, constraints, and opportunities. Public relations practitioners found they could greatly facilitate this adaptive process if they could become trusted, two-way communicators seeking to establish rapport and mutual understanding between groups.

From External Counselor to Internal Team Member

The field of public relations was established as a legitimate occupation and worthwhile field of study by a handful of ex-newspapermen and press agents in the early decades of the 20th century. These pioneers, for the most part, set up their own firms and frequently succeeded in building larger-than-life reputations for themselves as well as their clients. This external, independent counselor model of public relations practice quickly became the ideal taught in our textbooks and university classrooms ever since.

The actual practice of public relations has evolved far beyond this original model. Although counseling firms have flourished, a new breed of practitioner has emerged, primarily within the structures of large complex organizations. Public relations staffs now work for amorphous organizational entities with vast managerial hierarchies that can seldom produce a personality like J. D. Rockefeller. They must be concerned with internal communication as well as external publicity and must provide managerial leadership as well as communication expertise. They are essential members of the management team. Moreover, these new organizational practitioners are achieving, through their anonymous managerial accomplishments, the kind of influence the pioneers only dreamed about.

Public relations specialists in organizations must understand the concerns and attitudes of customers, employees, investors, managers, special interest groups, and a vast array of other publics. The job cannot stop with an understanding of these complex issues; public relations practitioners must be able to integrate this information into the organization's managerial decision-making process. Public relations practitioners of today and tomorrow must continue to exhibit high-quality communication skills to do the jobs for which they are hired. They must also understand both their role as managers in affecting the actions of an organization and the importance of public relations input into that process.

Public relations is increasingly the responsibility of managers themselves. Rather than having a public relations specialist to deal with the media or the community, managers often have that duty. In some cases public relations departments have shrunk because the managerial aspects of the public relations efforts are accomplished by managers and the marketing dimensions are farmed out to outside public relations agencies.

Not very long ago, the primary justification for public relations was its effort to sell products. Public relations was seen as an adjunct to the sales effort, concerned primarily with product publicity, special events coordination, and getting free advertising.

From Marketing to Management

The trend that has seen public relations move from a marketing adjunct to the management mainstream is a by-product of the changes in both areas. The development of the marketing concept that stresses organizational responsiveness to markets rather than sales efforts has changed the direction of information flow related to the development and sale of products. Management's task has also changed dramatically. Once, the job of management was to keep an established production organization smoothly functioning. Now, management seeks constantly to adapt a flexible organism to dynamic and complex environments.

Naturally, public relations has changed in conjunction with these changes in marketing and management. While still contributing to the marketing effort, the prime responsibility of public relations today is providing the information and environment in which management can function most effectively.

Traditionally, public relations has placed tremendous emphasis on programs and products, specific tangible outputs of public relations efforts. The job of the public relations practitioner has consisted of a progression of discrete tasks—media releases, publications, public service announcements, publicity campaigns, and the like. Such products and programs are still a time-consuming responsibility of public relations departments. They are the bulk of the expanding work of public relations agencies. One of the clearest observable trends in public relations, however, is the growing view that organizational communication is a continuous process, not just a succession of programs.

From Program to Process

Although public relations practitioners will still develop and deliver specific products and programs, they will be increasingly involved in broader, less discrete responsibilities. They will spend more time and effort developing communication objectives that are consistent with an organization's overall objectives. They will act as counselors to management and serve on teams with managers and other organizational specialists, working closely and cogently on a broad array of organizational programs. They will adopt a long-term, general perspective instead of a short-term, specific perspective.

In conjunction with the traditional emphasis on producing specific products and programs, public relations practitioners have been viewed as possessing a specific set of skills. Writing ability has always led the list, followed by speaking, interpersonal skills, and a potpourri of other abilities, including photography, graphic design, and the like. These skills are important, but stressing them exclusively leaves the fledgling public relations person in danger of becoming a narrowly specialized craftsperson or technician when trends demand a broadly experienced communication manager.

From Craftsperson to Manager

A young public relations practitioner with less than 10 years of experience put it this way:

> We're yearning to learn all we can about financial statements and effective management techniques. While many of us still write, edit, layout and design, we have also moved up to greater responsibilities demanding a broad knowledge of business, international affairs, and the issues affecting the industries in which we work.

She learned about writing, editing, layout, and design in school, but not the rest.

From Items to Issues

In times past, public relations practitioners sought to place "items" in the media and measured their effectiveness by their success. The current trend carries public relations away from that stage, through defending against negative publicity, and toward issues management.

Issues management is the identification of key issues confronting organizations and the management of organizational responses to them. This process involves early identification of potential controversies, development of organizational policy related to these issues, creation of programs to carry out policies, implementation of these programs, communication with appropriate publics about these policies and programs, and evaluation of the results.

The issues management process is an area in which public relations has its greatest potential in terms of contributions to managerial decision making (see chapter 4). Organizations can avoid negative publicity and gain positive public notice by adapting in advance to environmental demands. In this way, they are able to reap benefits by being perceived as responsible leaders. Public relations practitioners must be prepared to identify and deal with the issues that confront their organizations.

From Output to Input

The traditional emphasis of public relations has been on output—the creation of messages for external publics. Increasingly, however, public relations practitioners are realizing that their most important messages constitute input—messages to internal publics from external and internal publics. The trend line indicates the rising importance of employee and managerial audiences for public relations messages.

Ultimately, public relations enters into the very core of organizations, bearing the information and perspectives that influence fundamental decisions of policy and strategy. Public relations practitioners increasingly provide input and participate in such decisions. Thus, it is necessary too for them to understand the managerial perspective, while maintaining an independent viewpoint that considers social as well as economic variables.

From Firefighters to Fire Preventers

Among the most fully established trends affecting public relations practitioners is the evolution of their role from being "firefighters" to "fire preventers." Effective public relations does not exist merely to clean up messes once they are made, but seeks to avoid such dilemmas. Preventive public relations is a widely held ideal among practitioners.

The confluence of many of the trends just described makes preventive public relations possible. Public relations practitioners are moving into positions that allow them to more fully recognize areas of potential danger, to be equipped to deal with those dangers, and to possess sufficient power and influence to effect needed changes before potentials become realities. Once again, managerial skills take precedence over media skills.

Continuing debates about professionalism notwithstanding, and despite the efforts of PRSA and others, public relations has always had an air of illegitimacy about it. Public relations has been a bastard child, a waif that was not really wanted even by those who temporarily took it in. Journalists often treat public relations professionals like cousins who have fallen from grace. Thus, as long as public relations practitioners seek their legitimacy from the working press, they will remain unfulfilled.

From Illegitimacy to Legitimacy

Public relations has, however, rapidly gained legitimacy in the eyes of organizational managers and executives. Executives recognize and accept the responsibilities of being their organizations' chief public relations practitioners. The trend of legitimacy developed because of all the other trends discussed. Members of the profession who help organizations adapt and respond to the demands and opportunities present in society, who provide working linkages between organizations, and who play a critical role in the effective management of our crucial problem-solving organizational systems are not only legitimate, but are deserving of honor and esteem.

The last decade has seen worldwide expansion of public relations as U.S. business activity has increasingly become global. Cultural, language, and legal differences make global public relations more difficult, but rapidly evolving communication technology has made these barriers less of a factor. Marshall McLuhan's "Global Village," which he predicted more than 30 years ago, has finally arrived. The future of public relations must take into account the global community in all its efforts.

From U.S. Profession to Global Profession

As public relations educator and historian Scott M. Cutlip wrote in his book, *The Unseen Power,* "The essentiality of public relations as a management function that Ivy Lee envisaged in the early 1900s becomes clearer each passing day as our global society becomes even more dependent on effective communication and on an interdependent, competitive world."[31]

Persuasion and public opinion are forces that have always played a role in human events, but widespread practice of public relations as a necessary and respected organizational function is largely an American product of this century. Ever evolving and in transition, public relations practice has experienced three distinct stages: manipulation, information, and mutual influence and understanding.

Summary

The future of public relations can be understood through 10 trends that emphasize the practice's ongoing management role in helping to shape organizations' responses to their environments.

Wreck on the Pennsylvania Railroad, 1906

By Craig E. Aronoff
*Kennesaw State College
Marietta, Georgia*

Case Study

S evere railroad regulations passed in 1903 and 1906 caused Alexander J. Cassatt, president of the Pennsylvania Railroad, to seek the counsel of Ivy Ledbetter Lee concerning how to deal better with the press and the public.

Lee went right to work. He believed in absolute frankness with the press. Veteran railroad men were distressed at Lee's behavior. They were convinced that revealing facts about accidents would frighten customers.

A golden opportunity for Lee to put his ideas into practice soon arose. A train wrecked on the Pennsylvania Railroad main line near the town of Gap, Pennsylvania. As was its time-honored practice, the company sought to suppress all news of the accident.

When Ivy Lee learned of the situation, he took control. He contacted reporters, inviting them to come to the accident scene at company expense. He provided facilities to help them in their work. He gave out information for which the journalists had not considered asking.

The railroad's executives were appalled at Lee's actions. His policies were seen as unnecessary and destructive. How could the propagation of such bad news do anything but harm the railroad's freight and passenger business?

At about the time of the wreck on the Pennsylvania, another train accident struck the rival New York Central. Sticking with its traditional policy, the Central sought to avoid the press and restrict information flow concerning the situation. Confronted with the Central's behavior, and having tasted Lee's approach to public relations, the press was furious with the New York line. Columns and editorials poured forth chastising the Central and praising the Pennsylvania. Lee's efforts resulted in positive publicity, increased credibility, comparative advantages over the Central, and good, constructive press coverage and relations. Lee critics were silenced.

Earl Newsom, himself a public relations giant, looked back at this accident nearly 60 years later and said:

> This whole activity of which you and I are a part can probably be said to have its beginning when Ivy Lee persuaded the directors of the Pennsylvania Railroad that the press should be given all the facts on all railway accidents—even though the facts might place the blame on the railroad itself.*

When Ivy Lee died in 1934, among the many dignitaries at his funeral were the presidents of both the Pennsylvania and the New York Central railroads.

Questions

1. Were Lee's actions in response to the railroad accident consistent with Stage 1, Stage 2, or Stage 3 of public relations development? Explain your answer.

2. Had the New York Central accident not occurred, what do you think would have happened to Ivy Lee and his relationship with the Pennsylvania

Railroad? Do you think the course of public relations development would have been affected?

3. In certain totalitarian states, news of accidents and disasters is often largely suppressed. What do you consider their reasons to be for retaining a posture given up by American public relations practice more than 80 years ago?

*Earl Newsom, "Business Does Not Function by Divine Right," *Public Relations Journal* (January 1963), 4.

Source: Material for this case was gathered from Ray Hiebert's *Courtier to the Crowd* (Ames, Iowa: Iowa State University Press, 1966), 55–61, and Eric Goldman's *Two-Way Street* (Boston: Bellman Publishing Co., 1948), 8.

Notes

1. Philip Davidson, *Propaganda and the American Revolution, 1763–1783 (Chapel Hill, N.C.: University of North Carolina Press, 1941), 3.*

2. Allan Nevins, *The Constitution Makers and the Public, 1785–1790* (New York: Foundation for Public Relations Research and Education, 1962), 10.

3. Quoted in James L. Crouthamel, "Did the Second Bank of the United States Bribe the Press?" *Journalism Quarterly* 36 (Winter 1959): 372.

4. Richard Overton, *Burlington West* (Cambridge, Mass.: Harvard University Press, 1941), 158–159.

5. Marc Bloch, *The Historian's Craft* (New York: Knopf, 1953), 168.

6. Merle Curti, *The Growth of American Thought,* 3rd ed. (New York: Harper & Row, 1964), 634.

7. Forest McDonald, *Insull* (Chicago: University of Chicago Press, 1962), 44–45.

8. Marshall Fishwick, *American Heroes: Myths and Realities* (Washington, D.C., 1954), 70–71.

9. "Ladies and Gentlemen, Presenting—Kenneth Feld," *Business Week* (8 June 1987): 76.

10. Edward L. Bernays, *Propaganda* (New York: Horace Liveright, 1928), 41.

11. Eric F. Goldman, *Two-Way Street* (Boston: Bellman Publishing Co., 1948), 21.

12. Quoted in Sherman Morse, "An Awakening on Wall Street," *American Magazine* 62 (September 1906): 460.

13. Theodore Dreiser, "The Railroads and the People," *Harper's Monthly* 100 (February 1900): 479–480.

14. Ray Morris, "Wanted A Diplomatic Corps," *Railroad Age Gazette* (27 January 1909): 196.

15. James H. McGraw, "Publicity," *Electric Railway Journal* 39 (27 January 1912): 154.

16. Ray Morris, *Railroad Administration* (New York: Appleton & Company, 1910).

17. N. S. B. Gras, "Shifts in Public Relations," *Bulletin of the Business Historical Society* 19, No. 4 (October 1945): 120.

18. B. C. Forbes, "Flashbacks," *Forbes* (7 September 1987): 314.

19. Harold D. Lasswell, *Propaganda Techniques in the World War* (New York: Knopf, 1927), 220.

20. Allan R. Raucher, *Public Relations and Business, 1900–1929* (Baltimore: The Johns Hopkins Press, 1968), 4–5.

21. George V. S. Michaelis, "The Westinghouse Strike," *Survey* 32 (1 August 1914): 463–465.

22. Ray E. Hiebert, *Courtier to the Crowd: The Story of Ivy Lee and the Development of Public Relations* (Ames: Iowa State University Press, 1966).

23. National Industrial Conference Board, *Employee Magazines in the United States* (New York: National Industrial Conference Board, Inc., 1925).

24. Samuel M. Kennedy, *Winning the Public* (New York: McGraw-Hill, 1920).

25. George Griswold, Jr., "How AT&T Public Relations Policies Developed," *Public Relations Quarterly* 12 (Fall 1967): 13.

26. Raucher, *Public Relations and Business,* 80–81.

27. Sidney A. Knutson, "History of Public Relations Programs of the U.S. Army" (masters thesis, University of Wisconsin, 1953).

28. David Finn, "The Media as Monitor of Corporate Behavior," in *Business and the Media,* Craig E. Aronoff, ed. (Santa Monica: Goodyear Publishing Company, 1979), 117–121.

29. "The Corporate Image: PR to the Rescue," *Business Week* (22 January 1979): 47.

30. Ibid., 60.

31. Scott M. Cutlip, *The Unseen Power: Public Relations. A History* (Hillsdale, N.J.: Lawrence Erlbaum Associates, 1994), 761.

CHAPTER 3

A Theoretical Basis for Public Relations

By Rick Fischer, Ph.D., APR
University of Memphis

Preview

Theories present an understanding of the relationship between or among various actions or events. Theories are used to explain or predict the way things work or happen. As a public relations practitioner you will need to build a set of theories to use and refine as you apply professional skill to the task of doing public relations.

Unfortunately, there is no single theory to guide you. This chapter looks specifically at 10 theories, which are categorized by function in three areas: relationships, cognition and behavior, and mass communication.

Another way to build an understanding of public relations is by using typologies. This chapter divides practitioners' roles into managers and technicians and suggests more specific roles for each broad category. As individuals have roles, so do organizations. Noted public relations researcher Jim Grunig describes four models that public relations has used: press agentry, public information, two-way asymmetrical, and the two-way symmetrical models.

hat would happen if . . . ? Why did those people . . . ?
Questions like these should sound familiar. We ask them all the time—
about the routine and not so routine.

When someone knows answers to routine questions we say that person has "common sense." When someone can correctly answer the nonroutine, we say that person is smart or educated. To answer either type (routine or nonroutine) assumes that the person answering the question understands relationships among actions and events. If you were a scientist, you might call these actions and events *variables.*

For example, if you put a pot of water on the stove and turn the burner under the pot to high, what will happen? After a time the water will heat up, start bubbling, eventually come to a boil—and, if the pot is full, will likely spill water on the stove. If you don't intervene, the water level will begin to go down from spillage and evaporation and, eventually, you will burn your pot. Maybe you learned this from experience. Maybe someone told you, or you read about what happens when a pot of water sits on the stove unattended with the heat on high. However you learned it, you have some notion about the way heat interacts with pots full of water. We call that understanding a **theory.** A theory is a statement about the relationship among variables.

We have theories about many things, and individual theories can have any number of variables. Some serve us well because we get to test them regularly and observe the same relationship each time. Other theories are used only occasionally and with mixed results. Some of our theories have good predictive value; others may be no better than flipping a coin.

This chapter is about explaining and predicting the things public relations people work with regularly. As a public relations manager you are expected to know what works and what doesn't. You can learn it the hard way—by trial and error—or you can learn from others. In any case, your value to your employer or client will be directly related to the quality of your advice.

No single theory covers all you need to know in public relations or any other discipline. The only question is: How are you going to organize the theories you need to know? We will look at theories by function, that is, we are going to group theories according to how they are used. We will start with theories of relationships, then move to how people come to know things and what moves them to act. Next, we will consider two theories of mass communication. Finally, we will look at ways to describe what public relations people do and how organizations approach public relations.

Theories of Relationships

Systems Theory

Systems theory is especially useful to public relations because it gives us a way to think about relationships. It captures the notion of parts and wholes, allows us to look at structure, and provides insight into how the parts are related. When we formulate statements about how the parts of this model interact, we can use the model itself to clarify our thinking and predict outcomes.

Let's start with a hypothetical organization—United Fratchworks. This organization is depicted as an oval at the center of figure 3.1. Moving out from the organization, you can see that it has an environment—the area between the large

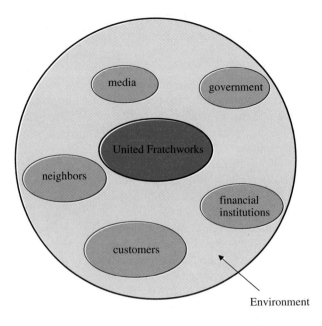

Figure 3.1 Systems model of an organization and its task environment

circle and the organization. In that environment are most of the publics considered in chapter 1: customers, suppliers, the community (neighbors), the media, financial institutions, and government. This is sometimes called the *task environment*. Whether we acknowledge it or not, we have a relationship with each of these publics. The question is: Will we manage these relationships or just let them happen?

We can also use systems theory to look at the parts of an organization— salaried employees and managers, departments and shops, staff and line. It's up to us to decide the most appropriate way to subdivide the whole.

The environment imposes constraints on our organization. Customers can boycott our products. The courts can make us pay damages to people who are injured by our products. Banks can choose not to lend us money. Public relations practitioners must know what is going on in the environment and maintain a balance between the organization and the environment.

That monitoring task is a major one for the public relations staff. We might think of the public relations function as straddling the edge of an organization— looking both within and outside the organization. Public relations practitioners explain the organization to its publics and interpret the environment to the organization. Public relations people warn of problems in the environment and help the organization develop responses to those problems.

Fortunately, organizations are adaptive. When they allow for the two-way flow of resources and information between themselves and their environment, they can use that information for self-change. Many organizations also use such information as the basis for plans to change the environment. That is a much more difficult task.

Using the concepts of organizations and environments, we can begin to create theoretical statements about the relationship. For example, we might say: The more turbulent the environment, the more flexible the PR department needs to be. This gives us a way to explain and predict organizational behavior at a macro level.[1]

Situational Theory

It would be shortsighted to identify key publics and then ignore the rest of the environment. We also need to be alert to the possibility of a new public popping up in the environment—one that might help or challenge us. Grunig and Hunt propose what they call a situational theory of publics to explain how and when we might expect to see such a group.[2]

Grunig and Hunt say that an active public is one that seeks and processes information about an organization or an issue of interest to an organization. They describe three variables that predict when individuals will seek and process information about an issue.

The first is *problem recognition.* People who face an issue must first be aware of it and recognize its potential to affect them. *Constraint recognition* describes how individuals perceive obstacles that may stand in the way of a solution. If they believe they have a real shot at influencing the issue, they will tend to seek and process information on that issue. The third variable is *level of involvement,* which refers to how much an individual cares about an issue. Those who care a lot would likely be active communicators on an issue. Those who care little would likely be more passive in seeking information and processing it.

From these three variables Grunig and Hunt describe four responses that follow from being high or low in these dimensions. The responses range from fatalism (doing nothing) to problem-facing (taking direct action). Situational theory also helps explain why some groups are active on a single issue, others are active on many issues, and others are uniformly apathetic. The specific relationship is determined by the type of group and how an organization is linked with the issue.

Approaches to Conflict Resolution

If we start with the notion that conflict is just one of many states a relationship can take, we will be making a good start in understanding conflict and how to deal with it. All of us have a common-sense understanding of conflict. It involves an individual or group actively opposing another owing to differences in values or goals.

Some people take the view that conflict is a phenomenon to be avoided. If you operate from this point of view, you must be alert to potential conflicts and attempt to handle them before they become unpleasant. Others see conflict as a natural stage that some relationships pass through and, therefore, something to be managed.

What we know about resolving conflict exists largely as a list of techniques and skills that negotiators have found useful. Fisher and Ury suggest four things to keep in mind when trying to resolve conflict.[3]

    1. *Separate the people from the problem.* Try to start from a position of respect for those with whom you disagree. Remember, it is the goals and values that you disagree with, not the person holding the position. The next three steps suggest ways to do this.

2. *Focus on interests, not positions.*   It is normal for both sides to stake out positions and try to convince the other side of the wisdom in adopting their point of view. It is natural but not productive. Instead, try to move beyond positions to find out what the other side really wants. A position is just one expression of what someone wants, but they may be able to satisfy their goals in other ways. Until you explore the possibilities, you won't know.

3. *Invent options for mutual gain.*   You may know this as creative problem solving. The idea is to explore ways you can both meet your goals. Plan on generating lots of solutions before you reach an agreement. It sounds like an impossible task, but for many issues it just requires the will to move beyond the conflict in a way that respects the interests of both sides.

4. *Insist on objective criteria.*   Seek early agreement on what a fair solution would look like. Is there a standard or index on which you could base a solution? Finding one makes evaluating solutions easier.

Public relations practitioners skilled in conflict resolution often can use personal interaction to build trust and improve the communication environment.

These guidelines are not expressed as formal theory, but those who use them regularly would likely agree that using this framework increases the chances of resolving a conflict early, results in higher-quality solutions, and preserves the integrity of the relationship between those involved in the conflict. That is theory any practitioner can understand.

Theories of Cognition and Behavior

Public relations practitioners find it useful to think about effects—how products, services, and policies affect others. What we say and what we do are given meaning by others, and sometimes that meaning is not what we intended.

Typically, we talk about getting people to know something, or to do something. Cognitive theories deal with the knowing, and behavioral theories cover the doing. There are many more approaches to thinking, behavior, and communication than are discussed here. It is a good idea for public relations students to take courses in general psychology, cognitive psychology, communication theory, and persuasion.

Action Assembly Theory

All behavior is logical to the person behaving. If that is true, then before we can understand behavior, we have to understand how people think. That sounds like an incredibly hard task, and at one level it is, but communication scholar John O. Greene believes thinking can be explained at an abstract level by three constructs: structures, content, and processes.[4]

Cognitive structure defines the form of our thought. Some call this form a script, some call it a schema, others call it a frame. It's like a storyboard that defines how we expect a story to unfold. Over time we build up a set of expectations. These expectations affect what information we process and store.

Content refers to the specific characters, details, and plot twists within the basic structure.

Cognitive processes are the operations we use to take in, transform, and store information (the content).

That's all very abstract. How does that help us understand how people think? Let's look a little closer.

People are great observers. We see that certain actions result in predictable outcomes in similar situations. Over time we develop expectations about these relationships. In fact, the expectations become so strong that we may fail to notice when the details or outcomes vary from what we expect to see.

For example, if we are used to seeing clutter and useless information on bulletin boards, then our script says "don't bother to read bulletin boards because it is a waste of time." That script guides our behavior, and we ignore information on bulletin boards—even if the information on it would be useful. Consequently, when we communicate with our publics we must put our messages in places where people look for important information. Maybe, too, we ought to think about putting out only important information—as perceived by the people who read our messages. Newspaper reporters who receive several dull press releases a week from a source will likely miss the good one that finally comes along. They already associate that source with dull content and will likely throw away all messages from that source without ever reading them.

Another part of understanding cognitive structure is understanding how content is stored in the mind. We don't record all that passes our senses as if they were hooked to a flight data recorder. We abstract data, filtering information based on what we think is important or useful. We determine this by checking to see if the new information is similar to information we labeled "important" in the past.

Have you noticed that when your teacher says, "there are seven . . . ," everybody begins writing? Students know from experience that lists are typically important at test time. The key is to decide whether you want to tap into your public's existing memory structures or try to establish and reinforce entirely new cognitive structures.

When 7-Up decided to position itself as the "uncola," it was taking advantage of our pre-existing beliefs about and responses to cola beverages. The uncola could be enjoyed in all the same settings as a cola; it would just look and taste different.

Oldsmobile recently tried to tell youthful car buyers that "It's not your dad's Oldsmobile." Here they tried to break the script that the Olds is a sensible family car—and boring!

Social exchange theory uses the economic metaphor of costs and benefits to predict behavior. It assumes that individuals and groups choose strategies based on perceived rewards and costs. This theory, developed by John Thibaut and Harold Kelley, has been used at many levels, including interpersonal, small-group, and organizational levels.[5]

Social Exchange Theory

Social exchange theory asserts that people factor in the consequences of their behavior before acting. In general, people want to keep their costs low and their rewards high. Get-rich-quick schemes have been using this principle for a long time.

But what does this have to do with public relations? Let's say we want people to respond to a survey. Remember, we want to keep costs to potential respondents low and perceived rewards high. What can we do to keep costs low?

Keep the instructions simple.

Keep the survey short.

If mailing is required, provide a post-paid return envelope.

If returning by fax, use an 800 number.

Avoid open-ended, complex, and personal questions.

Now, how can I increase the rewards for the respondent?

Make the survey interesting.

Emphasize that the person is being "consulted" for his or her thoughts and that his or her ideas are important.

Tell them how the results will be used—presumably to contribute to something worthwhile.

Offer an opportunity for a tangible reward, for example, a copy of the results or a chance to win something of value.

This same logic can be applied to more complex behavior by using a payoff matrix. Let's say our company, United Fratchworks, becomes aware of a defect in a batch of screws that has already shipped to its aerospace customers. The defect puts them outside acceptable contract specifications for hardness.

Figure 3.2 Pay-off matrix showing costs and rewards involved in a recall decision

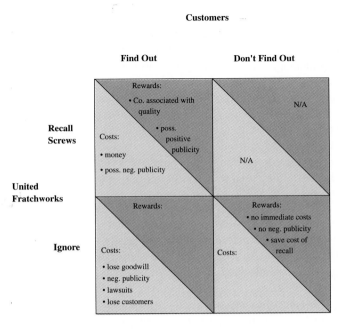

We can look at this situation as a set of possible decisions, with each decision having costs and rewards. In figure 3.2 the upper part of each cell contains perceived rewards and the lower part, possible costs. Some of the consequences, like recall costs, are certain. Others, like the possibility of lawsuits and negative publicity, have some probability associated with them.

Now, if the head of United Fratchworks could see the decision in this way, the company would recall the screws and accept the short-term loss. The trouble is, human nature can blind us to the information in the cells associated with customers finding out. Some people would bet they could get away with ignoring the problem. Have you ever done something at home or at school and immediately looked for ways to keep your parents from finding out? The PR practitioner's job is to let the decision maker see a whole range of options along with the associated costs and rewards.

Diffusion Theory

Diffusion theory is another way to look at how people process and accept information. Diffusion theory says that people adopt an idea only after going through the following five discrete steps (or stages):

1. *Awareness.* The individual has to have been exposed to the idea.

2. *Interest.* The idea has to arouse the individual.

3. *Evaluation.* The individual must have considered the idea as potentially useful.

4. *Trial.* The individual tries out the idea on others.

5. *Adoption.* This represents final acceptance of the idea after having successfully passed through the four earlier stages.[6]

This theory is useful for explaining how we reach important decisions—not acts of impulse. We know from testing this model that mass media are important in the first two stages; personal contacts are important for the next two.

Let's take an example. United Fratchworks's annual family picnic is two weeks away. You are selling tickets at $1 per family as a way to plan how much food to order. Ticket sales have been slow. You tell the boss at the morning staff meeting. If your boss is typical, he or she will say "Make sure every employee gets a flyer."

Sending out more flyers virtually guarantees awareness, but you are still three steps away from getting people to decide to go (adoption). By knowing how people accept and process information, you can plan systematically to move the employees through the remaining stages. To do this you will need lots of people at the shop level to talk to their fellow workers. Think about what precinct organizers mean to a political campaign.

We will return to the diffusion theory again in chapter 8.

Social Learning Theory

So far, we have discussed theories that consider the receiver to be actively involved in information processing. Social learning theory attempts to explain and predict behavior by looking at another way individuals process information. This theory helps us understand that personal example and mass media can be important in acquiring new behaviors.

Social psychologist Albert Bandura says that we can learn new behaviors merely by observing others.[7] When we see behavior that interests us, we note whether that behavior seems to be rewarding to the actor. These rewards can be external, as in praise, or internal, as in "it looks cool." Bandura says that we vicariously try out the behavior in our minds. If we agree that the behavior is potentially useful to us, it can lie dormant for long periods until we need it. The likelihood that a specific behavior will occur is determined by the expected consequences from performing that behavior. The more positive and rewarding the consequences, the more likely the behavior will occur.

Knowing this, public relations people shouldn't be surprised when employees model the inappropriate behavior of more experienced employees, particularly if that behavior is rewarded. If chronic complaining keeps someone from having to work a double shift or a weekend, you can bet others will copy this tactic. If a company promotes people who are cold and rigid, you can predict that those wanting to get ahead will model those same behaviors. If company publications run pictures that show people violating safety procedures or breaking company rules, readers of those publications are not likely to take those policies seriously.

Remember: You get the behavior you reward. Social learning theory explains one of the routes to this behavior.

Elaborated Likelihood Model

The notion of "routes" is central to a theory that describes two ways that people are influenced. Richard Petty and John Cacioppo describe the first route as the "central route"—the situation in which people actively think about an idea.[8] Relying on this route presumes people are interested in your message, have the time to attend to your arguments, and can evaluate your evidence with an open mind. This is how public relations people usually attempt to influence attitudes and behavior.

But, what if the target group is not interested, is too busy, or just can't understand the issues? How do you proceed?

The elaborated likelihood model proposes a "peripheral route" in which people are influenced by such things as repetition, a highly credible spokesperson, or even tangible rewards. Advertising people frequently use this route when designing their messages.

Candidates for local office can't engage all the voters in a discussion of the issues, so they take the peripheral route and blanket the town with yard signs. Message repetition provides familiarity with the candidate's name, and sign location suggests that many of your neighbors actively support that candidate. People who are not politically active don't have to think about the issues; they just vote for the obvious popular choice.

When long-distance phone companies claim they can save you money on plans that are not easily compared, it becomes difficult to make an informed decision. That's when the credibility of the spokesperson may be the deciding factor on which plan you select.

Today, rewards can involve valuable premiums, such as those offered for opening a bank account or donating money to your favorite charity when you use a certain credit card.

Theories of Mass Communication

Uses and Gratifications

It's important to recognize that people do not uniformly read the daily paper, watch the 6 o'clock news, or listen to talk radio as a mass audience. While papers, TV, and radio are called mass media, it is the individual person that determines how and when media are used.

Similarly, you shouldn't presume that employees uniformly read internal publications or view company videos. Even a note in every pay packet, could go straight from the pay envelope to the wastebasket.

What explains this behavior? Uses and gratifications theory asserts that people are active users of media and selective in the media they use.[9] Researchers have found that people use media in the following ways:

as entertainment,

to scan the environment for items important to them personally,

as a diversion (as when the TV is on and no one is in the room),

as a substitute for personal relationships, and

as a check on our personal identity and values.

For public relations people this means that not everyone will see or hear the bad news about a company or product. It also means you can't count on people seeing or hearing the good news. Just because a message is available in some medium does not mean that people attend to it and remember it.

We know from the O. J. Simpson trial that the media can focus attention on an event. The question is: Can it also convince us of such things as guilt or innocence?

In spite of a constant barrage from news analysts, Jay Leno, and *Saturday Night Live,* polls showed that throughout the O. J. Simpson trial those who initially believed him guilty maintained that belief, and those who believed him innocent were equally steadfast. How can we explain this?

Bernard Cohen noted that although the media can't tell people what to think, they are stunningly successful in telling them what to think about.[10] It was an interesting idea but not widely accepted in 1963. About a decade later journalism scholars Maxwell McCombs and Donald Shaw demonstrated Cohen was onto something.[11] During the 1968 presidential campaign, they followed public opinion and media reports of the key issues in Chapel Hill, North Carolina. They found that there was a strong positive relationship between what voters said was important and what media were reporting as important. Since the issues were evident in the media several weeks before they appeared in public opinion, McCombs and Shaw were reasonably sure media set the agenda and not the reverse. What was more amazing was that voters were more likely to agree with the composite media agenda than with the position of the candidate they claimed they favored.

McCombs and Shaw do not say that simple agreement with the media changed voting behavior. What they demonstrated was that the media can set the agenda for what we talk and think about.

Following Jim Grunig's and Todd Hunt's suggestion, this talking and thinking could lead to information seeking and processing, but only if other conditions are met. That's an important point for public relations people to remember when their organization is taking a beating in the press. People may be talking about you, but it doesn't necessarily mean that strong opinions about your organization will be changed. You will need to do some research before you can draw a conclusion.

More typically, public relations people attempt to influence the media agenda by providing news items for public consumption.[12] To accomplish this, they identify subjects editors and news directors consider news, localize their messages, and help media representatives cover the story.

Agenda Setting Theory

If you were to visit the public relations department of a large organization you would see a lot of activity. Some individuals would be on the phone. Others would be writing. A few would be working at computers. You would miss seeing some because they would be working away from the office. What you see are activities—things people do.

At another level we can describe their roles.[13] Roles define a collection of activities people regularly do. Glen Broom and David Dozier use public relations roles to describe and predict such things as the relative power of the public relations unit, public relations participation in strategic decision making, salaries, and job satisfaction.[14]

They see two broad roles in public relations: technician and manager. The technician is the writer, the layout person, the photographer. This is the journalist-

Useful Typologies in Understanding Public Relations

Practitioners' Roles

Theories Used in Public
Relations

Public Relations Spotlight 3.1

The 10 theories highlighted in the chapter are summarized as follows:

I.   Theories of Relationships
   1. *Systems theory*—evaluates relationships and structure as they relate to the whole.
   2. *Situational theory*—situations define relationships.
   3. *Approaches to conflict resolution*—include separating people from the problem; focusing on interests, not positions; inventing options for mutual gain; and insisting on objective criteria.
II. Theories of Cognition and Behavior
   4. *Action assembly theory*—understanding behavior by understanding how people think.
   5. *Social exchange theory*—predicting behavior of groups and individuals based on perceived rewards and costs.
   6. *Diffusion theory*—people adopt an important idea or innovation after going through five discrete steps: awareness, interest, evaluation, trial, and adoption.
   7. *Social learning theory*—people use information processing to explain and predict behavior.
   8. *Elaborated likelihood model*—suggests decision making is influenced through repetition, rewards, and credible spokespersons.
III. Theories of Mass Communication
   9. *Uses and gratification*—people are active users of media and select media based on its gratification for them.
   10. *Agenda setting theory*—suggests that media content that people read, see, and listen to set the agenda for society's discussion and interaction.

in-residence, the person who has a nose for news and works with media outlets to get the story out. Technicians carry out the broad plans of managers.

Public relations managers are problem solvers and advisors to senior management. They are responsible for broad program results. Broom and Dozier identify three manager roles:

expert prescriber operates as a consultant to define the problem, suggest options, and oversee implementation.

problem-solver process facilitator partners with senior management to identify problems and solve problems.

communication facilitator the person on the periphery between the organization and its environment who keeps two-way communication flowing.

Public relations managers tend to adopt all three roles when functioning in their organizations. Much depends on the style of the practitioner, the expectations of senior management, and the type of issues faced.

Just as individuals have roles, so can whole departments. Jim Grunig has given us four roles or models that public relations departments can assume while carrying out their collective duties.[15]

Press agentry describes the model where information moves one-way from the organization to its publics. It is, perhaps, the oldest form of public relations and is synonymous with promotions and publicity. Public relations people operating under this model are constantly looking for opportunities to get their organization's name favorably mentioned in the media.

Public information differs from press agentry because the intent is to inform rather than to press for sales, but communication is still essentially one-way. Today, this model is practiced in government and educational organizations, nonprofit organizations, trade and member associations, and even in some corporations. Practitioners operating under this model respond to queries from their various publics and become proactive when they believe their publics need to know something important.

The third model, the *two-way asymmetric* model, is best described as scientific persuasion. The two-way asymmetric model employs social-science methods to increase the persuasiveness of its messages. Public relations practitioners use polls, interviews, and focus groups to measure public attitudes so the organization can design public relations programs that gain the support of key publics. Although feedback is built into the process, the organization is much more interested in having the publics adjust to the organization rather than the reverse. This model of public relations applies to most goods-producing businesses where public relations programs are geared to short-term attitude change.

Finally, the *two-way symmetric* model represents a public relations orientation in which organizations and their publics adjust to each other. It focuses on mutual understanding and two-way communication rather than one-way persuasion. The two-way model is used often in regulated businesses like public utilities that strive to build long-term relationships with their publics. Practitioners operating under this model are as likely to suggest internal changes as to recommend repairing something in the environment.

In 1990 a group of public relations scholars completed a five-year study, underwritten by the International Association of Business Communicators (IABC), of excellent public relations departments. Not surprisingly, the two-way symmetric model emerged as the distinguishing feature of excellent programs. Thus, Grunig and Grunig considered the two-way model both a normative one expressing how public relations work should be conducted and a positive one explaining things as they are.[16]

Grunig's Model of Public Relations

Summary

Obviously, there is a lot to learn about human nature, organizations, and the practice of public relations. The approaches noted here are presented to get you thinking about theory and the implied relationship among variables.

As you can see, theory operates on many levels: between individuals, groups, and organizations. You will need to be able to conceptualize issues at each of these levels to be successful. The theories you use in public relations are your tools. Keep them handy and learn to use them well.

Communication Stages
in a PR Campaign

By James VanLeuven
Professor and Chairman
Department of Technical
Journalism
Colorado State University
Fort Collins, Colorado

Case Study

T he following case study serves as a conceptual illustration of how we might go about systematically influencing individuals and groups on an issue. More importantly, the case outlined in figure 3.3 spells out the types of public relations decision making and programming taking place when public relations campaigns are broken down into communication stages.[17]

Recall from the earlier discussion of systems theory that organizations try to maintain balanced relationships with their various publics, but that not all publics are treated equally because some create greater obstacles for organizations and vice versa. Thus, publics or audiences form at different stages as issues develop and the public relations practitioner must learn how to respond appropriately to each group at each stage. The key notion to grasp from this case is that the changing nature of the publics attending to a developing public issue shapes the way public relations practitioners operate and respond on behalf of their organizations.

Four types of publics are likely to emerge over the course of an issue's development. (See chapter 6 for further discussions of publics and public opinion.) At one extreme are active publics who get involved early because they make a practice of understanding issue dimensions and the issue's relevance to them, and because they perceive no barriers precluding active engagement.

Next are the aware-but-not-yet-active publics to whom public relations practitioners are quick to peg publicity and information campaigns. Latent publics become associated with an issue somewhat later as they see a connection between the issue and their established interests, social relationships, and values. Inactive publics (i.e., most people) are not likely to become aware of an issue until it's almost impossible to ignore.

The media coverage or center column of the figure shows how media adapt their coverage to the dominant publics at each communication stage of the process. Public relations practitioners use the mass media, but they also communicate directly with publics through speeches, newsletters, position papers, and so on. Thus, practitioners direct their efforts to different publics according to their changing assessments of the publics' relative importance. Stated theoretically, public relations practitioners match the intensity of the programming to the capabilities of different publics for achieving different levels of communication and behavioral effect.

Let's consider the five stages in the context of trying to pass the local school bond issue.

1. *Awareness Stage.* Plans for the school bond issue typically are confined for some time within the school board and perhaps a citizens' group before the issue moves onto the public stage when the school district's public relations practitioner announces the drive in the form of news tips to reporters, news releases, press conferences, a special rally in front of the

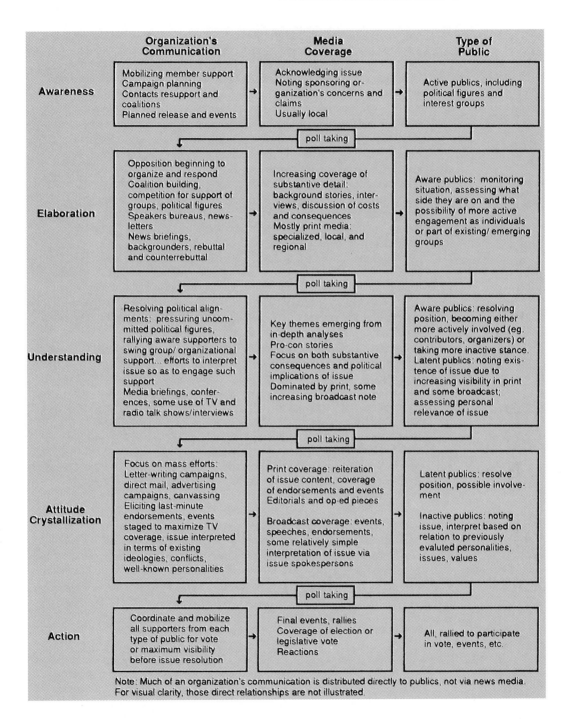

	Organization's Communication	Media Coverage	Type of Public
Awareness	Mobilizing member support Campaign planning Contacts resupport and coalitions Planned release and events	Acknowledging issue Noting sponsoring organization's concerns and claims Usually local	Active publics, including political figures and interest groups
		poll taking	
Elaboration	Opposition beginning to organize and respond Coalition building, competition for support of groups, political figures Speakers bureaus, newsletters News briefings, backgrounders, rebuttal and counterrebuttal	Increasing coverage of substantive detail: background stories, interviews, discussion of costs and consequences Mostly print media: specialized, local, and regional	Aware publics: monitoring situation, assessing what side they are on and the possibility of more active engagement as individuals or part of existing/emerging groups
		poll taking	
Understanding	Resolving political alignments: pressuring uncommitted political figures, rallying aware supporters to swing group/organizational support... efforts to interpret issue so as to engage such support Media briefings, conferences, some use of TV and radio talk shows/interviews	Key themes emerging from in-depth analyses Pro-con stories Focus on both substantive consequences and political implications of issue Dominated by print, some increasing broadcast note	Aware publics: resolving position, becoming either more actively involved (eg. contributors, organizers) or taking more inactive stance. Latent publics: noting existence of issue due to increasing visibility in print and some broadcast; assessing personal relevance of issue
		poll taking	
Attitude Crystallization	Focus on mass efforts: Letter-writing campaigns, direct mail, advertising campaigns, canvassing Eliciting last-minute endorsements, events staged to maximize TV coverage, issue interpreted in terms of existing ideologies, conflicts, well-known personalities	Print coverage: reiteration of issue content, coverage of endorsements and events Editorials and op-ed pieces Broadcast coverage: events, speeches, endorsements, some relatively simple interpretation of issue via issue spokespersons	Latent publics: resolve position, possible involvement Inactive publics: noting issue, interpret based on relation to previously evaluted personalities, issues, values
		poll taking	
Action	Coordinate and mobilize all supporters from each type of public for vote or maximum visibility before issue resolution	Final events, rallies Coverage of election or legislative vote Reactions	All, rallied to participate in vote, events, etc.

Note: Much of an organization's communication is distributed directly to publics, not via news media. For visual clarity, those direct relationships are not illustrated.

Figure 3.3 The emergence of public opinion roles of organizations, media, and publics

crumbling high school building, or perhaps from a newsletter distributed to teachers. As the initial announcements reach the public, the school district's goal is to get the issue on the media agenda, and in so doing, to assess how the issue is perceived. At the same time, the public relations practitioners assess how the media interpreted their presentation. From the public relations standpoint, the most important publics are the active ones who already see the connection of the issue to their collective interests.

2. *Elaboration (or knowledge gain) Stage.* The issue and its implications are developed more fully during the elaboration stage as the bond issue's impacts on children and taxes are learned. The school district's public relations programming—whether done by the district or through a citizen committee—gears up with position papers, a speaker's bureau, and mailings to targeted groups. Stories are planned with various community media along with story placement in newsletters and other in-house publications of key interest groups.

     For the most part, the elaboration stage of the communication process relies on newspaper and specialized publication coverage along with direct mailings, and these are directed to members of active publics (school booster groups, PTA's) as well as to aware publics (teachers, chamber of commerce members) who gather more information about the issue and its implications for group action.

3. *Understanding Stage.* The issue's political, social, and economic ramifications get synthesized, condensed, and integrated at the understanding stage. Then, as issues are cast as two-sided contests, members of groups begin to take collective stands, and, in turn, align themselves with other groups to form more organized publics. A group of residents in a neighborhood whose school will be closed decide to pool their time and resources with an anti-tax group to defeat the measure.

     At this time, the focus of media attention advances beyond reporting opposing views toward defining the consequences of the emergent issue. School public relations specialists, loaned PR executives, or agency practitioners hired for the campaign organize editorial conferences with the local media. Moreover, public relations efforts begin to target the more latent publics with television talk show appearances and drive-time radio interviews. Practitioners organize their publics at the local level.

     Latent publics become a primary audience at this stage along with active and aware ones. The latent publics, such as adults without school-age children, may start to recognize the issue due to increased media prominence, mention in the church bulletin, or discussion during volleyball practice. As a result, members of latent publics may adjust their individual stances in line with those of organizations and groups to which they belong.

4. *Attitude Crystallization Stage.* The complexion of the process changes considerably now that the primary participants have emerged, and their interests, implications, and consequences have been clarified. Attention from the public relations practitioners shifts to a much broader set of relatively passive, uncommitted voters and audience members. The emerging community involvement around the issue makes it easier for television to cover. Public relations practitioners and the citizens' group buy

full-page endorsement ads in the local paper, orchestrate rallies, letter-writing campaigns, media events, and other activities. Issue polarization prompts the print media to declare their stands and hence more time and space goes to editorials, op-ed pieces, letters to the editor, and guest columns.

5. *Action Stage.*   Because there's so little time before the election to correct misunderstandings, public relations practitioners employ all of their talents to maintain constant liaison with key publics. Sometimes they motivate desired behavior by arranging rides to the polls or providing sample ballots.

In summary, this model breaks down a campaign into more or less discrete communication phases in order to show how public relations practices change as issues emerge and new publics come into play.

Questions

1. Briefly describe how the two-way symmetric model might be working at each stage of this campaign.
2. How is agenda-setting theory used in this campaign?
3. What parallels do you see between diffusion theory and the model presented in figure 3.3?

Notes

1. For more theoretical statements useful to PR practitioners, see James D. Thompson, *Organizations in Action* (New York: McGraw-Hill, 1976), 70–72, 89.

2. James E. Grunig and Todd Hunt, *Managing Public Relations* (New York: Holt, Rinehart, Winston, 1984).

3. Roger Fisher and William Ury, *Getting to Yes: Negotiating Agreement Without Giving In* (Boston: Houghton Mifflin, 1981).

4. John O. Greene, "A Cognitive Approach to Human Communication: An Action Assembly Theory," *Communication Monographs* vol. 51 (1984): 289–306.

5. John W. Thibaut and Harold H. Kelley, *The Social Psychology of Groups* (New York: John Wiley and Sons, 1959).

6. Herbert F. Lionberger, *Adoption of New Ideas and Practices* (Ames: Iowa State University Press, 1960), 32.

7. Albert Bandura, *Social Learning Theory* (Englewood Cliffs, N.J.: Prentice-Hall, 1977).

8. Richard E. Petty and John T. Cacioppo, *Communication and Persuasion: Central and Peripheral Routes to Attitude Change* (New York: Springer-Verlag, 1986).

9. Elihu Katz, Jay G. Blumler and Michael Gurevitch, "Utilization of Mass Communication by the Individual," in eds. J. G. Blumler and E. Katz, *The Uses of Mass Communications: Current Perspectives on Gratifications Research* (Beverly Hills, Calif.: Sage, 1974), 19–32.

10. Bernard C. Cohen, *The Press and Foreign Policy* (Princeton, N.J.: Princeton University Press, 1963).

11. Donald E. Shaw and Maxwell E. McCombs, *The Emergence of American Political Issues: The Agenda Setting Function of the Press* (St. Paul, Minn.: West, 1977).

12. Judy V. Turk, "Information Subsidies and Influence," *Public Relations Review* vol. 11, no. 3 (1985): 10–25.

13. David M. Dozier, "The Organization of Roles of Communications and Public Relations Practices," in J. E. Grunig, ed. *Excellence in Public Relations and Communication Management* (Hillsdale, N.J.: Lawrence Erlbaum, 1992), 327–356.

14. David M. Dozier and Glen M. Broom, "Evolution of the Manager Role in Public Relations Practice," *Journal of Public Relations Research* vol. 29 (1995): 3–16.

15. Grunig and Hunt, *Managing Public Relations.*

16. James E. Grunig, *Excellence in Public Relations and Communication Management* (Hillsdale, N.J.: Lawrence Erlbaum, 1992).

17. James K. Van Leuven and Michael Slater, "How Publics, Public Relations, and the Media Shape the Public Opinion Process," *Public Relations Research Annual* 3 (Hillsdale, N.J.: Lawrence Erlbaum, Spring 1991): 165–178.

CHAPTER 4

Public Relations in Organizational Decision Making

Preview

To play a serious role in organizational decision making, public relations practitioners must: gain management support and understanding; be more than technicians by broadening their knowledge, interests, and perspectives; learn to think like managers while retaining an independent perspective; and become issue-oriented.

Issues management is a process by which organizations can have a voice in influencing public policy. It is also a way by which public relations staffers can play a more effective role in their organizations' decisions.

The opinion of the public is a judgment which the honest man should never entirely accept and which he should never reject.

—Nicholas Chamfort

T hroughout this book, we stress that the contribution of public relations to organizational decision making is among its most important functions. We do not claim that public relations practitioners actually make the decisions that determine organizational purpose, direction, coordination, and control. We do maintain, however, that all managers can and should take public relations considerations into account when making decisions, and that public relations practitioners can and should make direct contributions to fundamental organizational decisions. Lawrence Foster, former vice-president of public relations for Johnson and Johnson, believes, "The public relations factor can help influence important business decisions." Foster also suggests that "to gain management's confidence public relations professionals must lead instead of follow. Be ready with an analysis of the public relations problems being faced, and offer solutions . . . don't wait for the roof to cave in."[1] Executives who are sensitive to public relations considerations are "public relations-minded," a valuable perspective in today's complex environment.

In future chapters, we will discuss how the contributions of public relations to organizational decision making affect employee relations, local community opinion, financial activities, and dealings with the government. By active participation in managerial decision making, public relations people can gain the commitment and understanding necessary for effective communication.

In a sense, this chapter is a pivotal one in the book. It deals with decision making, which is the essence of the managerial process, and with the position of public relations in that process. The chapter explains the role and function of public relations in organizational decision making. It discusses the nature of public relations inputs and the constraints on those inputs. It tells how public relations can be most influential in organizational decision making.

Staff and Line: Where Public Relations Fits in Decision Making

The most common type of organizational structure is called **line organization.** In its most basic form, line organization can be thought of as a sequence of ascending levels of responsibility connected by direct vertical links. All functions and activities are directly involved in producing goods or services. Line structures can be found in churches, charities, museums, not-for-profit clinics, and business organizations.

As line organizations grow in size, however, various specialists are added, creating a line and staff organization. These **staff** functions provide advice and support to line management and are designed to contribute to the efficiency and maintenance of the organization. Staff functions might include research and development, personnel management and training, accounting, legal services, and public relations.

As a staff function, public relations must support management. The entire reason for the existence of public relations is to help create an environment of public opinion in which management can function. It provides counsel that management may ignore or consider, follow or reject. Part of being an effective adviser, however, is taking actions to assure that your advice is heard, heeded, and frequently acted on. In this way, public relations makes its contribution to organizational objectives and prosperity and earns management's support. Bob Thompson, public relations director of Spring Mills, Inc., points to the bottom line: "In the end, public relations in an organization is what top management says it is."[2]

Corporations are seeking to increase efficiency by cutting staff. This trend affects planners, economists, marketers, human-resources specialists, and others who provide executives with advice and counsel. Recent government figures show that more than nine million workers lost their jobs between 1991 and 1993. The *Fortune* 500 companies reduced their workforce by about four million workers in the 10-year period ending in 1992.[3] A report on the third quarter of 1995 by the *Daily Labor Report* found layoffs up 43 percent. Lockheed Martin Corporation recently laid off 15,000; General Motors laid off 5,000; and MCI 3,000.[4] Downsizing is increasingly becoming a way of life in corporate America. As it does, public relations advice becomes even more necessary.

> ### The Importance of Public Relations in Organizational Decision Making

Edward Gubman of Hewitt Associates notes this trend is "unlikely to change."

> Employers are not shedding jobs today because of a recession or slow economic growth. They are doing so because technology and global cost pressures are changing the way people work—requiring fewer people to do far more work than ever before . . . Pacific Bell, for example, served twice as many customers with half the employees in 1994 as it did in 1984 when the AT&T Bell system was broken up.[5]

The current need for public relations to become more thoroughly integrated into the organizational decision-making process cannot be questioned. Indeed, public relations is increasingly the responsibility of executives rather than the province of public relations staffers. Government agencies at all levels retrench in the face of new fiscal limitations. Hospitals struggle with regulations, rising costs, new technologies, and changing customer demands. Arts organizations seek new sources of funds as Congress plans to reduce or withdraw government support. Businesses deal with global competition, economic conditions, and a skeptical public. Successful managers in today's environments are those who maintain "a high batting average in accurately assessing the forces that determine the most appropriate behavior at any given time . . . and in actually being able to behave accordingly."[6] The contributions of a public relations specialist often enable managers to assess such forces accurately.

Even the initiation of organizational decision making can depend on public relations input. "The organizational decision-making process is activated when information is received indicating changes in an organization's internal or external environment calling for an organizational response."[7] Information gathered by the public relations staff can promote the organization's ability to adapt to changing political, social, economic, and cultural conditions. "Public relations should occupy one of the most strategic positions in the organizational structure," James N. Sites explains, "if for no other reason than that it sits squarely astride the communication channels that are absolutely vital to the effective operation of an organization."[8]

Chief executive officers of major corporations are well aware that public relations contributes to decision making. Sir Gordon White, who as chairman of Hanson Industries made a career of buying companies and eliminating their corporate staffs, had a staff of only 12—but it included a public relations officer.[9]

To blend public relations goals with organizational goals, public relations information must be part-and-parcel of the organizational decision-making process and must include intelligence regarding likely reaction and response by relevant publics. Moreover, the commitment and understanding that come through participating in organizational decision making are invaluable assets when communicating decisions to the organization's publics. Perhaps the most important task of public relations is to ensure the public relations–mindedness of management officials so that public relations considerations are in the mainstream of managerial decision making.

Entering the Management Mainstream

Acknowledging the importance of public relations in organizational decision making is one thing. Ensuring that public relations is part of the management mainstream is quite another.[10] To make public relations an effective part of an organization's decision-making process and to be taken seriously in a decision-making role, the public relations practitioner must observe the following five interrelated steps:

1. Gain management support and understanding.

2. Be more than a technician.

3. Broaden personal knowledge, interests, and perspectives.

4. Learn to think like a manager while retaining an independent perspective.

5. Become issue-oriented.

Gaining Management Support

"Early in his career every public relations practitioner finds to his surprise—and often distress—that he must . . . communicate . . . with those key centers of influence and power within his own organization."[11] Management is one of the key publics for public relations. Like that of any other public, the support of management must be earned. Like those of any other audience, management's needs, wants, attitudes, values, and perceptions must be considered. "Public relations counselors should be involved in all top management decisions, including mergers, acquisitions and downsizing," according to J. Handley Wright, retired vice-president for the American Association of Railroads.[12]

The public relations function cannot be taken as a given by those who practice it, for management generally does not view the communications function in that light. Traditionally, public relations has been first on the budgetary chopping block, precisely because management has not perceived it as essential to long-term organizational health. Only in the recession in the early 1980s did this tendency begin to fade. Tom Ruddell, former president of the International Association of Business Communicators (IABC), explained, "In past recessions public

Management is a key public for the public relations professional. Management must be sold on public relations plans before they are implemented.

relations and communication departments were too often the first to suffer from staff and budget cuts. This time management seems to be getting the message that communication is a necessity, not a luxury."[13]

Unfortunately, as organizations worked hard to reduce costs and get "lean and mean" in the late 1980s and 1990s, public relations staffing was affected. With many major businesses merging to produce more efficient operations, some found that one larger business required fewer public relations personnel than two smaller ones. Some public relations activities, like production of annual reports, were "outsourced." In other words, public relations staffs were reduced by turning certain tasks over to outside specialists.

Like all other staff specialists within organizations, public relations practitioners must be prepared to explain and justify their existence to managers and to convince them that public relations "is an investment in the privilege to operate . . . perhaps more an investment in the future than an operating expenditure for the present."[14] Most important, public relations can influence organizational action by demonstrating the ability to produce results in accordance with the organization's goals. An example of this ability is shown in mini-case 4.1.

Many communicators regard themselves as communicators first, last, and always. They think of their relationship to management in terms of "Tell me what you want to say and I'll tell you how to say it." Communication skills are essential to effective public relations. An attitude like that just described, though, simply encourages management to think of public relations as a tool with which to implement policy rather than as a crucial part of the policy-making process.

Whether holding the title "staff writer," "editor," "speechwriter," or "audiovisual specialist," a public relations practitioner must learn to think of the role as

Being More Than a Technician

Mini-Case 4.1

Communication Improves Silicon Wafer Quality at Monsanto

Monsanto Company's electronics division held a comfortable leadership role in the production of silicon wafers for many years. Suddenly, the company was being challenged by aggressive Japanese and German manufacturers who said their products offered superior quality.

Silicon wafers are used by producers of electronic chips for computers, video games, and digital watches. The manufacturing process is very labor-intensive, and quality control is critical. The product can be rejected for as little as a stray fingerprint or a speck of dust.

The problem was defined: How can Monsanto Electronics achieve and maintain the highest possible quality level? The answer: Develop in the employees, who are scattered in widely separated geographic areas, a single-minded dedication to a consistently high level of quality.

The challenge of achieving that goal was turned over to John Mason, Monsanto's corporate communications director. Mason explains:

> Our department at Monsanto tries to avoid concentrating on the traditional aspects of communications—such as the production of magazines, newsletters and videotapes. We use them but don't stress them. Instead, we offer ourselves to various divisions and departments as internal corporate communications consultants. The traditional approach is to say communications can increase employee involvement, thus leading to productivity gains. We say communications can help produce a product superior to that of the competition.

In response to the need for quality improvement in silicon wafer production, Monsanto's corporate communications department developed a communications program to be used with groups and one-on-one. Video, print, feedback, and recognition methods were employed. Mason insisted on two provisions: that the communications department be held accountable for measurable results and that once started, the program be turned over to the electronics division, freeing communications for new projects.

After its first year, the silicon wafer communications project reduced late shipments from 3 percent to 2½ percent. Moreover, the company saved $200,000 in reworks and penalties.

Mason concludes: "I am convinced that we can use communications to produce business results. However, you must look for opportunities to inject yourself into a business decision—don't wait around to be asked."

Source: Based on "Communicating for Bottom Line Results," a talk delivered by John Mason, Monsanto's corporate communications director, at the International Association of Business Communicators International Conference, Atlanta, Georgia.

more than that of a technician and the job as more than that of a communication medium. A writer writes, but a public relations practitioner helps solve problems. An editor reacts to management requests, but a public relations practitioner helps diagnose problems and opportunities while planning solutions and strategies. Writers and editors are typically concerned with the content and techniques of communication; public relations practitioners are concerned with the results. As one public relations professional put it, "Be an architect, not a bricklayer."

The two differing perspectives will lead individuals working in public relations jobs to ask different questions in the performance of their duties, to seek different insights, and ultimately, to offer different kinds of programs and solutions. One reacts, the other anticipates. One responds to decisions after they are made, the other is an essential part of decision making.

Communication consultant Ron Weiser tells of an incident that illustrates this distinction. Early in his career, when he was an editor at a factory in Pennsylvania, Weiser was told to communicate a change in safety policy to plant employees. Everyone in the plant would have to wear safety glasses at all times and in all locations. Instead of simply writing a memo to announce the change, Weiser started asking questions. Why everyone? Why everywhere? How was the policy decided? What prompted the change? What was management's objective? The answers he received demonstrated clearly that management had not really thought the policy through—that the main consideration was ease in administering the rule.

Management then decided to rethink the policy and invited Weiser to help out. The newly formulated policy required safety glasses in areas of the plant where specific hazards justified the requirement. Instead of a memo, a six-week, multimedia program introduced the change. The policy was implemented smoothly, and Weiser gained the respect of management and was allowed to take part in future decisions.

Being more than a technician earns the public relations practitioner management's respect. According to management consultant R. Edward Freeman, the communicator who sticks with traditional tools is in potential jeopardy. "Armed with the traditional weapons of the vitriolic press release, the annual report, a slick videotape, corporate philanthropy, etc., today's PR manager is a sacrificial lamb."[15]

Broadening Knowledge

To be valuable to management in a decision-making role, the public relations practitioner must have the appropriate knowledge, background, interests, and perspectives. Public relations practitioners, no matter what their training or background, must learn everything they can about business and government in general; the specific industry (or areas) in which their corporation (or agency) operates; and the organization itself. To be successful, public relations practitioners should know the functions, viewpoints, and problems of all parts of the organization. They should know its products, markets, internal structures, and external social, economic, and political pressures. New York public relations counselor Chester Burger says it this way:

> A deep and broad knowledge of the business in which we are employed remains an essential requirement for any public relations professional. We simply can't get by with public relations expertise alone. We need to inform ourselves about every aspect of our companies and organization: their history, their economics, their technology, their markets.[16]

More than any other executive except the chief executive officer, public relations people must understand what is going on inside the organization and how all activities and functions interrelate. They must do their homework and know the why, who, what, where, when, and how of whatever comes up for managerial consideration. They should also be prepared to present and evaluate a variety of alternatives and contingencies related to organizational problems and opportunities.

Increasingly, practitioners must learn about disciplines that would have seemed unrelated to public relations a few years ago. Required reading may include anything from archaeology to zoology. Drawing on such knowledge, the public relations practitioner is in a position to contribute creative ideas and sound judgment in clarifying and accomplishing organizational objectives.

Thinking Like a Manager

To influence management, public relations practitioners must learn to understand the managerial point of view, realizing at the same time that the greatest asset for public relations in decision making is its access to viewpoints not traditionally included in managerial deliberations. In other words, the public relations practitioner must think in terms of results, accountability, and accomplishments necessary to achieve organizational objectives while retaining a broader perspective that considers social as well as economic variables.

A results-oriented perspective is particularly important in competitive organizations that have moved away from the classic pyramid management style. Those who "advise, counsel or coordinate" are seen as less and less crucial. Those who demonstrably contribute to organizational success retain their positions and gain power and rewards.[17] Many corporations now let operating managers decide what corporate services to pay for out of their own budgets. If the corporate public relations staff fails to convince line managers that its services are valuable, it will fail to attract the resources to keep it operating.[18]

Former *Fortune* editor Max Ways points to what he calls the "danger inherent in any kind of concentrated framework of decision." He explains:

> "The public" cannot decide . . . where to put a paper mill. For that decision special competence in pursuit of narrowly defined goals is necessary. Yet if this power is not somehow related to interests outside the framework of competent action, the results will reflect a larger incompetence.[19]

To use Ways's example, the public relations practitioner involved in deciding where to locate a paper mill must understand the economic and geographic considerations of such a decision. But he or she must also understand social considerations, such as displacement of existing houses and pollution of waterways. Moreover, the practitioner must effectively communicate those concerns to other decision makers. If such issues are not resolved early in the process, a mill could be built on a site judged appropriate by economic criteria, only to be prevented from operating by community protests.

Similarly, when planning communication strategy, managers are often faced with the question of how truthful and open they wish to be about a given matter. In such circumstances, the public relations practitioner who does not think like a manager typically will counsel openness, honesty, and the people's right to know. In short order, such individuals are labeled "Johnny-one-notes" who really do not understand the big picture. Their advice and counsel are rejected as impractical or preachy.

The public relations practitioner who thinks like a manager seeks the same goals of openness and honesty, but takes a different approach. Instead of preaching, he or she helps management weigh the pragmatic risks of communicating or not communicating. By pointing out the costs and benefits that could result, this practitioner is much more likely to provide constructive and acceptable advice, to retain credibility in a decision-making role, and to steer the organization toward the course of openness and honesty.

William W. Weston, public relations director of Sun Company, has observed, "How well the public relations practitioner succeeds in retaining some distance and objectivity, resisting the almost irresistible pull toward total absorption into the view of the world held by the leadership of his institution, will critically affect his ability to be truly useful."[20]

Jim Osborne, a public relations consultant agrees, suggesting that senior managers are too often isolated from the outside world. "Consequently," he says, "CEOs require highly skilled communications and issue support. They also need candid advice and feedback that tells them what they need to know, not what they want to hear."[21]

All of this suggests that effective public relations practitioners who take part in organizational decision making must frequently tell their executives what they do not want to hear. They must ask hard, probing questions and raise points that may not have been considered. To do so takes a certain amount of assertiveness and guts. It is a role that, while essential, may certainly lead to alienation and ineffectiveness if it is not tempered by understanding of managerial thinking and commitment to organizational goals.

Developing a broadened base of knowledge and perspective helps elevate public relations to a central role in identifying and managing the key issues that confront an organization. Issues management is an important means of integrating public relations into organizational planning and operations. The management of issues involves identifying controversies early, ranking issues in terms of importance to the organization, developing policy related to issues, developing programs to carry out policies, implementing programs, communicating with appropriate publics about organizational policies and programs, and evaluating the results of such efforts.[22] Issues may range from ethical standards for organizational behavior to energy conservation, from solid waste disposal to immigration policy.

Becoming Issue-Oriented

Spring Mills board chairman H. W. Close explains:

> Meeting issues head-on is perhaps the biggest challenge facing management today. . . . If misunderstandings about the motives for business damage our freedom to run our businesses in the best interests of everyone concerned, then we won't be in business long and everyone loses. That's why this area of issue identification and response is so important. And it's why top management is looking to public relations pros for assistance.[23]

Public relations practitioners must develop the formal and informal research skills necessary to survey their organizations' internal and external environments. Such surveys help determine what issues their organizations must confront and how those issues can be successfully dealt with. Each organization must determine for itself which issues are most crucial at any given time. The issues management process, however, is an area in which public relations can make one of its greatest contributions to managerial decision making. Public relations counselor Ralph Frede agrees, "Interpreting our publics and anticipating future issues in order to recommend positions, actions, policy changes is equally, if not more, important than how well we select and use the channels of communication."[24]

W. Howard Chase is given credit for coining the term *issues management*. One of the nation's leading public relations practitioners, he sees issues management as "the highway by which public relations professionals can move even more significantly into full participation in management decision making."[25]

Issues Management

Issues management grew out of the same reality and recognition that led organizations to practice public relations originally. Organizations have been blindsided for too long by protest groups who gain public support by striking public chords through protests or other tactics. To avoid unpleasant surprises, organizations should scan, monitor, and track external forces. Some public relations practitioners say issues management is "analogous to establishing a radar system to help management anticipate and prepare for issues—any condition or pressure that if continued will significantly impact the mission of an organization."[26] These forces must be analyzed in terms of their effects on an organization's image, profit, and ability to act. Based on that analysis, an organization's policy must be developed, strategy planned, and action implemented.

The issues-management process initially serves as an early warning system. Much like the rangers who staff spotter stations in our nation's forests, the idea is to locate the smoke and take action before a major fire develops. In this way, the organization has a better opportunity to shape, rather than react to, public

Issues management is important to avoid such problems as Disney faced in this protest at the White House over a planned historic amusement park in Haymarket, Virginia.

discourse and decision making. There are two major goals of the issues-management function: (1) identify issues early that may have an effect on the organization; and (2) influence the issues to prevent them from causing a major consequence to the organization.[27]

The term *issues management* can be slightly misleading. No one can manage issues in a free society. Organizations, however, can manage their own actions and statements in relation to public issues. They can determine which issues to become involved in, and when and how to make statements or take action. Like marketing, issues management is an effort to manage an organization so that it can effectively interact with its changing external environment. In short, it is the systematic coordination of an institution's efforts to participate in the public policy process.

Although this area of public relations grew quickly in the 1970s and early 1980s, it has remained fairly constant in recent years. Reasons for the slower growth in this area of public relations are largely a result of tight corporate budgets; issues requiring organizational change as well as communication; professionals needed with a broad, interdisciplinary background; and little professional development assistance in this arena. Still, it is a function that many argue must be developed. "We've failed to advance the concept because we insist on viewing ourselves as professional communicators instead of management professionals experienced with communication and management principles," according to Ray Ewing, retired public relations director for All State. "We invented it [issues management], we developed the techniques, and no one is better equipped to staff issues management than we are. . . . Issues management runs parallel in value to strategic planning among top management, and we should never give it up," he said.[28] (See public relations spotlight 4.1.)

What are issues? An issue is a problem, question, or choice being faced. A *public issue* is a problem, question, or choice being faced by society or some segment of society that involves actual or potential governmental action. When public issues impact on an organization's investments, operations, or ability to act, that organization needs to become actively involved with those issues.

Public issues may involve a particular company, as when Minute Maid was accused of taking advantage of migrant labor. More often, issues affect specific industrial categories, such as the chemical industry. Manville Corporation was forced into bankruptcy in the 1970s because of the asbestos problem. It has emerged from bankruptcy and is one of the leading proponents of issues management today.

One of the early issues management examples involved Bank of America. An issues analyst identified a potential issue that it called "holds on deposits," a practice where banks will not give depositors credit for their deposit until the check or checks have cleared. This issue eventually was the focus of NBC's *Meet the Press* and an article in the *San Francisco Examiner.* Following the media pressure, U.S. House and Senate committees held hearings on the issue. Bank of America was ready at the hearings and able to provide Congress with facts showing only .03 percent of their deposits were held this way. Senator Christopher Dodd from Connecticut praised Bank of America for its plan and foresight to deal with the issue long before it became public.[29]

<table>
<tr><td>

How Can Issues
Management Be
Re-Energized?

</td><td>

Public Relations Spotlight 4.1

- Reposition issues management as a bridge between public relations and strategic planning with an eventual evolution to the planning function.
- Create a career path for issues management.
- Create an issues-management master's degree program.
- Create a new professional society or re-energize existing groups.
- Create a professional certification program.
- Create a new curriculum to meet the mandate of the American Assembly of Collegiate Schools of Business to include more social sciences.
- Develop continuing education programs for business organizations.
- Integrate the issues-management body of knowledge.

Source: "Managing Issue Acts as Bridge to Strategic Planning," *Public Relations Journal* (November 1993): 39.

</td></tr>
</table>

Perhaps most common, however, are issues of general concern affecting organizations across the spectrum. Such issues include environmentalism, consumerism, unionism, feminism, energy, health and safety, human resources, productivity, and the list goes on. (See figure 4.1 to see how Bridgestone dealt with an issue concerning their product.)

The Issues-Management Process

The issues-management process consists of five steps: identification, analysis, strategy, action, and evaluation.

1. *Identification* When identifying issues, organizations use various methods to scan the external environment for potential areas of threat or opportunity. An issue should be identified in the earliest stages of its life cycle—while still unnoticed or of only awakening interest to others. If an issue is not dealt with until it has reached the crisis stage, efforts to influence society's resolution of the problem often prove futile.

   The initial identification effort usually points out in excess of 100 issues that might have an impact on a given organization. Issues can be generated in a number of ways, including media scanning, polling of the public or special publics, or use of consultants. Alcoa, for example, explores issues considered important by governmental, academic, and activist organizations. John Naisbett, author of *MegaTrends,* gained his fortune by helping organizations identify and track important trends.

2. *Analysis* Issue analysis is the second step of the issues-management process. In this phase, priorities are set by determining an issue's potential and publics. Obviously, organizations cannot effectively manage hundreds of issues at one time. The list must be narrowed to the most important. The importance of an issue is determined by its timing and impact. To establish priorities, six questions must be asked:

   a. How quickly will this issue unfold?

   b. How will it impact our products and operations?

NEWS RELEASE
NEWS RELEASE
NEWS RELEASE

BRIDGESTONE TIRE
One Bridgestone Park
P.O. Box 140991
Nashville, TN 37214-0991
Phone: 615-391-0088

Figure 4.1 Bridgestone Tire took a proactive approach to provide help for novice customers, especially women. *continued on page 84*

"TIRE TIPS...TO KEEP YOU ROLLING"
A SUCCESS WITH WOMEN

NASHVILLE, Tenn., July 11, 1990 -- When it comes to tires, Bridgestone is a woman's best friend. And more than 440,000 women who have received the company's free tire-care brochure since it was first printed in 1989 will probably agree.

Offered through Bridgestone's U.S. independent tire dealer network as well as an 800-number, the brochure, "Tire Tips . . . To Keep You Rolling," is a guidebook to assist the novice--female and male--in understanding the basics of purchasing and caring for tires.

Developed by female race car driver, mechanic and Bridgestone consultant Pat Lazzaro, the brochure explains the basics of tire care in an easy-to-understand, visually appealing format. It's one part of a multi-faceted Bridgestone campaign designed to help women feel more comfortable making tire-buying decisions and to help tire dealers better assist novice customers.

"Studies have shown that many women often feel uncomfortable buying tires, in part because they have not been given the information necessary to make confident purchase and maintenance decisions," said Jerry Nunn, vice president of Bridgestone brand tire sales.

"The response to our brochure has been terrific. We have heard from many women saying they now are prepared to deal more confidently with the issue of tires as well as car maintenance as a result of our program."

The first section of the brochure is a list of things consumers can check themselves to ensure they get the most mileage from their tires. For example, step-by-step instructions are given for checking a tire's air pressure, tread depth and how to look for other problems.

Because there are thousands of tires on the market today, choosing the right ones for a particular car might be considered a chore. The section "10 tips for the tire buyer" offers some basic information consumers need to have before and during their visit to a tire dealer, including the make and model of their car, and what they want from their tires, such as a comfortable ride or performance capabilities.

"Making consumers experts in tire technology is not the intent of our
program," Nunn said. "Our goal is to give them practical information they
need--and want--to help them and their dealer select tires with confidence
and get the most for their money."

Bridgestone's "Tire Tips . . . To Keep You Rolling" is available from
local Bridgestone tire dealers or by call calling, toll-free, 1-800-382-
0600.

The Bridgestone division of Bridgestone/Firestone Inc. is based in
Nashville, Tenn., and markets a complete line of passenger, high performance,
light truck, truck and bus, off-the-road, industrial, agricultural, rally,
kart, motorcycle, and motorsport tires, as well as a variety of industrial
rubber goods, and aviation tires.

Bridgestone brand radial passenger, truck and bus tires are manufactured
in La Vergne, Tenn. A new $350 million radial truck tire plant is under
construction in Warren County, Tenn.

Bridgestone/Firestone Inc., headquartered in Akron, Ohio, manufactures
and markets Bridgestone, Firestone and Dayton brand tires, and a wide range
of industrial and synthetic rubber goods. Bridgestone/Firestone Inc. is a
wholly owned subsidiary of Bridgestone Corporation, a global tire and rubber
manufacturer with headquarters in Tokyo. Bridgestone Corporation is one of
the world's largest tire and rubber companies and markets its products in
more than 150 nations and territories around the world.

                                    # # #

c. How likely is it that this issue will come to fruition?
d. How would our stakeholders expect us to act in relation to this issue?
e. What is our ability to have an impact on this issue?
f. What are the costs of not dealing with the issue?

Ultimately, the organization seeks to determine whether a given issue potentially impacts its success or survival. Those issues with the greatest bottom-line impact should receive the most attention.

Different organizations view and prioritize different issues in different ways. Environmental issues may threaten Midwestern coal-burning electric utility plants, but present opportunities to companies in scientific waste disposal. The debate over the effects of cigarette smoke on nonsmokers may affect work practices in a bank, but impact the ability of a tobacco company to sell its product.

3. *Strategy* The third step in the issues-management process, developing strategy, is usually accomplished by a committee that includes top management and others in areas affected by the issue. Based on input by those affected and those who would be involved in implementing the

Pat Lazzaro offers tips on proper engine care to Jeanne Bentley (right) of San Diego, Calif.

Pat Lazzaro shows Jeanne Bentley (right) of San Diego, Calif., how to measure for low tread depth. "Insert a penny with Abe Lincoln's head upside-down into the tread. If you can see the top of his head, you need new tires."

Pat Lazzaro tells Jeanne Bentley (right) of San Diego, Calif., that "maintaining proper air inflation is one of two key factors in gaining the maximum investment from your tires. The other is keeping your car properly aligned."

Race car driver and certified mechanic Pat Lazzaro of Sonoma, Calif.

Seminars for women help them become more knowledgeable customers.

organization's response, position papers and plans are developed by staff subject to the approval of senior executives.

4. *Action* An organization's action program is an orchestrated, integrated response to the issue of concern. A campaign is developed and implemented that coordinates the efforts of lobbyists, media relations, general management, advertising, employee communications, and whatever other organizational units need to be included. While some efforts are of relatively short duration, many represent substantial commitments of energy and resources over time.

5. *Evaluation* Evaluation, the final step in the issues-management process, seeks to determine the effectiveness and impact of the program. Evaluation may help establish how long the program should continue or whether changes need to be made.

Summary

In this chapter, we have looked at how public relations considerations fit into the organizational decision-making process. We have pointed out that these considerations are playing an increasingly important role in all areas of organizational decision making, particularly through the issues-management process. Indeed, being public relations–minded is a critical perspective for line managers to possess. However, general trends toward reducing corporate staffs have jeopardized some public relations specialist positions.

As we continue through this book, we will consider the public relations practitioner as someone who does much more than write media releases or plan publicity stunts. The expanded role now includes harmonizing an organization with its environments by analyzing those environments; advising management and participating in decisions affecting all areas of organizational activity; and communicating with various corporate publics concerning policy, programs, activities, ideas, and images. Emphasis is placed, however, on achieving clear results relating to organizational goals. In the fullest sense, public relations practitioners are more than communication technicians. They are an integral part of the management team possessed with special skills, training, and sensitivities in the area of communication.

Case Study

Neighbors

By Dulcie Straughan
University of North Carolina
Chapel Hill, North Carolina

You are public information director for a city mental health department. Your department plans to open a group home for eight adults who are cognitively disabled. Group homes, in which a small number of clients live together with counselors, are designed to serve as an alternative to institutional living for some people who have cognitive disabilities. A house located in a middle-class subdivision was privately donated to the city for use as a group home. This is to be the first group home in your state; other states have been using the group-home system for years, while still others have not begun community care programs.

The clients (four men and four women) will live in the group home with a married couple who are trained counselors. All eight residents have full-time jobs in the city at places such as McDonald's. The money they earn working will go towards food bills, their clothing, and pocket money.

A few months ago, some general stories about the concept of group-home care for people who have cognitive disabilities appeared in the local newspaper. One story contained a statement by the city director (your boss) that said a group home was planned in the city "at a future date." After this article appeared in the paper, the director received a few letters from citizens objecting to the idea of "mentally retarded" persons living in group homes. One concern was that property values would be lowered in neighborhoods where group homes were located.

The director, fearing negative reactions from residents in the neighborhood where the group home is to be located, tells you he wants to keep a low profile about the opening of the group home. In a memo, he tells you not to generate any publicity about the group home's opening. When the counselors and residents arrive at the group home a few days later to move in, they find hand-lettered signs posted on the trees in the yard, saying that they are not welcome in the neighborhood.

The counselors call the director, who calls you to say that something has to be done before the situation gets out of hand. He asks for your advice.

Questions

1. Do you think the city director made the right decision in deciding not to generate any publicity about the group home? What would you, as public information director, suggest doing now?

2. How would the situation have been different had the public information director been involved in the original decision rather than being brought in after the fact?

Notes

1. Quoted in "Pursuing Professional Excellence," *Public Relations Journal* (October/November 1994): 27.

2. H. W. Close, "Public Relations as a Management Function," *Public Relations Journal* (March 1980): 12.

3. Edward Gubman, "People Are More Valuable Than Ever," *Compensation Benefits and Review* (January/February 1995): 7.

4. "Layoffs Surge 43% Led by Chemical and Chase Bank Merger," *Daily Labor Report* (7 September, 1995).

5. Gubman, "People Are More Valuable," 7.

6. Tannenbaum and W. H. Schmidt, "How to Choose a Leadership Pattern," *Harvard Business Review* (May/June 1973): 162–180.

7. O. W. Baskin and C. E. Aronoff, *Interpersonal Communication in Organizations* (Santa Monica, Calif.: Goodyear Publishing Co., 1980), 118.

8. James N. Sites, "Solving Problems That Keep Your Boss Awake at Night," *Public Relations Journal* (August 1974): 6.

9. Thomas Moore, "Goodbye Corporate Staff," *Fortune* (21 December 1987): 68.

10. The authors are indebted to Ron Weiser of the consulting firm Meidinger, Inc. for the phrase "management mainstream" and for some of the ideas contained in this section.

11. Sites, "Solving Problems," 5.

12. "Pursuing Professional Excellence," 27.

13. Quoted in "Communicators Outline Recession Strategies," *Communication World* (November 1982): 1.

14. Robert D. Ross, *The Management of Public Relations* (New York: John Wiley and Sons, 1977), 10.

15. R. Edward Freeman, *Strategic Management: A Stakeholder Approach* (Boston: Pitman, 1984), 221.

16. "Pursuing Professional Excellence," 28.

17. John A. Byrne, *Business Week* (12 September, 1988): 88.

18. Moore, "Goodbye Corporate Staff," 72.

19. Hill & Knowlton Executives, "Critical Issues," *Public Relations* (Englewood Cliffs, N.J.: Prentice-Hall, Inc., 1975), xxv.

20. William W. Weston, "Public Relations: Trustee of a Free

Society," *Public Relations Review* (Fall 1975): 13.

21. Jim Osborne, "Getting Full Value from Public Relations," *Public Relations Journal* (October/November 1994): 64.

22. R. P. Ewing, "Issues," *Public Relations Journal* (June 1980): 14–16.

23. Close, "Public Relations as a Management Function," 13.

24. "Pursuing Professional Excellence," 29.

25. H. W. Chase, "Adjusting to a Different Business/Social Climate,"

Public Relations Quarterly (Spring 1980): 24–26.

26. Kerry Tucker and Bill Trumpfheller, "Building An Issues Management System," *Public Relations Journal* (November 1993): 36.

27. Max Meng, "Early Identification Aids Issues Management," *Public Relations Journal* (March 1992): 22.

28. Quoted in "Managing Issues Acts As Bridge to Strategic Planning," *Public Relations Journal* (November 1993): 38.

29. Meng, "Early Identification," 22.

CHAPTER 5

Ethics and Professionalism

Preview

Legal and ethical issues are closely related in public relations practice; however, they are not identical. Even when no violation of law can be proven, a practitioner can be sanctioned for unethical conduct under the code of the Public Relations Society of America (PRSA). The law is the base; ethical conduct should rise well above that minimum standard. Ethics means more than being honest and obeying the law; it means being morally good.[1]

The history of public relations is filled with allegations and confirmations of unethical behavior. While this may be no different in any other profession, public relations practitioners are especially sensitive to any suggestion of misconduct. This sensitivity may exist because public relations is frequently called on to generate ethical statements and policies for an organization, as well as often to promote socially responsible action within the organization. To help provide guidance in ethical decisions, both PRSA and the International Association of Business Communicators (IABC) have established codes for ethical behavior. While both encourage professionals to demonstrate a commitment to ethical behavior, only PRSA has an enforcement procedure.

Ethical questions often arise in professional relationships with clients, news media representatives, financial analysts, and others. Increased professionalization is one possible answer to questions regarding ethical practice. Even with the legislative force of licensure, though, ethical practice is still a function of individual behavior.

Unless you are willing to resign an account or a job over a matter of principle, it is useless to call yourself a member of the world's newest profession—for you are already a member of the world's oldest.

—Tommy Ross

The Challenge of Ethical Practice

Everyone faces ethical dilemmas throughout life. What is ethics? What are common standards or criteria? What are ways to avoid and handle ethical dilemmas?

Mark McElreath, in *Managing Systematic and Ethical Public Relations,* defines ethics as "the set of criteria by which decisions are made about what is right and what is wrong."[2] He continues to suggest that the function of the public relations manager is "to establish criteria by which decisions are made in the organization."[3] Thus, managers establish guidelines that help employees decide what is right and what is wrong.

Ethics is an area of particular concern for public relations for four reasons: (1) Practitioners are aware that, to some, public relations has a reputation for unethical behavior; (2) public relations is often the source of ethical statements from an organization and the repository of ethical and social policies for that organization; (3) practitioners have struggled to create suitable **codes of ethics** for themselves; and (4) practitioners should act on behalf of their organizations as the ethical ombudsmen for the publics they serve.

The practitioner, then, should be the most ethical person in the organization. As we shall discuss in this chapter, public relations practice is based on trust. Members of the profession who violate that trust harm their colleagues as much as themselves.

Public relations practitioners are very sensitive, even defensive, about allegations of unethical behavior. The term *public relations* is sometimes used as a synonym for lying, distortion, selective disclosure, or coverup. A *Wall Street Journal* article points to the ethical shortcomings of public relations, quoting the former public relations vice-president for United Brands. "The more I thought about it, and the more I looked at events around me, the more certain I became that PR was helping to screw up the world," he said. "I could see the hand of the PR man pulling the strings, making things happen, covering things up. . . . Everywhere I looked it seemed as if image and style had taken the place of substance."[4]

While several limited studies have ranked the profession low in honesty and ethics, a recent study by Lynne Sallot asked the general public what they thought about public relations practitioners. The survey elicited both good news and bad news. "Overall, the good news—which, given public relations' bad press, is a pleasant surprise—is that among the general public, the reputation of public relations practitioners is better than many think."[5] Public relations practitioners have a reputation that is "better than average" for occupations, the study found.[6]

Like any other group or profession, public relations has ethical as well as unethical practitioners. However, because public relations as an emerging profession attempts to represent the public as well as the organization in business decision making, its practitioners are frequently held to a higher standard. The media and various publics will quickly point out deception in behavior that might be considered normal for members of other competitive businesses.

Ethics as Standards of Social Conduct

Ethics is what is morally right or wrong in social conduct, usually as determined by standards of professions, organizations, and individuals. Ethical behavior is a major consideration that distinguishes the civilized from the uncivilized in society. Allen Center and Patrick Jackson argue that five factors regulate social conduct:

1. *Tradition:* Ways in which the situation has been viewed or handled in the past.

2. *Public Opinion:* Currently acceptable behavior according to the majority of one's peers.

3. *Law:* Behaviors that are permissible and those that are prohibited by legislation.

4. *Morality:* Generally, a spiritual or religious prohibition. Immorality is a charge usually leveled in issues on which religious teachings have concentrated.

5. *Ethics:* Standards set by the profession, an organization, or oneself, based on conscience—what is right or fair to others as well as to self?[7]

Because morality is actually the basis for ethics, it is difficult to separate them. Many issues of right or wrong are not ethical issues. For instance, whether or not to jaywalk is a question of right or wrong, but it is not an ethical question. If the question is not one of moral right or wrong, then it is not an ethical issue; moral content is what makes an ethical issue.

Individual Ethics

Ralph Waldo Emerson, the American philosopher, once said, "What you are stands over you the while, and thunders so that I cannot hear what you say." This same philosophy was evident in the work of Ivy Lee, who became recognized as the "father of public relations" because he considered the public relations **actions,** not the words, more important. Lee's 1906 Declaration of Principles was the first code of ethics for public relations. More important than ethical codes of public relations conduct, though, is the nature of the individual, private ethics of the practitioner. When it comes right down to it, the public relations practitioner must have a high personal standard of ethics that carries over into his or her work. James Grunig, a proponent of public relations professionalism, argues that the practitioners must have two basic guiding ethical principles:

1. They must have the will to be ethical, intending not to injure others but rather to be honest and trustworthy.

2. They must make every effort to avoid actions that would have adverse consequences for others.[8]

At the heart of any discussion of ethics in public relations are some questions that are deeply troubling for the individual practitioner. For example, will he or she . . .

1. Lie for a client or employer?

2. Engage in deception to collect information about another practitioner's clients?

3. Help conceal a hazardous condition or illegal act?

4. Provide information that presents only part of the truth?

5. Offer something (gift, travel, or information) to reporters or legislators that may compromise their reporting?

6. Present true but misleading information in an interview or news conference that will mask some unpleasant fact?

Many public relations practitioners find themselves forced to respond to questions like these. Even though most report that they are seldom pressed to compromise their values, the questions are still asked. By conscientiously considering their ethical standards, practitioners can avoid difficult and embarrassing situations. Maintaining ethical standards is the key to establishing relationships of trust with employees, employers, clients, media contacts, and others. Because of the importance of ethical behavior to the general practice of public relations, attempts have been made to impose **sanctions** against individuals who violate professional standards.

While many practitioners consider it generally unethical to criticize each other's actions publicly, it is often necessary to raise the issue to meet the ethical obligations of the profession. When some public relations professionals spoke out against the Firestone Tire Company's stonewalling of accurate information about defective radial tires and when others denounced conflicting statements released to the press during the Three Mile Island nuclear accident, they themselves were criticized. For example, both *PR News* and *Public Relations Journal* labeled Firestone's critics unprofessional.

Thomas Bivins suggests that the individual practitioner has five moral obligations:

1. *To ourselves*—to preserve our own integrity;

2. *To our clients*—to honor our contracts and to use our professional expertise on our clients' behalf;

3. *To our organization or employer*—to adhere to organizational goals and policies;

4. *To our profession and our professional colleagues*—to uphold the standards of the profession and, by extension, the reputation of our fellow practitioner; and

5. *To society*—to consider social needs and claims.[9]

Unfortunately, most ethical situations are not black and white. When obligations to some of Bivins's five major stakeholders collide over an ethical issue, the practitioner must decide whose claim is most important or entails the least harm to the fewest people. Thus, when the employer's policies are different from those of the profession or the dictates of individual conscience, which should take precedence?

Some practical tips for ethical decision making are given in public relations spotlight 5.1.

More controversial than the question of personal ethics is the general issue of business ethics. It is relatively easy to agree in abstract terms that individual

---

Public Relations Spotlight 5.1   Ethical Tips

1. Never accept a client or a job with an organization or person whose character or conduct doesn't measure up to your personal ethical standards.
2. Always be honest with everyone, especially the media.
3. Don't handle competing clients.
4. Don't make unfair comments about competitors.
5. Keep the public interest in mind at all times, including your responsibility to represent the various stakeholder groups to management.
6. Respect confidences.
7. Make sure all your financial activities are "above board."
8. Use organizational codes—such as the PRSA Code given in this chapter—as a starting place, but build your own standards on top of these.

---

professionals have a duty to behave ethically. Unfortunately, translating these abstract concepts into rules governing business practice in a competitive environment has not been so easy. The Public Relations Society of America has established a Code of Professional Standards for the Practice of Public Relations (see public relations spotlight 5.2). In general, this voluntary code calls for truth, accuracy, good taste, fairness, and responsibility to the public.

The code, like the U.S. Constitution, is open to many interpretations. To deal with this problem, PRSA has supplied official interpretations of several of the provisions.[10] For example, article 6 says, "A member shall not engage in any practice which has the purpose of corrupting the integrity of channels of communication or the processes of government." Does this mean that you cannot give a small gift, such as a $10 pen with the company logo and your phone number, to reporters at an open house? No, it does not. The interpretation says that gifts of "nominal value" are acceptable. Does article 6 mean that "junkets" are prohibited? No, as long as the special media event has *legitimate news value* and there is *no pressure* to do a story or—especially—to give a story a particular slant. This article likewise does not prohibit giving legitimate sample products or services to media representatives who have a *bona fide interest* in the product. It is also permissible under the code to offer complimentary or discount rates to the media if the rate is for *business* use and *available to all* writers.

On the other hand, the public relations practitioner must be aware that many media representatives have their own codes of ethics that prohibit accepting anything free from public relations people. For example, Scripps Howard Inc.'s ethical policy prohibits "freebies." If the company has a legitimate news interest in the event or product, reporters and editors must pay their own way or risk being fired.[11]

Business Ethics

More and more, companies will be held to the same standards of behavior that people are, and more and more this will mean people answering for companies. The CEO will be expected to articulate his or her position on all these issues, and to the senior PR person will fall the duty of analyzing public opinion and advising on such positions. . . .

PRSA Code of
Professional Standards
for the Practice of
Public Relations

Public Relations Spotlight 5.2

Declaration of Principles

Members of the Public Relations Society of America base their professional principles on the fundamental value and dignity of the individual, holding that the free exercise of human rights, especially freedom of speech, freedom of assembly, and freedom of the press, is essential to the practice of public relations.

In serving the interests of clients and employers, we dedicate ourselves to the goals of better communication, understanding, and cooperation among the diverse individuals, groups, and institutions of society, and of equal opportunity of employment in the public relations profession.

We pledge:

To conduct ourselves professionally, with truth, accuracy, fairness, and responsibility to the public;

To improve our individual competence and advance the knowledge and proficiency of the profession through continuing research and education;

And to adhere to the articles of the Code of Professional Standards for the Practice of Public Relations as adopted by the governing Assembly of the Society.

Code of Professional Standards for the Practice of Public Relations

These articles have been adopted by the Public Relations Society of America to promote and maintain high standards of public service and ethical conduct among its members.

1. A member shall conduct his or her professional life in accord with the **public interest.**
2. A member shall exemplify high standards of **honesty and integrity** while carrying out dual obligations to a client or employer and to the democratic process.
3. A member shall **deal fairly** with the public, with past or present clients or employers, and with fellow practitioners, giving due respect to the ideal of free inquiry and to the opinions of others.
4. A member shall adhere to the highest standards of **accuracy and truth,** avoiding extravagant claims or unfair comparisons and giving credit for ideas and words borrowed from others.
5. A member shall not knowingly disseminate **false or misleading information** and shall act promptly to correct erroneous communications for which he or she is responsible.
6. A member shall not engage in any practice which has the purpose of **corrupting** the integrity of channels of communications or the processes of government.
7. A member shall be prepared to **identify publicly** the name of the client or employer on whose behalf any public communication is made.
8. A member shall not use any individual or organization professing to serve or represent an announced cause, or professing to be independent or unbiased, but actually serving another or **undisclosed interest.**
9. A member shall not **guarantee the achievement** of specified results beyond the member's direct control.
10. A member shall **not represent conflicting** or competing interests without the express consent of those concerned, given after a full disclosure of the facts.

11. A member shall not place himself or herself in a position where the member's **personal interest is or may be in conflict** with an obligation to an employer or client, or others, without full disclosure of such interest to all involved.

12. A member shall **not accept fees, commissions, gifts, or any other consideration** from anyone except clients or employers for whom services are performed without their express consent, given after full disclosure of the facts.

13. A member shall scrupulously safeguard the **confidences and privacy rights** of present, former, and prospective clients or employers.

14. A member shall not intentionally **damage the professional reputation** or practice of another practitioner.

15. If a member has evidence that another member has been guilty of unethical, illegal, or unfair practices, including those in violation of this Code, the member is obligated to present the information promptly to the proper authorities of the Society for action in accordance with the procedure set forth in Article XII of the Bylaws.

16. A member called as a witness in a proceeding for enforcement of this Code is obligated to appear, unless excused for sufficient reason by the judicial panel.

17. A member shall, as soon as possible, sever relations with any organization or individual if such relationship requires conduct contrary to the articles of this Code.

Again, it is the public relations professional who will be responsible for monitoring . . . controversial issues and ensuring that the company responds to the expectations of its consumers, acting almost as the corporate conscience.[12]

Some practitioners have been fired arbitrarily for refusing to write news releases they felt would be false and misleading. One practitioner worked for a company that wanted him to prepare and distribute a release listing company clients before the clients had signed contracts for services. The practitioner refused, believing that to comply would violate the PRSA code, and was fired. He subsequently sued the company for unlawful dismissal, receiving almost $100,000 in an out-of-court settlement.

The question of **whistle-blowing** has become prominent in recent years. What is an ethical practitioner's correct response when an employer or client refuses to exercise public responsibility? The PRSA Code of Ethics says that he or she should quit. Some practitioners, however, believe they can accomplish more good by staying on to argue for more responsible action. Realistically, few practitioners can afford to quit and therefore choose to stay in the face of questionable activities. Out of frustration, they become whistle-blowers. That is, they secretly inform the media about irresponsible actions in order to bring public pressure on their organizations. Although whistle-blowing can halt the unethical practice, it usually costs the whistle-blower his or her job in the long run. Thus, the decision to quit is a more direct means to the same end.

Another public relations professional resigned after initially participating in several ethically questionable practices with a multinational fruit conglomerate.

He charged the company with manipulation of press coverage as well as with political and military action involving a Latin American country in which it was operating. The increased attention of many corporations to the ethical dimensions of business can be traced back to Watergate and Koreagate. These major national scandals were followed by a 1975 investigation revealing that dozens of U.S. companies had made payments to government officials in foreign countries in order to gain lucrative contracts. The Lockheed Aircraft Corporation was the most publicized among more than 400 firms eventually admitting such practices. Opinion polls conducted soon after the scandal revealed that Americans felt only about 20 percent of business executives had high ethical standards. Most observers believe that these revelations were significantly related to the erosion of public confidence in American business and its leaders.

A study conducted by one of the authors solicited a copy of the ethics policy of each of the *Fortune* 500 companies. Of the organizations, 421 responded with ethics procedures ranging in length from a single page to 47 pages. Most not only affirmed the corporation's intent to do business in an ethical manner but also provided for dismissal of employees who violated the policy. However, closer examination of these documents revealed a tendency to rely on legal rather than ethical standards. Some *Fortune* 500 companies and other firms are providing ethics training for their managers and other employees. Companies increasingly are using outside consultants or panels to examine systematically the social and ethical implications of impending decisions. Some also use internal experts or ethics committees to review major decisions.

One recent study indicates that public relations professionals who are willing to take ethical positions are more likely to participate in top-level management decisions. Table 5.1 shows that 52 percent of the practitioners in the study who made frequent recommendations for socially responsible actions were also frequent participants in policy decisions within their organizations. In an Arthur W. Page Hall of Fame Lecture in 1989, W. Howard Chase predicted that "the next important stage in public relations service—its edge of the new unused—will be the management of values, the disciplines inherent in ethical corporate conduct."[13]

When public relations practitioners participate in organizational decisions, they bear a heavy ethical responsibility—not only to themselves and their organizations but also to their profession and the public. They must weigh all these

TABLE 5.1 Frequency of Recommending Social Responsibility and Frequency of Participation in Policy Decisions

	Participate in decisions more than 50% of the time	Participate in decisions 50% or less of the time
Very often or often recommend social responsibility	23 (52%)	21 (48%)
Not very often or never recommend social responsibility	17 (30%)	39 (70%)

considerations when helping to make organizational decisions and communicate decisions once they are made.

The examples cited here show that ethical behavior is ultimately an individual decision. Professional codes, corporate policy, and even law cannot ensure the ethical practice of any profession; only the application of sound personal values can guarantee ethical behavior. Nevertheless, professional codes, sound business policies, and appropriate legislation can serve as valuable guidelines for public relations practitioners who desire to maintain high ethical standards.

Ethical Dealings with News Media

Perhaps the most critical relationships managed by public relations practitioners are those concerning the news media. Here, anything less than total honesty will destroy credibility and, with it, the practitioner's usefulness to an employer or client. All news media depend on public relations sources for much of the information they convey to viewers, readers, and listeners (see chapter 10). Although public relations releases are sometimes used simply as leads from which to develop stories, at other times reporters and editors rely on the accuracy and thoroughness of public relations copy and use it with little change.

Trust, the foundation of all public relations practice, is achieved only through ethical performance. Therefore, providing junkets for the press that have doubtful news value, throwing extravagant parties, giving expensive gifts, and doing personal favors will ultimately destroy a practitioner's effectiveness. Even if journalists ask for favors, the ethical public relations professional must find a way to decline tactfully. In the long run, establishing a reputation for honesty and integrity will yield dividends in media relations.

Although several studies have consistently shown that public relations practitioners and journalists hold similar professional values and make similar news

News media depend on public relations practitioners for much of the information they convey to the public.

judgments, the same studies show that journalists strongly believe public relations practitioners lack professional values. The unwillingness of a few practitioners to uphold ethical standards could be the reason for this misconception.

Ethics and Laws

Ethical and legal issues frequently evolve from similar circumstances, but the public relations professional must understand the difference. Keeping to the letter of the law does not guarantee ethical action because the law is written to cover only the worst—or at least the most general—offenses. Many unethical claims and promotions have been structured to stay within legal limits, even though their intent was to trick or deceive. Although an understanding of the law is important, a professional must rely on a higher standard for decision making.

Public relations practitioners working for publicly held companies have both an ethical and a legal obligation to release promptly news about dividends, earnings, new products, mergers, and other developments that might affect the value of securities. A delay in releasing such news could allow insiders to derive unfair financial benefits. The Securities and Exchange Commission and the individual stock exchanges strictly enforce these regulations.

Corporations are also prohibited from using public relations techniques in connection with the sale of new issues of securities (see chapter 14). Public relations personnel must be thoroughly aware of Federal Trade Commission and Food and Drug Administration regulations regarding the promotion of products and services. Such practices as unsubstantiated claims, fraudulent testimonials, deceptive pricing, so-called independent surveys, and rigged contests are regulated through these agencies.

Establishing Standards for a Developing Profession

For any occupation to become a profession, it must meet four criteria:

1. Expertise
2. Autonomy
3. Commitment
4. Responsibility[14]

Expertise comprises the specialized knowledge and skill that are vital requirements for the profession to perform its function in society. *Autonomy* allows the practitioner to practice without outside interference. *Commitment,* the outcome of expertise, implies devotion to the pursuit of excellence without emphasis on the rewards of the profession. Finally, *responsibility* means that the power conferred by expertise entails a trust relationship with the practitioner's stakeholder groups.

Though all four criteria are important, the last one, responsibility, is operationalized through codes of ethics, professional organizations, and licensure. Thus, to be considered fully professionalized, an occupation needs a well-developed and well-enforced code of ethics, active professional organizations, and some means of controlling who is allowed to practice. It is the licensure issue that continues to prevent public relations from being a fully professional occupation.

James Grunig and Todd Hunt list five characteristics of a professional group. As a relatively young profession, public relations has made remarkable progress in each area, but its practitioners still need to do more and to encourage others to accept these norms:

1. *A set of professional values* In particular, professionals believe that service to others is more important than their own economic gain. Professionals also strongly value autonomy.

2. *Membership in strong professional organizations* Professional organizations provide professionals the contact with other professionals they need to maintain an allegiance to the profession.

3. *Adherence to professional norms* A true profession has a code of ethics and a procedure for enforcing it.

4. *An intellectual tradition and an established body of knowledge* A profession must have a unique and well-established body of knowledge.

5. *Technical skills acquired through professional training* Professionals should have the technical skills needed to provide a unique and essential service.[15]

Ethical Codes

As Grunig and Hunt indicate, true professions have strong professional organizations with codes of ethics and the ability to prohibit violators of their codes from practicing. Public relations has several professional organizations, and most have codes of ethics; however, no single central organization can control access to the practice. Therefore, enforcement of these codes is difficult, and the effects of sanctions that can be imposed are questionable. Many argue that for public relations to mature from an emerging profession to a fully professionalized occupation, some licensure or certification process is necessary.[16]

The PRSA Code

The code of the Public Relations Society of America is the most detailed and comprehensive in the field (see public relations spotlight 5.2). When PRSA was founded in 1948, one of its first actions was to develop a code of ethics so members would have some common behavioral guidelines and managers would have a clear understanding of their standards. This code became the tool used to distinguish professionals in public relations from shady promoters and publicists who had been quick to appropriate the term *public relations* to describe their activities.

The PRSA Code was adopted in 1954 and revised in 1959, 1963, 1977, 1983, and 1988. Because the code seeks to establish specific standards for public relations practice, it must be changed periodically to address new problems. In 1963, revisions were designed to toughen the standards for financial public relations after an investigation by the Securities and Exchange Commission resulted in a public revelation of the corrupt actions of some practitioners. In 1977, under threat of antitrust litigation by the Federal Trade Commission, certain provisions of the code barring contingency fees and banning one member's encroaching upon another member's clients were changed. This revision of the code also removed sexist concepts and language from the document.

In 1983, articles 1 and 5 of the code were revised to cover potential as well as past and present clients. This change was the result of a grievance board hearing about a practitioner's disclosure of a potential client's plans to a competitor. In the wake of a scandal involving the newly elected president of the society, who had been charged with insider trading and violations of a client's confidence, the code was revised again in 1988. This revision gives the ethics board more freedom to communicate its actions and those of members who resign before their cases can be considered. The need for this change was made apparent when a front-page story in the September 26, 1986, *Wall Street Journal* revealed to many PRSA members for the first time the resignation under fire of their president.[17]

Code Enforcement

Because professional organizations' codes of practice do not have the force of law, enforcement is problematic. Investigation of charges independent of those who make them is an expensive process that most organizations cannot afford. Moreover, the legal and ethical responsibility to avoid unwarranted damage to someone's reputation and livelihood requires that any group proceed cautiously in enforcing a code of practice. The American Society of Newspaper Editors encountered so many legal problems and other difficulties in its attempts to censure members that it suspended further enforcement attempts soon after its code of ethics was adopted in 1923. However, Allen Center, author and former vice-president for public relations at Motorola and Parker Pen, believes that "we need to stake our claim to the moral high ground, and not tolerate anyone among us who breaches our code of ethics."[18]

Guidelines for Ethical Practice

As noted earlier in this chapter, codes, policies, and even laws are not the answer to achieving ethical practice in public relations. Only the individual professional can ensure his or her ethical behavior. In an article titled "Hope Springs Eternal for Good Use of PR," W. M. Shaffer put it quite simply: "Customers and prospects long ago recognized ethics as an aspect of individual character, not collective industry. PR professionals would do well to emulate customer and prospect wisdom; good ethics is just good business."[19] Lee Jaffe, retired public relations director for the New York Port Authority, states that "integrity is the key to the proper practice of public relations."[20] Those who exemplify the best of any profession develop personal philosophies that allow them to deal with individual cases as they occur.

"What is needed is an approach to ethics that combines 'moral conviction and tolerance'," according to the Excellence study in public relations.[21] While practitioners won't always agree on what's right or wrong or on a practical interpretation of a moral principle, they should strive to be tolerant of other viewpoints.[22]

Chester Burger, president of a New York–based management consulting firm, revealed his own philosophy in a *Public Relations Journal* article concerning ethics in public relations. The following statements encapsulate what he learned during a newspaper reporting and public relations career spanning more than four decades:

Lesson 1 Communicators must trust the common sense of their audience. More often than not, the public will justify our trust by seeing accurately the issues, the contenders, and the motivations. Communicators should not resort to clever headlines, gimmicks, distortions, or lies; they should not underestimate the public's perceptiveness.

Lesson 2   People generally will know or care very little about the issues that concern you. You need to inform, to clarify, and to simplify issues truthfully and in ways that will relate to your audience's self-interest.

Lesson 3   Don't compromise your own ethical standards for anyone. Don't take the easy way out. Don't say what you don't really believe, and don't do for the sake of expediency what you think is wrong. It isn't worth it. Ask yourself how your action would look if it were reported tomorrow on the front page of your local newspaper. Who would absolve you from responsibility if you said you had written or said an untruth because your boss told you to?

Lesson 4   Choices for communicators between right and wrong are rarely black or white, yes or no. Questions of ethics involve degrees, nuances, differing viewpoints. Too many times in my life I have been wrong to feel sure that I know the right answer. A bit of uncertainty and humility sometimes is appropriate in considering ethical questions.[23]

The Question of Licensure

Some believe that codes of behavior will lack wholly effective means of enforcement until practitioners are required to be legally certified. Controlled access is the hallmark of a recognized profession. Therefore, controlled access, through **licensure,** to the title of "certified public relations counselor" is viewed as the only way to separate the frauds and flacks from legitimate practitioners. Proponents such as the late Edward L. Bernays, who was instrumental in formulating the modern concept of public relations (see chapter 2), believe that licensing can protect the profession and the public from incompetent practitioners.

Those who argue for licensure see it as the only effective method of enforcing professional standards, but efforts to impose such standards are highly controversial. The Public Relations Society of America has commissioned several studies on licensure but has never endorsed it. Even if licensure were implemented, many practitioners would probably not be affected because they work in corporate departments. In the legal and accounting professions, many trained practitioners never sit for bar or CPA examinations because they are not required to represent their firms in official capacities.

Both PRSA and IABC offer accreditation programs for experienced practitioners who pass a comprehensive examination. These programs are the closest existing approximation to licensing procedures. Less than half the memberships of both associations are accredited. Despite efforts by PRSA, few people outside the profession have any notion of the accreditation process and what it means.

The issue of ethical practice in public relations is closely tied to efforts toward accreditation and licensure. While no amount of testing or education can guarantee ethical behavior on the part of individuals, the potential removal of accreditation or license can give professional codes of practice more leverage. By promoting professional responsibility and recognition, public relations organizations can encourage ethical behavior and awareness among their members.

Summary

Public relations professionals frequently face ethical questions during the course of their daily business with clients, the media, and others. Practitioners are often called on to issue ethical statements on behalf of the organizations they represent. Thus, public relations professionals are especially sensitive to any suggestion of misconduct.

To encourage commitment to ethical standards, both PRSA and IABC have established codes for ethical behavior, and PRSA has set up an enforcement procedure as well. Some believe that practitioners would be further influenced to abide by ethical standards if they were required to become legally certified, but licensure is still a controversial issue and has not been implemented. Codes, policies, and laws alone cannot achieve ethical standards; the ultimate responsibility lies with each individual practitioner.

Case Study

Critical Incidents: The Practical Side of Ethics

By Donald B. McCammond, APR
*Former Chairman
Board of Ethics, PRSA*

Sometimes, in everyday practice, situations arise where the proper thing, the ethical thing, even the legal thing to do is not always immediately clear. Following are several such situations.

1. A well-known athlete is charged with selling drugs and planning and carrying out, with others, the death of a young married couple. His attorney calls you, a close friend, to advise and assist him in handling the intense media interest in the case. During the period before trial, you learn that the athlete was, in fact, a drug dealer and did participate in the murder. The lawyer tells you that the information is privileged. You decide to await the outcome of the trial. The lawyer is able to get his client acquitted. What should you do?

2. Your firm is one of six under consideration by a manufacturer planning to introduce a new service into your area. You are given confidential information as to the service and the plans of the company. You are aware that the company will face severe opposition from certain groups and politicians and that the job will entail overcoming this resistance. Your firm is turned down by the company, and the assignment is given to a competitor. Can you disclose the information you have learned to the manufacturer's opposition in your area?

3. Your public relations firm publishes a newsletter directed to brokerage houses. A corporate executive asks your help in making his company better known among the brokerage community. A subsequent issue of the newsletter carries a highly optimistic forecast of the company but omits some information. Nothing in the story indicates any relationship between you and the company. Were you under any obligation to disclose this relationship, and should you print a retraction?

4. You are a corporate public relations director. Your employer tells you to set up a supposedly independent organization to introduce and promote the use of

a new product made by your company. This new organization is to be financed secretly by your company and some of its suppliers. Is there anything wrong with establishing this organization?

5. A distributor of medicinal products arranges with your firm to put on a press conference for an independent British scientist who has tested the products and written favorably about them. You also arrange speaking engagements for the visiting scientist. After the press conference, you learn that the scientist was actually an employee of the research arm of the manufacturer of the products. What actions should you take?

6. A client asks you for help in a financial merger situation. You decline because the matter is outside your expertise and refer the company to a fellow practitioner who is knowledgeable in financial affairs. The fellow practitioner is so appreciative he sends you a check for $500. Can you accept the money without telling the client?

7. One of your clients calls you to assist in a takeover situation. You tell a friend who had originally helped you get the client. Several days later, your friend buys 5,000 shares in one of the companies involved in the takeover. You do not buy any yourself. The day after the merger announcement, your friend sells the shares, at a profit of $15 a share and a total profit of $75,000. Are you guilty of insider trading, even if you made no profit?

8. Your employer asks you to give a series of talks in communities served by your company regarding its new plant and the service it will provide. On a visit to the plant to acquaint yourself with its operation, you get clear evidence that it cannot fulfill the expectations outlined in the talk prepared by your company. Can you give the talks as originally prepared?

Questions

1. Which articles of the PRSA code (spotlight 5.2) apply to each incident description?

2. List the ethical questions involved in each.

3. Describe any legal questions raised by these incidents.

Notes

1. Don Wright, "The Philosophy of Ethical Development in Public Relations," *IPRA Review* (April 1982): 22.

2. Mark McElreath, *Managing Systematic and Ethical Public Relations* (Madison, Wis.: Brown & Benchmark Publishers, 1993), 320.

3. Ibid., 320.

4. J. Montgomery, "The Image Makers," *The Wall Street Journal* (1 August 1978): 1.

5. Lynne Sallot, "Doing Good Is a Hustle, Too," paper presented to the Association for Education in Journalism and Mass Communication in Atlanta, Ga. 11 August 1994, 21–22.

6. Ibid., 22.

7. Allen Center and Patrick Jackson, *Public Relations Practices: Managerial Case Studies and Problems, 5th Edition* (Englewood Cliffs, N.J.: Prentice-Hall, 1995), 476.

8. James Grunig and Todd Hunt, *Managing Public Relations* (New York: Holt, Rinehart and Winston, 1984), 72.

9. Thomas H. Bivins, "A Systems Model for Ethical Decision Making in Public Relations," *Public Relations Review.* (Winter 1992): 375.

10. "Official Interpretations of the Code," *Public Relations Journal* (June 1995): 22–25.

11. Angus McEachran, editor of *The Commercial Appeal,* speech to SPJ Memphis Chapter, April 1994, Memphis, Tenn.

12. Paul Holmes, "Public Relations," *Adweek* (11 September 1989): 235.

13. W. Howard Chase, "The Edge of the Unused?" *Public Relations Review* (Winter 1989): 10.

14. Dan Lattimore, "Professionalism and Performance: An Investigation of Colorado Daily Newsmen," Ph.D. dissertation, University of Wisconsin, 1972; and Blaine McKee, Oguz Nayman, and Dan Lattimore, "How PR People See Themselves," *Public Relations Journal* (November 1975): 47–60.

15. James E. Grunig and Todd Hunt, *Managing Public Relations* (New York: Holt, Rinehart and Winston, 1984), 66.

16. McKee, Nayman, and Lattimore, 47–60.

17. Joanne Lipman, "PR Society Receives Some Bad PR from Ex-Chief Anthony Franco," *The Wall Street Journal* (26 September 1986): 1.

18. "Pursuing Public Relations Excellence," *Public Relations Journal* (October/November 1994): 28.

19. W. M. Shaff, "Hope Springs Eternal for Good Use of PR," *Marketing News* (25 September 1989): 4.

20. Ibid., 35.

21. Quoted in James Grunig, ed., *Excellence in Public Relations and Communication Management* (Hillsdale, N.J.: Lawrence Erlbaum Associates Publishers, 1992), 59.

22. Ibid., 59.

23. Chester Burger, *Public Relations Journal* (December 1982).

PART II

Public Relations

The Process

It isn't enough to know what public relations is and what purposes it serves. To practice public relations, one must understand the process by which public relations operates. As we have already discussed, public relations goes far beyond the task of producing messages. An effective public relations effort is the result of mutual understanding between an organization and its publics. The development of this understanding can be regarded as a four-step process:

1. *Research*   An initial fact-finding stage defines the problem areas and differentiates among publics.

2. *Planning*   Once the facts have been gathered from the various publics, decisions must be made regarding their importance and their potential impact on the organization. After these decisions are made, strategies must be developed to enable the organization to achieve its goals.

3. *Action and Communication*   Strategies are implemented as new organizational policies and/or projects. Messages are then constructed to reach target publics.

4. *Evaluation*   Once a public relations campaign is developed and implemented, it should be followed by an evaluation of its effectiveness in meeting the criteria that were set. The results of the evaluation are used both to assess the effectiveness of the effort and to plan future action. For open-system responses, evaluation information becomes a self-correction mechanism; feedback of this type allows plans to be fine-tuned as they are carried out. The results of closed-system evaluations should be stored for use in similar projects in the future.

These four steps are essential to any effective public relations campaign. They are not, however, four independent functions. Each step overlaps the others; if any one is neglected, the entire process will be affected. The next four chapters will discuss each of these steps in detail. To help you keep in mind the interdependence of the steps, an integrating case study will open each chapter. The case of Cedar Springs Community Hospital will illustrate a complete public relations project as it progresses through each stage, from research through evaluation. You may find it useful to turn back and review the previous case segments as you read through the next four chapters.

CHAPTER 6

Research: Understanding Public Opinion

Preview

Research is a crucial part of the public relations process. Information gained through careful research can be used to guide planning, pretest messages, evaluate results, and direct follow-up efforts.

Effective research techniques for public relations practice include both formal and informal methods.

The use of research data to evaluate current practice and forecast future events is well accepted in most organizations today. Public relations practitioners must be able to evaluate their efforts and demonstrate effectiveness.

Good public opinion research must be sensitive enough to identify publics as definable groups rather than as unrelated masses.

Public relations audits, social audits, communication audits, and environmental monitoring are effective research methods for public relations planning and evaluation.

T he process of issues management, which has become a major part of public relations practice, must be informed at every stage by research data. The early identification of issues that may impact a client or organization is most thoroughly accomplished through research methods designed to scan the environment for potential issues. Analysis to determine which issues have the greatest possible impact requires various research methods designed to determine both the strength of opinion about an issue and its perceived centrality to the client or organization. Likewise, the selection of potential actions and the evaluation of their implementation can be determined through well-planned research activities.

Research is a vital function in the process of public relations. It provides the initial information necessary to plan public relations action and to evaluate its effectiveness. Management demands hard facts, not intuition or guesswork. Public relations practitioners, like their colleagues in every area of management, must be able to demonstrate convincingly their ability to "add value" in producing a product or service. The economic realities of modern organizations make it necessary for public relations to incorporate data-gathering techniques into every phase of the process. The Cedar Springs Hospital case study that follows shows how a public relations effort can utilize research in identifying and dealing with an organizational problem.

The Need for Research in Public Relations

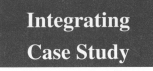

Integrating Case Study

Cedar Springs Community Hospital

Segment 1

Problem Identification

T he Cedar Springs Community Hospital, Inc., was formed by the merger of two formerly competing hospitals. Two years later, a new management team was brought in to help resolve concerns about the ability of the newly formed hospital to serve its patients' needs. Soon after the new administrator and his seven assistants assumed their duties, they began to hear reports of low employee morale and declining quality in patient care. Much of this input came from physicians who felt that the changes since the merger had produced an environment that was more routine and less personal. Many doctors felt that their relationships with other hospital employees had been undermined by the new organization's attempts to eliminate duplication and build a more efficient structure. In general, the growing consensus among the physicians was that the quality of patient care had declined significantly since the merger.

Informal and Secondary Research

Because physicians are a significant public for any hospital, their concerns received immediate attention from management. The physicians had suggested mounting a campaign to make employees more aware of their responsibility for quality patient care. However, the public relations director felt that more information was needed in the form of **secondary research** before an effective communication campaign could be planned. He began to look into the background of the merger and the relationships between hospital employees and the medical staff.

A careful review of hospital records and local newspaper files, plus conversations with several long-time employees, revealed the complexity of the situation. Not only had the hospitals formerly been competitors, they had also been founded by two very different religious groups and thus had developed two distinct constituencies. Although the religious affiliations of both hospitals had been discontinued long before the merger, an atmosphere of rivalry remained. This rivalry had been most obvious when the hospitals had attempted to outdo each other in terms of benefits for physicians.

Primary Research

One important public, the physicians, clearly believed that the quality of patient care was not acceptable. However, employees' and patients' views were not as easily defined. The public relations department devised a **primary research** plan to measure the opinions of each group. A random sample of hospital employees was asked to fill out a questionnaire about various aspects of patient care. Simultaneously, a telephone survey was conducted among recently released patients to gauge their opinions on the same issues.

The results were surprising. On a scale ranging from 1 (poor) to 10 (excellent), employees rated the hospital's performance a disappointing 6.6 overall. However, the survey of former patients produced an overall rating of 8.5. Other questions concerning the quality of patient care also elicited significantly lower marks from the employees than from the patients.

Qualitative Research

To understand the reasons for the low ratings given by employees, a focus group was assembled to respond to the survey findings. This five-member panel was composed of three representatives from nursing services and one each from ancillary support and business services. The members were interviewed as a group concerning their responses to the questionnaire. The interview revealed that while employees believed that the hospital in general delivered mediocre patient care, they felt that the care was significantly better in their specific areas than in the rest of the hospital and that they, personally, were slightly above average within their departments. These employees also indicated that their co-workers sensed that something was wrong in the organization but were not sure what. This led to feelings of individual helplessness and produced high levels of stress and frustration.

In the Cedar Springs case, what originally seemed like a rather straightforward employee communication problem was a complex situation involving three important publics. Research showed the physicians' concerns to be overblown. Had Cedar Springs management acted on the physicians' original recommendation without doing further research, the situation would have just gotten worse, increasing employee frustration and stress.

As you read about the different types of research methods public relations practitioners employ, refer to this segment and notice how several of the techniques were applied. A quick comparison of the Cedar Springs case with the first step in figure 6.1 will confirm that each of the basic elements of research is present

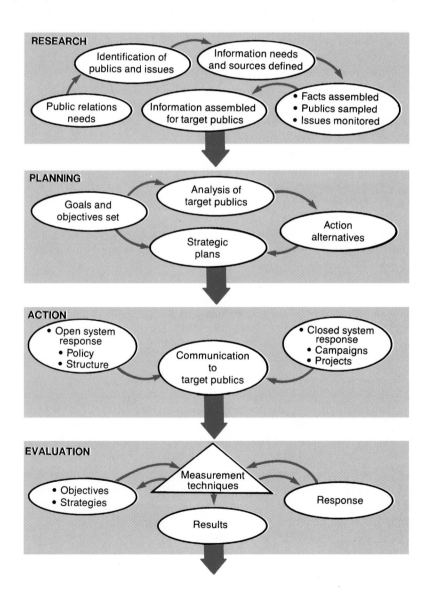

Figure 6.1 A process model of public relations

in this example. The surprising nature of the findings in this case illustrates the need for research in public relations.

Proving the Worth of Public Relations

Because public relations professionals have traditionally been doers rather than researchers, they often assume that others see the value of their function. That assumption places public relations necks squarely on budgetary chopping blocks. Even when economic conditions are not critical, public relations may be perceived as window dressing. Media, regulatory agencies, consumer groups, and many managers doubt that public relations has a useful purpose in American business. Typically, public relations professionals respond by claiming that they contribute to better understanding between publics and organizations, but they do not present tangible evidence of this contribution. When the Cobb County, Georgia, Chamber of Commerce went to the city council with a request for $100,000 to promote tourism, they took the council members out to dinner and made an appeal based on generalities. The council agreed to provide $10,000. While the chamber was disappointed, communication chairman Dave Kaplan was circumspect. "We'll have to spend that $10,000 on something that gives us measurable results," he said. "Then we'll come back next year and show them what we can accomplish."

Public relations practitioners must speak with authority when asked to prove their value to business and society. This authority can come only through an ability to conduct research and apply the results to public relations campaigns. Public relations professionals must maintain good media relations, produce employee publications, release financial information, and conduct community relations programs. In addition, those who succeed must also be able to measure the effects of their programs, provide sound forecasts of future needs, and account for the resources they consume.

An independent public relations counselor was seeking a new client. "What can you do for me?" asked the prospective client.

"I can get you exposure," explained the public relations person. "I can get you speaking dates and get you in the newspaper."

"*I* can do that," said the prospect (who was rapidly becoming a less likely client). "What I need is someone to help me make money."

"That's marketing," said the public relations counselor. "I do public relations."

"You do nothing if you don't contribute to my bottom line," was the response. "All my expenditures make me money or they don't get made. No sale."

Informal Research Techniques

Research means information gathering. Research can range from looking up the names of editors of weekly newspapers in Nebraska to polling those people to discover their opinions about farm export policy. Research is not always elaborate or highly structured. We want to begin this section by considering a few informal research methods and sources that practitioners use.

One of the most important skills necessary for the successful practice of public re-   *Record Keeping*
lations is the ability to keep comprehensive and accurate records. Practitioners are
frequently asked to produce critical information at a moment's notice for use inside and outside their organizations. Thus, when an editor or manager calls for information, the public relations practitioner must produce the needed data within a
relatively short time or suffer loss of credibility. By earning a reputation as a
source of valuable information, the practitioner can develop a network of internal
and external information contacts.

Frequently, individuals who are opinion leaders in the community, industry, or or-   *Key Contacts*
ganization act as **key contacts** for the public relations practitioner. Others who
possess special knowledge or who communicate frequently with significant
publics are also good sources. For a community college, for example, key contacts would be significant business, political, student, and community leaders.
However, while these people can provide valuable information, they may not represent the majority opinion. Because they are leaders or individuals with special
knowledge, they must be regarded as nontypical of their groups. Their special insight may give them greater sensitivity to an issue than most people would have.
Therefore, the practitioner must be careful not to overreact to feedback from these
sources or plan major responses based solely on such information. Key contacts
are best used to provide early warning about issues that may become significant.

To help obtain necessary information, many public relations practitioners orga-   *Special Committees*
nize special committees. Internal and external committees of key communicators,
decision makers, and opinion leaders can point out issues before they become
problems and suggest alternative courses of action. Such an advisory group can be
formed for a specified length of time, such as the duration of a campaign, or it can
be a permanent board that replaces members periodically.

Qualitative research offers an informal way to gain in-depth understanding of an   *Focus Groups*
audience without the rigor of more formal research methods. The most widely
used technique for qualitative research is the **focus group.** As we saw in the Cedar
Springs case, a focus group is a small number of people who share some demographic characteristic. Group members are interviewed, with open-ended questions used to encourage interaction and probe the nature of their beliefs. Focus
groups are generally assembled only once, and their responses are videotaped or
observed from behind a one-way mirror. This procedure enables researchers to
take into account not only what is said but also gestures, facial expressions, and
other forms of nonverbal communication that may reveal depth of meaning.

   Although ethical and legal considerations require researchers to inform
focus groups that they are being recorded or observed, experience shows that participants are seldom reluctant to discuss their feelings. Frequently, people selected
for focus groups are glad someone is willing to listen to them. Sometimes the
process of asking can be just as valuable as the information gained because the organization is perceived as being responsive to its publics.

Person-to-person interviews are usually the best survey research method but also the most expensive.

Recently, Syracuse University used several focus groups composed of alumni to help plan a major fund-raising drive. The centerpiece of the campaign was to be a promotional film stressing the scientific and research emphasis at the university. However, feedback from focus group participants revealed that such presentations turned them off. This realization prevented Syracuse from making a costly error in communication. Larissa A. Grunig reported on the use of focus groups to help plan a program for a county mental health department designed to reduce the stigma existing in the community regarding chronic mental illness. In addition to focus groups, a larger sample-size telephone survey of county residents was conducted. According to the departmental administrator, however, results of the phone survey provided fewer and shallower responses for designing the subsequent communication campaign. Focus groups allowed researchers to discuss why residents felt the way they did; the survey did not provide that opportunity.[1]

Casual Monitoring

Many practitioners find it helpful to screen systematically material that regularly comes through their offices. Monitoring of news reports in both print and broadcast media should be done to allow consideration of the quality and quantity of coverage. Carefully tracking incoming mail, telephone calls, and sales reports can also provide valuable information. Like all information collected through informal research methods, however, these techniques have built-in biases because the data are not collected from representative samples of the target publics.

Formal Research Techniques

The growing importance of formal research in public relations has in recent years prompted several studies that attempt to assess research techniques preferred among professionals. In one such study, Walter K. Lindenman sampled 253 practitioners, among them public relations executives from *Fortune* 500 companies, public relations

TABLE 6.1   Research Techniques Respondents Claimed They Used Most Frequently

Literature searches/information retrieval
Publicity tracking
Telephone/mail surveys with simple cross-tabs
Focus groups
PR/communications audits
Secondary analysis studies
Consumer inquiry analysis
Depth interviews with opinion leaders
Readership/readability studies
Pre- and posttests (before and after polls)
Sophisticated techniques (conjoint/factor analysis)
Psychographic analysis
Mall intercept/shopping center studies
Content analysis studies
Experimental designs
Unobtrusive measures (role-playing, observation participation)
Model building

agencies, nonprofit organizations, and academic institutions. A summary of his findings is listed in Table 6.1. Formal research procedures topped the list.[2]

Library and Data Bank Sources

Public and private libraries are sources of data that would be impossible for the practitioner to collect personally. Reference librarians are helpful in finding information, and many libraries now subscribe to computerized data retrieval networks that can obtain information from anywhere in the world. Census data and other types of public information are available at libraries that are designated as government depositories. In addition, a number of independent research organizations, such as the Survey Research Center at the University of Michigan, publish information that may be valuable to the public relations practitioner.

Media guides, trade and professional journals, and other reference books may be useful items in a public relations practitioner's personal library. Following are further sources that should be noted and can be valuable in researching a future employer or a competing organization:

Dun and Bradstreet Million Dollar Directory

Dun and Bradstreet Middle Market Directory

Standard and Poor's Register of Corporations, Directors, and Executives

Thomas' Register of American Manufacturers

Fortune Magazine's "Directory of Largest Corporations"

Fortune Magazine's "Annual Directory Issues"

Black Enterprise Magazine's "The Top 100"

As you read the next section, keep in mind that secondary sources like those mentioned should be exhausted before a primary research effort is planned. Researchers should review the information available to make certain the questions to be asked have not already been answered by others.

Content Analysis

Content analysis is a research method that allows the researcher to code systematically and thereby quantify the verbal content of written or transcribed messages. This technique provides a method of systematic observation for informal research efforts, such as the analysis of transcripts from focus groups. News clippings can be analyzed for quantity and quality of coverage. Many organizations analyze the contents of the annual reports and other publications of their competitors to discover strategic plans.

Survey Research

The practice of public relations employs all types of research processes, but the survey method is the most common. Cedar Springs Hospital used survey research to answer some critical questions. Laboratory and field experiments, as well as various types of simulations, can have a place (like pretesting a message) in a public relations research effort. However, surveys are the most effective way to assess the characteristics of publics in a form that allows the data to be used in planning and evaluating public relations efforts. Surveys should provide a means of separating publics rather than lumping them together into one amorphous mass.

The term *survey,* as applied in public relations research, refers to careful, detailed examination of the perceptions, attitudes, and opinions of members of various publics. The general purpose of a survey is to obtain a better understanding of the reactions and preferences of a specific public or publics. For public relations efforts, we divide survey data into two types: *demographic* and *opinion.* Demographic data are those characteristics (age, sex, occupation, etc.) of the people responding to the survey that help a practitioner classify them into one or more publics. Opinion data are responses to the questions a practitioner raises concerning the attitudes and perceptions of certain publics about critical issues.

Experimental Research

Experimental research is generally divided into two categories: *laboratory experiments* and *field experiments.* Laboratory experiments take place in carefully controlled environments designed to minimize outside effects. Field experiments take place in real-world settings. The trade-off between field and laboratory experiments is essentially one of authenticity versus purity.

In a field experiment, the researcher sacrifices a great deal of control over the setting to obtain reactions in a real environment. In a laboratory setting, however, the researcher can control many outside stimuli that might contaminate the results of the study. For example, a public relations practitioner might decide to pretest a particular message by inviting people into a room to view the message in several forms and then measuring their reactions. A church foundation attempting to raise funds for a chaplain in a local cancer hospital used this method to test the graphics and photographs in its brochure to avoid negative effects before publication. The laboratory setting ensured that the subjects' responses were based on the message being studied and not on other stimuli that might exist in a normal environment. To test the effects of a message in a more authentic setting, a field experiment such as a test-market study could be arranged, using a specific group of people in their normal environment.

We have described several methods of research. Now we will look at ways to actually collect information.

Formal research information can be obtained in a variety of ways that may be classified as either descriptive or inferential. **Descriptive data** are used to characterize something, like a particular group of people (a public). If the public relations practitioner in an organization asks the personnel department to prepare a demographic profile of its employees (average age, gender breakdown, years of education, experience level, etc.), he or she is requesting descriptive data. Such studies use averages, percentages, actual numbers, or other descriptive statistics to summarize the characteristics of a group or public.

   Inferential data do more than describe a particular public. Inferential data identify indirectly (infer) the characteristics of people not included in the specific group from which the information was obtained. Through sampling, which we will discuss later in this section, it is possible to select a relatively small number who represent a larger population. Using inferential statistics, a public relations practitioner can infer the characteristics of a very large public, such as a consumer group, from a relatively small but representative sample of that population.

Whether research is classified as descriptive or inferential, survey or experimental, and regardless of the sampling technique employed, the three basic means for collecting research data are *observations, interviews,* and *questionnaires.*

   Observational techniques are easily misused in public relations research because of the informal nature of many observations about publics. A practitioner's personal observations are severely limited by his or her own perceptions, experiences, and sensitivity. These limitations can lead to decisions based more on gut feeling than on reliable information. Structural techniques make personal observations more reliable because observers are trained within established rules to observe and record data systematically, but this is normally an expensive and complex process.

   Interviews can be a successful way to get information from a public. Skilled interviewers can elicit information that subjects might not otherwise volunteer. Interviews may be conducted face-to-face as well as over the telephone; they are generally classified as structured or unstructured. A structured interview uses a schedule of questions with specific response choices ranging from yes/no to multiple choice; unstructured interviews allow subjects to respond to open-ended questions however they wish. Although interviews are frequently employed, they have disadvantages. For example, the interviewer's personality, dress, and non-verbal cues may bias the response. To minimize such problems, it is necessary to use expertly trained interviewers, the cost of which can be prohibitive.

   Questionnaires are the most common form of data collection because they are stable in presentation and inexpensive to use. Once a questionnaire is printed, each subject is asked the same questions in exactly the same way. Questionnaires are generally designed to measure one or more of the following: attitudes, opinions, and demographic characteristics of the sample. Figure 6.2 is an example of

Collecting Formal Research Data

Descriptive and Inferential Methods

Methods for Obtaining Information

Public relations practitioners input responses from telephone interviews directly into the data base for study, making data analysis almost instant.

a questionnaire used to measure the effects of certain messages on the public images of political candidates. Note that it seeks information in all three categories.

The decision about whether to use questionnaires or interviews to gather data for public relations research must take into account the study's budget, purpose, subjects, and a variety of other considerations. Questionnaires can be distributed by mail and may be administered to either individuals or groups. They provide anonymity and present a uniform stimulus to all subjects. On the other hand, interviews are more flexible, elicit a higher percentage of responses in some situations, and can be used with relatively uneducated publics.

Sampling Methods

A sample is a subset of a population or public. Public relations researchers use samples because in most instances it is impractical to collect information from every person in the target public. Sampling techniques are numerous, but the best methods rely on the theory of probability to portray a miniature version of the target public. Although the theory of probability is too complex to discuss here, it is the basis of all inferential statistics. The following sampling methods rely on the theory of probability to ensure a sample that is representative of the public from which it is drawn.

Simple random sampling is a technique that allows each member of a public an equal chance of being selected. If the sample is large enough (some experts say at least 30 to 60 people) and is selected totally at random, it will accurately reflect the characteristics of its public. Probably the most common example of simple random sampling is drawing names from a hat. If the slips of paper are mixed thoroughly enough, each one has an equal chance of being drawn.

Systematic sampling uses a list, like a telephone directory or mailing list, to produce a sample at random. Generally, a table of random numbers is used to find a starting point on the list and a selection interval. For example, a researcher

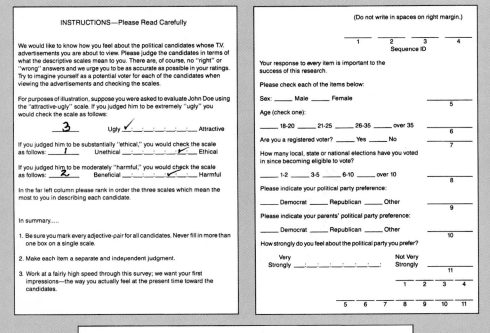

Figure 6.2 Sample questionnaire used to measure effects of political advertisements on candidate images

The diversity of individuals in our society presents a unique challenge for the selection of target audience groups.

might randomly pick the number 293006 from a table of random numbers. Using the first three digits, the researcher could start on page 293 of the telephone directory; then, using the last three digits, he or she could select every sixth name for the sample. This method is more practical than simple random sampling in most public relations research.

Stratified random sampling is a two-stage process that first divides the public into two or more mutually exclusive categories (such as males and females) and then randomly selects samples from each stratum. This method is used to guarantee that each subgroup of a particular public is adequately represented in the sample. For example, if a practitioner wanted information about all ethnic groups in a particular geographical area, it would be necessary first to divide the population into ethnic categories to ensure that the sample included representatives from each group.

Cluster sampling involves the random selection of groups rather than individuals for a sample. For example, if we wanted to measure the attitudes of United Auto Workers members, we could randomly include local unions in our study rather than individual UAW members.

Quota sampling randomly selects a fixed number of people from each of several distinguishable subsets of a public. For example, a researcher may decide to select 50 subjects from each of the following groups by sex and age, regardless of what proportion of the actual public they account for: males 18 to 25, males 26 to 40, males over 40, females 18 to 25, females 26 to 40, and females over 40. This technique would allow accurate assessment of the opinions of each subgroup.

Measuring Public Opinion

Most organizational goals and objectives dealing with public relations depend to some extent on the concept of **public opinion.** Therefore, the first step in public relations research is to sample public opinion. It is important to recognize at the outset that an organization does not have a single indistinguishable public. The practitioner who relies on so-called public opinion polls to provide insight into the characteristics of a potential audience may be operating with erroneous data. Most polls of this type are not very useful from a public relations point of view because they actually measure **mass opinion** rather than public opinion. Before using a survey, the practitioner should understand the difference between measuring mass opinion and measuring public opinion.

Mass Opinion

Mass opinion represents an average taken from a group with many different opinions. Averages by nature tend to blur the strength of some attitudes. When substantially different opinions are averaged together, the result may be very different from the original opinions stated. For example, if we conduct a poll asking about the image of a particular organization, we might find that 60 percent of our sample give it very high marks while 40 percent feel very negatively. Looking at the average of these responses, we might deduce that the organization in question has a moderately positive image; however, this average would hide the substantial negative feelings that exist.

Our hypothetical survey has actually uncovered two publics—one that has a very positive image of the organization and another that has a very negative image. In fact, no one in our sample holds the moderately positive view the average implies. To respond properly, we should construct communication strategies for two groups of people with very strong but opposite opinions. Public relations must be concerned with the strength as well as the direction of public attitudes.

Many mass opinion polls are useful for little more than predicting political election results. They do not shed much light on the complexities of public opinion that an effective public relations program must address.

Public Opinion

Public opinion polls involve carefully targeted populations. The public relations professional must break the audience into meaningful subgroups and design a specific communication campaign for each segment. Public opinion sampling is not useful unless it reflects accurately the feelings of each significant audience subgroup and provides some insight into the reasons behind these feelings.

Identifying Publics

John Dewey, in his 1927 book *The Public and Its Problems,* defines a public as a group of people who

1. Face a similar indeterminate situation.

2. Recognize what is indeterminate in that situation.

3. Organize to do something about the problem.[3]

A public, then, is a group of people who share a common problem or goal and recognize their common interest. In the remainder of this chapter, we will discuss specific methods for measuring public opinion and applying the results effectively in public relations work.

Traditional public opinion polling methods typically sort their results into demographic categories that seldom identify groups of people with common interests. Because of this inadequacy, James Grunig proposed and tested three categories for the identification of publics based on Dewey's definition:

Latent public A group faces an indeterminate situation but does not recognize it as a problem.

Aware public The group recognizes a problem—what is missing in the situation—and becomes aware.

Active public The group organizes to discuss and do something about the problem.[4]

Such categories group together people who are likely to behave in similar ways. This grouping enables public relations practitioners to communicate with each public regarding their needs and concerns rather than attempting to communicate with a mythical "average" public. Researching public opinion in appropriate categories can help direct the public relations process. For example, it may be possible to situate the primary audience for a public relations campaign in one of Grunig's three categories and to develop specific messages for that audience. In the Cedar Springs case, physicians were an active public. However, if management had not taken care to determine the view of a latent public, the patients, costly errors could have resulted.

Uses of Research in Public Relations

A recent study funded by the Foundation for Public Relations Research and Education considered 28 public and private organizations and concluded that "the use of public relations research by corporations is on the rise and its function and contribution are becoming better defined and recognized."[5] The study points out that the term *public relations research* no longer describes specific types of research methodology such as content analysis, public opinion polls, or readership surveys. Instead, the term as now employed refers to any type of research that yields data for use in planning and evaluating communication efforts.

The same survey revealed that most public relations research activities fall into four basic categories: environmental monitoring, public relations audits, communication audits, and social audits. These activities may incorporate any or all of the techniques already mentioned, furnishing public relations practitioners with information that is useful in every phase of their task. Table 6.2 illustrates how these categories of research provide useful information in the various areas of public relations practice.

TABLE 6.2 Categories of Public Relations Research Activities

External Environment	Organization	Publics	Message	Media	Effects
I. Environmental monitoring					

	II. Public relations audit
	  A. Audience identification
	  B. Corporate images
	III. Communications audit				

		1. Readership survey			
			2. Content analysis 3. Readability survey		
IV. Social audits					

Source: Otto Lerbinger, "Corporate Use of Public Relations Research," *Public Relations Review* 3 (Winter 1977): 13.

The study by the Foundation for Public Relations Research and Education revealed that **environmental monitoring** is the most rapidly growing category of public relations research.[6] Organizations today recognize themselves as dynamic, open systems that must react to changes in the environment; keeping track of those changes is important.

Environmental Monitoring

Public relations practitioners can use formal systems for observing trends and changes in public opinion and other areas of the environment to guide many phases of organizational planning, including public relations. Issues management, discussed in chapter 4, is one application of environmental monitoring. Another technique is scanning.

Scanning Liam Fahey and W. R. King described three basic scanning models—irregular, regular, and continuous—that various organizations employ to track environmental changes. Table 6.3 lists some characteristics of each model.[7]

Irregular model The irregular model of environmental study is an ad hoc approach. Generally, its use is precipitated by a crisis situation like an oil embargo or the introduction of a significant new product by a competitor. Once the unanticipated event occurs, the scanning process begins, focusing on past events that may help explain what has happened. The model is useful for identifying immediate reactions to problem situations, and it can provide input for short-range planning. The model does not help detect incipient crises or form long-range plans for future occurrences.

Regular model More comprehensive and systematic than the ad hoc model, the regular model generally entails an annual appraisal of environmental situations. Typically, the focus is on specific issues or decisions facing the organization.

TABLE 6.3 Scanning Model Framework

| | Scanning Models | | |
	Irregular	Regular	Continuous
Media for scanning activity	Ad hoc studies	Periodically updated studies	Structured data collection and processing systems
Scope of scanning	Specific events	Selected events	Broad range of environmental systems
Motivation for activity	Crisis initiated	Decision and issue oriented	Planning process oriented
Temporal nature of activity	Reactive	Proactive	Proactive
Time frame for data	Retrospective	Primarily current and retrospective	Prospective
Time frame for decision impact	Current and near-term future	Near-term	Long-term
Organizational makeup	Various staff agencies	Various staff agencies	Environmental scanning unit

Source: Liam Fahey and William R. King, "Environmental Scanning for Corporate Planning." Reprinted from *Business Horizons* (20). Copyright (1977) by the Foundation for the School of Business at Indiana University. Used with permission.

Automobile companies use this model in conducting annual research on consumer attitudes to help them develop advertising appeals for the automobiles they have already designed. Obviously, the regular model is still directed toward the recent past and the current situation and can develop only limited plans for the future. However, the regular model is an improvement over the irregular model: Current issues and decisions are examined in reference to the environment, and predictions are made about future impacts on those issues and decisions. Basically, the difference between the regular and the irregular model is a matter of degree and regularity.

Continuous model The continuous model emphasizes the ongoing monitoring of various environmental elements rather than specific issues and decisions. Any number of environmental segments—including political, regulatory, and competitive systems—may have input into this model. Auto companies that conduct consumer research to analyze preference trends are using continuous environmental scanning when the data collected become input for future automotive designs. Continuous scanning requires that the system be designed into the organization. Irregular (and to some extent regular) scanning methods can be managed by the concerned division or department, but an agency like the public relations department or another subunit must function as a clearinghouse for environmental data that are appropriate for several areas of the organization. In addition, computerized management information systems (MIS) are generally needed to store, evaluate, and integrate the vast amounts of information generated.

The continuous scanning model supports organizations' strategic planning efforts. Other models support specific issues or decisions, but the continuous model yields data to support the various issues and decisions an organization may face. For example, the American Council of Life Insurance developed a Trend Analysis Program (TAP), which "seeks to identify the direction of major social and economic trends so that companies may plan for the years ahead with greater confidence."[8] The program operates as a cooperative effort, with over 100 life insurance executives monitoring the specialty press and other publications where emerging social and economic trends might first become evident. Reports are issued whenever the data in a particular area are sufficient. For example, one report issued by TAP provided an in-depth survey of possible changes in American culture in the coming years.

The most frequently used type of public relations research is the **audit.** The public relations audit is essentially a broad-scale study that examines an organization's internal and external public relations. Many of the research techniques we have already discussed are used in public relations audits. The purpose of the audit is to provide information for planning future public relations efforts. Carl Byoir and Associates, one of the pioneers of public relations auditing, describes it as follows: "The Public Relations Audit, as the name implies, involves a comprehensive study of the public relations position of an organization: how it stands in the opinion of its various publics."[9] We can identify four general categories of audits in relation to organizations and their publics.

The Public Relations Audit

Relevant Publics   The organization's relevant publics are listed, and each is described according to its function—stockholders, employees, customers, suppliers, and the like. Also included are publics that have no direct functional relationship but are nevertheless in a position to affect the organization—for example, consumer, environmental, community, and other social action groups. The procedure is basically one of audience identification to aid in the planning of public relations messages. Some audits stop with this step.

The Organization's Standing with Publics   Each public's view of the organization is determined through various research methods, most commonly image studies and content analysis of newspapers, magazines, and other print media. Both of these research methods were discussed earlier in this chapter.

Issues of Concern to Publics   Environmental monitoring techniques such as those already mentioned are used to construct an issues agenda for each of the organization's relevant publics. These data identify publics according to issues of interest and their stands on those issues. The findings are then compared to the organization's own policies. This is a vital step in the planning of public relations campaigns for various audiences.

Power of Publics   Publics are rated according to the amount of economic and political (and therefore regulatory) influence they have. Interest groups and other activist organizations are evaluated according to size of membership, size of constituency, budget size and income source, staff size, and number of qualified specialists (lobbyists, attorneys, public relations professionals, etc.).

Public relations audits are becoming regular components of many public relations programs. They provide input data for planning future public relations programs and help evaluate the effectiveness of previous efforts. Several public relations counseling firms offer audit services to their clients. Joyce F. Jones of the Ruder Finn Rotman Agency describes the audit process in four steps:[10]

1. *Finding out what "we" think* Interviews with key management at the organization's top and middle strata are conducted to determine company strengths and weaknesses, relevant publics, and issues and topics to be explored.

2. *Finding out what "they" think* Research is conducted with key publics to determine how closely their views match those of company management.

3. *Evaluating the disparity* A public relations balance sheet of assets, liabilities, strengths, weaknesses, and the like is prepared on the basis of an analysis of the differences found between steps 1 and 2.

4. *Recommending* A comprehensive public relations program is planned to fill in the gap between steps 1 and 2 and to correct deficits revealed in the balance sheet of step 3.

Organizational Image Surveys Attitude surveys that determine a public's perceptions of an organization help the public relations manager obtain an overall view of the organization's image. Generally, such research seeks to measure (1) familiarity of the public with the organization and with its officers, products, policies, and other aspects; (2) degrees of positive and negative perception; and (3) characteristics various publics attribute to the organization. Frequently, organizations use such surveys as planning tools to compare existing images with desired images. Once the differences are assessed, image goals can be set and strategic plans made to overcome the identified problems. Cities seeking to attract convention and tourist business periodically check their images as perceived by key groups, then use these data to evaluate their attraction techniques.

Although several organizations conduct their own image studies, many employ outside consultants or research organizations to supply them with data. Some major organizations that provide such data are Opinion Research Center, Inc., Louis Harris and Associates, and Yankelovich, Skelly and White.[11]

Communication Audits

The communication audit, like the public relations audit, is applied in many different ways. Generally, it attempts to monitor and evaluate the channels, messages, and communication climate of an organization. Sometimes audits are applied only to internal organizational communication systems; however, the same technique can be used to evaluate external systems as well. Frequently, a communication audit reveals problems of distortion or lack of information.

Communication audits package various research methods for specific applications. The following research methods are used in appropriate combinations to audit organizational communication and investigate specific problem areas:

1. *Communication climate surveys* These attitudinal measurements are designed to reveal how open and adequate the publics perceive communication channels to be.

2. *Network analysis* This analysis reveals the frequency and importance of interactions in a network, on the basis of the most frequent linkages. These patterns can be compared to official organizational charts and communication policies to determine disparities between theory and practice.

3. *Readership surveys* These surveys identify which articles or sections of publications are read most frequently. While this method is strictly quantitative, it is an excellent way to determine the reading patterns of various publics.

4. *Content analysis* This quantitative tool, discussed earlier, can analyze the content of all types of messages. It is frequently used to describe the amount of favorable and unfavorable news coverage an organization receives.

5. *Readability studies* Several methods may be employed to assess how readily written messages are understood. Most of these methods are based on numbers of syllables in words and on length of sentences. These formulas—to be discussed in more detail in chapter 9, where evaluation techniques are examined—help determine the clarity of a written message and its appropriateness to an audience's educational level.

Social Audits

The concept of social auditing emerged in the early 1960s when businesses and other organizations were challenged to recognize their obligations to society. Social audits are generally attitude and opinion surveys that measure various publics' perceptions concerning an organization's social responsiveness. This technique attempts to quantify the organization's impact on its public in much the same way that a public relations audit does. However, social audits are generally confined to issues of social responsibility.

Social auditing was common in the mid- to late 1970s. In recent years, social issues have been addressed in other types of research, such as environmental scanning and public relations and communication audits. One of the best and most complete examples of a social audit was conducted for a city government and published in 1975 by Professor Robert D. Hay.[12]

Summary

Research is a vital part of any public relations effort. It supplies the initial inputs to guide strategy and message development, and it provides a method for predicting effectiveness and assessing results. In most organizations today, public relations professionals must be able to measure the effects of their work and make reasonable predictions about future success if they wish to influence managerial decisions.

Many public opinion surveys are not useful in public relations planning and evaluation because they tend to average responses in a way that disguises the relative strengths of attitudes. Good public opinion research must be sensitive enough to segment publics according to the strength of their opinions. Four basic categories of research in public relations are sufficiently sensitive: environmental monitoring, public relations audits, communication audits, and social audits.

Designing the Student Union

By James VanLeuven
*Professor and Chairman of the Technical Journalism Department
Colorado State University
Fort Collins, Colorado*

Case Study

Before hiring an architect to design a new student union building, University of Idaho student leaders commissioned an attitude study of student leisure interests. The leaders wanted to know which kinds of students used which kinds of facilities. Study the following data and then answer the questions.

Sampling Methodology

The researchers selected 384 students from a student body of 7,000 by taking every 17th name in the student directory. Each respondent was asked to complete a four-page mail questionnaire that utilized several question formats. Some 225 students, or roughly 60 percent, completed the procedure. The following table presents the results of the survey.

Year in School:	Respondents	Actual Student Body
Freshman	21.9	21.3
Sophomore	18.3	19.0
Junior	21.0	20.2
Senior	17.9	18.6
Graduate/law	20.9	20.9
Residence:		
Fraternity	12.1	12.0
Men's hall	22.9	20.6
Sorority	4.0	5.2
Women's hall	5.4	8.2
UI married housing	1.3	1.4
Off-campus	54.3	52.6
Sex:		
Male	68.4	59.2
Female	31.6	40.8

Participation in Activities	Involved: 4/more hrs/wk	Slightly Involved: Up to 4 hrs/wk	Not Involved: No time	Groups Most Involved
ASUI committees	0.9	1.4	97.7	f,s,m,2,3
ASUI senate	0.0	0.9	99.1	f,m,s,3,4
ASUI communications (Arg, KUOI, etc.)	2.3	3.7	94.0	m,w,2,3,4
Other ASUI activity	1.5	2.0	96.5	f,s,2,3
Living group officer	6.9	7.8	85.3	f,s,m,w,3
Living group social activity	17.9	25.5	56.5	f,s,w,1,2,3
Living group recreation activity	11.8	28.4	59.7	f,s,w,m,1,2
Visiting with members of living group	31.4	17.6	51.0	f,s,1,2,3,4
Live off campus, still take part in living group	3.3	10.6	86.1	f,1,2,3,4,5
Campus religious organization	5.2	10.0	84.8	s,w,m,1,2
Religious study group	5.7	12.7	87.3	s,w,m,1,2,3
Campus/community craft groups	0.5	3.8	95.8	o,4,5
Music performance group	3.8	2.3	93.9	m,w,1,2,3
International student organization	0.0	2.5	97.5	m,3,4,5
Other cultural group	11.4	8.9	79.7	m,w,o,3,4
Hunting and fishing	23.0	35.7	41.3	m,f,o,3,4,5
Camping and backpacking	19.3	41.5	39.2	m,o,3,4,5
Campus intramural sports	16.2	25.0	58.8	f,m,s,w,1,2
Swimming and water sports	7.3	38.0	54.6	w,o,3,4,5
Golf and tennis	8.7	33.0	58.3	f,0,2,3,4,5
Handball and gym sports	13.6	28.8	57.6	m,o,4,5
Bowling	4.1	19.8	76.1	m,w,1,2
Skiing	19.5	30.2	50.3	f,s,o,1,2,3
Other sports	31.5	24.3	44.1	
Television viewing	30.7	42.7	26.6	u,m,w,o,1,2,3,4
Movies and films	8.9	59.8	31.3	u,f,m,s,w,o,1,2,3
Bowling and billiards	8.1	29.9	62.0	m,1
Visiting over coffee or soft drinks	37.7	47.0	15.3	f,s,w,1,2,3
Service clubs and organizations	3.5	12.4	84.2	f,s,o,2,3,4
Honoraries, clubs in student's major	7.2	22.5	70.3	u,o,4,5
Political organizations	0.0	8.0	92.0	f,m,w,1,2,3
Other organizations	21.4	14.3	64.3	m,o,3,4

Participation key: 1 = freshman   4 = senior   m = men's hall   u = UI married student
2 = sophomore   5 = graduate/law   s = sorority   housing
3 = junior   f = fraternity   w = women's hall   o = off-campus

Questions

1. In which eight activities are nearly half or more than half of the respondents involved?

2. How representative of the total campus population are the respondents?

3. If this were your survey, would you feel comfortable suggesting to management that they act on these findings?

4. In general, what is the relationship between a student's year in school, living arrangements, and participation in student activities?

Notes

1. Larissa A. Grunig, "Using Focus Group Research in Public Relations," *Public Relations Review* (Summer 1990): 36–49.

2. Walter K. Lindenmann, "Research, Evaluation and Measurement: A National Perspective," *Public Relations Review* (Summer 1990): 10.

3. John Dewey, *The Public and Its Problems* (Chicago: Swallow, 1927).

4. James E. Grunig, "A New Measure of Public Opinions on Corporate Social Responsibility," *Academy of Management Journal* 22 (December 1979): 740–741.

5. Otto Lerbinger, "Corporate Use of Research in Public Relations," *Public Relations Review* 3 (Winter 1977): 11.

6. Ibid., 12.

7. Liam Fahey and William R. King, "Environmental Scanning for Corporate Planning," *Business Horizons* 20 (August 1977): 47–51.

8. Lerbinger, "Corporate Use of Research," 15.

9. Ibid., 16.

10. Joyce F. Jones, "The Public Relations Audit: Its Purpose and Uses. *R&F Papers,* no. 3 (New York: Ruder Finn Rotman, Inc., 1975). Reprinted in *Public Relations Journal* 31 (July 1975): 6–8.

11. Lerbinger, "Corporate Use of Research," 12.

12. Robert D. Hay, "Social Auditing: An Experimental Approach," *Academy of Management Journal* (December 1975): 872.

CHAPTER 7

Planning for Public Relations Effectiveness

Preview

Public relations effectiveness depends on planning. Good planning is the best way to practice preventive rather than remedial public relations.

Tactical and strategic plans help public relations coordinate its efforts with those of other areas of the organization.

Public relations units in organizations are generally considered expense centers when budgets are prepared because only the inputs or expenditures can be measured adequately. Therefore, to secure an appropriate share of the organization's resources, the public relations unit must do a good job of "selling" its activities to managerial decision makers.

Public relations practitioners can apply the basic four-step planning model discussed in this chapter to increase their effectiveness in organizational settings.

From now on, we will demand the same strategic plans from you that we expect from production and marketing and research—plans based on where the company wants to be . . . , what it needs to get there, and what the communications function can do to help.

—James Bere, Chairman and CEO
Borg-Warner Corporation

Public relations practitioners, like most other managers, tend to be action oriented. The constant changes both within and outside any organization produce an endless procession of public relations problems. Too often, because of the number of pressing problems, managers find themselves responding only to exceptional situations. Such situations are usually negative: They require the practitioner to intervene after a problem has already gotten out of control. Former media relations manager for the New York Yankees Ira Kase summed up his job as follows: "I have to come up with certain statements after the fact (and fend off nastiness in the press)." Thus, public relations managers frequently find themselves so busy putting out fires that they do not have time to prevent them from starting.

While putting out fires is certainly part of the public relations function, it cannot be allowed to dominate all actions. If it does, the practitioner becomes a victim of circumstances, able only to react to the situation at hand. Perhaps the most frequent complaint of public relations practitioners is that other managers request their services only after problems have become unmanageable. When damage to the organization's image has already been done, the public relations manager is often directed to "fix it." This may prove to be a no-win situation both for the organization and for the practitioner, who must engage in usually fruitless remedial public relations.

For a long time, practitioners have advocated preventive public relations to avoid such problems. Part of this approach involves the type of fact-finding research already discussed in chapter 6. If practitioners detect potential problems before they erupt into damaging situations, they can give management early warning and advice. At times, even early detection cannot forestall some negative impact. However, when advance warning is coupled with adequate planning, negative effects can be minimized, and public relations management can offer well-designed, positive actions rather than hastily conceived reactions. As we continue our integrating case study begun in chapter 6, notice how the pitfalls of hasty reaction were avoided.

The Importance of Planning

In the Cedar Springs case, research and careful planning prevented the loss of time and employee confidence that would have resulted from too quick a reaction to the first symptoms of the problem. Only through continuous advance planning can public relations practitioners avoid having to react after damage has been done. Even though many public relations managers feel they have no time to plan, the opposite is more accurate. The more time managers devote to planning based on adequate research, the less time they will need to spend putting out fires.

Planning actually creates the time needed to plan. It permits the development of integrated public relations efforts that support an organization's goals in a positive rather than a defensive manner. Planning provides the opportunity to involve management from other areas of the organization and to ensure their cooperation and support. One important cause of ineffective public relations efforts is the lack of planning. Through careful, detailed planning, public relations departments can make more efficient use of the funds and personnel allocated to them.

Integrating
Case Study

Cedar Springs
Community Hospital

Segment 2

Y ou may remember that the physicians at Cedar Springs Hospital (chapter 6) were calling for immediate action to correct what they saw as a potentially life-threatening situation in patient care. Reaction to the problem as it appeared at the time would have generated a campaign to heighten employees' awareness of the need for quality patient care and emphasize their responsibility for providing the best care possible. However, before taking action, the public relations director conducted some research to help him better understand the problem. The results were surprising and showed that the first action contemplated would have only made things worse. Employees already believed that the quality of patient care in the hospital was subpar, and they were frustrated because they felt that they personally were doing good work. In addition, research revealed that recently released patients rated the quality of care significantly better than the employees did.

The sizable difference between the employee and patient ratings pointed to a different problem than was originally suspected. The planning process based upon this research redefined the issue from one of actual care to one of perceptions about care.

Objective: The objective that emerged from the research findings was to improve employee and physician views of overall hospital performance. Obviously, because both doctors and individual employees felt they were personally providing the best care they could and because patients rated their performance high, the actual quality of care was good. However, their perception of poor performance was creating a morale problem for both doctors and employees.

Planning: Two basic strategies were devised to be implemented in a year-long campaign. The first strategy was continually to reinforce employees' feelings of worth as members of the hospital's medical team through positive feedback from management. The second strategy was to help both physicians and employees more accurately judge the overall quality of care through increased feedback from patients.

A budget of $6,000 was developed to conduct additional surveys of recent patients and communicate the message of quality care through a variety of media. Communication channels would be selected to let both internal and external audiences receive the message that hospital employees were a quality team. Policies were changed to allow letters with positive comments from patients to be routed first to the concerned departments before being filed.

Communicating with Management

Public relations efforts often fail because of communication breakdowns between practitioners and other managers within the organization. These breakdowns are frequently due to imperfect alignment between the public relations planning process and planning done elsewhere in the organization. Misunderstandings can usually be prevented if public relations practitioners analyze the organizational management as carefully as they analyze any other audience.

Public relations departments must prepare messages that communicate their needs and their potential contributions to other segments of the organization. Therefore, when planning, they must learn the terms and methods common to organizational management.

The Fundamentals of Managerial Planning

Managerial planning is generally classified into two broad categories: strategic and tactical. **Strategic plans** are long-range plans, usually made by higher levels of management. This type of planning involves decisions concerning the major goals of an organization and policies for their implementation. **Tactical plans** are specific decisions about what will be done at every level of the organization to accomplish the strategic plans. Strategic planners typically deal with future events and must therefore rely on relatively uncertain data. The use of forecasting techniques to predict the effects of economic and technical changes on an organization in the coming five years is an example of strategic planning. Tactical planners, on the other hand, are more concerned with the day-to-day operation of an organization and its immediate future.

Public relations plans are both strategic and tactical. Decisions concerning an organization's long-range future often take public relations into consideration. Of course, public relations develops tactical plans in support of strategic plans.

Strategic plans and tactical plans combined produce either **single-use plans** or **standing plans.** This hierarchy of plans is illustrated in figure 7.1. *Goals* refers

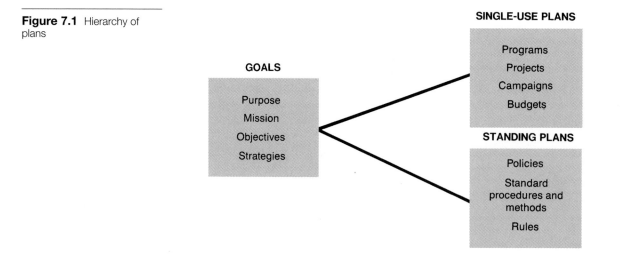

Figure 7.1 Hierarchy of plans

to the basic direction an organization is heading in. The purpose, mission, objectives, and strategies of an organization are all component parts of its goals. These terms are frequently used interchangeably; however, they may also be used in various combinations to indicate sublevels of planning. Because there are no universally accepted definitions for these terms, most organizations adopt their own very specific applications.[1]

In this section, we will discuss a four-step process that is characteristic of managerial planning. Understanding this process, along with the specifics of planning, should help public relations practitioners adapt their planning messages to other managers. The elements of the process are (1) establishing goals, (2) determining the present situation, (3) determining aids and barriers to goals, and (4) forecasting.

Establishing Goals

In the Cedar Springs case, patient care became the goal that unified physicians, administrators, and employees. Agreeing on a goal or a set of goals must be the first step in deciding what a public relations effort will need. Frequently, in a list of possible goals, two or more are mutually exclusive. When possible goals conflict, each must be evaluated to determine the long- and short-range effects of acceptance or rejection.

Resources often dictate the selection of goals. An organization may not be able (or willing) to devote the time, personnel, and capital necessary to accomplish some goals. Goals that are selected for the public relations function, however, must always relate to organizational purpose. When seeking approval for public relations goals, a manager will be more successful if he or she can relate them to the goals and objectives of the entire organization.

Determining the Present Situation

In reality, it is impossible to separate planning from research because they occur almost simultaneously. As a goal is considered, current data about the organization's environment must be collected and used to evaluate the likelihood that the goal can be reached. Information provided by the kind of fact-finding research discussed in chapter 6 is crucial at this point.

Again, the Cedar Springs example demonstrates the importance of taking appropriate steps to get accurate information before a plan is begun. It is useless to set goals that are unrealistic or that have already been accomplished. Even after the goal has been firmly set, data about the current situation must be monitored. If the situation changes, it may be necessary to alter the goal or goals. Goals must be set with a good understanding of the current situation, the available resources, and the limitations that must be placed on those goals.

Determining Aids and Barriers to Goals

After reasonable goals are determined, a more careful investigation of the environment must take place to identify aids and barriers to their attainment. An organization's resources in terms of people, money, and equipment are important aids for achieving any goal. Likewise, a shortage of any of these elements represents a barrier that must be overcome. Although money is frequently the first barrier to be considered, it is seldom severe enough to prevent the accomplishment of objectives. Many plans, like the one at Cedar Springs Hospital, can be carried out on relatively small budgets. The following are key questions that help identify aids

Computers are now the primary tool for tracking current data trends and developments.

and barriers: Do we have *the right individuals?* (rather than enough people) and Do we have *enough* money? (rather than how much money).

An organization's structure and policies can also form either aids or barriers. For example, the goal of creating a sense of unity between labor and management could be severely hindered by policies that prohibit informal communication between the company and its union. Other barriers and aids reside outside the organization—for example, with government, competitors, consumer groups, and other special interest groups.

Forecasting

Planning always involves the future. Predicting aids and barriers that will exist in the future is much more difficult than evaluating the existing situation, yet such predictions are necessary to determine the effects of anticipated conditions on the programs being planned. Such variables as unemployment, economic developments, and inflation can reasonably be predicted a year or more in advance by using quantitative techniques.

Econometric models and other statistical tools are used in most large organizations to predict future events. Public opinion surveys forecast reactions to initiatives or actions contemplated by politicians, government officials, and managers. In the early part of President Reagan's administration, various versions of his tax reform plan were aired publicly so that reaction could be measured prior to final congressional action. Public relations management must become familiar with these methods and use them to evaluate future effects on publics (see chapter 6).

Predictions should also be made concerning the effects of planned public relations activities on various publics and the corresponding effects of public reaction on the programs being planned. Often these judgments must be made by qualitative rather than quantitative means. Juries of executive opinion, sales force composites, and customer expectations are frequently employed. The following other forecasting methods may also be used:

The **Delphi Model** is a method developed by the Rand Corporation as a systematic procedure for arriving at a consensus among a group of experts. The panel of experts is usually separated by great geographical distances and never meets to interact about the topic. A series of detailed questionnaires is mailed to every panelist. The responses are used to construct subsequent sets of questionnaires that are sent to the same panelists. The process continues until a consensus is apparent.

Brainstorming is a group discussion technique used to generate large numbers of creative alternatives or new ideas. It has been used for some time by advertising agencies, public relations firms, and others who need to generate creative ideas. An example of brainstorming occurred recently when the Atlanta Chamber of Commerce held a breakfast for several top practitioners in the city and solicited their ideas on ways to revive the failing Peach Bowl game. Ideas were generated while the game's planning committee listened and took notes for later consideration.

The basic rule of brainstorming is that no one is permitted to interject negative feedback or criticism into the discussion. As the group proceeds to generate ideas, all are carefully recorded, to be critiqued later. No comment is considered too absurd or too simple because it could produce the spark necessary for a truly creative idea. Brainstorming can be effective with a group that is comfortable functioning in a freewheeling atmosphere.

Scenario construction has been used by "think tanks" like the Rand Corporation to create very long-range forecasts. A logical, hypothetical description of future events (a scenario) is constructed to explore the dynamics of various alternatives. For example, if a large auto company wanted to choose one of several manufacturing plants to close, a scenario could be constructed for each case to detail possible effects on the environment, the economic future of the community, the availability of replacement jobs, and other positive and negative results.

Developing a Plan to Reach the Goal

If the current situation has been described, aids and barriers considered, and forecasts completed, listing alternative courses of action should be relatively automatic. After as many alternatives as possible have been listed, the process of evaluating them should begin. Alternatives should be compared in terms of costs and benefits. In the following discussion, we will describe some management techniques that can be applied in public relations planning.

Management-by-Objectives

The term **management-by-objectives (MBO),** an approach to planning detailed in public relations spotlight 7.1, has lost popularity in management jargon. However, its basic elements are still widely used to describe management plans. Remember that the public relations plan is a message that must be communicated to an organization's executives. Whether or not that message is accepted depends not only on the effective execution of the planning process but also on the way the plan is communicated to the decision makers who must understand and approve it.

MBO is an administrative planning process that entails setting both long- and short-range objectives and then developing plans to accomplish those goals. Frequently, the process spreads to every level of an organization. Managers and their subordinates may begin the process by developing separate objectives and plans, then review each other's work and prepare a joint document as a final plan. This process can occur at every level up the organizational chart. Sometimes this flexible planning technique is called by other names. As we shall discuss in chapter 9, setting objectives before initiating action is critical to the ability to demonstrate effectiveness in public relations efforts.

PERT Network Analysis

Program evaluation and review technique (PERT) depicts a plan in network form by showing the sequence, timing, and costs of tasks needed to complete a project. PERT can be used in public relations for planning and controlling

---

Public Relations by Objectives

Public Relations Spotlight 7.1

Public relations often fails because managers do not understand what public relations people are saying and doing. This can be prevented if we talk in management's terms rather than trying to educate them in ours.

The Advantages of MBO
1. Communicates the way business people think in terms of business problems and objectives.
2. Raises the importance of public relations in the corporate structure.
3. Presents a structure for implementing effective communications programs.
4. Helps keep the public relations practitioner on target in solving public relations problems.
5. Contributes to the public relations body of knowledge.

The Process
1. Get a fix on the business problem: Analyze the business problem using all available research techniques, then develop a clear, concise statement of what the problem is.
2. Translate the business problem into public relations objectives: This is the most difficult part of the process. The objectives should be stated in measurable terms.
3. Determine the audience(s): Identify to whom your message will be directed. There may be several audiences. Examples: print and broadcast media, company employees, customers, government officials.
4. Determine program elements: Exactly what vehicles will be used to effect the program. Examples: TV, news clips, news releases, institutional ads, speeches, and publicity events.
5. Determine budget: The ideal situation is to fit the budget to the need, using an objective and task approach.
6. Evaluate the program: Utilize appropriate measuring instruments and techniques.

Source: Walt Seifert, APR, Professor Emeritus, School of Journalism, Ohio State University.

anything from single projects to entire campaigns. This technique is most appropriate when the effort being planned has definite beginning and completion points. After the planning phase is completed and action has begun, PERT can provide information about the status of the task and the alternatives available if the schedule or budget is not being met.[2]

PERT consists of four basic steps:

1. List all major tasks in a project.

2. Determine the required order of the tasks.

3. Estimate expected completion time for the tasks.

4. Draw a PERT network.

The application of PERT to public relations planning can be illustrated through the hypothetical case of Beverly James, a staff member in the public relations department of Alpha Corporation, who was asked to produce a new brochure for an employee community volunteer program.

Bev's first step was to develop a list of the major tasks required to produce a brochure. These tasks are usually called *activities* in PERT analysis. Public relations spotlight 7.2 includes the list of activities Bev developed for her assignment.

Public Relations Spotlight 7.2

PERT Time Network for Developing a Brochure

Activities Required to Develop a Brochure on the Employee Volunteer Program at Alpha Corporation

1. Begin the project.
2. Interview several employees who participate in the program to get details and personal interests.
3. Write copy for the brochure.
4. Obtain photos of employees serving the community through the program.
5. Integrate photos into copy.
6. Review similar publications from other organizations for ideas.
7. Prepare layout and finalize copy.
8. Prepare budget for project, including printing.
9. Get final approval of copy, photos, layout, and budget.
10. Make any necessary changes and prepare brochure for submission to print shop.

PERT Network Analysis for Brochure Project

$$t\epsilon = \frac{a + 4m + b}{6}$$

where $t\epsilon$ = expected time to complete an activity

a = optimistic time to complete an activity

m = most likely time to complete an activity (m is multiplied by 4 in the formula to give the highest weight to the most likely time)

b = pessimistic time to complete an activity

Figure 7.2 Time
calculations for PERT network

TIME CALCULATIONS FOR PERT NETWORK

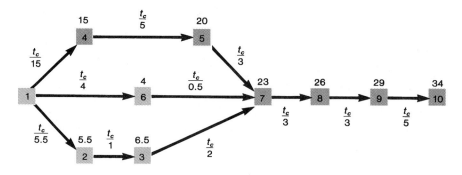

By simply listing the tasks in the order in which they must be accomplished, Bev had performed step 2, sequencing the activities.

Bev noted that some of the activities could be performed simultaneously. For example, she could meet with employees who were participating in the program (activity 2) while the staff photographer took pictures of employees at work in the community (activity 4). The PERT network in figure 7.2 shows some activities being performed at the same time.

PERT is especially useful in determining the time required to complete each activity. Note on the PERT diagram that each activity is preceded by a time line indicating the amount of time it is expected to take. When the task is fairly simple, experienced guesses can suffice. For complex projects, however, PERT offers a formula for computing expected times on the basis of three estimates: an optimistic time (*a*), a pessimistic time (*b*), and the most likely time of completion (*m*).

For example, Bev estimated that activity 2 (interviewing employees) could be completed optimistically in 3 days, pessimistically in 10 days, and most likely in 5 days. Using the formula illustrated in Public Relations Spotlight 7.2, Bev arrived at an expected time of 5.5 days to complete her interviews. She was able to calculate the time for the other activities in the same way.

PERT allows the planner to identify the *critical path* for completion of the project by discovering the longest sequence of events. The critical path for Bev's project is [1]—[4]—[5]—[7]—[8]—[9]—[10], showing that it should take a total of 34 days to complete the brochure. This tells Bev that if unexpected delays occur along the critical path, she must revise her estimated completion date; however, delays along the other paths probably will not affect the overall schedule. This information could be very important to the printing department that is scheduling Bev's job; an unexpected delay might necessitate starting another job ahead of hers.

Gantt Chart Time Analysis

Another tool for planning projects and campaigns is the **Gantt chart.** This method is widely used to plan any activity in which time is the critical variable. Unlike the PERT network, the Gantt chart does not use formulas for more sophisticated control and does not identify a critical path. It simply lists the separate activities or steps in the plan in the order in which they are to be performed and

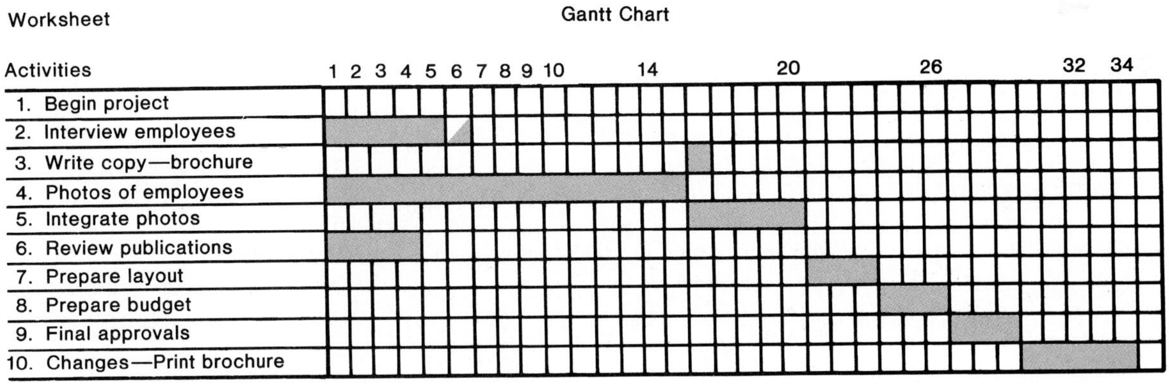

Worksheet

Gantt Chart

Activities	1 2 3 4 5 6 7 8 9 10	14	20	26	32 34
1. Begin project					
2. Interview employees					
3. Write copy—brochure					
4. Photos of employees					
5. Integrate photos					
6. Review publications					
7. Prepare layout					
8. Prepare budget					
9. Final approvals					
10. Changes—Print brochure					

NOTE: A calendar can be easily integrated into a Gantt chart with non-work days like weekends collapsed into a single cell per week.

indicates the time allotted to each task. A Gantt chart is a graph, with the activities listed along the vertical axis and the time listed along the horizontal axis. Time can be expressed in minutes, hours, days, or months, depending on the project. Figure 7.3 illustrates the use of a Gantt chart to plan Bev's brochure.

Figure 7.3 Gantt chart plan to develop a brochure on the employee volunteer program

Types of Plans

The three major types of plans used by public relations practitioners are budgets, campaigns, and standing plans.

Budgets

Budgets are perhaps the most common type of plan in any organization. Generally, they are short-range plans designed to project costs through the duration of a campaign or other period.

Campaign or *project budgets* are components of plans to accomplish specific public relations activities. They provide structure and discipline in terms of time and money costs. Budgeting for specific activities is a rather straightforward process. Public relations managers budget using a simple three-step model. First, required resources such as people, time, material, and equipment must be listed. Next, the extent to which these resources will be used is estimated. Finally, the costs of the resources are determined.

When Bev of Alpha Corporation set about producing her employee volunteer program brochure, she first had to develop a project budget. Table 7.1 shows her results. The left-hand column lists resources (step 1); the center column shows estimated quantities (step 2); and the right-hand column shows costs and how they are derived (step 3).

Project and campaign budgets are the building blocks for annual public relations departmental budgets and the basis for bids submitted by independent public relations counselors. In either case, budgets become instruments in the competition for organizational resources.

TABLE 7.1   Budget for Alpha Corporation Brochure

Resources	Quantities	Costs
1. Bev's time (interview, write, integrate photos into copy, administer project)	7 days	$ 700.00 (based on $26,000 yearly)
2. Photographer's time (freelance)	10 hours	$ 500.00 (at $50 per hr.)
3. Layout (graphics dept.)	8 pages	$ 200.00 (estimate, graphics dept.)
4. Printing (outside contractor)	1,000 copies, 2 colors, with halftone	$ 575.00 (estimate, printer)
5. Distribution costs (mailing and handling)	Postage for 1,000 copies Mailing lists of 500 names	$ 270.00 (bulk mail at $ 12 *and* cost of list)
		$ 2,245.00
	10% contingency	$ 225.00
	Total budgeted for brochures	$ 2,470.00

Competition for Resources   Because the annual budget represents the lifeblood of each subunit of an organization, there is inevitably competition for limited resources. One of the public relations manager's most important jobs, therefore, is to make certain the public relations function gets its fair share. This means that *the public relations professional must be able to understand balance sheets as well as galley proofs.*

In most organizations, the budgeting process is decentralized. Budgets are initially planned by those who must implement them. Supervisors submit their budget proposals to department heads, who in turn prepare department budgets to submit to their supervisors for approval. This process continues in an upward flow until the controller or budget director for the organization assembles all the budgets into one integrated package and submits it to the president or the budget committee. Finally, the master budget goes to the board of directors for approval. Negotiation and alteration occur at each step of this process.

The best writers, designers, and media relations experts cannot do their jobs without the necessary funding. As indicated in chapter 4, public relations staffs must fight continually to maintain influence within the organizational structure. Their skill in preparing budgetary proposals and getting them funded is often an important measure of their influence throughout the organization.

There is no substitute for a basic knowledge of financial planning and accounting procedures in understanding the budgeting process, but other factors enter into this process as well. Competition among subunits for funds involves certain vital aspects of organizational politics. It is most important to remember that public relations must constantly "sell" the value of its services to the organization. Unfortunately, too many public relations departments fail to understand the needs of their own internal publics and do not communicate with them as they should. The public relations practitioner in an organizational environment must maintain a professional image as a member of the management team.

Practitioners should identify the people in their organization who have both formal and informal power to influence budget allocations. They should then communicate with these individuals regularly, emphasizing the effectiveness and professionalism with which the public relations function is being carried out. Some ways to demonstrate and communicate effectiveness are discussed in chapter 9. If these people are ignored until just before the budget request is submitted, they cannot be expected to understand fully the needs of the public relations unit.

Preparing Budget Requests   Budget requests should consider and reflect continuing programs, new programs, and contingencies. Continuing programs are programs carried over from the previous budget period for completion. Such carryover must be justified. Was the duration of the program anticipated from the start? Was it included in the original plans? If so, this fact must be made explicit to avoid criticism for not finishing the job within the previous budget. If the carryover was an unforeseen circumstance, however, an explanation of the extension is in order. Though many activities are by nature continuous, an understanding of this fact should not be assumed. Those who make budgetary decisions must be reminded regularly, and especially at budget time, of the value of these continuous activities.

Requests for new programs must be well documented, particularly in slow economic periods. The need for each new program should be specified in terms that relate to the organization's most basic functions. Projections concerning the potential effects of a program should be secured from other departments as well as from the public relations staff.

Unexpected occurrences (contingencies) must also be accounted for in the budget request. Some organizations have a standard percentage that is acceptable for contingency funds; others do not permit such items in a budget. If an organization does not permit the direct budgeting of contingency funds, they are generally included as part of other budget items from which funds can be diverted if necessary. Many organizations also build an inflation factor into their budgets. Economic forecasts are used to establish a percentage figure that will minimize budget erosion due to inflation.

Budget padding is a common practice in many organizations. It usually occurs when the people who make budget requests know that top management will routinely cut every budget by a certain percentage. Budget requests are then increased enough to allow for cuts and still yield enough money to accomplish department objectives. Such political maneuvering is generally dysfunctional and should be discouraged by top management. Managers who do not understand how the "game" is played, however, may be left without sufficient resources to accomplish their assigned functions.

Types of Budgets   Organizations usually divide the budget planning process into two parts: operating budgets and financial budgets. **Operating budgets** forecast the goods and services the organization expects to consume, in terms of both costs and physical quantities (e.g., reams of paper). **Financial budgets** give detailed estimates of the amounts an organization expects to spend during the budget period

Figure 7.4 Budget components

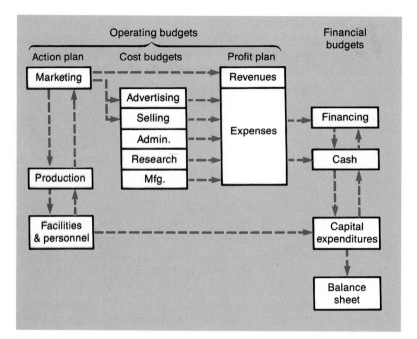

and where the funds will come from (i.e., cash or financing). Figure 7.4 illustrates the components of these two types of budgets. *Although public relations managers are typically responsible only for preparing their own operating budgets, an understanding of the entire process will make them more effective in defending their requests.*

Organizations are typically divided into four responsibility centers for purposes of budgetary control:[3]

1. *Revenue centers* These are organizational subunits, such as sales, in which outputs are measured in monetary terms but are not compared to costs of input because they have little influence over factors such as product cost and design.

2. *Expense centers* Budgets reflect only expenses for these subunits because only inputs (expenses) can be measured in monetary terms. These subunits (such as public relations departments) do not directly generate any revenues for the organization.

3. *Profit centers* Any organizational subunit that is charged with earning a profit will have its performance measured as the numerical difference between outputs (revenues) and inputs (expenditures).

4. *Investment centers* In addition to measuring monetarily the inputs and outputs of these subunits, depreciation and costs of capital investments are subtracted before profit is determined.

Public Relations Budgets Public relations units are generally considered *expense centers* because their budgets reflect only expenditures. The two types of expense centers are *engineered* and *discretionary*. Engineered cost budgets are most often used for manufacturing operations, while discretionary cost budgets are used for public relations and many other administrative functions.

Because their output cannot be measured with accuracy, expense center budgets are concerned only with inputs. At intervals during the budget period, comparisons are made between actual and budgeted expenses. Discretionary cost budgets cannot assess efficiency, however, because of the difficulty in setting performance standards for these functions. This fact often makes it difficult for the public relations manager to justify a budget request because normal control procedures cannot be used to evaluate performance. In chapter 9 we will discuss some alternative comparisons to help justify public relations expenses to top management.

Public relations budgets are typically concerned with two basic expenses: administrative costs (salaries, benefits, and overhead) and program costs (research, publications, special events, films, and other program-related activities).[4] Budgets are usually justified by one or more of the following factors:[5]

1. *Total funds available* Public relations is allocated a percentage of available revenue.

2. *Competitive necessity* Sometimes public relations receives a budget allocation designed to match or equal the public relations budget of a competing organization.

3. *Task to be accomplished* Public relations shares in an overall budget allotted for accomplishing a particular objective. Advertising and marketing promotion, for example, might also share in these funds.

4. *Profit or surplus over expense* The budget can fluctuate up or down depending on the amount of profit or surplus generated.

Campaigns are a frequent output of public relations planning. Because campaigns are usually designed to accomplish unique objectives, they must be planned using nonroutine procedures and unprogrammable decisions. Preparing a plan for a public relations campaign is a matter of following the process outline in figure 7.1. Some generally accepted guidelines for writing the campaign planning document include the following:

Campaigns

Problem statement This statement should reflect the research done to narrow the task to a manageable size. It should define the scope of the effort and recognize any special requirements of the organization, target audiences, and media.

Purpose statement This statement should present a realistic view of what the campaign is designed to accomplish. Clear objectives should be developed that can be measured against results to determine the effectiveness of the effort.

Audience analysis On the basis of preliminary research, the planning document should describe the primary target audience, identify appeals and points of interest that will attract attention, define audience lifestyles, and determine the relative strength of each possible appeal.

Recommended actions The planning document should tell how the purpose will be accomplished for the audience that has been identified. It should discuss specific tactics and alternatives; define expected outcomes; and specify communication media, activities, and channels to be used.

Time frame A schedule of activities should be developed. Any of the tools discussed earlier in this chapter (PERT, Gantt chart) can be applied to define the schedule of events.

Projected costs Plans cannot be evaluated unless they include a realistic budget. Enough documentation should be supplied to demonstrate that the projected expenses and fees are realistic.

Evaluation design A method should be set up in advance to determine the extent to which the objectives of the campaign have been attained. All objectives should lend themselves to an evaluation process that will have credibility with decision makers.

Standing Plans

Within all organizations, certain *programmable decisions* call for standardized, consistent responses. Standing plans provide routine responses to recurring situations. Once set, standing plans allow the manager to make more efficient use of planning time because he or she need not formulate a new plan for every similar situation. One note of caution is in order: Overuse of standing plans may limit an organization's responsiveness to its environment, a critical issue for public relations. Nevertheless, standing plans do have a place in the public relations function. We shall discuss three types of standing plans: policies, procedures, and rules.

Policies   Policies are generally established by an organization's top management as guidelines for decision making. The policy makers usually seek to guide decision-making activities in ways consistent with organizational objectives. Other purposes include improving effectiveness or imposing the values of top management.

Sometimes policies originate informally at lower organizational levels as a pattern of decision making occurs over a long period. In such cases, top management merely formalizes what is already happening. In other situations, policy may be established either as a result of recommendations from lower-level managers or directly as a result of top management's observation that a problem exists.

External organizations, such as governmental agencies, also set policies or at least influence them. Health and safety policies in most large organizations have changed considerably in recent years as a direct result of actions by government agencies.

Public relations departments, like all other subunits of organizations, must plan their daily operations to avoid conflict with policy. More important, the strata of policy makers in any organization should include public relations practitioners to ensure sensitivity to the interests of its publics. For example, policies that direct all contact with the press through the public relations department for approval and advice should be reviewed by the public relations staff.

Procedures Detailed guidelines for implementing policy decisions are called *standard procedures*. Standard procedures, or standard operating procedures, provide detailed instructions for performing sequences of actions that occur regularly. Most public relations departments have standard procedures for news releases, internal publications, site tours, media interviews, and many other activities that are carried on from year to year. In addition, every organization needs a standard procedure for emergencies.

Emergencies, although infrequent, should be handled through set procedures because of the need to respond quickly and effectively. When a disaster happens, it is too late to begin a deliberate planning process that will consider every alternative before responding. Nevertheless, coordinated, deliberate, and effective response is vitally important. When an emergency situation exists, time becomes the key element in communication; plans must be made in advance so that reaction can be immediate. Public relations spotlight 7.3 shows the set of disaster response procedures that was established by a major metropolitan hospital.

Public Relations Spotlight 7.3	A Disaster Response Plan

ST. LUKE'S EPISCOPAL HOSPITAL-Houston, Texas

GENERAL POLICY/PROCEDURE

Subject/Title: Staged Preparations for Anticipated Natural Disasters

Effective Date: April 1, 1989
Review Date: April 1, 1990
Developed by: Executive Office
Reviewed by: Policy Committee/Management Council
Management Central Approval:
Page 1 of 3

This policy/procedure rescinds all other policies/procedures and memoranda issued prior to April 1, 1989.

PURPOSE
To outline stages of preparation for anticipated natural disasters to assure adequate levels of preparation by all departments.

STATEMENT OF POLICY
It is the policy of St. Luke's Episcopal Hospital to establish written policies and procedures for response to disaster situations to assure adequate preparations and communications before, during, and after such situations.

PROCEDURES
1.00 Phase 1—General Preparations
1.01 The Emergency Preparedness Coordinator shall:

- Monitor weather broadcasts
- Establish a Communications Post from which department managers may obtain current weather information

- Assess current inpatient population to determine those that could be discharged in advance of severe weather
- Assess preparation of physical plant, including but not limited to:
  - Placement of storm shutters
  - Availability of flood stop logs
  - Securing of loose items on exterior of building
- Notify all department managers to begin making general preparations

1.02 Department Managers shall:

- Assess the current status of all essential supplies and make arrangements to restock as necessary.
- Determine, in consultation with the responsible administrator, which employees are essential to the operation of the department and which employees could be directed to leave early or not report to work, based on weather conditions. A written list of essential employees by shift shall be submitted to the department's administrator.
- Make any special preparations needed to meet their department's responsibility for disaster response.
- Assure that the department call list is accurate and up-to-date, to facilitate the calling of staff for coverage, should it be necessary.
- Discuss compensation, staffing, and other severe weather policies with employees. Obtain administrative clarification, as needed.

2.00 Phase II—Implementation of Disaster Response Plan

2.01 The Chief Operating Officer or his designee shall:

- Direct Nursing to begin census reduction by discharging patients whom the medical staff agrees may go home and consolidate remaining patients to free beds
- Notify Admitting to accept only emergency admissions
- Establish a central Command Post
- Notify Communications to begin paging "CARLA ALERT" or "CARLA," as applicable
- Notify department managers to implement their disaster response plans, including arrangements for essential staff
- Evacuate underground parking areas, order placement of flood stop logs, and notify the Emergency Department and Admitting of need to move emergency receiving site to Bates Street Lobby

2.02 Department Managers shall:

- Implement their department response plans, including calling in or holding over essential staff
- Direct non-essential staff members to leave for home even though their shifts may not be over
- Contact outpatients scheduled for visits or tests and cancel/reschedule appointments
- Report the above information to the Command Post

3.00 Phase III—Operation During Disaster

3.01 The Chief Operating Officer or his designee shall:

- Continue Command Post operations
- Evaluate need to move patients and staff from threatened areas (such as upper tower floors)

- Notify Communications to page physicians to the Emergency Department, if needed to handle incoming casualties
- Notify departments to curtail use of essential resources, if necessary
- Establish a Family Holding area and Press Center, as appropriate

3.02 Department Managers shall:

- Maintain necessary department operations
- Report any problems to the Command Post

Departmental Interface: All departments

Source: Reprinted by permission of St. Luke's Episcopal, Texas Children's Hospital, Texas Heart Institute.

Figure 7.5 shows how the same hospital implemented its disaster response plan in a simulated emergency.

Four areas of emergency planning should be specifically designed in advance.[6]

1. *Notification* Plan exactly who should be notified and in what order. Generally, this is handled on a "need to know" basis. For example, an accident within a particular department will generally be reported, as soon as it occurs, directly to the department head and then to specified individuals in management, including the appropriate public relations manager.

2. *Spokesperson* The best strategy to avoid conflicting reports and any appearance of attempting to conceal facts is to direct all inquiries, particularly those from the press, to one person or task force. Generally, this function is handled within the public relations department, which may also need to arrange for statements from others within the organization.

3. *News media* First, notify all media representatives listed in the emergency procedures file, and immediately issue all available facts to press representatives who request them. Never attempt to manipulate, delay, or conceal information. Anything less than full disclosure at such times runs the risk of being interpreted as a coverup. Mini-case 7.1 helps illustrate this point.

   Remember that reporters want to know all the information as soon as possible. If the public relations staff can facilitate this process, the organization will benefit by receiving objective coverage. If the organization's representatives appear to be holding back information, however, the press will react with suspicion. Help reporters get the kind of information they want within the limits of legal liability. Provide them with human interest material about the people involved and as much information as possible about the rest of the circumstances. While it is

Figure 7.5 Simulated disaster at St. Luke's Episcopal Hospital, Houston, Texas

important to work closely with the organization's legal counsel in such situations, remember that legal staff personnel may not be sensitive to the issues of public and media relations. They may react too conservatively and cause unnecessary problems if allowed to control the situation. Always be sure that public relations has a direct line to top management in emergency situations.

4. *Notification of families*   If the emergency has resulted in injury or death, inform the families involved before releasing any names to the news media. Handle such notifications with tact and concern, but because of legal questions regarding liability, take care when speaking to the families. Any acceptance of responsibility or indication of fault should first be cleared through the legal department.

Mini-Case 7.1

There were no reporters or correspondents from any media on hand at Cape Kennedy when the fire broke out. . . . The question of informing the public . . . was thus left entirely to the institutional machinations of NASA. The agency reacted predictably. It not only shut down all lines of communication, but, by either accident or design, issued statements that proved to be erroneous.

Although NASA knew within five minutes after the accident that all three astronauts were dead, the information was not released until two hours later. It was nearly midnight before UPI and AP received a NASA picture of two of the astronauts entering the capsule for the last time.

NASA claimed that the withholding of facts and its issuance of misleading and wrong statements resulted from the lack of a plan for handling information in emergencies. As hard to believe as this may be, coming as it does from an agency with a public information staff of 300, there is undoubtedly some validity to the claim.

NASA's information office has since maintained that an emergency plan was in effect and followed at the time of the Apollo 204 fire. NASA states that it has contingency plans for each mission.*

Early in 1986, tragedy struck the nation's space program again when millions of Americans and people all over the world witnessed live on television the explosion of the space shuttle Challenger. Many professional observers and news reporters in their critiques of NASA's handling of the disaster commented that little seemed to have been learned from the experience of Apollo 204. Although flight controllers knew the fate of the Challenger crew almost instantly, speculation about their ability to survive the accident was allowed to continue for about an hour while technicians "gathered data."

*Source: James Skardon, "The Apollo Story: What the Watchdogs Missed," *Columbia Journalism Review* 6 (Fall 1967): 13–14. Reprinted by permission.

Rules   While policies and standard procedures serve as guidelines for decision making, rules substitute for decisions. Rules are statements that specify the action to be taken in a particular situation. No latitude for application is provided other than the decision either to follow or not to follow the rule. Rules may be necessary when certain procedures are crucial. For example, it is often wise to have a rule requiring that signed releases be obtained before photographs or other personal information are used in publicity releases.

Summary

Good public relations practice demands good planning. As exciting as they may sound, public relations actions that arise from spur-of-the-moment decisions usually produce short-term gains and long-term losses. Even emergency situations that cannot be predicted must have planned response systems. The process of planning is slow, complex, and frequently boring. However, in public relations, as in other managerial functions, careful planning increases the effectiveness and decreases the frequency of future actions. Adequate planning also establishes a system of goals that can be used to measure public relations success. This aspect of planning will be expanded in chapter 9.

David M. Dozier summarized the significance of planning:

> The process of setting public relations goals and objectives in measurable form serves two purposes. First, the prudent and strategic selection of public relations goals and objectives linked to organizational survival and growth serves to justify the public relations program as a viable management activity. . . . Second, the specification of public relations goals and objectives in measurable form makes public relations accountable and makes program success or failure concrete and objective.[7]

Case Study

Lions Club Book Sale

By Artemio R. Guillermo
Assistant Professor of Speech
University of Northern Iowa
Cedar Falls, Iowa

Each spring the Waterloo, Iowa Lions Club holds a used book sale. The books, which are sold for as little as 10 cents, are donations from the public. Proceeds go to various sight-saving projects, including the cornea bank in Iowa City.

Since the Lions started the book sales, there has been only limited participation by its members. The most ever raised in one year has been $3,000. Still, the 1981 goal was set at $4,000. While the goal was raised, no changes were planned for promotion of the event. The Lions would use the same public service announcements, posters, and press releases that had not done the job before.

Fortunately, however, a group of senior public relations students decided to help the Lions. After analyzing the promotional efforts in the past year and determining target audiences, the team created a public relations plan using the communication tools used before and adding advertising and staged events. The target area was expanded to include Waterloo, Cedar Falls, and the surrounding communities within a 50-mile radius. The club provided $150 to the team for publicity expenses.

All promotional efforts centered on the slogan "Buy a Book and Help Someone See!" Simple announcements using two-color posters were placed in strategic places in shopping malls, dining centers at the university, and restaurants and other local businesses. Two students donned lion costumes and paraded in the shopping mall during the book sale week.

Local media supported the promotional effort by donating space and time. Expenses, including classified ads in the student newspaper, display ads in the local papers, rental of the lion costumes, and printing of posters, were carefully budgeted.

The five-day book sale was held in Waterloo's biggest shopping mall after target audiences had been saturated for four weeks. The receipts were counted. The Lions grossed $5,137—28 percent above their ambitious goal.

Questions

1. What made the difference between the 1981 book sale and the preceding sales?
2. How was public relations planning used to promote the sale?
3. Plan a similar campaign for a not-for-profit group.
4. What was missing from the public relations campaign described in this case?

Notes

1. L. J. Garrett and M. Silver, *Production Management Analysis* (New York: Harcourt Brace Jovanovich, 1966), 364–365.

2. James A. F. Stoner, *Management* (Englewood Cliffs, N.J.: Prentice-Hall, 1978), 99–139.

3. Ibid., 594–596.

4. Raymond Simon, *Public Relations: Concepts and Practice* (Columbus, Ohio: Grid, Inc., 1976), 95.

5. Scott M. Cutlip and Allen H. Center, *Effective Public Relations* (Englewood Cliffs, N.J.: Prentice-Hall, 1978), 175.

6. Lawrence W. Nolte, *Fundamentals of Public Relations* (New York: Pergamon Press, 1974), 317–318.

7. David M. Dozier, "Planning and Evaluation in PR Practice," *Public Relations Review* (Summer 1985): 21–22.

CHAPTER 8

Action and Communication

Preview

The public relations actions required in modern organizations have expanded to include managerial decision making in virtually every aspect of operation. Nevertheless, most public relations actions can be described as attempts to spread information within a target audience.

Public relations practitioners can benefit by following several basic steps in diffusing information. It is also possible to identify certain critical paths that facilitate the adoption of new ideas by target publics. These critical paths lead an idea through five basic steps: awareness, interest, evaluation, trials, and adoption.

Both primary and secondary critical paths are more sensitive to certain channels of influence or to certain media at each step in the adoption process. When a public relations plan is developed, it must take into account all five stages of implementation in order to have maximum impact.

The process of diffusion must be planned and executed separately for each target public. Therefore, a method such as stakeholder analysis should be used to plan actions appropriate to the needs and interests of each public. Publics can generally be categorized as primary, intervening, or moderating. After channels of influence are identified for each public, appropriate messages can be prepared within the basic functional areas of public relations.

Most public relations actions involve communication. Writing is the primary tool for constructing messages and is therefore a critical skill for practitioners. By applying the principles of effective writing, they can develop public relations messages for all audiences and media.

P ublic relations actions can be organized around three basic areas of planning: target audiences, channels of influence, and messages. These areas interact to provide a unique plan of action for every audience in every situation. Segment 3 of the integrating case study illustrates **action implementation** in the Cedar Springs Hospital case.

Integrating Case Study

Cedar Springs
Community Hospital

Action Implementation

Segment 3

I n the previous segment, described in chapter 7, goals, objectives, and basic strategies were developed for solving the hospital's problem. Next, the public relations staff turned its attention to the execution of those plans. It was clear from the patient surveys that the hospital's primary goal of quality patient care was already being achieved. Therefore, strategies were developed for improving employee and physician perceptions of the hospital's performance.

The two basic strategies for which action steps needed to be developed were (1) reinforcement of employee feelings of worth as members of the medical team and (2) increase in feedback from patients. Several tactics were implemented to address these needs.

Employee Team

A theme was developed to heighten all employees' awareness of their value as members of the medical team at Cedar Springs Hospital. The theme "Quality People, Quality Care" was communicated to employees, physicians, and other publics through five media:

1. Signs were displayed over the entrances to all three main buildings.
2. Mailing panels were printed for all publications.
3. Birthday cards for employees were redesigned.
4. Special employee name badges were designed for employees who had passed the 90-day probationary period, designating them as "Quality Providers."
5. T-shirts were printed with the theme and used as gifts for participation in the personnel department's annual Benefits Fair.

Hospital management also wanted to make a very public statement about the quality of the employees and their work. Thus, an existing "Employee-of-the-Month" program was revitalized. To give the recognition more visibility among patients, physicians, and the general public, a 24-inch display ad appeared in the local newspaper every month, featuring the honored employee and the "Quality People, Quality Care" theme.

Examples of communication
with various target audiences

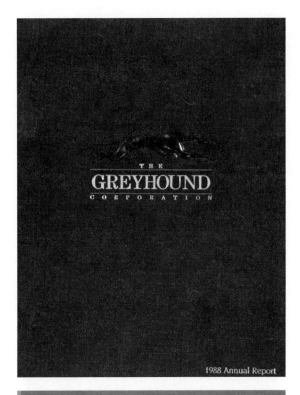

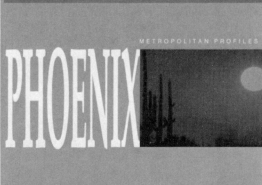

Patient Feedback

Three primary methods were used to increase feedback from patients to the hospital staff. First, the survey of recently released patients was repeated quarterly. Survey results were disseminated through various vehicles, such as the hospital newsletter and table tents in the staff cafeteria. In addition, a contest was established in which employees tried to guess the survey results before they were published. Second, positive letters from former patients were disseminated among hospital employees. Third, a regular feature called "Worth Sharing" was incorporated into the monthly newsletter to highlight patient success stories.

Public Relations in Action

Traditionally, public relations action has meant communication in some form, often a publicity release for print media. However, as the world has changed, so has public relations practice. Technology has altered the media practitioners must work with, and it is causing organizations to require an increasingly wide range of possible action alternatives from their public relations staffs. When Johnson & Johnson was ready to announce the return of Tylenol capsules to the market after the first wave of poisonings in 1982, satellite technology helped deliver the message.

Large organizations with access to space-age technology are not the only ones that require a variety of response mechanisms. Cedar Springs Community Hospital took several action steps, none of them press releases. While much of that action involved written communication, several important steps centered on managerial decision making.

Influencing Management Decisions

When it was first proposed that the "Quality People, Quality Care" theme be displayed over the entrances to the main buildings, many employees reacted negatively, feeling that "advertising" was too commercial for a medical facility. An ad hoc committee of department managers investigated the complaints and made recommendations regarding use of the theme. The committee eventually advised placing it above the entrances and sold the employees on the integrity of the idea. This group also suggested using the theme only on the name tags of employees who had passed the 90-day review period.

Management decision making was again the principal action leading to the wider dissemination of letters of appreciation from patients. This relatively simple action required a change in organizational policy that could have been politically explosive. Such letters normally had been routed to the personnel department and then to the manager of the department involved. This procedure meant that for a department to get any recognition, it would have to appear to "blow its own horn." Therefore, most letters of appreciation had been handled internally, without the knowledge of the rest of the organization. The private nature of this process was counter to the new objective of improving employee perceptions by sharing patient feedback. Thus, the policy was changed so that the original letter was routed first to public relations, where copies were made for the appropriate department manager and for personnel.

A policy change of this type, if not handled carefully, could have alienated both the personnel manager and the department managers. The public relations manager needed a good understanding of both communication and organizational dynamics to accomplish this objective.

Although managerial decision making was one of the public relations actions in the Cedar Springs case, the primary action process can be described as the **diffusion of information.** More often than not, the action implemented to accomplish a public relations plan can be explained as an attempt to spread information within a **target audience.**

Diffusing Information

Selecting a Target Audience   The action process begins and ends with the target audiences. Once each public is identified, its characteristics can be studied, and a *critical path* of influence can be planned for the issue in question.

When considering the individual characteristics of each target audience, it is helpful to categorize the audience as (1) primary, intervening, or moderating and (2) latent, aware, or active (see figure 8.1). A **primary public** is the group to which the action is ultimately directed. As we have shown, however, the critical path to this group frequently requires that other audiences be addressed. Individuals in **intervening publics** have direct contact with the primary audience and can pass messages along to them. All the channels of influence listed in figure 8.2, except personal experience, may constitute intervening publics. **Moderating publics** are groups that share a common goal or guiding philosophy and can make an impact on the primary public. These groups usually have high credibility with the primary public in specific subject areas.[1] In figure 8.2, only mass media and personal experience do not have the potential to be moderating publics.

As you will recall from our discussion in chapter 6, a **latent public** is not aware of a need to change or act. An **aware public** recognizes a need but is not prone to any action, such as accepting a new idea. An **active public** is aware and ready to do something.

The classification system just described helps determine the extent to which a given public is ready and able to respond to any planned action. The relationship between these classifications is diagrammed in figure 8.1.

The Diffusion Process   *Diffusion* is a term used to describe *the way in which new ideas are adopted in a society.* Sociologists and communication researchers

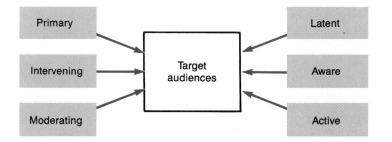

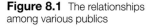

Figure 8.1 The relationships among various publics

Figure 8.2 Critical paths of influence in the adoption process

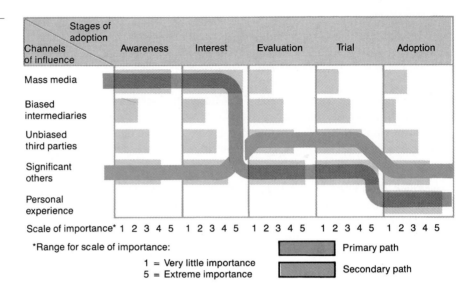

have long been fascinated by the paths that innovations follow as they make their way through a social system. Publics or target audiences are social systems that public relations practitioners seek to influence. Therefore, it is important that knowledge about the diffusion of information be applied to the public relations process.

Critical Paths   Figure 8.2 illustrates some of the critical paths for the adoption of innovations. Those who study the processes through which new products, ideas, and technologies spread have identified five steps that describe how people are influenced to change:[2]

1. *Awareness*   People are aware of the idea or practice, although their knowledge is limited.

2. *Interest*   People begin to develop an interest in the idea and seek more information about it.

3. *Evaluation*   People begin to apply the idea mentally to their individual situations. Simultaneously, they obtain more information and decide to try the new idea.

4. *Trial*   At this point, actual application begins, usually on a small scale. Potential adopters are primarily interested in the practice, techniques, and conditions necessary for application.

5. *Adoption*   Once the idea is proven worthwhile, it is adopted.

Channels of Influence   Researchers have tracked innovations through the adoption process and concluded that they use five basic channels of influence:

1. *Mass media*   Electronic and print media such as radio, television, newspapers, and magazines.

2. *Biased intermediaries* Individuals or groups (such as salespersons) that stand to benefit from another's adoption.

3. *Unbiased third parties* Consumer groups, government agencies, and other groups or individuals that have credibility.

4. *Significant others* Friends, relatives, and others who are admired by potential adopters.

5. *Personal experience* Actual use of the innovation.

Figure 8.2 traces primary and secondary paths of influence, following the most important and second most important channels at each stage of adoption. In the early stages of awareness and interest, mass media are most effective. In the critical stages of evaluation and trial, however, emphasis shifts to significant others. Finally, at the point of adoption, personal experience becomes the primary channel. The secondary or support path begins with significant others, moving to unbiased third parties at the evaluation and trial stages and then back to significant others at adoption.

The public relations practitioner can implement the critical path approach by attempting to create awareness and interest through press releases and other media coverage. From the start of the campaign, the practitioner should plan to communicate with other publics that are significant to the target audience. When the initial goals of awareness and interest are reached, public relations actions should move away from the obvious to more subtle forms of communication through significant others and unbiased third parties. After the evaluation and trial stages are passed, success can be measured by the extent to which the target public accepts the new idea.

Facilitating the Adoption Process

When Mountain Bell (new U.S. West) decided to introduce Local Measured Service in the Phoenix area, the media devoted a great deal of coverage to describing the advantages of the new system.[3] Because of the favorable publicity, the telephone company felt confident when the issue came up for approval before the Arizona Corporation Commission. When Mountain Bell representatives arrived at the hearing, however, they found senior citizens jamming the chambers and others picketing outside to protest the innovation. Obviously, one important public in the Phoenix area, senior citizens, had not adopted the idea. After its first request was turned down, the phone company began to work with senior citizen groups to win support from significant others and unbiased third parties. The proposal was approved without protest the next time it came before the commission. To secure the cooperation of various publics, Mountain Bell used an action strategy known as **stakeholder analysis.**

Pressure and Special Interest Groups Traditionally, much public relations practice has been based on a generally accepted *two-step flow of information* theory. This theory is built on the premise that certain people in our society are opinion leaders and that, if those leaders can be convinced to support a certain matter, they will influence others to support it also.

While the two-step flow theory contains a great deal of truth, both research and practice have shown that it is too simplistic. The theory allows for only two

Mothers Against Drunk Drivers (MADD) rally in St. Paul, Minn. A small but well-organized special interest group can sometimes influence decisions that affect the majority.

levels (leaders and followers) in any influence attempt. Further, it presumes a linear flow of information through a social system. From our discussion of systems theory in chapter 3 and the diffusion process in chapter 3 and this chapter, it should be apparent that society is much more complex. The proliferation of pressure groups demonstrates the flaws in the two-step flow theory. As more special interest groups appear on the scene, it is obvious that large masses are not always influenced by a few opinion leaders. Instead, issues may be fragmented by relatively small special interest groups, each with its own agenda. These groups have demonstrated an ability to pressure decision makers far more than the size of their constituencies would justify. Thus, a well-organized minority can (and frequently does) influence decisions that affect the majority.

Stakeholder Analysis   The concept of stakeholder management provides a more realistic framework for an organization to visualize its environment. Stakeholder analysis is a method for differentiating among publics. *Stakeholders are individuals who perceive themselves to have an interest in the actions of an organization.* They may be customers, shareholders, employees, or just members of society. They generally express themselves through groups that share a common purpose, such as environmental or consumer causes.

Applying the stakeholder management approach to public relations practice allows actions to be organized around an entire system of stakeholder groups. The goal is maximum overall cooperation between the stakeholders and the organization's objectives. To accomplish this goal, strategies are designed to deal simultaneously with issues affecting multiple groups.

The stakeholder approach does not fundamentally change public relations communication or other action processes. Instead, it organizes them for more efficient use. Stakeholder management can determine *who* should be the object of an action step, *what* that action should be, *what results* should be sought, and *how* each element will fit into the overall plan.

Traditionally, many public relations activities were managed through delivery systems like news bureaus, speakers' bureaus, and complaint departments. Because these systems focus on single actions, they have difficulty recognizing the differences between publics. In a stakeholder management system, however, action for each public is planned *separately*. The needs and interests of a given stakeholder group determine what actions are appropriate and how they should be implemented.

When Mountain Bell managers first attempted to begin Local Measured Service, they were trying to reach all consumers through the same action strategies. Their initial view of the problem is illustrated in figure 8.3. Further analysis led them to realize that the task required a more complex view of their publics (figure 8.4). The following stakeholders needed to be considered in the Local Measured Service issue:

1. *Internal stakeholders*   Employees and shareholders.

2. *Residence stakeholders*   Consumer advocates, the handicapped, minorities, low-income people, senior citizens, volunteer and service groups, educational organizations.

3. *Business stakeholders*   Those dependent on telemarketing, small businesses, large businesses.

4. *Other stakeholders*   Media, government, the Arizona Corporation Commission.[4]

Each stakeholder group was assigned to a project manager, who became familiar with the group's needs and interests and worked with functional departments such as media relations, the speakers' bureau, internal publications, and others to target messages to that audience.

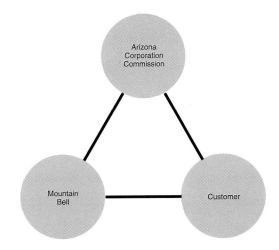

Figure 8.3 Mountain Bell's initial action plan

Figure 8.4 Mountain Bell's
revised view of its publics

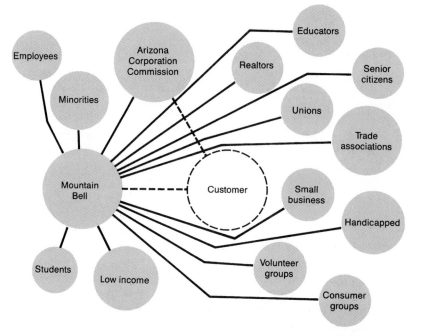

Senior citizens are important
stakeholders to many
organizations.

Designing the Public Relations Matrix

After the appropriate channels of influence are determined and target audiences
selected, messages are prepared within basic action categories. In a large organization, these functional areas or subspecialities within public relations are sometimes handled by different departments. Even if they are the responsibility of one
person, each action category must produce a distinct message. Frequently, different media are used as well. The result is a series of crossover or matrix relationships between target audiences and messages.

TABLE 8.1 Public Relations Matrix for Mountain Bell Target Audiences

Action Categories	Media	Residential Consumers	Employees	Business Consumers	Government
Press releases	Intervening	Primary	Moderating	Primary	Moderating
Speakers' bureaus	Intervening	Primary	Moderating	Primary	Moderating
Internal publications			Primary		Moderating
External publications	Primary	Primary	Moderating	Primary	Primary
Advocacy advertising		Primary	Moderating	Primary	Moderating

Reprinted through courtesy of Mountain Bell.

Table 8.1 illustrates the relationships between some of Mountain Bell's target audiences (stakeholders) and the action categories used to respond to the situation. In the case of Mountain Bell's response to the Local Measured Service protest, each target audience was assigned to a practitioner, while each action category was the responsibility of a functional department. For any message, at least two members of the public relations staff would be responsible for its design and implementation. For example, a news release prepared by the press relations group could have been initiated by the residential or business consumer manager and closely reviewed by other managers for potential impact on media, employee, and government stakeholders. Under this system, messages are prepared for primary audiences and checked for the desired effect on moderating and intervening audiences. This system allows functional specialists such as writers and editors to continue performing their tasks, while project managers assume the responsibility for making sure all messages received by their publics are prepared according to the public relations plan. A single manager can be responsible for supervising contacts with several publics in more than one project. These responsibilities change as projects are completed and new ones are added.

The Practitioner as Communicator

We began this chapter by illustrating the variety of action steps possible under a single public relations plan. While the actions that might be used are virtually limitless, one remains predominant: Most strategies involve communication.

Just as communication is the primary action step in a public relations plan, writing is the principal tool for constructing messages. Even messages that are primarily visual, like videotape or slide presentations, generally require well-written directions or scripts. Policies and other decisions are written as they are developed, transmitted, and preserved. Therefore, writing is a basic skill needed by all public relations professionals, regardless of the type or size of the organizations in which they work.

Principles of Effective Writing

Some people are born with an exceptional talent that cannot be explained or taught. The Ernest Hemingways of this world may not need to learn the principles of effective writing, but few of us are exceptionally gifted artists. Most people have to learn the craft of writing through study, practice, and hard work—that's the bad news.

The good news is that effective writing can be learned. People of average talent can learn to write effectively by practicing some basic principles. The following tips can help just about everyone effectively communicate technical and nontechnical information in letters, reports, news stories, booklets, and most other media that use the written word:

1. Use short, simple words.

2. Use short, simple sentences and paragraphs.

3. Write in the active, not the passive voice.

4. Avoid slang and jargon.

5. Use adjectives and adverbs sparingly.

6. Be brief; for example, keep most news releases to one or two typewritten pages.

Packaging Ideas   In a written document, sentence length is widely recognized as a key to clarity. Many of the readability formulas mentioned earlier use sentence length as the basis of measurement. Distinguished educator and journalist Harold Davis often tells the story of a journalist working with the American Press Institute in the late 1940s and early 1950s who helped firmly establish the link between clarity and length.

James H. Couey Jr. of the *Birmingham News* helped conduct seminars for working journalists at Columbia University. Before a seminar began, he would ask each participant to send him a writing sample so he could test it. The testing process was accomplished with the cooperation of several local civic organizations in the Birmingham area.

Couey would take a journalist's stories to a club meeting and ask the members to read them and answer some questions. The results would then be used to help the writers understand how well they communicated with the average reader.

One story submitted for testing, a description of an important breakthrough in the textile industry, was typical of material used in news releases. When Couey received the story, he noticed that it contained 271 words, but only five sentences, for an average of just over 54 words per sentence. The article is reproduced here:

American London Shrinkers Corporation has spent a year and a half experimenting and compiling data on the shrinking and finishing of man-made fibers used in combination with woolen and worsted yarns and is now equipped to handle all types of blends, it is made known by Theodore Trilling, president.

The trend toward blends in suiting and coating woolens and worsteds brought with it the need for a variety of alterations in the shrinking and sponging operation, Mr. Trilling adds, pointing out, for example, that the Orlon content in a fabric turned yellow, the rayon and acetate content tended to moire and the 15 to 20 percent of nylon now often used to give added strength tended to shine.

No new machinery is involved, just alterations in the processing, such as a change in the action or the weight of the apron or the leader, but it took a lot of trial and error observations, testing to make sure that further shrinkage would not take place, and tabulation of the data before the "we are now in a position" statement could be made, it was added.

Special reports of the tests and their results have been passed along to the mills and sealing agents of these blends, and in some cases, they have served as a guide in the correction and improvement of these fabrics, Mr. Trilling states.

He adds that his firm has been offering its 100 percent woolen and worsted finishing and shrinking service to the industry for the past 55 years and that with the alterations to handle blends now completed, an important step has been made.

Results of the preseminar test showed that readers gained little information from the story. Couey's questions and the reader's responses follow:

Who is making the statements? (26 percent knew)
What firm is doing the work? (18 percent knew)
How long have the experiments been going on? (30 percent knew)
What kinds of materials are involved? (11 percent knew)
What briefly is the story about? (9 percent knew)

To test his theory that the trouble with such stories was the average length of their sentences, Couey edited this one and then retested it. He used a mechanical editing technique that retained the original writer's style, grammar, and information. His corrected version (which follows), considered as literature, does not read any better than the original, but it now contains 265 words and 21 sentences, for an average of 12 words per sentence:

American London Shrinkers Corp. has come to the end of an 18-month search.

One year and a half ago, that firm set out to find a safe way to shrink, sponge, and handle blended materials without damage. Much experimentation was required. Many volumes of data were gathered. The trial and error method was given a thorough test.

And now—success.

Theodore Trilling, president of American London Shrinkers, has announced that the problem has been solved.

Exactly what was the problem?

The trend towards blends in suiting and coating woolens and worsteds created the necessity for developing some alterations in shrinking and sponging operations.

Mr. Trilling mentioned the "change color" problem. He pointed out that the Orlon content in a fabric turned yellow. The rayon and acetate content tended to moire. The 15 to 20 percent of nylon, used to give strength, tended to shine. The "color changes" do not occur in the new process.

No new machinery is needed, Trilling said. He made clear that only alterations in the processing are necessary. He referred to alterations such as a change in the action, the weight of the apron or the leader.

The firm's president emphasized that many tests were required to make sure no further shrinkage would occur.

Reports of the tests and results have been passed on to the mills and sealing agents of the new blends, Mr. Trilling said. In some cases, the new information has served as a guide in the correction and improvement of these fabrics, he said.

This is an important step in the industry, according to Trilling.

When another group was asked to read the edited version and answer the same questions, the results were very different:

> Who is making the statement? (68 percent knew)
> What firm is doing the work? (55 percent knew)
> How long have the experiments been going on? (71 percent knew)
> What kinds of materials are involved? (29 percent knew)
> What, briefly, is this story about? (64 percent knew)

If you were preparing a news release for your company or a client, a 37-percent increase in firm identification and a 55-percent gain in understanding of the story would be significant achievements. Couey repeated this experiment with dozens of articles. The results were always the same. A sentence is a package for ideas, and readers must struggle to get huge, bulky packages into their minds. By simply making the sentences shorter, he achieved large gains in understanding.

Couey continued to investigate the short sentence phenomenon and discovered some interesting facts:

1. Short sentences usually contained only one idea each.

2. A story could contain both long and short sentences for variety, as long as the average was short.

3. The optimum average for most sentences seemed to be about 17 words.[5]

Pyramid Power   Couey achieved tremendous gains in understanding by simply shortening sentences, but he never taught that sentence length was the only element in effective writing. Organization is another important skill that must be mastered.

Journalists use the inverted pyramid form (figure 8.5), which organizes a story so the most important points are covered first. The inverted pyramid is equally useful for other types of informative writing. A message should begin by answering five questions: who, what, when, where, and why? These questions are answered in the first one or two paragraphs, called the *lead.* Journalists begin with the question that is most important to the message and proceed in descending order. Each succeeding paragraph contains details that are less important than those in the previous paragraph.

The inverted pyramid offers several advantages. First, it puts the most important details near the beginning, where readers who skim the message will be more likely to see them. Second, an editor may cut the story from the bottom up if necessary without losing the more important details. Third, a strong opening gets readers' attention and directs them into the rest of the message.

Media Selection

Various media and their audiences will be discussed in detail in part III, but it is appropriate at this point to outline a strategy for media selection. Although it is crucial to construct each message carefully so it communicates the desired meaning to the audience, it is equally important to choose the proper medium to carry the message. For discussion purposes, media may be classified as controlled or uncontrolled.

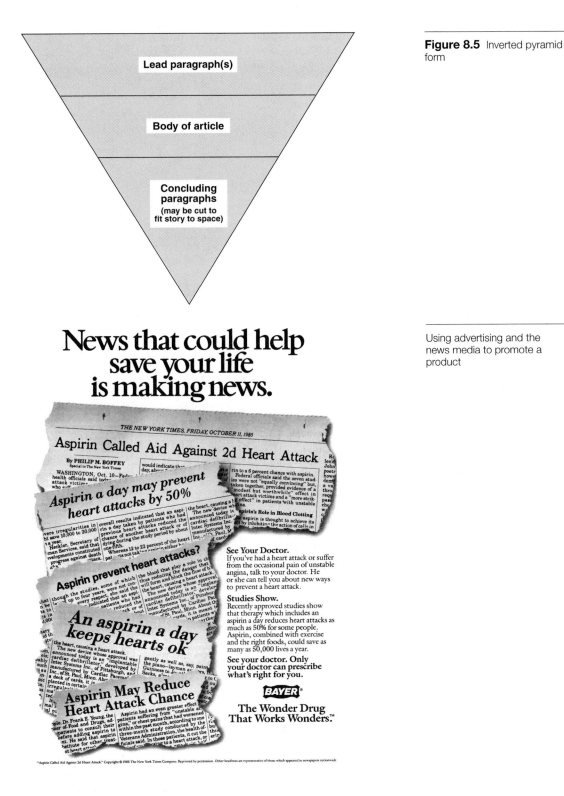

Using advertising and the news media to promote a product

The preparation of a news release is different from the preparation of an advertising message because news depends on a third party to select and deliver the message. This is the basic difference between controlled and uncontrolled media. **Controlled media,** such as internal publications, direct mail, posters (see chapter 10), and advertising, allow the public relations practitioner to dictate what is published and how it is delivered to the primary audience. **Uncontrolled media,** for which someone else makes decisions about content, include newspapers, television, and radio.

The three basic considerations in media selection are the audiences, the timing, and the available budget.

Audiences

Audiences must be the first consideration in any public relations effort (see chapter 6). You need to identify the publics you are trying to reach and determine what will interest them. Uncontrolled media present a special problem to the public relations practitioner because publicity releases must be planned for two audiences. The primary audience, the public for whom the message is intended, is the most important; however, the editor or reporter who selects or rejects the release for publication or broadcast is the first hurdle. Thus, although the release is designed to communicate a particular message to the primary audience, it must first attract the journalistic attention of an editor.

After identifying the target audience, you must next determine which media are likely to be interested in particular types of information. By researching available media carefully, you can become familiar with the types of stories they use and the audiences they attract. You may then select the best media for each release and package the information in a way that will attract the editor's attention. Chapter 10 discusses various strategies for media relations in greater detail.

Timing   Timing is the second important factor in media selection. Once the appropriate media are chosen, the time required to reach the primary audience is critical. Some publications have backlogs of material and may not be able to get a story out in time. Therefore, the question of *when* the primary audience receives the message may be just as important as whether or not it receives the message at all.

Budgets   Budgets, the third important consideration, are always limited, and frequently they, in turn, limit media selection. Usually the first decision is whether or not the message needs to be delivered by more than one medium. If a mix of media is desirable, it may be necessary to consider cost when deciding which ones to use. Remember that while the costs of controlled media, such as advertising, are obvious, costs associated with uncontrolled media must also be counted.

Table 8.2 contrasts advantages and disadvantages of several different media. Considering these points with regard to audiences, time, and budget will help public relations practitioners select the media most appropriate to their messages.

Summary

The job of public relations is to create a positive *universe of discourse* about the organization. It is this universe of discourse that creates the mental pictures publics develop about organizations. These public images are different for each

TABLE 8.2 Principal Media: Advantages and Disadvantages

	Advantages	Disadvantages
Television	1. Combines sight, sound, and motion attributes 2. Permits physical demonstration of product 3. Believability due to immediacy of message 4. High impact of message 5. Huge audiences 6. Good product identification 7. Popular medium	1. Message limited by restricted time segments 2. No possibility for consumer referral to message 3. Availabilities sometimes difficult to arrange 4. High time costs 5. Waste coverage 6. High production costs 7. Poor color transmission
Magazines	1. Selectivity of audience 2. Reaches more affluent consumers 3. Long closing dates 4. No immediacy of message 5. Sometimes high production costs	1. Often duplicate circulation 2. Usually cannot dominate in a local market 3. Offers prestige to an advertiser 4. Pass-along readership 5. Good color reproduction
Radio	1. Selectivity of geographical markets 2. Good saturation of local markets 3. Ease of changing advertising copy 4. Relatively low cost	1. Message limited by restricted time segments 2. No possibility for consumer referral to message 3. No visual appeal 4. Waste coverage
Newspapers	1. Selectivity of geographical markets 2. Ease of changing advertising copy 3. Reaches all income groups 4. Ease of scheduling advertisements 5. Relatively low cost 6. Good medium for manufacturer/dealer advertising	1. High cost for national coverage 2. Shortness of message life 3. Waste circulation 4. Differences of sizes and formats 5. Rate differentials between local and national advertisements 6. Poor color reproduction
Direct Mail	1. Extremely selective 2. Message can be very personalized 3. Little competition with other advertisements 4. Easy to measure effect of advertisements 5. Provides easy means for consumer action	1. Often has poor image 2. Can be quite expensive 3. Many restrictive postal regulations 4. Problems in maintaining mailing lists
Outdoor Posters (on stationary panels)	1. Selectivity of geographical markets 2. High repetitive value 3. Large physical size 4. Relatively low cost 5. Good color reproduction	1. Often has poor image 2. Message must be short 3. Waste circulation 4. National coverage is expensive 5. Few creative specialists

TABLE 8.2 *(continued)*

	Advantages	Disadvantages
Point-of-Purchase Displays	1. Presents message at point of sale 2. Great flexibility for creativity 3. Ability to demonstrate product in use 4. Good color reproduction 5. Repetitive value	1. Dealer apathy in installation 2. Long production period 3. High unit cost 4. Shipping problems 5. Space problem
Transit Posters (on moving vehicles)	1. Selectivity of geographical markets 2. Captive audience 3. Very low cost 4. Good color reproduction 5. High repetitive value	1. Limited to a certain class of consumers 2. Waste circulation 3. Surroundings are disreputable 4. Few creative specialists
Movie Trailers	1. Selectivity of geographical markets 2. Captive audience 3. Large physical size 4. Good medium for manufacturer/dealer advertising	1. Cannot be employed in all theaters 2. Waste circulation 3. High production costs 4. No possibility for consumer referral to message
Advertising Specialties	1. Unique presentation 2. High repetitive value 3. Has a "gift" quality 4. Relatively long life	1. Subject to fads 2. Message must be short 3. May have relatively high unit cost 4. Effectiveness difficult to measure
Pamphlets and Booklets	1. Offer detailed message at point of sale 2. Supplement a personal sales presentation 3. Offer to potential buyers a good referral means 4. Good color reproduction	1. Dealers often fail to use 2. May have a relatively high unit cost 3. Few creative specialists 4. Effectiveness difficult to measure

Reprinted by permission of Publishing Horizons, Inc. from *Advertising Campaigns, Formulations and Tactics,* by Quera, pages 71–74.

individual, yet they are highly similar. They are the collective impressions various publics use to judge the value and effectiveness of organizations in society. The first action step of public relations is to assess these images accurately and then to plan and execute communication programs based on that information. The final step in the process of public relations, measuring the effects of these messages, will be discussed in the next chapter.

Charlie Hustle

By Maryan Baskin
Pepperdine University

Case Study

F or most of his life, Pete Rose has been a hero. Born in Cincinnati and raised "blue collar," he made his professional baseball debut with the hometown team, the Cincinnati Reds, on April 4, 1963. Within two years he led the National League in hits—a performance he repeated often, in 1968, 1970, 1972, 1973, and 1976. He was also the League leader three times each in At-Bats, Runs, and Doubles. Over the span of his career, he set records for hits (4,256) and games played (3,562), and he broke Ty Cobb's batting record. He made the National League's All Star Team in 1965, 1967–71, and 1973–77. He was the 1963 Rookie of the Year and, in 1973, was selected Most Valuable Player by the Baseball Writers Association of America. During his years with the Reds, he managed to be the all-time leader in most of the batting statistics.

Pete endeared himself to many fans by not quitting baseball in his youth—he played into his forties, working for both Montreal and Philadelphia before returning to Cincinnati as player/manager in August of 1984. When he became the Reds' manager, they had finished last two years in a row and were in fifth place. The following season he moved them into second place and kept them solid contenders for the National League pennant. At one point in his career, it was said Pete Rose *was* baseball. He was definitely destined for the Hall of Fame.

Along the way, though, things began to go wrong in the private and professional life of "Charlie Hustle": a messy divorce in 1978, a paternity suit he did not contest in 1979, and in 1988, an unprecedented 30-day suspension from baseball for hitting an umpire. By 1989 he was facing threats to his very livelihood. He was being investigated by then Commissioner of Baseball A. Bartlett Giamatti on charges of betting on baseball games, including Reds' games. Six months and 225 pages of evidence later, Pete Rose signed a settlement that banned him from baseball for life. In April of 1990 he pleaded guilty to felony tax fraud stemming from his gambling monies and was sentenced in July of that year to five months in prison, three months in a halfway house, and $50,000 in fines.

Earlier in the year Rose had hired a new press agent, Barbara Pinzka, to restore his shredded public image. He did not appear at the Kentucky Derby or the Indy 500 (unusual for Rose), and Pinzka was credited with pointing out to Pete that a man accused of having a gambling addiction could not restore his hero image by appearing with high rollers. Although he was generally keeping a low profile, Pinzka arranged for Rose to appear on a national television interview program and speak about his compulsive gambling. He even entered treatment and contritely admitted, at his sentencing, to being at fault.

No sooner had Rose been sentenced than people began to wonder whether it would keep him out of the Hall of Fame, the final defeat. Amid speculation that Rose had learned nothing and that his remorse was simply a well-orchestrated public relations campaign, Rose himself seemed to believe he still had a chance.

Now, several years later, he would be eligible for the Hall of Fame. Sometimes fans can forgive and forget.

Questions

1. What publics would you want to influence if you were Pinzka? Are there intervening and moderating publics in this case?

2. What role would written messages have in a campaign to restore "Charlie Hustle's" image?

3. What media would you use in your campaign? Do you agree with Pinzka's decisions to keep Rose away from the Indy 500 and the Kentucky Derby? Was the television interview a good idea? Would those tactics reach the publics you want to influence?

Notes

1. Frank Walsh, *Public Relations Writer in a Computer Age* (Englewood Cliffs, N.J.: Prentice-Hall, 1986), 10.

2. Herbert F. Lionberger, *Adoption of New Ideas and Practices* (Ames, Iowa: Iowa State University Press, 1960), 32.

3. *Mountain Bell Submission,* Public Relations Society of America Silver Anvil Awards Competition, 1983.

4. Ibid.

5. Craig E. Aronoff et al., *Getting Your Message Across* (St. Paul, Minn.: West Publishing, 1981), 28–31.

CHAPTER 9

Evaluating Public Relations Effectiveness

Preview

Evaluation is an essential step in a public relations program. It permits the practitioner to assess the effectiveness of the effort, demonstrate that effectiveness to management, and plan for future efforts.

Value is more important than volume in evaluating the effectiveness of public relations efforts.

Public relations effectiveness is best measured using an open-system model that takes into account environmental factors and before-and-after comparisons.

Open-system evaluation models include effectiveness measures of factors like administrative processes, employee publications, media relations, and advertising.

W e have *arbitrarily* separated the public relations process into four related functions: research, planning, action, and evaluation. In reality, however, the methods outlined in chapter 6 and the material in this chapter are simply different applications of the research function. For illustration and emphasis, we have separated the two chapters, but much of the discussion about evaluating public relations programs relates directly to the research methods mentioned in chapter 6.

The Need for Evaluation Research

Although presented last, **evaluation** is not the final stage of the public relations process. In practice, evaluation is frequently the beginning of a new effort. The research function overlaps the planning, action, and evaluation functions. It is an interdependent process that, once set in motion, has no beginning or end.

To help explain how evaluation can be involved in virtually every phase of a program, figure 9.1 shows three evaluation segments: implementation checking, in-progress monitoring, and outcome evaluation.

1. *Implementation checking* In this start-up assessment step, the central question is: To what degree is the target audience being reached? However complete the planning may have been, it will still be necessary to determine the difference between *planned* and *actual* implementation. Variations from the original plan must be analyzed and explained so that a decision can be made to either modify the plan or correct the discrepancies.

2. *In-progress monitoring* Periodically during the program, actions undertaken should be reviewed and, if necessary, modified. Reviews at regular intervals can be planned to determine the program's effectiveness in meeting its objectives. Any unanticipated results can be assessed and factored into the evaluation. The variance between actual and anticipated progress at each point can be examined for its effect on the overall outcome. Regular monitoring helps determine why some results differ significantly from the original plan, and it prevents unwelcome surprises.

3. *Outcome evaluation* The final step is to assess the program's end results. Again, objectives and results are compared to determine the variance. At this point, all prior evaluations become important for explaining the context in which the program was implemented and for interpreting the results. An evaluation report transmits this information, along with suggestions for planning future efforts, to an appropriate decision maker. Research in public relations should be ongoing, continually evaluating the process and its environment and providing new information to sustain it. Learning about the failures and successes of a public relations campaign provides information that can be used in more precise planning for the next effort. Evaluation research is also valuable in assessing an existing campaign. This point is illustrated in the Cedar Springs Community Hospital case, where research made a tremendous impact on the planning and action steps taken. In the following final segment, research helps determine the effectiveness of the total effort.

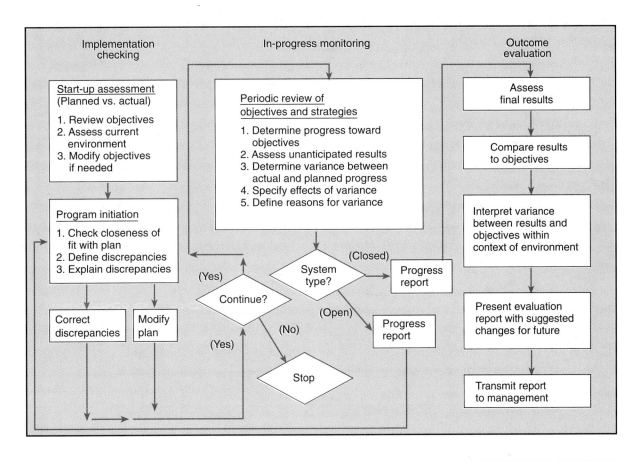

Figure 9.1 Components of an evaluation plan

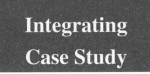

Cedar Springs
Community Hospital

Segment 4

A pproximately one year after the start of the program to improve the employees' perceptions regarding the quality of patient care, follow-up research was conducted. This evaluation process began at the same point as the original research. The methodology of the initial employee survey was used, and 300 names were again chosen at random from the 1,226 employees. Each individual selected received a mailed questionnaire similar to the one used to launch the process.

Four key factors from the original survey had been selected as objectives for improvement during the preceding year. These same factors were measured again in the evaluation survey to determine how much progress had been made. The following comparisons were produced:

Factors	Average Ratings (10-pt. scale)	
	Start	End
1. Quality of care	6.6	7.0
2. Patients' understanding of procedures and tests	5.7	6.2
3. Courtesy and respect shown to patients	7.4	7.8
4. Patient call lights answered in less than five minutes	56%	81%

Obviously, a noticeable and positive shift in employee perceptions of the hospital's overall performance had taken place. In addition to the quantitative evidence, which showed gains in every category over the previous year, qualitative indicators also supported this conclusion. Another focus group demonstrated considerable improvement in employees' feelings about the quality of care available. This finding was reinforced through letters from employees and comments made during monthly employee group meetings.

Although employee perceptions of quality did not rise to the same level as those of recently released patients participating in earlier surveys, the improvements were consistent and strong. Therefore, management concluded that continuation of feedback to employees from patients would be an important part of future employee communication programs.

Another important reason evaluation research is a necessity for public relations programs is that it enhances organizational support. Public relations professionals must assume the same responsibility for effectiveness as do their management colleagues. Organizational resources are always limited, and competition for them is keen. Public relations managers must be able to demonstrate effectiveness in ways that can be measured against other competing functions, as Robert Marker, manager of press services for Armstrong Cork, reveals in mini-case 9.1.

Mini-Case 9.1

The Importance of Evaluation

I remember an occasion, some years ago, that started me thinking about the need for some kind of measurement device and internal reporting system to help explain the public relations function. I was asked by a marketing executive at Armstrong to come to his office and inform him, as succinctly as possible, just what it was he was getting for what he was spending on public relations. It really didn't bother me at the time, because we had had these inquiries before, and I was pretty sure I could handle it. I came prepared with a considerable volume of newspaper clippings, magazine features, and case histories that we had produced in support of his product line that year.

I laid all this out in front of him. . . . After an appropriate interval, I pointed out that all this publicity—if strung end to end—would reach from his office located in the west wing of the building, clear across the center wing to the east wing, down the stairs, and out into the main lobby, and there'd still be enough leftover to paper one and a half walls of his office. (That was a favored "measurement" device back in those days. We used to have our secretaries total the column inches, and then convert it all into linear feet of hallway space.) And then it came, the question no one had ever asked before: "But what's all this worth to us?"

I stammered for a moment and said something to the effect that I thought the material spoke for itself. After all, this was highly coveted editorial space we were talking about. . . . I said it would be difficult to attach a specific value to it.

He smiled. "My boy," he said, "I have to attach a value to everything in this operation. . . . Why don't you go back and write me a memo outlining clearly what this function does for us, and then we'll talk about your budget for next year."

Source: Robert K. Marker, "The Armstrong/PR Data Management System," *Public Relations Review* 3 (Winter 1977): 51–52.

Too many public relations programs have been eliminated or severely cut back because no "value" could be attached to them. The harsh realities of corporate existence make it necessary for public relations practitioners to demonstrate the worth of what they do. Particularly in difficult economic situations, every aspect of organizational activity is measured by its relative benefit to the firm. A public relations department that cannot demonstrate its value to the organization will not be in a position to influence the policy decisions that affect its own fate.

Measuring the Worth of Public Relations Efforts

The concept of measurement itself is not new to the practice of public relations. The problem, as Robert Marker discovered, is that the rest of the business world has been using different standards. Marker's measurement system was quantifiable (linear feet of hallway), and it accurately reflected the effort that had been expended. In response to the devastating question of "worth," however, the measurement strategy could not provide any data. Because public relations is by nature intangible, assigning a value to its activities is difficult. Often the problem leads practitioners into the use of erroneous measures or measures incorrectly applied.

Measurement Strategies

Like every aspect of public relations practice, evaluation needs careful planning. Ideally, the evaluation effort should be planned from the inception of the program. An evaluation attempt that is tacked on after a program is finished will produce incomplete and generally inappropriate data. When evaluation is part of the overall plan, each component can be constructed with an eye toward later measurement of its success.

Measurement-by-Objectives The use of management-by-objectives (MBO), or any similar planning process, will alleviate the measurement problem facing public relations. Although MBO is most frequently used for evaluating individual employees, its basic elements can also be applied to programs, projects, and work groups. The object is to prepare advance statements, usually during the planning phase, concerning legitimate expectations from a given effort. These statements must be mutually agreed on by all those involved before the action occurs. When the set time for evaluation arrives, objectives can be compared to accomplishments to assess the degree of success. The process used varies among organizations, but the basic MBO steps include the following:

1. *Work group involvement*   If more than one person will be working on the project, the entire group should be involved in setting the objectives. This ensures that no portion of the task is overlooked and each contributor feels committed to the effort.

2. *Manager-subordinate involvement*   Once the group's objectives are established, each subordinate should work with the project manager to define a set of individual objectives. These keep the project moving by making certain that everyone understands his or her role.

3. *Determination of intermediate objectives*   This step defines a series of objectives along the way toward the overall target. Setting intermediate objectives permits more precise in-progress evaluation and makes it possible to consider mid-course corrections before the project gets out of hand.

4. *Determination of measures of achievement*   The point at which the effort will be considered complete should be specified in terms of either a time element or the achievement of a stated objective.

5. *Review, evaluation, and recycling*   Because no objective can be defined with absolute precision nor achieved perfectly, it is important to use information gained from each evaluation process to improve the planning for the next public relations effort.

Impact Analysis   Measuring the impact or results of a public relations effort is always difficult and never totally objective. As we have emphasized in this chapter, however, the more public relations practitioners can quantitatively measure the effects of their work, the better they will be able to plan future efforts and demonstrate their value to organizational decision makers. In this section, we offer four dimensions of measurement that can be applied to assess the impact of any public relations campaign, regardless of its size. These are *audience coverage, audience response, campaign impact,* and *environmental mediation.*

Audience Coverage   Perhaps the first point that must be addressed in any evaluation is whether or not the intended audiences were reached. Other questions that should be answered in the initial phase are: To what extent was each target audience exposed to the various messages? Which unintended audiences also received the messages?

Two basic measures are used to help answer these questions. First, accurate record keeping must detail what messages were prepared and where they were sent. Second, a system must be employed for tracking which releases were used and by whom. While the first measure is the easiest to obtain, it is worthless without the second for comparison. Massive amounts of publicity have no value unless some of it actually reaches the intended audience. Therefore, some method must be devised to measure accurately the use of publicity and the coverage of events.

Essentially, such measurement can be accomplished if the practitioner and/or other staff members keep a careful check on target media and maintain clipping files. This process, of course, is easier for print than for broadcast media, but some radio and television stations give periodic reports to public relations practitioners if requested. In addition, clipping services that monitor both print and broadcast media provide regular reports for a fee. Such a service must be selected carefully, on the basis of other users' recommendations concerning its accuracy.

The measurement of audience coverage involves more than just the ratio of releases sent to releases used. The practitioner must also be able to specify what audiences (both intended and unintended) were reached through which media. Data of this type are available from **readership surveys** and audience rating information obtainable through media advertising sales departments. Audience profiles for each publication or broadcast station can be calculated with the amount of space or time used to yield a complete measure of audience coverage. Such data can be reported in terms of total column inches (for print media) or amount of air time per audience (for broadcast media) for each release or event (see table 9.1). John Pavlik et al. used a readership survey at a medical center to determine that employees who were more integrated into the organization were more likely to read a company newsletter—the newsletter could then be designed to meet the needs of this public.[1] For more of a bottom line effect, however, many practitioners translate media time and space into dollar values based on prevailing advertising rates.

Audience Response   Once it is determined that a message has reached its intended audience, the practitioner must evaluate that audience's response. Frequently, this type of information can be obtained through various message pretesting methods like those discussed in this chapter and in chapter 7. Samples of each target audience are exposed to various messages before they are released. The resulting data help predict whether the message will elicit a favorable or unfavorable reaction. It can also determine if the message attracts attention, arouses interest, or gains audience understanding. With good sampling techniques and questionnaire design (chapter 6), accurate predictions are possible, and problems can be corrected before messages are released. Some messages, however, such as spot news or stories written from releases, cannot be measured in advance because they are not controlled by the practitioner. Thus, it is necessary to measure audience response using the survey techniques discussed in chapter 6. Frequently, the practitioner can predict audience response by tracking media treatment of stories in terms of favorable, neutral, and unfavorable tendencies, as we shall see later in this chapter.

Messages can also be pretested using **readability studies.** The basic premise of these tests is that written copy will be ineffective if it is too difficult to read. Most methods for measuring readability generate an index score that translates to an approximate educational level required for understanding the material. For example, *Time* and *Reader's Digest* are written at what is termed an 11th- or 12th-grade level. This indicates that their readers are primarily persons with education at least through high school. Though a great deal of controversy surrounds

TABLE 9.1 Some Available Measures of Audience Coverage

Column Inches of Space / Air Time in Seconds	Audience Type I	Audience Type II	Audience Type III	Audience Type IV	Magazine A	Newspaper B	Radio Station C	Television Station D	Wire Sercie
Release 1	271	450	175	206	250	375			400
	600	1320	480	540			1250	300	
Release 2									
Event 1									
Release 3									
Event 2									

which formula is the most accurate and what factors are necessary to compute readability, readability tests may be useful in public relations efforts to tailor writing styles for target publications. The index score of a news release compared to the score of the publication for which it is intended should indicate whether or not the two are compatible.

Four standard readability instruments are described here:

1. The *Flesch Formula* produces both a reading ease score and a human interest score.[2]

2. The *Gunning Fog Index,* one of the simplest methods, measures reading ease only (see table 9.2).[3]

3. The *Dale-Chall Formula* computes both sentence length and the number of infrequently used words.[4]

4. *Cloze Procedure* is a technique designed to measure readability and comprehension of both spoken and visual messages.[5]

Remember that the simplest writing is not always the best. Meaning may be lost through oversimplification as easily as through complexity. Abstract or complex concepts cannot be adequately expressed in simple, short sentences using one- and two-syllable words. The important point is to match the written message

TABLE 9.2 Computing the Gunning Fog Index

To check the reading ease of any passage of writing, compute:

1. The number of words in the copy.
2. The number of complete thoughts in the copy.
3. The average sentence length. [number of words ÷ number of complete thoughts]
4. The percentage of difficult words (words having three or more syllables except: proper names, combinations of short easy words, and verb forms made three syllables by adding -ed or -es). [number of difficult words ÷ total number of words]
5. Average sentence length + percentage of difficult words.
6. The figure derived in Step 5 is multiplied by .4 to get the Fog Index Score, the grade level at which the copy is easily read.

to the publication and audience for which it is intended. This textbook, for example, was written for college students who are studying public relations, not for casual readers. Frequently, editors of internal publications for highly technical organizations must avoid talking down to their readers as much as they avoid "fog."

Campaign Impact   In addition to considering audience response to individual messages, the practitioner must be concerned with the impact of the campaign as a whole. In this case, the whole is not equal to the sum of the parts. If a campaign is correctly researched and planned, its elements will interact to produce an effect that is much greater than the sum of the response to the individual messages. If the mix is not right, however, the combined elements of the campaign, no matter how individually excellent, may fall far short of the goal.

For this reason, it is important to measure the cumulative impact of a public relations campaign, keeping in mind the goals developed in the planning phase. This measurement can be made only after the campaign has been in progress long enough to achieve some results. Effects are generally attitudinal, although they can be behavioral as well. If one campaign goal is to maintain or increase favorable attitudes toward an organization among members of certain publics, research methods such as organizational image surveys described in chapter 6 can be used to gauge success. Usually this calls for both pretests and posttests or for a series of surveys to track attitude trends. In addition, the practitioner can measure certain actions by members of a public like complaints, inquiries about services, and requests for reprints.

Environmental Mediation   Practitioners must realize that public relations campaigns do not exert the only influence on the attitudes and behaviors of their publics. Any campaign exists in an environment of social processes that can have as much or more effect on the attainment of its goals as the prepared messages do. Therefore, the measured results must be interpreted in light of various other forces. Failure to reach a goal may not be failure at all when unforeseen negative conditions have arisen. Likewise, a striking success may not be entirely attributable to the public relations campaign when positive environmental forces were also present at the time. Techniques such as environmental monitoring and others discussed in chapter 6 should be used to evaluate the results of a campaign.

One method the practitioner can use to monitor environmental influences, even with a modest budget and a small staff, is focus group interviewing. Focus groups are composed of individuals randomly selected from a public who meet to discuss the campaign. The group should be presented with the elements of the campaign and then directed through a discussion of its effects and the causes of those effects. A skillful interviewer will keep the discussion on the subject without compromising candor or disrupting the free flow of ideas. Focus groups should be asked to discuss their reactions to the elements of the campaign and assess the campaign's overall effect. They can also help interpret data obtained in the campaign impact stage in relation to historical, social, and political events that may have had influence.

These four stages of measurement can help a public relations practitioner more completely assess the results of a campaign and plan effective future efforts. These stages of measurement also yield the kind of real-world data that managers in other areas of an organization use to support their activities.

Sources of Measurement Error

Following are some common mistakes in the measurement of public relations effectiveness:

1. *Volume is not equal to results.*   Too often, the working assumption is that if one press release is effective, three will be three times as effective. As Marker learned, a large stack or even a long chain of press clippings may be proof of effort. But results in terms of the effect of those clippings on the publics for which they were intended cannot be measured by volume. Even audience measurement devices designed to count the number of people exposed to a message do not show whether or not those exposed actually paid any attention or, if they did, what effect the message had on them.

2. *Estimate is not measurement.*   Relying on experience and intuition to gauge the effectiveness of public relations efforts is no longer acceptable as objective measurement. Experts know that appearances, even to the trained eye, can be deceiving. Guesswork has no place in a measurement system. It can be appealing and comfortable because it is easy to accomplish and flattering to the expert. However, when it comes to budget requests, managers like the one Marker encountered demand hard facts.

3. *Samples must be representative.*   Many wrong decisions about the future of a public relations campaign have been based on a few favorable comments that were either volunteered or collected unsystematically. Several pitfalls exist: Only those with positive (or negative) comments may volunteer them; some people, when asked, tend to give the response they think the interviewer wants to hear; or the selection of interviewers may be unintentionally biased. Samples must be selected scientifically and systematically to avoid such errors.

4. *Effort is not knowledge.*   One of the most common public relations objectives is to increase the public's knowledge about a particular

subject. Sometimes practitioners assume a direct relationship between the amount of effort they expend in communicating a message and the amount of knowledge a public acquires. This erroneous assumption leads to a problem similar to the volume error discussed earlier. The study of human learning suggests that after a certain level of knowledge is reached, the rate of learning slows in most people. Therefore, in spite of any communicator's best efforts, all publics will eventually reach a knowledge plateau at which very little additional learning occurs.

5. *Knowledge is not favorable attitude.* Communication is often deemed successful if the public has gained knowledge of the message content. However, even when pretest and posttest results indicate an increase in knowledge, it cannot be assumed that more favorable attitudes have also resulted. A high degree of name recall or awareness is not necessarily an indication that the public relations effort has been effective. Familiarity does not necessarily lead to positive opinion.

6. *Attitude is not behavior.* While positive public opinion may be a legitimate goal of public relations, it is incorrect to assume that favorable attitudes will result in desired behaviors. When members of a particular public hold favorable attitudes toward a client or organization, they will probably not consciously oppose that person or group. On the other hand, they still may not actively support the goals of the public relations campaign. Our discussion of latent, aware, and active publics in chapter 6 emphasized this point. Practitioners must be aware of the need to predict behavior, or at least potential behavior, when measuring public opinion.

Mark P. McElreath describes two models of public relations research into which most measurement efforts can be categorized: open and closed evaluation systems.[6] A **closed-system evaluation** limits its scope to the messages and events planned for the campaign and their effects on the intended publics. This is the model of public relations evaluation most frequently employed. Its purpose is to test the messages and media of a public relations campaign before they are presented to the intended publics. This pretest strategy is designed to uncover miscalculations that may have gone unnoticed in the planning stage. The posttest evaluation is conducted after the campaign has been underway long enough to produce results. Posttest data can be compared to pretest results and campaign objectives to evaluate the effectiveness of the effort. These results also provide input for planning the next campaign.

Closed-System Evaluation

Factors normally considered in the standard pretest and posttest evaluation design are as follows:

Pretest/Posttest Design

1. *Productions* The evaluation includes an accounting of every public relations tool used in the campaign (press releases, press kits, booklets, films, letters, etc.). The amount of material actually produced and the

total cost of production yield important cost-effectiveness information. The amount of time and money devoted to each segment of a public relations effort can be reassessed with this type of data.

2. *Distribution*   The evaluation examines the channels through which the messages of the campaign are distributed. Clippings collected by professional services are often used to measure how many stories were actually printed. The number of radio and television stations that picked up the story can be important information. These kinds of data are perhaps most frequently used to evaluate public relations campaigns. Note that although distribution data provide a reasonable measure of the campaign's efficiency, they do not really address the issue of effectiveness.

3. *Interest*   Reader interest surveys determine what people read in various types of publications. A representative sample of the total potential reading audience is surveyed for a quantitative measure of which items attract more interest. These surveys are relatively good measures of what readers actually consume, but they do not measure comprehension or the effect of the message on the reader. Television and radio use similar survey methods to determine what programs and times people prefer.

4. *Reach*   Reader interest surveys not only reveal whether or not a story was read but also describe the people who read it. This information can be valuable because messages frequently reach publics other than those for whom they are intended. The efficiency of a message is the extent to which it actually reaches the intended audience. A reasonably accurate measure of which audiences are being reached by which messages is imperative to any evaluation effort. Television and radio rating services provide information concerning the characteristics of audiences at various times of day.

5. *Understanding*   While it is important to determine whether the target audience is being reached, it is equally important to know whether or not the audience understands the message. A public relations campaign cannot be considered successful if the public does not get the point. Frequently, readability tests are applied to printed messages to measure their accessibility. As we have already discussed, readability measures are based on sentence length and number of syllables in the words used. While much criticism has been directed at such tests, they remain standard instruments for pretest evaluation.

6. *Attitudes*   Creating and maintaining positive attitudes or changing negative ones is a central purpose of all public relations activity. Therefore, measurement of attitudes, or preferably of attitude change, is a highly prized form of evaluation. Frequently a pretest/posttest measurement is conducted to determine the degree of change in the attitudes of target publics that can be attributed to the public relations campaign.

Attitude measurement is a sophisticated behavioral science technique that presents many opportunities for error. Few practitioners attempt major attitudinal studies without the help of professionals who specialize in this type of measurement. Several of the research techniques discussed in chapter 6 (for example, the public relations audit) use some form of attitudinal measurement. Professional research organizations frequently provide attitudinal data for public relations evaluation. Many factors, ranging from the need for a scientifically selected sample to the construction of a questionnaire that will not bias results, make attitude measurement a difficult task for most practitioners.

Disadvantages of the Closed-System Method

While closed-system evaluation is the model most widely used by public relations staffs, it has two major drawbacks. First, as we have already discussed, the fact that a message was transmitted to the intended audience in an understandable form and that it produced favorable attitudes does not mean the campaign goals were reached. Second, the likelihood that desired results will occur, especially in terms of actual behavior changes, is influenced by a number of factors external to the campaign. Failure of a public relations effort to achieve its goals may not mean that the elements or the plan of the effort were faulty. A number of environmental factors such as economic, political, and social change can nullify what might otherwise have been positive results.

During the early 1970s, oil companies caught in the grip of an embargo that caused escalating prices, shortages, and long lines at the gas pumps experienced losses in favorable public opinion in spite of massive public relations efforts. The effectiveness of their messages was undermined by events outside the control of any public relations campaign. Therefore, these events had to be factored in when the public relations efforts were evaluated. While the companies experienced losses rather than gains in positive public opinion, the campaigns may still have been effective. In the absence of workable public relations plans already in place, the losses in favorable public opinion could have been even more devastating.

Open-System Evaluation

Although a pretest/posttest design may be appropriate for evaluating short-range projects, many public relations programs are too complex for simple before-and-after measures. Continuing or long-range programs, such as changes in organizational policy, require an evaluation method that can provide feedback throughout the process, before the end results are available. **Open-system evaluation** models attempt to account for factors outside the control of the public relations campaign when assessing its effectiveness.

The open-system model emphasizes the extent to which the public relations function is encompassed by numerous other aspects of an organization and its environment. Factors like unintended audiences and organizational administration and effectiveness are also included.

In chapter 6, we discussed the growing use of environmental monitoring and social audits as data-gathering methods. These same techniques yield valuable information for evaluating effectiveness in public relations campaigns. The impact of public relations efforts on various environmental factors can be one useful measure of results. In turn, environmental data can help explain the effects of a campaign. Because most of these factors are outside the organization's control, they may operate as confounding variables in a closed-system evaluation. Economic conditions, for example, can have a significant effect on consumers' attitudes toward an organization. Thus, results from a public relations effort that do not seem positive when viewed alone might really be significant when the negative effects of certain economic conditions are considered.

Internal climate data are also useful for evaluating public relations campaigns. Public relations messages should be expected to have as much effect on the managers and employees of an organization as they do on other publics. In chapter 6, we suggested that organizations research their internal climate for public relations planning information, and the same holds true for evaluation. Public relations practitioners should look inside and outside their organizations to measure the effects of their efforts. Like environmental factors, the internal climate of an organization can help explain the effect of a public relations effort. Union activities, management perceptions, and changes in company policy can all affect the results of a campaign.

Many of the factors included in the open-system evaluation model are difficult to measure accurately. Nevertheless, recognizing these factors is itself an important step toward evaluating public relations efforts. The value of open-system evaluation is that it considers public relations within the broader context of overall organizational effectiveness.

An Open-System Plan in Actual Practice

James F. Tirone, public relations director of AT&T before the company's breakup, maintains that public relations is a managerial as well as a creative effort.[7] Tirone believes that public relations should meet the same tests of performance as other management functions. This belief is reflected in the classic measurement techniques developed by the Bell System to be applied uniformly in a wide variety of public relations situations. Although they are dated in content, the following examples from the Bell System program still represent an excellent attempt to implement an open-system evaluation model in three areas: administrative processes, employee publications, and media relations.

Evaluating Administrative Processes　To measure the effectiveness of public relations administrative processes, Tirone used information already available from standard organization sources to make some unique comparisons. Figure 9.2 shows the correlation between the size of the public relations budget of each of the companies included in the study and the company's revenues. The graph shows a clear positive correlation (0.91) between the public relations budget size and sales income. Figure 9.3 demonstrates an even greater correlation (0.913) between the number of telephones in service and the size of the public relations budget. By relating public relations budgets to these standard measurements in the industry, Tirone was able to show a "return" on public relations expenditures.

Figures 9.4 and 9.5 extend this analysis by comparing increases in public relations budgets with increases in revenues over a five-year period. Figure 9.4 shows that the percentage growth in public relations expenditures did not exceed

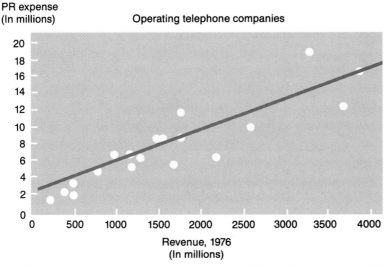

PR expense
(In millions)

Operating telephone companies

Revenue, 1976
(In millions)

Figure 9.2 Revenue and public relations expense, 1976

Telephone company revenues compared with public relations expenses, 1976

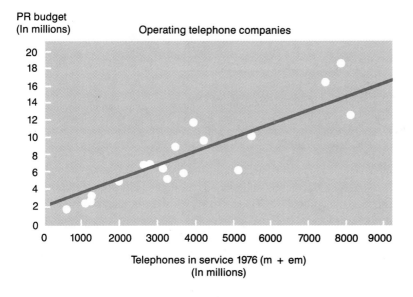

PR budget
(In millions)

Operating telephone companies

Telephones in service 1976 (m + em)
(In millions)

Figure 9.3 Telephones in service and public relations expense, 1976

the percentage growth in revenues. Taking this comparison still further, Tirone demonstrated that when compared to the increase in the consumer price index (one way to measure inflation), the general public relations budgets fell significantly behind, while the advertising budget stayed even (see figure 9.5).

Evaluating Employee Publications   The success of employee publications in the Bell System was measured against corporate objectives for those publications: to "reach all employees, create awareness, establish a reputation for reliability, be

Figure 9.4 Increases in
revenue and public relations
budgets

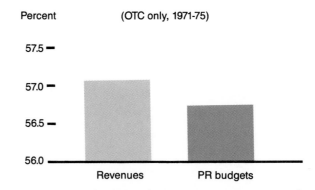

A comparison of the growth of Bell Telephone Company revenues with the growth of
public relations budgets from 1971 to 1975

Figure 9.5 Percent
increases in operating
telephone company public
relations accounts and
Consumer Price Index,
1971–1975

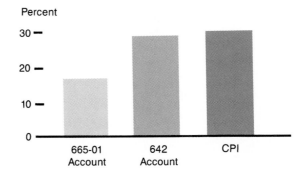

Comparison of the increase in total Bell Telephone Company public relations (665-01)
and advertising (642) expenses with growth of the Consumer Price Index

written so the material can be understood, and be readable at an educational level appropriate to the audience."[8] These objectives were translated into the following measurement criteria: "how effectively the publication was distributed within forty-eight hours, an average estimate of reader awareness of stories, a reliability index, understanding, and readability (as measured on the Gunning scale)." Table 9.3 reports the ability of a sample of employees to recall (without any help) certain stories that appeared in the company's weekly newspaper. Table 9.4 reports measures of all the components of publication efficiency as operationally defined.

Distribution   Percentage of issues delivered in a 48-hour period.

Awareness   Average of recall data.

Reliability   Average response to three questions about the newspaper. Is it: very understandable, excellent at presenting both sides, and an excellent source of information?

Understanding   Percentage of those recalling and comprehending the corporate planning seminar story.

TABLE 9.3   Top Recall by Employees of Company Newspaper Articles (Three Issues of the Publication)

Subject Matter	Unaided Recall
Employment office hiring (1)	56%
Defending the company (3)	42%
Pioneer circus (1)	40%
Marketing/competition (3)	36%
Corporate planning seminar (3-week average)	6%
Averaged recall	36%

Source: James F. Tirone, "Measuring the Bell System's Public Relations," *Public Relations Review* 3 (Winter 1977): 29. Reprinted by permission.

TABLE 9.4   Employee Publication Scoring

Component	Score
Distribution	67%
Awareness	36%
Reliability (average)	34%
Very understandable	61%
Both sides/Excellent	12%
Source/Excellent	30%
Understanding (CPS only)	40%
Readability (CPS only)	16.5 (Years)

Source: James F. Tirone, "Measuring the Bell System's Public Relations," *Public Relations Review* 3 (Winter 1977): 30. Reprinted by permission.

Readability   The Gunning score for the corporate planning seminar story, which is roughly equal to the number of years of education required for comprehension.

Evaluating Media Relations   Measuring the effectiveness of an organization's relationships with media representatives is a difficult task. Tirone reports three aspects of these relationships that can be measured to some degree: "the media's views of those relationships, the consequences which follow from news release output, and the activity of our (Bell System) media representative."[9] As a first step toward accomplishing these measurement objectives, Tirone proposed a nationwide survey of news media representatives to estimate their ratings of the quality and quantity of Bell System releases. He also initiated an analysis of the media to determine what was actually being said about Bell.

To launch the second phase of the process, Bell hired PR Data Systems, Inc., to code and computerize information collected from clippings and electronic media reports. Figure 9.6 summarizes the percentages of favorable, unfavorable, and neutral news articles about Bell companies in the media surveyed. Figure 9.7 sorts the news items into 10 categories relevant to Bell operations and provides favorable, unfavorable, and neutral data for each category. Figure 9.8 reports the

Figure 9.6 Total news
stories by tendency

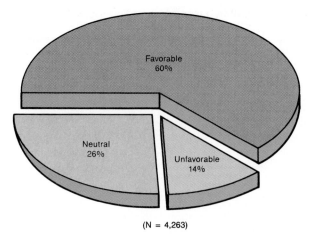

(N = 4,263)

Central tendency of all news items during one-month period

Figure 9.7 Stories by
tendency

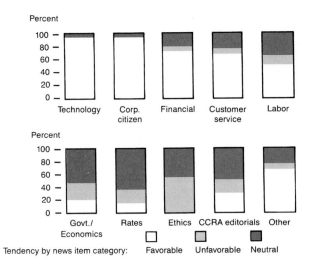

Figure 9.8 Rebuttal ratio

Relationship of
unfavorable
news items with
opportunities
for rebuttal

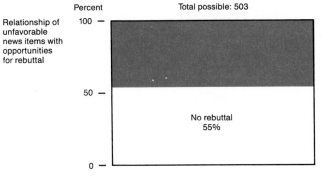

TABLE 9.5 Newspaper Stories by Region (Total: 3,848)

	Favorable	Unfavorable	Neutral	Totals
Northeast	14%	5%	5%	24%
South	18%	5%	8%	31%
North Central	18%	3%	10%	31%
West	9%	2%	3%	14%
	59%	15%	26%	100%

Source: James F. Tirone, "Measuring the Bell System's Public Relations," *Public Relations Review* 3 (Winter 1977): 34. Reprinted by permission.

TABLE 9.6 Treatment by Media Services

	Favorable	Unfavorable	Neutral	Totals
AP	61%	18%	21%	100%
UPI	19%	33%	48%	100%
Syndicates	43%	22%	35%	100%

Source: James F. Tirone, "Measuring the Bell System's Public Relations," *Public Relations Review* 3 (Winter 1977): 34. Reprinted by permission.

number of rebuttals by Bell representatives that were incorporated into the 503 unfavorable stories included in the sample. Tirone explains that Bell news people are expected to maintain the kind of relationships with news media that will encourage a reporter or editor to call for a company reaction before printing an unfavorable story. Figure 9.8 shows that 45 percent of the unfavorable stories included rebuttal statements from Bell representatives. Over a long period, this type of data could help measure both access to Bell spokespersons and the quality of their relationships with media representatives. Tables 9.5 and 9.6 report the percentages of favorable, unfavorable, and neutral stories according to region of the country and media service, respectively. From these data, certain discrepancies can be discovered that are useful in pinpointing problem areas and in planning future efforts.

Summary

Frequently, evaluation is assumed to be the final step in the public relations process; however, it is really best described as a new beginning. Measuring the effectiveness of a public relations effort frequently provides new direction and emphasis for an ongoing program. Even when the project being evaluated does not continue, the lessons learned concerning its effectiveness will be useful in numerous future activities. Knowledge gained through careful evaluation is an important payoff to any public relations effort. Evaluation of projects that are obvious failures can help prevent future mistakes. Careful measurement of successful efforts will help reproduce positive elements in future programs.

Public relations can no longer afford to ignore the question, "But what's it all worth to us?" Practitioners must be ready to respond with appropriate methods, solid data, and accurate predictions.

Case Study

American Red Cross
Centennial Celebration

By Artemio R. Guillermo
*Assistant Professor of
Speech
University of Northern Iowa
Cedar Falls, Iowa*

Anniversary celebrations can be major public relations events in the life of an organization. Celebrations are especially significant when they mark centennial observances that not only generate mass media coverage but also produce activities highlighting the image of the institution.

Although the planning of most celebrations follows the four-step process of public relations, evaluation is often neglected during the enthusiasm of planning. After activities and programs have been executed, how can planners know whether the celebration was a success? How can they know to what extent their celebration affected their target audience's attitudes toward the organization? What information can the planners get that could be used to evaluate the results of the celebration?

These questions were posed to a public relations student team that undertook to help the Hawkeye Chapter of the American Red Cross celebrate its centennial. When the team volunteered its assistance, the program and activities had already been planned. The overall objective was to project the humanitarian service of the American Red Cross and encourage volunteer participation.

The plan called for a week-long celebration. There were 20 events and activities, including a hot air balloon, a mock disaster, a historical display, a speakers' bureau, an open house, an annual meeting and banquet, a centennial blood donor day, a birthday party, and the like.

Printed communications, including a 16-page historical booklet and a 6-page newsletter, were sent to local institutions and community leaders. The local papers gave the celebration full-page pictorial coverage with the headline "Happy Birthday." Billboards, media releases, and public service announcements on radio and television were also used to publicize the event.

Although the Red Cross centennial committee planned an evaluation, they did not quite know how to proceed. When the students became involved, they decided that their first task was to develop an evaluation instrument.

After consulting with several professors, they devised a form on which to note the following terms:

Project name:
Description:
   Time—
   Place—
Has project been done before? If so, describe:
Intended publics:
   Primary—
   Secondary—
Goals and objectives:
   Strategies—

Cost:

Possible public relations problems:

Method of evaluation:

Results:

Conclusion:

When the centennial celebration started, the public relations team monitored the activities. Out of 20 projects/activities, 12 were evaluated.

When all the evaluations were compiled, the students had some interesting findings. One of the hottest items in the celebration as a crowd-drawer was the hot air balloon. An evaluator stated, "Such an event draws attention (biggest advantage); location was good."

On the other hand, a leaflet enclosed with monthly bank statements, describing the centennial activities, received a low evaluation. An evaluator's comment on the possible public relations effect was: "Confusion by general public as to purpose of stuffer." And the conclusion was that it had low visible response from customers.

All of these evaluations were placed on file with the Hawkeye Chapter of the American Red Cross for future reference as a record of its 100th anniversary celebration.

Questions

1. What is the value of an evaluation of this kind of program?

2. How would you improve the evaluation instrument used in this project?

3. What other forms of evaluation described in this chapter might be appropriate in this situation?

Notes

1. John Pavlik, John Vastyan, and Maj. Michael F. Maher, "Using Readership Research to Study Employee Views," *Public Relations Review* (Summer 1990): 50–60.

2. Rudolph Flesch, *How to Test Readability* (New York: Harper and Row, 1951).

3. Robert Gunning, *The Technique of Clear Writing,* rev. ed. (New York: McGraw-Hill, 1968).

4. Edgar Dale and Jeanne Chall, "A Formula for Predicting Readability," *Educational Research Bulletin* 27 (January/February 1948).

5. Wilson Taylor, "Cloze Procedure: A New Tool for Measuring Readability," *Journalism Quarterly* 3 (Fall 1953): 415–33; "Recent Developments in the Use of 'Cloze Procedure'" *Journalism Quarterly* 33 (Winter 1956).

6. Mark P. McElreath, "Public Relations Evaluative Research: Summary Statement," *Public Relations Review* 3 (Winter 1977): 133.

7. James F. Tirone, "Measuring the Bell System's Public Relations," *Public Relations Review* 3 (Winter 1977): 21–38.

8. Ibid., 31.

9. Ibid., 31.

PART III

Public Relations

The Publics

A public is a group of people with certain common characteristics. A public can be very large—college students, Republicans, blue-collar workers, even the entire population of the United States. A public can also be quite small—the city council, the budget committee, newspaper editors, or even a single person. Different organizations have different publics. Big businesses have publics different from those of small businesses. The publics for the steel industry are different from those for the computer industry or agriculture. Not-for-profit organizations have publics different from those of profit-seeking organizations. Different levels of government organizations deal with different publics.

Part III describes six general types of publics that most public relations professionals face on a regular basis. Chapter 10 discusses the media, one of the most basic publics that practitioners deal with. Chapter 11 focuses on the organization's relationship with its employees, and chapter 12 delves into the complex relationships between an organization and its community. Chapter 13 covers the importance of consumers to modern organizations, and chapters 14 and 15 discuss the impact of financial markets and government agencies on public relations practice.

CHAPTER 10

Media Relations

Preview

The media are businesses that gather, package, and sell information. Journalists have mixed feelings toward public relations practitioners—suspecting them of manipulation while depending on them for information. Public relations practitioners view journalists as an audience, as a medium through which to reach the broader public, and as gatekeepers representing and responding to the public's need to know.

When public relations practitioners build relationships of confidence and trust with journalists, much mutually beneficial interaction can result. Three direct ways of intentionally reaching the media include news releases, discussions with journalists (particularly interviews), and news conferences.

The press will go after anything, and that is the way it should be.

—Ben Wattenberg, coeditor, *Public Opinion*

W hen many people consider the function of public relations, their first thought is "Those are the folks who deal with the media." And although public relations does far more than deal with the media, that certainly is an important aspect of the job. Media coverage can have significant positive or negative impact on every aspect of an organization's operations. Public confidence and public support are often determined by the treatment an issue or organization receives in the media.

Gene Grabowski, director of media relations for the American Council of Life Insurance, says, "You cannot wage a successful campaign without media relations. . . . It is the one essential element in any serious public relations program."[1]

If a public relations practitioner is to work effectively with the media, he or she must understand how the media function and how reporters work. Insights into journalists' views of public relations and into the working relationship of journalists and public relations practitioners are also essential. Public relations practitioners must be prepared (and must prepare others) to deal with the media face-to-face. Finally, practitioners must be proficient in the art and craft of publicity and knowledgeable about the tools used to gain media attention.

Understanding the Media

The mass media are a pervasive part of modern society. There are 1,548 daily and 7,600 weekly newspapers currently operating in the United States. Over 5,000 U.S. magazines are published for a large variety of well-defined audiences. More than 11,700 radio stations provide entertainment and information to people on the go. The 1,520 television stations in the United States are watched in more than 84 million households an average of more than seven hours every day. More than half of these television households subscribe to cable systems that further expand the available programming.[2]

The mass media put us in touch with the world beyond our immediate experience. They shape significantly our perceptions and beliefs—particularly in relation to events and topics with which we have little direct contact. While providing greatly simplified and edited versions of the happenings in our complex and dynamic world, they give us a feeling of participation and understanding. Most newspapers, magazines, and broadcasting stations are businesses. The publishing and broadcasting industry is about the same size as the automotive industry in terms of market value. Only the beverage and tobacco industries show more profit in terms of return on equity. In short, the media are big, highly profitable businesses.

As businesses, the media sell information and entertainment. They gather and package them in ways that stimulate audiences to spend money or time to read, listen, or watch. Perhaps more important, the media sell access to their audiences to advertisers.

Journalists who gather and organize information for the media tend to take their responsibilities to society very seriously. They view themselves as having a sacred public mission: to serve as the public's eyes and ears, to be watchdogs on public institutions doing the public's business. They see their job as seeking the truth, putting it in perspective, and publishing it so that people can conduct their affairs knowledgeably.

That the media's goals of providing truth and making a profit sometimes conflict is an issue that will not be pursued here. Anyone who deals with the media, though, especially public relations practitioners, must recognize that both goals are constantly sought.

Journalists' devotion to their goals causes their view of facts to be quite different from those of their sources. The journalist considers news a highly perishable commodity, while the source of the news is more concerned about the lasting impression a story will make. To the journalist, a story is a transient element in the ongoing flow of information; to the source, it is a discrete event. The journalist is usually uninterested in the positive or negative flavor of the story, as long as it presents the facts fairly; the source always wants to be cast in a favorable light.

Yet, for all the concerns organizations manifest about how their stories are covered, the media's power does not lie in their ability to slant material one way or another but rather in what words, deeds, events, or issues they choose to define as news. It is this concept, or theory, of *agenda setting* that you examined in chapter 3. Douglas Cater, special assistant to President Lyndon Johnson and author of *The Fourth Branch of Government,* put it this way:

> The essential power of the press is its capacity to choose what is news. Each day in Washington tens of thousands of words are uttered which are considered important by those who utter them. Tens of dozens of events occur which are considered newsworthy by those who have staged them. The press has the power to select—to decide which events go on page one or hit the prime-time TV news and which events get ignored.[3]

The Reporter's Job

The journalist's job has been greatly glamorized since reporters Bob Woodward and Carl Bernstein unraveled the political scandals of Watergate in the early 1970s. The handsome men and women of local and network television news are accessible and admirable role models. On a day-to-day basis, however, the job can

Journalists often work in a stressful environment such as these reporters covering a Senate Republican budget meeting.

be highly demanding, very stressful, and quite unglamorous. Working in a bullpen atmosphere, without so much as a secretary or office of their own, reporters need all the help they can get.

Journalists collectively maintain that they have the responsibility not only to provide information to the public but also to provide feedback from society at large to the administrators of public institutions. As society becomes more complex and institutions have greater impact on private lives, journalists hold that more reporting and investigating are necessary to determine the extent to which these institutions measure up to their social and moral obligations. This process, they argue, will ultimately have a positive effect on society as a whole.

Reporters, in general, have an overwhelming desire to get facts. Joseph Poindexter points out, "To a reporter, a fact has an inherent worth, in and of itself. To a businessman, a fact is an asset to be invested."[4] Reporters resent anything and anyone they perceive as standing between them and the facts. Anyone who seeks to keep a secret is regarded with deep suspicion. Organizations in business, government, and other fields that conduct themselves in ways considered less than open invite journalistic scrutiny.

Journalists sometimes have difficulty getting the information they need. They claim that highly placed news sources are generally overly insulated, secretive, and sensitive, recognizing neither the public's right to know nor the value of the media's role in exposing questionable practices. Reporters feel that those who complain about media coverage often engage in the ancient practice of seeking to slay the bearers of bad tidings. Besides, say journalists, we don't criticize—we just report what others say.

Still, working journalists echo some of the complaints registered against them by the institutions they cover. Reporters recognize that they frequently have insufficient education and experience to cover complex issues and institutions adequately. They are frustrated by the lack of time, space, and staff needed to do their jobs thoroughly.

In the pursuit of facts, etiquette, civility, and even legality are sometimes forgone. Public relations practitioners and others who deal with journalists must remember that when reporters ask "nasty" questions, it is not necessarily because they are antagonistic or ignorant; they are just doing what good reporters are supposed to do.

The Relationship Between Journalists and PR Practitioners

The Reporter's View of the Public Relations Practitioner

Journalists often view public relations practitioners as people who make their living by using the media to their own advantage. Sometimes considering them parasites and referring to them as **flacks** or worse, editors often alert young reporters against public relations wiles. As one guidebook for newspaper editors warns, "Your job is to serve the readers, not the man who would raid your columns."[5]

However, in recent years the relationship has improved as many broadcast and print newsrooms have cut staffs. This trend has resulted in a greater dependence on public relations professionals for sources as well as for material. Another reason has been the increased number of practitioners who have graduated from university programs in public relations and who are prepared better than their predecessors to relate to the media both technically and ethically. Twenty years ago it was rare for a news organization to hire a person who had studied public relations; now the opposite is true. In spite of these developments, there is still an adversarial relationship between some journalists and some public relations practitioners. In certain situations that should and always will be the case.

The Public Relations Practitioner's View of the Journalist

From the public relations practitioner's perspective, the journalist is at once an audience, a medium through which to reach the larger public, and a gatekeeper representing and responding to the public's need to know. Because of this dependence, practitioners' selection and presentation of information often conforms more to journalistic standards than to the desires of their superiors in their own organizations. In a sense, both the journalist and the practitioner, in their mutual dealings, are caught between the demands of the organizations they represent and the demands of the opposite party. Public relations practitioners, as boundary spanners, are often caught in the middle between journalistic and other institutions, trying to explain each to the other.

Mutual Dependence

The relationship between public relations practitioners and journalists is one of mutual dependence. Although journalists like to picture themselves as reluctant to use public relations information, economic considerations force them to do otherwise. A news staff capable of ferreting information from every significant organization in a city without the assistance of representatives for those organizations would be prohibitively expensive. Public relations' contribution to total news coverage has been estimated in excess of 50 percent. Moreover, the public relations practitioner makes the journalist's job much easier, saving time and effort and providing information that might otherwise be unavailable.

To a considerable extent, the purposes of the news outlet and of the public relations practitioner overlap. Both wish to inform the public of things that affect them. This commonality provides the basis of a cooperative system for disseminating information. In this sense, public relations practitioners function as extensions of the news staff. They play a specific, functional, cooperative role in society's information-gathering network, even though they owe no loyalty to specific news outlets, are not paid by them, and may never set foot in the buildings in which the news is produced.

Communications between certain public relations practitioners and journalists are massive. Some public relations offices send out news releases daily. Additionally, personal contact and communication may be initiated by either party. The amount of communication between journalists and public relations practitioners is a measure of their interdependence. In some instances, public relations practitioners provide more useful information to specific media than do the journalists those media employ.

Through the efforts of public relations practitioners, the media receive a constant flow of free information. Facts that journalists might not have acquired otherwise become available in packaged form. The reporter or editor, as we have noted, can then decide what is newsworthy. As the editor of an Ohio daily newspaper remarked with relish, "I'm the guy who says 'yes' or 'no'; the public relations man has to say 'please'."

That editor's assessment of journalists' power is strictly accurate only when public relations practitioners and journalists share no dependence. When interdependence exists, journalists retain nominal veto power over incoming information, but they abdicate much of their decision-making responsibility to public relations practitioners who select and control the material disseminated. While journalists may reject one or another news release, they depend on the constant flow of information from representatives of important institutions. To a large extent, journalists are processors of information passed on by public relations practitioners who do the primary gathering.

Under these circumstances, journalists' main means of control becomes their ability to refuse to deal with public relations practitioners who fail to meet subjective standards. Even such rejection is impossible, though, when the public relations practitioner is firmly entrenched in the institution. As much as Washington journalists would have liked to avoid using material from Ron Ziegler, press secretary in the final days of the Nixon presidency, they did not have that option.

Building Positive Relationships

While much may be said about the art and craft of preparing materials for media consumption, perhaps nothing is so important to successful publicity as the relationships established between public relations practitioners and journalists. A reporter for the Austin, Texas, *American Statesman* was discussing his work. "I *never* accept information from PR flacks," he said. When it was pointed out to him that during the past week he had used material from corporate, university, and political publicity people, he replied: "Those aren't PR flacks, those are reliable sources."

When public relations practitioners take the time and make the effort to establish good personal relations with journalists, they are much more likely to attract positive news coverage for their organizations. Good public relations begins with good personal relations.

Tips for Getting Along with Journalists As in all walks of life, it is good for public relations practitioners to get to know the people they work with. Sometimes the direct approach is effective. Call a journalist with whom you know you will be working. Introduce yourself. Suggest lunch or a drink. Another approach is to hand deliver a news release to provide an opportunity for a brief introduction and meeting. Some journalists appreciate the effort. Says one: "I like to meet new PR types just to see who they are. I like to tell them what I want and don't want."

Other journalists, however, would rather not be bothered. With them, an indirect approach is required. Belonging to the local press club, attending meetings of the Society for Professional Journalists, or becoming involved in community activities in which journalists also participate are ways of getting to know media counterparts. Indeed, journalists are often hired for publicity jobs not only for their writing skills but also for their networks of media contacts. Cliff Webb, a TV reporter, says that one of the key things a public relations person can do to better his or her media relations is "to establish a good rapport with reporters."[6] He continues giving this advice: "Try to get to know the assignment editors. Encourage those people to come to your workplace. Good human interest stories can be developed from these types of visits."[7]

These media contacts have their own sets of constraints, of which you need to be aware as you deal with them on a continuing basis. G. A. Marken, writing in *Public Relations Quarterly,* stresses the following editorial constraints:

Time—It is in short supply for you and theirs is just as critical because they face daily, weekly or monthly deadlines that *must* be met.

Editorial integrity—These people are professional, so present your information in a professional manner and let them do their job.

Audience service—Their job is to serve the publication's audience based on their editorial guidelines rather than your wishes.

Editorial objectivity—They may like you and love a certain product or service but as much as possible they try to be objective in the articles they write.[8]

Once relationships are established, protect and cherish them. Do not squander valuable relationships by using them for small favors or one-shot story placements. Do not ruin a relationship by expecting a reporter always to do what you want. Take no for an answer. Do not insult your relationship with inappropriate gifts—journalists are sensitive even to the appearance of conflicts of interest.

Cultivate your relationships with journalistic colleagues by giving good service. Provide sufficient and timely information, stories, and pictures, when and how they are wanted. Be on call 24 hours a day to respond to reporters' needs and questions.

Nothing will destroy a relationship faster or more completely than an affront to the truth. Accuracy, integrity, openness, and completeness are the basis for trust bestowed by journalists. Once trust is broken, it can rarely be regained.

Finally, to ensure good relations with journalists, the practitioner should behave in a professional way. Live up to expectations. Don't play favorites among the media. Return phone calls promptly and with respect to deadlines. Don't beg for favors, special coverage, or removal of unfavorable publicity.

Lucy Caldwell, in an article in *Government Communications,* suggests:

Once they (the media) trust that I actually return calls . . . the media will wait for me to confirm the information they have received from "sources" or scanners prior to releasing it themselves. It seems a simple enough task, but building these relationships requires time, patience and the right attitude.[9]

Working with the Media

With a basic understanding of the complex relationships between public relations practitioners and journalists, we can outline a few general principles for working with the media. In the first place, managers must reconcile themselves to the legitimacy of the media's role in monitoring the performance of their organizations and leaders. Managers and institutions must understand and accommodate the unique position of the media, realizing that, on one level, an adversarial relationship is normal.

The best advice for dealing with the media is to give journalists what they need in the form and language they want. Respond quickly and honestly to media requests for information. By working to establish a relationship of mutual trust with particular journalists, you can defuse many potentially antagonistic encounters.

Consider the following situations:

> You are the chief public relations official for a major company. A reporter calls your office at 9 A.M. She wants to see you for an interview at 11 A.M. She wants your company to respond to allegations made by a source that she is not at liberty to disclose. All she will say is that the charges deal with corporate finances and questionable conduct of certain corporate officials.

> As the public relations director of a major private university, you decide to hold a press conference to announce the initiation of an important fund-raising effort. A prominent alumnus has donated $5 million to kick off the campaign. You know that recent media coverage has criticized the university's budgetary problems, tuition hikes, and incursions into neighborhoods around the school that displaced poor people and eroded the community tax base.

> You are the community relations director of the local police force. A reporter calls to request a meeting with your chief about low police morale resulting from the city's inability to meet rank-and-file demands for pay raises. When you attempt to arrange an interview for the following afternoon, the chief berates you, saying, "It's your job to keep the press off my back. Why can't you handle the guy's questions?" You convince the chief that the reporter would not talk to you because he said he was tired of the chief hiding behind his "flack." You tell him departmental integrity and morale depend on his willingness to deal with the press. You promise to help him prepare. He reluctantly agrees to the interview.

In each of these cases, a meeting with the media represents a critical challenge to the organization. Some organizations see such challenges as problems to be overcome. It is more constructive, however, to view them as opportunities. Publicity cannot replace good works or effective action, but it can gain attention for issues, ideas, or products. It can spotlight an organization's personality, policies, or performance. It can make something or someone known.

Every media contact is an opportunity to get feedback, to tell your story, to create a positive response to your organization. Of course there are dangers—but what opportunity presents itself without risk? And what opportunity can be taken without preparation?

Preparation to meet the media is essential for both individuals and organizations. Preparation means more than getting psyched up about a particular interview because when the opportunity comes, there may be little time to prepare, as the preceding cases suggest. In the first example, a company official would have only two hours to gather information and prepare strategy to deal effectively with some very sensitive issues.

Before anyone in the organization meets with the media, the first step is to develop the proper set of attitudes. Meeting the media is an opportunity, not a problem; therefore, defensiveness is not appropriate. There is no need to feel intimidated—particularly if your objective is worthy. In the case of the university's fund-raising campaign, the purpose of the press conference must be kept firmly in mind. The public relations director should refuse, in a friendly way, to be dragged by reporters' questions into subjects other than the donation and the campaign.

The attitude of the interviewee toward the journalist should be one of hospitality, cooperation, and openness. At the same time, the interviewee should realize that the reporter need not be the person in control. The interviewee should decide what needs to be said and say it—no matter what the reporter's questions may be. In other words, have your own **agenda** with the points you want to make, no matter what the journalist may want. A positive mental attitude is essential. Once this attitude is established among everyone in an organization who may be called on to be interviewed, it becomes much easier and less traumatic to prepare for specific interviews. After the chief of police completes one interview successfully, the next will be more easily handled.

Before looking further at how individuals can interact successfully with the media, we will discuss how organizations can publicize themselves effectively.

Research and Planning in Media Relations

The old saying "Success is when opportunity meets preparation" is never truer than when applied to publicity. As we showed in earlier chapters, preparation indicates research and planning.

In media relations, research means knowing who you are dealing with and what they are interested in. Media relations specialists deal primarily with their own management and with the media, so they must understand both parties well. The managements of various organizations differ in their attitudes toward media relations. The oil company Amerada Hess does not return calls from the press. Procter & Gamble encourages coverage of its products but not its manufacturing processes. Bank of America during recent financial problems, Johnson & Johnson during the Tylenol panic, and AT&T during deregulation all benefited from their candor and openness in difficult times.[10] In each case, media relations strategy was based on an understanding of management's desired approach. Adolph Coors Company provides another example in mini-case 10.1.

After understanding the organization, the publicist must study the specific media with which he or she will work. This means finding out the interests and needs of the people affiliated with the various media outlets. Media guides can provide some of this information. Effective media relations specialists also maintain their own file systems, Rolodexes, computer programs, and charts to keep track of the personal qualities and preferences of the media people with whom they interact.

Planning for publicity follows the processes discussed in chapter 7. Publicity plans can deal with an organization's overall efforts or with a specific situation or campaign. In general, media plans will describe the circumstances facing the organization, lay out goals or objectives, identify key audiences, specify strategies, list action steps, identify special media to be contacted, and provide for evaluation.

Mini-Case 10.1

Silence Is No Longer Golden at Coors

"A quality product will speak for itself." That low-profile philosophy guided the communication efforts of Golden, Colorado, brewer Adolph Coors's company until the late 1970s. That philosophy was partially the result of the tragic kidnapping and death of Adolph Coors III in 1960. Before 1976, the company had a three-person public relations staff charged with the responsibility of saying, "No comment."

However, things changed. A variety of external and internal pressures—including an emotional 1977 strike charging Coors had discriminated against African Americans, Hispanics, and females—made Coors more conscious of using communication to accomplish company objectives. Also, Coors went from an entirely family-owned business to a public corporation. The media relations, corporate communications, and other public relations functions at Coors increased staff size considerably. Coors representatives made hundreds of media visits to introduce themselves and explain that "silence is no longer golden at Coors," according to Shirley Richard, former director of corporate communications. In April 1982, the communication staff was put to the ultimate test. The television program *60 Minutes* called. Investigative journalist Mike Wallace would do a feature on Coors and its labor problems.

Complete openness was the operating philosophy of Coors' corporate communications department.

Not long ago, when you called Coors with a question, you could only cross your fingers and hope for an answer.

You see, mum was the word in Golden, Colorado.

It wasn't that we had some deep, dark secret. Or that we broke out in hives when faced with a microphone or a reporter's pad.

Quite the opposite.

We're proud of the way we do things here. And to put it simply, we thought that was all that mattered.

So we kept our silence.

Then we looked at the other side of the coin. And saw that others were genuinely interested in what we were doing. And how we were doing it.

We saw that talking about our programs on the environment, energy, and minority hiring wouldn't be self-serving. It would be serving everybody.

So now when you call us with a question, make sure you have a pencil handy. We've taken "no comment" out of our vocabulary.

And that's good news for both of us.

Coors
Corporate Communications Dept

LET'S TALK (800) 525-3786
In Colorado (800) 332-3725

Adolph Coors Company, Golden, Colorado 80401

The corporate communication department went to work. A written plan with clear objectives was developed. Complete openness was the operating philosophy. Bill and Joe Coors were sent to New York for public relations training by an executive training staff that specialized in teaching executives how to deal on camera with the tough investigative TV reporters. The CBS-TV team was invited to the brewery and given access to all workers. The communication staff responded immediately to any request for information.

"We couldn't have told the story any better ourselves," Richard explained after the feature was broadcast. "We accomplished all the objectives we set." The investigative report delighted the people of Golden, generated pro-Coors editorials, and eased labor tensions. Public relations practitioners point to this case as a classic example of how to prepare to deal with the electronic media. It was the first time an American corporation had come away from a Mike Wallace interview looking good.

Richard reviewed the lessons learned in the Coors experience with *60 Minutes:*

Be open and honest and never refuse to respond to a reporter's request for information.

Set clear message objectives so you can tell your company's best stories.

Educate your company executives on how to work with the news media and familiarize them with your media objectives.

Be prepared.

Sources: Shirley Richard, "Coors Cans the 'No Comment' Media Response," *Communication World* (September 1983): 18; personal interviews with Coors communication staff 1993–95.

Publicity

Publicity is a broad term that refers to the publication of news about an organization or person for which time or space was not purchased. The appeal of publicity is credibility. Because publicity appears in the news media in the form of stories rather than advertisements, it receives what amounts to third-party endorsement from the editor. Since the editor has judged the publicity material newsworthy, the public is not likely to perceive it as advertising. Publicity may, therefore, reach members of an organization's publics who would be suspicious of advertising.

Publicity can be divided into two categories: **spontaneous** and **planned.** A major accident, fire, explosion, strike, or any other unplanned event creates *spontaneous publicity.* When such an event occurs, news media will be eager to find out the causes, circumstances, and people involved. While spontaneous publicity is not necessarily negative, it should be handled through standing plans such as those for emergencies discussed in chapter 7.

Planned publicity, by contrast, does not originate from an emergency situation. It is the result of a conscious effort to attract attention to an issue, event, or organization. Time is available to plan the event and the way it will be communicated to the news media. If a layoff, plant expansion, change in top personnel, new product, or some other potentially newsworthy event is contemplated, the method of announcing it is a major concern. How an event is perceived by an organization's publics can determine whether publicity is "good" or "bad."

The method by which an event is communicated can determine its impact. Three direct vehicles for intentionally reaching the print media are a release, a discussion (conversation, phone call, meeting, or interview), or a news conference. The broadcast media can be reached through Video News Releases, satellite interviews, or satellite media tours. Nonprofit organizations can also reach the electronic media with public service announcements (PSAs).

How to Reach the Media

The publicity, news, or press release is the heart of any publicity effort. It is the simplest and least expensive way to reach the media. Releases can be duplicated and sent to dozens, even thousands, of news outlets. They should be used to convey routine news, to provide potential feature or background material, or to provide follow-up information.

Preparing Publicity Releases

Publicity releases take many forms, depending on the audience and the medium for which they are intended. Still, some general rules apply in most instances. A publicity release should always conform to accepted journalistic style. The opening paragraph (lead) should generally be planned as a complete account that can stand by itself. If the lead answers the five basic questions (who, what, when, why, and where), an editor with very limited space or time can still use the story. The following are tips for writing a news release:

1. Answer the basic questions of a news story (the five "W's" and "H"— who, what, when, where, when, why, and how) early in the news release.

2. Use the inverted pyramid form, emphasizing the most important or interesting facts first in the story.

3. Often use a summary lead though you may need to vary this practice by selecting the most important element for the lead and letting the other facts follow. Keep the lead to 25 words or less. Featurize releases that lend themselves to human interest and are not timely news stories.

4. Avoid the "time" (when) lead because it is not a strong lead; emphasize the more important elements.

5. Be accurate. Spell all names correctly; get the facts straight and the quotes correct.

6. Be specific, not general. Use examples; show your point.

7. Do not editorialize or advocate a viewpoint.

8. Vary paragraph lengths. The rule of thumb is that a paragraph may be as short as one sentence but should not be more than six typed lines. Sentences should also be varied in length but should average no more than 20 words.

Some stories can lose their impact if too many facts are forced into the lead. In such a case, the writer should select one or two major facts that will attract the reader's (and editor's) interest. If the release concerns someone who is not prominent, the writer may choose not to mention the person's name in the opening; this technique is known as a *blind lead*. Chapter 8 covers more specifics about writing news stories. Once the essential facts have been organized into an opening paragraph, details and elaboration should follow in descending order of importance to allow editors to cut the story to fit the space or time available. Attention to the following general guidelines will result in more effective publicity releases.

Format

1. Use standard format with 8½- by 11-inch plain white paper typed double-spaced on only one side.

2. Identify the organization with name, address, and telephone number. The public relations contact person's name and telephone number should also appear in the top portion of the release.

3. Give a release time. Most releases should be noted "For Immediate Release." If there is a compelling reason to specify a time and date, write, "For release at noon, September 21." Be sure to include the date on which the release is prepared, either in the top portion of the release or in a dateline.

4. Put a summary title or headline above the story (optional). Some editors prefer titles; some don't. You include it to let the editor see at a glance what the story is about, not to suggest a headline to the editor.

5. Start your story approximately one-third down the first page.

6. Begin with the dateline. Today wire service datelines include only the name of the city and in the state where the story originated; however, you may include the date if you prefer. The state is needed if the city of origin is under one million in population. A larger city, such as Chicago, does not need the state name appended.

7. Complete a sentence before going to the next page. Put "more" at the bottom of each continued page. Place page numbers on succeeding pages, along with a two- or three-word "slug" identifying the story. This usually goes in the upper left corner of the page. At the end of the story type "-30-." Or, you may use "###" or "END" to indicate the conclusion.

8. Include, when appropriate, quality black-and-white photographs with your release. Each photo should have a caption attached to the bottom border. The back of the photo should be marked with felt pen giving the name, address, and phone of the contact person. When writing on the back of a photo, be careful not to ruin it with a pen that will create a mark on the reverse side.

Content

1. Keep releases direct and factual. Supplemental information can be provided on a separate fact sheet included with the release. Focus on one subject in each release.

2. The information included should be appropriate to the medium to which it is sent. Do not bother editors with material you know they cannot use.

3. Write clearly, concisely, and with correct grammar. Releases rarely should exceed two pages.

4. Use inverted pyramid form, with the most important information in the early part of the story.

5. Avoid clichés, jargon, technical terminology, and foreign phrases.

6. Be accurate with everything—facts, names, addresses, quotes.

Figure 10.1 shows a sample release illustrating these guidelines.

Always check each publicity release carefully for accuracy. One practitioner suggests, "The reasons that bad, poorly written, non strategic, self-serving, too long releases go out is because people who call themselves professionals write, approve and authorize them."[11] Errors in fact or omission of important

Federal Express Corporation
Public Relations
2005 Corporate Avenue
First Floor
Memphis, TN 38132

U.S. Mail: PO Box 727
Memphis, TN 38194-1850

Telephone 901-395-3460

Figure 10.1 Sample news release

Contact: Federal Express
Sonja Whitemon
(901)395-3484

FOR IMMEDIATE RELEASE

FEDEX LAUNCHES NEW 8 A.M. DELIVERY SERVICE
Full range of services meets any customer need

MEMPHIS, TN (July 31, 1995) -- Federal Express Corporation today announced plans to launch a new service that will provide delivery by 8 a.m. to major metropolitan markets in the United States.

The new service, called FedEx First Overnight^{SM}, offers delivery by 8 a.m. from any U.S. ZIP code to more than 90 major markets, nearly 80 more markets than anyone in the industry.

The service, which will be available September 5, comes with two money-back guarantees: FedEx offers a money-back guarantee if the package is not delivered by 8 a.m. or if the status of the package cannot be reported within 30 minutes of inquiry. Customers around the nation will be able to request a package pick-up by calling 1-800-Go-FedEx. First Overnight rates are competitive with others in the industry.

FedEx has traditionally offered the most flexible delivery options in the industry. The company has long offered an early 9 a.m. hold service at no additional charge for customers who wanted to receive their packages at many of the company's nearly 2,000 locations around the world. This new service provides an early option for those who prefer to have their packages delivered.

-more-

FedEx First Overnight -- 2/2

"FedEx First Overnight offers our customers a complete range of services which meet every need. This new 8 a.m. delivery option allows customers to fit their delivery schedule to their own needs, whether it is for same-day, overnight or two-day delivery," said T. Michael Glenn, senior vice president, Worldwide Marketing, Customer Service and Corporate Communication for FedEx.

"Our research tells us that our customers will be excited about the opportunity to use FedEx for their most urgent shipments. For example, we deliver many repair parts for machinery to manufacturers who are depending on them to keep their production processes operating. We are pleased that we can now offer FedEx First Overnight and FedEx SameDay services to meet these urgent demands," said Glenn.

In addition to manufacturing industries, FedEx expects the 8 a.m. delivery service to appeal to other industries that ship highly time-sensitive packages, including the manufacturing, banking and entertainment industries.

Federal Express is the world's largest express transportation company, providing fast and reliable services for nearly 2.4 million items in over 200 countries each working day. The company employs more than than 110,700 people and operates more than 500 aircraft, 35,000 vehicles and nearly 180,000 Powership® and FedEx Ship® automated systems in its integrated global network. Federal Express reported revenues of $9.4 billion for its fiscal year ended May 31, 1995, including $2.6 billion in revenues and more than $125 million in operating profit from international operations.

##

details can be embarrassing to both the public relations manager and the organization. Some common errors are described in the following excerpt:

> One of our volunteer reporters scooped up at random an armful of press kits at the recent National Boat Show in New York's Coliseum, scanned them with the professional eye of a seasoned public relations executive, then sent them along to us with some interesting—if discouraging—observations. After checking his comments against material in the kits and adding a few findings of our own to the list, we came to the conclusion that some product publicists in the marine field are careless, some are lazy, and some simply don't know how to put together a proper news release. For example:
>
> 1. Three-quarters of the releases were undated.
> 2. At least half either lacked any follow-up press contact information (gave only name and address of manufacturer) or the information was incomplete (no telephone number, or PR firm name but no individual to ask for).
> 3. Some picture captions were stapled to photographs, while others were so flimsily attached they came apart when handled.
> 4. One company's release was single-spaced flush left, contained quotes without attribution, and misspelled "Coliseum."
> 5. The lead in another company's nine-page release was exactly the same this year as last except that the date had been changed. The president's statement about the new product line also was precisely the same in both years; and the

balance of the nine pages closely followed the previous pattern—word for word in some short paragraphs.

6. In one almost unbelievable case, a PR firm handling the publicity for three marine equipment companies (two are competitors, incidentally) not only single-spaced all the releases but left practically no margins and then framed the stories with a heavy rule. Included in the kit were several unidentified photographs. Compounding the agony, every release had a return card attached so the editor could report when and how he planned to use the story.[12]

Timing   The planning process for any public relations campaign should take into account the best time to issue publicity releases for maximum impact. Many considerations affect the timing. Information should not be released too far in advance of an event because it may become lost on an editor's desk or, if published, may be forgotten before the event occurs. On the other hand, release too close to an event can be a problem if editors do not have enough notice to plan for the material. Time of day can be an important factor in the delivery of a release. It is always wise policy to check with editors about deadlines. These will differ depending on the medium. Some newspapers and broadcast media have days that are lighter than others, and these are good times to get a release used.

Releases should be cleared with appropriate people in your organization before they are sent to the media. Public relations spotlight 10.1 suggests some guidelines for clearing releases.

Public Relations Spotlight 10.1

Clearing Publicity Releases

News releases and other publicity material are designed to create positive perceptions of your organization or client in the minds of target publics. Even the most experienced practitioner, however, cannot foresee all the potential consequences of any message. Thus, it is important to plan a system of checks for any message before it is released from your office. The following are some suggestions:

1. *Preparation stage*

   Preliminary approval of your first draft should be secured from the person(s) involved or in charge.

   A later draft should be sent to the top officer of the organization who is responsible for public relations activities.

   After any further revisions, the next draft should go to the legal department for review.

   In some cases, other managerial personnel should receive draft copies with an opportunity to comment before publication. This decision must be based on responsibilities and sensitivities in the organization.

2. *Distribution of final copy of release*

   An internal distribution list should be prepared for each release to target important internal publics. Those who should receive copies include:

   All personnel mentioned by name in a release;

   Editors of local and national internal publications;

   Everyone involved in the draft approval stage;

   Public relations and advertising firms associated with the organization; and

   All target media representatives.

Types of Releases

The most common type of publicity release is the **news release** (figure 10.1). Any occurrence within an organization that may have local, regional, or national news value is an opportunity for publicity. Sometimes this news is not favorable to the organization; even in such a case, however, a release is necessary. The news will always get out when something goes wrong. The role of the public relations practitioner is to be certain that the full story is told and that corrective actions are reported.

Business features An important form of publicity, and one highly prized by many organizations, is the feature article carried by a professional, business, trade, or technical publication. Specialized periodicals that target narrowly defined audiences have increased dramatically in recent years, and they allow public relations practitioners to focus on particular audiences for maximum effectiveness. Some analysis of feature articles will provide insight into the type and style of story an editor prefers. These specialized publications tend to publish articles that define problems common to a particular profession or industry and describe organizations' attempts to deal with them. Unique uses of existing products, or products developed to address old problems, are also frequent subjects. Public relations professionals often employ freelance writers who specialize in the particular field of the target publication. Most organizations have numerous other outlets for this type of publicity, including in-house technical reports, speeches discussing new technology or products, and papers prepared for professional societies.

Consumer service features Many newspapers and magazines, as well as some television stations, publish or broadcast material designed to assist consumers. Information about almost any consumer product or service can become a vehicle for both product and institutional publicity. Stories that provide consumer-oriented information concerning food, travel, fashion, child care, books, home management, and numerous other topics are in demand by many publications. Frequently, the recipes, food photographs, travel stories, and fashion news contained in special newspaper sections are provided by public relations practitioners representing various manufacturers and industry associations.

Financial features Most newspapers and television stations, and some magazines and radio stations, carry financial news and feature articles, and a growing number of publications specialize in that area. Such publicity can be an especially effective tool for shareholder relations (see chapter 14) because current and potential investors assign more credibility to information when an independent editor selects it for publication. Potential sources of financial publicity include dividend announcements, mergers, profit reports, expansions, new product lines, major orders, changes in top personnel, research breakthroughs, and many other events that might be of interest to the financial community in general.

Product features Product publicity can frequently be newsworthy enough to be selected for use by news editors. Stories about products should be directed to periodicals, newspaper sections, and television and radio programs specializing in consumer product information. Editors and others who use this type of material are interested in information about the features, composition, performance, and application of product—information that will help consumers with their purchasing decisions.

This type of publicity can build goodwill, foster customer loyalty, and create product awareness among manufacturers, distributors, and retailers. In addition to exploiting unique product features, the public relations practitioner can create newsworthy events to dramatize and illustrate product performance for media representatives.

Pictorial features   The increasing popularity of photojournalism has made more newspapers and magazines receptive to newsworthy or unusual photographs that can communicate messages by themselves. Such photographs are often used with only a caption line and no accompanying story. Because these high-quality, unique photographs are difficult for assignment editors to plan, they provide an excellent opportunity for publicity. A public relations manager should always be alert for photographs that might be good enough for this purpose.

Many organizations employ staff photographers, and their work should be examined constantly for exceptionally good or unusual shots. Photographs taken for in-house publications, annual reports, or even advertising may present opportunities for publicity. Special events should always be planned with good publicity photographs in mind. Frequently, newspaper and television editors assign photographers to special events if they know in advance of good possibilities for getting unusual or newsworthy photographs.

Publicity photographs should normally be printed on 7- by 9-inch or 8- by 10-inch paper, depending on the editor's preference. Print media prefer high-gloss photographs with caption lines attached, while television stations prefer slides instead of prints, but specifications should be determined in advance. Photographs for television should always be in color. Newspapers and magazines sometimes use color photographs, but black-and-white photos are standard. See public relations spotlight 10.2 for photography tips.

Public Relations Spotlight 10.2

Tips for Getting Good Photographs

Whether or not you must actually take the photographs that will accompany your releases, consider these tips to make them more effective:

1. Avoid busy, cluttered backgrounds that may detract from your subject.
2. Don't photograph subjects head-on. Photographs taken from a slight side angle are more natural.
3. Candid shots of subjects are better than posed "mug shots."
4. Too much space around a subject can be distracting. Try to keep your photographs tightly framed.
5. Photograph a group in a natural cluster, never in a stiff row.
6. Avoid the temptation to photograph too many people in a group.
7. Generally, faces should be at least as large as the nail of your little finger.
8. Ask for proof sheets from the processor before selecting negatives for printing.
9. Make sure the people in your photographs receive prints.
10. Always obtain a release, even for internal publications and file photos. A release should contain the following:
    Subject's name
    Signature of subject (parent or guardian for minors)
    Statement granting permission for all photographs taken
    Date, time, and place photographs were taken
    Statement that photos may be used for either publicity or advertising
    Name of the organization

*Packaging News
Releases*

Packaging in the form of **media kits** can frequently increase the probability that information from a publicity release will actually be used by an editor. A media kit, sometimes called a press kit, includes a collection of publicity releases, fact sheets, brochures, and photographs or other information pieces enclosed in a cover or some other packaging device (see Figure 10.2). However, though attractive packaging can be helpful in gaining the attention of a busy editor whose desk is covered with competing releases, design is not the primary consideration in

Figure 10.2a
Communications, or media, kits are helpful when you initiate a public relations program or campaign.

Communications Kit

The Power of Community
Just think of all we can do together . . .

United Way of Metropolitan Atlanta

Tips For Use

Tips For Use
....
Effective, consistent communication to employees about how they can impact community problems
through United Way is invaluable to the success of your campaign. This kit has been prepared to
help you explain to your fellow employees how United Way works.

This kit contains information on United Way and camera-ready articles and graphics that you can
use in your existing communication vehicles or that you can use to create these vehicles. Other tips
for success include:

- Work closely with your company's campaign manager and United Way liaison.

- Incorporate these messages and materials in all your employee communications —
  through newsletters, bulletin boards, video news and electronic mail.

- Involve other employees — ask employees to tour a United Way agency and to
  report on their experience in your newsletter, profile a group of employees who do
  a group volunteer project, feature employees who are involved in the community
  on posters or company bulletin boards. This involvement makes it easier on you
  and more meaningful for everyone.

- Camera-ready materials are easy to use — just cut, paste and copy.

- Customize materials and articles to fit your company, perhaps adapt to your
  campaign theme or include your corporate logo.

- Personalize the United Way message — find employees who volunteer or who
  have received help.

Ideas and additional information, stories and materials are available. Please contact your United
Way campaign liaison or Elizabeth McBride, director of workplace communications, at 527-7227.

compiling a media kit. News releases, photographs, fact sheets, background information, and features should be packaged in an organized and readable form to enable the editor to select the information he or she wishes to use. The strategy behind any media kit should be based on the understanding that most major media will not use a release verbatim but will instead select information to be rewritten into stories unique to their publications. A media kit should be designed to help editors select the information they need.

Jane Paley, a former vice-president of Manning, Selvage & Lee Public Relations, lists the following standard components of a media kit:

A lead story   The strongest news piece you have. Keep it short; one page is
    terrific; don't exceed two.

Backgrounders   These may run five to seven pages and should offer depth,
    detail, and well-documented facts and figures.

Photographs, diagrams, graphs   Should be 8″ × 10″ black-and-white
    glossies designed to reproduce clearly. Each should be captioned to
    identify and clarify subjects. Photos of products, personalities, and action
    shots are all acceptable.[13]

The basic rules for preparing any release apply to preparing the media kit. Always check your facts, avoid being overly commercial, never lie or deliberately misrepresent, and use only credible sources for value judgments and quotations. While photographs and artwork help attract an editor's attention, they must be appropriate to the subject of the release. Folders, binders, and other packaging devices must be functional for the editor as well as unique and attractive. Mini-case 10.2 provides an example of a creatively designed media kit that was strategically planned for maximum effectiveness.

Media kits need not be as elaborate and costly as the example in mini-case 10.2 to be effective. Releases can be packaged in simple but well-designed

Mini-Case 10.2

Quality Kit Produced for Johnson Wax U.S. Consumer Products

The objectives of producing this kit were (1) to communicate the scope and diversity of the company's product lines, (2) to emphasize the quality of the products, (3) to offer consumers a host of free resources available through the consumer services division, and (4) to apprise the consumer of the economic benefits of buying quality products and using them correctly.

The phrase "Quality Is $ in the Bag" was developed as an umbrella or overall theme for the kit, which was housed in a brown paper shopping bag that included product samples, consumer literature, and the kit, whose graphic elements complemented the grocery bag theme.

In fact, the kit's hardbound laminated folder contained vertically bound shopping bags complete with serrated edges. On each bag was printed a calendar month with ample space for appointments and deadlines. And each bag held releases with consumer information geared to surviving in tight money times.

"Quality Is $ in the Bag" press kit prepared for and distributed by Johnson Wax

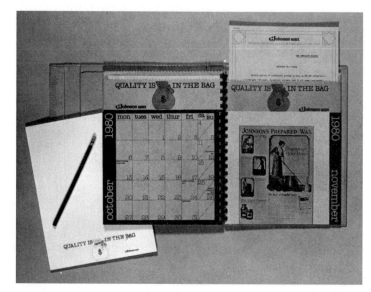

Each kit also contained a response card for feedback which was incorporated into follow-up mailings. Each month, a news release and product sample followed, as a reminder of the initial mailing, and more significantly, as a means of continually expanding editorial awareness of Johnson Wax products and services.

Source: Jane Paley, "The Press Kit: Staple of the Public Relations Cupboard," *Sky,* a publication of Delta Air Lines (June 1980): 36. Reprinted by permission.

one- or two-color folders, as long as they are adaptable to a variety of media needs. The basic role of a press kit is to provide editors information that would otherwise take many hours to research. Press kits can provide a service for the media by saving research time and identifying important information for consumers and others. The organization, of course, stands to gain favorable publicity.

Press kit used in "Great Balls of Foil" campaign by Amann & Associates Public Relations

Distributing News
Releases

News releases have typically been mailed or hand carried to the media. They still are; however, many releases are now either faxed or sent by e-mail directly to the editor or person targeted by the release. Broadcast fax, which is the material sent electronically to all fax machines set up on your computer to receive the material, is being used more and more often by media relations departments. Additionally, though, more journalists are looking to electronic mail. "A growing number of journalists prefer e-mail because they can address it without the interruption phone calls cause," according to James Horton.[14]

Use of the new technologies by journalists is growing rapidly. A survey titled "The Media in Cyberspace" by Don Middleberg and Steven Ross found that 16 percent of journalists surveyed used on-line services every day, with one-third signing on weekly. It also found that 22 percent of managing editors and 17 percent of business editors preferred electronic communications.[15] "These numbers are expected to double, or even triple."[16] Steven Ross, a professor at Columbia University Graduate School of Journalism, summed up his survey results this way: "The most dramatic finding is the speed in which the media is adapting to computer technology."[17]

Setting Up a
Newsroom

Getting media representatives to cover an event is only the start. The quality, quantity, and favorableness of their coverage, as well as their willingness to come back the next time they are invited, may depend on the facilities you provide for their use. A **newsroom** is simply an area set aside to provide information, services, and amenities to journalists covering a story. You often need to set up a newsroom at a large convention involving your organization or during a major crisis. Whatever the reason, if you need to set up a newsroom, the following tips should help:

1. Information must be accessible. All fact sheets, releases, photos, and people to be interviewed must be readily available.

2. The staff must be qualified and experienced. Media representatives' impressions of the organization and the event are influenced by the competence of those who are assigned to help them.

3. A convenient yet insulated location is important. The newsroom, interview rooms, and other media facilities should have easy access to the events but be separated enough to prevent interference.

4. Both print and broadcast facilities should be provided. For example, three separate interview rooms should be set up for television, radio, and print media.

5. The newsroom must be well supplied, containing the following:

   Telephone lines and any special hookups needed for broadcasts, computers

   Copy machines

   Individual stations (desks, tables, cubicles) for reporters

   Adequate lighting and electrical outlets

Computers and supplies

Fax machines

6. It is accepted custom to provide refreshments. These can range from meals and cocktails to coffee and donuts. The event and the length of time media representatives must stay in the newsroom should be considered in determining what is appropriate. The objective is to encourage representatives to stay close to the action.

The second direct way of dealing with the media is through discussion. In the place of information presented in written form, direct oral interaction occurs between the journalist and the public relations practitioner in the form of simple conversations, phone calls, meetings, or interviews. Whether these interactions appear informal or formal, they should never be taken lightly. Any interaction with a journalist is an opportunity for positive publicity.

Communicating Orally with the Media

While public relations practitioners often serve as the journalist's source of information, they also often provide a link between journalists and organization executives. It is the public relations person's role to coach and assist an executive who is not accustomed to dealing with the media. Thus, the following advice relates to two possible situations: (1) when the public relations practitioner is being interviewed and (2) when the practitioner is advising someone else in the organization about being interviewed.

Specific Interviews   The first step in preparing for a specific interview is to determine exactly what message you want to get across to the ultimate audience—those who will read the article or listen to the news on radio or television. The interviewee should establish in his or her own mind the major point of the interview, the *bottom line.* In the example presented earlier concerning allegations of questionable conduct, the bottom line might be that the company takes great pride in its honesty and integrity and will do everything possible to maintain its good name. In the case of the major gift to the university, the bottom line might be that the university is a great institution that makes significant contributions to its community and deserves the support of all its publics. In the case concerning police morale, the bottom line might be that despite a problem, the city's police consider themselves professionals devoted to safety and service.

Once the bottom line for the interview is established, gather information to support that position. Plan to relate all items of information to the basic message. Organize material for the interview around the major point, and be prepared to return to it consistently. In this way, you may control the interview rather than allowing it to control you.

The second step is to consider the audience—both the particular journalist who will conduct the interview and the ultimate audience who will read or listen to what the journalist writes. Does the reporter have a particular approach, hypothesis, or philosophy? How can messages be phrased to appeal to the interests and needs of the reporter and the ultimate audience?

Third, anticipate the interview. Many organizations even rehearse interviews—with the public relations practitioner playing the reporter, while the executive who is to be interviewed plays herself or himself. Remember the reporter's basic questions: who, what, when, where, why, and how. Try to organize material as a journalist would. Do not consider a chronological presentation; rather, try to think in the reporter's inverted pyramid form, with the broadest, most important points first, followed by the details. Try to visualize the first paragraph of an article developed from the interview as it would appear in print.

Fourth, have at your fingertips as much information as you can accumulate. It is almost impossible to overprepare. Develop alternative angles and backup facts. Also be prepared to suggest the names of other people to whom the reporter might talk, and inform those people that their names will be used so that they can prepare.

Finally, develop an interview strategy. This plan will depend on both the nature of your material and the interview situation. Should a balanced approach be used? How should negatives be dealt with? How explicit and specific should you be? How can the practical consequences of the issues in question be demonstrated?

Before and during interviews, try to keep these guidelines in mind:

1. Start with the news, then provide the details. Have your own agenda.

2. Answer direct questions directly—do not hedge or be evasive, but if you feel a question is unfair, you may say so. If you do not know an answer, say so—but promise to get the answer, and follow through on your promise.

3. Do not lie or exaggerate.

4. Do not argue with reporters—even if you win an argument, you will lose in the long run.

5. Do not let reporters put words into your mouth. Frequently reporters ask, "Would you say . . . ?" Either "yes" or "no" leaves you open to an embarrassing quote. It is better to respond, "You said that, I didn't."

6. Do not talk off the record. Reporters may use **off-the-record** information in a variety of potentially damaging ways beyond the interviewee's control.

7. Approach the topic from the viewpoint of your public's interest, not from that of your organization. Do not talk about "capital formation"; talk about "jobs."

8. Follow up. Be sure to provide promptly any additional information you have promised. Do not be pushy or meddlesome, but if you think a point needs clarification, do not hesitate to provide it.

You will never be satisfied with every interview as it is published or broadcast, just as you cannot expect to hit a home run every time you go to the plate. Your ability to take charge of an interview and control it depends on preparation in terms of attitude and information. If you take the time and make the effort to prepare, your batting average will be significantly higher.

A final note on interviews: Protect yourself. When an interview is agreed to, it is legitimate for all parties to concur in advance on certain ground rules. The rules may deal with the range of subjects to be covered, the conditions under which direct quotes may be used, and other matters of mutual concern. For example, the interviewee may agree to reveal certain information off the record so that the reporter can understand a situation. A reporter must agree in advance to accept information on that basis. Other ground rules include "not for attribution," when information may be used but its source not revealed; "background," when information may be used and attributed to a general source (such as "sources close to the company"); or "indirect quote," when remarks may be used in substance and attributed but not used verbatim.

One other ground rule that is sometimes of great value concerns the use of tape recorders. Reporters often use tape recorders and typically ask permission to do so. The interviewee also is well advised to tape the proceedings. An audiotape will provide a record should disputes emerge later.

News Conferences   A news conference is a structured opportunity to release news simultaneously to all media. It should be used only when the news is important and when interaction is required to promote understanding of complex or controversial topics. Unless the event is extremely newsworthy and simply cannot be handled through releases, or unless there is someone newsworthy to interview, do not call a news conference.

For those rare occasions when news conferences are appropriate, the following guidelines will help ensure success.

1. *Plan the event carefully.*   Invite all representatives of all potentially interested media far enough in advance for editors to plan to send reporters and photographers. Select an appropriate site close to the event being covered and convenient for major media (hotel, press club, airport, boardroom—never a public relations office). Check for enough electrical outlets and telephones. Time the conference to accommodate major media deadlines. Make certain you prepare enough handout material for everyone. Prepare any visuals that may be used so that they will photograph well from any place in the room. Prepare a poster of the organization's logo or name to place over the one on the speaker's stand if you use a rented facility. Plan to phone major media the morning or afternoon before the conference as a reminder. Simple refreshments are generally a nice touch.

2. *Prepare executives and others to be interviewed.*   Make certain they understand the topics that will be discussed. Help them anticipate and prepare for difficult or touchy questions. Advise them to be completely honest. If they don't know certain answers they should say so and offer to find out. If the answer to a question is considered proprietary information, they should state that it is not for public disclosure. Cultivate a pleasant, cooperative attitude among those who will be interviewed. If they are afraid of or resent the media, it will show. Advise them to avoid off-the-record comments.

3. *Public relations practitioners are the directors and stage managers.* Keep the meeting moving and interesting, but don't take over the jobs of

the media representatives. Try to keep relationships cordial and professional even in the heat of questioning. Never take obvious control of the meeting unless things get out of hand.

Electronic Media
Video

Video has become a major method for delivering an organization's news to the broadcast media. Budget cuts in TV news operations and new broadcast technology have both contributed to an increasing use of video by public relations practitioners in the 1990s. Until the late 1980s, when broadcast technology made it economically feasible to produce and distribute Video News Releases nationally, public relations practitioners had limited success in getting their stories told in the broadcast media. They were usually limited to providing "visual tips" for news crews or writing releases in broadcast style, with a few colored slides provided. Electronic News Gathering equipment providing field videotaping capability, along with satellite transmission, has made instantaneous delivery possible.[18]

VNRs have become the medium of choice in several major crises. In the summer of 1993, Pepsi-Cola used VNRs to show the nation that its cans could not be tampered with after a Tacoma man touched off a panic by claiming to find a hypodermic needle in his Pepsi can. A second VNR was produced showing a store surveillance camera catching a customer tampering with a can to perpetuate the hoax. Generally, though, a VNR is used to shape a message and tell a story. Dan Johnson, president of DWJ Television, gives 10 reasons to do a VNR in public relations spotlight 10.3.

Reasons to Do a VNR

Public Relations Spotlight 10.3

1. A VNR seen in the context of a TV newscast offers credibility not afforded by commercials.
2. A 90-second VNR shapes your message and tells your story.
3. A VNR can get your company name, logo, product or spokesperson in the news.
4. A VNR can help position your company as the authority on a certain topic, issue or industry.
5. You can get key product placements. By producing a VNR relating to an ad campaign or a new trend, your product can be featured legitimately as the "next, best, biggest" thing without looking like a commercial plug.
6. Your client or company can take a stance on a controversial issue. Using VNRs, you can spell out your company's or your industry's side of an issue.
7. Several hi-tech tracking systems are available to measure audience viewership.
8. You can reach specific target markets. It is easy to produce one skeleton VNR and then insert local cues/spokespeople/shots to impact your chosen target audience.
9. Producing and distributing a VNR is cheaper than producing a commercial.
10. VNRs can be used alone or to add credibility to an advertising, marketing or PSA campaign.

Source: Dan Johnson, president, DWJ Television, in "Beginner's Guide to VNRs," *Public Relations Journal* (December 1993): 16.

VNRs typically cost from $5,000 to $20,000 for preparation and distribution.[19] They are often prepared under contract by outside video firms and then distributed by one of several national distributors. The VNR is usually distributed by satellite, but videos and scripts sometimes are mailed or carried directly to TV stations. When transmission is by satellite, notice is usually given the TV station by fax, e-mail, or wire service. Often a summary of all VNRs is sent, along with a script for each one (see figure 10.3). The VNR contains the main story, or "A-Roll," which is the complete package in 90 seconds or less with sound on tape. However, "B-roll" footage, or extra taped shots, is sent for the station to develop its own story and perhaps customize it with local interviews, using the "wild shots" to illustrate the points made.

Electronic video titles, or "supers," should not be used because some stations will refuse to run a VNR if they can't put their own style electronic graphics on the tape.[20]

FEDEX OVERNIGHT-#1837
FRIDAY
APRIL 21, 1995

VIDEO	AUDIO
SHOW OPEN	----------------SOT-------------
TEASER	
A-1 WELCOME	--------------V/O--------------
TAPE # shots of explosion	
TRT=	The death toll continues to rise following
	an explosion at the Federal Building in
	Oklahoma City.
ANCHOR SUPER: LL	Our BSC is located just two blocks away.
	Fortunately no FedEx employees were
	injured although one employee lost a
	nephew in the blast.
	The explosion was felt for miles.
	As you know Fed Ex is working with the
	RedCross in disasters and we have already
	begun shipping emergency items into
	Oklahoma City.
	Once again, however, we want to report to
	you that our FedEx employees in
	Oklahoma
	City were not hurt. Everyone is, however,
	impacted by the tragedy.
B-1 EXPLOSION	Incue: The aftermath of the carbombing...
tk sot--TRT:	
incue:	
super: Linda Roberts	
super: Colleen Dickson	
super: Doug White	
outcue:	Outcue: for your prayers.
Anchor tag	Right now FedEx is transporting 30
	pounds of lime lights to the diaster area.

Figure 10.3 The video script used in a "FedEx Overnight" broadcast to employees can also be repackaged into a Video News Release for external distribution.

We are also bringing in 600 pounds of
work gloves for emergency crews.
We'll keep you updated on our activities
with the Red Cross and how our FedEx
employees are coping in the disaster area.

C-1 FAST FACTS (Sat Svc.)   -----------------SOCD----------------
TK ENG/CG/CD FULL
ENG/CG/CD OUT
D-1 WONDERS EXHIBITION
ANCHOR EFX WONDERS EXHIB.   We've told you about the Imperial Tombs
of China exhibition that you can see if
you're visiting Memphis for business or
pleasure.
We helped transport the ancient treasures.
During this week's opening ceremonies
the Chinese Golden Dragon Acrobats
performed. As we leave you
we want to let you see a portion of their
show. We think you'll find it fascinating
and wonderfully entertaining.
Have a great weekend and we'll see you
Monday.

TK Tape #
TRT=   ************SOT************
In: **Incue: (Chinese acrobats)**
Super:
Out: **Outcue:**
E-1 CLOSE
TK CG FULL
E-2 EC LOGO
CG OUT/TK ENG FULL   ---------------SOT----------------
end

Including the Video News Release, which is the most popular application of video, there are at least four particular uses of video for public relations:

1. *The Video News Release* is a short news package presenting a news item from the organization's viewpoint. The most popular VNR is about 90 seconds long but is accompanied by "B-roll" material (background video) with audio on separate channels. It is usually ¾-inch broadcast-quality videotape.

2. *Electronic media kits* are similar to the conventional media kit except that they include VNRs, perhaps a longer version than normal, giving more background material. They also include typical background print materials such as still photos, news releases, brochures, background papers, fact sheets, or other pertinent information.

3. *Satellite press conferences* provide an opportunity for TV journalists to participate in question-and-answer sessions via satellite with an

organization's representatives. Often the organization makes a presentation preceding the press conference. Some participants may be in studios with interactive uplink facilities, but some watch the satellite feed and phone in questions.

4. *Satellite media tours* provide individual interviews with a guest personality in a remote studio. Each interview is exclusive; some are carried live. Guests may be able to appear on two or three dozen stations per day this way.[21]

Public Service Announcements

Nonprofit organizations have an additional major electronic media outlet—the public service announcement (PSA). While radio and television stations aren't required to use PSAs, they have historically made available about 10 percent of their commercial time to provide announcements for nonprofits in the "public interest."

The public relations practitioner must work with the public service director at the broadcast station to determine the particular station's requirements for PSAs. Often the station will assist the organization in actually producing a PSA. TV stations in Denver, for example, allow an organization four TV spots a year. All Denver TV stations contribute to the production, which is done at one station. The spots must conform to 10-, 20-, and 30-second time frames for commercial breaks. Radio PSAs usually are produced for that time frame or an additional 60-second spot; some radio stations prefer to have their disc jockeys read the announcements and don't require specific timed copy.

One problem with PSAs is that they may be played at any time of the day or night. Your spot may air at 6 A.M. or 2 A.M. If you're lucky, however, it might air during prime time.

Summary

The relationship between journalists and public relations practitioners is a difficult one. If practitioners understand the media and the reporter's role, however, positive relationships can be developed that are beneficial to all.

Once positive relationships are established, practitioners should take several steps to use them effectively. Developing appropriate attitudes, setting goals, planning, and performing adequate research are essential aspects of successful media relations.

Specific techniques for communicating with the media include publicity releases, news kits, newsrooms, interviews, and news conferences. All of these approaches must be used judiciously, for publicity may backfire. Inappropriate publicity efforts can injure the relations that have been built over time with the media and the public. Electronic media have become especially important in the 1990s, with VNRs, electronic media kits, satellite press conferences, and satellite media tours leading the way. Public Service Announcements provide a means for nonprofits to communicate through radio and television.

Toxic Shock Syndrome

Case Study

A t Denver's Children's Hospital, a new public relations director made a plea to doctors and staff members to let her know if anything happened that might be considered news. She briefly explained to them what "news" was. A few days later, a doctor sheepishly came to her with an item he thought might be newsworthy. "I think I've discovered a new disease; do you think that's newsworthy?" he asked the public relations director. After she told him it was newsworthy, he continued by saying, "I think I'm going to call it Toxic Shock Syndrome." He wanted to announce it. She readily agreed but wanted to plan how to release the information so the hospital could get the maximum benefit from the exposure.

Children's Hospital in Denver is a major regional referral and research hospital for states in the West. It depends a great deal on its support from fund-raising efforts. If you were the public relations director, what would you do?

Source: Kyla Thompson, *Non Profit Public Relations,* interview by Dan Lattimore, videocassette, Colorado State University, 1986.

Questions

1. How would you announce the new disease?

2. How would you handle the requests from more than 500 media calls you would receive in the few days after the announcement?

3. If you had just been named public relations director for the hospital when this occurred, how would you proceed to develop your media contacts to help the hospital?

4. How could you use the discovery of Toxic Shock Syndrome in the years to come in your public relations efforts?

Notes

1. Gene Grabowski, "The Seven Deadly Sins of Media Relations," *Public Relations Quarterly* (Spring 1992): 37.

2. "Circulation of U.S. Daily Newspapers," *Editor and Publisher International Year Book* (New York: Editor and Publisher, 1995), preface; "Television," *Broadcasting and Cable Yearbook* (New Providence, N.J.: R.R. Bowker Co., 1995), C1–C226.

3. Douglas Cater, *Press, Politics and Popular Government* (Washington

D.C.: American Enterprise Institute, 1972), 83–84.

4. Joseph Poindexter, "The Great Industry-Media Debate," *Saturday Review* (10 July 1976): 22.

5. Associated Press Managing Editors Guidelines, 44.

6. Cliff Webb quoted in Lucy Caldwell, "Maintaining Media Relations: One Perspective with Tips for Radio, Print, and TV Personalities," *Government Communications* (June 1995): 16.

7. Ibid.

8. G. A. Marken, "Press Releases: When Nothing Else Will Do, Do It Right," *Pubic Relations Quarterly* (Fall 1994): 11.

9. Lucy Caldwell, "Maintaining Media Relations: One Perspective with Tips for Radio, Print, and TV Personalities," *Government Communications* (June 1995): 15–16.

10. Walter Guzzardi Jr., "How Much Should Companies Talk?" *Fortune* (4 March 1985): 64–68.

11. Doug Williams, "In Defense of the (Properly Executed) Press Release," *Public Relations Quarterly* (Fall 1994): 5.

12. *PR Reporter* (12 February 1973): 1.

13. Jane Paley, "The Press Kit: Staple of the Public Relations Cupboard," *Sky* (June 1980): 34–36.

14. James L. Horton, APR, "The ABC's of External E-Mail," *Public Relations Tactics* (March 1995): 9.

15. Adam Shell, "In Search of Scoops in Cyberspace," *Public Relations Tactics* (March 1995): 16.

16. Ibid.

17. Ibid., 16–17.

18. E. W. Brody and Dan Lattimore, *Public Relations Writing* (New York: Praeger Publishers, 1990), 166.

19. Adam Shell, "VNRs: Who's Watching? How Do You Know?" *Public Relations Journal* (December 1993): 14.

20. Diane Orr, "Incorporating VNRs into Your Public Relations Program," *Public Relations Quarterly* (Spring 1994): 24.

21. Brody and Lattimore, 165.

CHAPTER 11

Employee Communication

Preview

When an organization achieves effective employee communication, the results may include more satisfied and productive employees; improved attainment of organization goals; and better customer, community, investor, and public relations.

Effective employee communication depends on the establishment of a positive organizational climate. Feelings of trust, confidence, openness, candor, supportiveness, security, satisfaction, involvement, and high expectations characterize ideal organizational climates.

Public relations efforts should help employees become well informed about their organizations and encourage them to express their views to management.

What people say behind your back is your standing in the community in which you live.

—Henry Wadsworth Longfellow

ichael H. Mescon, a management consultant and former business professor, tells the story of an experience aboard a Delta Air Lines jet:

I was just settling into my seat when I casually remarked to the fellow sitting next to me about the skyrocketing cost of airline tickets. The fellow didn't take my remark very casually. "Do you know why that ticket costs what it does?" he asked.

"No," I said, "And I don't really care." "Well, you ought to care," he said. "Because what that ticket pays for is your safety, comfort and convenience." Well, by now I knew I was in for it. The guy told me what the carpet on the floor cost and why that particular kind of carpet had to be used. He explained the construction of the seat I was sitting in. He talked about support personnel on the ground for every plane in the air and, of course, he dealt with the costs of jet fuel. Finally, I stopped him.

"I know the president and several of Delta's vice presidents," I said. "You must be one of the vice presidents I don't know." "No," the fellow said, "I work in the upholstery shop." "Well, how do you know so much about Delta's operations?" "The company keeps us informed."

When organizations commit themselves to effective communication with their employees, a number of important benefits can result. Well-informed employees are usually satisfied employees. They are better, more productive workers who get more out of their work and do a better job for the company. Where communication lines are open, organizational goals are more easily achieved. Moreover, as the Delta Air Lines example shows, well-informed employees interact with the public and can have significant positive effects on relations with customers, the community, investors, and the general public. An unprecedented result of positive employee relations was the gift of a $30 million Boeing 767 to Delta from its employees. Wrapped in a giant red ribbon, the plane was presented to the airline at Christmas. The gift had the additional benefit of generating tremendous positive publicity worldwide.

Achieving effective employee communication is no simple task. Amid the corporate changes of the last few years, including corporate takeovers and mergers, downsizing, cost cutting, and developments in technology, public relations faces immense new challenges in dealing with employees.

Lynn Martin, former congresswoman from Illinois and labor secretary from 1991 to 1993, made these observations about the changing workforce to public relations practitioners at the 1994 PRSA convention in Baltimore:

1. We look at employees today as assets, not costs.

2. Individuals will have from four to six careers in a lifetime.

3. More than 84 percent of employees do not have unions or representation.

4. More than half of the women with babies are working.

5. Last year, more than five times as many women started businesses as men.[1]

Public relations efforts begin before an employee is hired and continue past the point where the employee separates from the organization. Thus, from recruitment to termination, public relations has a major role to play in the employee's work experience.

To understand the process by which the job is accomplished and the role of public relations in that process, we must first discuss in some detail the concept of organizational climate or culture.

The Concept of Organizational Climate

More than 50 years of research in organizational behavior has demonstrated that the most powerful forces in the workplace are psychological. The collective psychological forces at work in an organization make up its **organizational climate** or *culture.* Jim Grunig's massive study, *Excellence in Public Relations and Communication Management,* identifies a "strong, participative culture" as one of the 12 characteristics of an excellent public relations department.[2] He says that "employees of excellent organizations share a sense of mission."[3]

Several definitions of organizational climate exist. Here are two of the most widely accepted:

> Organizational climate is a relatively enduring quality of the internal environment of an organization that (a) is experienced by its members, (b) influences their behavior, and (c) can be described in terms of the values or . . . characteristics of the organization.[4]
>
> We might define (organizational) climate as a set of attributes specific to a particular organization that may be induced from the way that organizations deal with their members and their environments.[5]

In effect, organizational climate consists of employees' subjective perceptions of such organizational realities as policy, structure, leadership, standards, values, and rules. It is sometimes identified as "the way we do things here." Various researchers have noted important connections between climate and motivation[6] and between climate, creative ability, and performance.[7]

Two types of organizational climate are often seen—authoritarian and participative. In the Excellence study, Grunig and his research group concluded that

> participative cultures foster organic structures, symmetrical communication systems, and organizational excellence and effectiveness. Authoritarian cultures, in contrast, foster mechanical structures, asymmetrical systems of communication, and mediocrity and ineffectiveness.[8]

The ideal organizational climate is characterized by feelings of trust, confidence, openness, candor, supportiveness, security, satisfaction, involvement, pride in the organization, and high expectations. To a large extent, successful employee relations in general, and effective employee communication in particular, depend on positive organizational climates. William Whyte makes this point very clearly:

> Only with trust can there be any real communication. Until that trust is achieved, the techniques and gadgetry of communications are so much effort. Before employees will accept management's fact, they must have overall confidence in its motives and sincerity.[9]

Grunig makes a similar point specifically related to company media: How much employees use company media and how they evaluate them is more a function

Communicating changes in organizational climate

EXECUTIVE SUITE reprinted by permission of United Feature Syndicate, Inc.

of what they think of the company and their role in it than of anything the communications professionals do.[10]

All of this suggests that the crucial prerequisite for effective employee relations and communication is the creation of a positive organizational climate based on feelings of trust, confidence, and openness. Creating such a climate is not an easy job. Claude Taylor, chief executive officer of Air Canada, explains: "A good atmosphere, particularly for internal communication, doesn't blow in overnight, or even in one or two years. It takes a great deal of patience and listening—with no small investment in human and financial resources."[11] The way this is accomplished and the role of public relations in its accomplishment will be our next focus of discussion.

Public Relations and Organizational Climate

The primary responsibility for organizational climate belongs to line management—from the chief executive officer to the supervisors. Many organizations are consciously trying to change their cultures or climates. In the steel industry, for example, companies are trying to substitute a culture of cooperation for decades of adversarial relations between plant workers and management. Climates have been improved through better communication with employees and establishment of labor-management teams that give workers a voice in decisions.

Ford Motor Company is one organization deliberately pursuing a better climate. The company once known for its strong personalities and autocratic management (exemplified by Henry Ford and Lee Iacocca) is now emphasizing teamwork and mutual caring. Procter & Gamble has also been building trust while decentralizing.

Members of the public relations staff can make significant contributions to a positive organizational climate through their inputs to organizational decisions, their roles as internal communication consultants, and perhaps most important, their efforts to establish organizational communication policy based on a goal-oriented approach. Practitioners have also helped design and implement organizational change programs.

In terms of decision input and internal consultation, public relations managers must constantly remind line managers that nothing an organization says to

its employees can communicate more effectively than what it does to or for them. Explains Bank of California communications vice president Joelle Yuna,

> Companies have not lived up to the promises their communicators made several years ago. They told employees about quality of worklife, quality circles and participatory management, and workers began to expect more job satisfaction. We need to get off the buzzword bandwagon. . . . If you tell employees that companies are going to do this or that one year and then it's a totally different story the next year, employees and other constituents stop believing what you are saying.[12]

Donald R. Whitlow, vice-president for employee relations at Alcoa, a company with an excellent reputation for employee communication, says simply, "You always must make your actions back up your rhetoric. You can't talk about the state of the business unless you have credibility."[13]

To ensure an understanding of the organization's philosophy, policies, and actions, the public relations staff must consistently stress the need for effective two-way communication. Employees must be well informed and must have the means of expressing their views to management about organizational affairs. Says Terrance Deal, coauthor of *Corporate Cultures: The Rites and Rituals of Corporate Life,* "Communicators play a central role in interpreting the corporate culture to both internal and external audiences."

Establishing a Communication Policy

An important factor in improving organizational climate is the establishment of a communication policy. According to communication expert Norman Sigband, top management generally recognizes the need for and sincerely desires two-way communication.[14] The bottleneck in corporate communication is usually found in the middle of the corporate hierarchy. Breakdown in the communication process is most often at the first-line supervisor level. In a major IABC survey of 32,000 employees from 26 business organizations, half felt their company's communication was accurate, two-thirds felt it was incomplete, and half considered it only one-way communication from the top down.[15]

Although they may want to communicate, middle- and lower-level managers often find it difficult because they have no parameters, no boundaries, and no policies to guide them. Public relations managers can do much to foster positive organizational climates by convincing top management that communication—like finance, personnel, marketing, promotion, and almost every other area of organizational activity—should have established, clearly stated policies. Unstated policies leave dangerous vacuums that rumor and misinformation fill rapidly.

Communication policies must be goal oriented rather than event oriented. In other words, rather than addressing specific issues or topics, policies should help employees understand, contribute to, and identify with organizational objectives and problems. Successful communication policies must be based on management's desire to accomplish the following:

1. Keep employees informed of organizational goals, objectives, and plans.

2. Inform employees of organizational activities, problems, and accomplishments or any subject they consider important.

3. Encourage employees to provide management with input, information, and feedback based on their experience, insights, feelings, creativity, and reason.

4. Level with employees about negative, sensitive, or controversial issues.

5. Encourage frequent, honest, job-related, two-way communication among managers and their subordinates.

6. Communicate important events and decisions as quickly as possible to all employees, especially before they learn from media. They must be told first.

7. Establish a climate where innovation and creativity are encouraged.

8. Urge every manager and supervisor to discuss with each of his or her subordinates the latter's progress and position in the firm.

When such communication guidelines are accepted and practiced at all levels of management, the organization's climate will improve. Honeywell is an example of a company with a clear employee communication policy. Its Corporate Policy and Practice #157 ensures that employee communication is two-way, open, and timely; considers all sides; and presents bad news as well as good. The policy gives special attention to promoting upward communication, describes the responsibilities of various corporate levels, and explains a formal employee communication network. Employees want information first from their immediate supervisors, as shown in table 11.1. The last place they want to hear the company news is in the media.

Effective employee communication is crucial to organizational success. Public relations staffs can make great contributions in this realm of communication.

"Employee communication, the Johnny-come-lately of the public relations/ communication business, continues to inch its way into corporate executive thinking," according to a survey of corporate chief executive officers (CEOs)

The Importance of Employee Communication
CEO Perspectives

TABLE 11.1 Workers' Preferred Information Sources

1. Immediate supervisor
2. Small group meetings
3. Top executives
4. Annual report to employees
5. Employee handbook/other booklets
6. Orientation program
7. Regular local employee publication
8. Regular general employee publication
9. Bulletin boards
10. Upward communication programs
11. Mass meetings
12. Audiovisual programs
13. Union
14. Grapevine
15. Mass media

Source: IABC Study, quoted in Allen Center and Patrick Jackson, *Public Relations Practices,* fifth ed. (Englewood Cliffs, N.J.: Longman, Inc., 1995), 40.

conducted by the International Association of Business Communicators. The report continues, "In terms of corporate priorities, the vast majority of CEOs rated employee communication in the 'extremely important,' 'very important' or 'tops' categories."[16]

The survey report includes a variety of statements by CEOs about employee communication. Here is a sampling of their responses:

"The success or failure of everything from new products to advertising campaigns to reaching our goals for the fiscal year are affected by how well our employees understand what we are trying to accomplish and how we accomplish it."

"There is a direct correlation between employee communication and profitability."

"The best [business] plan is meaningless unless everyone is aware of it and pulling together to achieve its objectives."

"Employees can't be happy in their work or with their company unless they're well informed."

"If employees understand what you're trying to do and get involved in the process feeling like they're really a part of it, then the job gets done much more easily, and there are fewer grievances and fewer problems."

Not surprisingly, public relations managers share the concern expressed in these quotations. A survey of the public relations departments of the *Fortune* top 50 companies revealed the overwhelming consensus that employee communication is an area of expanding interest.[17] Public relations spotlight 11.1 emphasizes this increased interest from the CEO's perspective.

*Public Relations
Perspectives*

Rather than acknowledging the comprehensive nature of employee communications, public relations has traditionally viewed employees as just one of many publics. Today, employees are still considered a public, but a very special one. Public relations recognizes that employees are a medium through which other publics gain information and establish attitudes toward organizations.

Public Relations Spotlight 11.1

An increasingly competitive global marketplace, combined with one of the most unpredictable economic periods in this century, have served as a wake-up call for much of corporate America. To answer that call corporations are making revolutionary changes that are redefining the work place. Corporations are empowering employees, re-emphasizing and focusing on product quality and customer service, and intensifying efforts to improve productivity.

Crucial to the success of these initiatives is candid, ongoing communication with employees. This is a critical link to creating a corporate culture that can adapt and respond to the rapidly changing needs of the business environment. Managers trained in effective communication are needed to establish and manage this link, which in turn can have a positive and direct relationship to profitability.

At USG Corporation, our situation is typical of the tumultuous conditions under which many corporations have been operating. A Fortune 250 manufacturing company, USG has historically been a stable, conservative leader in the building products industry. However, in the span of eight years we have undergone dramatic changes. We sold $750 million in businesses. Our work force grew from 9,000 to 25,000, then fell to 12,500.

Obviously, these changes traumatized our work force. Our employees were used to a stable, secure environment which essentially offered lifetime employment. Now, faced with a new set of challenges, we must adjust our approach to business, redefine the corporate culture and become even more competitive and cost-conscious. We were historically accustomed to a somewhat authoritarian, hierarchical style of management, with business direction and decisions typically handed down from the top and communications primarily a one-way flow. Now, two-way communication is central to how we conduct business. Accountability is more broadly delegated and managers/supervisors function more as team leaders.

We needed our corporate communicators not only to help manage this shift in culture, but internal communications had to operate as an integral component of the corporate strategy. Today, as we emerge from the most challenging and frustrating period in our corporate history, we utilize internal communications to accomplish the following:

1. *Communicate the corporate goals.*   Our line and staff managers must ensure that hourly and salaried employees understand the corporate goals and the strategies designed to achieve them. This is especially critical because of the widespread changes that continue to occur both culturally and structurally throughout our organization. More importantly, we need to let each employee know how he or she fits within these strategies and how vital he or she is to USG's achieving its mission.

2. *Facilitate participative management initiatives.*   Although we have always valued our employees and their input, moving to a more participative management style has become an economic necessity. Giving people greater authority necessarily increases the need for strong internal communications. It is no secret that management expectations for employees are rising. As these expectations continue to rise, we must provide our work force with the information needed to meet them. Managers must establish consistent, efficient, cost-effective and credible channels through which this information can flow.

Equally important is seeking information back from our employees. They are closest to our products, customers and production processes. As responsibility is consistently delegated to all levels throughout the organization, it is necessary that bottom-up communication systems are in place so that senior management can receive meaningful input and feedback from the "front lines."

3. *Continually monitor the internal and external environment.* Employees at all levels of the organization must take personal responsibility for monitoring the environment and conveying that information where it can help the company compete more efficiently. However, it is not enough just to monitor the environment. Pertinent information must be effectively communicated to senior management. Strategies are needed that will answer employee concerns, correct misperceptions and optimize positive attitudes.

Employees' attitudes, perceptions, beliefs and concerns can have a tremendous impact on our productivity and ability to compete. As participative management initiatives become further entrenched in the workplace, the impact will become even more significant.

4. *Establish an environment of trust and credibility.* To enable effective leadership to take place, employees must believe, accept and support management decisions. If they don't, not only are trust and credibility at risk, but pride and morale can plummet. This typically results in reduced productivity which in today's competitive environment, can cause irreparable damage.

Corporate communicators must cross profit-center and staff organizational boundaries to reinforce trust and credibility. Employees' expectations must be set correctly and communicated honestly. Failure to meet them will undermine them and jeopardize the future support and confidence of the work force.

5. *Provide opportunities to interact with employees.* Some of the most complex problems corporate executives are facing today result from losing touch with their employees. At USG, with a continued shift to participative initiatives and the strain of financial challenges, maintaining strong relationships with our employees takes on increasing importance.

I, as chairman and chief executive officer, and other members of the executive team seek frequent occasions to interact with our work force. This enables us to keep in touch, firsthand, with our employees and the various functional areas of the corporation. It provides a forum for us to reaffirm and reassure employees, gauge morale and listen to their needs and ideas. In addition, it sends an important message: by taking part in open, two-way communication, each employee can positively affect change within the organization. Nothing has had such a profound effect on me than to hear directly, the issues and concerns of the minds of our workers.

Once you subscribe to the philosophy that an informed employee has a better opportunity to be a productive contributor to the success of the enterprise, each aspect of communication makes sense. Success inevitably hinges on the ability to communicate effectively. Our communication professionals, as members of the strategic team, have been striving to firmly establish sound principles of communication in our corporate culture.

The challenge before them is to continually find ways that communication can contribute more effectively to the overall productivity of the organization. They must identify communication barriers, both verbal and non-verbal, and break them down. And they must deliver important, meaningful messages to our employees efficiently and cost-effectively. Our competitive edge depends on it!

Source: Eugene B. Connolly, "A CEO's Perspective on Employee Communication," *Journal of Corporate Public Relations* (1992–93): 32–34. The *Journal of Corporate Public Relations* is a journal of theory and practice edited and published annually by graduate students in the Department of Integrated Marketing Communications in the Medill School of Journalism at Northwestern University. Courtesy subscriptions are available from Professor Clarke L. Caywood, Ph.D., 1908 Sheridan Road, Evanston, Ill. 60208 or jcpr@nuw.edu.

Good relations with the surrounding community or the general public originate through good employee communications. Neighbors, family, friends, and associates of employees are themselves potential customers, employees, and decision makers on issues crucial to the organization. A Gallup poll revealed that each employee influences an average of 50 people in the community. These facts are known to chief executive officers. In the IABC survey, one CEO stated, "We just had a survey commissioned on customer opinion. It found that where the customer knew a company employee, his attitudes toward the company were more favorable."[18]

Employee Communication Programs

Supervisors, working primarily through interpersonal and small-group communication, constitute the most critical link in employee communication. Public relations practitioners seek to improve, support, and reinforce this link through programs and media including small and large meetings, letters, periodicals, electronic mail, faxes, bulletin boards, exhibits, annual reports, advertising, handbooks and manuals, envelope stuffers, reading racks, public address systems, telephone hot lines, surveys, suggestion systems, videos, and other means.

Since the 1970s, several forces have combined to reshape organizational communication policies and practices. Employees now demand more challenging jobs and greater work flexibility. Consumer groups demand greater input and more product information. New government regulations have had impact in a variety of ways. As a result, more organizations are now concerned about their own responses. They are more receptive to incoming communication from their publics, more concerned about openness and truthfulness, and increasingly prepared to communicate with those publics.

Internally, organizations put greater emphasis on keeping employees informed about organizational positions on political issues, future plans, and economic status. Moreover, James Lahiff and John Hatfield found that organizations are more actively soliciting ideas from employees, listening to employee suggestions, and creating an atmosphere in which employees feel free to speak their minds.[19]

How Public Relations Can Help

Specific duties of public relations managers in relation to employee communications include the following:

Promoting awareness and understanding of organizational goals.

Interpreting management and personnel policies.

Fulfilling employees' informational needs.

Providing channels for and stimulating two-way communication.

Encouraging favorable employee attitudes and increased productivity.

Making all employees ambassadors from the organization to the general public.

What Communication Programs Can Accomplish

When communication programs work, they can be tremendously cost-effective. Sweetheart Plastics, for example, invested $7,000 in a communication program, hoping to increase productivity. The company realized a savings of $250,000 the first year and expects a 10-year savings of $2.5 million. Mini-case 11.1 cites another example.

Mini-Case 11.1

Communication Aids Productivity at Westinghouse

The Westinghouse major appliance division plant in Mansfield, Ohio, had an old physical facility and some old ideas about management. As a result, it suffered low productivity, rampant absenteeism, high unit costs, and sometimes hostile labor relations. Moreover, in a town where Westinghouse was the largest employer, press relations were indifferent at best. The plant had been losing money for years and had the highest production cost per finished unit in the fiercely competitive appliance market.

According to Tom Christensen, communication and training manager, "It was a 'produce-or-perish' situation." To deal with it, Westinghouse developed a program designed to accomplish five goals: increase salable hours, reduce defective product costs, reduce accident costs, increase cost improvement savings, and improve teamwork. Communication was the primary means by which these goals were achieved.

Communication efforts included the following:

Providing 60 hours of supervisor training in which information was shared on the nature of the plant's problems and ways in which supervisors might make positive contributions.

Holding (for the first time) face-to-face meetings between the plant's general manager and all employees. The manager explained the problems, goals, and ways each employee could help.

Beefing up the suggestion system to promote upward communication. In its first year, the system netted 67 percent more cost-saving ideas and 58 percent greater savings than in previous years.

Using company media to supplement and reinforce the program. The plant's publication, *The Conveyor,* featured articles in every issue on some phase of the program. Brochures, visual displays, and posters for bulletin boards were developed.

Improving labor relations through frank interaction between management and union officials. Union stewards were offered special training classes.

Discussing plant problems frankly with local media. The media responded by giving improved coverage that, in effect, reinforced management's message with headlines like "Future of Westinghouse in Workers' Hands."

The results of the program included productivity gains ranging from 10 to 17 percent, $100,000 annual savings in incentive plan subsidies, and a 20-percent drop in unjustified employee absences. Christensen concluded: "Now, if the economy would just pick up so that we could sell some of those appliances we're producing . . . "

Why Communication Programs Fail

When employee communication programs are ineffective, the negative impact is immeasurable. Inefficiency, waste, higher costs, low morale, absenteeism, strikes, turnover, and accidents are just some of the ways poor employee communication can adversely affect sales, profits, productivity, public image, and individual employees.

A recent survey of 705 employees in 70 companies by the Council of Communication Management found that only half the employees feel employers are communicating effectively about changes in the workplace such as layoffs and downsizing. About two-thirds said they don't believe what management says. And 40 percent don't even believe that their companies make a "sincere effort at honest and open communication."[20]

Some reasons for ineffective communication have already been indicated: unclear corporate images, negative organizational climates, lack of employee communication policies, and lack of mutual trust and respect between employees and management. Another common reason for failure is that employee communication too often attempts to "sell" management's line to employees. Interested only in getting their own messages accepted, managers may neglect employee input. One of the CEOs participating in the IABC survey emphasized this point:

> If we are making an attempt to communicate with our employees specifically to sell them something, our effort is going to fail. If we are attempting to communicate, to tell them something and invite feedback, then our effort will be successful, even if we make mistakes."[21]

Richard Nemec offers a more unsettling explanation of the failure of employee communication, returning, in effect, to the concept of organizational climate: "If you had to condense modern corporate communication problems into one word," he maintains, "it would be 'fear.' Fear of reprisal . . . fear of being innovative . . . fear of honesty."[22]

Special Employee Communication Situations

Communicating with an Organized Workforce

Understanding the evolution and role of organized labor in the United States is essential to understanding the American economic and business system. Such crucial matters as inflation, productivity, quality of life on and off the job, and international trade are strongly influenced by the collective bargains struck by businesses and unions. Union activities in the political arena—sometimes in conjunction with business and sometimes in opposition to business—exert a powerful influence on the government's role in the economy.

Unions are active in many kinds of organizations. The crushing of the air traffic controllers' union by the Federal Aviation Administration in 1981 showed that bad management-union relations can be as costly in the public sector of the economy as in the private sector. Teachers, nurses, municipal employees, police and fire personnel, and other employees of not-for-profit or government organizations are increasingly unionized. Indeed, these organizations represent the areas of fastest union growth. Virtually no organization is immune from the costs of poor labor relations, as the AFL-CIO learned when its own clerical employees went on strike.

Many organizations attempt to use effective employee communications to ward off union efforts to organize the labor force. The threat of unionization, in effect, scares management into instituting communication policies and programs that should have existed in the first place. Unfortunately, the timing and motivation of efforts to establish the proper communication climate and facilitate upward communication have sometimes engendered perception of those efforts as antiunion techniques.

Unionization of an organization's workforce places employee communication and public relations in a slightly different light, but basic practices of effective employee communication still hold. As personnel specialist Don Crane states, "Progressive organizations, whether unionized or not, encourage employees to express their complaints, questions, or job problems; insist they be given a fair hearing; and give them a timely answer."[23]

Why Workers Join Unions   Conventional wisdom holds that unions exist because of management failures, and although other variables play a role, in many cases this is true. Workers join unions to gain the power necessary to pursue their needs and goals more effectively. Increased pay, shorter hours, and improved working conditions are common reasons for unionizing. However, other factors, including the opportunity to be heard and the need to be recognized and respected, also motivate them.

Why Management Resists Unions   Unions are not inherently evil, as some might have you believe. Some corporate managements even prefer to deal with unions that offer consistency, predictability, control, and a pool of qualified workers. However, initial efforts at union organization are almost always resisted. When management is accustomed to making decisions alone, making decisions with others is a difficult adjustment. When unionization occurs, management's discretion is limited and its freedom constrained. What were once unilateral decisions become shared.

Management has considerable but not unrestrained freedom in its efforts to resist unionization. Communication activities often play an important role. The National Labor Relations Act, however, requires that communications by management trying to resist unionization not be coercive. Charles Coleman explains:

> Management's right to communicate its position is protected as long as the communication is not coercive. Outright threats or promises of benefit are prohibited. The law does not permit management to threaten a plant closing upon unionization, or to offer a special wage increase during a representation campaign. . . . Management may question the union's statements, explain to workers the nature of the benefits they already have, call to their attention the strike record of the union or its record in securing terms less favorable than those already enjoyed by the employees, or offer comparisons with other organizations. Written communication may be sent to employees' homes, posted on bulletin boards, or placed in company newspapers.[24]

Public Relations in Collective Bargaining   When union representation has been established, management is required to bargain in good faith with its agents. All matters relating to a previously established set of issues are resolved through a process known as **collective bargaining.** Harold Davey defines collective bargaining as "a continuing institutional relationship between an employer . . . and a labor organization . . . concerned with the negotiation, administration, interpretation, and enforcement of written agreements covering joint understandings as to wages or salaries, rates of pay, hours of work and other conditions of employment."[25] Davey's phrase "continuing institutional relationship" is an important one. The general public has a poor understanding of collective bargaining, associating the process with strikes, labor unrest, or protracted negotiations. In fact, these are exceptional circumstances. In 98 percent of negotiations, the parties agree on contracts without resorting to strikes or lockouts.

Contract negotiations and strikes often draw intense public scrutiny. At such times, the public relations function becomes very important, and practitioners really earn their pay. Nevertheless, as Harold Marquis points out, "One area in which large corporations and industry groups have been singularly ineffective is their public relations during labor controversies."[26] Part of the problem is the sensitive nature of negotiations underway. Management and labor usually agree that public disclosure of the negotiating process would result in increased posturing, disruption, and intransigence. Abe Raskin, who covered labor relations for several decades for *The New York Times,* puts it another way:

> Outside the realm of diplomatic negotiations between the great powers no field compares with collective bargaining in reluctance of the parties to let the public know what is really going on. The settled conviction of labor and management is that the only time the rest of the world is entitled to any useful information is when an agreement has been reached. Until then the statements issued by both sides are self-serving flapdoodle intended to mislead much more than to illuminate.[27]

A journalist by profession, Raskin favors opening bargaining to the media and the public, a view that gets little support from labor or management. During negotiations, then, public relations is left with the thankless task of disclosing nothing of the proceedings while at the same time avoiding alienating journalists like Raskin who operate on a primary assumption of the public's right to know.

When negotiations are successfully concluded, the public relations spokesperson should tell the story of that success and explain the terms of the contract to the public. The contract and its impact on the local or national economy are matters of critical public interest and importance. Even after a strike, when the ending of conflict seems to be the main story, information concerning these factors should be spelled out clearly in organizational and mass media.

Public Relations in Strikes   Although strikes are rare, their effects can last for years. Moreover, as we mentioned earlier, public sentiment can have significant influence on their ultimate outcomes.

Communication plays an important role in determining whether or not there will be a strike, how the strike will be perceived, and how it will conclude. Strikes occur when workers' needs, wants, and ideas are unheard and unheeded, with tremendous frustration the result. Effective communication can go a long way toward making strikes unnecessary. Cadbury Schweppes employees in the United Kingdom belong to 29 militant unions. Nevertheless, because the company has communicated consistently, keeping employees informed on costs and profits, it has been able to install high-tech machinery and cut jobs without labor strife.[28] Mini-case 11.2 presents another example—how effective communication at American Airlines prevented a strike.

The impact of public opinion was clearly demonstrated in one case when the local community became antagonistic toward a union because a prolonged strike was adversely affecting the local economy. Community leaders were attempting to pressure the union into a settlement. As the pressure increased, a

Mini-Case 11.2

Getting Wage Concessions in a Profitable Company

American Airlines was the first major profitable airline to gain significant concessions from its unions. Two years before negotiations, company president Robert L. Crandell began to tell employees that the airline had to earn a five-percent return on revenues to be competitive under deregulation. His message was reinforced in the company newspaper and in videotape presentations. He also met with groups of employees throughout the American system.

Thanks to his persistent, coordinated, multifaceted approach, Crandell won the changes he wanted without provoking a strike. Crandell says that the hardest part of his communication program was convincing employees that deregulation made "change absolutely essential." Communication continues to be critical at American Airlines because, as Crandell says, "We want to make sure that people continuously understand the changing environment we deal with."

---

union spokesman approached the company's representative and proposed arbitration of the unresolved issues. The company resisted, but the spokesman offered to permit a three-member arbitration panel consisting solely of businesspeople to rule on the issue. All three proposed arbitrators were customers of the company. The union representative was betting that the company would never place its clients in the difficult position of judging one of their suppliers; he bet right. The next day's newspaper carried the headline "Company Refuses Union Proposal to Have Businessmen Settle Strike." The resulting shift in public sentiment forced the company to concede.[29]

Unions frequently have the public relations edge in strike situations. As Abe Raskin observes:

> Unions locked in battles with corporations win more often than they lose in the propaganda exchange . . . unions have become adept at getting their story across whenever anyone is interested enough to listen.
>
> Union leaders are almost invariably more accessible than their industrial counterparts. . . . The other great union asset in a strike is its members and their families. When a strike turns into a siege, it is standard practice for newspapers to carry sob stories detailing the hardships the strikers are suffering and proclaiming their determination to stay out until the flint-hearted bosses meet demands of elementary justice. . . . The human factor—little people fighting a faceless profit machine—is a plus for the union which the company's image-makers can't match.[30]

Successful organizational public relations in a strike situation consists of humanizing the organization's position while clarifying the strike's impact on the local economy. Management's intrepid efforts to maintain operations, the strike's impact on local merchants, and the inflationary implications of the workers' demands are angles that can build sympathy for organizational positions. In recent years, management's public position has been improved by what often appears as union greed. When the worker is already making $15 per hour or more, much of the public responds with envy rather than sympathy. News reports showing air traffic controllers' prosperous houses and swimming pools during their strike did nothing to win them public sympathy. One note of caution should be added: The portions of the Taft-Hartley Act that are still in effect do regulate to some extent the communication that management may have with employees who are union members. See chapter 19 on the legal environment.

Communicating Employee Benefits

A major area of misunderstanding in most organizations is the employee benefit program. **Employee benefits** are services an organization provides as part of employees' compensation. Benefits may include health and life insurance, sick leave, vacations, employer-paid social security, retirement programs, and a variety of other services ranging from day care to prepaid legal advice to physical fitness programs. Benefits attract and retain employees and promote employee productivity.

With respect to their benefits, managers often claim that employees "just don't appreciate what they have." Often this lack of appreciation is the result of poor communication on the part of management, as the following episode illustrates:

> Workers at a corporation had just voted for union representation, and one of the strongest appeals the union offered was its benefits package. Management could not understand what had made the package so attractive to employees. "Those benefits offer no substantial improvements over the package we already had," complained one executive. Closer examination, however, revealed that the company had never prepared publications to explain its package. Employee meetings to discuss benefits were irregular, almost nonexistent. No employee handbook or guide had been published; no orientation program for new employees had been established. There is little doubt that when the employees cast their ballots for the union, they were not voting for better benefits but for communication and a plan they understood.

Another company, which had a really outstanding benefit program, was alarmed by inaccurate rumors about its benefit package. Consultants called in to investigate found that the firm's communication program consisted of a confusing booklet on group insurance and a dull monthly newsletter. The newsletter never discussed or rebutted rumors circulating through the grapevine. The communication void in that company was a breeding ground for misunderstanding, mistrust, and dissatisfaction.

Other organizations have become highly creative in communication about benefits. United Technologies developed a 17-minute film/video featuring comedian Jonathan Winters to discuss six benefit areas: retirement, health care, disability, life insurance, dental care, and savings plans. Bankers Land Company of Palm Beach Gardens, Florida, devised a game board to explain health benefits. Exxon Coal USA put together its 81-page *Guide to Your Employee Benefits* in the style of a magazine or annual report. Readability, vitality, and richness stimulated employee interest and readership.

U.S. Chamber of Commerce figures show that from 1991 to 1992, the cost of benefits to American companies increased 3.8 percent. In 1993, fringe benefit payments in organizations throughout this country amounted to 40.2 percent of total payroll, or about $13,631 per employee. Richard Huseman and John Hatfield suggest, "What is paradoxical about these expenditures is that organizations seem to be accruing few advantages from them."[31] The authors attribute this failure at least in part to employees' lack of knowledge and understanding of their own benefit programs.

Helping employees understand their benefits has always been an important area in public relations work. But it is increasingly difficult to win gratitude and appreciation for a standard benefit package. Traditionally established on the single-breadwinner model, benefit programs are hard pressed nowadays to respond to changing gender roles; new realities of divorce, marriage, and nonmarriage; flexible retirement age; career interruptions; childless and smaller families; and multi-income families. Jerry Rosenbloom, professor of insurance at the University of Pennsylvania, observed in *Business Week* that the more sophisticated employees realize that many of the benefits they receive at present "run exactly counter to people's needs."[32] For example, both partners of a working couple may be offered group health coverage, but neither may be provided with child care benefits.

The role of corporate communicators in dealing with employee benefits can be vital. Public relations practitioners working in this area need not be limited to disseminating information about existing programs. Perhaps more important, they can serve as conduits for the expression of employees' needs and desires and thus play a significant part in determining and evaluating benefit programs. Figure 11.1 is a Huseman/Hatfield model of the benefit communication process, demonstrating the various points at which corporate communicators can be useful.

One response to changing employee needs in the benefits area has been a "cafeteria" approach, which by 1993 was being used by about 18 percent of companies in the United States, according to the U.S. Chamber of Commerce 1993 Employee Benefits Survey. This approach allows individuals to choose the benefits

Figure 11.1 A model of benefits communication

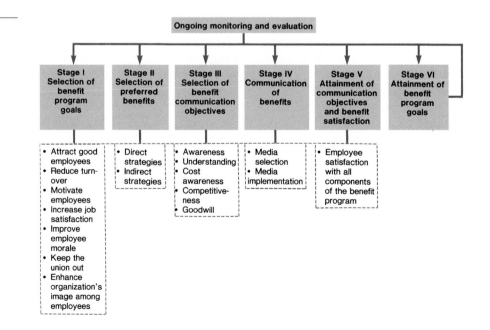

most appropriate to their own lives. At Bankers Trust Company, for example, 8,000 employees receive personalized allowances that vary according to length of service, salary, and age. When spending their allowances, employees may choose among seven life insurance, five medical, and three dental plans; varying degrees of disability coverage; dependent care provisions; and extra vacation time.

Flexibility is the key to cafeteria-style plans, but if they are to work, effective employee communication is essential. SCM Corporation, the New York City conglomerate, spent $100,000 just on an information campaign to explain its new benefit plan to employees.

In addition to responding to varying employee needs, cafeteria-style plans are one way of combatting the soaring costs of benefits. SCM expects to save over $1 million a year with its program. The health care component of benefit programs has caused the greatest headache in terms of escalating costs. In organizations like CIBA-GEIGY, Pacific Power & Light, and the Hartford Insurance Group, employee communication specialists have played a vital role in developing and disseminating health cost containment plans.

The Wisconsin Association of Manufacturers and Commerce produced a *Primer on Managing Health Care Costs.* That publication states: "A strong and ongoing communication campaign is a vital element of an employer's health education program. Communication tools take a variety of forms, but all support the major thrust of acting as constant reminders from the employer encouraging employees to help reduce the cost of health care." With changing employee needs, government regulatory requirements, and the tremendous corporate resources devoted to employee benefits, this promises to be a continuing issue of great importance to organizational communicators.

The Media of Employee Communication

In the first part of this chapter, we took a general approach to employee communication. We discussed a positive organizational climate supported by an appropriate communication policy as prerequisite for effective employee communication. We also discussed employee communication under special circumstances and for special purposes.

This section is devoted to the technical aspects of employee communication media—how to get your message across. Internal media, audiovisual media, and computers are means for reaching large numbers of employees on an ongoing basis. Personnel and resources devoted to these media have increased markedly in the past decade. This is the most rapidly growing aspect of the overall public relations effort. It is also the effort we have the most control over. That's why internal media are often called "controlled media."

Internal Media

Internal media take about as many forms as the organizations and individuals producing them (figure 11.2). Effective, professionally written messages may be found in photocopied newsletters, newspapers with editorial staffs of various sizes, glossy full-color magazines, company videos, computer home pages, or any variation on these. They have a common purpose: to give the organization a chance to tell its story the way it wishes. This is one reason controlled media are

Figure 11.2 Some internal publications including corporate, nonprofit, and government

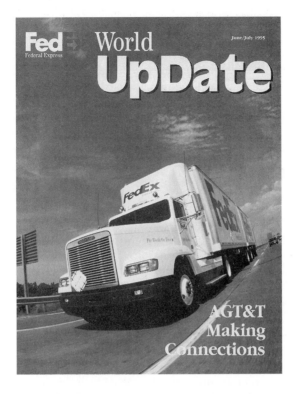

popular; it is also the reason so many fail to meet their objectives. When management speaks only from its own point of view without considering the intended audience, in-house media are only propaganda instruments. However, like the other media examined in this book, in-house media can be effective if produced with the needs of their intended audiences in mind.

The more than 50,000 in-house publications in the United States have a combined circulation of more than 460 million. Many large organizations have more than one publication. One auto maker, because of its size and the variety of its audiences, has 38. More and more large organizations use electronic media. Most such media carry internal messages not intended for the general public. Occasionally, however, the messages are distributed to influential people outside the organization or used as marketing tools.

Purpose and Potential   Organizations inevitably communicate imperfectly with their employees. A corporation preparing to honor an employee for 25 years of service discovered that he knew shockingly little about the organization he had served for a quarter century. The employee did not know the name of the company president, the location of headquarters, the number of plants the company had, the year the firm was founded, or the source of the raw material used in the manufacturing process—and he could name only two of his firm's 200 products.

Such examples are not uncommon. The standard response from managers, "What we have here is a problem of communication," does no more than label the situation. Even deciding to increase communication does not guarantee a solution; communication problems cannot be solved by a simple increase in the flow of printed messages. Printed media have their advantages, but they are not the appropriate response to every problem. Printed communication must take its place as a part of an overall program that also includes interpersonal communication, meetings, use of other media, and employee exposure to organizational officials, all within the context of establishing appropriate climate and policy. In-house media can do good work within an organization, but they can never take the place of person-to-person manager-subordinate relationships.

Communication Functions   *Downward communication* is the most common function of in-house publications (figure 11.3). Management's need to inform its employees is the justification behind most company media. Internal publications are well suited for this purpose because they publish regularly and can report news and information in a timely and relatively inexpensive way.

Internal media can, however, be counterproductive. There is a fine line between telling intended audiences what management would like them to know and providing them with the information they want and need. The former is the leading cause of failure for in-house publications; the latter ensures success. If an in-house medium appears limited to the "management line," it loses audience. Those who do read it do not take it seriously, and the publication becomes a communication liability.

Upward communication is an equally important, but sometimes overlooked, function of in-house media. It can help avoid the propaganda problem just mentioned. Letters to the editor, question-and-answer columns, articles written by

Figure 11.3 Downward
communication

NEWSPAPERS, COMMUNITY & LEADERSHIP 4

Alan Simpson, Dewey Knight, moderator Clark Hoyt, Joel Fleishman, Nancy Kassebaum : *Newspapers must be more involved*

Lessons in leadership

Though editorials are often read, they aren't often heard. Too often, nameless writers offer tepid opinions concealed in dense prose on uninviting pages deep inside the newspaper. Their pages are out of touch with most people and therefore aren't of much value to leaders.

"I have never cast my vote because of an editorial viewpoint," U.S. Sen. Nancy Kassebaum (R-Kans.) says.

"The time has come for editorial pages to be the voice of the people," says Sidney Haifetz, a small-businessman and neighborhood leader in Philadelphia.

"We in newspapers aren't exactly on the same wavelength with readers," Washington Post ombudsman Richard Harwood says.

Eight speakers — all in close contact with typical citizens, most with a track record of success in motivating them — assured editors that people *do* want to get involved, but that editorial pages aren't providing much help.

They offer these suggestions for sending clear messages that will be heard:

■ **Get closer to people.** "I wouldn't even think about" calling an editorial page editor with a question or comment, says Philadelphia businessman Michael Karp, describing the typical editorial as "ivory tower — I don't even know who wrote it."

Miami community leader Dewey Knight and U.S. Sen Alan K. Simpson (R-Wyo.) advocate town meetings, with the newspaper as the catalyst. "You can't isolate yourself," Knight advises.

On the need for establishing better rapport with readers, Simpson says, "I did 1,500 divorces when I was in practice (as a lawyer) and every one of them ended because of the ice treatment."

"Part of your relevancy is determined by how much you care," Kassebaum says. "Caring involves an investment of time and emotion that people don't seem to have today."

■ **Write with clarity and conviction.** Above all, avoid arrogance, Simpson cautions: "People of any education level know what bullshit is." But also be aggressive on issues: "If you're not gutsy, you're doomed. Who would want to read you?"

■ **Educate.** Philadelphia teacher and community activist Brenda Person recommends a standing "What You Should Know" column about issues, the way local government works and how to contact elected officials. "Repeat it, repeat it, repeat it. That's the only way you're going to get the public involved."

■ **Promote editorials.** "Part of the problem with editorials is that they are on the editorial page," says Duke University Senior Vice President Joel Fleishman. An editorial should appear on Page 1 every week, Karp agrees. "You have to sell the concept of thinking about issues."

And editorial pages need much visual improvement. "Every other section has a dramatic presentation, but not the editorial page," Karp observes. "The format has been taken for granted...If a poster had nothing but little words, you'd never read it."

Brenda Person and Michael Karp: *Educate, promote, listen*

employees, and other devices like readership surveys give information about issues important to employees (figure 11.4), and this information is valuable—even vital—to management decision making.

Lateral communication represents a growing need in modern organizations. Hierarchical organizations are usually designed only to pass information up and down, yet management needs some plan for communication among employees at the same level. Horizontal communication flow increases employee knowledge about the organization's overall operations and helps create a sense of community

Figure 11.4 Upward communication

A.I.D. and Mississippi State University: Partners in Seed Technology

by James C. Delouche Department of Agronomy, Mississippi State University and Frank Mertens, Bureau for Science and Technology, Office of Agriculture (S&T/AGR), U.S. Agency for International Development (A.I.D.)

Seed technology plays a major role in economic development. Improved seed provides more food, increases income and raises the living standards of the world's rural poor. Countries that have developed their seed industry like India, Thailand, Colombia, Brazil and Taiwan are now largely self-sufficient in food crop production.

In the development assistance era that began in the 1950s, seeds became a basic ingredient in agricultural improvement strategies such as: new crop introduction; crop diversification; improvement of existing crops; and, in recent years, sustainable agriculture.

As the catalytic role of seed in agricultural development was recognized early in U.S. foreign aid programs, U.S. agronomists have made significant contributions to economic development through assistance in seed production and supply systems and the introduction of improved crop varieties. Caribbean maize varieties, for example, were introduced into Thailand, Indonesia and other areas in the Far East and South Asia while better varieties of wheat and forages were introduced into the highlands of South America.

The partnership between Mississippi State University (MSU) and the U.S. Agency for International Development (A.I.D.) and its predecessors has, since 1956, played a leadership role in the development of seed programs and industries in the developing world. Mississippi State University serves as an informational resource and a center of expertise, applied research and training. The A.I.D./MSU partnership has been involved in many of the key advances in crop agriculture in the last three decades and exemplifies the wide ranging impact of a successful long-term collaborative relationship.

The partnership has contributed to the multiplication and widespread distribution of many high-yielding seed varieties, supported extensive technical assistance and training efforts and has resulted in the development of numerous successful seed improvement projects.

Mississippi State University has, for example, provided short-term assistance to more than 51 countries and long-term assistance in seed-industry development to Brazil, India, Thailand, Indonesia and Egypt. The University has contributed to increased seed production and supply in more than 22 countries and provided in-depth and short-term training to specialists from 72 countries in the developing world. As a result, centers of seed expertise in many countries today are staffed by MSU trained specialists who also occupy important positions in the seed program or industry of the various countries.

A number of seed improvement projects have generated major benefits. In Thailand, for example, where MSU has trained seed technologists for more than 30 years, a seed project, established in 1976, has produced $130 million in benefits to about 200,000 Thai farmers. The project has also stimulated the development of six private seed companies, which are now concentrating on corn, sorghum and vegetable seed production. Other private companies are now trying to enter the seed industry and other donors have made substantial contributions.

With better seed, peanut production in Cameroon should increase by 15,500 tons per year, corn by 23,400 tons and sorghum by 22,900 tons—a net benefit of $25 million. The Cameroon seed program was both assisted

Continued on page 7

Improved seed provides more food, raises income and living standards of the world's poor.

among its divisions. Moreover, lateral information can help develop new ideas and prevent duplication of effort. In-house media should include lateral communication as a primary goal. Giving employees information about operations outside their immediate spheres can create a broader understanding of the functions and goals of the whole organization (figure 11.5).

Objectives In the broad sense, the goal of in-house media is the improvement of relationships between their audiences and management. Setting policy and defining more specific objectives for those media is a complicated undertaking. Without

Figure 11.5 Lateral communication

specific guidelines, however, it is hard for an in-house medium to be successful, and it is even harder to measure its success.

As we have said, in-house media must fulfill the needs of both the organization and its employees. The information in the medium must be seen by the audience as useful and meaningful. Small talk and management propaganda undermine effectiveness. Most important to success is the selection of content that combines the common interests of management and employees. Following are some broad topics that are frequently treated in successful publications:

1. *Recognition of employee achievements*   both on the job and in the community can encourage internal cooperation by helping management and employees become better acquainted with other members of the organization (figure 11.6). Such recognition also serves as an official commendation for outstanding service and sets an example for others in the organization. Social activities can also be recognized but should not take precedence over job-related and community service accomplishments. Appropriate employee recognition can promote various objectives, including

   Strengthening positive relationships in the outside community.

   Building a sense of accomplishment in individual employees.

   Stimulating new ideas for company and community service.

2. *Employee well-being and safety*   can be promoted through information on safety practices, rules, and procedures. Worker safety is always an appropriate area of concern for management and employees. In some organizations, addressing safety involves little more than ensuring that everyone knows the location of fire exits. In others, however, the success of the operation—and indeed the operation itself—may depend on adherence to safety procedures. Internal publications are one outlet for the constant safety reminders necessary to such organizations.

   There is an endless need to explain benefits, vacations, holidays, taxes, workers' compensation, affirmative action, and equal employment opportunity policies. Employees can also be informed of community issues and educational and training opportunities. Objectives of this type include

   Encouraging employee advancement.

   Demonstrating the organization's concern for workers' health and safety.

   Interpreting local, state, and national news as it applies to the company and the well-being of its employees.

3. *Employees' understanding of their roles in the organization*   can be improved (figure 11.7). An in-house publication can stress the importance of each worker's job in meeting company goals. Information about the eventual use of products illustrates the importance of everyone's part in the process. Internal publications should promote the idea that each employee is a salesperson for the company. They should pay attention to

   Building loyalty to the organization.

   Improving cooperation and coordination.

   Improving production and efficiency.

   Reducing expense and waste.

   Getting everyone involved in and aware of the importance of public relations.

Figure 11.6 Employee recognition

Eagle Recognition PROGRAM

7

Customer satisfaction. Profitability. Positioning for the Future.

These goals drive AT&T's Southern Region marketing people. And those who soared to success in those areas in the fourth quarter of 1985 recently received Eagle awards.

The Southern Region recognizes its top marketing performers with two major Eagle award programs. The Team awards go to the region's marketing teams who show the best results among any or all of those three measures of success. Each quarter three teams are selected for the awards. An annual team winner in each category will be chosen from the year's quarterly winners.

The Eagle Challenger Award is presented quarterly to individuals demonstrating excellent performance in any of the corporate values. Eight winners are usually named each quarter, one from each major segment of the marketing department.

Winners of the region's Eagles are those who meet criteria based on the AT&T Communications corporate value system. Components of the value system are:

•A focus on customer satisfaction. Service is not good until perceived so by the customer.

•Recognition of the importance of people. Employees are intelligent, creative and want a positive role in making the business successful.

•A drive toward profitability. Employees must be conscious of how their job impacts the bottom line.

•A bias for action with an orientation to goals, commitments and credibility.

The 'Challenger' Award
Fourth Quarter — Individual Winners

Primary Account Sales Center

Brenda Simms, assistant manager, Ft. Lauderdale, Fla.

Simms captured a fourth-quarter Eagle by helping to improve the profitability of the Ft. Lauderdale primary account sales center (PASC). She developed an occupational "salespertise" course for the inbound telemarketing sales specialists. The 30-day program enhanced the employees grasp of business functions and data gathering skills and improved their ability to overcome customer objections and employ data analysis to make proper recommendations for closing sales. Class participants agreed that the program had changed their approach to selling. The program's initial success has led to plans to offer it to the entire inbound sales force in 1986.

General Business Markets

Judy Vice, assistant staff manager, Atlanta, Ga.

Vice helped position AT&T for the future in her role as staff coordinator for the reduction of unidentified and unbilled WATS and 800 services usage. She was instrumental in the recovery of nearly $1.7 million in revenue since June 1985. The Eagle-worthy accomplishment was achieved through her active participation in joint meetings with AT&T and local exchange company (LEC) staffs that were held to identify and resolve problems related to AT&T services. She also established close working relationships with comptroller personnel at the LECs in order to monitor the progress in resolving these problems.

Select Account Sales Center

Ledger Davis, sales manager, Tucker, Ga.

As sales manager of the national telemarketing account center (NTAC), Davis won an Eagle for his efforts to use telemarketing to provide better account management for national accounts. Under his guidance, NTAC provided effective support to 22 national accounts, maintaining effective market presence with 12,000 customer locations. In addition, NTAC was able to expand its initial role of revenue base protection to include application, upgrade, growth and winback sales. Since becoming operational in March 1985, NTAC has provided $1.4 million in growth revenue, $376,000 in application revenue, $474,000 in winback revenue and $2.4 million in product migration revenue.

National Markets

Ralph Stanze, account executive/industry consultant/acting national account manager, Creve Coeur, Mo.

In the fourth quarter of 1985, Stanze led AT&T's national account team for General Dynamics to successful sales of AT&T MEGACOM℠ Service to replace SBS services at two customer divisions. The winbacks represent $1,495,100 in extra revenue for AT&T so far and the effort is paving the way to win back an additional $2 million in annual revenue. The team was not only able to provide the customer with improved network quality at lower cost but supplied the sold services within two months rather than the normal nine-month interval.

Consumer Markets

Charles Francis, manager, Irving, Texas

Francis was both inventor and project manager in the acquisition and subsequent conversion of an AT&T Information Systems consumer sales and service center in Parsippany, N.J., to an AT&T Communications consumer markets sales center (CMSC). In terms of customer satisfaction, the new Parsippany CMSC immediately improved the ability of AT&T customers to get sales assistance. In addition, the acquisition of the office provided an opportunity for 172 surplused AT&T-IS employees to continue employment with the company. Moreover, opening the center saved AT&T $5.5 million in close-down costs and saved the company even more in training expenses because of the transition of already-trained employees.

Majors West

Brenda Popovich, communications systems consultant, Springfield, Mo.

Popovich led a team effort to solve the mystery of a lot of unanswered calls at Bass Pro's inbound calling center. Popovich discovered a problem with unanswered call volumes during the customer's peak season by comparing AT&T network reports with the customer's reports for its switch. She realized that several thousand more calls were being sent than were actually received at Bass Pro's switch. After more investigation, the source of the problem was found. It centered around a misinterpretation of procedures in a standard industry technical reference that dealt with timing between local phone company switches and customers' automatic call distributors (ACDs). With the problem solved, Bass Pro expects to

improve its call completion rate by 15 percent during the peak season and gain $150,000 to $250,000 in revenue from its customers.

Majors East

Bill Hastings, account executive/industry consultant, Nashville, Tenn.

Hastings demonstrated outstanding performance and drive toward profitability on the Northern Telecom account. Competing against SBS, MCI and ITT, Hastings protected a multi-million dollar revenue base and secured opportunities for future competitive winbacks. In addition, his MEGACOM℠ Service sale to Northern Telecom will provide AT&T with an additional $515,328 in annual revenue. Finally, his close attention to Northern Telecom's needs will also help the customer save $147,728 in telecommunications costs during the coming year.

In the profitability category, the fourth quarter Team award was awarded to Don Evans' team in Tucker, Ga. From left to right are Evans, Pamela Earle, Maureen Caine, Dave MacFarlane, Dennis Duensing, Carol Zeisler, Frank Grizas, Tracy Lehmberg and Sharon Perry.

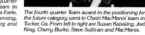

The fourth quarter Team award in the positioning for the future category went to Cheiri MacManis' team in Tucker, Ga. From left to right are Susan Kaissiing, Joel King, Cherry Burke, Steve Sullivan and MacManis.

Jim Donnelly's Exxon national account team in Houston won the fourth quarter Team award in the customer satisfaction category. From left to right are Stan Miller, Esther Viveros, Felix Dukes, Donnelly, Laura McGarth, Jim DiBona, Sara Grier and Dennis Carter.

'Eagle Challenge' Award
Fourth Quarter — Team Winners

Customer Satisfaction

Team Manager: Jim Donnelly, national account manager, Houston, Texas

Donnelly's national account team won its Eagle for its ability to satisfy the complex and demanding telecommunications needs of Exxon. The dedication to customer service resulted in the application of AT&T's new Software Defined Network (SDN) Service to Exxon's internal network. The account team also helped Exxon prepare its 10-year communications plan by outlining AT&T's plans in SDN, the Integrated Services Digital Network (ISDN), packet switching, satellite transmission and regulatory issues management. In addi-

tion, the team demonstrated other AT&T services of potential value to Exxon, including MEGACOM℠ and MEGACOM 800 services and video teleconferencing.

Positioning for the Future

Team Manager: Cheiri MacManus, sales manager, Tucker, Ga.

MacManus and the four members of her team were successful in positioning AT&T for the future with target customers in the financial industry. They established a comprehensive long-range plan whose goals are to position AT&T at the highest management levels of the accounts, to ensure that

AT&T is perceived as an integral part of the customers' long-range planning efforts, thwart competitive inroads and demonstrate AT&T's value-added capabilities. Initial customer reaction has been excellent.

Profitability

Team Manager: Don Evans, sales manager, Tucker, Ga.

Evans led his 10-person team to successful sales resulting in a 30 percent improvement in revenue results, $430,000 in winback revenue, a competitive sale worth $6 million in 1986 revenues and the execution of a co-marketing agreement with a shared tenant services provider worth $18 million to $20 million in annualized revenues by the end of 1987. The team also sold customers telemarketing training for 200 of their employees and sold the select account sales center's (SASC) first college/university resale application.

Figure 11.7 An in-house publication can enhance employees' understanding of their roles within the organization.

4. *Clarification of management policies* should consider the viewpoints of both management and employees. The workforce has changed. "Employees don't want trivial news. They're looking for what the company's business direction is, how it's performing financially," according to a study at Boston University's School of Management. The workforce feels management owes them that information.[33]

Employees must be accurately informed about business activities if management expects them to support its programs. In-house media can enhance employees' understanding by

Explaining policies and rules.

Building confidence in management.

Combatting rumors and misunderstandings.

An in-house medium can accomplish these objectives if it meets the needs of employees, conveys information that employees want to think and talk about, and is attractive and easy to read. (See mini-case 11.3.)

Mini-Case 11.3

Employee Communication at FedEx

FedEx uses an approach to employee communication that integrates face-to-face, management-to-employee communication with print and broadcast communication. This approach allows the company to target information according to employees' interests and needs for information and to reinforce critical information by using variations of available media.

FedEx managers are expected to keep an open two-way channel of communication, always identifying and sharing information of relevance to their employees. In addition, all U.S. managers are expected to have planned, organized meetings lasting a minimum of 20 minutes, with their direct reports at least every two weeks.

The company's internal media network includes several print publications, many of which are targeted by job function, allowing the company to channel information to specific audiences. In addition to print media, the company regularly produces several taped broadcast programs designed to address employee issues. Many of these programs are also targeted according to job function. FedEx also uses an internal television network (FXTV) to facilitate communications with its rapidly growing employee population. The FXTV network includes 1,200 satellite connections in the U.S., Canada, and Europe. The network allows the company to air live telecasts that include phone-in question and answer sessions between officers and employees on a variety of topics. Major announcements (such as the acquisition of The Flying Tigers) are made via FXTV to employees before the external media are informed.

In addition to its television and video productions, the company uses electronic media such as e-mail to reach its massive employee audience quickly. E-mail is used almost daily to inform and remind employees of critical information. It is also an effective means of communication in situations requiring rumor control.

Source: Sonja Whitemon, Media Relations, Federal Express.

Managing Internal Media   Who will be the audience for the medium is a decision that will shape all others. Do not try to be all things to all people. Do not try to rival *The New York Times*. An internal medium serves the needs of the organization that sponsors it. Successful in-house media are those that identify, acknowledge, and stick to a purpose: serving their audiences.

Identifying the audience may not be as simple as it seems. Although the primary audience is usually limited to people inside the organization, these people can often be divided into several groups. A large petrochemical company employs blue-collar workers who each belong to one of several unions. It also hires engineers and research scientists with professional affiliations, as well as white-collar middle management and clerical personnel. Each group has different interests and needs different information.

When only one medium is available, you should identify a primary audience and treat the other groups as secondary, serving them through special columns or stories. Secondary audiences might also include suppliers, distributors, other company plants or divisions, competitors, and the surrounding community. Because many of these external secondary audiences will read or see your

medium even if you do not want them to, the contents should reflect good judgment. The medium must address issues of substance if it is to have credibility.
This is not the place, however, to air dirty laundry that will embarrass the organization and its employees. Some large companies have begun using media aimed
at such outside groups as the community, suppliers, and industry.

What type of publication does your organization need? Once the primary
and secondary audiences are identified, decide what kind of publication or other
medium will best meet their needs: a newsletter, a tabloid newspaper, a magazine,
a home page, or some other format. Sometimes audience needs change. Frequency of publication and methods of distribution should also be decided in advance and tailored to the requirements of the primary audience. Most in-house
publications are published monthly, but some appear quarterly or even weekly.
The easiest, cheapest, and simplest method of distribution is to make copies available for pickup around work areas. To get wider distribution, some organizations
hand publications directly to employees, use in-house mail, or send them to employees' homes. All of these matters are interdependent. The format (size and
shape) of the medium may limit the possibilities for distribution.

Other considerations in determining the medium are budget and audience
needs. Once a budget for the medium is established, information about audience
needs must be gathered. Interviews and questionnaires can tell a great deal about
content, frequency, and distribution needs. To help select a format, many companies ask employee panels to review sample publications from other organizations.
The panel can also evaluate data obtained through the interviews and questionnaires. The results of such planning efforts should be recorded and saved to help
plan future issues and evaluate past ones.

Starting Internal Media   Producing an internal medium takes organization and
coordination. It must appear at scheduled regular intervals, and such consistency
requires budget and staff. Putting out a medium on a shoestring may be worse
than doing nothing at all. A medium that cannot be properly maintained creates
negative attitudes by building expectations it cannot fulfill. Therefore, organizing
the details of production is important to success.

What makes news? The content of an internal medium will vary from one
organization to another. Some employees will not read certain items, and even
more do not have time to read anything at all. Extraneous topics, even when educational, are not proper for an in-house publication. Topics appropriate to your organization will attract the interest of even the busiest executive or blue-collar
worker. These topics should form the backbone of your medium.

News is everywhere. Any topic that concerns what people do, feel, or
think is interesting. Select topics that grow out of the activities within the organization. Potentially, every job, group, program, and employee has news value.
To identify possible stories, the editor or writer should consider the topic from
the intended reader's point of view. Include items that will interest many groups
within the organization. You should consider the needs of your primary audience first, but you may expand the audience by publishing items of interest to
others as well. Look for stories that inform and entertain. No one will attend to

everything, but almost everyone will see something. A rule of thumb for an appropriate mix is

50 percent information about the organization—local, national, and international

20 percent employee information—benefits, quality of working life, and so on

20 percent relevant noncompany information—competitors, community, and the like

10 percent small talk and personals

Remember, company information must satisfy the needs of the employees, not just those of management. If the publication is to serve the goals of the sponsor organization, readership or viewership is essential. Table 11.2 shows topics of interest to employees, ranked in order of importance, as determined by an IABC survey. An increasing employee concern for job security is evident in the study's top-ranked item, "organizational plans for the future." The workers' wishes are clear: They want to know where the organization is headed, what its plans are for getting there, and what that means to them.[34]

Set and maintain strict policies about what will be published and how space will be allotted. The following criteria can help you evaluate a topic's newsworthiness:

1. *Timeliness* Is the topic timely enough to interest most of the readers?

2. *Scope* Does it affect enough people directly or indirectly?

TABLE 11.2 Subject of Interest to Employees

Rank	Subject	Scale (1–10)
1	Organizational plans for the future	8
2	Job advancement opportunities	7
3	Job-related "how-to" information	7
4	Productivity improvement	6
5	Personnel policies and practices	6
6	How we're doing vs. the competition	6
7	How my job fits into the organization	6
8	How external events affect my job	5
9	How profits are used	5
10	Financial results	4
11	Advertising and promotional plans	4
12	Operations outside of my department or division	4
13	Organizational stand on current issues	4
14	Personnel changes and promotions	4
15	Organizational community involvement	4
16	Human interest stories about other employees	2
17	Personal news (birthdays, anniversaries, etc.)	2

Source: IABC Study, quoted in Allen Center and Patrick Jackson, *Public Relations Practices*, 5th ed. (Englewood Cliffs, N.J.: Longman, Inc., 1995): 39.

3. *Noteworthiness*   Does the topic involve something or someone important or well known?

4. *Human interest*   Does it deal with matters vital to the interests of the readers or the people involved?

A tickler file is used by newspaper editors to "tickle the memory" about future news stories. The editor of an internal publication can also use this method by starting a futures book or file with headings such as "use next issue," "if space available," and "short fillers." Updating the file yields ready material for each issue.

Writing for Internal Media   Most internal media use two types of articles: news stories and human interest features. They serve different purposes, but both are important. News stories concentrate on information about market conditions, safety, company-sponsored events, current events that affect organizational policy, and other happenings. Articles that focus on people and their lives are called *feature* or *human interest* pieces. A balance between these two types should be determined on the basis of reader feedback. Both, however, must meet the criterion of general interest.

Internal media are not daily metropolitan newspapers; their writers should not try to be investigative reporters. Objectivity is an important goal, but in-house media should have a more personal tone than public newspapers or magazines. They should reflect a sense of closeness and common interest that says to the reader, "We're all in this together." One writer says an in-house publication "should look and read like . . . a letter from home . . . a pat on the back . . . a friendly handshake." Most important, the tone of in-house publications must never be condescending or frivolous.

Staffing Internal Media   All editors know that producing a good publication requires more than sitting in an office and waiting for stories to come in. A system is needed for gathering information and preparing it for timely publication. The editor is someone who does more than write and rewrite stories: Editors of internal publications are managers in the best sense. Managing is generally defined as "getting things done through other people," and the editor's task includes getting others to provide information and write stories for the medium. Even when an editor has a paid staff, it will never be large enough to cover all the sources of information in the organization, nor would a publication written entirely by the public relations staff always be desirable. Readers of house organs are often more interested in articles written by their co-workers. Thus, there are good reasons to develop an external network to provide information and articles.

Enlisting auxiliary writers is not difficult. The only reward is a byline, but even that is a powerful inducement for many people. Others will provide information and news tips just to help out. Following are some ways to organize the news-gathering process:

1. *A "beat" system*   The organization can be divided into territories and a reporter assigned to cover each. This is an excellent system if enough people are willing to serve as reporters. One way to recruit

correspondents is to identify the people in each area who have been there longest. Ask them whether they will help you. Then ask their supervisors if they can be reporters for the house publication. This support is valuable motivation. After all the reporters are selected, invite them to participate in a news clinic on company time.

2. *A telephone network* If you cannot recruit enough reporters, people willing to phone in information can be used. You should stay in constant touch with every link in this network even if there is no news. Regular conversations may turn up information that the contact did not realize was newsworthy.

3. *News request forms* Memos or notices asking for information are seldom effective. Most people do not understand what news means. They seldom think what is happening to them is important. A news request form that asks for information about promotions, awards, achievements, or other specific topics, however, can produce excellent articles.

A house publication needs columnists, feature writers, photographers, and artists. The potential to pay for these skills depends on the funds available. Recognition, however, can often substitute for pay. Printing the names of all who contribute to an issue is one way to recognize those who do not receive bylines.

Controlling Internal Media Every medium should periodically evaluate its progress toward its objectives. Purpose, content, and frequency of publication should all be examined in terms of the needs of the target audience. The panel that originally identified the target audience can be used again to evaluate progress. Surveys and questionnaires also yield useful information about how well a medium fulfills expectations. National magazines have found that even simple surveys can provide excellent insight into readers' interests. To pretest the potential readership of planned articles, for example, an editor can prepare a questionnaire that lists various headlines and asks a sample of the intended audience which articles they would read. The feedback indicates the probable success of certain stories.

Most organizations prepare publications on miscellaneous topics at irregular intervals. Forms range from one-sheet leaflets to books by professional writers. Responsibility for these publications often rests with the personnel department, but other areas may also become involved because of legal requirements, government regulations, or company policy. These publications generally can be divided into three categories, according to purpose:

Occasional and Special Media

1. *Orientation literature* indoctrinates new members of an organization. It can help a new employee get off to a good start by setting forth the ground rules. Organizational goals and objectives are often included to give a sense of where the company is going and the employee's role in achieving those objectives.

2. *Reference material* is designed to be kept for future use. Because of the nature of reference publications, it is unlikely that anyone will ever read

them from cover to cover, and they must therefore give fast and easy answers. This information sometimes changes; thus, the publications should be designed so that supplements or other materials can be added later. Reference materials deal with subjects like benefits, insurance, and recreation programs.

3. *Position or special-topic publications* are put out only once. They deal with specific subjects or occasions the organization feels it should discuss. The most frequently treated subjects include the free enterprise system, charitable and social commitments, history, awards, and scientific or technological developments. Occasional publications have more impact than regularly scheduled newsletters, and they allow an organization to convey specific messages. The requirements of credibility and interest that apply to newsletters must be followed if special-topic publications are to present their messages effectively.

Leaflets, Inserts, and Enclosures Inexpensive publications that may be read and thrown away are often printed on single sheets that can be folded to produce any of several formats. Leaflets or handbills printed on a laser printer and duplicated on a copying machine are inexpensive and fast to prepare. With a little more effort, single-sheet publications can be folded into brochures for display on information racks, in-house distribution, or direct mail. Many organizations use them as inserts in pay envelopes. Credit card companies and utilities use inserts as an effective and inexpensive means of communicating with their customers.

Booklets and Manuals Because of their expense, booklets and manuals are made to be read and saved for reference. Their greatest shortcoming is that they can be hard to read and use if not designed properly. Employee orientation manuals or insurance plan booklets need indexes, and their information can be more accessible if they incorporate tabs or color-coded pages. No matter how much information a book contains, employees will remain uninformed unless they can locate what they need when they need it.

Booklets and manuals must be written with employees' needs in mind. Such publications will be useless if management allows them to be written in technical language or the jargon of insurance, law, accounting, or finance. The reading levels and interests of the intended audience must be considered before copy is prepared for a booklet or manual. Too often, publications meet the regulations of insurance companies or government agencies rather than the needs of employees. Booklets and manuals can be used successfully to do the following:

1. Orient new employees.

2. Explain safety regulations as they comply with Occupational Safety and Health Administration standards.

3. Explain the benefit plan and its value to employees.

4. Explain company policies and their compliance with government regulations.

5. Explain the costs and benefits of the organization's insurance package.

6. Explain the company retirement plan and its requirements.

7. Give information helpful to the employees in the performance of their jobs.

8. Give information about social or community issues.

9. Explain organizational compliance with environmental standards.

Printed Speeches and Position Papers   Speeches and position papers are sometimes distributed as publications. Organization officials frequently speak to professional, community, or other groups on topics of interest to employees. It may be useful to print such addresses for distribution within the organization since copies have usually been made available to news media anyway.

Reprints of magazine articles of concern to the organization and its employees are often available at low cost. Magazine reprints have the advantage of outside credibility. If articles from general interest magazines are used, their readability will probably make them suitable for wide distribution. If articles are drawn from more technical or professional publications, however, writing style may limit their use.

Message Displays

A growing body of laws and regulations require that notices be posted where employees can see them, and many organizations find this a quick, inexpensive way to reach large numbers of people. Message displays include bulletin boards, posters, billboards, information racks, and exhibits.

Bulletin Boards   Bulletin boards display messages in established locations with minimum effort and expense. The board remains a much used and effective means of communication within organizations. It often fulfills a supplementary or follow-up function because notices that have been mailed or handed to employees can also be posted as reminders. Details of announcements previously made in meetings or in the internal publication can be posted for those who wish more information. The bulletin board is an appropriate location for information that has value but does not warrant publication, and of course, the law requires that certain information be posted on bulletin boards.

Bulletin boards are fast and effective when used and maintained properly. To ensure credibility and readability, they must be carefully planned and kept current.

Location is a primary consideration. No matter how professionally written and designed bulletin board information may be, if hidden in a corner, it will not be read. Management must pick locations convenient for most of those who should read the bulletin board, rather than for the manager charged with keeping it current. Too many bulletin boards are outside supervisors' offices.

Bulletin boards should be placed in or near areas of heavy traffic. As many employees as possible should pass by the message. The boards should be at eye level, where the light is good and where employees can stop and read without blocking traffic. Bulletin boards should never be placed where they could present safety hazards.

Neatness will improve readability and increase readership. Order and arrangement invite reading. If a board becomes cluttered, even with important notices, it will no longer communicate its messages. Someone should check each board regularly to be sure it has not become overloaded and disorganized. Boards containing information on more than one topic should be organized so that all messages on a given subject are together. When possible, a separate board for each topic is desirable.

Timeliness is a key to credibility in bulletin boards. Out-of-date notices kill interest. If an organization's bulletin boards always have current information, employees will regularly check their contents. Constant attention is required to post up-to-date material and take down old messages. The wear-out potential of a message must also be considered. Even if content is still current, the notice itself should be changed periodically. Once employees have read a notice, they are likely to skip over it when next checking the board. If the information is repackaged, it will again attract notice. This method can keep employees alert to long-term issues.

Interest of the intended readers can be assured if management selects messages that meet their needs. Like any other medium, posted items should reflect the interests of the targeted audience. Personal items, advertisements, and entertaining odds and ends should be kept to a minimum. The presence of nonofficial information can create a relaxed atmosphere, but an overabundance of nonessential items destroys credibility.

Responsibility for the upkeep of each bulletin board should be delegated to one person. Bulletin boards are important media and should not be assigned to a secretary or clerk. Decisions about what information should be posted and how it will be conveyed are the job of the public relations staff.

Posters and Billboards Like bulletin boards, posters and billboards offer fast, effective communication. They are most appropriately used to emphasize ideas; they are not intended for careful reading or study. Posters and billboards convey messages that can be grasped quickly; details can be published in other media. Posters and billboards should be in high-traffic areas where most employees can see them easily. Here again, wear-out potential is a consideration. Messages should be changed or revised periodically.

Information Racks You can combine the effects of posters, bulletin boards, brochures, and booklets by using an information rack. It should incorporate a poster to draw attention and invite the reader to take the brochures or booklets displayed. (Figure 11.8 shows an example of informational materials that might be found in racks or displays.) Racks provide information that cannot be handled in short messages. Because the materials are selected by readers without pressure from management, interest is likely to be higher. The economic advantage of information racks is that only interested employees are likely to take material.

Information racks work best in places where employees can look over the material in a leisurely way; lunchrooms, break areas, waiting rooms, and dressing areas are good locations. Empty information racks suggest that management is uninterested, so regular maintenance is needed.

Exhibits and Displays Exhibits and displays rely primarily on visual messages. Their effectiveness lies in showing a sample or model of what is being discussed.

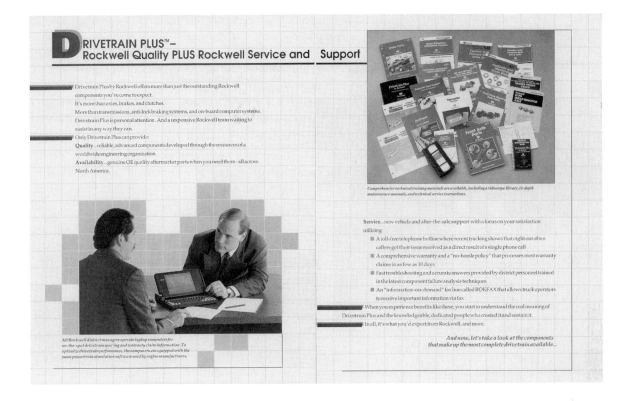

Figure 11.8 Informational materials prepared for corporate display

Displays and information provided at trade shows and other exhibits are often important ways to reach a target audience.

Many organizations recognize the value of exhibits and displays at industrial meetings or in sales-related contexts, but they are equally valuable in employee communication. Exhibits and displays can show how production facilities work, display products, honor award recipients, or depict the history of the organization.

Electronic Media   New technology has spawned at least three major electronic approaches to employee communication. Electronic mail, computer home pages, and internal video are fast becoming the media of choice among employees.

E-mail   Because of its immediacy, ease of distribution, and virtual lack of added cost, electronic mail has become a major employee communication tool. It is even relatively inexpensive for organizations that have facilities spread throughout the world.

Home Pages   A rapidly growing controlled medium is the computer home page. With graphic and sound capability, coupled with the advantages of e-mail, this medium may soon replace the company newsletter as the employee communication tool of choice (see figure 11.9).

Internal Video   For the last 20 years larger companies, especially those encompassing several distant locations, have turned to internal video to keep employees informed about organizational matters (see figure 11.10). Other media, such as audio magazines as shown in figure 11.11, are also used.

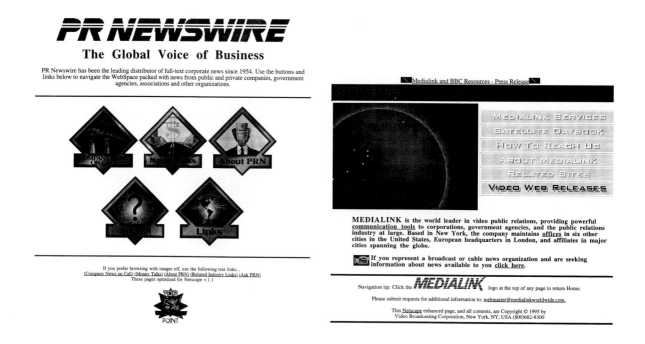

Figure 11.9   Home pages can provide useful communication links to employees as well as others.

Figure 11.10 Internal video is popular in large corporate settings where employees are spread out widely in the country, or even globally.

Figure 11.11 FedEx audio magazine is a specialized communication tool.

Summary

Employee communication is a large and complex aspect of public relations practice. Many different topics and issues confront practitioners working in this area. Not surprisingly, it is the most rapidly growing segment of the public relations field in both numbers and perceived importance. In this chapter, we discussed the importance of keeping employees informed, creating the proper organizational climate to facilitate proper communication, establishing communication policy, and building employee communication programs. We also considered the special issues of employer communication with a unionized work force and communication of employee benefits. Finally, we detailed production of employee newsletters and other media. Armed with this knowledge and these tools, public relations practitioners can make great contributions to their organizations' success.

The Beer Barrel Layoff

By Robert Taylor
*Professor of Journalism and
Mass Communications
University of
Wisconsin–Madison
Madison, Wisconsin*

Case Study

The Madison Cooperage Company, founded in 1861, one of the town's oldest firms, is the current employer of 1,200 people who "make the best kegs in the world," according to its nationally advertised slogan.

Having weathered the change from wooden to aluminum beer kegs, the firm now has come upon hard times because of the swing from wood to steel and plastic in vats and kegs for wine making.

Company president Harry R. Jones made the difficult decision to eliminate the second shift and lay off 500 people at the end of this month.

Harold Storm, president of Amalgamated Coopers Union Local 5, after pledging his secrecy, has been informed and has given the company president this statement and permission to release it if the company so desires:

> This is tough on our workers, but I've been assured by President Jones that every effort has been made to avoid it, and every effort is being made to abide by the seniority specified in our contract; that the severance pay provided in the contract will be paid in a lump sum to each employee; that hire-backs will be made strictly in seniority fashion; and that workers hired back won't have to refund severance payments but will begin accumulating severance pay time when hired. This last is not in the contract and indicates, I think, that the company's heart's in the right place.

While talking the situation over with Storm, Jones makes the following points:

> Madison Cooperage is a good and responsible employer and corporate citizen of Madison and, as a unique sort of business these days, has attracted a lot of national attention.
>
> We love our workers. They're mostly good and devoted, and some of them have been with us 50 years. My grandfather, Oscar Jones, who started this company, hired some of their fathers—old-world artisans.
>
> It's hell that this is coming at this time of year.
>
> Although we hate to lose some of our older workers, we are going to reduce our retirement age from 65 to 60, for those who want to leave, and provide those 60 and over the same retirement pay that they would get if they were 65 on the day they leave.
>
> Those on the second shift who have more seniority than those on the first will be able to bump (take the jobs of) people of lesser seniority on the first shift. Thus, some of those we have to let go may come from the first shift—though that's mostly made up of people of higher seniority.
>
> We are providing full severance pay—one week at present pay for every year served— to all those who are let go, except the ones who take early retirement.
>
> My guess is that of the 500 jobs we have to cut, about 50 may be made up by either regular retirement or early retirement. Ten of the 500 jobs are supervisory night foremen, but some of them also may take the early retirement.
>
> I will be in my office during all of next week, and those who receive notices are welcome to make appointments to see me if they have some question about the layoff. They should remember, however, that we must do this strictly by seniority since that is what their union contract demands.

This will be the first time since President Roosevelt brought back beer that we won't have a night shift at the plant—our first big layoff, though we have been dropping in employment since our high of 2,000 in 1945 when the aluminum keg came into the beer business. We have tried to diversify some in our plant—butter vats, flowerpots, and things like that—but they make up only 10 percent of our business today. We still have about 5 percent in beer, cider, and vinegar kegs, but 85 percent of our business is with the wineries—and that's been declining now for 10 years.

Madison Cooperage has a once-a-month employee newsletter distributed to employees, which has traditionally contained an abundance of bowling scores and birth announcements.

Questions

1. What is the best strategy for informing employees about the layoff?
2. What information should be provided to employees and the public?
3. Within the ranks of current employees, are there different audiences that must be communicated with? What is the basic message that should be communicated to each group?
4. What ongoing communication efforts would you recommend implementing for remaining employees?

Notes

1. Quoted in Larry Waltman, "Organizational Survival: Connecting with the New American Values," *Government Communications* (January/February 1995): 14.

2. James Grunig, ed., *Excellence in Public Relations and Communication Management* (Hillsdale, N.J.: Lawrence Erlbaum Associates, 1992), 16–17.

3. Ibid., 17.

4. R. Tagiuri and G. H. Litwin, eds., *Organizational Climate: Explorations of a Concept* (Boston: Harvard University Press, 1968), 27.

5. J. Campbell, M. D. Dunnette, E. E. Lawler, and K. E. Weick, *Managerial Behavior, Performance, and Effectiveness* (New York: McGraw-Hill, 1970), 390.

6. D. R. Hampton, C. E. Summer, and R. A. Webber, *Organizational Behavior and the Practice of Management,* 2nd ed. (Glenview, Ill.: Scott, Foresman, 1973), 520.

7. L. G. Hrebiniak, *Complex Organizations* (St. Paul: West Publishing, 1978), 273.

8. Grunig, *Excellence in Public Relations and Communication Management,* 565.

9. William Whyte, "Is Anybody Listening?" *Fortune* (June 1951): 41.

10. James Grunig, "Some Consistent Types of Employee Publics," *Public Relations Review* (Winter 1975): 35.

11. Quoted in "Rapid Change Increases Communication Need," *Communication World* (May 1983): 8.

12. Quoted in Bill Hunter, "PR '84: Fourteen Experts Tell What's Ahead," *Communication World* (January 1984): 14.

13. "How Companies Are Getting Their Message Across to Labor," *Business Week* (24 September 1984): 58–60.

14. This discussion is based on Norman B. Sigband, "What's Happening to Employee Commitment?" *Personnel Journal* (February 1974): 133–135.

15. Bill Cantor, ed., *Experts in Action,* 2nd ed. (New York: Longman, Inc., 1989), 74–75.

16. Louis C. Williams, "What 50 Presidents and Chief Executive Officers Think About Employee Communication," *Journal of Organizational Communication* (Fall 1978): 7–10.

17. Paul Keckley, "The Increasing Importance of Employee Relations," *Public Relations Review* (Fall 1977): 70–76.

18. Williams, "What 50 Presidents Think," 8.

19. James M. Lahiff and John D. Hatfield, "The Winds of Change and Managerial Communication Practices," *Journal of Business Communication* (Summer 1978), 19–28.

20. "Companies Fail to Communicate Change, Survey Shows," *Public Relations Journal* (October/November 1994): 10.

21. Williams, "What 50 Presidents Think," 9.

22. Richard Nemec, "Internal Communications—A Scary Science," *Public Relations Journal* (December 1973): 28.

23. Donal P. Crane, *Personnel: The Management of Human Resources,* 2nd ed. (Belmont, Calif.: Wadsworth, 1979), 79.

24. Charles J. Coleman, *Personnel: An Open Systems Approach* (Cambridge, Mass: Winthrop Publishers, 1979), 392.

25. Quoted in Crane, *Personnel,* 80.

26. Harold H. Marquis, *The Changing Corporate Image* (New York: American Management Association, 1970), 141.

27. Abe H. Raskin, "Double Standard or Double-Talk?" in *Business and the Media,* C. E. Aronoff, ed. (Santa Monica, Calif.: Goodyear, 1979), 252.

28. "The Payoff on Ethics," *Forbes* (17 November 1986): 8.

29. Based on a portion of "How Companies Are Getting Their Messages Across to Labor," 58–60.

30. Raskin, "Double Standard," 251.

31. Richard C. Huseman and John D. Hatfield, "Communicating Employee Benefits: Directions for Future Research," *The Journal of Business Communication* (Winter 1978): 3.

32. "New Benefits for New Lifestyles," *Business Week* (11 February 1980): 112.

33. Mary Young and James E. Post, "Managing to Communicate, Communicating to Manage," *Journal of Management Advocacy Communication* (July/August 1995): 99.

34. Cantor, *Experts in Action,* 74–75.

CHAPTER 12

Community Relations

Preview

An organization's community relations may be affected by such diverse factors as its recruitment methods, employee relations, waste disposal, energy use, design and maintenance of buildings and grounds, marketing and advertising strategies, and corporate philanthropy.

The quality of an organization's employees, the cooperativeness of citizens and governmental agencies, the patronage of community members, the ability to attract financial support—indeed, the success or failure of an organization may depend on the effectiveness of its community relations.

Special audiences for community relations include women, nonreaders, and minority groups.

Today, no matter how large, small, or important an institution may be, it can be undermined if its community relations are haphazard.

—Wilbur J. Peak

I n an age when marketing, technology, resource acquisition, and management are increasingly international in scope and the federal government is the most conspicuous aspect of many organizations' operating environments, concern for community seems almost anachronistic. Indeed, certain sociologists and political scientists have maintained that our communities are dissolving in the face of increased mobility and communication.

The community cannot yet be declared dead, though; some strange things have begun to occur. Neighbors are banding together on small-scale issues like schools, security, and community services. Back-to-the-city movements are repopulating many metropolitan areas; downtown businesses are reviving after years of inactivity; people are interested in genealogical and community roots. Strong chauvinistic pride in cities and communities is widespread. Slogans modeled after the "I love New York" campaign are commonplace, and the citizens of Buffalo, Cleveland, and Terre Haute rush to the defense of their much-maligned hometowns.

The lesson for organizations in this trend is simple: Regional, national, and international concerns may preoccupy you, but do not forget the folks next door. In the past, constructive community relations programs were characterized by phrases like "corporate citizenship" or "good neighbor." These terms still apply, but they oversimplify today's complex relationships between organizations and their communities.

The urban problems that were recognized as matters of public concern in the 1960s cast **community relations** in a new light and forced institutions to pay more attention to their relationships with surrounding communities. Throughout the last three decades, equal employment opportunity and training, employment of the disadvantaged, stimulation of minority business enterprises, elimination of substandard housing, and many other issues have caused companies and other organizations to become more involved in community activities.

Community relations has long been a business priority. Morrell Heald, in a history of the social responsibility of American business, points out that since the beginning of this century,

> American businessmen fully shared the social concerns and preoccupations of their fellow citizens. Although they have often been depicted—indeed caricatured—as single-minded pursuers of profit, the facts are quite otherwise. The nature of their activities often brought them into close contact with the harsher aspects of the life of a rapidly industrializing society. Like others, they were frequently troubled by the conditions they saw; and, also like others, they numbered in their ranks men who contributed both their ideas and their questions to redress social imbalance and disorganization. . . .
>
> From the outset, self-interest combined with idealism to foster sensitivity to social conditions on the part of the business community.[1]

Often organizations have viewed community relations as an extension of employee relations, tying programs together. Employees who are treated well represent their organization favorably through volunteer activities and informal communication. Employee volunteer activities have become a major community relations tool in the last decade as large corporations such as Federal Express even provide some compensation time for employee volunteer efforts in the community. (See public relations spotlight 12.1.)

Public Relations Spotlight 12.1

Employee
Volunteerism: A
Complement to
Corporate Philanthropy

Throughout our nation's history, a willingness to help those in need has defined "America" to the rest of the world. The spirt of volunteerism continues to flourish today, as evidenced by a recent Gallup poll indicating that nearly half of all Americans spend about five hours volunteering each week. In total, all that time and energy is worth more than $150 billion every year.

Voluntary efforts on the part of any business organization will win that institution favorable media coverage. Companies will be pleased to grant media interviews about their volunteer efforts and the positive, far-reaching effects associated with them.

In addition, a strong history of employee volunteerism speaks well to a company's shareholders. Stockholders who are satisfied with a company's service to the community are more likely to think favorably about the organization and continue to invest in its future performance. Similarly, potential investors are impressed by a business's commitment to society, and almost nothing is a more accurate indication of these commitments than an active volunteer force.

Volunteer programs and projects also have the ability to unite employees by focusing them toward a common goal, by bringing them together in a more relaxed setting, and by providing an environment conducive to the development of friendships outside the workplace.

Improved employee relations, as well as improved relations with stakeholders, the media, and special interest groups, are not the only auxiliary benefits a company may enjoy as a result of its volunteer programs. As any volunteer will explain, the real rewards of volunteering stem from the knowledge that someone else has benefited from your efforts.

Employee-volunteer programs are becoming increasingly common in corporations; more than 1,000 companies currently have employee-volunteer programs in place. Like any other aspect of a business, such a program must be managed effectively to prove successful.

Ideally, one employee should be responsible for overseeing and coordinating the program. This volunteer coordinator must carefully match the interests and talents of the volunteers to the needs and requirements of the nonprofit entities.

Once the company has successfully matched its volunteers with appropriate organizations, it must continue to stimulate employee interest in the program through newsletters, bulletin board displays, seminars, and other continual reminders. Luncheon meetings will encourage volunteers from various departments to share their experiences with one another and may serve to create informal volunteer networks to reinforce recruiting through word of mouth. Constant recruitment of new volunteers is vital to the success of any employee-volunteer program and will help prevent employee burnout.

The company must not forget to recognize its employee-volunteers, whether by giving extra vacation days, certificates of appreciation, or awards. In some businesses, extra monetary compensation is offered as a thank-you for outstanding volunteer work. A company must never take its volunteers for granted; volunteerism is not part of employees' job descriptions but a service provided in addition to regular duties.

If managed properly, employee-volunteer programs constitute a "win-win-win" situation for all involved: Nonprofit organizations, companies, and company employees all benefit in numerous ways.

Source: Elizabeth R. Bunta, "Employee Volunteerism: A Complement to Corporate Philanthropy," *Journal of Corporate Public Relations,* vol. 3. (1992–93): 38. The *Journal of Corporate Public Relations* is a journal of theory and practice edited and published annually by graduate students in the Department of Integrated Marketing Communications in the Medill School of Northwestern University. Courtesy subscriptions are available from Professor Clarke L. Caywood, Ph.D., 1908 Sheridan Road, Evanston, Ill. 60208 or jcpr@nuw.edu.

Most organizations in the 1990s understand that the community relations effort must be much more organized and proactive. The key to any effective community relations program is positive, socially responsible **action** to help the community on behalf of the organization. While the organization must be on guard against negative acts and must also work to maintain existing relationships, proactive, positive actions are crucial to giving the organization the desired good-citizen image.

An appropriate basis for institutional efforts toward good community relations is derived from an understanding of the nature of a community. William Gilbert defines the word "community" as

> a place of interacting social institutions which produce in the residents an attitude and practice of interdependence, cooperation, collaboration and unification . . . a web of social structures all closely interrelated.[2]

In this chapter, we will first discuss the complex relationships between organizations and their communities before considering the process and practice of community relations. We will also address several subjects generally associated with community relations, including corporate philanthropy, local government relations, business and the arts, and business and education.

An Interdependent Relationship

Effective community relations depends on a recognition of the interdependence of institutions. Management helps establish social balance when it recognizes the many ways organizations can have impact on their local communities and the extent of reciprocal dependence.

Organizations of all types practice community relations. Schools, churches, hospitals, museums, and groups like the Red Cross and the Boy Scouts depend on community relations the way businesses depend on marketing—as the primary means for attracting "customers." Prisons, military bases, and universities (where "town versus gown" conflicts are common) must strive for community acceptance. Except for corporate philanthropy, however, the process of community relations is the same whether or not the organization seeks financial profit. Every community has a vital stake in the economic health and prosperity of its institutions; every organization has a vital stake in the health and prosperity of the community it inhabits. Quite naturally, therefore, organizations and their communities develop mutual interest in each other's successful and effective operation. At this level, the connection between institutional interest and public interest is most clear.

At the very least, an organization expects the community to provide adequate municipal services, fair taxation, good living conditions for employees, a good labor supply, and a reasonable degree of support for the company and its products. In addition to employment, wages, and taxes, communities expect from their institutions attractive appearance, support of community institutions, economic stability, and a focus for hometown pride.

Good community relations aids in securing what the organization needs from the community and in providing what the community expects. Moreover, it helps to protect organizational investments, increase sales of products and stock, improve the general operating climate, and reduce costs of dealing with government agencies. Positive community relations can affect worker productivity when an organization sponsors community health and education programs. Also, favorable community attitudes may influence worker attitudes toward the organization. The best community relations programs are those that flow naturally from organizational resources. Woodward Governor in Fort Collins, Colorado, has beautifully landscaped acreage around its plant. The company decided to make landscaping its community relations effort and has provided landscaping when new additions were made to the city hospital, to new municipal buildings, and to various other civic projects.

Community Relations is a growing specialty area of Public Relations. See public relations spotlight 12.2 for the latest survey by Boston College's Center for Corporate Community Relations.

The clarity of the mutual interest of organizations and their communities, however, does not imply that community relations can be practiced without careful planning and execution. Effective community relations does not just happen, nor

The Community Relations Process

Public Relations Spotlight 12.2

Community Relations: A Growing Area

In an initial survey in 1987, The Center for Corporate Community Relations at Boston College found that only 16 percent of respondents worked full time in a separate community relations department. However, in the latest survey in 1995, researchers found the number had increased to 22.3 percent. In addition, 65 percent of the respondents who considered themselves to be in community relations work full time.

Among the highlights of the survey were these:

- In spite of downsizing, there has been only a slight decline in the numbers of fulltime CR professionals, indicating that CR remains a priority for corporations.
- Although women make up about two-thirds of CR professionals, the trend over the past eight years toward feminization of the industry has leveled off.
- More CR professionals, 22.3 percent, are working in community affairs departments, suggesting that CR is establishing a presence in the corporate environment.
- CR professionals continue to devote the largest amount of their time, 30 percent, to contributions activities.
- Salaries for CR professionals increased to an estimated mean of $63,490, but when adjustments were made for inflation, men received an increase in purchasing power of $2,966, while women experienced a decline of $1,240.
- Indices of job satisfaction show improvement and are high.

Source: The Center for Corporate Community Relations at Boston College, *1995 Profile of the Community Relations Profession.* For further information about the center and this report, contact Dr. Edmund Burke, Director, The Center for Corporate Community Relations at Boston College, Chestnut Hill, Mass. 02167-3835.

Mini-Case 12.1

Norton Simon Puts Action in Community Relations

Norton Simon Inc.'s commitment to community relations goes beyond good words, high ideals, and moral pressure. Based on performance in four areas of community involvement, company managers' bonuses can be increased by as much as 20 percent.

The four areas of the company's concern are equal employment opportunities, encouragement of minority businesses, charitable contributions, and involvement of managers in community organizations. Norton Simon's managers are assessed on performance in these areas by their immediate supervisors as part of their normal performance appraisals. The company regards corporate citizenship as a central plank in its strategic plan. By doing this, the company provides an example of corporation-wide commitment to community relations backed by its resources and managerial experience.

---

is it an inevitable by-product of a well-run, civic-minded organization. In effect, community relations must be built into the structure and culture of an organization, as is illustrated in mini-case 12.1. Community relations is not based on pure altruism; it looks to the organization's self-interest. W. J. Peak offers the best definition of community relations we have seen:

> Community relations, as a public relations function, is an institution's planned, active, and continuing participation with and within a community to maintain and enhance its environment to the benefit of both the institution and the community.[3]

The community relations process embraces all aspects of an institution. In some ways, good community relations simply means good performance. A company that offers poor products and unsatisfactory service is unlikely to benefit from positive community relations. Prisons that allow their inmates to escape rarely enjoy their neighbors' support. Beyond this, Robert Ross explains, "Good community relations consists of recognizing and fulfilling the organization's responsibilities in and to the communities in which it operates."[4]

Recruitment, employee relations, production processes, marketing and advertising strategies, design of the organization's building and facilities, and many other organizational activities affect community relations. George Sawyer maintains that even the internal standards of the organization have a bearing on its community relations:

> A community becomes to a large extent an expression of the values, aspirations and achievements of its businesses. Thus, the internal standards a corporation sets for itself and for the members of its organization have an influence that carries down through the work force and out into the community.[5]

Arguably, community relations is an organizational attitude or state of mind, rather than any specific process or practice.

Some organizations publish special Community Relations Reports to describe their activities to the public.

EDUCATING OUR YOUTH

Quality education is fundamental to the growth of any community. As a corporate citizen, we play a major role in assisting our educational institutions. We are dedicated to providing a wide range of educational programs for our youth to familiarize them with MLGW operations, facilities and services. We also provide educational opportunities for career advancement.

Our Public Education Program (PEP) provides speakers and guided tours of MLGW facilities. Employees also visit schools as speakers on Career Day programs and are available to discuss career opportunities with students.

A full-time staff of Home Economists in our Consumer Education department makes learning a fun event for elementary school students. They visit the schools and teach the students interesting tips and methods to safely use and conserve energy.

COOPERATIVE EDUCATION

Cooperative Education is an innovative approach that combines academics with on-the-job training to reinforce classroom theory and enhance professional and personal growth. We provide opportunities for co-op students to integrate academics with practical experience by alternating periods of employment and classroom studies. Students can test their career interests through a series of progressive work experiences. Computer science, engineering and accounting are just a few of the fields at MLGW in which students obtain invaluable work experience.

CAREER DAY

Careers in the Utility Industry is an annual program held in the lobby of the MLGW Administration Building. Junior and senior high school students visit to learn about career opportunities at MLGW. Approximately 200 students attend the event each year. Area colleges and universities are also available to explain their admission procedures to them.

Cal Gill speaks to Booker T. Washington High School students at a Role Model Extraordinaire program.

ADOPT-A-SCHOOL

Through our partnership with the Memphis City Schools, MLGW participates in the Adopt-A-School program. This program matches a business with a school to provide career guidance and to motivate the students. MLGW's adopted school is Carver High School. Our employees serve as facilitators and trainers in several special programs such as Athletes Speech Seminars, Leadership Training, Job Readiness and Toastmasters. The programs are designed to improve the communication skills of athletes, develop potential leaders, prepare students for the world of work, and improve their public speaking skills. We are counselors and tutors for students who need individual attention and assistance, or are experiencing difficulties with their studies. We provide technical assistance to Carver's newspaper and yearbook staff.

SCOPE

In 1987, MLGW began a program, SCOPE (Shelby County Opportunities for Potential Engineers). The program offers students an overview of engineering, on-the-job training and special workshops. The objective of the program is to familiarize students with the types of jobs available in the engineering profession, provide information on sources for engineering scholarships for minorities, provide information on college admission requirements in engineering, provide counseling on preferred high school subjects and to expose students to industries that employ engineers.

When the Memphis City Schools system needed role models for students at Booker T. Washington High School, we were there. Some of the 15 MLGW employees participating in the Role Model Extraordinaire program had graduated from the school and were able to provide the students unique insights into their experiences as students at the school.

MLGW is one of the 19 Memphis businesses participating in INROADS, a nationally-recognized career development program for minority college-bound students. The idea behind INROADS is to increase business opportunities for minorities by providing them internships. We provide internships and sponsor a four-year scholarship for two students.

Junior Achievement is another example of the partnerships MLGW has formed with other Memphis businesses and the Memphis City Schools system. Our employees serve as Business Consultants at various schools and teach economics to students.

Training teachers is yet another example of MLGW's commitment to educating our youth. We participate in the Urban League's Memphis Urban Mathematics Collaborative, a program in support of teachers, where working mathematicians reach across organizational boundaries to help make mathematics teaching less isolated. With the improvement of mathematics teaching in our inner-city schools as a goal, MLGW gladly accepted the challenge of playing a major role in this Ford Foundation pilot program through the local Urban League. MLGW provided three Resource Associates, several speakers and a summer internship for a teacher.

*Determining
Objectives*

In a very general sense, community relations seeks to inform the community about the organization and its products, services, and practices. It should correct community misconceptions and reply to criticism while gaining favorable opinion and support. Following are other general community relations objectives:

> Obtaining support for legislation that will favorably affect the operating climate in the community.
>
> Determining community attitudes, knowledge, and expectations.
>
> Supporting community health, educational, recreational, and cultural activities.
>
> Gaining better local government.
>
> Assisting the local economy by purchasing local supplies and services.

General objectives, however, will not suffice for specific institutions. Every community relations program should have a written policy clearly defining management's view of its obligation to the community. Specific community relations objectives should be spelled out so efforts can be coordinated and concentrated. Failure to set forth concrete objectives kills too many community relations programs before they get started.

Community relations policies and objectives are not determined according to idealistic principles. They arise from assessments of organizational needs, resources, and expertise on the one hand and community needs and expectations on the other. Before meaningful policies and objectives can be developed, the organization must know its community.

*Knowing the
Community*

While community relations usually stresses communication from the organization to the community, the success of such efforts rests on the communicator's knowledge of the audience. The effective communicator always listens before acting. Stated simply, "A basic ingredient of every good community relations program is the necessity for officials up and down the line to know their community.[6]

Of course, standard information about the community is useful to management. Demographic, historical, geographic, economic, and other readily accessible data are essential, but real knowledge of the community is not found in almanacs or chamber of commerce fact sheets. The solid community relations program must be built on the answers to questions like these:

1. *How is the community structured?*

   Is the population homogeneous or heterogeneous?

   What are its formal and informal leadership structures?

   What are the prevailing value structures?

   How are its communication channels structured?

2. *What are the community's strengths and weaknesses?*

   What are the particular problems of the community?

   What is the local economic situation?

   What is the local political situation?

What are the unique resources (human, cultural, natural) possessed by the community?

3. *What does the community know and feel about the organization?*

   Do the organization's neighbors understand its products, services, practices, and policies?

   What are the community's feelings about the organization?

   Do misunderstandings about the organization exist?

   What are the community's expectations regarding the organization's activities?

The answers to such questions are not necessarily easy to get. Moreover, answers change over time and thus require frequent monitoring. Good information can be acquired in several ways. Many organizations engage in survey research to determine community knowledge, attitudes, and perceptions. Professional polling organizations are often employed to provide such services. Close contact with community leaders provides an extremely important source of information. Professional, civic, religious, or fraternal leaders; political officials; and media editors can generally be reached through membership in local organizations or through face-to-face meetings on a variety of subjects. Some organizations formalize such input by including community leaders on their task forces or committees that deal with important community issues. See public relations spotlight 12.3 for suggestions for community relations efforts.

Public Relations Spotlight 12.3

Ten Commandments for Community Relations

1. Know your community.
2. Develop an organizational community relations policy.
   Spell out specific objectives. Base the policy on assessment of organizational needs, resources, and expertise and on community needs and expectations. Following are some sample objectives: attract more employment applications from women and minorities; improve community awareness of the organization's contributions; improve relations with local government; improve the local school system to make the community more attractive to potential executives and professional employees; improve the quality of local colleges for more effective recruitment; and so on.
3. Review your organization's policies, practices, and procedures. Are they consistent with sound community relations?
4. Consider especially the following issues: waste disposal; employee recruitment; employment policies (layoffs, compensation, overtime); noise or traffic problems; maintenance of organizational facilities and grounds; advertising, signs, marketing; and energy sources and energy waste.
5. Utilize all means to communicate with the community. These may include employees, local media, open houses, local clubs and organizations, local advertising, direct mail, newsletters, brochures, annual reports, movies, exhibits, and so on.

6. Involve your organization in local organizations. Do this by sponsoring employees who wish to join civic and professional groups, providing speakers for meetings, lending facilities for meetings or activities, sponsoring contests and programs for youth, supporting fund-raising activities, and so on.

7. Distribute corporate donations according to community relations policies and objectives. Philanthropy is an important aspect of community relations.

8. Use local merchants, banks, insurance agencies, lawyers, and other professionals for goods and services.

9. Offer aid to local governments. Make organizational resources available to governments by loaning employees and materials.

10. Evaluate the community relations effort. Measure to determine the extent to which objectives have been achieved. Be prepared to develop new strategies if current programs fail to meet expectations.

Guidelines for Effective Community Relations Programs

Once the means are established for receiving ongoing community inputs, the following guidelines should be used to develop an effective community relations program:

1. Careful effort should be made to specify the objectives top management wishes to achieve. The organization may seek many objectives—reputation, experience with a potential future payoff, stability of environment, and so on—but whatever it seeks should be established in realistic and concrete terms.

2. Alternative strategies should be explored and choices made. If an organization wishes to improve housing conditions in a city in which it operates, for instance, possibilities for action range from partially funding research into new ways to build low-cost housing to actually building such housing.

3. Impacts of community relations programs on the organization and the community should be anticipated. Offering training for jobs that will not exist when the training is concluded helps no one.

4. Attention should be paid to the likely total costs of a not-for-profit action and to the volume of the organization's resources that may legitimately be allocated to community relations. It is not advantageous to either the organization or the community if the organization suddenly discovers a given program is costing too much and abruptly stops all community service.

5. Many managers have found that certain types of involvement in urban affairs require knowledge and understanding that go beyond the usual managerial and technical business talents. Political skills, deep understanding of community problems, and the ability to resolve difficulties in an unfamiliar cultural setting are requisites for some activities. Special expertise may have to be acquired.[7]

Community . . . refers not only to a group of people living in the same locality, but to the interaction of those people. . . . In the past, the tendency was to treat a community as a rather simple entity—a collection of people, a "home town." Today we are beginning to recognize each community as a complex dynamism of diverse, constantly changing, often powerful, and always important forces.[8]

Community communication has no single audience. Messages reach communities through employees, their families, and local media. Other important communication channels consist of a community's opinion leaders: teachers, clergy, public officials, professionals and executives, bankers, union leaders, and ethnic and neighborhood leaders. Hewlett Packard held an open house to show employees' families and community residents what was going on behind its newly built plant. Caterpillar Tractor staged an open house for barbers, bartenders, and librarians because the company found them to be significant disseminators of community information. Another company hosted cab drivers for the same reason.

Local organizations provide another important channel of communication in communities. Fraternal, civic, service, and social clubs; cultural, political, veterans', and religious organizations; and youth groups all provide platforms for institutional messages and ample opportunities for informal communication. Organizational managers should be encouraged to belong to such groups and should make themselves available to speak before those groups as well.

Channels of Communication   The communication channels through which community audiences are reached may range from an informal chat over lunch at a Kiwanis Club meeting to advertisements in local mass media. In-house publications, brochures, and annual reports can easily be shared with community leaders. Some organizations create newsletters specifically for their neighbors. Upjohn Company, for instance, distributed a special report on the company's economic and social involvement in its headquarters city (Kalamazoo, Michigan) to 20,000 people. Abbott Laboratories circulates 85,000 copies of its quarterly publication *Commitment* to employees; shareholders; customer groups; local, state, and national leaders; and community groups. Institutions frequently make organizational films available to local groups and set up exhibits at local airports, shopping centers, and civic centers. Consumer's Gas System in Scarborough, Ontario, makes available a 15-minute slide show entitled *Consumers and the Community* to explain gas pricing and supply and to improve understanding of the company's role in the community. The show's modular format allows regional managers to insert slides of local facilities and services.

A uniquely community-oriented method of organizational communication is the open house, which can be very effective if well planned and executed. Successful open houses provide small group tours of organizational facilities with knowledgeable guides. They include films, displays, and brochures and usually provide product samples or mementos for guests to take home. The major message of such activities, of course, is the interdependence between the institution and the community.

In some cases, industrial or company tours become major tourist attractions. Tours of Heineken's Amsterdam brewery, for instance, win the company "thousands of loyal friends who speak well of us throughout the world."[9] Boise Cascade gives "plant tour" a whole new meaning. Advertisements in major national magazines invite readers to visit the company's working sites (see figure 12.1). The benefits of plant tours, however, must be weighed against possible organizational objections. One of the authors had his film confiscated at an open house for St. Regis Paper Company's plant in Lake Mills, Wisconsin. Officials were afraid that photos of his father-in-law standing by a tank the father-in-law had designed might be used by a company spy—or worse, that the son-in-law *was* a company spy.

Figure 12.1 Boise Cascade's invitation to a plant tour

The community relations person spends the greatest proportion of his or her time (29.6%) dealing with corporate philanthropy. Program administration (20.3%), other public relations activities (19.3%), government relations (17.8%), corporate communications (16.9%), and volunteerism (16.7%) account for the other tasks, according to the 1995 survey by The Center for Corporate Community Relations at Boston College.[10]

Community relations is particularly critical when an organization moves into a new community or leaves an old one. While virtually any major organization was once welcomed with open arms, communities now ask questions before they accept new businesses, industries, or even not-for-profit undertakings. Community response to an organization should be an important factor in the location decision.

Once the decision to locate in a particular community is made, it is essential immediately to provide local media with factual information on appropriate events and project stages. Familiarize key groups with the organization and its products, activities, policies, and people, using all available media and methods.

The dependence of a community on its organizations is never clearer than when a plant or facility leaves town. Plant shutdowns may raise levels of psychological depression, alcoholism, drug abuse, marital stress, child abuse, and even suicide among former employees, and the effects on the community can be severe. The organization that fails to prepare appropriately for its departure only invites increased government regulation to prevent such irresponsible activity in the future. General Foods, Brown & Williamson Tobacco Corp., and Olin Chemical provide examples of successful departures from communities highly dependent on them.

When the General Foods Jello Division left LeRoy, New York, it provided full information on its plans. The company aided the community by supporting an industrial survey and the formation of an industrial development council to attract new industry to the town. Employees were offered the choice of transfer to the new plant in a neighboring state or termination allowances and assistance in finding new jobs.

When Brown & Williamson closed a 51-year-old Kentucky plant, even the Tobacco Workers' Union praised the company. After giving workers three years' notice of the closing, the company relocated 350 of 2,700 employees and provided six months' separation pay, health care coverage, financial counseling, and vocational training for all others. The effort succeeded because all parties worked together to phase the closing gradually.

Olin Chemical was forced to close its Saltville, Virginia, plant when new pollution regulations made production inefficient. The company carefully explained the reasons for its actions. Employees were offered the chance to relocate to other plants, and arrangements were made for special retirement and severance benefits. According to *Life Magazine,* "The people were disappointed but not bitter as the company left; the company dealt generously in its settlements with the town."[11]

In Philip Lesly's *Handbook of Public Relations* several criteria are suggested that organizations might apply to community relations activities. These criteria are presented here, with case examples showing how organizations have used them to establish community relations programs.[12]

Specific Functions of Community Relations

When an Organization Moves

Criteria for Community Relations Activities

1. *Creating something needed that did not exist before.*   Hospitals have established "Health Lines" to provide health information services to people in the community who need such information. Originated by the University of Wisconsin, Health Lines have been adapted to the needs of communities all over the country. Some add their own services to the basic informational audiotapes.

2. *Eliminating something that is a community problem.*   Kiwanis International has been a champion of disseminating information to alleviate the drug problem. Many organizations, including PRSA, have worked with literacy programs in communities.

3. *Developing a means of self-determination.*   When American Oil Company moved out of Neodasha, Kansas, it gave its land and buildings to the town for an industrial park. The town would then be able to create jobs to replace those lost when the oil company left town.

4. *Broadening use of something that exists to include "have-nots."*   American Airlines' "Operation Grace and Glamour," a program designed for young women in poor urban areas to teach them how to dress and improve their appearance, helped give the young women self-confidence.

5. *Sharing equipment, facilities, and professional expertise.*   McDonald's lets groups use its juice machines for parties, many banks let groups use their seminar rooms for meetings, and professional groups such as the American Bar Association provide free professional advice to the poor or elderly. Local CPA groups often provide free tax consultation to the elderly at tax time.

6. *Reconstituting, repairing, and dressing up.*   Woodward Governor Company in Rockford, Illinois, and Fort Collins, Colorado, provides landscaping for government buildings and hospitals as its contribution to the community.

7. *Tutoring, counseling, and training.*   Many television stations sponsor "homework hotlines" to give community children expert tutoring during the school year.

8. *Activating others.*   St. Jude Research Hospital has worked with corporations such as Federal Express in Memphis to put on the Federal Express–St. Jude PGA Golf Tournament and to provide thousands of dollars through the efforts of the volunteers for cancer research.

Typical community relations activities reflecting these criteria include open houses, speakers' bureaus, service by employees on nonprofit boards of directors, and monetary support and volunteer support for community events. Community relations activities also include making facilities and any extras available, undertaking social projects to attack major community problems, and establishing employee volunteer programs. Publicity and promotion for such community relations programs must be seen as tools supporting the actual programs, not substitutes for them.

Community relations goes beyond mere communication. It requires action on the part of the organization in relation to community health and welfare, education, government, culture, recreation, and other areas.

Local Government and Political Action

Business/government relations will be discussed in much greater depth in chapter 15, but community relations and governmental relations clearly overlap in the area of local government and politics. In fact, the term *public affairs* is usually defined in public relations as two related activities—government relations and community relations.

As previously stated, local political officials can supply invaluable input to corporate community relations programs. Corporations have a great stake in effective local government since they are major taxpayers and users of municipal services. Part of the community relations effort, therefore, must be devoted to building solid relations with city officials, county commissions, and other agencies of local government. Corporations accomplish this, in part, by making organizational expertise available to governments through loan of managerial personnel or through service on panels, commissions, or committees established by or for local government.

As political activity becomes more important to organizations, community relations plays an increasingly critical role. Institutions must mobilize on the local level those who recognize the importance of their contribution to the health and prosperity of the community and those who will speak out for policies in the best interests of their community and its institutions. This is true whether the institution is a hospital, art museum, university, or business. Moreover, political experts now recognize that strength in Washington is derived from organized, localized grass-roots support. In an era when virtually all legislators are looking out for their own districts and careers, local people making local demands and representing local interests are far more effective than Washington-based lobbyists. In this regard, community relations may be not only an end in itself but an integral part of national efforts.

Great controversy has raged over corporate philanthropy for many years. Only in the past 50 years has corporate charity been recognized as a legal use of stockholders' funds. Even with its legality established, questions remain as to whether or not and to what extent the practice is appropriate and useful. Beyond these issues lie questions of proper motivations, goals, and criteria for corporate giving.

Corporate Philanthropy

Some maintain that corporate managers have no business giving away profits that rightly belong to stockholders. If stockholders wish to donate their money to what they consider good causes, it is argued, that is their right—but managers should not make such decisions for them. Berkshire Hathaway Corporation solved this dilemma by making two dollars per share available to stockholders to contribute to their favorite charities.

Clearly, however, the corporate entity incurs obligations and responsibilities of its own and needs to engage in activities traditionally considered philanthropic as a matter of long-term self-interest. W. J. Baumol explains:

> The company pays a high price for operating in a region where education is poor, where living conditions are deplorable, where health is poorly protected, where

property is unsafe, and where cultural activity is all but dead. . . . These
circumstances are all more expensive than corporate giving.[13]

By law, corporations are permitted to donate up to 10 percent of earnings to
charitable organizations. In practice, however, very few corporations give to the
limit. Overall, about 1 percent of corporate profits is actually given away. Though
corporations could legally give more, they obviously feel that it is not in their interest nor in the interests of their stockholders to do so.

With these limits established, however, debates over the legitimacy of the
practice have ended. As Richard Eells points out:

> The whole activity of corporate giving has now become an accepted part of good
> corporate management. The donative decision, as we are now coming to appreciate
> more and more, is part and parcel of the whole decision process in managing a
> business.[14]

The motivations and goals for such decisions are, however, still matters of
considerable debate. Despite the fact that the legal rationale for corporate donations rests on the notion of self-interest, some maintain that the term *philanthropy*
should be taken literally, with giving done strictly for the love of mankind. Irving
Kristol represents the opposite view:

> Some corporate executives seem to think that their corporate philanthropy is a form of
> benevolent charity. It is not. An act of charity refines and elevates the soul of the
> giver—but corporations have no souls to be saved or damned. Charity involves
> dispensing your own money, not your stockholders'. When you give away your own
> money, you can be as foolish, as arbitrary, as whimsical as you like. But when you
> give your stockholders' money, your philanthropy must serve the longer-term interests
> of the corporation. Corporate philanthropy should not be, cannot be, disinterested.[15]

In practice, research indicates that self-interest prevails. According to Baumol, surveys show that patterns of corporate giving fit in well with the doctrine
that corporations should provide funds to causes that serve the broadly conceived
interests of the firms.[16] Similarly, Neil Jacoby has found that "corporate giving is
generally in proportion to the extensiveness of local public contacts which generate social pressures.[17] He points out the extensiveness of the charitable activities
of banks as an example of this phenomenon.

Corporate giving can serve many corporate interests, including recruitment,
sales, and employee morale, but it inevitably serves that interest called public relations. Consequently, corporate public relations personnel are almost always involved in, if not responsible for, charitable decisions.

Unfortunately, in some cases, corporate charitable decisions are still made
capriciously and without adequate planning. In the development of a coherent approach to corporate giving, several factors should be considered:

1. *Do no harm.* Contributions should not be made to any cause that may
   be contrary to the best interest of the donor.

2. *Communicate with the recipient.* Effective grant making requires a
   close partnership between donor and recipient.

3. *Target contributions toward specific areas.* Gifts should achieve maximum impact on the community and maximum benefits for the donor. In this regard, donations should go to areas where individual corporations have unique expertise not available in the voluntary, nonprofit sector.

4. *Make contributions according to statements of corporate policy.* Fully developed policies of this nature should include the charitable aims and beliefs of the company, the criteria to be used in evaluating requests for funds, the kinds of organizations and causes that will and will not be supported, and the methods by which grants will be administered.

5. *Plan within the budget.* Corporate giving should be tied to set percentages of net earnings.

6. *Inform all persons concerned.* Employees and the community at large should be fully aware of corporate activities.

7. *Do a later follow-up.* The corporation does a valuable service by demanding of recipients high levels of performance and proper financial accounting.

8. *Remember that more than money may be needed.* An effective corporate contribution requires more than checkbook charity. Volunteer participation managerial expertise, and corporate leadership are essential elements of an effective program.

Two trends in corporate giving hold the promise of making such philanthropic programs more effective. Rather than reacting to public issues and public pressures, more firms—particularly the larger ones—are taking greater initiative in channeling dollars and corporate talent into problem areas that they deem significant and in which they wish to make an impact. Other corporations are attempting to broaden their philanthropic programs through decentralization and employee participation. By asking local managers of corporate facilities to make decisions about allocation of donations, large corporations ensure that they are in touch with the needs and desires of local communities. Federal Express, for example, has an employee committee that decides where the company's contributions go. As a result, those nonprofit activities in which FedEx employees are involved as board members and volunteers often stand the best chance of being funded.

Many corporations now match employee contributions to educational institutions, museums, orchestras, public broadcasting facilities, hospitals, and ballet companies—thus, in effect, permitting their contributions to reflect those of their employees. Xerox even gives employees paid leave to work on worthwhile community projects. IBM encourages top executives to teach at colleges and universities. Such practices allow employees to be the motivating force behind their companies' charitable donations.

At the same time, corporate giving is increasingly being integrated into the overall corporate goals of businesses in what might be called "strategic philanthropy."[18] This approach is a result of business understanding that "now, more than ever, philanthropy is good business."[19]

Figure 12.2 Corporate giving of $5.9 billion in 1991 went primarily to education and health activities.

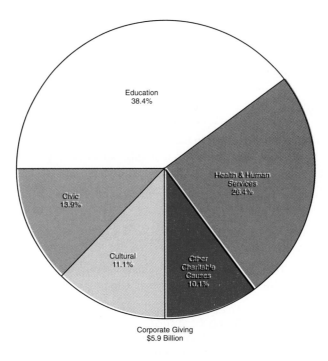

Education
38.4%

Health & Human
Services
26.4%

Civic
13.9%

Cultural
11.1%

Other
Charitable
Causes
10.1%

Corporate Giving
$5.9 Billion

In 1991 (the year yielding the most recent data), corporations gave a record $5.9 billion to charitable causes. Of that amount, 38.4 percent went to education, 26.4 percent to health and human services, 13.9 percent to civic activities, 11.1 percent to cultural activities, and 10.1 percent to other charitable causes (see figure 12.2). Beside cash contributions, corporate giving includes sponsorship of events, pro bono work, in-kind contributions, and cause-related marketing.[20]

Education   The largest portion of corporate philanthropy supports education. Businesses have long made contributions to educational institutions. Again, self-interest is evident. Skilled, intelligent workers and university-generated research are directly beneficial to business. A better-educated population creates a more congenial economic, political, and social environment for business. Corporate contributions to educational institutions can improve public relations, recruitment, and marketing. Increasingly, corporate contributions support efforts to improve students' and teachers' understanding of the private enterprise system.

Education is one area in which corporate support calls for more than money. With school budgets stretched to the breaking point, donations of classroom and recreational materials are extremely important. Examples of contributions include pencils and pads, printing of high school newspapers, automobiles for driver training, and sophisticated computers and equipment for advanced research. Donations of equipment represented one-sixth of corporate giving to higher education in 1984. Businesses can also provide plant tours for student field trips, speakers for classes and assemblies, internships for high school and college students, and managerial and financial expertise for school administrators. Bridges built between the corporation and the classroom are among the most important relationships in any community.

The level of business concern about education has increased in recent years. Business organizations and associations have taken many actions and made many statements on the subject. The Committee for Economic Development investigated the relationship between business and the public schools under the leadership of Owen Butler, former Procter & Gamble board chairman. The report describes the role of business as follows:

> Business has a major stake and a major role to play in the improvement of our public schools. Better schools can mean better and more productive employees and a boost toward restoring the nation's international competitiveness.[21]

Business can do many things to improve public education. Among them are

Working with local school districts to define goals for business involvement based on mutual needs.

Engaging in local business-school partnership programs utilizing proven techniques.

Encouraging employees to serve on local school boards and providing flexibility in working hours to make this possible.

Permitting working parents and other employees to participate in local school activities.

Providing qualified volunteer help to assist the local school administration with training in modern management and administrative methods.

Helping redirect vocational education programs to provide students with strong academic and real job-related skills.[22]

Many businesses, large and small, are committing not only money but time and other resources toward concrete action. Some are establishing direct relationships with public education through "adopt-a-school" programs.

Health and Human Services   The self-interest of corporations in their philanthropic efforts is perhaps most obvious in the community health and welfare area. Donations to hospitals and medical schools are very common. Classic examples of corporate community action are found in relation to health and welfare. Professors Keith Davis and Robert Blomstrom offer the following example:

> In the first decade of this century, Birmingham, Alabama, was menaced by serious health problems. Malaria, typhoid fever and other diseases were prevalent because of unsanitary community conditions. This city was the site of a United States Steel subsidiary, Tennessee Coal and Iron Co., whose productivity was lowered by illness. Tennessee Coal and Iron organized a health department and hired a prominent specialist in the offending diseases from the Panama Canal Zone. In its first year of operation the health department spent $750,000 for draining swamps and improving sanitary facilities. This amount was 30 times the total health budget of the entire state of Alabama.[23]

A more contemporary example of corporate resources being used for human problems is called CAN (Corporate Angel Network). CAN provides free rides on corporate aircraft to cancer patients. The organization has more than 270 corporate participants, including American Express, Norton Simon, AMF, AT&T, Champion International, General Foods, Merrill Lynch, and Time Inc. Health and human service activities now encompass a broad range of efforts dealing with employment, housing, and the physical environment.

The Arts   Of all corporate contributions, about 10 percent are currently devoted to cultural activities. This is the most rapidly growing area of corporate philanthropy, however, and one in which corporations can make their most significant impacts. As government funds to support the arts are reduced, private sector contributions will become even more important. Moreover, the connection between community relations and arts patronage is very clear. "No city can count itself a quality-of-life city without the arts," says Bob Guyton, CEO of Atlanta's Bank South.

The arts as a target of corporate giving developed later than health and welfare or education because the advantages are less obvious. By the 1960s, however, business leaders like David Rockefeller were appealing to their colleagues' self-interest on behalf of the arts. "Support of the arts by business amounts to nothing less than a prudent investment in community survival and growth," Rockefeller claimed. By the mid-1980s, business had become so thoroughly involved in the arts that *Newsweek* reported on what it called "the museum-industrial complex."

On a practical level, international cultural exchanges have paved the way for expanded trade relations. Theater, museums, dance, music, and architecture promote tourism. Former Philip Morris chairman George Weissman points out: "More people go to museums than to ball games." He has made his company one of the nation's most generous arts patrons.

Former Bristol-Myers-Squibb executive Gavin K. MacBain points to the utilitarian aspects of art—advertising, packaging, design, and marketing. He maintains:

> The use of art to move products in the marketplace would be impossible if there were no art museums, composers, orchestras, painters, filmmakers, writers, playwrights, and choreographers who are dedicated exclusively to their arts.[24]

Gideon Chagy puts his rationale for business support of the arts on a higher, more philosophical plane:

> If our society is to be both affluent and humane, the competitive drive and the sense of community must be kept in balance. Without a widely shared sense of community there would be nothing to restrain the logic and dynamics of business competition from leading to a system of exploitation. . . . While art is not a panacea for society's problems, it is a restorative for the sense of community.[25]

Themes of "excellence" and "quality" have been adopted by many companies. These themes fit naturally with artistic endeavors. Says Alvin Reiss, editor of *Arts Management,* "The arts represent excellence, a reflection of which rubs off on businesses that help arts groups."

Collective and individual corporate efforts related to the arts are very impressive. Several organizations now have multimillion-dollar annual arts budgets managed by executives who are highly knowledgeable or even professionally trained in the arts. Dayton Hudson, the Minneapolis retailer, is one company that has a full-time director of cultural affairs. Philip Morris, Equitable Life Assurance, Georgia Pacific, and Champion International have all established art museum annexes in the most accessible parts of their office buildings, forgoing as much as $1 million in annual rent.

The extent of corporate arts activities sometimes requires outside public relations counsel. Ruder and Finn Public Relations established a consulting program in business and the arts over 25 years ago. Today, Ruder, Finn and Rotman advises corporations on cultural support programs. The firm develops and implements corporate public relations programming keyed to cultural activities. It assists in managing corporate-sponsored museum exhibitions, performing arts presentations, symphony tours, and other arts-related activities.

To encourage further participation by business in the arts, more than 160 top business leaders have established the Business Committee for the Arts. The committee assists companies of all sizes in their efforts to establish arts programs that can enhance corporate image, benefit employees, or provide tax breaks. The committee also cosponsors, with *Forbes Magazine,* annual "Business in the Arts" awards.

Whether consciously or not, corporations routinely act as art patrons whenever they engage the services of architects. The community relations aspect of architectural decisions should not be overlooked. The late publisher Malcolm Forbes said, "The architecture that houses a company is a more visible statement than the president's in the annual report."[26] Cummins Engine has transformed Columbus, Indiana, into an oasis of architectural excellence by paying top architects to design new buildings and restore old ones in the town. Included are 12 schools, two churches, a fire station, a library, a golf course and clubhouse, newspaper and telephone company offices, a mental health clinic, the city hall, and more. Others in the town have been inspired by Cummins's effort and have followed its lead. Architects used include Eero Saarinen, I. M. Pei, Kevin Roche, and Richard Meier.

Every company can make an important contribution to its community by considering appropriate location and design for its plants, warehouses, showrooms, and offices. The public is served well by distinctively designed buildings that enhance their surroundings.

Cause-Related Marketing   A fairly new way in which businesses aid community organizations is cause-related marketing. In an effort to do well by doing good, businesses give their customers a chance to be altruistic by relating products to causes.

American Express is one of the leaders in cause-related marketing. From 1992 to 1995, American Express raised more than $25 million for its nonprofit partner Share Our Strength (SOS) through its national sponsorship of programs including Taste of the Nation, Writers' Harvest, and Charge Against Hunger (see figure 12.3). Charge Against Hunger was a national fund-raising, volunteer, and consumer awareness campaign to help fight hunger in the United States. Each

Make a Charge, *Make a Change.*

Everytime you use the American Express® Card in November and December you'll help provide a meal for someone who is hungry.*

Last year, over 500,000 hungry kids ate breakfast at school every day thanks to *you.* Please continue to help. Everytime you shop, dine or travel with the Card in November and December, American Express will make a donation to Share Our Strength, one of the nation's largest anti-hunger relief organizations. In turn, they will contribute these funds to local and national hunger relief agencies, providing support where it is needed most.

The fight against hunger begins with a charge - *your American Express charge.*

*American Express will donate up to $5,000,000 to Share Our Strength based on $.03 per Card purchase, between November 1 and December 31, 1995. Donation is not tax deductible for Cardmembers.

CAH CM/95

Figure 12.3 American Express "Charge Against Hunger" cause-related marketing campaign

year between November 1 and December 31, every time the American Express® Card is used, American Express donates three cents to SOS. From 1993 to 1995, the campaign raised) more than $15 million with the help of American Express cardmember transactions and merchant support.[27] In earlier years American Express used this effort to aid the Statue of Liberty restoration. Says Jerry Welch, then head of marketing for American Express's travel-related services, "Social responsibility is a good marketing hook."

More companies are developing creative ways of simultaneously selling products, helping community organizations, and generating positive publicity.

Citibank initiated its CompuMentor program to support its move into the Atlanta market. The program was designed to help high school and middle school students with career planning by providing special computer systems to inner-city school counselors. The bank donated one computer system for every 50 Citibank financial accounts opened with specially coded brochures. Suddenly, the bank's services were being sold from pulpits and PTA platforms. In four months, the program resulted in 800 new accounts and placed computer systems in 16 schools.

General Foods, Merrill Lynch, American Airlines, Ford Motor, and other companies use cause-related marketing to aid museums, symphonies, theaters, zoos, community service organizations, and health research groups.

Special societal and community circumstances give rise to special publics, problems, and opportunities for community relations efforts. For example, in certain Pittsburgh-area mill towns, steel-related unemployment hit 40 percent in the early 1980s. Food banks were established to provide staples for stricken families. Pittsburgh Brewing Company raised $13,000 for the food banks in two months by sponsoring personal appearances by professional football players and charging $5 to drink beer with a pro.

Special Publics and Problems

Some special publics, such as women and urban minority groups, represent ongoing concerns.

Women Women's important roles as employees, consumers, business owners, and voters have gained increasing recognition in recent years. Clear distinctions between work life and family life have blurred, and communication with audiences of women has become both more important and more difficult.

Over half of all women now work outside the home. Nearly a quarter of small business owners are women. Women are more likely to vote than are men. Perhaps most dramatic, it is estimated that women do 85 percent of retail buying in the United States. The large increase in direct economic participation by women has been called the greatest social revolution of the 1970s.

These changes have raised several issues of concern and opportunity for community relations specialists in businesses and other organizations. Compliance with equal economic opportunity laws is required, of course, for any business with more than 15 employees. Moreover, organizations must deal with affirmative action policies. To eliminate discriminatory practices is not enough. Organizations must take positive steps to ensure that minorities and women are hired, developed, promoted, and appropriately meshed into the entire organization. Successful programs depend on effective communication with current and potential employees to clarify policies and highlight opportunities.

Other women-related issues often requiring attention from organizational communication staffs include the following:

Comparable worth This issue is based on the contention that equal pay for equal work is not an adequate formula. Because, on average, women earn only 60 percent of what men do, and men and women still characteristically move into separate areas of employment, some groups have agitated in favor of equal pay for so-called *comparable worth*. Jobs may differ for janitors and secretaries, for example, but they can be compared in terms of skill requirements and worth to the organization. Rather than depending on the marketplace to determine pay, some contend that compensation should be adjusted according to a comparable worth scenario.

Day care   The percentage of working women with children under age six increased from 32 to 52 percent between 1970 and 1984. By 1985, 2,000 employers provided some form of child care assistance—a threefold increase in only three years. Companies have responded to the situation because child care problems can short-circuit recruiting efforts, injure productivity, and increase absenteeism and turnover.

Sexual harassment   If an organization cannot provide a working environment free from sexual threat, that organization has failed to give equal opportunity to all employees. Moreover, such organizations are extremely vulnerable to legal and publicity problems.

Volunteerism   Programs that use extensive volunteer workforces must reduce their traditional dependence on women. In some cases, previously voluntary tasks must become paid employment. In others, organizations may look to senior citizens rather than women for volunteer help.

Urban Minorities   The urban poor, including minority groups, cannot be considered a major market for many businesses, but they are an important public. Urban poverty is a negative factor in the business environment of any city. Business controls the distribution of capital and employment in our society; therefore, the cycle of poverty cannot be broken without its help.

In many ways, favorable business environments, because they hold the promise of jobs, are responsible for the concentration of poor in our cities. This responsibility must be met by all organizations. Public relations practitioners, because of their unique training, are the logical choice of most managers to monitor urban problems and recommend actions for their organizations to take.

Many of the efforts to improve conditions for inner-city residents have been conceived and initiated by concerned business leaders who feel that their organizations have certain responsibilities to the surrounding society. After more than two decades of programs and policies designed to meet the needs of the urban poor, both business and government have evaluated their efforts. Such evaluations always uncover inadequacies, waste, and misplaced emphasis. Yet, in spite of some obvious failures on the part of both business and government, the outlook and role of organizations in the United States has unquestionably changed.

The need for sensitivity to community problems and open communication with many segments of society has not diminished. As a result, the role of managers responsible for public relations has become critical. Public relations practitioners must be able to translate their companies' concern and actions into messages that are meaningful to the publics involved. More important, the corporate public relations staff must be able to detect social problems in the community and make management aware of them. In its role as facilitator of two-way communication between the organization and its publics, public relations can be key to the effectiveness of business response to urban problems.

Most problems that have haunted our large cities since the 1960s can be traced to poverty in one way or another. Although statistics show that only about one-third of America's poor families live in the central cities, they are probably the best-known disadvantaged group in our society. The urban poor who live in central city areas are more concentrated and thus more visible than other impoverished groups. The nature of the inner city itself makes the conditions of poverty even more devastating for the people who live there.

Concentrations of poor families have developed in most of our large cities, with minority groups disproportionately represented. The ghetto and barrio areas of major cities are centers of poverty, unemployment, pollution, and crime. In addition, civic functions such as sanitation, police and fire protection, and transportation are often inadequate.

Identifying and reaching minority publics should be no more difficult than reaching other publics. Blacks, for example, constitute a distinct market psychologically, geographically, socially, culturally, and economically. While television is the black community's medium of choice, blacks can be more efficiently reached through the black-oriented print and radio media.

Carol Torres of the Minority Media Syndicate gives advice on what minority media want. Editors are particularly interested in stories about minority members who have made it, programs that helped them make it, possible effects of upcoming government decisions, and tips for stretching modest budgets. "A good story is a good story," Torres says, "and minority media need good stories."

The difficulty in dealing with the black urban public arises from the diversity of opinions and outlooks within that public. Various individuals and groups claim to represent black interests.

Increasingly, black and Hispanic groups are using their clout as consumers to gain concessions from major corporations. The Reverend Jesse Jackson, for instance, through his operation PUSH, negotiated $275 million in concessions to black businesses from Coca-Cola, R. J. Reynolds, and Philip Morris. When Jackson attempted a boycott of Anheuser-Busch ("Bud is a dud," he said), the company fought back. The firm pointed out that it was already sponsoring aggressive minority programs, including $18 million spent with minority suppliers and $7 million spent on advertising in minority media. Moreover, the black community of St. Louis, home of company headquarters, opposed Jackson's effort. Anheuser-Busch prevailed.

Aetna was less fortunate, however. When the company developed a program to finance rehabilitation of inner-city housing, residents in three of the seven affected cities got very upset. The company ran head-on into conflicts over who should decide what is best for neighborhoods. "Aetna or any big company that wants to help with housing should first canvass the people who live around the proposed development and see how they feel about it," explained a Chicago city official.

Many major corporations have implemented programs to develop and support minority suppliers. Major franchisors, including McDonald's, Burger King,

Pizza Hut, Taco Bell, Kentucky Fried Chicken, and Baskin-Robbins, have established programs to encourage minority ownership of retail outlets. Hunt-Wesson and other food companies have minority home economists on staff.

Summary

Community relations as an organizational activity is as diverse as the communities in which organizations operate. It may be carried out by an officially designated community relations staff, by a general public relations staff, or by various departments throughout the organization.

Community relations publics, programs, and activities are united only by the creativity, energy, and budgets devoted to them. One thing, however, is certain. As the boundaries between communities and organizations become more permeable, the importance of the community relations function will continue to grow.

Case Study

The Deserted Hospital

By Walt Seifert, APR
Professor Emeritus
School of Journalism
The Ohio State University
Columbus, Ohio

You have been named public relations director of St. Christopher's Hospital. The facility has 500 beds at a downtown location in a major city.

You have your first meeting with your boss, the chief hospital administrator, Mr. Winston. Winston has been with St. Chris's for about two decades, and he is proud of his hospital's accomplishments. In the course of the conversation, you conclude that Mr. Winston has great confidence in his own conclusions. He gives you these "facts":

St. Chris's recently built a high-rise building on its inner-city site. Although the new building has been open two years, most of its rooms are unoccupied because of a lack of interest on the part of physicians and a shortage of patients. The administrator attributes this to a fear of crime. "We are in the high-crime area. Most people are afraid to come here," he says. "Also, a nurse was raped and murdered en route to this hospital. Although this happened quite far away, because she worked for St. Chris's, most people think it happened right here."

On the positive side, he mentions that St. Chris's has an outstanding speech clinic and the only teen alcoholism program in the state. He says the hospital would be willing to give physicians free office suites on the top floors of the tower if they would come.

Questions

1. How would you go about establishing objectives, both general and specific, for a community relations program at St. Chris's?

2. What kind of information would help you understand the community?

3. Describe some ways you might communicate with the community. Suggest specific channels.

Notes

1. Morrell Heald, *The Social Responsibilities of Business: Company and Community, 1960–1990* (Cleveland: Case Western Reserve University Press, 1970), 1, 2.

2. William H. Gilbert, *Public Relations in Local Government* (Washington, D.C.: International Management Association, 1975), 103.

3. W. J. Peak, "Community Relations," in Philip Lesley, ed., *Handbook of Public Relations,* 4th ed. (New York: AMACOM, 1991), 117.

4. Robert D. Ross, *The Management of Public Relations* (New York: Wiley, 1977), 170.

5. George Sawyer, *Business and Society: Managing Corporate Social Impact* (Boston: Houghton Mifflin, 1979), 316–317.

6. Peak, "Community Relations," 120.

7. Adapted from Jules Cohen, "Is Business Meeting the Challenge of Urban Affairs?" *Harvard Business Review* (March/April 1970): 81–82. Reprinted by permission of the *Harvard Business Review.* Copyright 1970 by the President and Fellows of Harvard College. All rights reserved.

8. Peak, "Community Relations," 117.

9. Gerald Tavernier, "Is Your Company Worth a Visit?" *International Management* (June 1974): 24–28.

10. Edmund M. Burke, director, and Richard Barnes, research director, *1995 Profile of the Community Relations Profession,* The Center for Corporate Community Relations at Boston College, 7.

11. "End of Company Town: The People of Saltville, VA, Lose Their Plant to Pollution Laws," *Life Magazine* (26 March 1971): 37–45.

12. Peak, "Community Relations," 130.

13. W. J. Baumol, "Enlightened Self-Interest and Corporate Philanthropy," in *A New Rationale for Corporate Social Policy,* W. J. Baumol, R. Likert, H. C. Wallich, and J. J. McGowan, eds. (Lexington, Mass.: Heath, 1970), 19.

14. Richard Eells, "A Philosophy for Corporate Giving," *The Conference Board Record* (January 1968): 15.

15. Irving Kristol, "On Corporate Philanthropy," *The Wall Street Journal* (21 March 1977).

16. Baumol, "Enlightened Self-Interest," 6.

17. Neil Jacoby, *Corporate Power and Social Responsibility* (New York: Macmillan, 1973), 199.

18. Rhonda J. Luniak, "The Art of Giving: Strategic Corporate Philanthropy," *Journal of Corporate Public Relations* (1992–93): 35.

19. Ibid.

20. Ibid.

21. From *Investing in Our Children: Business and the Public Schools,* New York: Committee for Economic Development, 1985.

22. Ibid.

23. Keith Davis and Robert L. Blomstrom, *Business, Society, and Environment,* 2nd ed. (New York: McGraw-Hill, 1971), 277.

24. Quoted in Gideon Chagy, *The New Patrons of the Arts* (New York: Harry N. Abrams, N.D.), 87.

25. Ibid., 82–83.

26. *Forbes Magazine* (4 June 1984): 19.

27. Gregory Tarmin, Public Affairs, American Express, correspondence and interview, October 1995.

CHAPTER 13

Consumer Relations and Marketing

Preview

The relationship between the consumer and the public relations practitioner in an organization is a natural one because consumers are one of the publics to which organizations must respond. Therefore, public relations and marketing functions in any organization must be supportive of each other.

One function of public relations involves basic product promotion, and its ability to contribute to the organization's overall marketing plan must not be overlooked. Public relations' support for the overall marketing mix, including product design, distribution, communication, and pricing, can greatly increase the effectiveness of any marketing strategy.

Complaint handling must be quick and effective, but it cannot be an organization's only response to consumers. Practitioners must find ways to improve two-way communication between an organization and its consumer publics.

Information about consumer concerns must be communicated to manufacturing and service personnel so that problems can be corrected before they affect public opinion. Public relations practitioners use their skills to help organizations provide consumers with appropriate, useful information.

Integrated communication is a total communication effort within an organization linking marketing, advertising, and public relations in an organizational unit.

Public relations can help the organization take smart risks and avoid the bad ones.

—Judith Rich

T hough it is wrong to view public relations as simply another method of product or service promotion, promotion is one of the most powerful ingredients in any organization's marketing mix. Public relations and marketing functions have some fundamental differences, but they share one significant goal. Both attempt to help an organization respond to a very significant public: the consumers of its products and/or services.

"Relationship marketing" has drawn the disciplines of marketing and public relations closer together in organizational strategy and structure. Customers want to be served, not sold. Public relations can help make an organization's corporate climate conducive to customer service. Marketing is concerned with the quality, availability, and affordability of the product or service; it concentrates on selling. Public relations, on the other hand, emphasizes relationships with all stakeholders, including (but not limited to) consumers, suppliers, and competitors. The two disciplines are similar in that both conduct extensive research, identify target publics, and develop communication action plans. However, public relations differs from marketing because it deals with the following key concerns that marketing does not:

1. Internal publics such as employees, stockholders, and management

2. Reputation, or image building

3. External publics (other than consumers) such as government

4. Crisis management

5. Public opinion change; social issues

6. Issues management

The primary goal of the marketing function is to "build and maintain a market for an organization's products or services."[1] Public relations can be an important part of this process. Problems with the Ford Pinto, Audi 5000, and Suzuki Samurai, are all examples of consumers' quick responses to negative information about a product. More than advertising and other traditional marketing tools is needed to restore customer confidence and sales in such situations. Likewise, product publicity can augment advertising efforts and make other marketing techniques more effective.

For public relations, however, sales and profits must be subordinate to long-term goals for positive relationships with consumers and other publics. Therefore, the primary goal of public relations is to "build and maintain a hospitable environment for an organization."[2] While this distinction can be stated rather easily, it is not so clear in practice. In many organizations, the structure of departments and divisions confuses the relationships between public relations and marketing to the point that the terms are almost always linked. Recent trends in the mergers of public relations firms and advertising agencies have further clouded this issue in the minds of many managers and others, leading some organizations to create Integrated Communication (IC) departments or Integrated Marketing Communication (IMC) departments.[3] This development is discussed later in the chapter.

Applying Public Relations Techniques to Marketing

Robert J. Ristino, vice-president of public relations for the Medical Center of Central Massachusetts, described the relationship of public relations to the marketing mix as illustrated in table 13.1. In this relationship, public relations provides support to the organization's overall efforts to market goods or services. Because public relations is integrated completely into the marketing process, it is easy to understand why many have trouble grasping the distinction between the two functions.

Product/Service Design

Because public relations practitioners maintain constant contact with their organizations' various publics, they can provide valuable insight into consumer behavior issues. This type of informal research can be an important check on other data used in the design of products and services. The frequent monitoring of mass media, the use of social forecasting services, and other forms of environmental surveillance discussed in chapter 6 make public relations practitioners important sources of information in the marketing process.

Any product or service has a life cycle that must be a part of the marketing plan. Public relations can help extend that life cycle at several stages. When a new product is launched, special events and publicity can help foster a positive reception. During the product's growth stage, publicity can help increase consumer awareness. When the product has achieved its market share potential, public relations can help maintain its visibility among competitors. Other communication activities can help delay a product's decline in the market.

The public relations information base regarding a wide range of publics, including but not limited to consumers, can be instrumental in determining product name, style, and packaging. Marketing texts are filled with examples of ill-chosen names that doomed or delayed the success of perfectly good products. The Ford Edsel may be the most famous of these legends. Beyond their names products and services are viewed by consumers as bundles of utility or collections of attributes that hold value. Packaging and style must add to that perception of utility. Because

TABLE 13.1   Public Relations Support of the Marketing Mix

Product/Service	Distribution	Communication	Price
Informal research	Physical access	Educating the market	Strategy
Environmental surveillance	Time access	Advertising message and media	Image
Product life cycle	Informational and promotional access	Sales promotion	
Naming or branding			
Style and Packaging			

Source: Robert J. Ristino, "Public Relations Marketing: Applying Public Relations Techniques to the Marketing Mix," *Health Care Management Review,* 14, 1989, p. 80.

of their skill in communicating and understanding publics, public relations practitioners can help guide the proper styling and packaging of products and services.

Distribution

Public relations people, and the information they provide, can assist marketing in deciding how and where a product or service will be offered to the consumer. Issues of logistics related to location and time availability must be thoroughly analyzed for target markets before a product or service is released. Because banks learned that automated teller machines must be safe to use and close to customers' homes and workplaces, ATMs are now available in most supermarkets and convenience stores instead of only after hours at banks. In distribution as in design, communication and promotion concerning product and service availability is important for success.

Communication

Communication is such an obvious role for public relations in the marketing mix that it is frequently considered the only role. Consumer understanding of new products is often a complex process that involves dealing with third parties such as reviewers and editors. These are the same "significant others" that public relations practitioners deal with in all other aspects of their work. Therefore, public relations becomes the natural focus for programs designed to educate specific audiences about the benefits of new services or products. Though the domain of public relations is usually nonproduct advertising, input from practitioners on advertising messages and campaigns can facilitate coordination with other product promotion efforts. Trade shows, special events, exhibits, displays, and other techniques discussed in this book all become a part of the effort to communicate with potential consumers.[4] Microsoft's introduction of Windows 95 used nearly all imaginable techniques to announce the new product. (See the case study featuring Windows 95 at the end of the chapter.)

Public relations practitioners must analyze issues related to attitude, access, and effectiveness when promoting goods and services. Here customers have the choice of four languages when using an ATM machine.

Development of Consumer Relations Issues

As our society has moved from an agricultural base to a service-oriented structure with highly interdependent elements, perceptions of business have also changed. The corporation, which once was perceived as a totally private entity, is now considered responsible to the public as well.

When the variety of available products was still rather small, consumers could rely on face-to-face relationships with merchants and tradespeople. Trademarks, grading, and other forms of standardized product identification were not needed. The relatively narrow product selection enabled both buyer and seller to be knowledgeable in their transactions.

Toward the end of the 19th century, the relationship between seller and buyer began to change. Manufacturers found it necessary to expand their markets and began to ship goods over great distances, thereby separating the purchaser from the source. Lengthening the channels of distribution led to the use of preservatives like formaldehyde and other harmful food additives. A large segment of the U.S. business community adopted the philosophy that customers had the responsibility to look out for their own interests (buyer beware). This belief created a gap between buyer and seller that engendered many unethical business practices.

Recent Trends in Consumer Issues

The recent consumer movement has applied social organizing principles to combat the growing power and influence of the giant corporations that dominate American business. Because businesses wield more power than individuals, consumer advocates believe the entire U.S. economic climate is biased in favor of big business. They claim that

> Legal remedies in cases of corporate liability or criminal action are insufficient.
>
> Prototype research and development in the interest of consumer safety and health are lacking.
>
> Consumer information systems are inadequate.
>
> Corporate executives are not required to answer to Congress on consumer issues.
>
> Government has failed to provide for an effective system of handling consumer complaints.[5]

In fact, recent court awards to consumers in **product liability** cases, coupled with a new recognition of consumer power in increasingly competitive markets, have led to the gradual replacement of the traditional adage *caveat emptor* (let the buyer beware) with a new one, *caveat venditor* (let the seller beware).

In the 1990s, however, corporations have reacted against organized consumerism and sometimes against individual consumers who have criticized a company's products, services, or actions by filing lawsuits against individuals or consumer groups. These suits, popularly known as SLAPPs (Strategic Lawsuits Against Public Participation), are used to squash the criticism of activists. The companies use vast corporate resources to involve the public interest groups or activists in expensive legal battles. Fear of such litigation is likely to reduce consumer activism.

The rising educational level of American consumers has contributed to their increased awareness, knowledge, and expectations of business and its products and services. As a result, consumers

Better-Educated Consumers

Place greater emphasis on product performance, quality, and safety.

Are more aware of their rights.

Are more responsive to political initiatives to protect those rights.

Have more self-esteem.

Want to be treated more as individuals.

Are far less tolerant of organizational restraints.[6]

Consumers today demand more information about products and services and more voice in business decisions that affect them. Increasingly, businesses are trying to accommodate consumers before product defects or other problems get out of hand. Dayton Hudson, parent of Target stores, has a policy of "keeping close to customers" (see public relations spotlight 13.1).

Public Relations Spotlight 13.1

Keeping Close to Customers

At Dayton Hudson our CEO spends at least one day a week in stores. Throughout our corporation, we keep close to our customers in three ways:

First, by having high standards for serving the customer that are clearly spelled out and monitored against.

And made public because our customers should know what we stand for. For us, it's things like values, clean stores, a liberal return policy. For schools, it's discipline, standards of competence, skills learned, and so on. For banks, it's minimizing procedures for customers, how soon telephones are answered, the length of time you wait in line. You get the idea.

Second, by focusing our entire organization on how the customer is changing.

Times change. Society changes. Your customer's needs change. And you must be able to change with them. To keep close to the customer you must know the direction of change and—be ready for it. Only then will we be able to get out ahead of change and manage it.

And third, by changing our business strategies to meet changing customer needs.

So whether you speak in terms of clients, or buyers, or patients, or constituents, taxpayers or students, we're talking about the same thing . . . customers.

Source: Ann H. Barkelew, vice-president of corporate public relations at Dayton Hudson, "Building Bridges: The Public Relations Challenge in the Public and Private Sector," Vernon C. Schranz Distinguished Lecture, Ball State University, 1993.

A White House study indicates that soliciting consumer comments may be good policy, as only one in six dissatisfied customers actually registers a complaint, while 90 percent of them switch brands. That figure contrasts with 54 percent who will stick with a company if their complaints are handled well.[7]

Common Consumer Complaints

Consumers constantly hear of product warnings, hazards, and recalls in the media. Manufacturers claim defective products are the exception; they make news, while routinely good products do not (see figure 13.1). That may be true statistically, but every consumer has had a bad experience with some product and

Figure 13.1 Advertising message from Procter & Gamble (Courtesy of the Procter & Gamble Company. Reprinted by permission.)

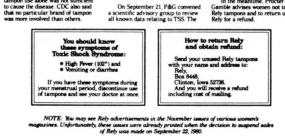

can easily identify with the news reports. One manufacturer-sponsored survey, though, says that 48 percent of consumers think the quality of American goods has improved in the last few years.[8] In addition to defective goods, two other common consumer complaints concern (1) inadequate repairs and guarantees and (2) unfair and deceptive advertising.

Inadequate Repairs and Guarantees Consumers often encounter numerous frustrations in getting products repaired. In response to this problem, many major manufacturers have set up their own service units. In fact, a Whirlpool-sponsored survey found that 72 percent of Americans believed most manufacturers would be willing to replace or repair defective products.[9] However, another survey indicated that service was getting worse,[10] and several earlier surveys pointed out repair problems such as fraud or incompetence in independent repair shops. Sears settled out of court for $8 million in a California lawsuit that accused the Sears automotive centers of selling unnecessary repairs and service to individual consumers. Mini-case 13.1 describes the Sears problem.

Mini-Case 13.1

The Sears Automobile Repair Problem

"Trust shaken is not easily taken back," one customer said about the Sears automobile repair shop scandal in 1992. Sears is the largest retailer of tires and batteries in the United States. It operates 776 tire and battery centers nationwide. In 1990, Chairman Edward A. Brennan sought to make every employee focus on profits. The company instituted commissions and product-specific quotas for auto service employees nationwide. Some employees attempted to achieve their goals or quotas with the aid of unnecessary repairs.

In 1990, customer complaints to the Consumer Affairs Department in California increased 29 percent and rose another 27 percent in 1991. While Sears refused to acknowledge fault, an undercover investigation by the Consumer Affairs Department found that on 34 of 38 visits, the customer was charged an average of $235 for unnecessary repairs. Sears ran an ad in most California newspapers that said, "With over two million customers serviced last year in California alone, mistakes may have occurred. However, Sears wants you to know that we would never intentionally violate the trust customers have shown in our company for 105 years."

Nevertheless, on September 2, 1992, the largest settlement in the history of the California Consumer Affairs Department was announced. Governor Pete Wilson announced that Sears, Roebuck and Co. had agreed to an $8 million out-of-court settlement for unnecessary repairs and service sold to California customers. When the consumer affairs group had filed accusations in June of 1992, Brennan had announced a change in compensation policy.

Despite the change in pay policy, the publicity hurt Sears nationwide. Sales dropped 15 percent in the month after the charges were announced. The Sears Merchandise group reported a third-quarter loss of $36.4 million that year compared to a $54.4 million profit the same quarter the previous year, a decline of more than $80 million.

Since 1992, Sears has not only changed the way its technicians are paid, it has also "farmed out" some of its service operations. Jiffy Lube is expected to open as many as 456 units in Sears Auto Centers 1998. Under this agreement, Jiffy Lube will remodel, equip, and operate oil change and lube centers in Sears Auto Centers. Sears will continue to use its other service bays.

Still, the earlier publicity haunts Sears. In August of 1995, a $100 million class action suit was filed in Federal Court against Sears in Tampa, Florida, alleging that tire balancing from its "AccuBalance" made $400 million from 1989 to 1994 but that it failed to perform the service 30 percent of the time. Sears denies the charges, saying that it discontinued AccuBalance in 1992.

Sources: *PR NewsWire,* 2 September 1992, 23 March 1995, and 17 October 1995; *Newsday,* 30 September 1992; *Compensation & Benefits Review* (American Management Association), May 1994; *Denver Post,* 4 August 1995, p. D7.

The issue of product warranties is probably the most highly charged consumer concern. Claims that manufacturers either fail to honor warranties or phrase them so that they actually guarantee nothing have created a consumer credibility gap. A presidential task force report described the situation this way:

> It is not uncommon for the manufacturer to ignore the appeal altogether and make no response. Some do respond and advise the consumer to contact the dealer. . . .
> Others recommend contact with a distributor or area service representative. This often leads to what is described as the "runaround," with a considerable exchange of correspondence, broken appointments, and nothing being done, with the manufacturer, distributor, and retailer all disclaiming any blame or ability to solve the problem.[11]

Mini-case 13.2, which centers on General Motors, relates to large-scale mishandling of consumer concerns.

Mini-Case 13.2

General Motors Consumer Concerns

General Motors has had its share of product liability situations. The 1960s witnessed the safety concerns surrounding the Chevrolet Corvair. In the 1970s, GM experienced numerous and continuing quality problems with its vehicles and dealers. In the 1990s, issues of quality, safety, corporate responsiveness, and dealer support still persist.

Recently, the safety of GM pickup trucks equipped with side-saddle gasoline tanks has been questioned. These safety issues related to the engineering of the GM vehicles involved can be defined as a long-term corporate crisis. The safety of any vehicle goes to the heart of the most basic consumer wants. Neglecting the customer's concerns can be detrimental to the long-term image and success of a company. In the case of General Motors, the corporate response to safety issues over the past 30 years has been viewed by some consumer activists as corporate arrogance. In fact, consumer advocates have roundly criticized GM for its handling of safety-related issues.

Voluntary safety recalls on a large number of GM products occur yearly. Some recent examples: In 1994, General Motors recalled 400,000 Cadillac DeVilles prone to engine fires. In 1995, GM recalled 34,000 Chevrolet Cavaliers and Pontiac Sunfires for steering problems; 206,000 Buicks, Cadillacs, and Chevrolets for leaking fuel tanks and poorly designed seat belts; and 91,000 Pontiac LeMans cars for faulty brakes. Finally, Secretary of Transportation Frederico Peña threatened a mandatory recall of some six million C/K pickup trucks manufactured by GM from 1973 to 1987 for gasoline tanks suspected of leaking after side-impact collisions. Consumer advocates have labeled the vehicles "rolling firebombs."

The yearly costs to General Motors of these recalls can be staggering. In 1994, GM reportedly spent $220.6 million on product recalls. This figure did not include $51 million spent to settle government charges for the C/K pickup. In addition, the company faces numerous lawsuits concerning the design of the fuel tanks on the C/K pickup truck.

The long-term costs to General Motors are much harder to pinpoint. According to a 1993 survey completed by Porter/Novelli, consumers remember mishandled corporate crises. In the survey, the gasoline tank danger of GM pickups ranked third, behind only the Exxon Valdez oil spill and the savings and loan crisis of the 1980s. The survey also found that consumers do not trust companies to be truthful in times of crisis and that they are angered by a company's refusal to accept responsibility for a crisis.

Obviously, it is crucial for companies like General Motors to realize how a crisis can have a compelling effect on public opinion. Failure to build trust and confidence among customers can lead to a long-term decline. General Motors once held over 50 percent of the U.S. market for automobiles. The most recent statistics show that the firm's current market share hovers around 30 percent. These are stark figures that illustrate the hazards of neglecting to respond to consumer concerns.

A corporate crisis will continue to haunt a company well after management has declared it over. Even as GM has rebounded with new cars, better quality, improved safety features, and competitive pricing, consumers have failed to return General Motors to its former domination of the U.S. automobile market. A failure to respond adequately to safety issues that surfaced over 30 years ago will continue to hamper GM's current attempts to win back the U.S. consumer.

Source: Greg Robitaille, University of Memphis, public relations graduate assistant.

Unfair and Deceptive Advertising   Further damage to the buyer-seller relationship occurs when products are promoted through unfair or deceptive means. Again, the business community points out that deceptive advertisers are a highly publicized minority, and government-sponsored research seems to back up that claim.

Research done for the U.S. Food and Drug Administration by an agency of the National Academy of Science found that only 7 percent of drugs tested failed to live up to the advertising claims of their manufacturers. One of the products deemed ineffective was mouthwash, which is widely used in the United States and grosses more than $200 million in sales each year.[12] Clearly, even though only a small percentage of advertisers may actually be guilty of false or deceptive practices, their fraudulent claims can still have direct impact on the majority of U.S. consumers.

In this era of mass marketing, a small number of businesses can have a great impact on public opinion. Seemingly minor infractions can do major harm to an entire industry because of the large numbers of consumers affected. Although only a small percentage of goods do not live up to their advertising, enough consumers have had bad experiences with these products to make dissatisfaction a common occurrence.

Public Relations and Consumer Affairs

In the past three decades, consumer affairs units have become fixtures in most organizations that have direct links to consumers. This function goes by a variety of names: public affairs, customer relations, consumer relations, consumer advocate, or public relations. Whatever the title, the relevant staff members usually work both inside and outside the organization. Their goal is to improve the organization's relationships and communication with consumers by investigating consumer issues and conveying the findings to management. Responsibilities of the consumer relations unit may include resolving customer complaints, disseminating consumer information, advising management on consumer opinion, and dealing with outside consumer advocacy groups.

Frequently, the consumer relations unit is linked to the public relations department of an organization. This connection is natural, since consumers are one of the publics that public relations practitioners have traditionally served. The exact placement and design of the consumer relations units vary, depending on the size and nature of the organization and the diversity of products or services. The different approaches do share one common characteristic: The vast majority of consumer relations units report directly to top management; they thus enjoy the autonomy needed to investigate issues and identify problems early, with easy access to those who make policy decisions.

Organizational Structure

The consumer relations unit at JCPenney, the Educational and Consumer Relations Department, is a separate entity under the supervision of the public relations manager, the vice-president of public relations, and the vice-president of public affairs (see figure 13.2.). This organizational substructure includes all the other functions and staff specialists normally associated with public relations. A separate consumer

Figure 13.2 Where consumer relations fits in the total structure of JCPenney Company, Inc.

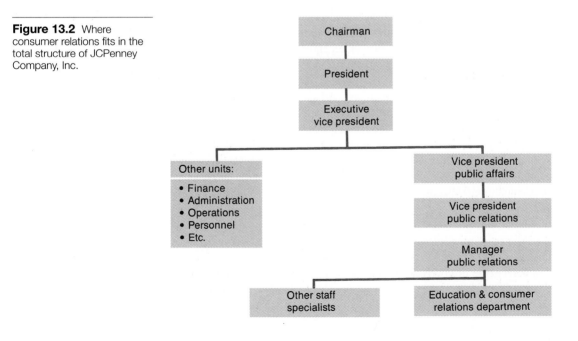

relations unit within the public relations department can respond and do follow-up in its own specialized area. Three functional groups are within the Educational and Consumer Relations Department. One group handles the various publications dealing with consumer issues that are sponsored by JCPenney. A second coordinates and develops the annual consumer issues programs for educators operated through local stores. A third team organizes and develops various consumer information programs.

The Chase Manhattan Bank's consumer affairs group has even more immediate access to top management, as figure 13.3 shows. Organized under the public relations vice-president and director and the corporate communications senior vice-president, the consumer affairs group at Chase Manhattan has a direct line to the chairman and chief executive officer. Because of this structure, the consumer affairs division operates as a consumer consulting service to top management as well as handling complaints directed at senior management. Frequently, the complaints have already gone through regular channels without resolution. In such situations, consumer affairs personnel can deal directly with the vice-president in charge of the division where the complaint originated.

Most divisional firms like Chase Manhattan locate their consumer affairs groups at the corporate level rather than in the divisions. This structure provides for a consumer voice in overall organizational policy, and the consumer affairs unit becomes more than a complaint department. A few very large organizations have consumer affairs groups at both the corporate and division levels.

The staffing of consumer affairs units varies tremendously. Some organizations have only one consumer affairs specialist; others have more than 100. Frequently, the staff is divided into groups responsible for certain functions, such as complaint

Consumer Affairs Staffs

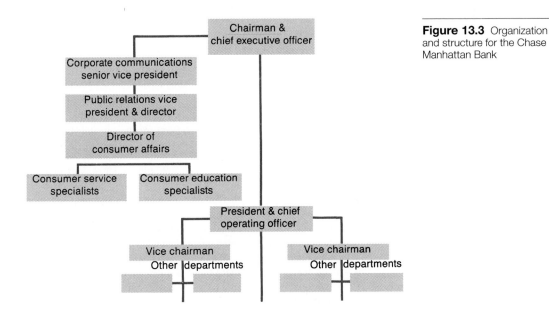

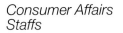

Figure 13.3 Organization and structure for the Chase Manhattan Bank

handling, publications, consumer education, and so on. Their activities are frequently integrated with those of other public relations groups within the organization that share similar functions.

Organizations frequently staff their consumer affairs units with employees who have enough prior experience in the company to handle complaints and investigate problems effectively.[13] One study revealed that among chief consumer affairs officers, public relations was the area of previous experience most often cited.[14]

Complaint Handling

Customer complaints are one of a growing list of responsibilities assigned to the consumer relations professional. Even the rare consumer affairs unit not directly involved in handling complaints still helps determine procedures for complaint routing and response. Consumer relations departments also monitor policies and procedures and their effects on consumers.

To ensure fast and uniform processing of consumer complaints, many organizations have developed elaborate complaint control systems. Consumer affairs specialists generally hold the following views:

1. Consumer complaints should be solicited.

2. All complaints should be logged when received.

3. The complaining party should be notified at receipt as to how the problem will be handled.

4. Action to resolve the complaint should follow quickly.

5. Affected company personnel and departments should be notified promptly and their responses monitored.

6. Ongoing analyses of complaint patterns should be aimed at preventing future problems.

The most common communication feedback from customers is the complaint. Don Peppers and Martha Rogers, in *The One to One Future,* suggest that we must learn to use customer dissatisfaction as an opportunity for collaboration. They argue that we should make complaining easier and try to resolve complaints in a collaborative fashion. The use of toll-free numbers for complaints is one measure that facilitates customer complaints. Communication through World Wide Web pages is another example. In order to hear more complaints, and thus establish relationship marketing on a one-to-one basis, you should take these steps:

1. Design your satisfaction questionnaire with the knowledge that its primary function is not research, but the discovery of complaints. . . .
2. Always ask your customer to identify himself or herself. . . .
3. Be sure you do get back to a complaining customer. Don't simply ask him to contact you. If your first effort to contact him doesn't succeed, get back to him again and again until you've reached him and made an effort to solve the problem, together. . . .
4. If you have a product that is sold in a store, encourage complaints by asking, on your package or inside it, for comments of any kind. Your package probably represents the only real customer-contact point available. . . .

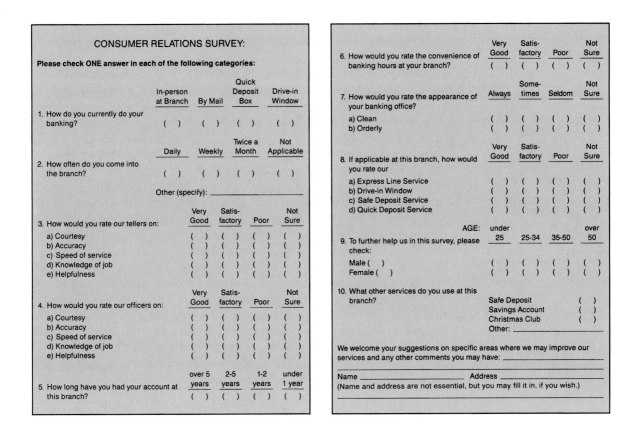

Figure 13.4 Questionnaire sent to customers of Chase Manhattan Bank

5. The economics of complaint handling will almost always work out to your benefit, as long as you pay attention to resolving one problem at a time, in a collaborative fashion, with each individual customer. . . .[15]

The consumer affairs operation of the Chase Manhattan Bank illustrates how a comprehensive complaint resolution system works. The consumer affairs office divides complaints into about 25 categories and prepares monthly reports on the effectiveness of each division and of the entire company. From these analyses, preventive measures are recommended. A summary of typical complaint letters, including direct quotations, is also prepared and submitted with the monthly reports. Top management has found these summaries particularly revealing and informative. For example, one analysis showed that the tone of collection letters sent out by the bank's credit department was irritating to some patrons. Management reasoned that irritating a customer was not likely to speed up payment and would only harm the bank's image; thus, the letter was revised.

Frequently, the consumer affairs unit at Chase Manhattan solicits grievances. The bank realizes that for every dissatisfied customer who writes, many more are complaining to others but not to the bank. To discover these hidden complaints, Chase sends out questionnaires and letters signed by the president to customers of each branch bank (figure 13.4). The information collected is compiled in a statistical summary and reviewed by top management. Organizations with aggressive consumer affairs policies are integrating this kind of information into their production and service decision making.

General Motors discovered and corrected a flaw in its Pontiac Fiero windshields within a few months of the car's release by having worker volunteers call owners to solicit complaints and suggestions. Sony redesigned its televisions within three months of hearing via the customer service center that consumers needed an easier hookup when using the sets as home computer monitors.[16] Consumers' letters to Scott Paper Company stating that their paper napkins emitted a strange odor started an investigation that turned up a leaking valve.[17] At Coca-Cola, consumer complaints overturned management's most controversial decision in the company's 99-year history, leading the Atlanta giant to return its traditional soft drink to the market, albeit in new packaging, within four months. In each situation, a potentially costly mistake was averted or corrected by quick attention to information from the consumer affairs unit.

Consumer Information

The principal tenet of consumer advocacy is that consumers lack adequate information for making purchasing decisions. The complexity of the business system and the proliferation of products contribute to this difficulty, but many consumer problems result from product misuse or improper maintenance. Consumer relations units have responded to the need for fuller and clearer information by providing simplified warranties, clarified product use instructions, and educational programs to help consumers select the right products for their needs and use them properly.

Consumer Education   Most people don't understand how businesses operate, what company policies are, or how complaints are resolved, according to market research for Coca-Cola.[18] A satisfied customer may share that satisfaction with another 5 to 8 people, but a person with a complaint will probably tell 10 to 16. To keep word of mouth on its side, JCPenney launched a massive consumer information effort consisting of improved labels, publications to explain labels and warranties, educational programs for consumers at local stores, and information and materials for educators. Coca-Cola gained esteem with its brochure on how to resolve consumer complaints.

Toll-free numbers are one way consumers can reach companies with their complaints, questions, and suggestions. Johnson & Johnson, Kentucky Fried Chicken, Pizza Hut, Whirlpool, Kraft, Sony, American Express, General Electric, and Procter & Gamble are among companies that use toll-free lines as consumer communication tools.

Regardless of the content, consumers usually value a message more if it comes from the media than from company representatives. Recognizing that fact, managements work with their consumer and public relations staffs to schedule new product releases and major announcements for times when they will gain maximum publicity. When Microsoft introduced Windows 95, for instance, Bill Gates's company used a multiplicity of channels and techniques to announce its new product. As a result, the Windows 95 release (see the case study at the end of this chapter) was a top story in magazines, newspapers, and the electronic media.

Mini-Case 13.3

Winning Consumers Over

Public relations practitioners call it "brandstanding." Management calls it a way to promote products and corporate identity without paying for extensive media advertising. **Brandstanding,** the new label for corporate sponsorship, has become increasingly popular. Sponsors of the 1984 Olympics in Los Angeles covered nearly 25 percent of the games' half-billion-dollar cost. They also provided the official Olympics soft drink, Coca-Cola; the official credit card, American Express; the official fast-food restaurant, McDonald's; and the official film and photo processing house, Fuji Photo Film Co.

Concerts and sporting events are natural focuses for brandstanding. Corporate sponsorship of cultural events is nothing new, but Kool cigarettes (Brown and Williamson) opened a new era by underwriting jazz festivals in 20 cities. Schlitz underwrote the 10-day New Orleans Jazz Festival (where the company sold 400,000 cups of its beer). It then helped sponsor national tours of the rock groups Fleetwood Mac and The Who, following up with "Schlitz rocks America" media advertisements.

Companies clearly like the publicity and goodwill return on their brandstanding investments. Cigarette companies, banned from advertising over the electronic media, lead the way. American Tobacco's vintage brand, for example, is seeking a comeback by sponsoring bowling tournaments with the slogan "Lucky Strikes Again."

Time magazine reports that brandstanding is credited with giving companies $10,000 in free publicity for each $1,000 spent.

When audiences are difficult to reach through traditional media, organizations must be extra creative. Mini-case 13.3 shows how some companies provide information to difficult-to-reach publics.

The Corporate Liaison

The role of consumer affairs within corporations has become one of consumer spokesperson to management. Most consumer affairs specialists consider it part of their jobs to influence decision making actively by speaking out for the consumer. They solicit consumer opinion and make management aware of the potential effects on consumers of various decisions. The in-house ombudsman must balance the needs of the actual customers, the demands of consumer activists, and the goals of the organization. This liaison role has always been the highest calling for public relations professionals.

Those who understand the purpose of public relations realize that the practitioner must do more than echo the company line. Public relations professionals should help senior managers stay in touch with their various publics. Doing so is especially critical in emergencies, when public relations professionals must serve as management's bridge to the media and the public.

Integrated Communication

Integrated communication (IC) is the concept that all of an organization's communication efforts, including public relations, advertising, and marketing, are either merged within a single unit or are closely coordinated. Several names and acronyms have been suggested for this concept. Integrated Marketing Communication (IMC),

Integrated Communications: Advertising and Public Relations (ICAP), Integrated Communication (IC), and Total Communication (TC) are often proposed. Public relations practitioners have resisted the IMC designation because it implies that public relations and advertising are subsumed under a marketing umbrella.

Several factors underlie the recent movement of some organizations toward this integrated approach. First, mergers, acquisitions, downsizing, and an increasing concern for the bottom line have caused management to look at ways to reduce expenses. High advertising and marketing costs can be lowered to some degree with greater emphasis on product publicity and other public relations communication tools. In one case, Goodyear sold 150,000 new Aquatred tires before any advertising was released because advance publicity had generated considerable interest in the product. Windows 95 generated 58 percent profit in the quarter in which the product was introduced, with considerable publicity accompanying the advertising.

Second, mergers and acquisitions of public relations firms by advertising companies have created a natural tendency to consolidate functions that overlap between advertising, marketing, and public relations.

A third reason is the movement to "one-to-one" marketing and "relationship marketing." This approach resembles the relationship building that is a cornerstone of public relations strategy in work with stakeholder groups or primary publics. It requires development of a good reputation, or image building, another public relations activity. Because these are aspects of communication that public relations brings to the communication mix with advertising and marketing, it is essential to include the public relations practitioner in the integrated approach. A final reason for favoring integrated communication may be the realization that government relations, a public affairs function of public relations, is also an important aspect of an organization's communication efforts. Laws and regulations at the federal, state, and local levels often affect a firm's sales and marketing aspects. Some municipalities may strictly regulate signage, for example, requiring McDonald's, BP, or other companies to alter their signs if they want to do business there.

Many public relations professionals have not enthusiastically endorsed the integrated concept. Often practitioners fear they will be subsumed under marketing and will lose their ability to counsel management directly regarding company issues, to be prepared to deal with crises, or to continue developing effective internal communication programs. These are all functions not typically related to marketing communication. However, other advertising and some public relations professionals see the need to support integrated marketing communications as a total effort within an organization. They realize the current practice of integrated communication "makes sense and that to survive in their careers they will need to have skills to do both advertising and public relations assignments within their organizations."[19] In fact, some argue that the movement is toward generalization instead of specialization of the workforce. Boyett and Conn suggest this in *Workplace 2000:*

> As American companies restructure themselves into small business units, and small companies grow, employees in greatest demand will be those who are flexible and can perform a wide variety of jobs. Small companies can afford few specialists. Everyone

in a small company must be willing to and able to do everything, or at least a wide variety of things.[20]

Tom Harris, one of the leading advocates of marketing public relations and author of *The Marketer's Guide to Public Relations,* argues that public relations and marketing "can, should and must be compatible."[21] He writes:

> I make the distinction between those public relations functions which support marketing which I call MPR and the other public relations activities that define the corporation's relationships with its non-customer publics which I label CPR. I believe that in today's business climate both have an unprecedented opportunity to become more valuable than ever.[22]

Amelia Lobsenz, public relations counselor for the New York–based firm Lobsenz and Stevens, agrees that public relations and marketing have a great deal in common but observes that they are different and require different approaches. "The sooner we recognize how we can supplement each other, the better off we'll be,"[23] she says.

Bill Ehling, Jon White, and Jim Grunig conclude their chapter on public relations and marketing practices in the *Excellence in Public Relations* study with the following proposition: "The public relations function of excellent organizations exists separately from the marketing function, and excellent public relations departments are not subsumed into the marketing function."[24] This sums up the public relations side of the issue. While public relations practitioners need to be able to work in a total or integrated communication environment, they don't want that effort to be called Integrated Marketing Communication and/or subsumed under the marketing function. Public relations has too many other functions to be relegated to a role of publicity in support of marketing. At the very least, coordination among the three major communication efforts of an organization need to be improved. Public relations can and should support marketing in the organization's effort to meet its goals and objectives.

Summary

As consumers become better informed and products more complex, consumer relations plays a more prominent role in public relations practice. No longer can retailers, manufacturers, and service providers simply respond to complaints from their customers. Sophisticated public relations techniques must be applied to understand the needs of consumers and solicit their comments. In addition, organizations must be prepared to respond to consumer action and other special interest groups who take notice of their products or services. Because of increased awareness and government interest, the consumer relations function of many organizations has grown to occupy a substantial managerial role. More important, good relations with consumers have demonstrated their value to the bottom-line productivity of many businesses. These changes have opened new opportunities for public relations practitioners in consumer-oriented organizations.

Integrated communication is a total communication effort within an organization linking marketing, advertising, and public relations in an organizational unit or at least coordinating those efforts more closely.

Windows 95 Rollout

E. W. Brody, APR, Fellow
Professor, Department of Journalism
University of Memphis
Memphis, Tennessee

Case Study

M icrosoft Corporation's introduction of Windows 95 will stand, at least for a time, as the most elaborate and most costly new product rollout in history. Microsoft spent some $300 million in advertising, public relations, and sales promotion to introduce the new operating system. Among the more noteworthy expenditures:

- $12 million for rights to the opening chords of the Rolling Stones' hit "Start Me Up."
- £350,000 ($537,000) to sponsor rollout day's edition of the *Times* of London, which was distributed free of charge to 1.5 million readers.
- Undisclosed sums to Jay Leno to serve as co-host (with Microsoft chairman Bill Gates, the world's richest individual) of an unveiling ceremony at Microsoft's Redmond, Washington, headquarters and to the managers of the CN Tower in Toronto and the Empire State Building in New York, which were decorated in bunting and lights for the occasion.

While arguably a component of product testing rather than promotion, the introduction of Windows 95 was preceded by what almost certainly was the most extensive software beta testing program in history. The 50,000 beta sites used in the official beta program were supplemented by an estimated million users at 400,000 sites participating in a Windows 95 preview program.

Microsoft's corporate efforts were supplemented by a broad range of retailer promotions. Many opened at 12.01 A.M. on rollout day. Some offered incentives ranging from free long-distance service to discounted airline tickets. A CompUSA store in Philadelphia hired waitresses from a nearby Hooters restaurant to attract customers.

How efficient and effective was the effort, which *The Washington Post*'s David Segal described as "software's glitz blitz?" The jury is still out and is likely to remain so for some little time.

The rollout was not without problems from Microsoft's perspective, although others in the microcomputer industry fared relatively well. Viruses, inadequacies in customer support, and operating software incompatibilities diminished the initial impact.

The virus problem afflicted disk no. 2 in the 13-disk Windows 95 set. Microsoft blamed the difficulty on viruses resident on buyers' hard drives but agreed to replace the disks free of charge.

The company was prepared to handle 20,000 customer calls daily—10 times the number received for Windows 3.x—but callers who were able to get through found themselves waiting for hours to speak with support engineers. Support forums on CompuServe and other on-line services were similarly inundated. Microsoft was forced to turn on busy signals to limit the sizes of customers' long distance bills, and response times on CompuServe ranged from days to a week or more.

The company's greatest problems, however, came from software incompatibilities, especially those that occurred when Windows 95 users accessed the company's new Microsoft Network, a new computer utility designed to compete with CompuServe, America Online, and Prodigy. The Windows 95 installation process prevented users from subsequently accessing competing Internet access software, with predictable results. Users complained. Competitors cried "foul." Microsoft promised to fix the problem.

Perhaps more significant were the potentially dampening effects of less-than-impressive versions of Microsoft applications for Window 95. Among the first to ship was an upgrade of Word for Windows that offered only networking enhancements. Individual users found no significant improvements and were left without the many shareware improvements available for Word for Windows.

Incompatibilities between Windows 95 and application software produced by other vendors proved equally troublesome to users of earlier Windows versions. Many elected to remain with those earlier versions.

While Microsoft declined comment on sales, industry observers predicted that 20 percent of the 100 million computer users who had previously relied on earlier versions of Windows would upgrade within a year. The ultimate profitability of Windows 95 inevitably will be governed equally by sales of the operating system on the one hand and applications software on the other.

Sixty days after the Windows 95 rollout, only one industry group was unanimously applauding the product. These were hardware manufacturers, who enjoyed record sales as Windows 95 adopters upgraded or replaced computer systems to meet the demands of the new operating system.

Questions

1. What does the Windows 95 promotional effort imply as to underlying objectives? What do you think Microsoft was trying to accomplish? What corporate objectives were implied by the promotional push? What do you think were the company's promotional objectives?

2. Given the scope of the Microsoft promotional program, how would you have expected the planners involved to have defined target audiences? List the audiences you believe the Windows 95 rollout addressed.

3. To what extent do you believe Microsoft achieved its objectives? Do developments that occurred after the rollout suggest that Microsoft was adequately prepared to cope with audience responses? Have Microsoft's promises for Windows 95 been fulfilled?

4. What impact would you expect the Windows 95 rollout and subsequent events to have on the introduction of Microsoft applications for Windows 95?

Notes

1. Glen M. Broom and Kerry Tucker, "An Essential Double Helix," *Public Relations Journal* (November 1989): 40–41.

2. Ibid., 41.

3. Debra Miller and Patricia Rose, "Integrated Communications: A Look at Reality Instead of Theory," *Public Relations Quarterly* (Spring 1994): 14.

4. Jordan Goldman, *Public Relations in the Marketing Mix* (Lincolnwood, Ill.: NTC Business Books, 1984).

5. Robert D. Hay, E. R. Gray, and J. E. Gates, *Business and Society* (Cincinnati: South-Western, 1976), 297.

6. Ibid., 301.

7. "Making Service a Potent Marketing Tool," *Business Week* (11 June 1984): 165.

8. Research & Forecasts, Inc., *America's Search for Quality: The Whirlpool Report on Consumers in the 80s* (Benton Harbor, Mich.: Whirlpool, 1983), 5.

9. *America's Search for Quality,* 14.

10. "Service a Potent Tool," 170.

11. G. A. Steiner, *Business and Society.* (New York: Random House, 1975).

12. E. F. Cox, R. C. Fellmeth, and J. E. Schultz, *The Nader Report on the Federal Trade Commission* (New York: Richard W. Baron, 1969).

13. E. P. McGuire, *The Consumer Affairs Department: Organization and Functions, Report No. 609* (New York: The Conference Board, 1973).

14. R. T. Hise, P. L. Gillett, and J. P. Kelly, "The Corporate Consumer Affairs Effort," *MSU Business Topics* (Summer 1978): 17–26.

15. Don Peppers and Martha Rogers, *The One to One Future* (New York: Currency Doubleday, 1993), 85–87.

16. *Business Week* (11 June 1984): 165, 167.

17. "Disgruntled Customers Finally Get a Hearing," *Business Week* (21 April 1975): 138.

18. Virginia H. Knauer, "Customer Education Pays Off," *Enterprise* (October 1984): 22.

19. Debra Miller and Patricia Rose, "Integrated Communications: A Look at Reality Instead of Theory," *Public Relations Quarterly* (Spring 1994): 14.

20. Quoted in Tom Duncan, Clarke Caywood, and Doug Newsom, *Preparing Advertising and Public Relations Students for the Communications Industry in the 21st Century,* Report of the Task Force on Integrated Communications, December 1993, p. 8.

21. Thomas Harris, "How MPR Adds Value to Integrated Marketing Communications," *Public Relations Quarterly* (Summer 1993): 14.

22. Ibid.

23. Amelia Lobsenz, "How Public Relations Can Support Your Marketing Efforts," *Public Relations Quarterly* (Spring 1991): 9.

24. Bill Ehling, Jon White, and Jim Grunig, "Public Relations and Marketing Practices," chapter 13 in Jim Grunig, ed., *Excellence in Public Relations and Communication Management* (Hillsdale, N.J.: Lawrence Erlbaum Associates, 1992), 390.

CHAPTER 14

Financial Relations

Preview

Financial public relations creates and maintains investor confidence. It builds positive relationships with the financial community by providing corporate information. Growing interest in investor relations following the Texas Gulf Sulphur case has greatly increased public relations involvement in the financial reporting of corporate information.

Strong financial relations programs, characterized by responsiveness, openness, and regular communications, help lower the cost of capital for businesses.

A key function of financial relations is to provide prompt disclosure of corporate news that is significant to the financial community.

Hostile takeover attempts, whether through tender offers or efforts to take over management via a proxy fight, are two key financial public relations crises that corporate management may face. Public relations must become intimately involved in the battle for control when such crises occur.

Publics for financial relations include individual stockholders, financial analysts, and the financial media. Major tools of financial relations include annual reports and annual stockholder meetings.

Effective financial relations gives a business increased support for its management, higher stock prices, and greater ease in attracting new capital.

Markets run on information. Financial markets run on financial information.

—Jay Sarmir, Merrill-Lynch broker

T he success of any organization depends on its ability to attract resources from its environment. Among the most important of these resources is capital—the money with which other resources can be purchased. Corporations raise money in a variety of ways, including selling stock, issuing bonds, and securing loans from financial institutions. In all cases, a company can attract capital only if investors have confidence in the business and its management.

Bond ratings, interest rates, and stock prices are not just a matter of negotiation between a corporation's financial officers and its bankers or brokers. Such negotiations are preceded by and based on the business's current performance and future prospects. These facts must be persuasively communicated, and that is where public relations comes in.

Growing Interest in Investor Relations

Since 1968, when the Texas Gulf Sulphur case was decided by the Supreme Court, business has had an increased interest in improved investor relations. Company executives were fined, and some served jail time, in the first major case of insider trading since the formation of the Securities and Exchange Commission (SEC) in 1934. That landmark case was the "wake-up call" to U.S. corporations that the SEC meant business with its rules on insider trading and related disclosure of information.

Other catalysts have vaulted investor relations into a multibillion-dollar-a-year operation. Among these factors have been a growing number of firms "going public" in the last three decades, high visibility of corporate mergers and acquisitions, efforts to stop hostile takeovers of companies, and much tougher requirements for disclosure imposed by the SEC and the stock exchanges. In addition, the expanding importance of global financial markets and the growing understanding of need for expert public relations guidance in view of court cases such as the Texas Gulf Sulphur case have heightened management's interest in financial public relations.[1]

In this chapter we will first examine the tasks of financial public relations. Then we will consider disclosure of information and the major issues facing the financial public relations practitioner. We will also look at the role of the financial public relations practitioner, the audiences, and the appropriate communication strategies, including the annual meeting and the annual report.

Maintaining Investor Confidence

The first task of **financial public relations** is to create and maintain investor confidence, building positive relationships with the financial community through the dissemination of corporate information. Executives who fail to do this may be unable to attract capital investment. They may lose control over their organizations and even lose their jobs.

Financial public relations is much easier to relate to the proverbial bottom line than are other kinds of public relations. Relative stock prices, bond ratings, and interest rates on loans are direct measures of confidence in a company. When confidence is high, stocks are worth more, and bonds and borrowing cost less. When confidence is low, stock is worth less, and higher interest is demanded by

Mini-Case 14.1

Financial Relations Saves a Small Business

Guardian Industrial Services, a family-owned business with $3 million in sales per year, was having a rough time. Sales were down. Certain expenses were up. More money was needed to get the business through the slow season. Guardian president Jim Gladden went to his banker, seeking to extend his credit line. The banker said no, not one more penny.

To stay in business, Gladden needed money, and he needed it quickly. Family sources had all been tapped. Potential private investors wanted too much from the business in exchange for too little in funds. Gladden needed a bank willing to extend a more substantial credit line.

Over the years, Gladden had played an active role in his community. He served on the chamber of commerce board. He was in Rotary Club and supported scouting. He was known, trusted, and respected by others in the business community, including other bankers.

Within three weeks, Guardian Industrial Services had established a relationship with a new bank that increased its credit line substantially. "I always knew credibility was important," Gladden explained, "but it is rarely as important as when credibility equals 'creditability'."

---

those who loan funds to the business. Most corporations consider their financial relations programs effective if they have been able to reduce the cost of funds or obtain capital at the best cost.

Financial relations is most often associated with large corporations, but it can be critically important to small businesses, too, as mini-case 14.1 shows. Fund raising by not-for-profit groups is also a form of financial relations.

The practice of financial public relations touches on diverse areas like finance, accounting, law, public affairs, community relations, marketing, and employee relations. Consequently, its list of objectives is a lengthy one. Practitioners are charged with all these responsibilities:

Specific Objectives for Practitioners

Building interest in the company.

Creating understanding of the company.

Selling company products.

Broadening the stockholder base by attracting new investors.

Stabilizing stock prices.

Winning stockholder approval for management.

Increasing the company's prestige.

Creating favorable attitudes in the financial community.

Developing political sensitivities of stockholders on issues relating to the company.

Improving employee relations.

Building loyalty of stockholders.

Arthur Roalman best sums up the purpose and rationale for financial public relations:

> An individual is not likely to invest money . . . in a corporation's stocks, bonds, commercial paper, or other financial pledges unless he believes strongly that he understands fully what is likely to happen to that corporation in the future . . . most investors' willingness to invest in a corporation is influenced by their trust in its management. Trust isn't built overnight. It is the result of long-term actions by the corporation to provide factual financial information in proper perspective.[2]

He continues:

> Strong investor relations programs emphasizing a full and continuous flow of information about the company can help lower the cost of capital in the securities markets and develop and maintain goodwill among shareholders.[3]

Providing Public Information

Investors bet fortunes on what they believe to be true about particular enterprises. Fraud and deception could part gullible investors from their funds. These dangers have been largely (but not completely) eliminated by government law and regulation, stock exchange policies, and the voluntary disclosures of corporate management. The importance of corporate information to investor decisions, however, highlights the second major function of financial public relations: prompt provision of public information required by law, regulation, and policy.

SEC Regulations

Many aspects of financial public relations are affected by law and regulation. The Securities Act of 1933 was passed "to provide full and fair disclosure of the character of securities . . . and to prevent frauds in the sale thereof." The Securities Exchange Act of 1934 supplemented the previous year's legislation and was intended "to secure for issues publicly offered, adequate publicity for those facts necessary for an intelligent judgment of their value." These and other **Securities and Exchange Commission (SEC)** regulations apply to all companies that are listed on any of the 13 largest United States stock exchanges or that have assets of $1 million and 500 stockholders. Other regulations require that corporations "act promptly to dispel unfounded rumors which result in unusual market activity or price variations."

SEC regulations are copious and subject to frequent changes. It is therefore impractical to present them all here. The commission routinely requires submission of three kinds of reports: annual reports (**Form 10-K**), quarterly reports (**Form 10-Q**), and current reports (**Form 8-K**). Form 10-K asks for descriptions of a corporation's principal products and services; assessment of competitive conditions in its industry; the dollar amount of order backlog; sources and availability of raw materials; all material patents, licenses, franchises, and concessions; and the estimated dollar amount spent on research. The form also requires reporting of the number of employees, sales and revenues for the past five years in principal lines of business, a description of principal physical properties and a list or diagram of parent and subsidiary firms, pending legal proceedings, and changes in outstanding securities.

Other information required by Form 10-K includes the names, principal occupations, and shareholdings of the corporation's directors; remuneration, including amounts accrued in retirement plans, of each director and principal officer; stock options outstanding and exercise of stock options; and interest of officers or directors in material transactions. All of this information must be accompanied by corporate financial statements prepared in accordance with SEC accounting rules and certified by an independent public accountant. Moreover, the entire form must be submitted to the commission no later than 90 days from the close of the fiscal year. Finally, the 10-K must be made available free of charge to anyone upon request.

The 10-Q quarterly report is much less detailed. It asks primarily for the corporation's summarized profit and loss statement, capitalization and stockholders' equity at the end of the quarter, and sale of any unregistered securities.

In its effort to gather all relevant investment-related information on a continuous basis, the SEC also requires filing of Form 8-K, the current report. This document must be filed when an unusual event of immediate interest to investors occurs—for example, the acquisition or sale of significant assets or changes in the amount of securities outstanding.

These SEC reports are prepared largely by accountants and lawyers. They are described here, however, because public relations professionals should (1) recognize the extent to which SEC-regulated corporations must share information, (2) understand the kinds of information deemed significant by investors, (3) realize the extent of federal regulation in this aspect of business, and (4) avail themselves of the information contained in these documents.

Policies of various stock exchanges also influence the activities of financial public relations. The New York Stock Exchange states, for example, that news about matters of corporate significance should be given national distribution.[4] What is significant is a matter of some debate. The American Stock Exchange considers the following kinds of news likely to require prompt disclosure and announcements:

Stock Exchange Policies

(a) a joint venture, merger or acquisition;

(b) the declaration or omission of dividends or the determination of earnings;

(c) a stock split or stock dividend;

(d) the acquisition or loss of a significant contract;

(e) a significant new product or discovery;

(f) a change in control or a significant change in management;

(g) a call of securities for redemption;

(h) the borrowing of a significant amount of funds;

(i) the public or private sale of a significant amount of additional securities;

    (j) significant litigation;

    (k) the purchase or sale of a significant asset;

    (l) a significant change in capital investment plans;

    (m) a significant labor dispute or disputes with contractors or suppliers;

    (n) establishment of a program to make purchases of the company's own shares; and

    (o) a tender offer for another company's securities.[5]

To facilitate *timely* national disclosure, financial relations practitioners use several news wire networks. Associated Press (AP) and United Press International (UPI) are well-known general wire services. Dow Jones and Reuters Economic Service specialize in business and financial news. PR NewsWire and Business Wire charge fees for their services but guarantee that corporate news is carried promptly. The key point is that the information must be disclosed simultaneously to all audiences.

The Disclosure Issue

One other SEC regulation of particular interest to the public relations practitioner is Rule 10B-5, which renders it unlawful "to make any untrue statement of a material fact or to omit to state a material fact . . . in connection with the purchase or sale of any security." In the landmark case, *SEC v. Texas Gulf Sulphur Co.* 401 F.2d833 (2nd E.r. 1968), this regulation was applied to press releases.[6] In subsequent suits, public relations counsel has been named as a defendant when press releases and other materials "contained false and misleading statements and omitted to state material fact."[7]

Two later cases sharply focused on the disclosure issue, although financial relations officers were left in confusion by their outcomes. One involved the 1984 merger between food giants Nestlé and Carnation. The other involved Chrysler Corporation's struggle to survive in the early 1980s.

Nestlé was bidding secretly for Carnation. Rumors were flying, and Carnation stock rose nearly 50 percent before Nestlé announced the purchase for $83 per share. Throughout the negotiations, Carnation's spokesperson refused to comment. A year after the merger, the Securities and Exchange Commission ruled that by saying "No comment" during negotiations, Carnation had been "materially false and misleading." Since the company no longer existed, however, the SEC took no action to back its ruling.

Chrysler was saved by an unissued press release. One day in early 1981, Chrysler was down to $8 million in liquid assets. Company lawyers held that Chrysler was obligated to issue a press release to disclose its near insolvency, but company officials risked being charged by the SEC rather than destroy what little confidence their creditors and customers had left. The release went unissued, and the company survived—its potential insolvency made moot by its renewed financial health.

No simple formula provides guidance in disclosure situations. While the Chrysler example is unusual, it shows the importance of judgment. Generally, however, disclosure is both required and desirable.

In the life of a corporation, several issues may arise that constitute crises in its effort to survive. In the last decade, we have seen mergers and acquisitions that have often been hostile takeovers. In efforts to thwart hostile takeover attempts, bitter proxy fights have often ensued. Win or lose, the company is often left with considerable debt, and if it can survive, it may have to spin off some of its assets.

Eugene Miller, executive vice-president of United States Gypsum Company, says, "The most stressful and crucial element of investor relations is in forestalling and defending against efforts of outside interests to take over the company."[8]

Takeover attempts assume two fundamental forms: the proxy fight and the tender offer. Both are efforts to persuade shareholders, but in different ways and perhaps for different reasons.

In a tender offer, money is the key factor. The tender offer is an offer that is high enough above the market price of the stock to entice shareholders to sell despite loyalty to the company or desire to keep the stock. For example, if a shareholder had bought stock at $20 per share and it was now worth $25 on the stock exchange, a party who wanted to get control of the company might make shareholders a tender offer of $35 per share to sell. Because of the potential financial gain for the shareholder, management would face a tough fight to keep control of the company. Mini-case 14.2 recounts Phillips Petroleum's classic fight against a hostile takeover by T. Boone Pickens, one of the world's foremost corporate raiders.

Crisis Issues in Financial Relations

The Tender Offer

Mini-Case 14.2

Lessons from Phillips Petroleum

Since the mid-1980s, merger mania has swept the corporate landscape. Raiders brought some of America's corporate giants to their knees with hostile takeover attempts. "Greenmail" and "golden parachutes" were the daily fare of business news.

Phillips Petroleum was the object of not one but two corporate raiders—Texas oilman T. Boone Pickens and New York financier Carl Icahn—and lived to tell about it.

C. M. Kittrell, Phillips executive vice-president, learned the hard way that a company must not lose touch with its investors. "Individual shareholders are generally loyal to their companies—and vote in favor of management. Yet they tend to get scared off in takeover battles," Kittrell explained. "With all the lawsuits, poison pills, and debt securities that surround a hostile raid—who can blame them for cashing in?" Individuals owned half of Phillips's stock before the takeover attempts. Afterward, they owned only 20 percent.

When the battle was over, the company set about rebuilding its investor relations program as a major function of the public affairs division. The company surveyed present and potential shareholders to learn their characteristics and attitudes. Stockholder publications were simplified and personalized; investors got more straight talk and fewer complex numbers.

Kittrell maintains that it is in a company's best interest to create a balance in ownership by catering to the needs of individual investors.

Source: Based on Lyn Allgood, "Investor Relations a Vital Defense Measure Now," *Atlanta Business Chronicle* (5 August 1985): p. 5A.

The Proxy Fight

In a proxy fight, the two (or more) contestants for control of management (or an issue) seek to persuade shareholders to let them vote in their stead. Shareholders are asked to give their "proxies," or absentee voting rights, to one side or the other. In this case, though, the shareholder does not sell the stock.

Public relations for the company under seige in a proxy fight can take several defensive measures. Primary, of course, is providing information to stockholders, the financial press, and investors about the present management's operation and strategic plans for the future and drawing a contrast with the proposals of the competing group.[9]

Laura Johnston, investor relations specialist at Citigate Communications, suggests that public relations practitioners in the financial arena need to prepare as far in advance as possible. If you anticipate a tough fight in the coming year, begin now to prepare. Johnston suggests these four strategies for the preparation stage:

1. *Don't procrastinate.* Start planning your investor relations strategy early.

2. *Begin by managing your shareholders' expectations. . . .* Pave the way for the proposal by informing shareholders about management's general line of thinking on that particular issue well before a proxy statement is produced.

3. *Involve investor relations people in drafting the proxy statement.*

4. *Hire a proxy solicitor* who will get down in the trenches and fight for every vote.[10]

Once the fight is underway, a number of tactics can help you win. You should use every means at your disposal to reach your shareholders. You may need to go on line or set up a World Wide Web page. Use all the available communication tools. Focus your message into a few key ideas, and repeat them throughout the proxy campaign. Your theme should be easily recognized by your shareholders. Rally your past supporters, and don't be afraid to use the endorsements of the media or other credible third-party sources to your advantage.[11]

Financial Relations Professionals

Financial relations professionals must have broad-based knowledge and skills to deal effectively with their many-faceted responsibilities. A survey of 300 senior financial relations officers in leading corporations showed that a broad financial background combined with marketing communication skills is considered the best preparation for the field.[12] The survey indicated that although financial and security analysts may enter the financial relations field, lack of marketing and communication backgrounds often impedes their success. Knowledge of finance, marketing, and law, coupled with public relations skills, are all important for those considering financial relations careers.

Audiences for Financial Relations

In addition to the Securities and Exchange Commission, parties interested in a corporation's financial information include investment firms with seats on the stock exchanges, investment counselors, financial writers, brokers, dealers, mutual fund houses, investment and commercial banks, institutional buyers, employees, and both current and future stockholders. For discussion purposes, however, these categories can be grouped into three broad audiences: individual stockholders, financial analysts, and the financial press. Following are examinations of these groups, their informational needs, the means by which they may be reached, and the best ways to secure positive relations with them.

Some corporations consider their **stockholders** a vast, untapped resource of potential customers and grass-roots support on political and financial issues. Harrison T. Beardsley recommends that financial relations efforts, particularly for smaller companies, concentrate on stockholders rather than on financial analysts.[13] Others dismiss stockholders as purchasers of stock for income and profit who are best ignored. John Kenneth Galbraith says simply, "The typical stockholder does not identify himself with the goals of the enterprise." In any case, stockholders are a group that must be communicated with and reckoned with. Figure 14.1 shows how one company used advertising to attract stockholders.

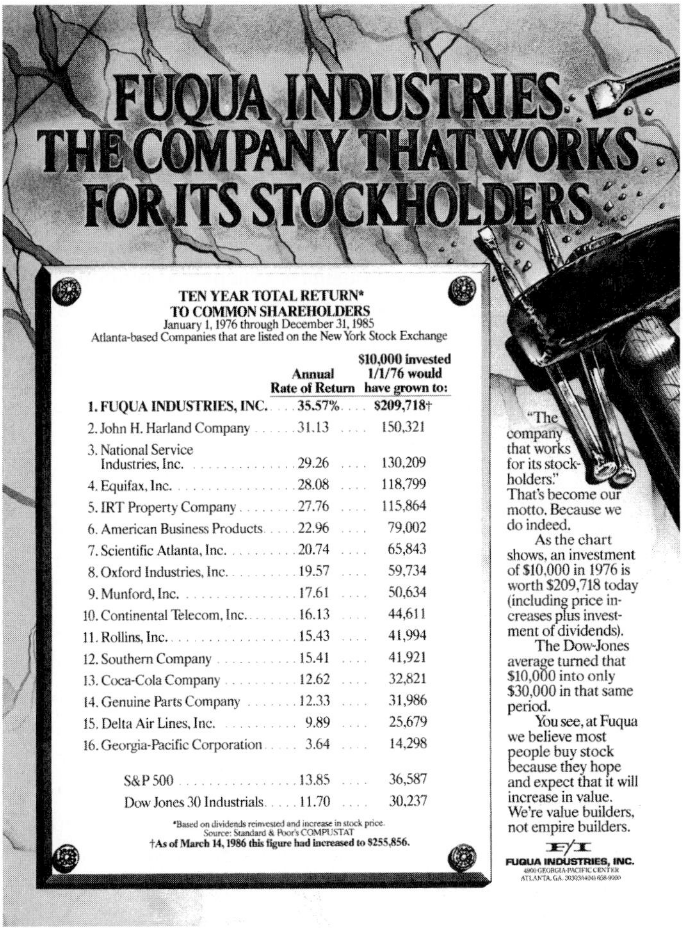

Individual Stockholders

Figure 14.1 Some companies advertise in the effort to attract additional stockholders.

Fuqua Industries

As discussed previously, the Securities and Exchange Commission requires companies to keep their investors fully informed. Management has learned the hard way that uninterested stockholders may be quick to sell their shares to even the most unfriendly entity attempting takeover. Moreover, stockholders themselves have become more vocal and active—initiating proxy fights or raising financial, social, and ethical questions in relation to environmental matters, sex discrimination, corporate political activities at home and abroad, labor relations, South African apartheid, and many other issues.

Most corporations now recognize that "a company's foremost responsibility is to communicate fully anything that can have a bearing on the owner's investment."[14] The extent and quality of their efforts vary widely, however. Informative annual and quarterly reports and well-organized annual meetings with follow-up reports are the basic tools of stockholder relations. We will discuss both in detail later in this chapter.

Sound stockholder relations are built on three principles: (1) Learn as much as possible about your stockholders, (2) treat them as you would your important customers, and (3) encourage investor interest from people who are predisposed toward your company. A basic principle of communication is *know your audience.* Consequently, learning as much as possible about stockholders makes excellent sense from a communications perspective. The stockholder survey, which solicits demographic and attitudinal information, is a readily available tool, but too few U.S. corporations actually use it.

Treating stockholders as important customers has a number of implications for financial relations officers. Communicating in readable, nontechnical language is a must. Welcoming new stockholders and writing to express regret when stockholders are lost is good business practice. Prompt and appropriate response to stockholder correspondence also helps maintain positive relations.

Sun Company follows a comprehensive stockholder relations plan. The company believes, "Shareholders are our business partners. It's helpful to us if management gets an insight on what they think of us." Each new Sun stockholder receives a welcoming note from the company's chairman. A very readable newsletter goes out with every dividend check. About 100 shareholders are selected at random six or eight times a year and invited to a dinner at which a top company executive speaks. Sun also maintains a toll-free telephone line to make corporate news available to stockholders and invites them to call the shareholder relations department collect with questions or complaints.

Sometimes going beyond the call of duty in stockholder relations reaps excellent benefits. Consider the case of William Comptaro of Pittsburgh, Pennsylvania, owner of 100 shares of Louisiana-Pacific. Comptaro was dissatisfied with management's decision to acquire Flintkote Corporation and expressed his views in a letter to Louisiana-Pacific's president. Comptaro received a reasonably prompt response from a woman in the stockholder relations department. She explained how much confidence she had in the company's officers and invited him to call if he had further questions. Comptaro wrote a letter of thanks and considered the matter unsatisfactorily closed.

But here the story takes an unexpected twist: One evening Comptaro's phone rang. The president of the company was calling to explain in detail why he considered Flintkote a good buy.

Louis Rukeyser, who reported Comptaro's story in his nationally syndicated column, made these comments:

> You don't have to be a skeptical professional securities analyst in order to recognize that there are plenty of other factors that ought to be considered by a potential investor, other than extraordinary courtesies shown him by the company's president . . . but surely there is a lesson here . . . for all those arrogant corporation bureaucrats whose cold form-letter responses frequently feed public cynicism.

Rukeyser continued:

> If capitalism is to survive in the face of ideological competition and muddled political management, it had better look to its own followers—and to its own failings. And while the company president can't be on the phone all day every day, a little more of the kind of communication related here could win the system a lot more friends.[15]

Finally, just as a company should seek new customers among the most likely segments of the population, it should seek stockholders from those predisposed toward buying stock. Employees, suppliers, dealers, and members of communities where the corporation is located are the most likely prospects. They should receive annual reports and other materials that encourage investment.

Financial analysts include investment counselors, fund managers, brokers, dealers, and institutional buyers—in other words, professionals in the investment business. Their basic function is to gather information concerning various companies; to develop expectations in terms of sales, profits, and a range of other operating and financial results; and to make judgments about how securities markets will evaluate these factors. They gather quantitative and qualitative information on companies, compare their findings to statistics from other companies, assess opportunities and risks, and then advise their clients. Corporate financial relations assists analysts by providing information and, in doing so, may positively influence expectations and judgments. The New York Stock Exchange gives its listed companies the following advice:

Financial Analysts

> Securities analysts play an increasingly important role in the evaluation and interpretation of the financial affairs of listed companies. Annual reports, quarterly reports, and interim releases cannot by their nature provide all of the financial and statistical data that should be available to the investing public. The Exchange recommends that corporations observe an "open door" policy in their relations with security analysts, financial writers, shareowners and others who have a legitimate investment interest in the company affairs.[16]

To secure relations with financial analysts, the basic method is to identify the prospects, meet them, establish interest and understanding, and then maintain the relationships. All dealings with professional analysts should be characterized by responsiveness, openness, and regular communication, but the practitioner should take care not to overcommunicate.

"Fluff and puff" will quickly sour an analyst's view of a corporation. When representations from a company's financial relations staff lead an analyst to become overenthusiastic and corporate performance fails to live up to expectations, the results can be disastrous. When Toys R Us announced that its Christmas sales were up 17 percent, its stock dropped 20 percent. On the basis of discussions with the company, analysts had expected a 30-percent sales gain and thus were disappointed.

The shoe manufacturer Nike lost half its value when it earned 88 cents per share rather than the anticipated $2. Rather than informing the financial community when it realized profits would be lower than expected, Nike management tried harder to live up to the inflated figures. The next year the company set aside more time for communicating with financial analysts.[17]

Analysts want to know the following: the background and nature of the business, primary factors affecting the business, current operating conditions, and estimates of future outlooks. Analysts are also vitally interested in management forecasts, pricing data, capital expenditures, financial data, labor relations, research and development, and any other information that may materially influence the quality of an investment. Annual reports provide much of the needed information. A survey of institutional investors showed the annual report to be the most useful and informative communication vehicle within a company's financial relations program.[18] Annual reports are discussed in detail later in the chapter.

A primary way to reach financial analysts is through **investment conferences,** meetings that investment professionals attend specifically to hear company presentations. These programs convey information on a company's performance and offer persuasive arguments for buying its stock. Although speeches by company executives are central, they are usually accompanied by slick publications and audiovisual support materials.

Theodore Pincus, chairman of the largest U.S. financial public relations firm, is critical of such presentations. He calls them "saccharin-soaked speeches . . . focus(ing) on a company's history and . . . present operations."[19] Pincus maintains that companies should candidly discuss their plans and goals.

The annual San Francisco investment conference sponsored by Montgomery Securities has a reputation for attracting powerful investors and analysts who hear pitches by some of the most promising companies around. Under such circumstances, companies have the opportunity for substantial financial impact.

Relationships with financial analysts are not all one-way. Analysts can provide valuable information to companies as well. When communicating with financial analysts, first be prepared to listen. They can give significant feedback about a financial relations program in terms of its adequacy, credibility, and sufficiency of information. Perhaps even more important, this exchange provides an opportunity for the company to understand how the market perceives its strengths and weaknesses and the behavior of the business as a whole.

The Financial Press

The third major audience for financial relations is the **financial press.** "The financial press provides a foundation and backdrop for any corporation's financial communications program," says Hill & Knowlton executive Stan Sauerhaft. "It develops credibility and it can add impressive third-party endorsement."[20]

Financial media are important publics for financial relations efforts.

Financial public relations practitioners deal with media much as other public relations specialists do. The major difference lies in the specialized nature of the financial media. Major daily newspapers carry financial items of local, regional, or national interest. Weekly newspapers generally carry items of local interest. The business press includes the *Wall Street Journal, Forbes, Barron's, Business Week, Fortune,* and other national publications as well as various local business-oriented publications (for example, the *Business Chronicle* in Houston, Atlanta, Los Angeles, San Francisco, and other cities). These periodicals are primary outlets for financial news, but they are deluged with information, so their channels of communication should not be cluttered with trivia or fluff.

Do not overlook the financial columnists. The Dan Dorfmans and Louis Rukeysers of this country carry great weight and can offer unique perspectives on particular companies. Trade magazines, usually devoted to particular industries, occupations, or professions, are also important outlets. They may reach such likely prospects as suppliers and producers.

Television and radio are limited but growing outlets for financial news. Some cable programming is devoted exclusively to business news. With channels proliferating thanks to direct satellite transmission and fiber-optic cable systems, such programming is likely to increase severalfold. Certain local and network programs are devoted specifically to business. Public broadcasting's '*Wall Street Week*,' Cable News Network's financial programs, and Associated Press Radio's *Business Barometer* are examples of such programs. Network or local major market news operations generally should be approached only with information that has news value for the community at large.

Finally, specialized financial media are extremely interested in corporate news. Market newsletters (often published by brokerage firms), investment advisory services, and statistical services (like Standard and Poor's, Value Line, or Moody's) frequently carry the greatest weight with potential investors.

Communication Strategies in Financial Relations

Strategies for communicating financial information, like those for implementing other plans (see chapter 7), must grow out of management's long-term view of the corporation. Communication strategy is a plan for getting from where you are to where you want to be. Thus, the perception of the company by its relevant publics should be compared with the way it hopes to be perceived in the future. Methods for implementing strategy include personal meetings, financial literature (correspondence, quarterly and annual reports, dividend enclosures), financial news releases, and annual meetings. Whatever a corporation's current status or ultimate objectives, its financial relations communication strategy must be characterized by responsiveness, regularity, and openness. Communication should never be evasive and must include bad news as well as good. Financial openness means "willingness to communicate honestly and forthrightly with . . . employees and external constituencies regarding economic matters."[21] Credibility is the key to a strong financial relations program.

Annual Meetings

The **annual meeting** is a kind of mandated ritual in which the actual owners of a business consider and vote on the effectiveness of management. In theory, stockholders have the power to do what they please (within the law) with their company. But in practice, issues are rarely discussed and even more rarely voted on because management collects proxies in advance to support its positions, appointments, and decisions.

Views on the annual meeting ritual are widely divergent. "At one end of the spectrum are those who regard the annual meeting as a hallmark of corporate democracy and an expression of our free enterprise system," says Arthur Roalman. "At the other are those who look upon the function as a meaningless corporate exercise."[22] The view held by management will influence the nature of a corporation's annual meeting. Whatever the case, the annual meeting presents certain opportunities and entails genuine risks; thus, careful planning and orchestration are essential. Most major public accounting firms publish guides for corporate executives preparing for annual meetings.

Besides trying to attract, inform, and involve the audience of stockholders, the annual meeting has other functions. It enables corporate management to reach all stockholders through pre- and postmeeting communication. It provides a showcase and a focus for corporate publicity. It permits personal contact between executives and stockholders through which actions can be explained, accomplishments recognized, and feedback offered. It is also a marketing tool, displaying products in their best light.

The annual meeting functions as a safety valve by which stockholders can let off steam. Its democratic nature makes the company vulnerable. Organized dissent may come from stockholders who have bought a few shares of stock just to gain a platform. Such individuals may intervene or disrupt—confronting management with embarrassing questions and drawing the attention of the news media. Chrysler Corporation, the third-largest U.S. auto maker, was confronted with the possibility of hostility at its 1995 annual meeting. Kirk Kerkorian, who holds a large block of Chrysler stock, was unhappy with the stock's performance. His concern led to actions by the Chrysler board to improve the stock price. G. A.

Marken suggests several ways to improve the chances for an effective, successful meeting:

CEO's presentation should be well prepared.

Provide displays highlighting company products, services, financial results.

Invite the media and representatives from the financial community.

Prepare an advance news release for the media to highlight the CEO's presentation at the meeting.

Have handouts such as annual reports, product literature, CD ROM, videos available.

Consider the meeting environment and amenities carefully (invitations, name badges, refreshments, tours, favors or speciality advertising gifts, etc.).

Develop an executive summary or digest of the meeting, if it is particularly unusual or controversial.[23]

Commenting on annual meetings, *Atlanta Journal* business editor Tom Walker observed tongue-in-cheek that corporations should retain consulting sociologists, "especially during the annual meeting season when managements are forced to line up before their shareholders and give an account of themselves."[24] Financial relations actually plays the role that Walker would assign to sociologists. By anticipating the concerns, issues, and even the mood of stockholders— on the basis of continuous interaction—financial public relations should be able to prepare management for most situations that could arise. With careful planning, the positive potential of the annual meeting may even be realized.

Annual Reports

Annual reports are prepared not only to publish the required SEC information but also to fulfill a public relations and marketing function. Reports are usually released in March, about six weeks before the company's annual meeting, which is often held in April or May. Annual reports represent a $8.5-billion-a-year industry.[25] The trend in annual report preparation is for more CEOs to write their own letters to shareholders, to include the bad news upfront, and to contract out actual production to consulting firms.

Annual reports come in a variety of shapes and styles. They average 44 pages long and cost $2.84 each to produce, according to Sid Cato, whose annual report newsletter office is in Kalamazoo, Michigan. Some reports, he says, "are spectacular, with glossy covers, creative art design, terrific color photographs and graphics, superior paper stock and easy to understand explanations of company performance."[26] Some are produced on CD ROM, some are on video, while others may be done as newspaper supplements. However, other companies produce only the 10-K report in black and white that is required by the SEC.

The pharmaceutical company Pfizer sends copies of its annual report to every physician in the United States. AT&T produces a braille version of its report. Some companies provide their annual reports on videocassettes to shareholders.

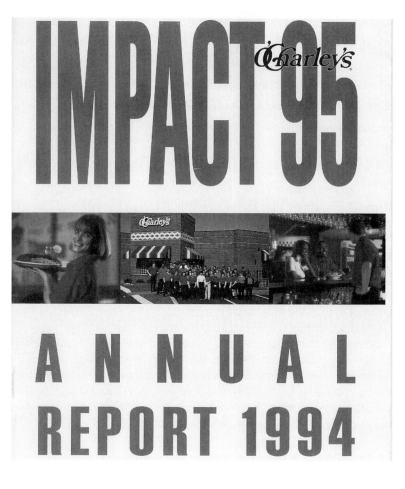

Oscar Beveridge calls the annual report "unquestionably the single most important public document issued by a publicly-held corporation."[27] Writing in *Fortune,* Herbert Meyer states: "Out of all the documents published by a Fortune 500 corporation, none involves so much fussing, so much anguish—and often so much pride of authorship—as the annual report to shareholders."[28] In short, the annual report can be considered the keystone of a company's financial relations program.

The History of Annual Reports   The Borden Company published the first corporate annual report in this country in 1854. It was a simple document, but its presence shocked corporate leaders, whose view of stockholders was best expressed as "the public be damned." By 1899, the New York Stock Exchange required every listed company to publish at least once a year "a properly detailed statement of its income and expenditures . . . and also a balance sheet, giving a detailed and accurate statement of the condition of the company at the close of its last fiscal year."

In 1903, United States Steel published what could be considered the first modern annual report. It included 36 pages of facts and figures and 22 pages of photographs. By the mid-1950s, the typical annual report was a slick, magazine-style publication. In 1964, Litton Industries commissioned the artist Andrew Wyeth to produce a painting for the cover of its report. What were once management scorecards have become management showcases.

The Purpose of Annual Reports   Fundamentally, the annual report fulfills the legal requirements of reporting to a company's stockholders. As such, it becomes the primary source of information about the company for current and potential stockholders, providing comprehensive information on the condition of the company and its progress (or lack thereof) during the previous year.

Some companies leave it at that. But nearly all large companies carry their annual reports considerably further, taking the opportunity to reinforce credibility; establish distinct identity; and build investor confidence, support, and allegiance. In this sense, the annual report becomes the company's calling card, a summary of what the firm has done and what it stands for. By accident or by design, the report usually conveys much about the personality and quality of corporate management.

Some companies get further service from their annual reports by using them for purposes of marketing, public relations, and employee recruitment and orientation. A report may also serve as an informational resource for financial advisers; a "backgrounder" for business editors; or even an educational resource for teachers, librarians, and students. General Motors uses its report to advertise its products. Goodyear Tire and Rubber puts out a special edition for classroom use. Increasing numbers of companies produce special editions for employees to gain their loyalty and support, build morale by stressing their contributions, and improve their understanding of company operations.

Another purpose of the report for some companies is to speak out on issues of social responsibility or state political positions. Paine Webber recently devoted part of its report to an essay extolling the virtues of economic growth and warning of the dangers of increased taxation. Columnist James J. Kilpatrick calls for much broader efforts of this nature:

> I have complained before, and will keep on complaining, about annual reports and other messages to stockholders. The annual reports that flow across my desk are often beautiful specimens of the graphic designer at work. There are four-color photos, pie charts that glitter like Keno-wheels, the last word in typography. But only a handful of top executives seize the opportunity to mobilize a constituency of stockholders, who presumably have some political clout, in support of the company's political positions. I am mystified by this failing.[29]

Some disapprove of the many faces of the annual report. James H. Dowling, for instance, maintains that the annual report should have only one purpose: to help investors decide whether to become or remain stockholders in a company.[30] Another dissenter is former SEC chairman Harold M. Williams, who claims that annual reports "often appear to reflect the results of a conflict between the desire to create a promotional document and the need to provide full and fair disclosure." Herbert Meyer takes the opposite view:

> What some people see as the great weakness of annual reports—their use as a soapbox to sell products, build managerial egos, and blast off against government regulations—is in a very real sense their considerable strength. Annual reports have become wonderfully clear windows into the personalities of corporations and the executives who manage them.[31]

Responding to both schools of thought, Lowe's Companies, the North Carolina materials retailer, sent out a postcard-sized, fill-in-the-blanks "generic" annual report (see Figure 14.2). For those wanting the full treatment, the company provided a set of five paperback books on Lowe's strategy, required disclosures, industry and company facts, and an essay on why people invest.

While accountants may decry verbal and pictorial embellishment of their ciphers, the communication opportunity presented by annual reports is too important to pass up. Moreover, with the cost of preparation and distribution sometimes reaching $10 per copy, financial considerations practically demand that these publications do double duty. Although a few companies have toned down their documents, annual reports are not likely to return to the minimum level of information required by the government.

Figure 14.2 Lowe's "generic" annual report

Date _March 1, 1994_

Dear Investor:

• We want you to be the first to know
  Lowes ___ results for _1993_ ___

• Sales were $ _1.43_ (billion, ~~million~~).
  This was a (record, ~~near-record~~, ~~not a record~~).

• Earnings were $ _50.6_ (~~billion~~, million).
  This was a (record, ~~near record~~, ~~not a record~~).

• Per share earnings were $ _1.40_
  This was a (record, ~~near-record~~, ~~not a record~~).

• Dividends paid were $ _.32_ per share.

• Share price in the year (increased, ~~decreased~~) by
  _12_ %

• Prospects for the new year look to be (~~great~~, good,
  ~~about average~~, ~~not so good~~, ~~poor~~ ~~just plain awful~~).

• Full Annual Report will be mailed about _April 25_

Chairman _Robert L. Strickland_

President _Leonard G. Herring_

Planning and Producing Annual Reports   Preparing the annual report is an elaborate undertaking requiring creativity, coordination, and the joint efforts of specialists in public relations, financial relations, accounting, law, photography, graphic design, and general management. Certain aspects of the report may require consultation and input from marketing, personnel, research and development, public affairs, or others. Although public relations may have overall responsibility for creating, producing, and distributing the annual report, it is necessarily a corporate effort.

The **first step** in planning and producing the annual report is to establish its objectives. What message should the document communicate? Objectives should be defined as specifically as possible. Once they are chosen, the **second step** is to select the means of achieving them. Often a theme is established. Growth, change, entrepreneurship, international competition, and high technology are examples of themes reflecting a report's specific objectives.

The **third step** in planning and production is to establish a budget and a schedule. Annual report budgets vary tremendously and depend largely on corporate means and desires. At least three months should be allowed for gathering material and information for the report, writing the copy, completing graphic design, collecting photos, and obtaining financial statements. Corporate attorneys and management must approve the copy. Adequate time for printing and distribution must be allowed. The total process usually requires a total of six to nine months. Much of the effort devoted to annual reports is aimed at attracting readers. F. C. Foy explains: "The annual report needs more than figures and tables, or even graphs, charts, or pictures. It needs candid, specific, readable statements of objectives, of difficulties and problems and how they are being attacked, of new products or services, and of how management envisions the future of the business."[32]

When business has had a bad year, annual reports often have tried to hide the news through evasive language or euphemisms. Not so today, though. Many of the top companies appear to have taken their public relations practitioners' advice and are meeting the bad news upfront, head-on. Phillip Knight, CEO of Nike, began his letter to shareholders in his 1994 report by saying, "So, it wasn't such a a great year."[33] Intel's annual report begins with "What a year . . . 1994 was the best of times and the worst of times."[34]

Why do these companies tell the shareholders the bad news right away? According to a report by Patrice Samuels of the New York Times News Service, the 1994 annual reports were less formal and more straightforward than previous reports because CEOs were afraid that otherwise they might "look out of touch to worried shareholders desperately seeking information"[35] Sid Cato, annual report newsletter publisher, says that "honesty has improved, nearly nine out of 10 annual reports will include any bad news up front, rather than burying it."[36] Whatever the format, good design and clear writing make annual reports attractive and readable.

The planners and producers of the annual report must be ever mindful of their audience's needs, while bearing in mind that annual reports reach a variety of audiences. Primary stakeholders, of course, are investors and the investment community. Generally speaking, the investing community is most interested in the auditor's report, financial highlights, changes in financial position, debt, and other data. Even among investors, however, desires for information differ. Potential and current employees also constitute an audience, but they may be more interested in the president's letter or the graphic presentation.

How can one document serve various stakeholders? Some companies, as we have noted, produce special editions for employees or students. Other companies, recognizing that annual reports need not be read from cover to cover, present information in layers so that various readers can take what they want. The layers consist of (1) cover, pictures, and captions; (2) the president's letter and financial highlights; and (3) detailed information about operations and financial developments, including footnotes. This presentation lets the reader decide just how deep he or she wants to go.

Contents of Annual Reports   The typical annual report consists of a cover; a president's letter (see public relations spotlight 14.1) financial and nonfinancial

---

The CEO's Letter for the Annual Report

Public Relations Spotlight 14.1

The following elements should be included in the CEO's letter that is part of the annual report:

1. In the opening paragraph, emphasize the most important aspect of the company's past year sales and earnings. Stress your preparations for achieving the best possible results in the year ahead given the economic and market conditions.
2. Recognize special contributions of employees and any key programs such as Total Quality Management or "reengineering."
3. Review briefly major accomplishments of the year.
4. Discuss your dividend policy and record.
5. Present the corporate outlook for the year ahead, both the positives and the problems.
6. In the concluding and—some consider most important—section, outline your strategies and plans to build on your strengths and overcome problems.

   Additional items that you may want to discuss may include these:

   - Improvement plans
   - Efforts to broaden market diversity geographically or in terms of new products
   - Initiatives to improve customer service
   - Ongoing research and development and increased use of technology
   - Any additional innovations that will give your company a competitive edge.

   The incorporation of these points should project your company as customer driven, cost-efficient, dynamic, technology oriented, and perhaps global. All of this must strike the right tone for the letter. Rather than a rigid style, the letter should have a conversational tone that is candid and enthusiastic.

Source: Based on Arthur J. Marino Jr., "Separating Your Annual Report from the Herd," *Public Relations Quarterly* (Summer 1995): 46.

highlights; a balance sheet and income statement; a description of the business (products and services); names and titles of corporate officers; names and affiliations of outside directors; location of plants, offices, and representatives; the address and telephone number of corporate headquarters; and reference to stock exchanges on which company stock is traded. The report may also include the company's history (particularly in anniversary issues), a discussion of company policies, a request for support of the company's stance on a political issue, results of stockholder surveys, and other reports or features. Figure 14.3 shows portions of diverse annual reports.

Photographs, graphic art, and color are increasingly important in annual reports. Award winner Michael Watras, president of Corporate Graphics and producer of annual reports for companies such as H. J. Heinz and Chase Manhattan Bank, explains, "Annual reports are more visual today than they were a few years ago. We're using larger pictures and more of them, and much more four-color. . . . Photographs are more likely to be tied into an overall theme."[37]

The annual report should always put corporate earnings in perspective and spell out prospects for the next year. It should answer these questions:

What is the major thrust of our company?

Where do we excel?

What are our weaknesses?

Why has the company performed as it has?

What are we doing about the future?

Financial highlights are a well-read aspect of annual reports. They generally include figures representing net sales, earnings before taxes, earnings after taxes, net earnings per common share, dividends per common share, stockholders' equity per common share, net working capital, ratio of current assets to current liabilities, number of common shares outstanding, and number of common stockholders. Other highlights include profit margin, percent return on stockholders' equity, long-term debt, and number of employees. Report designers are concerned not just with the numbers but with how they look. Financial data are most often integrated into the entire report and presented in interesting or unusual ways.

Herbert Rosenthal and Frank Pagani list eight elements of what they call "big league annual reports:"[38]

1. A meaningful or provocative pictorial cover

2. A well-designed format

3. Complete and understandable graphics

4. Unstilted photographs and artwork

5. Comprehensive text

6. Comparative figures

7. Tasteful presentation of products

8. Stylish printing

Figure 14.3a United Technologies emphasizes in their annual report the Pratt & Whitney division that makes engines for three-quarters of the world's aircraft.

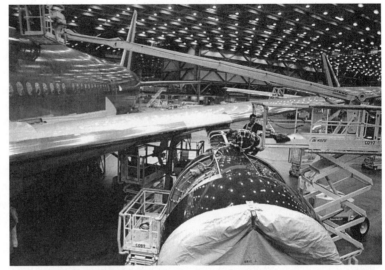

11:00 a.m. At the Boeing plant, another PW4084 engine is being installed.

6:00 a.m. Airborne. Flight test director Pete Smith (standing) and Pratt engineers monitor engine performance.

3:00 p.m. Post flight debriefing. Engines' performance during 90,000 lbs. thrust test is analyzed.

3:05 p.m. Boeing's 777 chief pilot John Cashman praises the engines' achievement.

2:30 p.m. Back in Seattle, inspecting the engine after the flight.

3:45 p.m. The next flight test begins.

JIŘINA MATOUŠKOVÁ
LIBRARIAN
THE FREEDOM FORUM NEWS LIBRARY,
PRAGUE, CZECH REPUBLIC

Matoušková has been librarian at The
Freedom Forum News Library at the
Center for Independent Journalism in
Prague since the library opened in
December 1992 — the first in a network
of Freedom Forum libraries in Europe
and Asia. They offer journalism texts and
reference books, on-line databases and
CD-ROMs. Matoušková answers more
than 5,000 information queries a year
from journalists, journalism students and
others on topics as diverse as Chilean
pension funds, Martina Navratilova,
"Jurassic Park" and journalism ethics.

" What people really love are
the CD-ROM archives.
When they see they can
search *The New York Times* in minutes,
it's just wonderful for them. Some of
them have never used a database like
that.

"Newspapers in Prague are thinking
about investing in CD-ROMs, but their
budgets don't allow them to. Not even
the English-language publications run
by Americans have these databases, so
they try to get the information from us.

"It is a lucky combination that the
library is free of charge and has such
valuable resources. Some of the few
information sources in Prague that I can
recommend cost money. And I can't name
any other source that offers such a unique
collection."

BORN: Oct. 10, 1948, Prague, Czech Republic
EDUCATION HIGHLIGHTS: Diploma in English, Russian and Czech, Prague School of
Languages, 1968; diploma in information systems, State Technical Library, 1975
CAREER HIGHLIGHTS: Czech/English translator, database indexer, Institute for
Agricultural Information, 1970-77; English instructor, Czechoslovak Ministry of
Finance, 1977-81; electronic librarian, Prague Research and Info Institutes, 1982-89;
assistant to the manager, U.S. Pfizer Co., Prague, 1989-91; press attache assistant,
U.S. Embassy, Prague, 1991-92; librarian, The Freedom Forum News Library, 1992 —
DIVERSIONS: Reading, bicycling, hiking, swimming, photography

Figure 14.3b The Freedom
Forum, for its 1994 annual
report, highlighted people
involved in its programs.

Figure 14.3c Brøderbund software, Inc. uses illustration integrated with text to tell its story.

Sound and video represent especially significant opportunities for Brøderbund to enrich consumer software, thanks to CD-ROM's huge data storage capacity. Video may be included as a separate presentation on the disk to help explain the program's use, or it may be integrated directly into the program. Either way, video involves all the normal issues of traditional film: concept, scripting, creating a shot list, hiring talent, camera crews and a sound stage.

The video-taped results are digitized in Brøderbund's video studio, then adjusted to balance image quality with screen size and frame rate on the computer monitor. The sound team comprises composers, musicians and audio engineers with computer experience. Their involvement usually begins in the pre-production stage in order to define broad sound characteristics. In the course of production meetings, they work with the animators to match audio effects with on-screen action, frequently drawing on libraries of classic cartoon sounds. Using Brøderbund's in-house studio, they record and edit volumes of dialog, which can exceed the amount written for an entire season of a television sitcom. They also write original musical compositions appropriate to the program's "environment."

Where in the World is Carmen Sandiego?® **Junior Detective Edition** turns world geography into fun on the run for 5- to 8-year-olds. Junior Detectives chase Carmen through seven regions of the world while learning about new cultures.

In his article "Separating Your Annual Report from the Herd," Arthur J. Marino suggests doing the following to make your report stand out:

Pack your information into less than 36 pages;

Prepare a simple graphic design on the cover, such as a few splashes of color;

Choose a theme that centers on your strategies for long-term success—through recessions as well as booms; and

Fashion a CEO letter of two pages or less that focuses on plans for the year ahead.[39]

"What a refreshing report that will be," Marino concludes.

Summary

The annual report is out. The annual meeting is over. Good communication links are established with financial analysts and editors. Stockholder correspondence is operating smoothly. How can you evaluate your efforts?

Good financial relations will usually result in increased proxy response, reduction of stock turnover, better attendance at stockholder meetings, appropriate price-to-earnings ratios, and greater ease in selling new stock issues. If you do not achieve this kind of success, you can always blame the economy.

Case Study

Proxy Fight at MC Shipping

M C Shipping Inc., an American Stock Exchange–listed company, was a limited-life company started in 1989 with a simple objective: buy a fleet of ships, operate it, distribute cash flow to stockholders, and sell once the ships' value had appreciated.

However, with a market decline in the shipping industry shortly after the company was begun, the objective could not be met. By 1993 the company management decided that the operating structure should be changed from a limited-life structure to a perpetual one. To allow this, debt and equity were to be increased so the company could operate more aggressively.

The perpetual proposal, though, had to be approved by two-thirds of the shareholders. Five similar proposals had been advanced by other companies, and only two had succeeded. Management knew it was in for a proxy fight. After a tough battle that included an annual meeting plus two adjournments and a final meeting, the proposal passed by a slim 1.1 percent margin.

Source: Case study is based on information in Laura Johnston, "How to Succeed in a Close Proxy Vote," *Public Relations Quarterly* (Spring 1994): 35–36.

Questions

1. If you had been a public relations account executive for the counseling firm handling the MC Shipping account, what advice would you have given MC Shipping once management determined it needed to change the structure?

2. What could you do to improve the chances for success in a proxy battle?

3. Once this battle had been won, what would be your priority financial relations advice for the company as it sought to begin its financial relations effort in earnest?

Notes

1. Eugene Miller, "Investor Relations," in Philip Lesly, *Lesly's Handbook of Public Relations and Communications,* 4th ed. (New York: AMACOM, 1991), 164–165.

2. Arthur R. Roalman, ed., *Investor Relations Handbook* (New York: AMACOM, 1974), iii.

3. Ibid., 31.

4. *NYSE Company Manual* (1 August 1977).

5. American Stock Exchange.

6. Henry Rockwell, "A Press Release Goes to Court," *Public Relations Journal* (October 1968).

7. G. Christman Hill, "Financial Public Relations Men Are Warned They're Liable for Clients' Puffery," *Wall Street Journal* (16 March 1972): 30.

8. Eugene Miller, "Investor Relations," 196.

9. Ibid.

10. Laura Johnston, "How to Succeed in a Close Proxy Vote," *Public Relations Quarterly* (Spring 1994): 35–36.

11. Ibid.

12. "Investor Relations Pros Downplay PR Skills," *Communication World* (May 1983): 15.

13. Harrison T. Beardsley, "Problem-Solving in Corporate Financial Relations," *Public Relations Journal* (April 1978): 23.

14. Oscar M. Beveridge, *Financial Public Relations* (New York: McGraw-Hill, 1963), 68.

15. Louis Rukeyser, *Atlanta Journal* (28 February 1980): 12–13.

16. Roalman, *Investor Relations Handbook,* 190.

17. Stuart Weiss, "Hell Hath No Fury Like a Surprised Stock Analyst," *Business Week* (21 January 1985): 98.

18. Holly Hutchins, "Annual Reports: Earning Surprising Respect from Institutional Investors," *Public Relations Review* (Winter 1994): 311.

19. Thomas Pincus, "How to Boost Your P/E Multiple," *Fortune* (10 November 1986): 183.

20. Stan Sauerhaft, "Won't Anybody Listen?" in Hill & Knowlton Executives, *Critical Issues in Public Relations* (Englewood Cliffs, N.J.: Prentice-Hall, 1975), 37.

21. Frederick D. Sturdivant, *Business and Society: A Managerial Approach* (Homewood, Ill.: Irwin, 1977), 358.

22. Roalman, *Investor Relations Handbook,* 43.

23. G. A. Marken, "There's More to Being Public Than Being Listed," *Public Relations Quarterly* (Fall 1993): 44–45.

24. Tom Walker, "J.P. Stevens Fights Catholics' Proposal," *Atlanta Journal and Constitution* (2 March 1980): 10.

25. Barnet D. Wolf, "Annual Reports Get Thumbs Down," *The Columbus Dispatch* (19 March 1995), 1F, Extra Dividends section.

26. Ibid.

27. Beveridge, *Financial Public Relations,* 137.

28. Herbert E. Meyer, "Annual Reports Get an Editor in Washington," *Fortune* (7 May 1979): 219.

29. James J. Kilpatrick, "A Short Course in Media Relations," *Nation's Business* (June 1979): 17–18.

30. James H. Dowling, "Main Job of the Annual Report, Wooing Investors," *Dunn's Review* (September 1978): 127.

31. Meyer, "Annual Reports Get Editor," 222.

32. F. C. Foy, "Annual Reports Don't Have to Be Dull," *Harvard Business Review* 51 (January/February 1973): 49–58.

33. New York Times News Service, "Annual Reports Less Formal; Shareholders Get a Dose of Candor from Companies," *Chicago Tribune* (17 April 1995), p. 6, Business section.

34. Ibid.

35. Ibid.

36. Sid Cato quoted in Barnet D. Wolf, "Annual Reports Get Thumbs Down," *The Columbus Dispatch* (19 March 1995): 1F.

37. "Annual Reports Help Sell Organizations," *ABC News* (December 1981): 1, 11.

38. Herbert C. Rosenthal and Frank Pagani, "Rating Your Annual Report," *Public Relations Journal* (August 1978): 12.

39. Arthur J. Marino Jr., "Separating Your Report from the Herd," *Public Relations Quarterly* (Summer 1995): 47.

CHAPTER 15

Public Affairs: Relations with Government

Preview

Government activity at every level has tremendous daily impact—positive and negative—on every kind of organization in the United States. Public affairs units help organizations anticipate or respond to issues affecting their activities or environments.

Business organizations in particular recognize the necessity of political adroitness and try aggressively to increase their public affairs effectiveness. Organizational political activities fall into three major categories: electoral, legislative, and regulatory.

The federal government's effort to return responsibility to local government increased the importance of state and local public affairs.

Change in the function of public affairs is evident—change in the direction of being proactive, anticipatory, and integrated into real decision-making.

—Lloyd B. Dennis
Executive Director of Public Affairs
Los Angeles Department of Water and Power

A regulation is changed, and a manufacturer goes out of business. A tariff is enacted, and an industry thrives. State revenues go down, and universities suffer. A county budget passes, giving libraries and cultural centers a shot in the arm. A zoning hearing opens the way for a major new development. A church acquires land for a new parking lot and seeks to convert the property to nonprofit status. Changes in the federal tax code shift $100 billion in liabilities from wage earners to corporations. A local ordinance bans smoking in the workplace. The unwillingness of a local government to promote a bond issue makes a proposed museum seek another city in which to locate. . . . Chernobyl, Bhopal . . . the recall of 160 million bottles of Perrier because of employee failure to clean filters . . .

The list goes on and on. Government activity at every level has tremendous daily impact—positive and negative—on every kind of organization in the United States. When an organization reviews the external forces that affect its operations, governmental bodies should be at the top of the list. Indeed, public opinion and media, employee, and community relations are considered important in part because of their potential influence on possible government action or inaction.

Public affairs, a term sometimes used to denote all of public relations, more often describes the aspect of public relations that deals with the political environment of an organization. Sometimes it is called government relations. Public affairs is related to issues management (discussed in chapter 4) in that it helps an organization anticipate or respond to issues affecting it's activities or environment. Public affairs efforts include seeking to shape public opinion and legislation, developing effective responses to matters of public concern, and helping the organization adapt to public expectations. Specifically, public affairs may be involved in monitoring public policy, providing political education for employees or other constituents, maintaining liaison with various governmental units, and encouraging political participation. "Access to lawmakers and their staffs is without a doubt the most important aspect of public affairs work in Washington. Without access your message will not be heard."[1] As shown in figure 15.1, public affairs facilitates the two-way flow of information between an organization and its political environment.

Public Affairs for Not-for-Profit Organizations

In the 1980s, public affairs was pursued as never before in terms of resources, executive involvement, sophistication, and openness. Large business organizations, particularly, awakened to the political process. When in the 1980s federal budget cuts made life more complex for not-for-profit organizations, these groups also became more sophisticated and aggressive in their government relations efforts.

Unions, schools, hospitals, libraries, cultural organizations, foundations, businesses, and other organizations have both the problem and the opportunity of dealing with government. All want to improve communication with government agencies and employees, monitor and influence legislative and regulatory actions, encourage constituent participation, and expand the awareness and understanding of people in power. Even the U.S. Navy has to deal with itself and the public, as illustrated in mini-case 15.1.

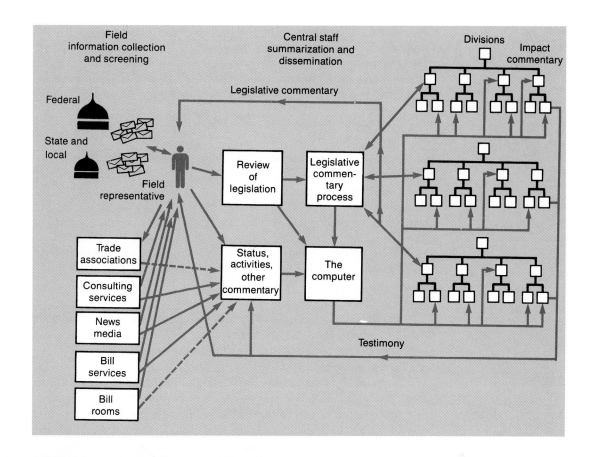

Figure 15.1 Field information collection and screening / Central staff summarization and dissemination / Divisions / Impact commentary

Figure 15.1 Two-way flow of political information

Mini-Case 15.1

Team Public Affairs

An article in *U.S. News and World Report* in 1992 asked, "What's Wrong With the Navy?" Another article nearly a year later said that the problem with the Navy was that it was made up of "many officers, not many gentlemen." Several unfavorable events, including the Tailhook scandal, cheating at the U.S. Naval Academy, sexual harassment, and the explosion on the USS Iowa, had led to this conclusion Enlistment was lagging as a result.

To deal with this problem, the Navy created Team Public Affairs, charged with changing the Navy's public image. A goal of Team Public Affairs was to reeducate the public about the Navy's changing role in the post–Cold War era.

Among the communication tools were two videos, including one for children, and a color brochure. An on-line Internet address broadened external communications. In addition, the Navy was featured on several television specials, and *U.S. News and World Report* ran a favorable cover story.

These position reports helped improve the Navy's image. Enlistments rose for the first time in several years.

Source: Based on Silver Anvil case study, "Silver Anvil Award Winners '95," *Public Relations Journal* (August 1995): 18.

These organizations realize that they can no longer even pretend to be above the political fray. Political activity has grown up and come out of the closet. Fundamentally, ours is a pluralistic society in which various interests compete in the political arena. Under these circumstances, business and other organizations recognize that their interests, indeed sometimes their survival, require political acumen and effort.

Public Affairs in Business

Because business practices public affairs most ardently and extensively, a deeper understanding of that practice will give insight into the application of public affairs in all organizations.

Background of Business/Government Relations

Our country's founding fathers were strongly influenced by the economic philosophy Adam Smith enunciated in his seminal 1776 work *The Wealth of Nations.* Smith advocated a very limited role for government in economic activities. Nevertheless, since their beginnings, the U.S. government and the various state governments have exerted more power over economic activity than is considered acceptable according to classical capitalistic theory.

Although the founding fathers took care to protect political freedoms with the Bill of Rights, they did not deem it necessary to protect economic freedom. Consequently, the preconditions for government intervention in the economy were present at our nation's birth.

In America's first century, business and government pushed forward together, promoting invention and westward expansion. When the captains of industry came to be known as robber barons, though, business leaders found out what it meant to be unpopular. By the turn of the century, muckrakers and trust-busters, socialists and populists made business their target in the courts, the voting booths, and the streets.

The passage of the Interstate Commerce Act in 1887 marked the beginning of 20 years of regulatory legislation aimed at curbing monopoly, stopping debilitating business practices, and controlling cutthroat competition. Unions were organized in response to abysmal working conditions; strike breaking, violence, murder, corruption of public officials, watered stock, and monopolistic practices were constantly in the public eye. Moreover, a nation of small individual businessmen was rapidly becoming a nation of employees.

In the 20th century, business's public support and government interaction waxed and waned. In the 1920s, the post–World War II period, and the 1980s, business enjoyed considerable popularity. The depression era of the 1930s, when bankruptcies, mass unemployment, and economic stagnation seemed to suggest that the American Dream was counterfeit, sank business to a low ebb of popular and political approval.

In the 1960s and 1970s, American society saw increasing complexity, a growing velocity of change, a heightening of risks, and a fragmentation of social norms and goals. The economic engines of business and government were both at full throttle. Social goals went beyond materialism, with demands for racial and sexual equality and the rise of environmentalism, consumerism, and other causes. Government began to use business to pursue social as well as economic goals.

In the midst of this era, business professor Neil Jacoby wrote:

> The profit-seeking corporation . . . has no choice but to be as politically influential as the law . . . and its resources . . . permit. Hedged in by a multiplicity of local, state and federal regulations affecting building, zoning, health, safety, insurance, employment, workmen's compensation, social security, wage and hour standards, equal opportunity rules, securities issuance, financing, fees and taxes, product and advertising, standards, et cetera, corporate business naturally takes political action to defend the freedom of action that remains to it.[2]

An article in *Time* pointed out government's power and the vigilance required to deal with that power. "A single clause tucked away in the Federal Register of Regulations (this year's version has already grown to a mountainous 32,000 pages) can put a small-town manufacturer out of business or rejuvenate an industry that was on the brink of bankruptcy."[3] As a consequence, business's presence in Washington grew rapidly. One-third of the public affairs units existing in corporations in 1980 had been created in the previous five years. In the 1980s, expansion continued but at a much slower pace. By the 1990s this expansion had largely ended.

In relation to business and the economy, government now plays a variety of roles: stimulant, referee, rule maker, engineer, pursuer of social goals, defender, provider, customer, controller. To be successful, business must be prepared to deal with government in any of these roles. That is why governmental relations is critically important and why public affairs has become, in the last 20 years, a crucial dimension of public relations.

Changing Roles Today

Government's enormous power and increased willingness to take an active hand in business management are further pressures for corporate involvement. Some have described the new and complex link between business and government as "a second managerial revolution . . . one in which the locus of real control over a corporation shifts from private executives to public officials."[4]

Another change in the relationship is the posture of business's political activity. Traditionally, business merely reacted to the threat of government action, whether that action took the form of taxation, regulation, legislation, or opposition to the efforts of labor, public interest groups, or even other business groups. Not until the danger was apparent did business, as a rule, enter into political activity (see figure 15.2). As Graham Moliter, president of Public Policy Forecasting, points out, business still often waits until too late to get into the political game:

> America's business environment is increasingly shaped by public policy dictates. Legislative, litigative and regulatory constraints grow daily. Yet, despite the enormity of government entanglement, the business community all too often waits until the last minute to focus on important issues. As a result, it comes up short in anticipating and adapting to changes in public policy.[5]

Recently, however, business has realized the value of developing continuing relationships with government at all levels that permit early involvement in

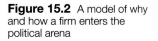

Figure 15.2 A model of why and how a firm enters the political arena

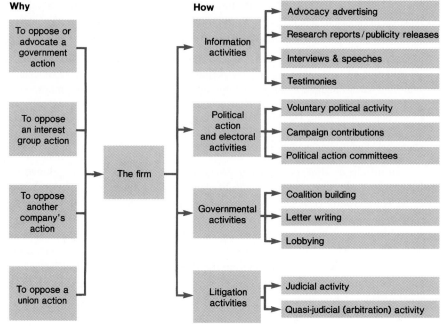

issues, policies, regulations, and legislation. Joseph Gleason, managing director of Manning, Selvage & Lee in Washington, says, "It's also important to develop relationships with policy-makers, many who know little about your client or organization prior to initial communication."[6] Advance notice can be a critical factor in political effectiveness. Moreover, early involvement makes provisions for crisis management less necessary when a critical bill comes to a vote later on.

Finally, the business-government relationship is changing because business senses changes in public attitudes toward government. As those become more critical and negative, success of business in specific and general political activity becomes more likely. F. Clifton White, president of Public Affairs Analysts, Inc., states:

> Because of growing negative attitudes toward government, it should be possible to convince people that the solution to specific economic and social problems does not lie in the direction of governmental action, but is quite the reverse.

Impact on Management   The growing importance of business public affairs and political activities has had substantial impact on management in general and public relations in particular. Because the issue is one of corporate control, top corporate leaders take an active role in public affairs efforts. Explains former Congressman Donald G. Brotzman, now president of the Washington-based Rubber Manufacturers' Association, "Involvement of top management is a most important principle. The chief executive officer and all top managers must be active participants." Grover Starling maintains, "The direct and indirect influence of government action on business changes the kinds and mix of skills that one needs to succeed as a manager."[7] The effect on top management, he feels, is even more pronounced: "Top managers must now be as concerned about public policy as they are about anything else they do."[8]

Nicholas F. Brady, chairman of the investment banking firm Dillon, Read & Co., served eight-and-one-half months in the United States Senate, filling an unexpired term. He makes the following suggestion to sensitize top management to public affairs:

> Why not hold one board meeting each year in Washington? All of us who serve on boards make trips to important plant locations where new products are being developed. Our government is as important a part of our business life as a new product. Why not hold one board meeting a year in Washington, finish up business promptly, then spend the rest of the time talking with government leaders? The gap in communication, in cooperation, in understanding is too deep to be conducted on a jet-in and jet-out basis.[9]

Today no public relations program is complete unless it includes provisions for dealing with government. This job is, in part, a complex sequence of information acquisition, processing, and dissemination. Fact finding and serving as a listening post may be the most important aspects of governmental relations. In gathering information, practitioners often do essentially the same things as journalists do.[10] In fact, many (though not all) public affairs activities resemble those undertaken by other public relations practitioners on a daily basis.

After gathering information, government relations specialists weigh and evaluate its potential impact on the company or industry. Information is then disseminated to corporate decision makers, employees, stockholders, and the public. Indeed, public affairs has its greatest impact on an organization when it aids corporate planning. At the same time, government relations staffs convey information to legislators, regulators, congressional staffers, potential political allies, and the public.

Public relations is also sometimes called on to fight fire with fire on the government relations front. Investigation and publicity lack the force of law, but they are clearly among the weapons government uses to influence business. Leaks to the media by "high-level sources," visits to the sites of supposed infractions, staged public hearings, and the like may be used against business by government officials. Businesses' public affairs efforts must sometimes entail responding in kind. Their public relations specialists must compete with the public information machines of government and the public relations operations of a variety of special interests. Honesty and forceful public communication is a crucial aspect of the government relations process.

The Job of Public Affairs

To operate effectively, government relations professionals must thoroughly understand the U.S. political process. In a general sense, political activities fall into three broad categories: electoral, legislative, and regulatory. Electoral activities involve the election of candidates favorable to an organization's interests and the

Understanding the Political System

development of plans for financially supporting selected political campaigns. Political action committees (PACs) are the major vehicles for fund-raising efforts.

Legislative activities work to create or increase support for favorable legislation and build opposition against unfavorable activities. Lobbying is the major avenue for legislative activities.

The primary goal of regulatory activities from a public affairs point of view is to foster an understanding of the day-to-day problems of a particular organization or industry. Regulators are more difficult to lobby because they are rarely elected officials. Nonetheless, many public affairs efforts related to regulatory activity take a form quite similar to lobbying.

Electoral Activities

A few wealthy cattle ranchers, logging companies, and mining concerns have used federal lands for tremendous gain while paying little to the government. Critics claim this use has damaged the environment and cost the taxpaying public billions of dollars. When President Bill Clinton sent legislation to Congress in early 1993 to raise rent for the use of federal lands, you would have thought it would pass easily. Not so: It was defeated soundly. Critics said this defeat was directly attributable to the $7 million contributed to key legislators by PACs.[11]

Although political action is often viewed in electoral terms, most organizations actually place less emphasis on electing candidates than on working with the winners after election. In 1974, however, the Federal Election Campaign Act legitimized the role of corporations and business-related groups in federal elections, greatly improving their position vis-à-vis labor and other special interests.[12] The law allowed the formation of business **political action committees.**

A political action committee is a group of people who raise or spend at least $1,000 in connection with a federal election. Members of a PAC usually have some common political concern, interest, or cause. To pool resources in support of favored candidates, PACs have been formed by unions, businesses, industry groups, church groups, professionals, and many others. In 1992, about 6,000 PACs gave away $179 million to candidates.

The goal of legislation allowing PACs was to reform campaign financing. Legal limits on and full disclosure of contributions are supposed to ensure fairness in the electoral process. However, numerous loopholes exist and have caused the concern that PACs may promote corruption or tip the political scales in favor of special interests. Some critics maintain that PACs are costly, time-consuming, and demeaning to candidates. Others say that since PACs multiply and therefore tend to neutralize one another, they should be abolished.

Supporters maintain that PACs are an example of citizens' rights to free speech, that they promote political awareness and involvement, and that they have brought campaign financing into the light. Table 15.1 shows the 10 PACs that made the largest contributions to the 1992 national election campaigns.

The money generated by corporate PACs goes to politicians of divergent views. The American Trucking Association PAC has given almost exclusively to incumbents regardless of party. Coca-Cola and Grumman PACs have favored Democratic incumbents. Ford and General Motors have tended to give to both

TABLE 15.1   Ten Largest PACs in 1992

1 American Medical Association	$3.25 million
2 National Association of Realtors	$2.95 million
3 Teamsters Union	$2.53 million
4 Association of Trial Lawyers	$2.36 million
5 National Education Association	$2.36 million
6 United Automobile Workers	$2.25 million
7 American Federation of State, County, and Municipal Employee's	$1.95 million
8 National Auto Dealers Association	$1.78 million
9 National Rifle Association	$1.74 million
10 American Bankers Association	$1.69 million

Source: Federal Elections Commission.

incumbents and challengers. Amoco and Corning Glass Works have favored Republicans. "Overall, business-related PACs split their donations about equally between Democrats and Republicans with most of the money going to senior incumbents in both parties."[13]

Corporate PACs get their money from employees or stockholders. Other PACs get funds from their members or constituencies. Thus, if a PAC is to be effective, it "must first educate its people and motivate them to participate."[14] Some have charged that PACs attempt to "buy" political officials or unduly influence legislators in relation to pet issues. Senator Edward Kennedy has claimed that PACs "are doing their best to buy every senator, every representative, and every issue in sight."[15] Typically, PACs contribute to candidates whose philosophies are consistent with their own. One PAC official explained that his group has two tests for campaign contributions: Is the candidate someone we agree with, and is he or she someone in the area of government that relates to the way we do business? In reflection of these criteria, a senator on the banking committee gets contributions from bank PACs, while one on the agriculture committee receives funds from the Associated Milk Producers.

What PACs typically seek is access. That is why funds more often flow to incumbents. PACs are so eager to back winners that they often do so retroactively—making contributions after the election is over. Funds contributed after the election are called "hundred percent money," meaning that none is wasted on losers. Many PACs switch sides after the votes are counted. When Senator Charles Hecht (R-Nevada) upset incumbent Howard Cannon, postelection contributions came from former opponents, including the American Dental Association, the American Bankers Association, and the McDonald's Corporation. The National Association of Realtors kicked into Hecht's campaign chest after opposing him in the primary and the general election. In many cases, PAC funds are used to keep from making enemies.

Because a PAC contribution may be as much as $10,000 per election, the gift generally helps open the door to a legislator's office. Indeed, the most important function of electoral activities is to provide support for legislative activities.

Legislative Activities

Most political decisions important to organizations are made long after elections are over. Consequently, business firms and other organizations concentrate their efforts on affecting legislation and regulation in relevant areas. These activities are known as **lobbying.**

Lobbying has been defined as "the practice of trying to influence governmental decisions, particularly legislative votes, by agents who serve interest groups."[16] Lobbying is an extensive and expensive activity. Although the term has acquired an unsavory connotation of graft and influence peddling, lobbying has long been recognized as a legitimate practice. James Madison, writing in 1788, held that an essential characteristic of a representative democracy is that the various interest groups in society are permitted to compete for the attention of government officials.

In recent years, lobbyists have cleaned up their acts. Lobbyists for business have adopted more restrained practices regarding gifts and entertainment. Old-time Washington business lobbyists have been replaced by carefully selected professionals who have business acumen, a thorough grasp of sometimes highly technical information, and lots of political savvy. Henry Ford II sums up the new attitude: "The problem with 'lobbying' activities is not to conceal their existence, nor to apologize for them, but to make sure they are adequate, effective and impeccably correct in conduct."[17]

The federal lobby reform act was signed into law in late 1995 and is scheduled to take effect in 1996. This reform measure came nearly 50 years after enactment of the original lobbying law in 1946. For the last four decades, reformists have been trying to change the law to give it more impact. The new law requires registration of all persons who earn more than $5,000 in a six-month period by contacting not only members of Congress but also their staffs and executive branch top officials. Corporations spending more than $20,000 in a six-month period are also required to report details of their activities. The law requires lobbyists to report their income and expenses, who hired them, and on what specific issues they have worked. Violators face fines of up to $50,000.

States often have stricter laws for registration of lobbyists than the federal government. Of course, those laws vary widely from state to state.

No accurate count of lobbyists exists because, while full-time lobbyists in Washington must register, many part-time ones do not. However, some estimates suggest that close to 100,000 people work in Washington for various firms and groups seeking to influence policy.[18] Pat Buchanan, political columnist, commentator, and sometimes candidate who is a critic of big government, said, "In 1950, there were several thousand lobbyists in Washington and 1,000 lawyers accredited to the D.C. Bar. In 1994, lobbyists number more than 90,000 and 61,000 lawyers are listed by the bar."[19]

The lobbyist's function is critical, though, from the perspective of business. Starling maintains:

> Because many government policies can have a sizable effect on company profits, the business manager who neglects the lobbying function is every bit as irresponsible as one who ignores the company's capital structure or level of employee motivation.[20]

Lobbyists are essential to the functioning of Congress. The mass of legislation introduced each session is so great that congressional staff simply cannot handle the load. Senators and representatives trying to judge the likely impact of legislation depend on the input of lobbyists who analyze proposed bills and point out potential consequences. *Time* assesses the impact of the lobbying process this way:

> On balance the relationship between the governors and the governed, even when the lobbyist does represent one of the nation's many special interest groups, is often mutually beneficial, and perhaps indispensable to the fullest workings of democracy. The increasingly knowledgeable and competent Washington lobbyist supplies a practical knowledge vital to the writing of workable laws.[21]

What do lobbyists do? Many things. They inform corporate executives about developments in legislation, report on the introduction and progress of specific bills, offer or arrange testimony to congressional committees, file statements, communicate with legislators, analyze policies and legislation, inform legislators about the potential effects of legislation, educate legislators about business and economics, help draft laws, publicize testimony, and develop strategy to support or oppose specific legislation.

Lobbyists dig out information from officials and records, then use it to inform corporate executives, persuade government officials, promote or oppose legislation or other governmental action, and obtain governmental cooperation. Lobbyists devote much time to creating contacts and programs that will improve communication with government and to monitoring legislators' activities regarding statutes and laws.

Lobbyists involve themselves in the earliest stages of the legislative process. Recognizing that lobbying can work only while the legislator is still in the decision-making stage, lobbyists provide information before bills are drawn up. Their emphasis is on information and advocacy, not pressure. Lobbyists seek to define issues in terms of the legislators' constituencies and the public interest, providing briefly stated, neatly organized facts that answer questions. Often, they must communicate through a legislator's staff or assistants.

Facts must be presented in a truthful, straightforward, and helpful fashion. Honesty is essential because credibility is the lobbyist's most important asset. As Walter Guzzardi wrote in *Fortune,* "Without credibility, try suicide."[22] Lobbyists who have achieved credibility are relied on by senators, representatives, and their staffs. When such relationships are established, the lobbyist is in a position to suggest legislation, prepare speeches, line up witnesses for congressional hearings, and provide research and position papers. Under such circumstances, it is difficult to tell where legislator leaves off and lobbyist begins.

Lobbying activities are carefully organized and integrated into corporate planning. Figure 15.3 shows the staff organization of Atlantic Richfield's Washington office.

Perhaps even more important than establishing the order of the staff is establishing an order of issues. Legislative battles must be carefully chosen and related to the overall objectives of the corporation.

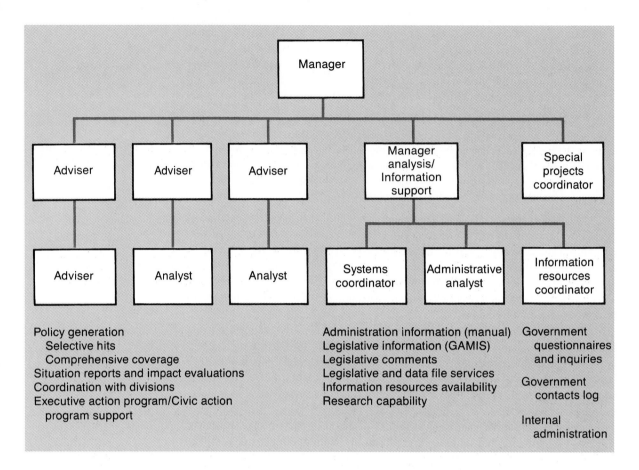

Policy generation
   Selective hits
   Comprehensive coverage
Situation reports and impact evaluations
Coordination with divisions
Executive action program/Civic action
   program support

Administration information (manual)
Legislative information (GAMIS)
Legislative comments
Legislative and data file services
Information resources availability
Research capability

Government
   questionnaires
   and inquiries

Government
   contacts log

Internal
   administration

Figure 15.3 Atlantic Richfield's government relations coordination and policies

Politicking from the Grass Roots   In a democracy, attempts to influence government occur in the context of public opinion and require dealing with an audience much broader than political officials. This broader audience is reached through **grass-roots lobbying** and issue advertising. "The chief weapon (for) all successful lobbies today is the mobilizing of support at the grass roots level."[23] As we have mentioned in other chapters, businesses increasingly seek to organize employees, stockholders, community leaders, and others as potent weapons in the political arena. Washington lobbyists must demonstrate that their positions are those of the legislators' constituents. This means the constituents must be organized to make their voices heard.

According to *Business Week*, "The wedding of lobbying and PR makes sense . . . because of the increasing need to win public support for their causes."[24] Top lobbyist Charles E. Walker maintains, "Lobbying has come to require strong grass roots efforts . . . I go to a congressman and he tells me 'You can sell me if you can sell my constituents.' "[25]

Different constituents can be mobilized to communicate in a variety of ways. The grass-roots approach may consist of flooding Congress with mail or getting just the right people to call their representatives. Grass-roots lobbying means establishing an organization at the local level by which support can be activated when needed. The Associated General Contractors, for instance, maintain a legislative network among their 113 chapters across the country. At least one person in each chapter personally knows his or her senator or representative. On one occasion, this network was invaluable in defeating a labor law reform bill.

The American Bankers Association (ABA) asks legislators which bankers they want to hear from. Then the ABA asks those bankers to transmit the ABA's positions on specific legislation. The ABA has 1,200 designated contact bankers, many of whom know members of Congress, have served as campaign treasurers, or have worked on campaigns.

The most striking aspect of grass-roots lobbying is the mail it generates. Congressional mail has more than tripled in the past decade. As much as 50 percent of congressional staff time is devoted to constituent mail.

For a mail campaign to be effective, the letters have to make an impression on the senator or representative. Letters that receive attention tend to be those written by constituents, local community leaders, or friends, or those dealing with subjects of particular interest to the legislators. Personal, persuasive, fact-filled letters are far more effective than canned or preprinted ones. "We are more impressed by personal correspondence than by mass-produced, engineered campaigns," says former California Senator S. I. Hayakawa.

In general, letters to legislators should be brief and confined to one subject. The piece of legislation at issue should be clearly identified. Of course, the letter should be typed neatly and should follow all rules of spelling, grammar, and punctuation (see figure 15.4). When writing to a legislator, state your case positively and politely, without criticism or threats. Ask the legislator to respond by explaining his or her position. Timing is perhaps the most important factor in determining the clout of your correspondence. If the letter arrives after the vote, it is useless. Letters should be timed to arrive during the early stages of pending legislation.

Issue advertising (or advocacy advertising) is a way of taking an organization's position straight to the people, with the anticipation that they will support it politically. This kind of advertising is not new. Organized labor, private voluntary groups, governmental agencies, and others have long used advertising to support their positions on public issues.

Mobil Corporation is perhaps the nation's leading issue advertiser. Under its vice-president of public affairs, Herbert Schmertz, Mobil pioneered corporate advocacy. The company spends $5 million annually to share its opinions on excessive government regulation, environmentalism, consumerism, nuclear power, and protectionism (figure 15.5).

Other issue advertising efforts seem more innocuous but still serve the sponsoring organizations' political goals. General Motors urges use of seat belts and attempts to ward off government efforts to make airbags mandatory. R. J. Reynolds calls for common courtesy on the part of smokers and nonsmokers, seeking in part to stem a tide of legislation against smoking in the workplace and in public buildings.

Figure 15.4 Sample letter from a paper company for its customers to use for "grass-roots lobbying"

Sample letter from customer to Senators and Congressmen

The Honorable (Name)
United States Senate   **OR**   The Honorable (Name)
Washington, DC 20510   United States House of Representatives
                                Washington, DC 20515

Dear Senator/Congressman/Congresswoman: _____

I am writing, as a customer of the paper industry, to urge you to call or write to EPA Administrator, Carol Browner, objecting to the unnecessarily high costs of the proposed Cluster Rules, and asking her to consider the alternative proposed by the U.S. paper industry.

The proposed rules will raise the operating costs of U.S. paper mills to the point that it will be hard for them to compete with foreign producers. There also will be a severe shortage of investment capital which will prevent them from investing in quality and productivity improvements to keep our industry competitive on a world-wide basis.

Industry-wide, the EPA's proposals will close a total of 33 mills, eliminate 21,500 mill jobs and 86,000 indirect jobs. As an indirect result, my business will be adversely affected.

EPA should re-evaluate its position in light of current data on complete substitution of chlorine dioxide for elemental chlorine in the pulp bleaching process. In addition, the Maximum Achievable Control Technology (MACT) portion of the rule should be withdrawn and reconsidered utilizing the up-to-date, multi-facility air emission data provided to EPA by the industry.

Please contact EPA Administrator Browner and recommend that EPA consider the paper industry's alternative proposal that is designed to protect the environment <u>and</u> jobs.

Sincerely yours,

Regulatory Activities

In an era of governmental growth, government regulation is the area in which the most dramatic expansion has occurred. During the 1970s, the period of greatest increase in government regulations, 22 new regulatory agencies were created, including the powerful Environmental Protection Agency (EPA), the Consumer Product Safety Council (CPSC), and the Occupational Safety and Health Administration (OSHA). A total of 120 major regulatory laws were passed during the decade. Regulatory outlays rose 53 percent, while regulatory staff increased from 27,600 to 87,500 in 10 years (figure 15.6).

"We have become a government, not of laws passed by elected officials . . . but a government of regulation," claimed former Congressman Elliott H. Levitas (D-Georgia). "A Congress . . . will enact 500 laws during its two-year tenure. During that . . . time, the bureaucracies will issue 10,000 rules and regulations."[26]

Almost every facet of business activity is subject to the rules, standards, or other controls of one or more federal agencies that have the power to review, inspect, modify, or even reject the work of private industry. Robert Lane explains business's response:

> Business objects to regulation not just on economic grounds but because it challenges the manager's belief systems, questions his judgments, deprecates the importance of

Protectionism: A persistent threat—II

What's wrong with H.R.4800

The House-passed omnibus trade bill—H.R. 4800—is 458 pages long and quite complex. It would shift the U.S. sharply toward protectionism and away from its current emphasis on free trade. And in the fine print, it would do even more. It would attempt to extend U.S. law to sovereign foreign nations, and open the door to a federally planned economy at home.

Here are some of the bill's protectionist provisions we found most troubling:

● The bill would, under certain circumstances, weaken the President's long held discretion in trade matters and force him to impose quotas and raise tariffs, shifting the balance from negotiation to confrontation. This would soon trigger retaliation from the nations involved.

● Some provisions clearly violate the rules of the General Agreement on Tariffs and Trade, which the U.S. first signed in 1947 and which the U.S. intends to help amend and update again at international meetings beginning this fall. How much clout will this country have in treaty negotiations if its trade policies are governed by a law that is inconsistent with the treaty?

● The bill is sometimes vague, sometimes overly specific. For example, it would allow special import quotas against countries whose exports to the U.S. are 175 percent of its imports from the U.S. At present, this provision would apply only to Japan, West Germany and Taiwan. It would not answer the need to broaden those markets to U.S. exports, and thereby create jobs in the U.S. Besides, in the normal course of business, trade balances are never equal; they rise and fall in accordance with the shifting tastes and needs of both parties.

Equally onerous are those fine-print provisions guaranteed to make our trading partners wince.

For example, the bill defines as an "unreasonable" trade practice by a foreign nation the denial of collective bargaining, the absence of laws protecting child labor, and the lack of health and safety regulations. These are termed "internationally recognized workers' rights," but to the governments of many nations that trade with the U.S., the provision will doubtlessly be seen as an attempt to impose American law on *their* people. What do we know of worker protection in a country like China, say, where trade with the U.S. is growing and welcomed by both parties?

We're also particularly wary of provisions that open the back door to the discredited belief that government should plan the economy. The House measure would establish agencies called Industry Adjustment Advisory Groups. With members drawn from business, labor, government and public interest organizations, the groups could review the requests for help not only from companies, but also from trade associations and employee groups that say they're in trouble from foreign competition.

The groups would define the problem and provide advice on the type of federal help needed, and then monitor the industry to see that the "readjustment plan" was being followed. The bill would also create a Council on Industrial Competitiveness with subcouncils for specific industries to develop long-term strategies for those industries. In other words, whether a company said it wanted help or not, a request by an outside organization could suddenly find the company knee-deep in unwanted and unsought "advice."

For a long time, those who would restructure American society along collective lines have advocated exactly this sort of central planning. They haven't gotten very far because Americans have seen no reason to impose central government planning on their industries when even the Socialist countries are abandoning grandiose central plans in favor of free-market solutions to their economic problems.

Perhaps, for political reasons, the Senate feels it will have to pass a trade bill this year. If it does, it ought to recognize how central to America's well-being is the free flow of goods and services all over the world. To curtail America's trade is to cost Americans jobs, and punish the American economy.

But if the Senate follows the route taken by the House, the promised presidential veto would be the best trade relief we can think of.

Next: A sound trade policy for America.

Figure 15.5 Mobil's issue advertising (Reprinted with permission of Mobil Corporation.)

Figure 15.6 A decade of federal regulatory growth

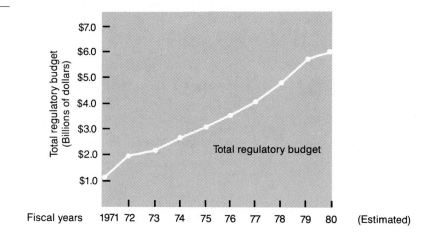

his role, limits his autonomy, and creates anxiety by introducing new uncertainties into an already unpredictable environment.[27]

A Conference Board study showed that the country's major corporations are seeking to reform the federal regulatory structure. Although they accept the need for virtually all regulatory agencies, "the vast majority of firms are demanding that companies and industries be given a larger voice in the formulation and execution of regulations."[28]

Business activities meant to affect regulation are often more the purview of the corporation's legal function than of its public relations function. The reasons lie in the structure of the regulatory process and in the way in which opportunities for challenge or intervention present themselves. For example, consider the government's attempt to develop safety standards for power mowers.

The Consumer Product Safety Commission began working on lawnmower regulation in August 1973. For six years, lawyers, economists, engineers, and technicians conducted research, oversaw oral presentations, attended public meetings, and debated foot-probe requirements and thrown-object tests. Having accumulated 35,000 pages of official record on the subject, CPSC decided to require that walk-behind power mowers be equipped with a clutch that would stop the blade three seconds after the operator let go of the handle.

The commission said this measure would prevent 60,000 injuries and cost $190 million per year. Of course, the industry had provided inputs during the investigative process. As soon as the CPSC published its requirements, however, the Outdoor Power Electric Institute, a trade association, sued the commission, challenging its data, its conclusions, and every aspect of the proposed regulation. The Fifth Circuit Federal Appeals Court heard the case on April 1, 1980—seven years after the regulatory process had begun. The Appeals Court decision was appealed.

"This saga is fairly typical of the way federal regulation works—or, to put it more accurately, doesn't work," one article stated.[29] Ultimately, regulations on lawnmower safety were not made by Congress, the president, the CPSC, or the industry. The final regulation was handed down by federal judges. In this process, public relations may prepare testimony or publicize a corporation or industry position, but the final job is usually the lawyer's.

Traditionally, most attention has been paid to interaction with government at the federal level, but the relative importance of local and state governments has increased recently for organizations of many types. While builders and developers have long sought to influence local zoning decisions, for example, the players in local and state government affairs are now more numerous and more intense.

State and Local Public Affairs

Deregulation, federal budget cutbacks, and Washington's determination to return government to the people have forced state and local governments to pick up the slack. As a result, state officials are now dealing more extensively with health care, environmental issues, labor legislation, bank deregulation, and international trade. Moreover, state and local funding for the arts, transportation, health care, education, and other areas has become more critical. Naturally, both profit-seeking and not-for-profit organizations have focused increasingly on the 50 state capitals in addition to Washington, D.C.

Covering 50 cities is more difficult, complex, and expensive than merely focusing on Washington. "In a two-year period almost 250,000 bills are introduced in the various state legislatures. For a company with nationwide interests this volume appears to create an insurmountable obstacle."[30] To deal with this insurmountable obstacle, some companies have established their own networks of private legislative information in all 50 state capitals. Others have monitored only those states where they have major interests. Another approach has been to rely on the industry's association for surveillance and lobbying efforts. Often companies use a combination of these approaches.

When national organizations seek to influence local affairs, they must understand local politics and culture. A major New York corporation dealing with a tax problem in a southern state got an audience with the chairman of the state senate's tax-writing committee. After an informative and persuasive 30-minute presentation, the senator asked, "Y'all aren't from around here, are you?"[31] Steven Markowitz, a state government relations consultant, explains:

> Corporate America's commitment to state government relations today is at the same point that federal government relations was in the late '60s and early '70s. The need to become more actively involved is generally acknowledged, but the organizational commitments and strategies needed to effectively deal with the issues are still emerging and taking shape.[32]

Staying on top of issues, tracking bills, knowing the right people, knowing which PACs to contribute to, cultivating the right media contacts, and all the other necessary lobbying activities may be approached in a variety of ways. Generally, goals and objectives, the scope of the effort, and key states must be identified. The corporation or association may then set up its own in-house operation, employ outside lobbyists or consultants on a retainer basis, or depend on industry or state business associations.

Despite the associated difficulty and expense, Markowitz says the trend is clear: "Corporations and associations will have to devote more time and resources to managing state government relations in the years ahead."[33]

Internal Political Communication

We have already discussed political action committees as a means of promoting employee and shareholder awareness and involvement. Beyond PAC activities, however, a public relations practitioner whose position involves monitoring government relations can also use in-house publications and other media to provide political instruction, increase employee awareness of political issues, and encourage employee political involvement.

Organizations stimulate employee political awareness in a variety of ways. Bliss and Laughlin Industries of Oak Brook, Illinois, provides work sheets with W-2 forms so employees can calculate how much of their wages have gone to taxes, what percentage of income goes to taxes, and how long each one must work to support the cost of government. The employees have learned that their biggest expense is not shelter or food but taxes. Dow Chemical maintains an extensive public affairs program for employees. The program rests on four objectives:

1. Informing employees about national and local issues that potentially affect the firm.

2. Making employees aware of governmental processes and legislative procedures.

3. Encouraging employees to take part in the political process and giving specific examples of approaches they might use.

4. Advising employees of the value of political contributions and providing the opportunity to contribute through political action committees.

Budd Company gives its managers a "discretionary bonus" of up to several thousand dollars based on evaluation in 11 categories, including "involvement in government affairs." Managers are judged on their ability to get their people involved in political campaigns, their willingness to write to government officials on issues affecting the company, and their ability to organize in-plant political education committees. All of these companies recognize that if business intends to remain a viable part of society, its leaders must encourage employee participation in the political process.

Does Business Conduct Its Government Relations Properly?

Some claim that American business holds inordinate political power. Undeniably, corporations possess the organization, financial resources, access, and prestige that tend to increase political effectiveness. It is important to remember, however, that business is only one of many interests seeking political favor. Indeed, from the mid-1960s through the late 1970s, businesses were notably unsuccessful in their political efforts. Moreover, as Neil Jacoby pointed out, "At any given time, business corporations are split on many national issues; there does not appear to be a monolithic 'business interest.' "[34]

Perhaps a more serious charge is that of "crosstown estoppel," or corporate political double-talk. Corporations seriously jeopardize their positions and images when they contradict themselves. *Business Week* warned, "Companies that have made conflicting statements to federal agencies could find those contradictions coming back to haunt them," and cited the case of the Sharon Steel Corporation as an example. When the Environmental Protection Agency moved to bar the company from government contracts because of noncompliance with federal regulations, Sharon Steel claimed that the penalty was "so severe that its imposition may destroy a going business." Yet in a prospectus filed with the Securities and Exchange Commission, the company said that if blacklisted, it did "not anticipate that the resulting loss of business, if any, would have a material adverse effort on its consolidated sales or results of operations."[35]

Sharon Steel was lying to someone, and unfortunately, it is not the only company that has engaged in crosstown estoppel. Such corporate behavior opens opportunities to business's political foes, invites congressional scrutiny, and almost begs for additional regulations.

Another example of such double-talk was found when the National Association of Home Builders launched a $250,000 campaign criticizing the 1984 federal deficit. The hypocrisy of such an effort becomes evident when one considers the extent of funds flowing into federal housing and mortgage insurance programs.

Summary

The relationship between government and business has been described in many ways. Depending on the observer's perspective, the pair are partners, adversaries, or strange bedfellows. In fact, as we have seen, the relationship is far more complex than any of these designations implies. It might be summed up as mutual dependence in structural terms and mutual hostility in emotional terms. The complexity and the schizoid nature of the dealings between government and business are not likely to lessen. The importance of government in the environments of business and other organizations is undeniable. For those organizations and for public relations, the public affairs challenge is clear.

Case Study

50th Anniversary of Normandy Invasion

By Joseph V. Trahan III, Ph.D., APR
University of Tennessee at Chattanooga

"Think not only upon their passing. Remember the glory of their spirit." These words are forever inscribed in the Normandy American Cemetery Chapel, where 9,386 Americans are buried on a magnificent bluff overlooking Omaha Beach. On June 6, 1994, thousands of World War II veterans, their families and friends, and media representatives stormed the hallowed beaches once again. Waiting for them were 2,342 military personnel, including the USAR 314th Press Camp headquarters from Birmingham, Alabama.

Figure 15.7 The Joint
Information Bureau
organizational chart

The Joint Information Bureau Organizational Chart:

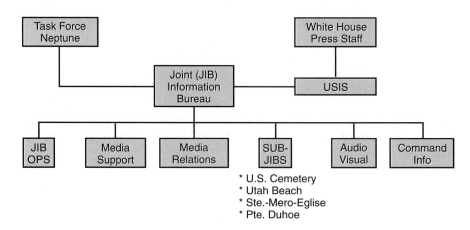

* U.S. Cemetery
* Utah Beach
* Ste.-Mero-Eglise
* Pte. Duhoe

Our mission was to establish and operate the Joint Task Force Information Bureau (JIB) near the American Cemetery. We were tasked to brief, credential, escort, and provide transportation for the thousands of media representatives from throughout the world who would capture the returning veterans' emotions and report on the national tributes paid to the heroes of "The Longest Day" (see figure 15.7).

The JIB and media village were fully operational on May 25, 1995. The media began registering with the main JIB from opening day. They were given ceremony information and historical data and directed to media opportunities that the JIBs had compiled.

Reporters were issued ceremony passes, and Col. Richard Bridges, JIB Director, issued ground rules, which concluded with the following statement:

> The estimated 20,000 veterans expected to attend ceremonies in Normandy on D-Day are VIPs. The estimated eight million veterans who will watch the ceremonies on television, listen to radio reports, or read about the events in their newspapers and magazines are also VIPs. Media coverage of these events will be the only means whereby the vast majority of these veterans receive the honors due them on this historic occasion. You, the media, are the primary conduit through which this story will be told. The JIB's goal is to assist you to the maximum extent possible in doing your jobs. The only dumb request is the one we never hear.

From May 25 to 2:30 A.M. June 7, 1994, over 4,500 media registered with the JIB, thousands of photos were shot and transmitted via satellite, thousands of TV packages and radio spots were broadcast live, and print stories were sent by the high speed of cellular phones and modems. David Brinkley, an American news icon, best described the scope of this operation in a National Public Radio interview at the conclusion of these emotional events. "I've never seen so much television equipment and media assembled in one place as I did in Normandy!"

Questions

1. Evaluate the media coverage of the 50th anniversary of Operation Overlord.

2. What key issues, challenges, and activities must you plan in order for an event of this importance to be successful?

3. Plan a 50th anniversary event for a nonprofit client.

Notes

1. Adam Shell, "Winning in Washington Takes Luck as Well as Skill," *Public Relations Journal* (February 1994): 6.

2. Neil H. Jacoby, *Corporate Power and Social Responsibility* (New York: Macmillan, 1973), 150.

3. "The Swarming Lobbyists," *Time* (7 August 1978): 15.

4. Grover Starling, *The Changing Environment of Business,* 2nd ed. (Boston: Kent Publishing Company, 1984), 95.

5. Graham Moliter, "Plotting the Patterns of Change," *Enterprise* (March 1984): 4.

6. Adam Shell, "Winning in Washington Takes Luck as Well as Skill," *Public Relations Journal* (February 1994): 6.

7. Starling, *Changing Environment of Business,* 96.

8. Ibid., 516.

9. *Forbes* (2 January 1984): 28.

10. R. C. Born, "Corporate CIA: In Washington, It Helps to Meet Business's Need to Know," *Barron's* (19 March 1979).

11. Herbert Buchsbaum, "Money Talks, Lobbying in Congress," *Scholastic Update* (5 November 1993): 10.

12. Edward M. Epstein, "An Irony of Electoral Reform," *Regulation* (May/June 1979).

13. Epstein, "An Irony," 5.

14. Edie Fraser, *PACs: The Political Awakening of Business* (Washington, D.C.: Fraser/Associates, 1980), 2.

15. Ibid., 15.

16. Starling, *Changing Environment of Business,* 531.

17. "The Swarming Lobbyists," 17.

18. Johnathan Rauch, "Growth of the Parasitic Economy; Criticism of Lobbyists," *USA Today Magazine* (January 1995): 22.

19. Patrick J. Buchanan, "War Drums Thump Along the Potomac," *San Diego Union* (24 October 1994): B-7.

20. Starling, *Changing Environment of Business,* 538.

21. "The Swarming Lobbyists," 22.

22. Walter Guzzardi, "Business Is Learing How to Win in Washington," *Fortune* (27 March 1978): 55.

23. "The Swarming Lobbyists," 17.

24. Christine Dugas, "Now, Madison Avenue Runs Straight to Capitol Hill," *Business Week* (4 August 1986): 27–28.

25. Ibid., 28.

26. Elliot H. Levitas, "Bureaucracy Stifling America's Right to Self-Govern," *Atlanta Business Chronicle* (9 June 1980): 4.

27. Robert E. Lane, *The Regulation of Businessmen: Social Conditions of Government Economic Control* (New Haven, Conn.: Yale University Press, 1954).

28. Alan Jenks, "Memos," *Atlanta Business Chronicle* (2 June 1980).

29. "Lawn Mower Regulations Taking Years to Develop," *Atlanta Journal* (5 June 1980): 28A.

30. Richard A. Armstrong, "Working with State Government," Philip Lesly, ed., *Lesly's Handbook of Public Relations and Communication* (New York: AMACOM, 1991): 99.

31. *Parade Magazine* (9 November 1986): 8.

32. Steven Markowitz, "On the Homefront," *Public Relations Journal* (June 1986): 16.

33. Ibid., 19.

34. Jacoby, *Corporate Power,* 155.

35. "A U.S. Drive to Curb Corporate Doubletalk," *Business Week* (12 May 1980): 35.

PART IV

Public Relations
The Practice

Public relations serves all types of organizations. Not-for-profit organizations, government agencies, and corporations have embraced public relations and set it to work, recognizing it as a means of increasing organizational effectiveness in a complex and changing environment.

To operate effectively within these organizations, the public relations practitioner must be thoroughly aware of all we have discussed to this point: the process of communication, the role of public relations in organizational decision making, the four-step public relations process, and the primary publics of public relations. Practitioners must also recognize the problems and publics that are specific to public relations in each organizational type.

In this section, we look first at the practice of public relations in three distinct types of organizations: chapter 16, not-for-profit organizations; chapter 17, government; and chapter 18, corporations. Next, in chapter 19, we examine the legal environment that governs public relations practice. We conclude in chapter 20 with a realistic look at careers in public relations and some helpful hints for finding your first job.

Public Relations in Not-for-Profit Organizations

Preview

Communication with members, government, and other publics is the bottom line for many not-for-profit organizations. Maintaining a positive public image, fund-raising, and cost containment are crucial public relations issues facing not-for-profit organizations in general.

Membership recruitment and retention is the chief public relations objective of many associations and religious organizations. Labor unions and trade and professional organizations sometimes prefer to work behind the scenes to influence government regulation rather than to address issues in more public forums.

Health care organizations are changing drastically. The advent of for-profit management companies and recent changes in medicare payment procedures have resulted in an emphasis on marketing and competition that has made a profound impact on public relations. Dealing with volunteers requires more attention to motivational factors than does dealing with typical employee groups.

In elementary and secondary schools, parents, alumni, and school board members represent both internal and external publics. The value of higher education may be the single most important public relations issue facing colleges and universities in the 1990s. Fund-raising is a primary public relations function in most not-for-profit organizations.

There is a tremendous opportunity for practitioners who think broadly and who welcome accountability. This is not an era for communications technicians.

—Frank J. Weaver, APR
Director of Public Affairs
Cleveland Clinic Foundation

N ongovernmental organizations that do not seek to make a profit are becoming more prevalent in our society. "More people work for nonprofit associations than the federal government and all 50 states combined: namely 8.6 million versus 6.8 million."[1] Numerous associations, societies, and labor unions promote the interests of their members and impose ethical, professional, or contractual obligations on the individuals or organizations they represent.

Hospitals, religious bodies, and volunteer organizations serve various constituent groups while relying on broad-based support to survive. Educational institutions, both public and private, must maintain effective relationships with a variety of professional and nonprofessional publics while serving society as a whole.

Accomplishment of these missions depends largely on the quality of the relationships a **not-for-profit organization** maintains with its publics. Fund-raising is a common concern shared by all these organizations and often becomes a priority of public relations practice.

Communication in Not-for-Profit Organizations

Communication is the primary mission of most associations, societies, unions, and religious organizations. Communication with members, government, and other groups becomes the basic product of many not-for-profit organizations. Even those with missions other than disseminating information find communication a necessary prerequisite to attainment of their announced objectives. Hospitals, charities, and educational institutions devote a great amount of time and energy to communicating ideas and soliciting volunteers and funds. We discussed in chapter 9 the need to relate public relations effectiveness to an organization's bottom-line objectives. In a not-for-profit organization, the bottom line is frequently measured in terms of new and retained members, dues collected, or funds raised. Effective communication programs are generally seen as the key to success in these areas.

Not-for-profit organizations rely much more heavily on publications in their public relations efforts than do corporations. Although the trend is toward expanded use of new communication technologies such as Video News Releases (VNRs), satellite interviews, fax machines, and World Wide Web pages, not-for-profit organizations have not branched into these areas as rapidly as their business counterparts have.

Formal communication programs with written goals and objectives are less prevalent in not-for-profit organizations. A survey of such organizations also found a distinct difference between for-profit and not-for-profit organizations with regard to the issues they believe should be addressed through their communication programs.[2] High on the corporate list of key issues were inflation and compensation, government regulation, and equal opportunity. Not-for-profit organizations pointed to maintaining a positive public image, fund-raising, and cost containment.[3]

Public Relations in Not-for-Profit Organizations

In the same survey, not-for-profit organizations indicated that their departments charged with public relations functions were called either public relations (20 percent) or public affairs (16 percent). Of the 81 organizations surveyed, 46 percent of the public relations staffs reported directly to the CEO, 19 percent to a vice-president, and 20 percent to a director. The sizes of public relations staffs vary as widely as the sizes of the organizations themselves; however, 35 percent of the organizations surveyed reported staffs exceeding 10 persons.

In the 1995 *Profile* of business communications issued by IABC, 13 percent of the communicators worked for nonprofit organizations (excluding government); this figure reflects an increase since the 1989 *Profile,* which showed 11.8 percent working in nonprofits. The nonprofit sector was second only to corporate communicators, with 44 percent.[4]

Despite differences in application, public relations is alive and well in not-for-profit organizations. In fact, we could argue that public relations is the business of many not-for-profit organizations. While the salaries for practitioners in these organizations have traditionally been lower than for those in corporations, they have improved. The median salary for all nonprofit public relations work is $43,388.[5] We will discuss the differences and opportunities specific to certain types of not-for-profit organizations in the remainder of this chapter.

Public Relations in Associations and Unions

Labor unions and the various trade or professional associations have one important focus in common: membership. Representing the interests of members to a number of different publics is the business of these not-for-profit organizations. Recruitment and retention of members is also a major function. Therefore, publics for unions and associations can be divided into two groups: members and nonmembers.

Member publics must constantly be kept informed about new developments in their field or area of interest. Nonmember publics must be told about the group's importance to society and the benefits of heeding its recommendations. Many associations and all labor unions mount strong efforts to influence local, state, and federal legislation. Membership may be the single most important factor all these organizations have in common, and it also accounts for their diversity.

Associations and Societies

Associations can be divided into two categories: professional and trade. A professional association, like the Public Relations Society of America and those listed in public relations spotlight 16.1, works to enhance the public image of the profession and disseminate knowledge among the membership and to society at large. In addition, many professional associations establish legal and ethical requirements for practice and certify the proficiencies of practitioners.

The public relations function of an association is complicated considerably when it plays the dual roles of advocate and regulator for a professional group. Besides professional associations, many learned societies, such as the International Communication Association or the Academy of Management, promote knowledge in certain fields without exercising any regulatory powers. Members of these organizations are individuals or organizations involved in research,

Public Relations Spotlight 16.1

Some of the Various Trade and Professional Associations

Agricultural Institute of Canada
American Association of University Professors
American Bankers Association
American Bar Association
American Dental Association
American Home Economics Association
American Hospital Association
American Hotel and Motel Association
American Institute of Architects
American Iron and Steel Institute
American Library Association
American Management Association
American Society for Personnel Administration
American Society for Training and Development
American Society of Association Executives
Canadian Bankers Association
Canadian Home Economics Association
Canadian Nurses Association
Canadian Pulp and Paper Association
Credit Union Executives Society
International Association of Chiefs of Police
Music Educators National Conference
National Association of Home Builders
National Association of Manufacturers
National Association of Realtors
National Industrial Recreation Association
National Secretaries Association
Retail Council of Canada
Texas Motor Transportation Association
Women in Communications, Inc.
Young Presidents Organization

practice, or teaching in the fields. Learned societies, for the most part, do not employ public relations professionals.

A trade association primarily represents organizations that produce a common product or service. Sometimes trade associations enforce ethical and legal standards, like the television and radio codes established by the National Association of Broadcasters. More frequently, they promote products or services and attempt to influence legislation and government regulations for the benefit of their members.

Sometimes trade association efforts are perceived as working against the broader interests of society. For example, the American Dairy Association conducted a massive television, radio, and print media campaign advertising milk as "the perfect food." After the campaign was in full swing, it was widely reported that drinking milk could in fact pose a threat to some individuals, primarily members of several minority groups who lack an enzyme necessary to digest milk products. The Dairy Association and its member cooperatives were suddenly in the position of promoting a product that could be harmful to minority children.

Association Diversity　Many associations and societies are divided into local, state, national, and sometimes international levels. Frequently, each level has a separate staff. The diversity that exists among the members of broad-based groups is not apparent. For example, the National Rifle Association is well known for its opposition to gun control laws, but not all its members support these efforts; this reality has caused criticism and even loss of membership within the organization. Member organizations within a trade association may range from small family businesses to giant conglomerates; obviously, these organizations will not hold the same views on all issues. Public relations skills are therefore important within associations to retain members, ensure that all points of view are represented, and build consensus.

Public Relations Practices　Some associations take very aggressive action to promote the interests of their members (figure 16.1). Many, like the American Dairy Association, spend millions of dollars a year on advertising. The Grocery Manufacturers of America bought time and space to inform consumers about the percentage added to rising food costs by growers, shippers, wholesalers, and retailers. The Toy Manufacturers of America also spend considerable sums to increase consumer confidence in the safety of their members' products.

Other organizations prefer to work behind the scenes to promote their members' welfare. Frequently, they attempt to influence legislation and regulation. Lobbying is a major activity of associations ranging from the American Medical

Figure 16.1 Sample association publications

Association to the National Association of Homebuilders. Many organizations maintain offices in Washington, D.C., and in some state capitals to support their continuous efforts to influence lawmakers and government officials.

Sometimes, lobbying efforts exceed legal limits. During the Nixon administration, three of the country's largest dairy cooperatives were convicted of making illegal campaign contributions in exchange for higher milk price supports.[6] Public relations professionals must be able to advise policy makers concerning the possible damage such activities may do to an association's image, whether the action is technically legal or not. Chapter 15 discusses more thoroughly the role of public relations in influencing government.

Communicating with members occupies the time of professionals in many associations. The need to attract new members and retain current ones is a constant issue facing most such organizations. The bulk of their budgets and professional talent may therefore be spent on association meetings and publications. Of course, large associations can afford to engage in membership recruitment, lobbying, advertising, and other activities simultaneously.

According to the Public Relations Society of America, practitioners in professional and trade associations can expect to participate in the following activities:

Preparing and distributing news and informational material to the press, radio, and television.

Preparing and disseminating technical and educational materials (publications, motion pictures, and audiovisual aids) to other publics.

Sponsoring conventions, meetings, educational seminars, and exhibitions.

Maintaining government relations, including interpreting the legislative and administrative actions of government agencies in terms of members' interests.

Compiling and publishing business and industry statistics.

Sponsoring public service activities (such as those related to health or safety).

Preparing and enforcing codes of ethics or professional standards.

Conducting cooperative research (scientific, social, and economic).

Issuing institutional and/or product advertising to better acquaint various publics with the products or services represented.

Media relations is, of course, an important aspect of nonprofit public relations. Often, though, nonprofit associations cannot afford media relations efforts. See public relations spotlight 16.2 for five tips for saving media relations dollars.

Most of these recommended activities underscore two basic values and functions of the association in the American economy and society. First, they provide a means of *experience sharing* for individuals and entities with common activities or interest. The benefits of shared experience accrue to all members and might be unobtainable otherwise. Second, through voluntary, cooperative support, they make possible *beneficial programs* that in most instances could not be

Tips to Save Media
Relations Dollars

Public Relations Spotlight 16.2

1. Call the local university journalism or communication department to see if students need hands-on experience through internships, practica, or class credit. A small sum of money will go a long way here. If you can pay $500 or $600 a semester as an honorarium or perhaps as a scholarship, you will see the level of work and responsibility rise considerably.

2. Submit articles to local company newsletters asking for volunteers when you need help.

3. Join the local chapter of PRSA, IABC, or Women in Communication. Contacts and ideas you get from the meetings will be invaluable.

4. Attend seminars and workshops where media personnel talk about what they want from public relations people. Universities, local chapters of professional organizations, and others often hold such seminars. If they don't, work with them to develop one.

5. Work with the public relations staffs of companies that have donated money to your nonprofit group. These professionals will often find time and resources to assist you with your major programs.

undertaken by individual companies or persons. Many medical, engineering, scientific, technological, and social advances affecting the lives of all Americans exist only because of such programs.[7]

Labor Unions

In many ways, the role of public relations in a labor union is much like its role in professional or trade associations. Communicating with current members, recruiting new members, and influencing legislation and regulation are all objectives of labor unions. Thus, the public relations professional will be involved with union publications, news releases, and lobbying efforts. Some unions, such as the International Ladies' Garment Workers, have mounted campaigns to encourage consumers to buy products with the union label.

For the most part, however, unions have avoided public discourse in favor of lobbying efforts and member communication. These tactics have made the labor movement, which represents less than 20 percent of the country's workforce, the major voice of working people in the United States.

While the voice of labor is powerful in political circles, its popularity with many publics has suffered in recent times. Economic problems like inflation and trade deficits have been blamed on organized labor. Public opinion surveys consistently place labor unions last among institutions holding the public's confidence.[8]

In recent years, the continued decline in the proportion of the workforce unionized, the loss of union political power, and the failure of union pay raises to keep pace with those for the nonunion workforce suggest that labor unions may be facing a crisis. Sensitivity to public opinion, though, does not appear to be spreading rapidly in the labor movement. In 1992, striking newspaper employees refused to settle a contract dispute with Scripps Howard Corporation even though it meant the death of the Pittsburgh Press.

Unions traditionally look to their own ranks for professional services. Frequently, individuals responsible for public relations policy in organized labor are promoted from the rank and file with little or no formal training in the field. This practice appears to be changing, however, and unions are employing more professionals. As a result, the aversion of labor unions to broader public discourse may also change.

Hospital public relations, like all other aspects of hospital administration, is a relatively new field. Not many years ago, professional managers in hospitals were very rare. A hospital typically was managed by a board of physicians, with one named as director. These physicians gave more attention to patient care than to details of administration. As hospitals became larger and more complex, managerial duties were turned over to professionally trained administrative personnel. As hospital management became increasingly professional, the need for public relations practitioners was perceived and met.

Hospital and Health Care Public Relations

Until recently, the vast majority of health care delivery systems in the United States were nonprofit organizations operated by government, charity, and religious organizations. Today, however, for-profit management companies like Humana, AMI, and Hospital Corporation of America are major players in the health care field.

The Volatile Health Care Industry

Nonprofit hospitals have been faced with several major changes in the health care system that have special implications for the practice of public relations. First, the federal government has changed its method of payment to health care providers; second, competition has increased dramatically; and third, marketing has become the watchword of the industry.

Federal and state reimbursement to hospitals for Medicare and Medicaid has changed. In 1983, the federal government decided to reimburse health care service providers under Medicare in a totally new way. Ailments were placed in categories called Diagnostic Related Groups (DRGs), with set fees for treatment. Thus, if a DRG #72 appendectomy has a set price of $1,000, the hospital receives that amount regardless of the procedure's actual cost.[9] Because the federal government is the single largest purchaser of medical services, this change revolutionized the health care industry. Some states have considered changes in Medicaid reimbursement. Tennessee, for example, has established its own program called TennCare. Suddenly, there were incentives for cost savings that had never been present before. This situation increased the demand for professional managers in health care organizations and injected a new word into the vocabulary of health care: **competition.**

New delivery systems have increased competition. Hospitals not only compete among themselves for patients but must also contend with a growing number of alternative delivery systems. Hospital occupancy levels have been dropping as health maintenance organizations (HMOs), surgicenters, and other minor care facilities have taken shares of the market once controlled by a few nonprofit hospitals. These alternative delivery systems have been successful in cutting costs and marketing their services to prospective patients directly rather than through physicians.

Marketing has become a dominant force. As a result of the increased competition in health care, marketing is now viewed as the key to survival. Markets are being segmented, and new products and services are being introduced as never before.

The marketing push in health care focuses on communication and promotion. This situation significantly raises the value of public relations and presents many new challenges to those in the field. Many public relations practitioners are now being called on to administer their health care organizations' marketing programs. Staffs are growing as an increasing array of new skills are demanded.

This boom also has its downside. In many health care organizations, marketing and public relations managers are locked in heated combat over who will control the communication function. Marketing has often been put in charge of public relations, rather than the two working as partners. Some public relations professionals are called on to manage a complete range of communication programs, including advertising and other consumer-oriented media. In hospitals, the lines between public relations and marketing will continue to blur.

Hospitals, nursing homes, convalescent care centers, HMOs, emergency care clinics, and all other health care organizations are caught in the bind of rising patient expectations for services. No one disputes the fact that health care has improved phenomenally over the past 25 years. Health care practices that were considered advanced only a few years ago are now obsolete. Yet, scientific, technological, and clinical advances have in fact contributed to the problems of health care organizations. Because the state of the art changes so rapidly, hospitals and other facilities are under constant pressure to update their services. The same publics who call for continuous updating, however, are shocked by the rapid rise in costs.

People also know more than ever before about their own health and the treatments available to them. When this factor is added to the cost/service dilemma, the credibility problems of health care organizations can be better understood. In spite of tremendous advances in medical practice, physicians are no longer relied on as completely as they once were. Today, it is not unusual for a patient to ask for a second opinion on a diagnosis or treatment—something almost unheard of a few years ago. In this rapidly changing environment, hospitals and other health care organizations need help communicating with a variety of publics (figure 16.2).

Health Care Publics   In simpler times, hospitals were the only source of most major medical services. Both physicians and patients had relatively little choice because hospitals were often large, centralized organizations that serviced entire geographical areas without any competition. For the hospital, public relations merely meant basic internal communication, a little pampering for physicians, and a strong volunteer organization. Today, however, the audiences for public relations are changing and expanding. Key internal publics include employees—doctors, nurses, medical technicians of all kinds, clerical staff, and maintenance and housekeeping employees.

Figure 16.2 Sample pages from a hospital publication (Used with permission of Hendrick Medical Center Foundation, Abilene, Texas.)

The hospital environment, frightening to many patients, places special demands on public relations practitioners in the health care industry.

Target external publics include patients and potential patients (the clients), government, business, and volunteers.

Even though public relations plays a clearly important role in health care organizations, the number of full-time practitioners is still rather low. As the professionalization of health care administration increases, however, the opportunities for public relations professionals in those organizations likely will increase also. Public relations practitioners are needed to advise administrators and professional employees in a variety of matters involving internal, community, and media relations.

Public Relations in Religious and Volunteer Organizations

Churches and other religious and charitable organizations depend on positive public images for their very lives. Most have relatively few employees and must rely on volunteer labor. The vast majority are funded solely by member contributions, public fund-raising drives, and/or philanthropic gifts. Public relations is an important part of the day-to-day operation of such organizations, but only the largest employ full-time practitioners.

Religious Organizations

The goals of most religious organizations require a great many activities that can be considered public relations. Churches and synagogues must communicate with their memberships and with local and even national publics regarding doctrinal and social issues. In the early 1970s, declines in church membership and rising costs forced many of the larger protestant organizations to cut back their mission operations and staffs. These circumstances led some denominations to realize their need for professional help in public relations.

Recently, a number of religious organizations have begun to expand their communication activities, especially those involving mass media. Some of these organizations have been able to exert considerable influence. The Moral Majority, a conservative group of fundamentalist churches, became active in electoral politics and is widely believed to have been instrumental in the election of Ronald Reagan. Other organizations, such as the church described in mini-case 16.1, have found that public relations skills and techniques can help them better accomplish their traditional missions.

The number of public relations practitioners employed in churches, synagogues, and other religious organizations is still very small. However, because the church is no longer the center of local communities and cannot automatically count on large weekly attendance, things may have to change. Indeed, the following examples indicate a new era of religious communication:

Baptist Press, the Southern Baptist Convention's news service for secular media, packages and distributes the work of five bureaus and material supplied by paid stringers, the staffs of 34 Baptist state papers, and some 350 public relations employees. The press service uses CompuServe to transmit the material to its subscribers electronically. Recently, because of controversy within the convention, a rival press service, *Associated Baptist Press,* has been formed to compete with the more traditional, fundamentalist-controlled Baptist Press.

The Church of Jesus Christ of Latter-Day Saints (Mormons) has a well-defined and well-organized communication function. The managing director of

Mini-Case 16.1

Advocacy Advertising for a Church in Trouble

An Episcopal Church in Minneapolis, Minnesota, found that techniques borrowed from corporate advocacy advertising campaigns could turn a dying congregation around. Their first set of ads was so successful that they prepared a second campaign as follow-up messages.

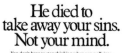

He died to
take away your sins.
Not your mind.

You don't have to stop thinking when you walk into
an Episcopal Church. Come and join us in an atmosphere where
faith and thought exist together in a spirit of fellowship.
The Episcopal Church

The Episcopal Church
welcomes you.
Regardless of race, creed,
color or the number
of times you've been born.

Whether you've been born once or born again, the Episcopal Church invites you to come
and join us in the fellowship and worship of Jesus Christ.
The Episcopal Church

Some approaches employed
by the Episcopal Ad Project

Is the Me Generation doing
to Christianity
what the lions failed to do?

If you think it's time people started thinking less about their own self fulfillment
and more about the needs of others, come and join us in the fellowship of the Episcopal Church.
The Episcopal Church

With all due regard to TV Christianity,
have you ever seen a
Sony that gives Holy Communion?

If TV Christianity makes you want to switch channels, come and join us this Sunday in
Christian fellowship and worship without commercial interruptions. **The Episcopal Church**

The Episcopal Ad Project sold about 200 sets of ads nationwide to other churches of several denominations. "They just stuck their own name in place of ours," said the Rev. George Martin, pastor of St. Luke's Episcopal Church.

St. Luke's was a shrinking church in a shrinking town when it decided to advertise itself—to "break out of the church advertising mold of just the sermon topic and time of services," Martin said. The project came up with ads that brought in both new church members and national awards.

"Now, we're a congregation with a good mix of 300 families and growing in a city that lost 100,000 people over the past few years," Martin said. The first ads were aimed at "what people are doing on Sunday morning. . . . They had striking visuals like a line drawing of Dante's Inferno with short messages." The church placed the ads in neighborhood newspapers.

The new set of four ads is aimed at people who "seem to fear any religious involvement, worrying they might turn into some kind of religious fanatic" or will lose themselves in church trappings, he said.

One of the ads shows a picture of Jesus with the caption, "He died to take away your sins. Not your mind."

Perhaps the most striking of the new ads again concerns television religion, raising the question, "Have you ever seen a Sony that gives Holy Communion?"

Martin said that while researching the new set of ads, "We were also concerned with what was happening to young people involved with some of the cults." The resulting ad notes, "There's only one problem with religions that have all the answers. They don't allow questions."

Tom McElligott Jr., of the Minneapolis office of the national advertising firm Bozell and Jacobs, worked on the ads, saying it was part of the free public service work "we feel we should do."

Source: Adapted with permission of Knight-Ridder Newspapers.

---

communication and special affairs supervises a public affairs, operations, and special affairs unit. Public affairs handles the writing, production, and placement of print and broadcast messages as well as media relations. The operations unit manages the local public relations efforts of approximately 1,400 volunteers at ward levels, and the special affairs unit maintains legislative relations and contacts with other groups.[10]

Volunteer Groups

It is estimated that some 500,000 gift-supported organizations other than hospitals, churches, and colleges exist in the United States.[11] Most of these organizations depend for their survival on donations of time and expertise as much as money (see mini-case 16.2). Corporate financial support has remained static (see table 16.1). However, volunteers have declined.

TABLE 16.1 Corporate Contributions

Year	Amount Given
1991	$ 6.00 billion
1992	$ 5.90 billion
1993	$ 6.05 billion

Source: *Employment & Training Reporter*, vol. 26, no. 42 (7 September 1994): 33.

Mini-Case 16.2

U.S. Army Supports National Scout Jamboree

"A Bridge to the Future" was the 1993 National Scout Jamboree's theme for 33,000 Boy Scouts and their adult leaders at Fort A. P. Hill, Virginia. Approximately 1,650 active, reserve, and National Guard Army soldiers in addition to 100 sailors, aviators, Marines, and Coast Guard members supported the Scout Jamboree with the U.S. Army theme: "America's Army: Defending Values. . . . Adding Value."

The Department of Defense has provided the support that the nonprofit Boy Scout group has needed for more than 50 years and that was authorized by Congress in 1972. Col. Conrad Busch Jr., director of public affairs for FORCES Command, Fort McPherson, Georgia, summarized the Army's support for the Boy Scouts this way:

> What we have is one great institution, The United States Army, supporting another great institution, the Boy Scouts of America. These two organizations instill similar values—leadership, responsibility, and service to our country.

The 314th Press Camp Headquarters' missions were to:

1. Provide command and control for the deployment of the public affairs detachments.
2. Tell the U.S. Army's support story to the nation through print news releases, VNRs, radio spot beepers, photos, hometown news releases, fact sheets, and other media channels.
3. Assist the U.S. Army's future recruiting efforts by instilling in today's Boy Scouts an understanding, appreciation, and support for the U.S. Army.

The 314th Press Camp Headquarters organized Army Media Center and Joint Information Bureau by integrating all public affairs detachments into the following sections: headquarters, media relations, media briefing, video section, print section, marketing, and logistics.

The press camp prepared for every possible crisis communication situation by developing a thorough crisis communication plan. This was extremely important because President Bill Clinton had just announced the U.S. Department of Defense's policy on homosexuality—namely, "Don't ask, don't tell, and don't pursue." The Boy Scouts of America had just reinforced its antihomosexuality stance in early 1993. The nation's media wondered how these two organizations, with different policies regarding homosexuality, could work together in August of 1993.

During the 12 hot, dusty August days of the Jamboree, the press corps accomplished the following: registered and briefed over 500 media representatives, took and distributed thousands of photos, wrote and distributed more than 2,000 hometown news releases, produced and transmitted to Soldiers Radio Satellite Network more than 100 radio "live break-ins," wrote and mailed out 300 news releases, produced an army adventure souvenir issue newspaper, answered more than 200 media inquiries, and made 33,000 impressions on future American voters.

Major General Richard Griffitts, deputy commander of First Army and the senior Jamboree officer, remarked, "This has been one of the most rewarding experiences I've ever had in the Army. To see the thrill Scouts get talking with soldiers, who really are role models for them, and to see the bond that developed between Scouts and soldiers was really impressive. The Jamboree has given us an opportunity to support America's future leaders, conduct mission training, and show America another facet of the military's domestic support role."

Source: Joseph V. Trahan III, Ph.D., APR, University of Tennessee at Chattanooga.

Unfortunately, volunteers, like church members, can no longer be taken for granted. As families move too frequently to become a permanent part of any community, and as more and more women enter the workforce, volunteerism is declining in the United States. Although volunteers are still important to the life and economy of many organizations, their future is uncertain.[12] To continue attracting volunteers in the numbers necessary to carry out their programs, organizations will need to take innovative approaches in communicating with their publics.

Although their full-time staffs are relatively small, volunteer organizations offer public relations students an excellent opportunity to gain experience. Volunteers with communication and other public relations skills are always needed, and the problems they confront are good preparation for full-time careers. The following are just a few of the many large volunteer organizations:

American Heart Association

American Cancer Society

American Lung Association

American Red Cross

American Humane Association

Advertising Council

March of Dimes

Sierra Club

Salvation Army

Girl Scouts of America

Boy Scouts of America

YMCA

YWCA

Public Relations in Educational Institutions
Public Schools

Anyone who doubts the need for public relations practice in the administration of elementary and secondary schools today need only glance at the headlines. School bond issues are being voted down, teachers are striking, AIDS patients are attending schools, gang activity is increasing, parents are demanding that curricula return to the "basics," students and teachers are being attacked in classrooms. . . . The list of problems in our schools could go on. Most large school districts now realize that part of their responsibility as publicly funded agencies is to keep taxpayers and other publics informed about their operations.

In some communities, few issues are as volatile as those relating to the public schools. The recent history of busing and other issues surrounding public school desegregation has proven in every region of the country that changes in the schools can result in catastrophic social upheaval. Any issue that affects public schools is likely to affect large segments of the community; even people without school-age children have an interest in the school system because their taxes support it, and it is a focus of civic pride and concern. Most people in our society feel it is their right to know and have a voice in what happens in the public schools. As the over-all educational level rises, more and more people feel they have not only the right but also the qualifications to express their opinions concerning every phase of public education.

Following are some of the many publics that must be addressed by public relations efforts in the educational environment:

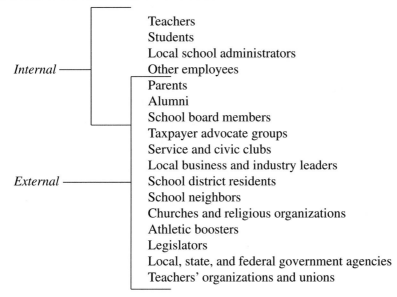

Internal
- Teachers
- Students
- Local school administrators
- Other employees

External
- Parents
- Alumni
- School board members
- Taxpayer advocate groups
- Service and civic clubs
- Local business and industry leaders
- School district residents
- School neighbors
- Churches and religious organizations
- Athletic boosters
- Legislators
- Local, state, and federal government agencies
- Teachers' organizations and unions

Each of these publics affects schools in a variety of ways, but four groups—teachers, students, parents, and district residents—are of particular importance and must receive special attention here.

Teachers are now a well-organized and influential force in many parts of the country. Teachers' unions and professional organizations are concerned with every phase of public school operation. These groups also exert influence with other publics like legislators, government agencies, and parents. The political na-ture of public school administration and the enormous size of many school dis-tricts have strained the naturally cooperative relationship that should exist be-tween teachers and administrators. With every segment of the population demanding a stronger voice in what takes place in the classroom, many teachers feel deprived of authority. Like other employee groups, teachers increasingly turn to unions to gain influence on what happens where they work. Any effective pub-lic relations effort in a school district must recognize the importance of the pro-fessional input teachers can offer and take appropriate steps to bring them into the communication system.

Students are now more active and vocal, even at the elementary and sec-ondary levels. Various student groups demand more say in the decisions that af-fect the educational environment. Individual students have brought suit against school districts over policies they considered discriminatory or unreasonable. Public relations efforts must be designed to inform students about the reasoning behind decisions that affect them. To be responsive to student needs, however, school public relations programs must be able to assess student opinion and predict reactions to decisions before they are made.

Parents function as both an internal and an external public. Because of their intense interest in everything that affects their children, parents are frequently as knowledgeable as students about school events. Many parents volunteer in their local schools through parent-teacher organizations or other programs. Parents often feel as involved in the school as the staff does, but their participation is indirect because it is not full time. Teacher organizations are quick to point out that parental cooperation is essential to good education. Public relations programs must be designed to win parental approval and cooperation in a team effort to educate children.

School district residents are concerned about public school operations even if they do not have children attending school. The quality and reputation of local schools have considerable influence on the property values of a community. In addition, the preparation of young people to become productive citizens is an issue that affects everyone. School public relations programs must be sensitive to the impact of their efforts outside the classroom. Those who pay taxes and vote on school bond issues must be kept informed about the needs, concerns, and contributions of local schools.

Higher Education

The practice of public relations is well established in higher education. Colleges and universities, both public and private, have long understood the necessity to cultivate favorable public opinion. The Council for Advancement and Support of Education (CASE), a national organization concerned with public relations, alumni relations, and fund raising, dates back to 1917.

In spite of its long history, however, public relations in higher education may be facing its most difficult era. The student activism of the 1960s brought numerous changes to college and university operations. Curricula were changed to meet the interests of politically and socially active students. Rules and entrance requirements were relaxed in response to student pressure. Students in the mid-1990s are much more pragmatic. They are often more interested in specific career preparation and maximum earning potential. The question now is whether a college education is really worth the time, effort, and expense involved.

The mid-1990s has also seen the bottom of the low-birthrate trend that has affected the public school system for more than a decade. High school graduation rates are at their lowest point. The trend has reversed itself in the last half of the decade, however.

Financial difficulties due to declining enrollments have been exacerbated by the pressures on state governments to increase funding for prisons, Medicaid payments, social services, mass transportation, and other important needs. Funding of public colleges and universities has in many instances been reduced, and this development in turn has put demands on private institutions. Colleges and universities have faced funding reductions, cutbacks in curricula, and even layoffs of tenured faculty.

Higher education has responded to these pressures by offering new career-oriented degree programs. In addition, colleges look for students other than the traditional 18-year-old high school graduate. Both degree offerings and nondegree continuing education programs have been expanded to meet the needs of students in all age ranges. Extended or distance learning has become a popular means to reach nontraditional students or those who cannot attend traditional classes. Interactive video, fly-in weekend or week-long classes, and on-line computer instruction have become important. Syracuse University, for example, offers its master's in public relations program in a special format: In lieu of traditional class meetings, the program includes a week-long session at the beginning of the term and assignments throughout the term often discussed via e-mail. The University of Memphis has begun the first master's program in public relations and journalism to be offered entirely on line (see mini-case 16.3).

Higher education has become a lifelong process instead of a brief training period. Continuing to meet the needs of a changing society without sacrificing quality will be the toughest challenge for colleges and universities in the late 1990s. Public relations practitioners must help institutions of higher learning

Mini-Case 16.3

On-Line Master's Program

The University of Memphis Department of Journalism launched the first on-line master's program in journalism and public relations in January 1995.

Classes meet "on line" through an arrangement with CompuServe twice a week, three hours at a time, for six weeks. The $1,000-per-course fee includes all tuition, books, and materials. Usually a professor uploads lecture material at the beginning of the week. Students can download the lecture and then be prepared to meet on line for discussion. A student can earn a master's degree in two years. Requirements for the on-line program are the same as those for the department's on-campus program, but computer technology has made possible extended or distance learning.

From the professor's office or home—or anywhere there is a phone connection—the class can be taught. Students can also connect with the class from wherever they may be. One student took his laptop to work with him, but he had to excuse himself twice to deliver babies. The student, a physician, was on call during class.

One problem has been time zones. While requests have come from Europe, Asia, and Canada, the program is not large enough at this point to schedule class meetings at times to accommodate distant time zones. In the United States, classes usually meet at 9 P.M. eastern time to accommodate students on the west coast who, at 6 P.M. their time, would likely be off work and free to go on line.

Begun by Dr. E. W. Brody, APR, PRSA Fellow, the program graduated its first two students in 18 months. In the first year the program enrolled about 24 students. Dr. Brody says the program is especially helpful for the midcareer student who is not near a university with a master's program in public relations, who travels a great deal, or who may have any kind of mobility problem. Students with disabilities may find this program attractive, he believes.

The University of Memphis president addressed a convocation of faculty, staff, students, and friends shortly after a major public relations campaign to change the university's name.

communicate their changing programs and needs to a changing audience. Following are some of these varied publics:

Internal
- Students
- Faculty
- Administrators
- Alumni
- Parents
- Trustees

External
- Federal government agencies
- State government agencies
- State legislators
- Professional associations and learned societies
- Accrediting agencies
- Textbook publishers
- Business and industries that employ graduates
- Local community

In the late 1990s, college and university public relations professionals will have to demonstrate (1) the value of postsecondary education, (2) justification for increased faculty workloads, and (3) the importance of their institutions' contributions to economic development through teaching and research.

Fund-Raising: A Common Task for Not-for-Profit Groups

All not-for-profit organizations face a common problem: the recurring need to raise money to support their operations. Even public institutions like universities and hospitals have discovered that they cannot continue to develop in these inflationary times without sources of private funds. Institutional advancement (or development) programs are big business in the United States. Much of the effort of most nonprofit organizations goes toward raising the funds necessary to carry out their missions.

Frequently, the job of coordinating fund-raising efforts falls to the public relations function of an organization because of the communication expertise required. John Price Jones, a pioneer professional fund-raiser, noted that:

> Fundraising is public relations, for without sound public relations no philanthropy can live long. . . . It takes better public relations to get a man to give a dollar than it does to convince him to spend a dollar. Favorable public opinion is the basis upon which American philanthropy has been built.[13]

Successful development campaigns require close attention to many details. Because they are massive projects, organizations frequently engage professional fund-raising firms to provide counsel or even to manage entire campaigns. John W. Leslie, an international authority on fund-raising, enumerates nine steps for a successful institutional advancement program:[14]

Step 1. Identify broad objectives and policies for the institutional advancement program. In this first step, the broad objectives and governing policies should be outlined for all activities designed to increase understanding of and support for the institution. Objectives, broad and specific, are designed to assist in achieving already established institutional goals. (We are assuming, of course, that the institution has a current concrete, understood, and accepted statement of purpose and goals.) Resulting from this step is a plan with both long- and short-range objectives.

Step 2. Define relevant trends that might affect the institutional advancement program. Careful consideration of such trends will ensure that the implementation of the plan is as appropriate as possible to the prevailing conditions. Examples of trends and external influences that would affect elements of the program are relations with various components of the institution's constituency, the condition of the national economy and of various industries important to the institution, congressional and legislative attitudes, current and anticipated campus problems, and so on.

Step 3. Identify specific communication and financial support activities, and group them into program elements. All institutional advancement programs are composed of a number of activities through which program objectives are pursued. All activities (regardless of departmental direction) should be itemized as to which are designed to communicate and ensure the financial support of the institution's educational goals. Activities may be unique and nonrecurring, like special events. Or they may be ongoing, like gathering and distribution of institutional news.

Discrete activities should be grouped into program elements. A program element is a logical grouping of related activities for purposes of management and budget control. It is administered by a director who supervises the activities and personnel within the program element.

Step 4. Determine the basic approach and designate administrators for discrete activities within the program elements. Broadly plan and outline the purpose, basic approach, and audience emphasis of each activity within each program element. The primary concern should be determining the type (personnel, funds, etc.) and amount of resources required for each program element.

When converting to a programmatic analysis of planning and budgeting (using information acquired from conventional accounting methods), a manager needs to keep several points in mind. Arbitrary allocations of staff time and expenditures will often have to be made for various activities. Travel, telephone service, and print materials are examples of expensive items that often serve multiple activities but are usually accounted for in lump sums.

Further, the manager should expect that in the beginning, allocation estimates will be crude. The key to effective program planning and budgeting in the future is establishing procedures to validate as well as possible the initial allocation estimates. Relevant literature and experience are substantial and can yield suggestions for keeping staff time records. For those who divide their time among several activities, the easiest method is to use the various activities as broad time category headings. Although procedures are crucial, assessing the time devoted to specific activities is not difficult; in fact, it is routine in consulting firms, advertising agencies, and similar groups that provide services to a number of clients.

Each major activity should be the responsibility of one administrator. It is not always possible or desirable to limit activity administration to professional staff personnel. More than likely, one person will administer several activities; this has for some time been common practice in the management of institutional advancement programs.

Step 5. Designate a person to direct and coordinate the various activities within each program element. This step is crucial to overall program success. The choice of director will depend on the following considerations:

Nature, purpose, and audience of the key activities

Principal source of funding for the key activities

Knowledge and experience deemed desirable

Management skills

Program element directors will report to the program manager concerning coordination and direction of the various activities—regardless of whom they report to in the departmental chain of command. Procedures must be established to facilitate good working relationships and smooth transfer of funds (when necessary) among budget authorities.

Step 6. Establish objectives of various program elements. Program element directors, in cooperation with the program manager, should determine long- and short-range objectives for each element. Objectives should be as specific and quantitative as possible and must reflect analogous objectives of other program elements.

Step 7. Review and revise various activities to conform to the objectives of their respective program elements. The entire rationale for programmatic planning and budgeting is summed up in this step. Undoubtedly, step 6 will point up a number of duplications—and probably some oversights—in programming.

To increase effectiveness as well as efficiency, the activities composing a program element must be streamlined. The cost of each activity in staff time and institutional funds must be assessed in relation to the exact results achieved or the estimated results desired. Likewise, the relative merit of each activity within a program element must be analyzed. Undoubtedly, opportunities for revision (and probable elimination) of some activities will be obvious to analytical judgment. Objective scrutiny and the courage to streamline decisions are crucial management tools for successful program planning and budgeting.

Step 8. Develop revised plans for each activity within each program element. Program element directors will need to work with each activity administrator to review and formulate new plans for the activities composing each element. The director must ensure that objectives established for his or her particular element will be met by the sum of the results of the activities. Directors and the manager may discover that a realignment of activities would be advantageous.

Revised program element plans must include resources required, sources of those resources, job descriptions, space requirements, time schedules, expected results, evaluation procedures, and revisions and future modifications expected in light of long-range objectives.

Step 9. Establish a control system. The control system should provide a periodic, systematic review of performance in relation to objectives. The control system is the manager's chief method of assessing progress toward objectives. Quality awards, such as the Malcolm Baldridge Award, are often used to focus on Total Quality Management. Figure 16.3 is a sample page from an entry for a quality award that is available to nonprofit agencies. Managers must allow sufficient calendar time—not continuous time—for implementing a program planning and budgeting system. Procedures must be thoroughly tested, and personnel must understand and adjust to the new methods.

Programmatic planning and budgeting is a management tool but not a philosophy of management. Its strength is its flexibility, but programmatic planning does not replace imagination, intelligence, and initiative.

Fund-Raising as a Public Relations Problem

No one questions the need for not-for-profit organizations to raise funds, but the methods they employ can lead to public relations problems. **Burnout** is always a risk in huge fund drives that employ mass media, direct mail, or telephone communication channels. Another issue that can trigger adverse public reaction is the proportion of funds raised that is spent on the campaign itself. Some national campaigns cost as much as 25 percent of the total funds raised. Unfavorable publicity about campaign costs can hurt future efforts for all organizations that depend on public generosity. Most professional fund-raising organizations advise that costs not exceed 12 to 15 percent of the amount raised. Fort Worth, Texas, prohibits nonprofit organizations from collecting funds in the city if their administrative costs exceed 20 percent of budget.

Marc Epstein suggests three major factors that affect the decline of corporate giving to nonprofit organizations. First, shareholders rank corporate giving low on their priority lists when looking for stocks to purchase. Second, economic decline

Figure 16.3 Youth Villages won the Tennessee Governor's Award for its quality improvement plan—one of the first nonprofit agencies ever to enter the program. This illustration is a sample page of Youth Villages' application.

Tennessee Quality Award
Building Partnerships for Continuous Improvement

7.0   Customer Focus and Satisfaction

7.1a Determining Expectations and Requirements
In keeping with our mission to provide high quality care and innovative services to emotionally troubled youth and their families, Youth Villages maintains regular communication with customers in all market segments. We collect and analyze our customers' input and identify customer needs, segment them by markets and develop appropriate services. We evaluate our services through customer input, resulting in continual service improvement. This ensures that short-term and future customer requirements are met (Figure 7.1.1).

7.1a (1) How Customer Groups are Determined
Customers are the core of Youth Villages' planning process (Figure 3.1). After market research in the states of Tennessee, Missouri, Kentucky, Mississippi, Alabama and Arkansas, we determined that our market niche was providing the most intensive level of service to the most severely emotionally disturbed youth. We surveyed suppliers (referral sources) who contract with other providers for services. Data included service trends, diagnosis patterns, service alternatives, cost, response time, licensing requirements and accreditation. Our customer groups are listed in Section 7.1.2.

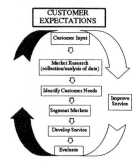

7.1a (2) How Information is Collected
Youth Villages seeks information frequently from customers in all target market areas. Although specific data collection varies slightly for each market segment, we compile customer information on a daily or weekly basis. We log customer visits and phone calls received by customer personnel.

Customer	Data Collection Methods
Children and Families	Telephone surveys Written surveys Personal visits
State Governments	Telephone surveys` Personal visits Focus groups
Mental Health Professionals	Focus groups Telephone surveys Written surveys Personal interviews
Licensing Agents	On-site visits Informal telephone Surveys
Accreditation Groups	On-site visits Informal telephone Surveys
Private Insurance Companies	Written surveys Telephone surveys Personal interviews On-site visits
Schools and Universities	Telephone surveys Personal interviews
Juvenile Court Judges	Informal telephone Surveys Personal interviews
Volunteers	On-site visits Informal telephone Survey Focus groups Comment cards
Donors	Written surveys Telephone surveys On-site visits Personal visits Comment cards Focus groups
Customer Partners such as suppliers	On-site visits

Opening a new facility, a 1000-acre youth treatment center near the Tennessee River, required a special public relations plan.

has sharply affected the margin from which corporate donations are drawn. Third, damage was inflicted by news about former United Way president William Aramony's salary, lavish spending by top officials, and general abuse of charity funds.[15] (See the case study featuring United Way at the end of the chapter.)

Summary

Not-for-profit organizations by nature rely on public relations for their survival. In spite of this fact, many of these organizations are slow to develop the public relations function within their professional staffs. Increasingly, however, the realization of the necessity for more consistency in their relationships with various publics is causing many not-for-profit organizations to expand their public relations efforts.

Membership recruitment/retention and fund-raising are the two major public relations objectives of most nonprofit associations. Labor unions spend much of their effort lobbying, as do trade associations. Health care organizations, religious groups, and public schools also have volunteer assistance as a key objective.

Case Study

Restoring Confidence in the Nation's Largest Charity

By Mark Dvorak
Director of Marketing Services
United Way of Metropolitan Atlanta

The nation's nonprofits received a wake-up call in early 1992 when the president and two top officers of United Way of America (UWA) were charged with mismanagement and lavish spending. Hardest hit were the 2,100 local, independent United Ways that raise more than $3 billion annually for human service programs in their communities.

Donors responded quickly to the allegations and intense negative publicity. Many believed their contributions had been mishandled and questioned United Way practices and accountability. Local United Ways and the agencies they support feared donations would decrease dramatically, with cuts in programs and services resulting. In Atlanta, where United Way raised $54 million in 1991, the organization moved quickly to rebuild confidence and trust within the community. Research revealed that 67 percent of Atlantans were aware of the controversy and that 38 percent said it would adversely affect their donations. Only half knew their money stayed in the metro area.

Ongoing, open disclosure with the local media was important in reaching a mass audience. However, United Way of Metro Atlanta also used direct communication strategies to reach its donor base with key messages: (1) Steps were being taken to make sure this could never happen again, (2) dollars raised locally stay at home to help people in need, and (3) the issue was never about the local charity (United Way of America is a trade group that provides advertising, training, and legislative advocacy for local United Ways). In Atlanta, the organization trained staff, volunteers, and agency representatives to present the facts to hundreds of employees and neighborhood and civic groups. An information line was established to answer questions and allow donors to air their concerns.

While many local United Ways saw large losses in contributions following the 1992 scandal, Atlanta's donations remained flat. Each year since, however, the campaign has grown—reflecting restored donor confidence in the organization and the charities it supports. Moreover, a 1995 survey showed that Atlantans rate United Way's trustworthiness the same as they did before the national problems surfaced.

An old adage says that every problem is an opportunity. In Atlanta and other communities, the heightened sense of accountability encouraged a number of nonprofits to review their practices. Over the long run, increased attention focused on United Way has reduced donor apathy—enabling the organization to share important messages about community needs and how funds are used. In many cases, years of goodwill gave United Way the benefit of the doubt with donors. But effective public relations helped to maintain credibility and, more important, to make United Way better prepared to meet the needs of the community in years to come.

Questions

1. What can the national United Way do to restore credibility with its local, independent United Way organizations?

2. If the national United Way does advertising, training, and lobbying, what would you suggest it do in each of these areas now?

3. If you were the public relations director for a major nonprofit youth services agency that had net revenues of $5 million over expenses for the year, what would you suggest it do with the surplus (not profit!)?

4. What would you suggest in regard to pay increases for the youth agency, given the United Way experience?

Notes

1. "Associations Advance America," *Government Communications* (July/August 1995): 14.

2. Rae Leaper, "CEOs of Nonprofit Organizations Agree: Communicate or Perish," *Journal of Organizational Communication 4* (1980): 9–17.

3. Ibid., 17.

4. *Profile: A Survey of IABC Communicators' Salaries and Responsibilities* (San Francisco: IABC and IABC Foundation, 1995), 29.

5. "Eighth Annual Salary Survey," *Public Relations Journal* (July 1993): 13.

6. "16 in Probe of Milk Fund Got Co-op Cash," *Chicago Tribune* (5 June 1974): 1.

7. Reprinted from *Association Public Relations,* with permission from Association Section, Public Relations Society of America, 1981.

8. James J. Kilpatrick, "Populace's Confidence on Upbeat," *San Diego Union* (5 January 1977): B-6.

9. Nancy J. Hicks, "Patients and Other Publics," *Public Relations Journal* 42 (3 March 1986): 28–32.

10. John Brice, "Guiding Lights," *Public Relations Journal* 42 (1 January 1986): 20–25.

11. Scott M. Cutlip and Allen H. Center, *Effective Public Relations* (Englewood Cliffs, NJ: Prentice-Hall, 1978), 467.

12. Leaper, "Communicate or Perish," 12.

13. John Price Jones, *The Engineering of Consent.* Edward L. Bernays, ed. (Norman: University of Oklahoma Press, 1955), 159.

14. John W. Leslie, *Seeking the Competitive Dollar: College Management in the Seventies* (Washington, D.C.: American College Public Relations Association, 1971), 44–46.

15. Marc J. Epstein, "The Fall of Corporate Charitable Contributions," *Public Relations Quarterly* (Summer 1993): 37–39.

CHAPTER 17

Public Relations in Government

Preview

Governmental public relations plays a crucial role in keeping the public informed about issues, problems, and actions at all levels of government.

Government public information officers seek citizen approval of government programs, help explain what citizens want from the government, strive to make government responsive to citizens' wishes, and attempt to understand and affect public opinion.

Public relations operatives are pervasive in political campaigns, promoting both public understanding of candidates and candidates' understanding of publics.

A popular government without popular information or the means of acquiring it is but a prologue to a farce, or a tragedy, or perhaps both.

—James Madison, President

T he framers of the U.S. Constitution believed that the American people were capable of governing themselves. To do so, however, citizens needed to be fully informed about issues and problems confronting them and actions taken by their government. Despite their belief, the founding fathers provided no specific means to disseminate information nor any assurance that citizens would be kept informed. It was assumed that government would maintain open communication channels with the public and provide sufficient information to enable citizens to make intelligent decisions about its policies and activities.

To a certain extent, these ideals have been realized through a system that evolved in response to public needs. The mass media struggle to serve our right to know. In providing information to the public about government affairs, they draw on the public relations arm of government—local, state, and federal—that offers the media a constant flow of information.

Government public relations practitioners are often called **public information officers (PIOs),** a designation suggesting that they simply transmit information in an objective and neutral fashion. In fact, they are no more neutral or objective than public relations professionals working in the private sector.

Because the success and stability of democratic governments are ultimately determined by continuous citizen approval, public information officers seek to ensure such approval. The democratic system implies that government will respond to the wishes of the governed, so public information officers work to determine those wishes, then strive to make government responsive to them. Because public opinion provides the climate in which public officials, agencies, and institutions succeed or fail, public information officers try to understand and influence public opinion. Given that a multitude of institutional interests coexist in any society, public relations practitioners both inside and outside government represent a comparable variety of perspectives. As a consequence, much of the significant dialogue needed to ensure democracy's proper functioning is generated, molded, and enunciated by public relations practitioners.

In short, in government—as in any other organization—public relations is a management function that helps define objectives and philosophies while also helping the organization adapt to the demands of its constituencies and environments. Public relations practitioners—whether called PIOs, **public affairs officers (PAOs),** press secretaries, or just plain administrative aides—still communicate with all relevant internal and external publics to make organizational goals and societal expectations consistent. Public information officers, like their counterparts in business and industry, develop, execute, and evaluate programs that promote the exchange of influence and understanding among an organization's constituent parts and publics.

Of course, because they work in a different context with different constraints and problems, government public relations specialists operate somewhat differently from their private sector counterparts. PIOs face unique problems. Their mission and legitimacy are questioned more extensively. Their constituents are forced to provide financial support through taxation. Red tape, internal bureaucratic situations, and political pressures hinder their efforts. Career development opportunities are limited.

In this chapter, we will explore the practice of government public relations and its background, importance, functions, and responsibilities.

The Background of Public Relations in American Government

As we stated in chapter 2, leaders have always courted the sentiments of their people. In this sense, governments have practiced public relations since the reign of the pharaohs. In the United States, however, its formal integration into local, state, and federal government programs has occurred largely since World War II. Before this time, public relations practice was confined mainly to the upper levels of the federal government.

As previously discussed, Amos Kendall served Andrew Jackson in the capacities of pollster, counselor, ghostwriter, and publicist. Use of such counsel, though, did not become established until the administration of Theodore Roosevelt. From that time forward, "Strong U.S. presidents have utilized the expertise of public relations to exploit the mounting power of the news media . . . to mobilize public support for their policies."[1]

Public relations pioneer Edward Bernays recognized that his own expertise could be applied to government and politics as well as to business and philanthropic endeavors. Having served as adviser to Presidents Coolidge and Hoover, he recommended in the 1930s the creation of a cabinet-level Secretary of Public Relations. His suggestion was not acted on; nevertheless, press secretaries of some recent presidents, although formally ranked merely as presidential staff, have been more influential than cabinet officers. When Gerald Ford took office, his first appointments were a personal photographer, a new press secretary, and a chief speechwriter.

Frequently, presidents are conscious of the public relations aspects of their highly visible job. Teddy Roosevelt talked of the presidency as a "bully pulpit." Harry Truman was characteristically more blunt; in a letter to his sister Mary, dated November 14, 1947, he wrote, "All the President is, is a glorified public relations man."

Outside of the presidency, public relations had tougher sledding. In 1913, the U.S. Civil Service Commission announced an examination for a "Publicity Expert." On October 22 of that year, Congress passed the Gillett Amendment (38 U.S.C. 3107), which stated:

> No money appropriated by any act shall be used for the compensation of any publicity expert unless specifically appropriated for that purpose.

Despite the law, the public relations function persisted. Most notable among government's early public relations endeavors was George Creel's World War I Committee on Public Information.

Public relations in the federal government came of age during the New Deal, when the creation of the so-called alphabet agencies "precipitated a flood tide of publicists into the channels of government."[2] The Office of War Information, created during World War II, gave further federal support to the profession. When the war was over, the office became the United States Information Agency (USIA). During the late 1940s, public relations activity was increasingly evident in state and local government. By 1949, nearly every state had established a state-supported public relations program to attract both tourism and industry.

Since 1970, at least 20 new federal regulatory agencies have been created. All of them have extensive public information programs.

Despite the limits placed on public relations activity by Congress, government publicity has always been necessary, if for no other reason than to tell citizens what services are available and how to use them. With the developing complexity of government has come a corresponding increase in publicity.[3]

The Importance and Scope of Governmental Public Relations

Ron Levy, counselor to government communicators, argues that government needs to do a better job of giving the public more information about what government literature is available, what services are available, and where to write for specific government information materials. He says government communicators also should provide wider dissemination for speeches by government leaders.[4]

They may be given different titles, but virtually every federal government agency maintains a public relations body. The Federal Bureau of Investigation (FBI) has an External Affairs Division. The Interstate Commerce Commission (ICC) maintains an Office of Communications and Consumer Affairs. The Environmental Protection Agency (EPA) has an Office of Public Awareness. Even the Central Intelligence Agency (CIA) employs a 20-person Public Affairs Group.

It is impossible to estimate the number of people involved or the money spent in government public relations. As William Gilbert states, "If you are in government, you are in public relations. . . . [There is a] public relations element in all the things . . . government . . . does."[5]

Government public relations ranges from simple publicity to global propaganda. The government spends more money on audiovisual services than does any film studio or television network. It prints over 100,000 different publications each year. K. H. Rabin quotes *U.S. News and World Report* in putting the size of the federal government's public relations expenditures in perspective:

> The federal government spends more money each year trying to influence the way people think than it spends altogether for disaster relief, foreign military assistance, energy conservation and cancer research.[6]

It is similarly difficult to know the numbers of people involved in federal public relations.

The major government information agency for worldwide communication is the United States Information Agency (USIA). Its activities are summarized in mini-case 17.1.

As impressive as federal government public relations employees and budgets may be, they do not include the personnel or expenses involved in city, county, state, or regional governmental agencies, programs, or authorities. Nor do they reflect the fact that the inputs provided by these tens of thousands of public relations officials grow more influential every year. In fact, it is at the state and local levels that public information has witnessed its greatest expansion in recent years. School districts, counties, and local governments have seen the need to tell

Mini-Case 17.1

The USIA

Sometimes the target of terrorists' bombs abroad and of political uproar at home, the United States Information Agency is the public relations arm of the United States in more than 125 countries. USIA's 1996 budget is an estimated $496 million. It has about 9,000 employees, including 1,100 foreign service officers; 4,000 foreign citizens employed to assist the agency, mostly in its posts abroad; and 4,000 civil service employees, mostly in the United States. This is the agency's mission:

> To support the national interest by conveying an understanding abroad of what the United States stands for as a nation and as a people; to explain the nation's policies and to present a true picture of the society, institutions and culture in which those policies evolve.

The Voice of America, the USIA radio operation, maintains 106 transmitters worldwide, broadcasting in 40 languages and reaching 75 million people a year. USIA also annually produces and distributes about 200 films, publishes 15 magazines in 31 languages, and mounts 50 major exhibits.

The agency maintains over 200 libraries and information centers in 90 countries and provides educational programs for 350,000 students per year.

Media relations is also an important USIA job. Like the Associated Press or United Press International, the agency functions as a wire service, providing film news clips for overseas television and moving information from 205 posts in 127 countries everyday.

Sources: *USIA: Its Work and Structure,* October 1987; also, the United States Budget for fiscal year 1996.

---

their stories to taxpayers to get budget increases, bond approvals, or tax increases. They have seen that a public relations (or public affairs/public information) specialist is essential in this process.

The Function of Governmental Public Relations

Government public information officers, like any other public relations practitioners, seek to achieve mutual understanding between their agencies and publics by following the four-step process explained in part II of this book. They must gauge public opinion, plan and organize for public relations effectiveness, construct messages for internal and external audiences, and measure the effectiveness of the entire process.

Serving Both the Public and Government

Like all organizational boundary spanners, public information officers jointly serve two masters—their publics and their employers. On the one hand, they provide the public with complete, candid, continuous reporting of government information and accessible channels for citizen inputs. On the other hand, Scott M. Cutlip maintains:

> The vast government information machine has as its primary purpose advancement of government's policies and personnel . . . the major objective is to gain support for the incumbent administration's policies and maintain its leaders in power.[7]

In a recent Brookings Institution study, former aide to Presidents Eisenhower and Nixon, Stephen Hess, observed the contradictory pressures on government press officers in the Departments of Defense, Transportation, and State; the Food and Drug Administration; and the White House. What he found was "a semibureaucrat/semireporter, in the bureaucracy but not truly of it, tainted by association with the press yet not of the press."[8] Hess found that press officers were trusted neither by the media nor by their own superiors. Because they are suspect in the eyes of their own political executives, according to Hess, "The career press officer is often the odd person out in the permanent bureaucracy."[9]

Moreover, the media perhaps underappreciate the press information officer's role. Says Hess, "If they were to be invited to view press operations from the inside, many reporters would be surprised to see the extent to which the press officer is their advocate within the permanent government."[10]

Currently, public information officers serve neither master very well, as evidenced by millions of Americans viewing their "government as distant and unresponsive, if not hostile."[11] Both the public and the politicians might be better served if public information officers could provide more active input for governmental decision makers. In his seminal 1947 report, *Government and Mass Communication,* Zachariah Chafee Jr. held that:

> Government information can play a vital role in the cause of good administration by exploring the impact of new social forces, discovering strains and tensions before they become acute, and encouraging a positive sense of unity and national direction.[12]

The most basic functions of government public relations are to help define and achieve government program goals, to enhance government responsiveness and service, and to provide the public with sufficient information to permit self-government. The goal of public information officers is to promote cooperation and confidence between citizens and their government. This in turn requires government accessibility, accountability, consistency, and integrity.

Planned, continuous governmental public relations programs may have any one or several of the following objectives:

Objectives of Governmental Public Relations

1. **To gain support for new laws or initiatives.** Jockeying for political support for particular laws and initiatives is evident in news reports every day. Whether the issue is a local ordinance related to land-use planning, a state effort to improve elementary and secondary education, or a federal tax reform, public information officers play an active role.

2. **To stimulate citizen interest and relieve public confusion about governmental agencies, processes, and programs.** When drought hit the Southeast, governmental agencies implemented various water conservation measures. Government public relations officials encouraged interest in water conservation and straightened out confusion about new water use rules.

3. **To facilitate voter decision making by providing factual information.** Particularly important in local government referenda, government public

relations practitioners provide accurate information about potential outcomes of various initiatives.

4. To enable citizens to use government services fully by providing continuous information. An example is promotion of state parks or dissemination of energy-saving tips during crisis power shortages.

5. To open channels of communication with government officials. PIOs serve as ombudsmen, establish hot lines, and set up public forums to promote information input and output.

6. To serve officials by helping interpret citizen attitudes and public opinion. At the highest levels of government, press secretaries and other communication operatives are members of the teams that seek to fathom public desires regarding legislation and governmental programs.

7. To gain voluntary obedience with laws, regulations, and rules. Public relations efforts support laws and rules related to everything from the automobile speed limit to drug abuse and from littering to compliance with tax laws.

8. To build generalized support for agencies or programs so that conflicts or negative events can be overcome. The National Aeronautics and Space Administration is mandated by law to provide the American public with full information about its programs. Throughout its history, it has done so with an eye toward building public support. The reservoir of public approval for NASA was evident in the aftermath of the Challenger space shuttle disaster. Although investigations were launched, no one seriously suggested dissolving the agency or its programs.

The Practice of Governmental Public Relations
Dealing with Unique Problems

The practice of public relations in government is much like that in other institutions, but government information officers do face some difficulties unique to their area. Because they are paid with public funds, their mission and legitimacy are questioned more than would be the case in private organizations. Gilbert points out that "the citizenry . . . regards government public information activities as wasteful of the taxpayers' money and essentially propagandistic."[13] This is why the Gillett Amendment has never been repealed and why government public relations practitioners ply their trade under euphemisms like "information officer," "public affairs officer," or "education officer."

Unlike the customers of corporations, the constituents of governmental entities are forced to support those entities financially through taxes. Thus, while government may be responsive to political forces, it is not directly responsive to market forces. "Government red tape" has become a sadly accurate cliché and a serious public relations problem.

David Brown points out other problems of public information officers: internal bureaucratic situations that hinder professional efforts; weak job standards; political pressure; and little career development or recognition. Moreover, he states, government public relations specialists are considered "after-the-fact operators, expected to put out fires started by others or to implement information about programs that we strongly feel will not stand the muster of the media."[14] The increasing complexity of government policies, rules, and practices; the widening chasm between citizens and their government; and the escalation of demands made by citizens without understanding of the political, legal, and financial constraints placed on government are additional difficulties public information officers face. Mini-case 17.2 relates how a county government recognized the need to improve its public relations effectiveness.

Devising Solution Strategies

To deal with these problems, public information officers may adopt several strategies. First, they should strive to be generalists in both public relations and management skills while becoming expert in the language and discipline of particular fields within government (health, education, transportation, welfare, defense, etc.).

Second, public information officers should practice preventive maintenance, providing policy guidance before programs are approved. Doing so requires them to enter government's management mainstream, as we discussed in chapter 4.

Third, government public relations must develop a service orientation—responding to a public made up of consumers of government services. Moreover, public relations should foster this perspective in all government employees, using established channels of internal communication.

Fourth, government public information officers should concentrate on inputs as much as outputs. As Rabin suggests, "The proverbial general audience . . . will be identified more and more as a consumer public."[15] This calls for getting direct feedback through citizen participation, surveys and questionnaires, and community meetings—feedback that will be used to adjust programs, messages, and media.

Finally, as the downfall of the Nixon administration so aptly demonstrated, great hazards confront governmental attempts to hide failures, ineptitude, or mistakes. Openness is essential to effective government public relations.

Fairfax County, Virginia, has worked to involve citizens in the open communication process that is needed for government to work well (see mini-case 17.2.).

Employee and Media Relations in Government
Employee Relations

Although employee and media relations are processes important to all institutions, certain aspects are specific to government public relations practice.

The impression citizens have of their government, particularly of local government, is often formed through routine day-to-day contacts between government employees and members of the public. Gilbert points out, "One dissatisfied employee can, by his or her deeds and words, do irreparable harm . . . if such actions are multiplied by several . . . the result can be devastating."[16]

Practitioners must foster attitudes of goodwill and respect for the public among governmental employees and officials. Particular attention should be given to face-to-face contacts, correspondence, and telephone conversations.

Mini-Case 17.2

Interactive Government: Involving Citizens on Many Fronts

Hundreds of citizens testify during budget deliberations. Homeowners join in associations in almost every neighborhood. Other citizens spend their evenings at local government board and commission meetings. Still others volunteer to help the police, the libraries, the animal shelter, the county's elderly.

This is participatory democracy at its best. And Fairfax County, Virginia, has the good fortune—and the challenge—to have all this citizen activism going for it.

Consensus is an important result of citizen involvement. In an era of government bashing and citizen distrust of institutions, citizens most often become either advocates of the process or positive catalysts for change.

When Fairfax County has needed major funding for schools or parks or other capital projects, it has placed a bond issue before the county's voters. The last county government referendum helped finance transportation facilities, including highways and subway/bus facilities. Informing citizens about the bond issue is a major challenge in logistics, usually met under time constraints and with limited resources.

In each recent bond referendum, a citizen task force has played a major and vital role in explaining to the electorate the projects to be funded. Task force members meet with editorial boards, citizen groups, reporters, and businesses, and provide a proactive conduit of information to the community. The task force remains neutral on the issues, advocating neither pro nor con. Its job is strictly to provide information.

The citizen bond task force reinforces the county's other information efforts: a cable TV program, a coordinated series of media blitzes, a bond pamphlet sent to all citizens, and major districtwide and countywide information meetings. As a result of this multipronged voter education effort, the vast majority of county bond proposals in recent years have won voter approval because the voters understood the issues.

Literally thousands of other opportunities exist for individuals to make a difference. In fiscal 1994, more than 17,000 volunteers assisted county government, contributing an estimated 850,000 volunteer hours.

Volunteers staff gyms for nighttime sessions, deliver hot meals to the homebound elderly and those with disabilities, work with victims of crimes, and assist at the county animal shelter. One volunteer helped set up the police department's electronic bulletin board, making crime reports available to anyone with access to a computer and a modem.

Electronic communications are beginning to grow in importance as a tool in the county's multifaceted communication efforts. The new Countywide Information Network Bulletin Board offers citizens details on county job openings, Board of Supervisors' agendas and meeting actions, budget and taxes, and requests for proposals on county contracts. The bulletin board becomes interactive when users ask questions via e-mail, and citizens can even download tax forms.

Electronic communications joins other ongoing programs such as the county's 24-hour telephone taped information system. In addition, the county's cable television channel offers a variety of information programming and a new bulletin board, and its *Weekly Agenda* newsletter highlights agendas of the Board of Supervisors and planning and zoning bodies as well as other county government news.

The county also targets specific groups in its communications efforts. Homeowners get special recycling news, and civic homeowner associations receive quarterly mailings of an anthology of county news they can pass along to their memberships. The association mailings are 20- to 25-page documents prepared—camera ready—for the more than 1,400 civic associations to use in their newsletters or on flyers. The material is also available on disk. In this way, the associations receive information that is important to them but may not have been picked up by the media.

As more and more sophisticated electronic means become available and affordable, the citizen-government interaction not only will become easier, it will become faster. The path ahead begins to look like one of the "alternative futures" the County Goals Citizens Commission envisioned eight years ago.

The groundwork, in fact, was laid for interactive government in a statement made by the Goals Commission in its report to the board and the citizenry:

> The Commission cannot stress enough its view that citizen participation is essential to good county government and to the public's support of that government. . . . In its ability to touch our daily lives county government is unique. To serve us well, the county must nurture the ability of its citizens from many diverse backgrounds to express their needs and then must respond to them.

Source: Marion M. Meany, "Interactive Government: Involving Citizens on Many Fronts," *Government Communications* (June 1995): 8–10.

Reception areas should be pleasant and well maintained, and public vehicles should be driven in a safe and courteous fashion.

Rabin puts it this way:

> If the image of the government is to be enhanced, the process must take place at the level of the individual employee—his or her productivity, and how he or she conducts encounters with individual citizens. . . . Focus will be more and more on internal communications . . . employees . . . will be sent more and more as media for communicating with external publics.[17]

Chapter 11 provides further discussion of the rationale and means for employee communication.

Media Relations

Some commentators seem to believe that media relations has lost importance as a priority of public information officers now that the public increasingly receives government information in more direct forms. J. M. Perry, writing in *The Wall Street Journal,* observes, "The press release is more or less a decaying institution in Washington . . . government communicators have turned more and more to sophisticated tools—orchestrated advertising campaigns, television commercials, videotape cassettes, full-color brochures and glossy magazines."[18] Although government information encompasses an ever-broadening range of media and techniques, plain old media relations still gets tremendous attention. Indeed, without government information officers, the news media could not report on governments as effectively and economically as they do.

Government public information officers outgun reporters in numbers and resources. Moreover, reporters often feel lost in local, state, or federal bureaucracies. Under these circumstances, says Cutlip, "An ever-increasing share of news content . . . is coming often unchanged from the government officer's typewriter. More and more of the governmental news reporting task is abandoned to the practitioner who supplies the information in professional ready-to-use packages."[19] The public information officer thus has an enormous opportunity for media access, but with that access comes the responsibility not to abuse it. Typically, government press officers accept that responsibility. According to Hess, "Releases are readable and competent . . . sometimes the press releases were more precise than the hurried accounts written by general-assignment reporters."[20]

Press officers work hard to serve the media and to do so with a high sense of ethical behavior. Hess describes the qualities of a good press officer: "stamina, curiosity, a helpful nature, a good memory, civility, coolness under pressure, and an understanding of human psychology."[21] Commenting on PIOs' ethical standards, he says:

> For all press secretaries the crux of unethical conduct is lying. Spokesmen are expected to tell the truth—it is U.S. government policy. They also prefer to tell the truth.[22]

Summing up his observations of governmental media relations, Hess explains:

> The view from inside a press office is that most energy seems to be devoted to trying to find out what the rest of the agency is doing (often unsuccessfully), gathering material that has been requested by reporters rather than promoting carefully prepared positions, and distributing information that is neither controversial nor especially self-serving.[23]

Using the Internet

Using technology to communicate with the publics is not new in government public relations, but the possibilities of the new computer-based technologies make inexpensive two-way communication a reality for the low operating budgets prevalent in government public relations.

One use of computer technology is the Internet, and especially World Wide Web pages. The World Wide Web is composed of home pages that make up web sites. These home pages often incorporate full-color photos or graphics and text that can be designed like a brochure or newsletter. To "navigate" or move between web sites once on the Internet, the user merely points and clicks the computer mouse. New software, sometimes called "browser software," is used to get people onto and through the Internet. This software makes using the Internet easy and fun for even the computer newcomer. With an estimated eight million users in the United States in 1995, the Internet is quickly becoming a mass medium.

Government web sites range from the White House to local city and county sites such as one in Hennepin County, Minnesota. (See figure 17.1 for a sample of government web sites.) Memphis is developing a network of city sites. See minicase 17.3 for a look at a network of city web sites.

Web sites can accomplish several objectives:

1. *Communicating with the public.* With the web you can bypass the media. The web site can supplement your media relations efforts and may eventually replace much of the media effort.

2. *Communicating with researchers, activists, specialists, and journalists.* People will use your site for information they need.

3. *Distributing large volumes of information.* Web users can pick and choose what they want from the information provided. A good web site, though, routes users to information that interests them.

U.S. Fish and Wildlife Service

The National Wildlife Refuge System
Refuges: A Wild Place For Wildlife!

The Blue Goose Server provides information about the National Wildlife Refuge System and topics of interest related to wildlife management and natural resources management.

Other U. S. Fish and Wildlife Service Resources

Information Relating To Natural Resources Management

Legislative Information - Federal Government

Tools to search the Internet

Reference resources on the Internet. Electronic publications of History of the Net, Surfing the Internet, Big Dummy's Guide, A Guide to Cyberspace, Frequently Asked Questions (FAQs) and more.

What's New On The Blue Goose Server, updated as of December 5, 1995.

Blue Goose Server Statistics

This page was revised on December 5, 1995

Your questions and comments will assist us to decide what features and information to add to this server. Send questions about the National Wildlife Refuge System and information being provided to Sean Furniss - Sean_Furniss@mail.fws.gov. Mail address: Division of Refuges, U. S. Fish and Wildlife Service, MS 670 ARLSQ, 4401 North Fairfax Drive, Arlington, VA 22203, USA

U.S. Department of Education
home page

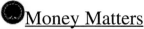
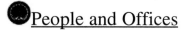

Welcome

What is the Department of Education? Read this brief introduction to learn about the Department, its mission and goals for American education, and also discover some of the special features that this Web site has to offer.

News

What's making the news at the Department of Education? Look in here for pointers to the latest information we've added, including: announcements of new funding opportunities, press releases, transcripts of speeches and testimony made by Secretary Richard Riley, and updates on current legislation and our budget.

Guides

If you are a **teacher** or a **researcher** you have specialized information needs and interests. What resources does the Department make available especially for you? The answer is "lots!" So much, in fact, that we publish two books about what we have to offer -- one for teachers (_Teacher's Guide to the Department of Education_) and another for researchers (_Researcher's Guide to the Department of Education_). We're also starting to collect links to ED-sponsored Internet resources for **parents**.

Money Matters

If you're interested in applying for a grant or contract, here's information you'll need to know. Department guidelines, regulations, and funding opportunities are available here. Interested in student financial assistance? That's in this section too. If it's about money, you'll find it in Money Matters.

Secretary's Initiatives

What are the programs highlighted by the Department? You'll find information and publications about our major initiatives, including Goals 2000, School-to-Work, School-Wide Programs, Family Involvement, Technology, Flexibility and Waivers, the reauthorization of the Elementary and Secondary Education Act, and the Individuals with Disabilities Education Act (IDEA).

People and Offices

Who's who at the Department of Education? Check the Department's organizational chart, which leads to information about program offices, organizational units, key staff, and a listing of programs managed by eac office. You'll also find where we're located -- both in Washington and around the nation. In addition, there': searchable phone directory so that you can find the person who has answers you need.

⬤Programs and Services

What programs does the Department sponsor? What services are available in your state? Check out the new dynamic map of the United States to identify resources and services in your area. Read about the Departmen major program themes and then use the *Guide to ED Programs* to lead you to as much detail as you want abc individual programs.

⬤Publications and Products

Have we got a document for you! You'll find the full text of many of our publications, all marked-up and ready to be read or searched. Other documents are available via our Gopher system, too.

⬤Other Sites

In addition to this site, there are many educational resources available online around the world. This section provides links to some public sites of interest to teachers, students, and researchers. We've also put together list of Department-funded or affiliated sites and services.

⬤Search!

Use great information retrieval tools to find documents at this site or elsewhere on the Internet.

⬤Picks o' the Month

We pick three great resources every month and highlight them here for you. Our picks are taken from three broad categories: ED-affiliated Internet sites elsewhere, newly available documents of merit, and new selections at this site focusing on individual ED programs and offices.

Last update December 6, 1995 (BNS).

Figure 17.1 U.S. Air Force home page

Notice: The AFIN Homepage has moved!!! Our new Home Page is located at URL http://www.afin.af.mil. Please make a note of it.

Welcome to AirForceLINK, the United States **Department of the Air Force Home Page,** your first source for Air Force news and information.

 First AF C-130 arrives at Tuzla

President accepts defense bill

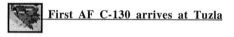 **December Airman Magazine**

AirForceLINK Search Gateway (News, People, Features, Fact Sheets, Speeches, Photo Descriptions)

Quick Search AirForceLINK

Search for: [   ] (Maximum of 50 Hits)

[Submit Query] [Reset]

Contents

- <u>News</u>: Current Air Force news and information
- <u>Fact Sheets</u>: Major weapons systems and Air Force commands
- <u>People</u>: Biographies of Air Force Leaders
- <u>Library</u>: Air Force Speeches, Air Force Issues and Air Force News Service Features
- <u>Pictures</u>: Photos of Air Force People, Operations, and Weapon Systems
- <u>Air Force Sites</u>: Links to other Air Force World Wide Web Servers
- <u>What's New</u>: Recently added AirForceLINK products
- <u>Overview</u>: How AirForceLINK is organized
- <u>Air Force FAQ</u>: Frequently Asked Questions

The <u>Mission</u> of the U.S. Air Force is to defend the United States through control and exploitation of air and space. The Vision: Air Force people building the world's most respected air and space force - global power and reach for America.

The Department of the Air Force is headquartered in the <u>Pentagon</u>, Washington D.C. The service is organized in eight major commands throughout the world which provide combat aircraft, airlift, refueling, reconnaissance and other support to the <u>Unified Combatant Commands</u>.

The Air Force also has more than three dozen Field Operating Agencies and Direct Reporting Units who directly support the mission by providing unique services.

Together with Air Force Reserve and Air National Guard forces, the United States Air Force is the best in the world.

The Secretary of the Air Force is <u>Sheila E. Widnall</u>. The Air Force Chief of Staff is <u>Gen. Ronald R. Fogleman</u>. Chief Master Sergeant of the Air Force is <u>CMSAF David J. Campanale</u>.

As you browse these pages, let the <u>Air Force Song</u>, (245K) play in the background. It is performed by the <u>Air Combat Command Heritage of America Band</u>.

AirForceLINK is provided through the cooperative efforts of the Office of the Secretary of the Air Force (Public Affairs), and the <u>Defense Technical Information Center (DTIC)</u>. This is a <u>government computer system</u>. We welcome <u>comments and suggestions.</u>

| News | Fact Sheets | People | Library | Pictures | Air Force Sites |

Mini-Case 17.3

American Community Network

Imagine turning on your computer to find an art show in Dallas, job openings in Denver, or the best flies to use while fishing in Montana in late July.

Under the American Community Network, a planned network of possibly 1,200 communities beginning in Memphis, Tennessee, you will be linked to a community information clearinghouse through a home page at a World Wide Web Site on the Internet (see figure 17.2).

Information on topics such as educational data, economic statistics, tourism, amenities, sporting events, or entertainment opportunities will be available for these 1,200 communities.

Figure 17.2 Memphis was one of the first cities to link its home page to various businesses, community organizations, and tourist attractions.

Information About Memphis

- Memphis Concerts - Current Week
- Memphis Theatre - Current Week
- Memphis Art Exhibits - Current Week
- Memphis Miscellaneous Events - Current Week
- MECCA - Memphis Educational Computer Connectivity Alliance
- Memphis Information
  Includes a map of Memphis
- Shelby County Web Site
- Representative Harold Ford
- City of Memphis Prototype Web Site
- The City of Memphis
- Memphis Mojo - The Insider's Guide to Memphis Music for the Outside
- MemphisNet
- Memphis Web Sites
- Radio-Free Memphis
- Tennessee.com
- Higher Education in Tennessee

Memphis Links

Businesses

- Federal Express
- Promus Corporation
- Towery Publishing

Community Organizations

- Jericho Road
  Jericho Road, Inc. is a non-profit Christian organization based in Memphis, Tennessee, whose purpose is to provide a centralized, ecumenical, global repository of ministry information. The churches and organizations listed serve the Memphis / Shelby County area.

Museums, Arts, Attractions, Bands

- Dixon Gallery & Gardens
- Mud Island

The network is being developed by New Media Publishing for The Chamber of Commerce Executives and Towery Publishing of Memphis. The basic web sites will be sponsored by local chambers of commerce.

Larger cities will be linked together for supersites that will provide a wider variety of information. Organizers plan to have 20 supersites and 200 others created by 1997. For local citizens, the hometown page will be a means of getting local information and keeping informed of city events and services. For the out-of-towner it will provide tourist-type information such as weather reports, sporting event schedules (and possibly tickets), and restaurant guides.

Initial access can be found at http://www.memphis.acn.net.

Source: Jody Callahan, "Memphis Will Be 1st City on Internet Data Finder," *The Commercial Appeal* (Memphis: 4 November 1995): C-2.

4. *Publicizing anything from a new policy to an upcoming event.* A web site is accessible all over the world, and it can be updated easily. You can also use other media to invite the public to your web site.

5. *Soliciting public comment.* The web provides a two-way communication medium. You can build in an e-mail option with a click of the mouse.[24]

The Presidential Press Secretary

The single most conspicuous and important government public relations practitioner is the presidential press secretary. As the chief public relations spokesperson for the administration, he or she communicates policies and practices to the public while providing input into governmental decision making. The unfortunate wounding of press secretary Jim Brady during an assassination attempt on President Reagan shows that the job even carries an element of danger. The following

The presidential press secretary is the most conspicuous and important government public relations practitioner. George Stephanopoulos was President Bill Clinton's first press secretary.

description of the press secretary's job can be applied to all government public relations duties in general.

Several times a day, the presidential press secretary stands before largely hostile media representatives and fields questions for the president. The smallest misstatement can lead the world to think there has been a change in White House policy.

According to William Safire, a speechwriter for President Nixon who became a political columnist for *The New York Times,*

> A good press secretary speaks up for the press to the President and speaks out for the President to the press. He makes his home in the pitted no-man's land of an adversary relationship and is primarily an advocate, interpreter and amplifier. He must be more the President's man than the press's. But he can be his own man as well.[25]

Gerald Ford's two press secretaries give differing perspectives on the relationship that should exist between the practitioner and the president. Gerald terHorst quit after Ford pardoned Nixon, commenting, "A spokesman should feel in his heart and mind that the Chief's decision is the right one so that he can speak with a persuasiveness that stems from conviction."[26]

Ron Nessen, who replaced terHorst, took a different view: "A press secretary does not always have to agree with the President. His first loyalty is to the public, and he should not knowingly lie or mislead the press."[27] Larry Speakes, spokesman for the Reagan White House agrees. "If I lose my reputation for being truthful," he says, "I've lost everything."[28]

Whether or not a practitioner must agree with her or his boss is a matter of personal conscience. Loyalty to the public and an ability to foster communications in both directions, however, are essential aspects of the job, just as they are for all public relations professionals.

Public Relations and Political Campaigns

Government really cannot be discussed without regard to political context. While government provides many and diverse services to its constituents, its policies are guided by politics. The political campaign is the most overt expression of politics. Public relations activity on behalf of political candidates is practically synonymous with the campaign itself.

Political campaigning is a nonstop industry, raising hundreds of millions of dollars from political action committees (see chapter 15) and others and spending that money to attract votes. Public relations plays a critical role in both raising and spending those funds.

The public relations practitioner in the political campaign is not just a spokesperson to the media but usually also a trusted adviser who helps formulate campaign strategy and positions on issues. Gaining votes first requires gaining funds, media exposure, and volunteers. Public relations works hard to attract all three. These resources must then be converted into political support.

Some campaign tasks in which public relations may be involved include the following:

Developing computerized mail campaigns.

Coordinating broadcast, print, and other advertising.

Scouting sites for speeches and other campaign events.

Staging events to increase candidate visibility.

Raising campaign funds.

Preparing news releases concerning candidates' activities, positions, and schedules.

Writing speeches and position papers.

Coordinating research on issues and voters.

Providing briefings and background sessions for the media and others.

Attracting and coordinating volunteers.

All of this activity is designed to get the candidate elected so that he or she can become a part of the governing process. Campaign press aides to successful candidates often join government as well.

Contemporary political campaigning is frequently criticized for the extent to which the process has become one of "packaging" and "selling" candidates. Public relations has received much of the blame for this perceived phenomenon. Indeed, public relations practitioners have changed the nature of political campaigns in both negative and positive ways.

Candidates are criticized for paying too much attention to polls and for trying to be what people want them to be rather than being themselves. When operating ethically, positively, and professionally, public relations practitioners facilitate two-way communication between candidates and constituencies. They help candidates gain public attention for themselves and their positions. Moreover, public relations people help candidates understand what voters want and expect. Such understanding is essential in a representative form of government.

The success of many government programs depends on the dispensation of adequate information about them to relevant publics. The president and the police officer, the legislator and the librarian all rely on public information officers to do their jobs effectively and efficiently. Government programs ranging from soil conservation to crime prevention, from anti-litter campaigns to army recruitment depend on public relations.

The Impact of Public Relations on Government

R. L. Rings demonstrated the dramatic impact of governmental public relations in a study of 70 Ohio school districts. Rings analyzed 35 school districts that employed public information officers and 35 that did not. The districts with public information officers received significantly more news coverage. Moreover, where public information officers were on staff, the news focused on student and public affairs; without public information officers, coverage consisted mainly of sports and administrative news. The most telling findings, however, concerned the finances of the school districts:

> Financial records indicated that the director systems' current average operating millage was two mills above the state mean, whereas the non-director systems average operating millage was four mills below the state mean. In local support per pupil, the director sample averaged $374 to the nondirector sample average of $275.[29]

It could be argued that only more affluent school districts can afford public relations directors, but it is probable that such directors in Ohio had impact on public support of education that directly translated into financial support.

Summary

Public relations is just as critical to governmental organizations as it is to other institutions. Since government activities depend so much on public opinion, public relations is the stuff of government. Rather than seeking to ban public relations from government, citizens should recognize its legitimacy, and public relations specialists should work toward making its practice ever more professional, responsible, and efficient.

Case Study

The Insurance
Company and the
Country Yokels

By W. F. (Fred) Kiesner
*Loyola Marymount
University
Los Angeles, California*

In early summer, officials from Kern County, California, contracted to have a "chip seal" of small rocks applied to the only road leading in and out of the mountain community of Frazier Park, about 75 miles north of Los Angeles. The chip seal would provide better road traction during icy and snowy conditions in the high mountain country. Several thousand people live in small isolated communities along the 15-mile stretch of road. The contractor began applying the rocks to the road, but something went wrong, and they did not stick to the tarry sealant. It was also reported that the contractor's heavyweight rolling machine had broken down, and thus he could not pack down the rocks and gravel.

The road became extremely dangerous, with cars encountering flying gravel and stones. Reportedly, the contractor's own trucks caused a great deal of damage as they roared up and down the road at high speeds, showering passing cars with rocks. During the next two days, approximately 600 cars suffered severe damage, including broken windshields and headlights and ruined paint. Irate local residents bombarded the country supervisor with calls, and he assured them that all damage would be repaired by the contractor's insurance company. He advised each caller to get two damage estimates, submit them to the insurance company, and wait until everything was paid.

The hundreds of local residents did that, then waited and waited and waited. After three months, with no action from the insurance company (a very large national firm, United States Fidelity and Guarantee—USF&G), residents contacted the firm's regional office in Fresno. Many were treated in a curt and rude manner, and a number of residents reported that the firm's officials had hung up on them.

Finally, in September, all residents who had filed claims received a form letter from the insurance company denying any settlement. The insurance firm said it had closely investigated the insured's behavior and had concluded that he had done nothing wrong. The denial letter also stated that all those sustaining damage had driven in a reckless and careless manner and thus had caused their own damage. Local residents were extremely angry and insulted that the big insurance company thought it was sloughing off a bunch of dumb mountain hillbillies! The fact that dozens of California Highway Patrol cars, county sheriff's cars, and U.S. Forest Service vehicles had also sustained severe damage made the insurance firm's claims of reckless driving a bit ludicrous! The total damage to local residents' vehicles was estimated at approaching $1 million.

One of the local residents called a public meeting in the town hall to discuss ways to fight the insurance company. Hundreds of irate citizens showed up, filling the hall to overflowing.

Questions

1. Did the county supervisor have additional responsibility beyond "passing the buck" to the insurance company? What was his responsibility after the insurance company refused to pay?

2. Obviously, the insurance company officials in this case mishandled the situation. What should they have done? If they were going to deny all claims, could they have used public relations techniques to ease the tensions? What would you have done differently?

3. Considering the heated situation the insurance firm, now finds itself in, what would you, as its public relations director, do next? Can you save the day for the firm?

4. Would "stonewalling" (attempting to prevent information from getting out) be a viable alternative for the insurance firm? What are the potential risks of such an action?

5. Do the local residents really have any power in fighting the big national company and its apparently arbitrary decision? Could the citizens use public relations techniques in their battle against the insurance firm?

6. If the local residents launched a negative publicity campaign against the insurance company in an attempt to equalize and neutralize its power and size, would this be fair or ethical?

Notes

1. Scott Cutlip, "Public Relations in Government," *Public Relations Review* (Summer 1976): 10.

2. William H. Gilbert, ed., *Public Relations in Local Government* (Washington, D.C.: International City Management Association, 1975), 9.

3. Ibid., 8.

4. Ronald Levy, "New Realities in Government Communications," *Government Communications* (November 1995): 8–9.

5. Ibid., 5.

6. K. H. Rabin, "Government PIOs in the '80s," *Public Relations Journal* (December 1979): 21.

7. Cutlip, "Public Relations in Government," 12.

8. Quoted in West Pederson, "Brookings Study Profiles Government Press Officers," *Public Relations Journal* (November 1984): 43–45.

9. Ibid.

10. Ibid.

11. Final Report of the 32nd American Assembly, Columbia University.

12. Zachariah Chafee, Jr., *Government and Mass Communication* (2 vols.; Chicago: University of Chicago Press, 1947), 2.736.

13. Gilbert, *Public Relations in Local Government,* 11.

14. D. H. Brown, "Information Officers and Reporters: Friends or Foes?" *Public Relations Review* (Summer 1976): 33.

15. Rabin, "Government PIOs," 23.

16. Gilbert, *Public Relations in Local Government,* 20.

17. Rabin, "Government PIOs," 23.

18. J. M. Perry, "Federal Flairs . . . ," *The Wall Street Journal* (23 May 1979): 1 ff.

19. Cutlip, "Public Relations In Government," 15.

20. Pederson, "Brookings Study Profiles," 43.

21. Ibid., 43.

22. Ibid., 45.

23. Ibid., 44.

24. Cliff Majersik, "Deciding Whether to Build a World Wide Web Site," *Government Communications* (September 1995): 7–8.

25. William Safire, "One of Our Own," *The New York Times* (19 September 1974): 43.

26. Robert U. Brown, "Role of Press Secretary," *Editor and Publisher* (19 October 1974): 40.

27. I. W. Hill, "Nessen Lists Ways He Has Improved Public Relations," *Editor and Publisher* (10 April 1975): 40.

28. Jeremiah O'Leary, "Firmly in the White House Hot Seat," *Insight* (1 September 1986): 51.

29. R. L. Rings, "Public School News Coverage With and Without PR Directors," *Journalism Quarterly* (Spring 1971): 62–65; 72.

CHAPTER 18

Corporate Public Relations

Preview

Public relations efforts designed to improve public attitudes toward private enterprise must address the credibility of corporations, corporate concern for individuals on a human scale, public understanding of economic realities, and corporate willingness to lead society toward change.

Renewed business credibility must be built on honest performance, open communication, consistency between performance and communication, commitment to problem solving, and establishment of feasible expectations.

To ensure public confidence in business, public relations should act as business's eyes and ears, as a receiver of the subtle information that signals societal demands, and as a purveyor of information that moves management toward effective response.

Small business owners and managers typically serve as their own public relations experts. They can and should be involved with media, community, employee, customer, supplier, financial, and political

relations. Such efforts promote and protect the small business and also improve its profitability.

Public relations is practiced more extensively and with more impact in large business organizations than anywhere else. Public relations is a means by which businesses seek to improve their ability to do business.

Other major issues of special significance for corporate public relations in the last half of the 1990s and into the early 21st century include globalization of business operations thus of public relations, increased emphasis on diversity issues, intensified crises and disasters, and unprecedented technological change.

Organizations that cannot understand the new era and navigate a path through the transition are vulnerable and will be bypassed.

—Don Tapscott and Art Caston
Paradigm Shift

B usinesses deal with and adapt to increasingly complex and dynamic environments. They manage relations with a variety of publics and balance behavior in response to many, often conflicting, demands. They confront numerous complicated and pressing issues, including business ethics, equal opportunity, the quality of work life, consumerism, environmentalism, global commerce, and others.

Large corporations have substantial resources available to invest in public relations efforts. They do not invest, however, unless they believe the amounts spent will yield even greater returns. Thus, while public relations is allotted great scope and resources in business organizations, it is also held closely accountable for producing desired results.

As indicated in earlier chapters, public relations is practiced by all managers in business, not just by those whose titles or job descriptions contain the term. Top-level executives are expected to spend substantial portions of their energies and efforts on public relations–related matters. Consequently, while the status of public relations has recently been elevated in business organizations, public relations specialists who possess only traditional skills risk being restricted to technical roles.

Obviously, all of the chapters in this book dealing with the practice, the process, and the publics of public relations apply directly to business public relations. Businesses use *media relations* to gain support and sympathy from print and broadcast outlets, to generate positive publicity, to tell business's side of the story, and to reduce negative publicity or at least keep it in perspective.

Employee relations is important to business as it contributes to harmonious labor relations and helps attract and retain good employees. Effective employee communication can also stimulate worker creativity and input, boost attitudes and morale, improve product quality and customer service, and enhance productivity.

Community relations is a business concern because it supports sales, attracts employees, improves the quality of public services, provides support for business initiatives, and improves the quality of life for employees and executives.

Business is greatly concerned with *consumer relations.* Corporations want to build positive relations with customers, respond effectively to consumer complaints and problems, and support sales and marketing efforts.

As our chapter on *financial relations* indicates, sound financial communication allows business to attract capital at the lowest possible cost. Other financial relations goals include ensuring that public firms' stock is appropriately valued, building knowledge and confidence in fund sources, and responding to investor questions or needs.

Finally, *public affairs* deals with business's interaction with government on various levels. Government relations have direct impact on a business's flexibility and manageability. Regulation, taxation, labor law, and international trade policies are only a few ways in which governmental actions constrain business decision making and success.

In short, public relations is a means by which businesses seek to improve their ability to do business. Effective public relations smooths and enhances a company's operations and eases and increases its sales. It enables a business to better anticipate and adapt to societal demands and trends. It is the means by which businesses improve their operating environments.

The Challenge of Corporate Public Relations Today

The demands placed on large corporations are great and diverse. Business organizations must fulfill a long list of domestic responsibilities and still compete effectively in domestic and international markets.

International competitiveness has possibly been the greatest challenge facing business in the last decade. Cooperative arrangements between business and government in Japan, West Germany, and other countries represent a competitive advantage over the often adversarial relations found in the United States. Public relations in business must help corporations and society accept and conform to two "Iron Laws:"

> The Iron Law of Responsibility: In the long run, those who do not use power in a manner which society considers responsible will tend to lose it.[1]

> The Iron Law of Cooperation: Those societies who do not establish cooperative relationships will tend to decline economically.[2]

To compete successfully in the global market, corporations must use and retain their power responsibly in relation to the demands of various domestic publics. Moreover, if our societal institutions cannot develop cooperative relationships, we will face economic decline. The job of public relations in large corporations is ultimately to ensure that corporate power is maintained through responsible use and to help develop cooperative relationships between corporations and other societal institutions. To successfully promote attainment of these goals, public relations practitioners must understand and deal with public opinion concerning business. In this chapter, we will consider what attitudes the public holds toward private enterprise; how corporate management responds to those attitudes; what corporations, trade associations, and others are doing about the situation; and what else might be done. We hope to produce an accurate picture of these problems and to suggest a role public relations can play in their solution. We will also examine several key issues facing public relations practitioners today and in the immediate future.

Attitudes Toward Business

The 1970s marked an era of decline in positive attitudes toward U.S. business; however, evidence of an attitude change came in 1980. The election of Ronald Reagan as president marked an upswing in those attitudes. Indeed, public attitudes—particularly among students—became much more favorable toward private enterprise. Once again, entrepreneurs were American heroes.

By the 1990s, however, the public opinion pendulum seemed to be swinging again. Massive trade deficits pointed to the weakness of American corporate competitiveness. Big business in particular received criticism from all sides. Government officials hurled charges of "corpocracy," while so-called "corporate raiders" vilified entrenched executives for selfishness and mismanagement. Insider trading scandals rocked Wall Street as record numbers of postdepression bank closings rocked Main Street in many U.S. cities and towns. Massive layoffs

Consumer confidence is often related to financial news reports.

due to corporate restructuring suggested that the little guy would be stepped on without feeling when the corporate titans began their dance.

Reasons for Negative Attitudes

Various reasons have been advanced for the unpopularity of American business: the unresponsiveness of business to customers; the mass media's treatment of business; a general distrust of institutions and power; the failure of business to tell its own story; unrealistic expectations of business; crimes, misdemeanors, and corporate misconduct; so-called economic illiteracy (a lack of public understanding of profits, productivity, and the laws of supply and demand); and many others. Most explanations contain some truth, but no single reason is sufficient to explain the phenomenon.

Effects of Negative Attitudes

The potential consequences of adverse public opinion are many and diverse. Business executives recognize that private enterprise enjoys no constitutional guarantee—private and corporate business are carried out at the public's pleasure. The ballot box, the media, and the marketplace are mechanisms through which U.S. citizens express their approval or disapproval of the ways, means, and institutions through which the nation's business is conducted.

Trends such as the environmental and consumer movements, increases in governmental regulations, and calls for social responsibility are direct consequences of negative public attitudes toward private enterprise.

Dealing with Negative Attitudes

The public's attitude toward business is an issue confronting all businesses and the professionals who represent them. Dealing with opinions concerning the whole private enterprise system, however, requires a substantial shift in orientation for the public relations practitioner. Instead of working on behalf of a particular and specific institution, organization, individual, product, or idea, the practitioner is asked to promote what could best be described as a way of life.

It is safe to conclude that public relations efforts designed to improve public attitudes toward *private enterprise* as a whole will not work. The real issue is not private enterprise; rather it is business attitudes and behavior. To be effective, corporate public relations efforts must focus on the following factors:

1. The credibility of corporations and corporate management.

2. Demonstration of corporate concern for individuals on a human scale.

3. A more thorough public understanding of the economic realities of corporate life including profits, productivity, pricing, and the distribution of the sales dollar.

4. A willingness on the part of business to help solve the problems of U.S. society and lead the country toward change.

In the next section of this chapter, we will discuss each of these factors in turn.

If business and private enterprise are to exert positive influence on public attitudes toward business, they must be perceived by the public as trustworthy. In a sense, businesses have and always will have one strike against them in this respect. Research into techniques of persuasion clearly demonstrates that disinterested parties are perceived as more credible than interested ones. As long as the profit motive drives business (that is, as long as business is business), spokespersons will be perceived as self-interested. Today, **caveat venditor** is directed as much toward business's words and deeds as toward its products. Hill & Knowlton executive William A. Durbin says simply, "The single most critical problem facing today is . . . lost credibility."[3]

> **Establishing Corporate Credibility**

Other reasons for the lack of corporate credibility include records of evading issues, disclaiming responsibility, exaggerating facts, or overpromising results. Perhaps the most devastating cause is the systematic violation of expected business behavior that has largely been built on an image projected by business itself. Business, in effect, has not lived up to the standards set for it by the American public (see mini-case 18.1). According to George A. Steiner, "Society expects business to help society improve the quality of life, and expectations are running ahead of reality."[4]

Areas where business has failed to meet public expectations run the gamut from economic performance (as it relates to improving living standards, combating poverty, controlling business cycles, fostering employment, etc.) to social performance (rebuilding cities, eliminating discrimination, promoting world peace, etc.) to scientific and technological performance (finding cures for disease, controlling pollution, reducing accidents, etc.). Richard Darrow explains that the public's inflated expectations are the result of what he calls business's "five big mistakes."

> *Meeting Public Expectations*

Mini-Case 18.1

How to Destroy Corporate Credibility

"Did you ever have one of those days when you felt like you were driving down the highway of life in a Ford Pinto on Firestone 500 radials?" What turns a good company into a bad joke?

In today's world, a corporation's success is a function not only of how it manufactures and markets its products but also of how it is viewed by its publics.

Firestone Tire and Rubber Company, second-largest in the industry, lost its credibility—and damaged the credibility of business as a whole—in what has come to be known as the "500 Fiasco." Shortly after Firestone introduced its "500" line of steel-belted radial tires, questions were raised regarding their safety.

Federal authorities charged that the tires were prone to blowouts, tread separations, and other dangerous deformities. Thousands of customer complaints, hundreds of accidents, and at least 34 deaths formed the basis of their allegations. In the process, profits became losses as customers deserted the company; millions of tires were recalled; stock prices plummeted; takeover attempts, once unthinkable, were sought.

Meanwhile, the company had been hit with over 250 lawsuits. In some cases, settlements exceeded $1 million. Through it all, Firestone steadfastly maintained that the company had been unjustly accused, that nothing was fundamentally wrong with the tire, and that tire failures could be blamed on consumer neglect (overinflating tires) and abuse (hitting curbs).

Firestone made every effort to avoid negative consequences. In fact, the company made too many efforts and became its own worst enemy. Firestone provoked hostility and doubt by failing to cooperate with government agencies, attempting to thwart investigations by regulatory agencies and Congress, trying to publicly impugn investigator motives, and engaging in legalistic maneuvering and hairsplitting. All of these activities were widely reported in the mass media (to which Firestone officials told blatant lies). Despite all the company's efforts, the government eventually forced recall of all "500" radials on the market.

Even before the massive recall, Firestone had lost not only the battle but the war. It now stands as an example of why government regulation is desirable and necessary. It is also an example of how not to deal with government and the public.

He argues that business formerly took credit—or permitted the American public to give it credit—for material prosperity

1. Furnished by mass production and mass marketing of products, some of which had defects that were only gradually detected;

2. Energized by a speculative stock market;

3. Based on underpriced fuel and raw materials from less developed countries, many of which have ceased to cooperate;

4. Provided at the cost of mismanaged solid, liquid, and gaseous wastes; and

5. Measured largely against the illusory statistics of spiraling wage and price inflation.[5]

In short, American business made promises it could not keep, accepted credit for accomplishments that were not really its own, pushed costs and problems into a future that has now arrived, oversold and underdelivered, and kept score with a crooked measuring stick. Whether such mistakes and misdemeanors are intentional or not, and whether business is the perpetrator or the victim of these circumstances, is not the point. What matters is that public and consumer expectations have been pumped up in thousands of small ways—through corporate statements, advertising, marketing techniques, and public relations—and that those expectations have not been fulfilled.

In the early 1930s, President Hoover and American business promised that "prosperity is right around the corner." When the promises proved false, the American public invited Franklin Roosevelt and the New Deal to change the face of American business, government, and society. Such is the power of promises perceived to be broken.

Credibility once lost is difficult to regain. Nevertheless, a number of policies, if implemented and practiced by businesses individually and collectively, can contribute substantially to the reestablishment of public trust.

Restoring Credibility

Openness and Honesty   As a first step, business must tear down the walls. The notion that public relations can be used as a shield is passé. The idea that the corporate domain is impervious to the prying eyes and ears of consumers, competitors, the media, and the regulators is an illusion. Honesty is no longer just the best policy, it is the only policy when even painful truths cannot be securely and permanently hidden. Procter & Gamble's handling of Rely tampons, Johnson & Johnson's Tylenol response, and the Pepsi-Cola hoax all show how businesses have become more open and forthcoming.

Complete candor and forthrightness is the only way to achieve credibility. This candor, though, must be active rather than passive. It is not enough to say, "I will answer any question," when you know that your audience does not necessarily know what questions to ask. Instead, businesses must listen to their constituents (including employees, customers, regulators, and other stakeholders) and respond to their incompletely articulated questions and concerns.

U.S. corporations, represented by their upper-level executives, must reach out to their communities directly and through the media on a regular and continuing basis, responding to public concerns and explaining the impacts of and rationales for corporate actions and decisions. Chief executive officers recognize in most cases that they should play the leading roles in public outreach. It is no longer uncommon for top executives to spend one-fourth to more than one-half of their time on externalities.

In responding to the public's desire and need to know, businesses must go further than ever before in releasing what was previously considered confidential information. Marshall C. Lewis, former head of Union Carbide's communication department, states: "I think we have no choice but to accept less confidentiality as the quid pro quo for greater credibility. Openness has become the name of the credibility game."[6]

Openness, in this case, refers again to many publics. Employees need more information on the finances, economics, and policies of their employers. Members of communities in which businesses operate should be informed in advance of decisions and actions that may affect them. Corporations have already learned painfully that voluntary disclosure of corporate problems, mistakes, or wrongdoing hurts far less than the later discovery of coverups by regulators or the media.

Consistent Actions   The second step in restoring the credibility of business is to resolve the glaring contradictions of business behavior. Too often, what business says and what it does fail to correspond. There are gaps between mouth and movement, code and conduct, espoused theory and actual practice. These inconsistencies undermine business credibility. For example, the promise is that private enterprise rewards individuals on the basis of ability rather than birth. Yet, being born on the wrong side of the tracks; belonging to a poor family rather than a rich one; being black or white, male or female, or having an accent still affects individual opportunities. In many cases, what you get—good or bad—does not correspond with what you do.

Some business people preach free and open markets while they seek to restrict freedom and act in secrecy. Even those who claim to fear for the future of private enterprise may only fear the loss of privileges they currently enjoy through abuse of that system.

Some business people who crusade publicly against government intervention and regulation are also quick to rush off to Washington or to the state capital to seek favorable legislation, treaties, tariffs, regulations, and policies. A steel company that resists the Environmental Protection Agency on ideological grounds one day but insists on protective tariffs on pragmatic grounds the next appears self-serving at best and hypocritical at worst.

Social Responsibility   Third, if business is to be treated and trusted as a central force in American society, it must address issues perceived as crucial to society. Although we will discuss this matter at greater length later in the chapter, we should note here that for the sake of credibility, businesses must be visibly involved in the public realm, making substantial commitments in time, energy, resources, and discipline toward solving problems of public importance.

In a sense, the focus of corporate concerns needs to be refined. As one former major corporate CEO put it:

> Companies like ours are public institutions with several publics to account to—not just shareholders. This requires a different type of informational approach. Part of my job is to be a public figure and to take positions on public issues, not just company activities.[7]

Mini-case 18.2 demonstrates how a relatively small action aimed at providing sound incentives to employees can build credibility, employee morale, and sales.

Public Education   Finally, business must strive to offer the public a better understanding of what it can do, what it cannot do, how it operates, and what are the constraints on its operations. Public expectations must be brought into line with reality.

Mini-Case 18.2

Chick-fil-A: Employee Scholarships Demonstrate Good Corporate Citizenship

Fast-food chains sometimes suffer from the public perception that they take advantage of undereducated, often underprivileged teenagers, working teens long hours for low wages. Chick-fil-A, Inc., the nation's third-largest quick-service chicken company operating 650 restaurants in 34 states and Canada, and with plans to open in 10 South African nations, counters the image by offering very attractive scholarship opportunities to its employees.

Since the program was initiated in 1973, the Atlanta-based Chick-fil-A has given $1,000 "Team Member" scholarships exceeding a total of $10 million to more than 10,000 outstanding restaurant employees who "have demonstrated a strong work ethic, determination, and commitment to the chain," according to S. Truett Cathy, founder and CEO. Cathy believes business is more than a matter of profits; it is a matter of social responsibility. "We're also in the people business. Young people are investments in the future. I consider each scholarship seeds well planted," he says. A 23-foot sculpture along Peachtree Street near the Georgia State University campus in downtown Atlanta commemorates the scholarships with the inscription, "No goal is too high if we climb with care and confidence."

To qualify for a scholarship, a restaurant employee must have completed high school, must have worked for Chick-fil-A for two consecutive years and 2,000 working hours, and must use the scholarship to attend any accredited school. To date, employees have received scholarships to more than 1,200 institutions, and they represent almost every profession—from engineers to veterinarians attending schools from Abilene Christian University to Yale. In 1984, Truett Cathy also founded the Win-Shape Centre Foundation, which annually awards 20 to 30 $16,000 joint scholarships, funded equally by Berry College, to students wishing to attend that institution in Rome, Georgia.

According to the Council for Aid to Education, no other company "does as much in the scholarship area in terms of the company's size; it's remarkable." And the "Team Member" scholarship program is growing. Chick-fil-A is on track to award $20 million in scholarships by the year 2000.

Source: Lynne M. Sallot, Ph.D., APR, Assistant Professor of Public Relations, University of Georgia, Athens, Georgia

Renewed credibility must be built on a firm foundation of honest performance, open communication, and resolution of inconsistencies between performance and communication. Business should reemphasize its commitments to problem solving in areas usually considered beyond its purview, and business should avoid raising or encouraging expectations that cannot be met. Restoring business credibility is, however, only a first step in the overall rehabilitation of public attitudes toward business.

Frequently, the public develops attitudes toward business neither by reading stories about business in the newspaper nor by listening to the pronouncements of executives in public forums. Most people develop their opinions as a result of their experiences as consumers, employees, or investors. Every interaction between buyer and seller or employee and employer has not only economic but educational and political implications.

Considering the Human Factor

Polls have revealed the widespread belief that business lacks concern for the consumer. Harris found that 71 percent of the population feels business will do nothing to help the consumer that might reduce its own profits—unless forced to do so. It is really not necessary, though, to go to the pollsters to discover consumer dissatisfaction. Everyone has not one but several horror stories about experiences as a customer, including battles with computers, insensitive salespeople, false and misleading advertising, abusive repair services, warranty problems, and so on. At the heart of all such difficulties is the consumer's perception that business is unconcerned and unresponsive. Business on too many occasions reinforces feelings of depersonalization and alienation—of being just a number. It is in this fertile ground of hostility and alienation that the roots of the consumer movement have grown.

At some point, the people say (as they did in the popular film *Network*), "I'm mad as hell and I'm not going to take it any more!" Consumer relations was discussed at length in chapter 13, but we will touch here on ways it can improve public attitudes toward private enterprise.

Consumer Relations

Researchers Z. V. Lambert and F. W. Kniffin analyzed the concept of alienation and concluded that it "provides important insights into the propelling forces behind consumerism." When looking at the feeling of powerlessness that is an important component of alienation, they found that:

> From a consumer standpoint, powerlessness is a feeling or belief held by a person that as an individual he cannot influence business behavior to be more in accord with his needs and interests.[8]

Since many dissatisfied consumers feel they cannot obtain redress through the offending companies, they either live with their anger or make their complaints and seek resolution at the institutional level. They turn to the courts, the regulatory agencies, or the mass media for action. Consequently, when businesses are continually unresponsive and insensitive to the problems of individual consumers, they invite public attitudes and actions that will eventually restrict the freedom of private enterprise.

Standard public relations techniques cannot address these problems. Educational efforts designed to inform consumers about their real clout in the marketplace cannot address these problems either. Lambert and Kniffin offer a five-point program that could be called "point-of-sale public relations." It addresses problems of consumer alienation by enabling even very large corporations to respond to individuals as individuals. Following are elements of the program:

1. A corporate mechanism and a willingness to implement consumer proposals;

2. An information system that monitors consumer concerns and irritants;

3. Corporate conditioning and mechanisms for rapidly alleviating consumer dissatisfactions;

4. A control system to prevent practices that inadvertently produce consumer dissatisfaction; and

5. Employee training, evaluation, and compensation methods that provide incentives for satisfying consumers.[9]

If attitudes toward business are to become more positive, the quality of the average individual's daily experiences with it must be improved. The role of public relations in this effort is to advise top management of appropriate responses to alienated consumers and to assist in implementing point-of-sale public relations.

Promoting Public Understanding

Many polls have shown that Americans severely overestimate average business profits on sales. In one survey, 10 percent was considered a just and reasonable profit on sales, although in reality, average profit is less than 5 percent.

When a poll stated, "Excessive profits are one of the most important causes of inflation today," 74 percent of the respondents agreed. Opinion was split equally regarding the statement, "The country would be a lot better off if the government put a tight lid on the percentage of profit any business can make." As many as 45 percent agreed that "most companies could afford to raise wages 10 percent without raising prices," while 29 percent disagreed.

When these opinions are analyzed, it is obvious that they are based on erroneous information about the magnitude of profits. Widespread misinformation, together with Americans' inflated expectations, suggests that mass **economic education** might remedy negative public attitudes toward private enterprise (see figure 18.1).

Economic Education Efforts

Several surveys have shown that many people lack the knowledge and skills to make intelligent individual decisions in the marketplace, let alone to comprehend or appreciate the private enterprise system as a whole. The term **economic illiteracy** is now widely used to describe this condition. Sylvia Porter has labeled this illiteracy "a fundamental threat to the survival of our capitalistic systems."[10] Still other studies underscore the need for economic education by showing a strong correlation between people's attitudes toward private enterprise and the amount of economic information they have (see figure 18.2).[11]

The battle against economic illiteracy is being waged on several fronts. With the support of thousands of businesses, centers for economic education and chairs of private enterprise have been established at colleges and universities throughout the United States and abroad to develop objective economic understanding among teachers, students, and others. Many states have mandated economics for high school curricula. The Advertising Council, the Chamber of Commerce of the United States, and the National Association of Manufacturers have developed programs that respond to this need, as have hundreds of major corporations, using their advertising and employee communication systems. In effect, economic education itself has become a minor industry.

Although it is difficult to assess the effect of all the activity aimed at reducing economic illiteracy, two conclusions can be drawn:

1. Those who claim that economic education is sufficient to correct the problem of negative public attitudes are mistaken. Economic education

Figure 18.1 Public interest report from GM tells how it addresses public concerns.

GENERAL MOTORS

PUBLIC INTEREST REPORT

NINETEEN NINETY-FOUR

as a remedy can be effective only in the context of the people's overall economic experience. Business credibility and individual responsiveness must be restored if economic education is to achieve its desired ends.

2. Those who claim that economic education is inherently inappropriate for achieving the goal of improved public opinion toward business are also mistaken. Real gaps of knowledge and understanding do exist and have helped created public attitudes. Thus, depending on the means and methods by which it is pursued, economic education can be an effective antidote to negative public opinion.

Public relations, always charged with providing information and building public sympathy for organizations and their activities, is in the thick of corporate efforts to improve public understanding of private enterprise. Its functions include

ABOUT GM

General Motors has operations in 53 countries and worldwide employment averaging 711,000 people. Best known as a full-line vehicle manufacturer, GM had worldwide factory sales in 1993 of more than 7.8 million motor vehicles, of which approximately 4.7 million were sold in the U.S. GM manufactures and sells cars and trucks worldwide through a variety of nameplates, including Chevrolet, Pontiac, Oldsmobile, Buick, Cadillac, GMC Truck, Saturn, Opel, Vauxhall, Holden, Isuzu and Saab. In 1993, GM's market share was 33.2% of the total U.S. vehicle market and 18.2% of the worldwide vehicle market. As of December 31, 1993, there were approximately 8,665 GM motor vehicle dealers in North America and approximately 9,200 dealers overseas.

GM also has other substantial business interests. GM's Automotive Components Group Worldwide (ACG-W) supplies components and systems to every major automotive manufacturer. General Motors Acceptance Corporation (GMAC) and its subsidiaries provide financing and insurance products to GM customers and dealers. GM Hughes Electronics Corporation (GMHE) is a specialist in automotive electronics, commercial technologies, telecommunications and space and defense electronics. Electronic Data Systems (EDS) is a world leader in applying information technologies around the globe. Electro-Motive Division is the second largest producer in the world of diesel-electric locomotives, and Allison Transmission is the largest U.S. producer of heavy duty vehicle transmissions. In total, GM's 1993 worldwide sales and revenues were $138.2 billion.

Although GM is an international corporation, this report focuses on the performance of GM's North American vehicle, parts and related financing operations, including North American Operations (NAO), ACG-W, Saturn and GMAC.

Figure 18.2 GM addresses economic contributions in its annual public issues report.

BACKGROUND ON THE U.S. AUTO INDUSTRY

ECONOMIC CONTRIBUTIONS

The domestic motor vehicle industry is a major factor in the U.S. economy, in terms of the value of its output, the jobs it creates, the income it generates and the taxes it pays:

Material Consumption by the Automotive Industry
(Percent of U.S. Total)

74%	Natural Rubber
23%	Zinc
49%	Synthetic Rubber
20%	Semiconductors
41%	Platinum
18%	Aluminum
40%	Machine Tools
11%	Steel
34%	Iron
10%	Copper
25%	Glass
3%	Plastic

SOURCE: American Automobile Manufacturers Association (AAMA)

franchises employing 650,000 people that sell and service the products of the domestic automobile industry and the more than 300,000 repair and service facilities that help to maintain the U.S. vehicle fleet.

❏ Among the three domestic automakers, GM's vehicles have the highest average U.S. and Canadian domestic content at 97%, and over 96% of the GM light vehicles sold in the U.S. are assembled in the U.S. and Canada.

❏ Over the last three decades, spending on new vehicles has averaged 4.4% of the U.S. Gross Domestic Product (GDP).

❏ Collectively, the members of the American Automobile Manufacturers Association (AAMA) — GM, Ford and Chrysler — employ over 600,000 U.S. workers in auto-related jobs, making the motor vehicle industry the largest employer among U.S. manufacturing industries. In addition, AAMA members support 900,000 jobs in the supplier industry, so that, in total, AAMA members support 19 out of every 20 jobs related to the production of cars and trucks in the U.S.

❏ The sale and service of completed vehicles generates further economic activity. This includes the 18,000 dealer

Taxes Generated by GM Activities -1993
(Dollars in Millions)

TAXES PAYABLE BY GM TO U.S. AND FOREIGN TAX AUTHORITIES	
Income Taxes	$ 109.5
Payroll Taxes	3,102.9
Property Taxes	603.7
Federal Excise Taxes & Import Duties/Taxes	271.6
Miscellaneous Taxes	129.4
Franchise, Sales and Use Taxes	65.4
TOTAL	**$4,282.5**
U.S. AND FOREIGN TAXES PAID BY CUSTOMERS PURCHASING GM PRODUCTS*	
Franchise, Sales, Use and Other Local Taxes	$1,203.6
Federal Excise Taxes & Import Duties/Taxes	3,529.4
TOTAL	**$4,733.0**
EMPLOYEE U.S. FEDERAL INCOME AND SOCIAL SECURITY TAXES WITHHELD BY GM	
Federal Income Tax	$2,899.3
F.I.C.A. Tax	1,289.7
TOTAL	**$4,189.0**

* These taxes represent only those taxes paid by customers that are collected by GM and remitted to the appropriate tax authorities.

advising corporate management, developing programs, and disseminating information. Unfortunately, many economic education efforts to date have been ineffective.

Preaching to the Choir   Economic education efforts have too often been directed toward audiences that already understand and agree with the points being made. Although such activities reinforce communicators, making them feel good, they serve little useful purpose in improving public understanding. "A lot of business people want to preach to the choir," says TRW, Inc.'s Richard A. Condon. "That does no good whatsoever."[12]

Perhaps even worse is the tendency to communicate as though you were preaching to the choir when in fact you are not. Critics of economic education have labeled such efforts propagandistic indoctrination. Preaching "the gospel of private enterprise" to nonbelievers will result in rejection of messages at best and in reinforcement of negative attitudes at worst.

Who are the nonbelievers? Many business people think that students constitute the major market for economic education; thus, they are content to support academics and teachers in traditional roles. The far bigger market, however, consists of people who have already left school. In fact, the primary audience for economic education may be business and its employees.

Economic understanding programs for employees should be built on the specifics of corporate finances, activities, and economics as they affect the individual. Bethlehem Steel, Dow Chemical, Firestone, GTE, Kemper, Owens Corning Fiberglass, Pitney-Bowes, TRW, and other companies have used that approach.

To be effective for any audience, economic education must be communicated objectively and the facts allowed to speak for themselves. Moreover, information should be presented in ways that are meaningful to the audience and related to their needs and values. Finally, while facts are important, they are insufficient. Most attitudes are at least in part emotionally derived. Consequently, affective as well as cognitive dimensions of learning must be addressed. In a strike situation, for instance, all the facts a company can muster will pale before the sight of one striker's suffering family. Economic education must be exciting and alive, appealing to the emotions and the intellect while walking the thin line between propagandistic manipulation and objective presentation of reality.

Cowboys and Indians   Often, economic education efforts are scare tactics in which the so-called enemies of private enterprise are reviled while its heroes are stridently defended. The "enemies" may be socialistic conspiracies, creeping socialism, consumer activists, government regulators, or simply critics of business behavior. It is important to remember, however, that little sentiment exists in the United States in favor of socialism, that consumer activism and government regulation are arguably necessary checks on business behavior, and that critics sometimes express legitimate grievances on behalf of the public. In any case, defensive postures lack both credibility and persuasiveness.

Moreover, if economic education is to be believable, it must resist the temptation to equate private enterprise with big business as it is practiced in the United States. As we noted earlier, opinion polls indicate that private enterprise has broad support. But private enterprise is in danger at least in part because it is too often identified with huge corporations—that is, collective organizations that are not private, involve little entrepreneurship, promote dependence and conformity, and have on many occasions sought to avoid risk and responsibility. If economic education is to present private enterprise in ideal terms, it must also point out areas where the ideal is not being achieved.

It is not the function of economic education to paint business as the good guy in the white hat. In fact, effective economic education can actually reveal to the public abuses of the private enterprise system by government, business, or other institutions. Individuals educated in economics and business will be able to recognize monopolistic and other unfair business practices. They will demand information and openness from business, not only about products but also about the ways business is conducted.

In short, when undertaking the economic education of the American public, business risks increasing scrutiny, demands to honor its promises, and most of all, change.

First Do No Harm   We have repeatedly mentioned polls showing that the public has an exaggerated notion of business profits. Where do people get their ideas about sales profits? Some have suggested that survey respondents have not understood the distinction between profit and markup. A more obvious reason, however, is a recent trend in business reporting. In the rush to impress investors with reports of quarterly earnings, public relations staffs can undo years of carefully nurtured economic understanding.

One example was a newspaper headline which reported a major company's "Profits Up 273 Percent." During the next few days, other corporations' second-quarter earnings were reported in similar terms: An auto maker's profits were up 313 percent; three chemical companies' profits were up 109 percent, 430 percent, and 947 percent, respectively. Various sources reported that all industries enjoyed average profit increases ranging from 31 to 36 percent. People who have business experience understand these figures and can immediately put them in perspective. Indeed, such statistics are designed to impress knowledgeable stockholders and investors. But these astronomically high figures also reach the general public, who interpret them as big, even "obscene" profits.

Admittedly, those who know what they are looking for and are willing to search for information or apply a calculator to a newspaper article can dig out the real story. One can learn, for instance, that one company's return on sales rose from 3.6 to 7.3 percent, figures that are impressive to the trained eye but not inflammatory to the untrained one. Of course, even these numbers can be manipulated. A company can still express the increase by claiming a 103-percent increase in profit as a percent of sales or simply stating it as an increase of 3.7 percent in profits as a percent of revenues. As Disraeli said, there are lies, damn lies, and statistics.

An insurance company offered another example of inflammatory rhetoric, reporting "operating earnings . . . almost four times greater than . . . a year earlier." Consumers who do not understand the statistics that follow this claim consider their higher insurance premiums and conclude that they are being ripped off. With the help of a calculator, however, one can see that the company's margins rose from .92 percent to 2.57 percent. An informed emotional response changes from hostility to sympathy. But the company cannot assume that the ordinary consumer will understand such figures.

If we want the public to understand profits or private enterprise, we must see to it that communicators present information in terms the public can understand. Statistics must illuminate, not exaggerate. Here again, public relations practitioners should heed the basic tenets of their creed: Consider the audience, word the communication carefully, and be consistent. We cannot achieve public economic understanding by blocking it with statistics, generalities, technical language, or the like. Frequently, such communication does more harm than good.

Helping Solve Societal Problems

As we mentioned in our discussion of credibility, the public expects business to play a leading role in pursuing solutions to societal problems and has been disappointed when business has not lived up to expectations.

At one time in the United States, business was broadly perceived as benevolent. From 1850 to 1887, there was probably less government regulation of business in this country than at any other time in any other nation. Business will never again be viewed in that way—as a means of solving society's ills while also pursuing profit. Society now expects business to improve the quality of life in ways that go beyond serving narrowly defined, if enlightened, self-interest. The popularity of business or government in the public mind is ultimately less important than society's choice of institutions to solve its problems. Since the New Deal, the United States has chosen government. The long-term efficacy of business and the well-being of private enterprise depend on society's view of business not as a problem but as a problem solver.

Business must adjust to a changing world, realizing that capitalism can no longer be based on an economy of unpaid costs. Profit must be measured by more than a bottom line; human and environmental costs must also be accounted for. Business has to find profitable solutions to such social problems as pollution, health care, housing, illiteracy, and urban decay. This will call for unparalleled creativity on the part of business and the private enterprise system.

If business begins to solve such problems, the old relationship of government aiding business rather than business serving government may be reestablished. The trend toward increasing government encroachment in the marketplace will be reversed if business demonstrates that it can fulfill the goals and aspirations of the American public.

The last decade has revealed a much-expanded social role for business. In particular, firms have assumed broader responsibility. They are more interested in ethical conduct and more involved with public policy and government. Moreover, large businesses are more sophisticated in planning, implementing, and controlling their social performance.

Ultimately, the case for private enterprise must be made in the marketplace. The present and the future of private enterprise depend on its ability to meet societal

An environmentally
responsible business
approach creates good
business for many companies.

demands, which in turn rests on the receptiveness, responsiveness, flexibility, and skill of business people. If business as a whole fails to meet market demands, it will go the way of any single business that fails. It will go bankrupt.

In the effort to restore public confidence in American business, the public relations practitioner must reestablish business credibility, reintroduce the human dimension to business corporations, and facilitate public understanding of business and economics. Most important, public relations must be business's eyes and ears—the receiver of society's subtle signals and the prod that moves management toward effective response.

Public Relations for Small Businesses

Small business owners and managers lack the luxury of in-house public relations staffs, and they rarely employ public relations agencies. Nonetheless, public relations efforts can make tremendous contributions to a small business's bottom line. As is typical in a small business, if you want something done, you do it yourself. Thus, small business owners or managers usually serve as their own public relations practitioners.

The potential value of public relations for a small business is substantial. Leone Ackerly started a business called Mini-Maid—at the time a unique service where a crew cleaned a house in a few hours. With women working outside the home in greater numbers and fewer people able to afford full-time domestic help, it was an idea whose time had come. Local publicity helped build sales by generating customer inquiries and receptivity. Tying the business to the "working woman" theme and persistently telling her story, Ackerly received national coverage on the *Today* show, in *Newsweek,* and in other publications. People throughout the country wanted to know how she handled her enterprise. Soon her main business changed from cleaning to franchising her successful formula. Ackerly became wealthy and received national recognition for her hard work, vision, and tenacity and (implicitly) for her skill at public relations.

Public relations in small businesses covers as broad a range as it does in large businesses. It is less systematic, however, because no one in a small business can concentrate solely on public relations. In effect, public relations becomes a way of life for many small business owners, who are concerned not only with media relations but also with community, customer, employee, financial, supplier, and political relations.

Although the subject is not treated elsewhere in this book, supplier relations is particularly important to small businesses. Smaller businesses may be highly dependent on their suppliers for materials or goods. Moreover, they often depend on suppliers' credit terms to finance their inventories, and it is not unusual for a small business to fall behind on its bills. Following are some ideas for maintaining good relations with suppliers:

Get to know your suppliers—not only salespeople but decision makers in the supplier organization.

Communicate with your suppliers, letting them know the advantages of doing business with you.

Give honest feedback to your suppliers on their products and services. If you can see ways suppliers can improve, let them know.

If you are having problems paying bills, tell your suppliers. It is often advisable to explain what the problem is, what you are doing about it, and when it will be straightened out.

By attending to relationships with media, community, employees, customers, sources of financing, politicians, and suppliers, a small business can be promoted and protected. New business opportunities may be identified and brought to fruition while risks and liabilities may be reduced—and that translates into profits.

Major Issues Facing Corporate Public Relations Professionals	Other major issues with special implications for corporate public relations in the latter half of the 1990s and into the early 21st century include (1) globalization of business operations with resulting globalization of public relations, (2) unprecedented technological change, (3) increased emphasis on diversity issues, and (4) intensified crises and disasters.
Global Public Relations	American business has expanded rapidly into global markets in the last decade and especially in the 1990s. The passage of the NAFTA and GATT treaties with the resulting lowering of trade barriers; the development of worldwide, almost instantaneous financial markets; and the acquisition of many U.S. businesses by foreign companies have led to the globalization of American business and the consequent globalization of public relations. Speeding the process have been major technological changes including the advent of the Internet, fax machines,

Global public relations requires careful attention to cultural communications.

and microwave telephone relays. The innovations have linked even remote parts of the world with businesses everywhere.

Much of the business expansion followed the fall of the communistic regimes in Eastern Europe and the creation in 1992 of the European Community of Western Europe, which seeks a single European business community.

Historically, American business has been disinterested in international trade. However, out of economic necessity in the last decade, U.S. companies have expanded rapidly into global markets. International trade is much more complicated than trade within the United States because differences in laws and cultural norms often cause considerable confusion. Conditions of competition are often quite different as well. Many barriers not found in American markets are present in international business.

The challenge of global public relations is to eliminate as many as possible of the barriers to effective communication. That communication must be able to transcend cultural as well as geographic barriers. Three major barriers that often confront business and public relations are differences in language, law, and culture. Other barriers in many countries include extremely bureaucratic governments, multiplicity of languages, and underdeveloped mass media.

Public relations for multinational corporations is a complex area of practice requiring all the skills discussed elsewhere in this book plus extraordinary cross-cultural sensitivity (see public relations spotlight 18.1).

Cultural adjustment is a key aspect of preparing employees to work in a foreign environment. Controlling the integration process eases new employees' adjustment to the environment while encouraging them to make unique contributions to the enrichment of the organization. In the cross-cultural adjustment process, the employee in a new culture is confronted with three situations (see table 18.1): the employee's culture of origin; the culture he or she must adjust to; and the third culture, which results from the integration of the two.

Cultural Adaptations:
Avoiding Cultural
Shock

Public Relations Spotlight 18.1

Culture is complex. There are so many things we take for granted that we tend to be unaware of the tremendous differences that exist across the world.

We're familiar with our own surroundings—buildings, streets, people, clothing, food, and everything around and part of us. The way we do things or put things together makes up our culture. Why do we eat with knives and forks? What's okay to eat with the fingers? Why? Who should you sit with? Who not? When do you smile? When do you remain silent?

What does it mean when someone belches? When someone laughs at you? When someone doesn't ask you to sit down? When someone shakes a stick at you? When the agreed-upon meeting time arrives and there's no one there but you? These questions have cultural meaning and, when you don't know the "code," you feel left out. Likely after a while it will get to you, and you will withdraw into a stupor. That's **cultural shock!**

Cultural shock is real. It may be one of several things, or a combination:

- Emotional anxiety from being in strange surroundings;
- Disorientation from not being able to predict what other people are going to do;
- Discomfort from not knowing what one should do to handle the situation;
- An overwhelming feeling of incompetence that comes from experiencing so many sensory stimuli that don't have clear meanings.

Reducing Cultural Shock

To reduce cultural shock or to make it more unlikely, there are three principal things that you may do:

1. **Empathy**—How you relate to others is the basic foundation for cross-cultural effectiveness. Can you trust others? Do you accept help from others? Americans often pride themselves on being independent. There are few places outside the United States and Europe where that will work very well. In most of the world, people are expected to need one another, especially within the extended family. This mutually dependent relationship is built on sensitivity to the needs and feelings of others. *You must be prepared to depend on other people.*

2. **Observation Skills**—You need to be more alert to what is going on around you. Practice in observing even the small things around you will help you see things and become more aware of your environment. *You must observe your environment.*

3. **Transactional Exploration**—You can relate to the unknown by experiencing it. As a child, this is the way you learn. You try something and see if it works. This is called discovery learning or inquiry learning. It is building inductively toward the generalized principles of the culture. It is better to act than to freeze up and do nothing. When you freeze up, you stop learning. *You must experience the unknown.*

Source: Information from United States Agency for International Development training seminar at the East-West Center, Honolulu, Hawaii.

TABLE 18.1 Cross-Cultural Adjustment

Culture I Come from	Culture I Have to Adjust To	Third Culture
1. What I shall keep 2. What I shall modify 3. What I shall give up	1. What I shall adopt as is 2. What I shall accept by adjusting 3. What I will reject	New Products of the interactions between members (all) of the culture (Innovation)

Source: Pierre Casse, *Organization Development and Cross-Cultural Training,* World Bank.

Cultural understanding is essential for effective global public relations.

The public relations function in multinational corporations has three distinct aspects. In one role, public relations practitioners represent multinational corporations at home, dealing with public opinion and governmental activities that relate both to specific corporations and to multinational enterprise as a whole. The second role of multinational public relations is to help bridge the communication gap that inevitably exists between foreign operations and top management in the world headquarters. Finally, public relations must be conducted in the corporation's various host countries. (Another aspect of global public relations is the propaganda efforts by various countries, which were examined in chapter 17.)

John M. Reed concluded that public relations in the host country "has to have three legs upon which it is built: cultural savvy; language savvy; a savvy use of the tools of the craft. Forget one leg and the edifice topples. Use them in balance and success is assured."[13]

Corporations often engage public relations agencies to handle their international interests. The increased demand for experts in international public relations accounts for a major portion of agency public relations income. "The 15 largest public relations organizations now generate more than 40 percent of their fees outside the United States."[14]

Agencies have found they need global presence to compete for U.S. clients. On the other hand, U.S. public relations firms are competing well for clients outside the United States. American-style public relations is highly regarded. One French practitioner is quoted as saying, "U.S. public relations is 10 years ahead of the brand practiced in this country."[15]

To increase effectiveness in dealing with host country public relations, the practitioner can do the following:

1. Be flexible. What works in Memphis, Tennessee, won't necessarily work in Columbo, Sri Lanka.

2. Use local public relations practitioners as an interface with the local culture. This can help avoid the kinds of major public relations catastrophes that have occurred much too frequently in recent years.

3. Work through local public relations agencies in dealing with local media to maximize your media relations efforts.

4. Develop community relations programs in the host country (including corporate contributions when appropriate).

5. Develop good relationships with government, business, and financial leaders in the host country.

6. Interface with U.S. trade, embassy, and other officials in the host country.

7. Work with higher education in the country to assist in research and evaluation.

Technological Change

Advancing technology is already revolutionizing the way public relations people do business. Don Tapscott and Art Caston in their best seller, *Paradigm Shift,* suggest that we all must be transformed or be left out. They claim:

> We are entering a second era of information technology in which . . . the applications of computers, the nature of technology itself, and the leadership for the use of technology are all going through profound change.[16]

Public relations practitioners must understand this new era to succeed in the years ahead. See public relations spotlight 18.2 for a discussion of ways the new technology can help public relations practitioners do their jobs more effectively.

While a variety of new technologies affect the public relations practitioner, those related to the computer are the most revolutionary. We are in the fourth decade of computers, and perhaps the fourth era. The 1960s saw the development

Public Relations Spotlight 18.2

New technologies are having profound impact on public relations, but in ways that relatively few in the discipline or in the business community recognize. The political community was first to perceive and act on the practical implications of facsimile systems, computer bulletin boards, information utilities, and the Internet. Would-be officeholders exploited them with singular success during the presidential campaign of 1992 and beyond. Before the end of 1995, every announced 1996 candidate had opened a home page on the World Wide Web and was deluging media with automated facsimile transmissions.

The rest of the world lags behind, in part because of the volume of "techno-hype" dispensed by hardware and software vendors and trade magazines. In pursuit of sales, they entice both "techies" and managers to "stay on the cutting edge" or, at minimum, to avoid being left behind. The resulting avalanche of messages obscures the fundamental change that new technologies are creating in public communication.

The postindustrial nations of the world have or soon will have moved beyond the age of one-way mass communication. Print and broadcast audiences continue to fragment, while new technologies feed explosive growth in one-to-one communication.

What are the new technologies? All are creatures of the microprocessor—the computer on a chip. It gave birth to the facsimile or fax machine and to the microcomputer. With the advent of the fax modem, the two merged, spawning **broadcast fax** and **fax-on-demand** systems. Sophisticated software enables computer owners to maintain fax telephone lists and distribute news releases, newsletters, and other information at will and in personalized form. The electronic "documents" involved, together with any other information an organization wants to make available to any group, then can be stored on the computer's hard drive and can be made accessible to prospective users via fax machine and modem.

The boom in desktop computers and high-speed modems produced a corresponding growth in consumer use of information utilities and the **Internet.** The utilities—CompuServe, America Online, Prodigy, and the Microsoft Network— serve as information sources and communication channels. All provide **electronic mail services.** Their forums, essentially electronically joined special interest groups, offer real-time conferencing as well as bulletin boards and data libraries.

The Internet is similarly but less formally organized. The Net, as it's called, links the computers of governmental agencies, educational institutions, and businesses. Most businesses are concentrated on the World Wide Web, essentially a group of electronic "store fronts" through which merchandise one day will be sold in volume. For the moment, security problems discourage credit transactions, but this obstacle soon will be overcome.

Colleges, universities, and others also may be on the Web, but their greatest value to "net surfers," as users are called, is in their links to **gopher** and **ftp** (file transfer protocol) sites, from which information of all kinds can be retrieved. The Internet also affords access to **newsgroups** and **listservs.** The former are akin to the information utilities forums. The latter are electronic information transmitters that Internet users can join and leave at will.

Collectively, these and other technology-based information exchange systems threaten the very existence of traditional mass media. They have broken the monopoly the media once held in mass communication. They enable individuals to transmit messages directly to large audiences across the nation and around the globe. Media have been responding to this challenge by adopting the technologies to their own use. Many newspapers sell the information they have gathered through computer data bases such as Lexis/Nexis. Some, such as *The*

Businesses find home pages are a good informational tool.

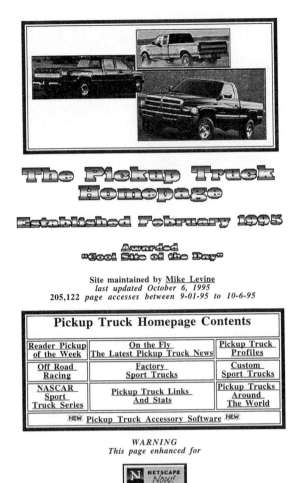

The Pickup Truck Homepage

Established February 1995

Awarded
"Cool Site of the Day"

Site maintained by **Mike Levine**
last updated October 6, 1995
205,122 page accesses between 9-01-95 to 10-6-95

Pickup Truck Homepage Contents		
Reader Pickup of the Week	On the Fly The Latest Pickup Truck News	Pickup Truck Profiles
Off Road Racing	Factory Sport Trucks	Custom Sport Trucks
NASCAR Sport Truck Series	Pickup Truck Links And Stats	Pickup Trucks Around The World
NEW Pickup Truck Accessory Software NEW		

WARNING
This page enhanced for

NETSCAPE *Now!*

Wall Street Journal, have developed and are offering subscriptions to electronic newspapers.

The public relations community, unfortunately, has been slow to react to these changes. Most practitioners continue to focus the bulk of their efforts on mass media publicity. They package the product electronically and deliver it through facsimile systems or Video News Releases, but the substance and underlying one-to-many communication principles remain the same. The practitioner needs to be skilled enough to:

- Design a World Wide Web home page in a way that will encourage "visits" by members of specific audiences.
- Create a library of documents that will encourage use of a fax-on-demand system.
- Publish a newsletter electronically, avoiding the expenses associated with printing and postage as well as the untender mercies of the postal service.
- Function in behalf of the clients or the employers in the new electronic environment popularly known as "cyberspace."

Operating in cyberspace arguably will be the most challenging of these functions. The Internet, privately operated bulletin boards, and computer utilities have been markedly inhospitable to commercial interests. Internet users are quick to condemn use of the net for commercial purposes. Computer utilities and many bulletin boards bar commercial messages of all kinds.

Public relations practitioners who would overcome these barriers must establish individual credibility with their electronic peers. On the western frontier of the United States, the gun was commonly known as an "equalizer." The computer fulfills that role in cyberspace. It is a world of equals in which social, political, and economic standing are valueless. Knowledge alone creates status.

Public relations practitioners who would succeed in this environment first must be wholly knowledgeable in the affairs of their employers or clients. They have no choice but to become involved on a personal level with computer utility forums, Internet news groups, and other components of the electronic community that may influence client or employer welfare. With demonstrated expertise comes the peer recognition necessary to function successfully in the electronic world.

Source: E. W. Brody, APR, Fellow, president, Resource Group, and professor, University of Memphis.

---

of the mainframe computers used by government, education, and large industry. In the 1970s the minicomputer was developed. Smaller and much less expensive, it was still a centralized system. The 1980s saw the invention of the personal computer—a relatively inexpensive tool that individuals can use on their desktops. Not only is the personal computer widespread in government, education, and business, but also the consumer has been able to afford it for home use. The 1990s has evolved into the decade of the network. While the Internet was actually in use in the earliest days of the computer, recent familiarity with it and its widespread use have changed the world dramatically.

Experts expect that the Internet, or some similar communication system, will become the focus of information technology in the next several years. This network orientation will eliminate platform dependence. Thus, it will no longer matter whether you use a Macintosh or a PC. By the end of the decade it won't matter what computer sits on your desk because it will be using software on a network and everything will be compatible. "The Internet wipes away differences in platforms, thanks to a standard communication language. All computers are equal on the Net,"[17] writes Kevin Maney in *USA Today*.

The Internet's usage increased 60 percent in 1995, to a total of about eight million users. The figure is expected to rise to 25 million by the end of the decade.[18] Usage has also grown worldwide, with increases of more than 40 percent in 1995 in Japan and Germany and 30 percent in Canada. Forrester Research predicts there will be 52 million users worldwide by the year 2000.[19] World Wide Web sites have also proliferated at an unbelievable rate. From 1,000 sites in April 1994, there was an increase to 110,000 by October 1995.[20] Learning to use the Internet, then, is a must for the public relations practitioner.

J. Donald Turk, public relations adviser at Mobil Oil Co., believes that in the future, "there will be greater diversity of employees, customers, and constituencies."   *Diversity*

Turk, who was the 1995 chair of the Corporate Section of PRSA, continues by saying that the global economy will be a place where "diversity will be characteristic of the work force and customer mix, as well as one in which diversity will be valued and even required to be a successful business."21

Diversity is a relatively new concept in American business. Rather than just denoting minority issues, diversity encompasses the mix of race, age, gender, religious beliefs, national origin, and disability. Most business workforces have had difficulty attaining optimum diversity. Public relations departments may have had even more trouble because of their relatively small size and the problem of finding people with the appropriate professional and educational qualifications.

Business, however, can perhaps borrow from the late Commerce Secretary Ron Brown's seven tenets for planning to achieve diversity. The census bureau uses the following guidelines for achieving a diverse workforce:

1. *Inclusion* Valuing all employees regardless of race, gender, color, religious belief, national origin, age, disability, or sexual orientation.

2. *Opportunity* Recruiting aggressively and developing career programs to ensure a diverse pool of qualified candidates for the job.

3. *Comprehensiveness* Considering diversity in business affairs such as training, seminar procurement, grant processes, trade missions, regulatory matters, business liaison, and "every other program of the department."

4. *Accessibility* Strengthening EEO complaint procedures to ensure fair and timely processing of complaints.

5. *Training* Encouraging participation of senior managers in training on diversity policies and conflict resolution techniques.

6. *Management* Adding diversity efforts as a factor to job performance evaluations of management personnel.

7. *Evaluation and communication* Establishing a diversity council to monitor, evaluate, and facilitate programs to implement diversity.22

Crisis Communication

Crisis management has emerged recently as a major corporate concern. Corporate America has been faced with a rising number of both crises and disasters in recent years.

While the terms *crisis* and *disaster* are often used interchangeably, there is a distinction. A crisis develops in predictable fashion. E. W. Brody says that a crisis is "a decisive turning point in a condition or state of affairs."23 Thus, an organization can anticipate possible consequences and put into effect a crisis plan to deal with the problem or issue. A disaster, of course, is either a natural disaster, such as a flood, or a human error disaster, such as an oil spill or gas explosion (see mini-case 18.3).

Two keys to crisis or disaster public relations are (1) having an up-to-date, workable crisis plan and (2) taking positive action that will move your corporation off the defensive and onto the offensive. *Action* can be what Standard Oil did

Mini-Case 18.3

In the Eye of the Storm: Hurricane Andrew

On August 24, 1992, Hurricane Andrew, packing winds of 165 miles per hour and greater, smashed into the Florida towns of Homestead, Florida City, and Kendall. The destruction was total, and chaos was everywhere.

Within 24 hours, hundreds of media representatives descended on south Florida with cameras, tape recorders, and computers screaming into operation. Our U.S. Army Reserve unit, the 314th Public Affairs Detachment (Press Camp Headquarters) out of Birmingham, Alabama, was voluntarily activated to handle the hundreds of media inquires that were rushing into the Joint Task Force Andrew Headquarters in Miami.

The 314th PAD (PCH) is one of only three military press camp headquarters in the Department of Defense's arsenal that briefs, gives media credentials to, and escorts media in a theater of operations.

Our six specific missions were as follows:

1. To handle successfully hundreds of media inquiries for Joint Task Force (JTF) Andrew.
2. To coordinate the media responses of all federal agencies involved in JTF Andrew's relief efforts. The following federal agencies were involved: U.S. Army, U.S. Navy, U.S. Air Force, U.S. Marines, U.S. Coast Guard, U.S. Army Corps of Engineers, FEMA, USDA, SBA, Department of Health and Human Services, IRS, and U.S. Forest Service, plus the American Red Cross.
3. To escort media into the hurricane-ravaged areas.
4. To prepare Transportation Secretary Andrew Card's daily media briefings.
5. To provide command and control for the U.S. Army Reserve Public Affairs Detachments (PAD) that were voluntarily activated to produce internal and electronic products.
6. To assist in the establishment and operation of Radio Recovery, which broadcast 24 hours a day in English, Spanish, and Creole. This radio station went to 50,000 watts with the coordination and assistance of the FCC and Miami's WINK.

Four simple communication objectives were established:

1. To ensure that the Hurricane Andrew victims were kept informed of where and how to get assistance.
2. To tell the American people what Joint Task Force Andrew members were doing to help the victims.
3. To keep Joint Task Force Andrew members informed of what was happening in and around the hurricane-ravaged areas.
4. To help keep morale high within Joint Task Force Andrew.

The following organizational lessons were learned:

1. Your organization must have an easy-to-understand and annually practiced crisis communication plan.
2. Your organization must have a mobilization readiness container with state-of-the-art communication and computer equipment.
3. Your communication channels must be successfully analyzed and properly utilized in order to get your message out and understood.

4. The public affairs/relations staff must establish a direct and credible working relationship with the operations and logistics personnel and other staffers.

5. The public affairs/relations senior staffers must be involved with the policy decisions and have direct and total access to the CEO.

6. All media inquiries must be routed and answered by one and only one media inquiry section.

7. You must remain flexible to the ever-changing situation! Think multicultural!

8. Be totally accessible to the media.

9. Be patient with the media's numerous and repetitive questions.

10. Finally, like a good scout, always be prepared.

Source: Joseph V. Trahan III, Ph.D., APR, University of Tennessee at Chattanooga. See also Joseph V. Trahan III, "Media Relations in the Eye of the Storm," *Public Relations Quarterly,* vol. 38, no. 2 (Summer 1993): 31–32.

---

following a tanker collision in San Francisco Bay in the late 1960s. Standard oil immediately spent whatever resources were necessary to clean up the mess. At the end newspapers editorials were saying things like, "Beaches never cleaner before." Also, it is possible to plan for crises and disasters, despite what Exxon president Booth Simon claimed when he said the Exxon Valdez disaster was "inconceivable." It could have been anticipated with knowledge of what had befallen Standard Oil in San Francisco and the Amoco Cadiz in 1978, when it spilled six times as much oil off the coast of France as the Valdez spilled off the Alaskan coast.

Crisis Planning   In a random survey of 200 of the *Fortune* 500 corporations, Debbie Walton found that 69 percent had crisis plans in place. Of those that didn't, however, 42 percent were currently developing plans, with the remainder either postponing their development or not even considering it.[24] Walton found that almost all of the plans addressed media relations and emergency personnel contact. However, fewer than half of the businesses' crisis plans addressed shareholder communication or vendor communication.[25] See Table 18.2 for a look at the plans' elements.

Planning must take place before any sign of a crisis appears or a disaster occurs. Philip Lesly suggests four actions that should be operationalized in the plan:

1. Establishing beyond doubt among everyone in the organization that it will put first the interest of all people concerned—employees, their families, neighbors, communities, personnel of sales outlets, investors, and so on.

2. Making it clear to all that the organization will be as open about what happened as the facts and conditions permit.

3. Giving priority to resolving the emergency and protecting the people affected until it is completely resolved.

4. Emphasizing that despite stress and danger to the company, it will be fair to all, including, to the extent possible, critics or opponents who may have instigated the problem.[26]

TABLE 18.2 Crisis Plan Elements (n=71)

Plan Element	Percent Addressing Element
1. Media Relations	88
2. Emergency Personnel Contact	88
3. Communication with Legal Department	82
4. Communication with Governmental Agencies	80
5. Communication with Customers/Consumers	69
6. Follow-up Communication	51
7. Shareholder Communication	49
8. Vendor Communication	43

Source: Debbie Walton, *A Study of Components and Variables Comprising Corporate Crisis Communications Plans,* master's thesis, University of Memphis (1993), 20.

Other more specific items and guidelines that should be in a crisis or disaster plan include these:

1. Have a designated spokesperson.

2. Gather all relevant facts and verify them.

3. Set up a media center, appropriately equipped if possible.

4. Don't release names of dead or injured until relatives have been notified.

5. Respond to all media inquiries, but if you don't know the answer, say so. Then promise to get back as soon as possible with the answer.

6. Do not speculate.

Public relations spotlight 18.3 is an example of an initial response statement. It illustrates what can be included in the plan to let the media know an emergency has occurred if your company spokesperson is not yet present at the crisis location.

Once the spokesperson is available, he or she should handle all media inquiries. A look at what can go wrong in these media interviews may help you avoid them (see public relations spotlight 18.4).

Communication Efforts   Technological changes have transformed the way we communicate in a crisis or disaster. While traditional communication tools may need to be used, Raymond Kotcher suggests that the following new techniques are useful in a crisis:[27]

Satellite communication: Local United Way agencies used teleconferencing to discuss leadership and other questions surrounding the national office during the Aramony case examined in chapter 16.

Video News Releases: Pepsi used this tool extensively to tell its story in the Pepsi hoax, as we discussed in chapter 1.

Fax technology: Ketchum Public Relations used a fax to help a high-tech company announce its filing for bankruptcy by faxing customized letters from the CEO to shareholders, customers, vendors, and elected officials within an hour of filing.

Initial Media Response Statement

Public Relations Spotlight 18.3

Instructions: Should a major emergency situation (fire, explosion, accident, etc.) occur when _____, the designated crisis spokesperson, and other managers are absent, the following may be used to respond to inquiries from news reporters who phone or come to the facility for information.

Fill in the blanks with the appropriate information, and select the most accurate injury statement as you *know* the facts to be.

Do not provide any other information to reporters. As soon as the designated crisis spokesperson is available, discontinue the use of this statement, and refer all media inquiries immediately to that individual.

At _____, (a/an) _____ occurred
    (time)   (fire, explosion, accident)

at_____ in the _____.
   (company name and facility)   (area affected)

Emergency services are responding.

    (Select most accurate statement—**DO NOT SPECULATE**)

    _____ We do not know whether injuries occurred.
    _____ No injuries have been reported.
    _____ There have been some injuries.

This facility _____.
                 (describe plant operation/products)

We have no further details at this time. Additional information will be provided

by _____ as soon as possible.
       (public information officer)

Keep a record of the names, organizations, and phone numbers of all reporters inquiring about the incident, and provide that list to the public information officer or his/her alternate as soon as he/she arrives at the facility.

The initial statement must **NOT** include:
A. Any discussion or speculation about the **CAUSE** of the incident.
B. Any discussion or estimate of the **AMOUNT OF DAMAGE**.
C. Any speculation about the **IMPACT** of the incident on the **FACILITY, EMPLOYEES, CUSTOMERS,** or **SUPPLIERS;** on the **COMMUNITY;** on the **COMPANY** generally; or on the **ENVIRONMENT**.

Source: Debbie Walton, *A Study of Components and Variables Comprising Corporate Crisis Communication Plans,* master's thesis, University of Memphis (1993), 98–99.

Public Relations Spotlight 18.4

1. **Failure to take charge.** The spokesperson must be a leader. His/her role is not just to answer questions but also to disseminate information.

2. **Failure to anticipate questions.** Don't just concentrate on assembling the factual details. Prepare for obvious questions. Remember, the public wants to know, "Is it safe?"

3. **Failure to develop key message.** This is your opportunity to communicate with the public. Make sure you can take advantage of it by having your organization's message prepared and ready for use.

4. **Failure to stick to the facts.** Speculating or answering hypothetical questions can get you in trouble. Avoid "What if" questions by confining your answers to what is known.

5. **Failure to keep calm.** By not letting questions get under your skin, you will show a willingness to cooperate with courteous journalists and convey an impression of candor. Keep cool.

Source: Debbie Walton, *A Study of Components and Variables Comprising Corporate Crisis Communication Plans,* master's thesis, University of Memphis (1993), 104.

Other tools: Improved video and print distribution services, and the use of the Internet to provide information on the World Wide Web or to send information by electronic mail, can speed communication.

Summary

Though all aspects of public relations practice apply to corporations, public relations practitioners must also deal with career issues related to the role of business in society. Corporate credibility and public confidence in business form the backdrop for all businesses' public relations efforts, but public relations is not the exclusive domain of large businesses. Although small business owners serve as their own public relations experts, the smaller enterprise can profitably employ a variety of public relations techniques.

Globalization of public relations, diversity, technological change, and crisis management are major issues facing the corporate public relations practitioner. How he or she prepares to deal with these issues may well be the margin of success or failure by the year 2000.

Snap-on Tools' Image
Campaign Pays Tribute
to Auto Repair Industry

By Lynne M. Sallot, Ph.D.
APR
*Assistant Professor of Public
Relations
University of Georgia
Athens, Georgia*

Case Study

I n 1994, Snap-on Tools of Kenosha, Wisconsin, realized that its customers—automotive repair dealers—needed help with a new public image. The *Fortune* 500 manufacturer and distributor of quality power tools and diagnostic equipment had a big idea, and it decided to lend a hand to the auto repair trade while taking a fresh public relations/advertising approach for itself. The idea was to elevate the image of auto repair mechanics from grease monkeys to "automotive technicians" in the public's mind by paying tribute to these highly skilled but unsung heroes.

Focus group research revealed a gap between consumer's perceptions and reality about mechanics. While consumers understood new car *features,* they did not comprehend advances in automotive technology, nor did they recognize the impact of complex new technology on the mechanics who keep their cars running. Instead, consumers persisted in seeing automotive service in terms of a simple tuneup, despite the fact that automobiles manufactured in the past 10 years are increasingly complicated technological works. Consumers did not recognize that, because of the advent of antilock brakes, fuel-injected engines, and other systems managed by on-board computers in today's cars, contemporary mechanics are highly skilled technicians who require countless hours of training and information and who spend thousands of dollars on high-tech tools and intricate diagnostic equipment.

"A lot of exceptionally bright people get dirt under their fingernails, and we all depend on them every time we put the key in the ignition to head for work, the mall, or the kids' soccer game," said Robert Cornog, chairman, president, and chief executive of Snap-on in *USA Today.* "Snap-on knows the importance of automotive technicians in our daily lives. We want the rest of the world to know it, too. Just about everyone has had an experience where he or she realized the value of a good mechanic. We're going to help people remember that experience."

Snap-on's comprehensive, integrated communications effort was directed at consumers by Ogilvy Adams & Reinehart of Chicago, with Sawyer Riley Compton of Atlanta. It was built around a tribute campaign theme of "When did you first learn the value of a good mechanic? A tribute to the automotive *technicians* that keep us moving from Snap-on Tools . . ."

Snap-on's first-ever consumer advertising with that tag line appeared in popular media such as *Time, People, Sports Illustrated, Motor Trend, Hot Rod,* and *USA Today.* Clever photography in the institutional ads underscored the theme. For example, one ad showed a frustrated father frantically trying to assemble toys in front of a Christmas tree. The ads also appeared on the tailgates of vans used by Snap-on dealers to call on the nation's one million mechanics weekly. Posters of the ads were made available to automotive service centers and dealerships nationwide. Major news stories about the tribute campaign appeared in *USA Today* and other media.

In addition, Snap-on hosted a series of educational "service update" conferences for consumer automotive writers and editors. Experts from a variety of associations covered what consumers should know about today's automotive service to save time and money and get better results. To complement and extend the value of the educational conferences, Snap-on began publishing a quarterly newsletter for consumer automotive writers.

Coincidentally, in the fifth month of its tribute campaign, Snap-on made the separate decision to discontinue distributing 1.2 million classic "pinup" calendars to its 5,000 worldwide dealers, who in turn passed them on to auto repair shops. With attractive female models displaying—among other things—a variety of Snap-on products, the calendars had become legendary among auto mechanics, who had hung them in their offices and repair docks for the previous 12 years.

News of the demise of the girlie calendars made the front page of *The Wall Street Journal*. Acting immediately, Snap-on's public relations firm was able to place information about the tribute campaign, including a print of one of the tribute ads, with the Associated Press wire coverage about the discontinued calendars. Subsequent coverage about the tribute campaign was carried by CNN, *Entertainment Tonight*, and TV and radio segments in 80 local markets.

Follow-up evaluation research, when compared with precampaign research, measured a marked increase in consumer awareness of Snap-on during the first year of the tribute campaign. The campaign generated a total of 400 million impressions through public relations and advertising efforts. Focus groups were conducted to measure the impact of the campaign on individual consumers. Results showed a positive impact, with consumers saying the ads made them stop and think that there are hard-working technicians who want to make a difference. Snap-on dealers reported consumers stopping them in parking lots to comment favorably about the tribute ads. Repair shop owners have reported positive reactions to the posters from customers. And Snap-on has received endorsements from several top automotive associations for its efforts.

By doing the auto repair industry a good turn with its consumer tribute, Snap-on Tools has strengthened its own relationships with its customers. To further strengthen those relationships, Snap-on Tools has expanded its tribute campaign to focus on profiles of individual skilled auto technicians.

"As cars continue to become more sophisticated, and as stringent new emissions testing takes on a national scope, consumers' reliance on qualified auto technicians will become increasingly important," said David Heide, manager of public relations for Snap-on, Inc. "We're hoping the campaign will have a positive effect on the future workforce. As the technology of cars become more complicated, the need for automotive technicians continues to grow. Through advertising and consumer education, Snap-on will increase awareness of automotive technology as a highly skilled, well-paying career option," he added.

Questions

1. What is the value of research in this kind of program? At what stage(s) is it valuable?

2. John Pavlik, in *Public Relations: What Research Tells Us,* defines public relations as "the business of relationship management." How does Pavlik's definition of public relations apply in this case?

3. As the Snap-on campaign moves into its second phase, focusing on profiles of individual automotive technicians, what additional communication strategies would you recommend to Snap-on?

4. What additional theme lines might complement and extend the campaign as it expands in its subsequent phases?

Notes

1. Keith Davis and Richard Blomstrom, *Business and Society: Environment and Responsibility,* 2nd ed. (New York: McGraw-Hill, 1975), 50.

2. Grover Starling, *The Changing Environment of Business,* 2nd ed. (Boston: Kent Publishing, 1984), 594.

3. Hill & Knowlton Executives, *Critical Issues,* 223.

4. G. A. Steiner, *Business and Society,* 2nd ed. (New York: Random House, 1975), 72.

5. Hill & Knowlton Executives, *Critical Issues,* 4.

6. Marshall C. Lewis, "How Business Can Escape the Climate of Mistrust," *Business and Society Review* (Winter 1975): 70–71.

7. William Agee, quoted in *Business Week* (22 January 1979).

8. Z. V. Lambert and F. W. Kniffin, "Consumer Discontent: A Social Perspective," *California Management Review* 18 (1975): 36–44.

9. Lambert and Kniffin, "Consumer Discontent," 37.

10. "Sylvia Porter Blasts Economic Illiteracy," *The Ann Arbor News* (17 October 1975): 26.

11. See W. Barlow and C. Kaufman, "Public Relations and Economic Literacy," *Public Relations Review* (Summer 1975): 14–22; and *National Survey on the American Economic System* (New York: The Advertising Council, 1978).

12. "The Corporate Image: PR to the Rescue," *Business Week* (22 January 1979): 50.

13. John M. Reed, "International Media Relations: Avoid Self-Binding," *Public Relations Quarterly* (Summer 1989): 15.

14. *O'Dwyer's Directory of Public Relations Firms, 1995,* quoted in Keith Greenberg, "Going Global," *PR Tactics* (September 1995): 1.

15. Keith Greenberg, "Going Global," *PR Tactics* (September 1995): 13.

16. Don Tapscott and Art Caston, *Paradigm Shift.*

17. Kevin Maney, "Networks May Topple Today's PC Leaders," *USA Today* (10 November 1995): 2.

18. In a speech at the Memphis PRSA meeting, Oct. 11.

19. Ibid.

20. Ibid.

21. J. Donald Turk, quoted in Susan Bovet, "Forecast 2001," *Public Relations Journal* (October 1995): 13.

22. Carol Shaw, "Achieving Diversity After Work Force Downsizing," *Government Communications* (November 1995): 18.

23. E. W. Brody, *Managing Communication Processes: From Planning to Crisis Response* (New York: Praeger, 1991), 175.

24. Debbie Walton, *A Study of Components and Variables Comprising Corporate Crisis Communication Plans,* master's

thesis, University of Memphis (1993), 24.

25. Ibid., 20.

26. Philip Lesly, "Policy, Issues, Crises, and Opportunities," *Lesly's Handbook of Public Relations and Communication,* *4th ed.* (New York: AMACOM, 1991), 25–26.

27. Raymond L. Kotcher, "The Technological Revolution Has Transformed Crisis Communications," *Public Relations Quarterly* (Fall 1992): 20–21.

CHAPTER 19

The Legal Environment
of Public Relations Practice

Preview

The public relations profession is constrained by a dynamic environment of laws and regulations designed to safeguard freedoms and provide guidelines for the secure pursuit of First Amendment rights.

Attorneys and public relations practitioners need to recognize and accept each other's expertise in their respective areas of practice. Legal counsel represents organizations before the court of law, and public relations counsel performs similar services before the court of public opinion.

Free speech is balanced against privacy, property, and other rights. Communication is limited to the extent that it may slander or libel an individual, invade an individual's privacy, infringe on trademarks or copyrights, breach contracts, or violate regulatory requirements.

Regulations of the Federal Trade Commission, the Food and Drug Administration, the Securities and Exchange Commission, the National Labor Relations Board, the United States Postal Service, the Federal Communications Commission, and other agencies impact the practice of public relations.

The Internet, while a great boost for the gathering and disseminating of information, is particularly vulnerable to libel and copyright violations.

The life of the law has not been logic; it has been experience.

—Oliver Wendell Holmes

"M"any public relations professionals may be placing themselves and client organizations at risk of legal liability because they have little or no familiarity with important legal issues that affect public relations activities," according to a recent survey of public relations practitioners by Kathy Fitzpatrick.[1] Public relations personnel are increasingly vulnerable to legal liability. It is thus more important than ever that a public relations practitioner be acquainted with key legal issues such as libel, privacy, copyright, conspiracy, contracts, and numerous agency regulations. However, in her survey, Fitzpatrick found that more than half of public relations practitioners had no familiarity with SEC regulations, more than 40 percent had no knowledge of commercial speech or financial public relations legal issues, and just over 21 percent reported no familiarity with laws governing access to information.[2]

In 1986, the chairman of Puritan Fashions, a clothing manufacturer, was sued by the Securities and Exchange Commission for making "false, overly optimistic" statements about the firm's performance during a recessionary period. Furthermore, the corporation's chief financial officer, an official of the financial public relations firm that represented Puritan, and two stockbrokers were accused of insider trading of the manufacturing company's stock.

The charges against Puritan's chief executive resulted from his failure to correct inflated projections of the company's 1983 performance although (the SEC alleged) he was aware of the inaccuracies. According to an article in *The New York Times,* the public relations official "learned of the alleged inaccuracy of the public projection and passed that information to . . . a stockbroker."[3]

In another case, the Food and Drug Administration ordered ICN Pharmaceutical, Inc. to correct a news release concerning the safety and effectiveness of Virazole, a recently developed drug used to treat respiratory viral infections.[4] ICN claimed the errors were unintentional, but it was forced to amend what the FDA considered exaggerated product claims in its press kit and suffered some unfavorable publicity because of the incident.

In October 1985, *The Wall Street Journal* reported that a $50 million, five-year public relations campaign initiated by Dow Chemical Company got off to a rocky start when it released the inaccurate information that an arrested member of a protest group had venereal disease. According to the news article, a local law official was "investigating how Dow Chemical obtained the information."[5] The error not only tainted an expensive public relations campaign but also left the company open to possible costly and embarrassing charges of libel and invasion of privacy.

Members of each business or profession are constrained by laws and regulations affecting their practice. Public relations practitioners are no different. Their advice and guidance to management should be consistent with relevant laws and regulations. Moreover, they must understand the legal and regulatory areas that can affect their own communication activities.

Discussing the legal environment of public relations can be both overwhelming and frightening to those not formally educated in law. Much of the fear originates from an inability to interpret legal jargon. Many people misunderstand the purpose of law in the United States, believing that law exists to restrict rights.

On the contrary: The purpose of law in this country is to safeguard freedoms. Laws offer guidelines under which rights may be securely pursued.

The legal environment of public relations is quite dynamic. Laws and government regulations are frequently changed or clarified. Court decisions may narrow, broaden, or reinterpret laws or regulations affecting public relations practice. Nonetheless, basic legal guidelines—most of which rest on the freedom of expression guaranteed by the First Amendment to the United States Constitution—remain fairly consistent. These guidelines should be understood by all who aspire to practice public relations.

Because public relations professionals' efforts are often concentrated in such sensitive areas as financial relations, product publicity, and labor relations, their work is scrutinized by government regulatory agencies. Lack of knowledge may lead to violations of Securities and Exchange Commission (SEC), Federal Trade Commission (FTC), National Labor Relations Board (NLRB), or other state or federal agency regulations.

Lawyers can be very helpful to public relations practitioners. Professional communicators should strive to develop close working relationships with attorneys, but they need to recognize that public relations and legal counselors may clash head-on when offering advice to organizational executives.

Public Relations and Legal Advisers

The public relations practitioner may have a basic understanding of laws and regulations, but certain sensitive or questionable areas require expert legal advice. Whether that advice comes from a corporate legal department or from outside law counsel is not important. What matters is that the attorney and the public relations practitioner recognize and accept each other's expertise in their respective areas. When major difficulties confront organizations and place them in the public eye, decisions need to represent a careful balance of public relations and legal tactics. Kathy Fitzpatrick came to the following conclusion in her survey of public relations practitioners:

> Although practitioners reported that in situations involving conflicts with legal counsel over the public release of information, decisions are generally made as a result of collaboration between the two advisors or by a company official, the reality is that the public relations professionals are not playing lead roles in these instances.[6]

Unfortunately, close working relationships between public relations practitioners and lawyers are rare. More often, the two find themselves in competition for the ear of top management, and their advice is often contradictory.

Public relations practitioners are sometimes envious of the status enjoyed by lawyers in the corporate world. Indeed, the term "public relations counsel" emulates the term "legal counsel." Early public relations specialists specifically compared their role to that of lawyers—one specializing in representing organizations before the court of law, the other performing similar services before the court of public opinion.

These courts, however, are not as distinct in practice as they are in theory. What an organization does in the name of public relations may well affect its legal position. Likewise, an organization's behavior in court may affect public opinion. The reason is that lawyers and public relations practitioners view public relations from different perspectives. The lawyer tends to look at the short-term, immediate action that must be taken. On the other hand, the public relations person should look at the potential long-term effect of the situation on relations with stakeholder groups, media relations, and the long-term image of the organization. Consequently, legal and public relations counsels often find themselves at loggerheads. As Ivy Lee put it, "I have seen more situations which the public ought to understand . . . spoiled by the intervention of a lawyer than in any other way."[7]

In discussing problems that occur between business and the media, David Finn, chairman of one of the country's largest public relations firms, suggests that disclosure of information is frequently impeded by legal counsel. According to Finn, this is "the least-known aspect of corporate communications, yet it is in all probability the most troublesome in achieving an open, constructive communication between business and the media."[8]

Conflict over Disclosure

Lawyers generally advise their clients to avoid making any public statements that could prove troublesome in future legal actions. Frequently, they recommend saying nothing. When an executive tersely says, "No comment," it is usually on the advice of the lawyer rather than the public relations counsel.

Finn comments:

> For the most part, I find that business executives would like to be open and candid about their affairs. They repeatedly make the point that they want the truth to be known, and that they would like to cooperate with the press as much as possible. . . . When public relations advisors tell their clients that the only way to avoid distortions is to answer all questions as fully as possible, the instinct of most businessmen is to do so. But when there are critical issues involved, legal counsel usually has a greater influence on business executives by making it clear that speaking too freely about matters that may have to be litigated can cause a great deal of trouble for the corporation and even for the executives personally.[9]

The damages that lawyers anticipate are very real. So are the damages that occur when a corporation appears unresponsive, unfeeling, defensive, or irresponsible and consequently loses the respect and trust of its publics. In either case, millions of dollars can be lost and careers can be ruined.

There are no simple solutions to the problems arising from the differences between lawyers and public relations practitioners. That public relations should speak of the potential practical consequences of various communication strategies rather than merely preaching truth and openness certainly applies in these sensitive areas. Procter & Gamble's Rely tampon case, Firestone's 500 radial tire case, and Johnson & Johnson's handling of Tylenol illustrate this point.

Lawyers' advice to clients not to speak is based on legal tactics, not on the law per se. We all recognize that individuals in the United States are guaranteed freedom of speech under the **First Amendment** to the Constitution. We also know that the media are protected by freedom-of-the-press provisions of the same amendment.

First Amendment Rights and Limits

Recent court cases have clarified that nonmedia corporations enjoy much the same freedom and protection. When the First National Bank of Boston wanted publicly to oppose and advertise against a Massachusetts personal income tax referendum, State Attorney General Francis Bellotti said a state law barred corporations from financial participation in referenda that did not affect them directly. First National sued the state for violating its First Amendment right to speak. In 1978, *First National Bank of Boston v. Bellotti* [435 U.S. 530] was resolved when the Supreme Court ruled in favor of the bank. A similar case in 1980, *Consolidated Edison Company of New York v. Public Service Commission of New York* [447 U.S. 530], reaffirmed the utility's right to issue advertising promoting electricity. Thus, the Supreme Court has diminished distinctions between the levels of First Amendment protection for political and social expression and for what has been called **commercial speech.**

The importance of commercial speech was made clear in yet another Supreme Court decision, *Virginia State Board of Pharmacy v. Virginia Citizens' Consumer Council, Inc.* [425 U.S. 748 (1976)]. In his opinion on the case, Justice Harry Blackmun wrote:

> So long as we preserve a predominantly free enterprise economy, the allocation of our resources in large measure will be made through numerous private economic decisions. It is a matter of public interest that those decisions in the aggregate be intelligent and well informed. To this end, the free flow of commercial information is indispensable.[10]

The Supreme Court decisions in these and other cases opened the door to issues-oriented advertising by corporations, as discussed in chapter 15. The broadened interpretation of free speech protection has resulted in increased corporate political activity through lobbying and political action committees (PACs). Free speech is not without limits. Most jurists today interpret the First Amendment to mean that free speech should be balanced against other human values or rights. Those other rights—for example, the right to privacy, the right to a good reputation, or property rights—can restrict the right to free speech (see mini-case 19.1).

The free flow of commercial information is indispensable, but the content of all public communications—news releases, company newspapers, speeches, and advertisements—must meet legal and regulatory guidelines. For instance, section 8c of the Taft-Hartley Act says:

> The expressing of any view, argument, or opinion or the dissemination thereof, whether in written, printed, graphic, or visual form, shall not constitute or be evidence of an unfair labor practice under any of the provisions of this Act, if such expression contains no threat of reprisal or force or promise of benefits.[11]

The last clause is the key—"no threat . . . or promise of benefits." This would mean, for example, that in an employee newsletter, you as editor could not promise workers a bonus if they would come back to work early from a strike or threaten that workers who didn't would likely be fired.

Public communication is limited to the extent that it may slander or libel an individual, invade an individual's privacy, infringe on existing copyrights or trademarks, breach contracts, or violate regulatory requirements.

Mini-Case 19.1

Commercial Speech in U.S. Healthcare Case

Blue Cross of Greater Philadelphia launched a major advertising campaign to reduce the attractiveness of HMOs to consumers. One HMO, U.S. Healthcare, objected. U.S. Healthcare sued Blue Cross of Philadelphia for libel, claiming that it had defamed the HMO through its derogatory advertising.

Departing from the concept of corporations being public figures, the Third Circuit Court of Appeals ruled in favor of the libel charge by U.S. Healthcare. In its departure, the court imposed the commercial speech doctrine into the determination of malice. The court looked first at the nature of the speech rather than the status of the parties.

Most corporate cases in the last two decades have assumed that the public figure status of a corporation makes actual malice unnecessary to prove under the 1964 *New York Times v. Sullivan* doctrine. The Third Court noted that the *New York Times* case opinion said that the advertisement was political and not commercial when it handed down its landmark ruling.

The Third Circuit Court ruled in the U.S. Healthcare Case that the commercial speech doctrine applied. This approach gives less First Amendment protection to the corporation. The ruling should give corporate public relations practitioners reason to consider more carefully any possibilities of defamation in publicity and advertising.

Source: Based on material in Matthew D. Bunker, "The Corporate Plaintiff as Public Figure," *Journalism Quarterly,* vol. 72, no. 3 (Autumn 1995): 597–609.

Defamation

The definitions of **defamation** are as diverse as have been its various legal interpretations through the years. Perhaps the simplest, most straightforward definition is that offered by Don R. Pember of the University of Washington. Pember says defamation "is any communication which holds a person up to contempt, hatred, ridicule, or scorn."[12] While "truth" is the best legal defense against defamation suits, Pember does not define defamation as a "false" statement. As he carefully points out, a true statement can still be held legally defamatory if its truth cannot be established in court. Proving truth can sometimes be more difficult than it seems. In at least one state, Colorado, truth is not a complete defense in criminal libel in two instances: blackening the memory of the dead and holding a handicapped person up to ridicule.

Libel is published defamation, and **slander** is oral defamation. Libel has two categories: criminal and civil. Although the Supreme Court has frequently overturned the convictions, individuals have been found guilty of **criminal libel** in cases involving "breach of the peace" or "inciting to riot." In some states, one can criminally libel a dead person, and in 1952, the conviction of a white racist for criminally libeling an entire race of people was upheld by the Supreme Court. Criminal libel suits are very rare today, but some states still carry criminal libel statutes on their books.

More important to public relations practitioners is **civil libel.** The attention generated by Carol Burnett's suit against the *National Enquirer,* General William Westmoreland's libel suit against CBS, and Israeli General Ariel Sharon's

Entertainer Carol Burnett in court, suing the *National Enquirer* for $10 million

defamation suit against *Time* may lead many people to think such charges apply only to the media. That assumption is erroneous. The vast majority of libel suits are filed against the media, but any corporation, organization, public relations practitioner, or private individual can be guilty of defamation through written material or through remarks made before any group of people. *Advertising Age* reported in its February 10, 1986, issue that an ex-employee of JWT Group had filed a libel suit against her former employers on the basis of the wording of a press release issued regarding her dismissal (see mini-case 19.2).

Mini-Case 19.2

A "Responsible" Play on Words

JWT Group is one of the nation's largest and most successful advertising agencies. However, in 1982, the company took a $30 million pretax write-off. An internal investigation revealed that the losses were due to irregularities in the corporation's barter syndication unit. The special investigation found several improprieties within the department, including fictitious accounting entries in the syndication unit's computer system. Marie Luisi, one of the overseers of the syndication unit, was fired.

In March, JWT Group issued a press release announcing the large write-off. The communication claimed that Ms. Luisi "was responsible for the improper activities" in the syndication unit and noted that she had been fired. The release quoted Don Johnston, JWT chairman and CEO, as saying, "As long as business depends on human beings, we will all be vulnerable to human frailty. We're not the first ones to discover that—we won't be the last. In today's world you are more than ever dependent on the personal integrity of the people involved."

Ms. Luisi took offense at the wording of the press release. She consulted an attorney and filed suit for libel against JWT Group and various JWT executives, including Mr. Johnston. Her suit sought damages of more than $20 million and punitive damages of $30 million.

Her lawyers contended that using the word *responsible* was the same as saying she had actively engaged in wrongdoing, which in fact had not been proven. They further argued, "The press release clearly tends to injure Ms. Luisi's business reputation. This is especially true in a profession such as advertising where, as defendant Johnston notes, personal integrity is crucial."

During the next four years, the suit made its way through the court system. A lower court held that "this press release may reasonably be understood as indicating that plaintiff Luisi is dishonest, incompetent, unethical, and has committed criminal acts."

JWT Group appealed, contending that the word *responsible* was meant in an organizational sense. Furthermore, JWT Group's attorneys argued, the meaning of *responsible* is open to a number of interpretations other than that advanced by Ms. Luisi.

In January 1986, an appeals court upheld the New York State Supreme Court ruling that Ms. Luisi had cause for action against JWT Group and its president. The ruling did not evaluate the merits of her libel claim, but it cleared the way for a trial.

Source: Based on "Luisi Wins Round in Libel Suit," *Advertising Age* (10 February 1986).

Elements of Civil Libel   For a statement to be libelous, it must contain certain elements. It must be published, it must be damaging, and it must identify the injured party. Negligence must be involved, and the statement must be defamatory. If the statement involves a public figure, another element becomes of paramount importance: It must involve **malice.**

Publication is considered to have occurred when the alleged defamation has been communicated to a third party. For example, it is "published" when the writer, the injured party, and one other person have seen or heard the remark.

Defamation deals with the words themselves or the implication behind the words. A person's reputation (not character) has been damaged. Libel can either be *per se* or *per quod.* Libel per se is libel "on the face of it," which means that the words themselves are defamatory. To call someone a thief, murderer, or labor agitator is libel per se. Libel per quod means that it is libel by the circumstance or by innuendo.

Damage has occurred if the remarks reflect poorly on one's reputation, impair one's ability to earn a living, or restrict one's social contacts.

Identification has occurred when readers or listeners are able to identify the person referred to, whether or not that person is specifically named.

Fault must be shown in order for the plaintiff to win a libel suit. If the wrong photograph is run with an article, if there is a typographical or mechanical error in the publication process, or if information is not carefully checked, then the defendant may be found negligent. First established by a 1974 Supreme Court ruling (*Gertz v. Welch,* 94 S.Ct., 2997), definitions of negligent conduct are still evolving.

Malice has occurred when the plaintiff can prove that the defendant knew the published material was false or showed a reckless disregard for the truth. Only public figures must prove malice. Politicians, elected government officials, and entertainers are obvious public figures, but the legal interpretation of who is or is not a public figure continues to evolve.

Defenses Against Libel Charges   There are three primary defenses against libel charges—truth, qualified privilege, and fair comment. The primary legal defense against libel is **truth.** That sounds simple enough, but truth and provable truth are often quite different. To know that John Smith is an incompetent manager is one thing; to prove it with evidence that would be admissible in court is another.

A second legal defense against libel is **privilege.** Privilege protects materials and remarks coming from official proceedings and actions of members in executive, legislative, and judicial branches of government, from the local to the federal level. However, this privilege is **qualified.** The qualifications are that the report must be a fair, accurate, and complete account of the proceedings. There is no guarantee of privilege related to proceedings from public, (but nongovernmental) meetings such as those of unions, political parties, and chambers of commerce.

The extent of privilege was examined by an Arkansas court in a defamation case involving an employee dismissed for theft. The court held that remarks made in the presence of the employee, his immediate supervisor, and another supervisor were privileged, as were accurate statements made to the employee's wife and to unemployment compensation officials. The company, the wife, and the unemployment compensation officials all had legitimate interest in the information, and the information given was necessary and factual. The court found, however, that the employee had been defamed by a supervisor who had made excessive, incorrect statements to co-workers. Although a company's right to inform its other employees of a co-worker's dismissal for theft could be privileged, the information released had to be both totally accurate and limited to only that necessary to protect company interests.

A third legal defense is **fair comment.** If communications involve matters of genuine public interest, expressing critical opinions is permissible. However, the opinions expressed must be limited to the public interest aspects of the matter and buttressed by the publication of factual material on which the opinion is based. This is the position assumed by book, restaurant, and film critics, but fair comment can apply equally well to consumer products and services or even to the work of charitable organizations—all of which are of public interest. Fair comment makes possible comparative advertising, in which one brand is weighed unfavorably against another. Using this technique, corporate advertising campaigns have pitted Pepsi against Coke, Burger King against McDonald's, and Hanes underwear against Fruit of the Loom.

For the public relations practitioner, the best defenses against libel are knowledge of the law, exercise of good judgment, and reasonable care in constructing all public communications. Practitioners should take time to research and verify controversial material and, if still in doubt, seek legal advice.

Defamation is not the only curb on the exercise of free speech. Defamation may be defined broadly as the issuance of untrue, derogatory information, but even the publication of complimentary information may break the law if it invades another's right to privacy.

Privacy is a word that probably has as many definitions as there are people. Individual notions of its meaning can differ markedly, and relevant laws may vary widely from state to state. Advance Machine Company was found guilty of breaking a New Jersey privacy law when it rummaged through the garbage of a competitor and retrieved valuable customer lists. The competitor was awarded damages of $500,000.[13]

As government bureaucracies grow, so does their penchant for collecting personal data about the citizenry. As society becomes more reliant on credit, more and more personal information is stored in the computer systems of retail credit agencies. Centralized health agencies disseminate data concerning the diseases, hospitalization, and treatment undergone by patients throughout the nation. Personnel files and school records contain information that many people consider confidential. Individuals feel that their privacy is being assailed by a number of sources, and perhaps because they feel a long-cherished right slowly eroding, lawsuits charging **invasion of privacy** have increased over the last few years.[14]

Public relations practitioners should be aware that the right of privacy extends not only to an organization's customers but also to its employees. A business does not have carte blanche to use an employee's picture or to divulge information about an employee's personal life in either external or internal communications.

Though privacy itself may be difficult to define, and though what constitutes an invasion may vary from state to state, most legal scholars agree that invasions of privacy fall into four categories: appropriation, publication of private information, intrusion, and publication of that material which casts a person in a false light.

Appropriation is the commercial use without permission of an entity's picture, likeness, or name. This area of the privacy laws is especially significant to public relations professionals involved in preparing organizational communications. Although John Doe is a mechanic for the Skiddo Brake Company, his name, picture, or likeness should not be used to advertise the company's products without his permission. Although customer Jane Smith wrote an unsolicited letter claiming Skiddo brakes saved her life, Skiddo should not use her name without permission either.

Equally important to public relations practitioners is the category known as **publication of private information.** While not recognized in all states, this area of privacy law requires the public relations person to be diligent. Private or personal information might be defined as true information not known by a great number of people. Banks and health care organizations possess a great deal of personal information about their clients, as do some charitable groups. The release of information without prior consent can be cause for an invasion-of-privacy suit, as happened to Midatlantic Banks, Inc. A Midatlantic banker made known a customer's lavish lifestyle to the customer's employer. When the customer was subsequently fired, he sued the bank, charging invasion of privacy. The judge ruled in favor of the plaintiff, declaring that bankers have an implied contract not to release customers' confidential financial information.[15] Release of information that a particular employee has AIDS would fall into this category as well.

Novels and films often feature detectives who invade privacy by **intrusion**—surreptitiously filming, bugging, or otherwise snooping into other people's private affairs. However, secretly recording the voice or actions of another or surreptitiously examining private documents is generally illegal.

False light is the fourth and final category of invasion of privacy. It would seem to fall under defamation laws; however, there are some differences. For example, much of the published information may indeed be factual, and it need not actually have damaged a person's reputation. Suits based on publication of false information claim that certain true facts have been embellished with falsehoods (fictionalization) or that certain true facts have been exaggerated or used out of context (false light). In fact, this is often called "false light" publication and can include distortions of the truth. A case occurred in Aspen, Colorado, where a news videographer shot random tape of houses of some celebrities and then talked about drug use in Aspen. One of the celebrities took issue that his house was featured. The case was settled out of court, with considerable money going to the celebrity.

Defenses Against Invasion-of-Privacy Charges   Written consent is the best defense against charges of invasion of privacy. In all instances in which a photograph, likeness, or name is to be published, a practitioner should get the individual's consent to the usage in writing. One can accomplish this most simply by keeping standard release forms on hand. (Figure 19.1 is an example.) Releases occasionally need renewal. Just as it makes sense for public relations professionals to update their photographic files continually, so too should they update the releases that go with the photographs.

While employees do not often sue companies for publishing private information in internal newsletters, the wisest course is either to limit the content to on-the-job subjects or to obtain written releases when private information is to be disclosed.

The Freedom of Information Act   Officials and organizations in the public sector enjoy much less privacy than do individuals and organizations in the private sector. The **Freedom of Information Act (FOIA)** opens the federal government to great public scrutiny.

Communicators employed by federal agencies need to be familiar with the public's general rights under the Freedom of Information Act. Adopted in 1960 and revised several times since then, the act allows for disclosure of certain information gathered by the government. In 1976, Congress passed the **Sunshine Act,** which opened to the public some previously closed meetings of federal boards, commissions, and agencies, including the SEC and the FTC. Many states and municipalities have similar statutes affecting their boards and commissions.

Generally, the materials mandated for disclosure under the federal act fall into the following categories: (1) opinions in settled cases, (2) statements of policy or interpretations not published in the Federal Register, and (3) staff manuals that affect the public.

Though public relations practitioners employed by the government need to know what materials must be made available, business practitioners should also

Adult Release

Figure 19.1 The use of a standard release form can protect against possible charges of invasion of privacy.

In consideration of my engagement as a model, and for other good and valuable consideration herein acknowledged as received, upon the terms hereinafter stated, I hereby grant _____, his legal representatives and assigns, those for whom _____ is acting, and those acting with his authority and permission, the absolute right and permission to copyright and use, re-use and publish, and republish photographic portraits or pictures of me or in which I may be included, in whole or in part, or composite or distorted in character or form, without restriction as to changes or alterations, from time to time, in conjunction with my own or a fictitious name, or reproductions thereof in color or otherwise made through any media at his studios or elsewhere for art, advertising, trade, or any other purpose whatsoever.

I also consent to the use of any printed matter in conjunction therewith.

I hereby waive any right that I may have to inspect or approve the finished product or products or the advertising copy or printed matter that may be used in connection therewith or the use to which it may be applied.

I hereby release, discharge and agree to save harmless _____, his legal representatives or assigns, and all persons acting under his permission or authority or those for whom he is acting, from any liability by virtue of any blurring, distortion, alteration, optical illusion, or use in composite form, whether intentional or otherwise, that may occur or be produced in the taking of said picture or in any subsequent processing thereof, as well as any publication thereof even though it may subject me to ridicule, scandal, reproach, scorn and indignity.

I hereby warrant that I am of full age and have every right to contract in my own name in the above regard. I state further that I have read the above authorization, release and agreement, prior to its execution, and that I am fully familiar with the contents thereof.

Dated: _____

_____

_____

_____

(Address)

_____

(Witness)

be familiar with government information. Businesses use the FOIA far more than do private individuals. Government statistics are important research and verification tools in the preparation of product news releases, brochures, and other forms of public communication.

Public disclosure of private information without proper consent is illegal, and so is the use of another's intellectual property. Tangible intellectual properties are protected under **copyright** or **trademark** laws.

Copyright Law

Why would a public relations practitioner need to be familiar with copyright law? Because most formalized methods of communication can be, and often are, copyrighted. Books, movies, plays, dances, songs, sculptures, pictures, and other original artistic works fixed in any tangible medium of expression are eligible for protection from unauthorized use by copyrighting. Ideas, news events, and utilitarian objects cannot be copyrighted. An original design of an annual report cover can be copyrighted once the idea has been transferred to paper, as can original brochures prepared by an organization. Music you can use in videos, PSAs, or slide shows is often copyrighted. You need to obtain permission to use it, to provide your own original music, or to use licensed music you have obtained by paying a fee. Material that is available on the Internet is also copyright protected.

Wendy's popular slogan "Where's the beef?" is protected by copyright law, a remedy the corporation had to seek in order to prevent the slogan's unauthorized use on T-shirts.[16] Mattel, Inc. was sued for copyright infringement when it produced a toy replica of the comic strip character Conan the Barbarian.[17]

Self-employed public relations consultants can copyright materials they produce unless they contractually sign away that right to their clients. Public relations staff members within organizations cannot copyright their work; it belongs to the organization, which can copyright it. The "fair use" provision of the Copyright Act allows use of material, with broad provisions addressing the following:

1. The purpose and character of the use, including whether such use is of a commercial nature or is for nonprofit educational purposes.

2. The nature of the copyrighted work.

3. The amount and substantiality of the portion used.

4. The effect of the use upon the potential market for or value of the copyrighted work.

This means that in the preparation of communications, a portion of copyrighted material may be used without the author's permission

1. If it is not taken out of context.

2. If credit to the source is given.

3. If such usage does not materially affect the market for the copyrighted material.

4. If the work in which it is used is for scholastic, news, or research purposes.

5. If the material used does not exceed a certain percentage of the total work.

    (No percentage is given in the law, but it depends on the work. One rule of thumb is: Don't use any music; use only a fraction of poetry; but you can use 100 to 200 words of a book or major article.)

Trademark Laws

Copyright laws do not apply to the names of businesses and business products. Just as the products themselves are often covered by patent laws, their names can be covered under trademark laws. For someone other than the holder to market a product with a name strongly resembling or suggestive of an existing trademark or trade name would constitute infringement.

Companies zealously protect their product brand name trademarks. Failure to do so allows the brand name to become generic for all products in its category, thus sacrificing its uniqueness and causing serious advertising and public relations problems. Trade name and trademark protection can be an uphill battle, its necessity an ironic confirmation of the success of marketing and advertising techniques. How many people think that Kleenex (brand) is the generic name for all facial tissue (see Figure 19.2), Band-Aid (brand) is a word denoting all small bandages, and Xerox (brand) is a verb that can be substituted for the word "copy"?

In a consumer survey conducted in connection with a lawsuit involving another trademark, 76 percent of those surveyed identified "Kleenex" as a brand name. Only 23 percent thought the name was generic for facial tissue.[18] Those results told Kimberly-Clark Corporation, the owner of Kleenex, that its trademark protection efforts were successful.[19]

The Minolta Corporation redesigned the logo for its new Maxxum camera. According to *The Wall Street Journal,* that measure settled a lawsuit in which

The Kimberly-Clark Corporation has successfully protected its "Kleenex" trademark through efforts like this.

Exxon Corporation had claimed the Maxxum logo was too similar to its own use of the "interlocking double X in the Exxon name."[20] Exxon contended that the Minolta logo constituted trademark infringement.

Contracts

Copyrighted and trademarked materials may be used if permission has been given by the copyright or trademark holder. Permission for use can constitute a **contract,** a legal instrument that protects the rights of two or more parties.

Public relations practitioners must often use contracts. Independent public relations professionals need contracts between themselves and the firms or individuals they represent. Special events may require contracts with hotels, musical groups, caterers, and others. Most practitioners work with outside publishing or printing firms, and those relationships should involve contracts. And, while perhaps not generally viewed as such, correctly prepared information and photographic release forms are also contracts.

For a contract to be binding, it must meet certain legal criteria. If they are not met, the contract is not valid. The essential elements of contracts include these:

A genuine, legal offer;

A legally effective acceptance;

An agreement that includes an exchange of acts or promises, which is called "consideration."[21]

Some but not all contracts must be in writing. Courts often consider oral contracts binding if all legal tests have been met in the process. Implied contracts may also be valid. If, for example, an employee is told that his picture will be used in a company newspaper to illustrate safety techniques and he then poses in hard hat and safety goggles, his behavior implies agreement, and a valid contract is in force.

If some of the obligations set out in a contract are not fulfilled, a possible breach of contract has occurred. Such disputes may be settled in court. To avoid unpleasant misunderstandings or possible breach of contract, all parties involved should make certain they understand the terms and conditions of the contracts they sign.

Conspiracy

Another area of criminal law with which public relations practitioners need to be familiar is **conspiracy.** If a public relations person (or anyone else) knows about a felony and fails to report it, he or she could be found guilty of conspiracy in the crime. Even the president can be affected. Richard Nixon resigned from the presidency because of the Watergate coverup and resulting conspiracy. If you were the public relations director for a bank and knew about a land fraud scheme financed by your bank, you would be obligated to report it to police or face conspiracy charges.

Laws related to contracts, copyright and trademark, invasion of privacy, defamation, and conspiracy constitute part of the legal environment of public relations. That environment is further complicated by a number of federal regulations that govern business conduct. While a public relations practitioner cannot always ensure that federal regulatory guidelines are met, an awareness of the principal agencies involved in the area of communication can help avoid problems.

Several years ago the Warner-Lambert Company's commercials for Listerine were required to include a disclaimer that its product would not prevent or cure common colds.

> Later, most television viewers noticed that Carter's Little Liver Pills suddenly became Carter's Pills, but they may not have known why.

> In both cases, the manufacturers had run afoul of **Federal Trade Commission (FTC)** regulations. The FTC is just one of the government agencies having regulatory powers over the conduct of business. Others include the **Food and Drug Administration (FDA),** the **Securities and Exchange Commission (SEC),** the **National Labor Relations Board (NLRB),** the **Federal Communications Commission (FCC),** and even the **United States Postal Service.** Public relations professionals need to be aware of the regulatory environment in which their employers operate.

> Regulatory complaints may originate within an agency itself, or they may be brought to the agency's attention by consumers or competitors. An alert public relations practitioner who stays informed about the corporation's publics can sometimes avert problems with regulatory agencies by making management aware of product problems as perceived by either consumer or competitor publics. Product or service deficiencies can be corrected, irate customers can be soothed, regulations can be complied with, and unfavorable media attention can be avoided.

> The NLRB and the SEC are covered in chapters 11 and 14. Two other powerful agencies with which many businesses must deal are the Federal Trade Commission and the Food and Drug Administration; another, the FCC, regulates the telecommunication businesses.

Government Regulatory Agencies

The FTC not only governs advertising, it also regulates product or service news releases. Advertising and news releases are illegal if they deceive or mislead the public in any way. Likewise, promotional practices are illegal unless they are literally true.

> Business must be able to substantiate all specific product claims. In 1984, the U.S. Court of Appeals upheld the FTC's ruling that Bayer Aspirin's advertising made deceptive and misleading claims; Bayer's assertion that it was better than other brands of aspirin had not been substantiated. The court also affirmed the FTC finding that the pain reliever Midol's claim to contain no aspirin was false.[22] Similarly, advertising claims for Bufferin and Excedrin were found to be unsubstantiated.[23] The claims could no longer be used in the marketing of the products.

> The FTC requires that unsubstantiated or false claims for products be omitted from future advertising, and some advertisers may also be required to run corrective ads. Both alternatives can be expensive.

> Nonspecific, subjective product claims may sometimes be permitted by the FTC. Regarded as product "puffery," claims that a brand of whole wheat bread is

Federal Trade Commission

the "best" or that a vacation on a tropical isle is a trip to "heaven" are regularly permitted.

Food and Drug Administration

The Food and Drug Administration (FDA) regulates labeling, packaging, and sale of food, drugs, and cosmetics. The regulations govern both product safety and product advertising. Many product recalls and the prohibition of some drug products in the United States result from failure to meet FDA safety regulations or guidelines. The FDA is responsible for the nutritional labeling on many food products.

Federal Communication Commission

The Federal Communication Commission (FCC) regulates broadcasting. However, beginning with the Reagan presidency, the FCC has engaged much less in regulating media *content*. This means, among other things, that public service announcements are not as closely scrutinized as they once were in determining if a broadcast station met the requirement that it be operating in the public interest. Most stations have continued to use PSAs anyway because of the community relations benefits the stations receive.

In 1987 the FCC decided to cease enforcing the *Fairness Doctrine,* which had especially affected political public relations. However, Section 315 of the Communications Act is still enforced. It specifically concerns fairness in political broadcasting and spells out precise regulations addressing that content. A public relations practitioner for a political candidate should be well acquainted with Section 315—especially Section a, which says:

> If any licensee shall permit any person who is a legally qualified candidate for any public office to use a broadcasting station, he shall afford equal opportunities to all other such candidates for that office in the use of such broadcasting station, provided that such licensee shall have no power of censorship over the material broadcast under the provisions of this section. No obligation is hereby imposed upon any licensee to allow the use of its station by any such candidate.[24]

While Section 315 doesn't require stations to provide broadcast time, Section 312(a7) does. It requires stations to sell "reasonable amounts of time" to legally qualified candidates for federal office. What is important to remember in these sections of the FCC regulation is that the stations aren't held accountable for content but that the candidates, their organizations, and their public relations people are accountable.

Legal Considerations Surrounding the Internet

The Internet has quickly entered the legal realm of our information society. Cyberspace is charting new territory in libel, copyright, and obscenity. Especially of interest to the public relations practitioner are the first two issues—libel and copyright infringement.[25]

Copyright and the Net

Public relations practitioners are using the Internet and on-line services to deliver breaking news, feature stories, photos, information about their agencies or organizations, and many other materials. Accessibility of research resources and multiple dissemination opportunities increase the likelihood of piracy on the Net.

The Internet is becoming an important communication vehicle for the public relations professional.

But all information in cyberspace is copyright protected, even without the optional copyright notice, and public relations persons should not use material without permission.[26]

Business Week calls copyright violation on the Internet "highway robbery," claiming that infringement goes far beyond the copy machine violations. A digital copyright code was being designed in 1995 to put a "cipher," or a code, identifying the owner in each copyrighted work on the Internet.[27]

Libel and the Net

Though a debate is raging in the courts and elsewhere about who is responsible for libel on the Internet, public relations practitioners would be held accountable for libel should they use the Net because the practitioner controls the messages sent to the public. Common carriers such as telephone companies, however, are not responsible because they don't control the statements. A New York court decided in 1995 that an Internet provider could be held responsible if it edited electronic messages posted by subscribers. The Long Island securities investment firm Stratton Oakmont Inc. sued Prodigy for $200 million because an anonymous user of Prodigy's "Money Talk" bulletin board falsely portrayed the company as criminals involved in fraud.[28] The court said that since Prodigy marketed itself as a family-oriented on-line service that screened new messages on its bulletin board, it was more like a publisher than like a common carrier.

Another 1995 case has added a new dimension to the debate. A Caribbean resort owner is trying to get America Online to divulge the name of a subscriber, identified on line only as Jenny TRR, so it can sue the subscriber. In June of 1995, the user put on the bulletin board a message suggesting that the "only white instructor" at a particular resort in the Caribbean was stoned when he gave her scuba diving lessons.[29] How the Cook County Court (and possible appeals courts) will rule on the request to reveal the name may have serious ramifications for libel as well as for privacy and freedom of speech on the Internet.[30]

Summary

This chapter does not constitute a complete discussion of the laws affecting public relations practice. It merely touches on some of the important legal areas with which professionals should be familiar. It outlines most of the legal protections for and the limitations on public communications. If public relations practitioners have a general knowledge of law as it affects their profession, take reasonable care to fulfill obligations and avoid legal transgressions, follow organizational procedures in handling sensitive information, and consult appropriate legal counsel when any question or doubt emerges, they can avoid most legal troubles.

The Internet has emerged as a legal problem area for users. Of particular concern to public relations personnel are issues of copyright and libel on the Internet. The legislative bodies and courts are trying to keep up with technology in developing legal models to regulate the Internet.

An Employee's Rights

By Mary B. Cawley
Kennesaw State College
Marietta, Georgia

Case Study

Officers of Pinetree Lumber Company,* a large corporation supplying the construction industry with wood products, noticed that its overall production figures were steadily slipping. After analyzing internal personnel figures, the officers determined that the majority of the slippage seemed to be occurring at its isolated raw materials production plant near Mt. Perkins. Among the plant's 50 workers, absenteeism and turnover were high, and supervisors reported an increased number of disciplinary problems. Several workers had been discharged for drinking on the job, and supervisors noted a large number of workers whose productivity was affected by their consumption of alcohol when off the job. Worker morale was extremely low.

Pinetree sent personnel director Jim Haskins and employee communications specialist Bob Burruss to the Mt. Perkins site to survey the problems and report back to corporate management. Haskins and Burruss spent two weeks observing the workers on site and conducted extensive interviews with both employees and management. The two skilled communicators successfully encouraged the interviewed workers to speak openly and honestly by assuring them of confidentiality. Their interviews yielded a great deal of personal information about many of the employees.

Haskins and Burruss's report to corporate management concluded that several factors were contributing to low productivity: boredom, alcohol, and the workers' sense of isolation. Haskins and Burruss felt that a large part of the problem lay in the living conditions at the plant. Workers were housed in large barracks, which were noisy and provided little or no privacy. The nearest town was 50 miles away, over often impassable, unpaved mountain roads. The closest outside contact was a small hunting supply store that also sold liquor and beer. There, the workers could sit and drink and visit with a few hunters who frequented the area.

The company quickly acted to improve worker facilities. While the remoteness of the site precluded the presence of families, Pinetree built more private, comfortable living quarters and some recreational facilities for the workers. An on-site clubhouse was equipped with cable TV, a small library, and a supply of fishing and hunting gear that the workers could use free of charge. At Burruss's suggestion, Pinetree's employee newspaper focused more attention on the workers at the Mt. Perkins site, praising both collective and individual accomplishments and introducing them to other Pinetree employees through articles on individual workers' interests and activities. Furthermore, the company initiated a monthly 21-day work schedule, with 10 days paid leave, allowing workers extended visits with their families.

The effect was immediate and dramatic. Productivity increased sharply, and absenteeism and turnover figures dropped. A residual problem remained, however. While the majority of the workers had decreased their alcohol intake, an unacceptable percentage continued to drink excessively. Pinetree was concerned for these workers and determined to institute an alcohol rehabilitation program for the problem drinkers.

Although Burruss and Haskins communicated the available program through a variety of channels, there were no takers at Mt. Perkins. Burruss decided that a true story on the ravages of alcohol might provide the needed incentive. After consulting with Haskins and reviewing their interview notes, Burruss chose to tell the story of one Mt. Perkins worker. Mack Frame, the youngest of three treetoppers at the facility, had revealed during his interview with Haskins that he had been a heavy drinker during his teenage years; in fact, he had been convicted of DUI and manslaughter and kicked out of his parents' house at age 18. He married at 19, had a son, and was divorced by age 20. He couldn't keep a job, he said, because of his constant drinking, and his wife grew fearful of his drunkenness around their small child. He confided to Haskins that he had never discussed his past with his co-workers because he was ashamed of his youthful behavior. Now nearly 30 years old, he had not had a drink since attending an alcohol treatment program after his divorce. He looked at his job at Mt. Perkins as a part of a new, sober life. His ex-wife had finally become convinced that he was no longer drinking and for the last several years had allowed him to spend his vacation time with his son. The prevalence of alcohol use among his co-workers provided a continuing test of the strength of his convictions, the young man told Haskins. In checking Frame's personnel file, Haskins found that the manslaughter conviction was noted there and that he had been an exemplary employee during his tenure with Pinetree.

Burruss contacted Frame's supervisor, who sought written permission to do a profile on the employee for the company paper. Frame, having seen the interesting employee profiles already published, readily granted permission. The finished news article was a straightforward retelling of Frame's story. While the article told of his bout with alcohol and the manslaughter conviction, it placed particular emphasis on his subsequent recovery and exemplary life. The publication of Frame's story had the desired effect: Nearly 50 percent of the problem drinkers at Mt. Perkins entered the alcohol rehabilitation program. Within one month of the story's appearance in the company newspaper, Mack Frame sued Pinetree Lumber Company, Jim Haskins, and Bob Burruss.

Questions

1. Under what law did Mack Frame most probably bring suit against Pinetree? What do you think were the elements of his suit? On the basis of information in the chapter, do you think he had cause for suit?

2. What actions could Bob Burruss and Jim Haskins have taken to avoid legal problems with Frame? How might Pinetree defend itself?

3. Do you think Burruss and Haskins could (or should) be liable as individuals?

*This is a fictional case. Neither the company nor any individual mentioned is real.

Notes

1. Kathy R. Fitzpatrick, "Public Relations and the Law: A Survey of Practitioners," unpublished paper presented at the Public Relations Society of America annual convention, Seattle, Wash., 31 October 1995, p. 1.

2. Ibid., 3–4.

3. *The New York Times* (10 January 1986): D3.

4. *The Wall Street Journal* (14 April 1986): 39.

5. *The Wall Street Journal* (4 October 1985): 23.

6. Fitzpatrick, "Public Relations and the Law," 7.

7. Ivy Lee, *Publicity: Some of the Things It Is and Is Not* (New York: Industrial Publishing, 1925), 58.

8. David Finn, "Media as Monitor of Corporate Behavior," in *Business and the Media,* Craig E. Aronoff, ed. (Santa Monica: Goodyear Publishing Co., 1979), 120–121.

9. Ibid., 122.

10. 425 U.S. 748, 771–72, N. 24 (1976).

11. Taft-Hartley Act, Section 8(c).

12. Don R. Pember, *Mass Media Law* (Dubuque, Iowa: Wm. C. Brown Publishers, 1977), 99.

13. *The Wall Street Journal* (9 November 1984): 33.

14. Pember, 171.

15. *The Wall Street Journal* (21 February 1986): 9.

16. *The Wall Street Journal* (13 March 1984): 33.

17. *The Wall Street Journal* (15 August 1984): 14.

18. Survey conducted in the case of *The Nestlé Company, Inc. v. Chester's Market, Inc., 219 U.S. Patent Quarterly,* 298 (Dist. C., D. Connecticut, 1983).

19. Ibid.

20. *The Wall Street Journal* (4 March 1985): 20.

21. J. Edward Conrey, Gerald R. Ferrer, and Karla H. Fox, *The Legal Environment of Business* (Dubuque, Iowa: Wm. C. Brown Publishers, 1986), 197.

22. *The Wall Street Journal* (29 August 1984): 37.

23. *The Wall Street Journal* (22 January 1985): 4.

24. Section 315a, Federal Communications Act.

25. Laurie Lattimore, "Legal Considerations," chapter 15 in Fred Shook, Dan Lattimore, and Jim Redmond, *The Broadcast News Process* (Denver: Morton Publishing Co., 1996).

26. R. Penchina, "Venturing On-Line: Protecting You and Your Product in Cyberspace," *Editor and Publisher* (24 June 1995): 122.

27. "Halting Highway Robbery on the Internet," *Business Week* (17 October 1994): 212.

28. P. H. Lewis, "Judge Allows Libel Lawsuit Against Prodigy to Proceed," *The New York Times* (26 May 1995): D4.

29. *Tuscaloosa News,* June 1995.

30. Laurie Lattimore, in "Legal Considerations."

CHAPTER 20

Public Relations as a Career

Preview

The demand for public relations practitioners is growing, primarily because of the need for all types of organizations to maintain effective relationships with their constituents. Public relations practitioners are gaining more influence in policy-level decisions made by their organizations and are more likely to be part of management teams.

Women represent a significant portion of the total number of public relations professionals in practice today. More practitioners are employed in corporate public relations than in any other type.

Today, of course, I would take courses in journalism and public relations, but I'd emphasize the liberal arts, particularly economics, philosophy and cultural history.

—David Ferguson, former PRSA President

T he term *public relations* covers a variety of occupations, as we discussed in chapter 1. Because of the variety of titles, government agencies have difficulty determining how many people are in the occupation. Moreover, budget cuts in most government agencies, with the resulting reduction in numbers of reports, compound the difficulty of obtaining accurate data on occupational employment. The *Handbook of Labor Statistics'* latest figures place the number of public relations practitioners in the United States at 151,000. The Office of Employment within the Labor Department projects public relations as one of the most rapidly growing industries through 2005, predicting a 69-percent total increase in jobs during the next decade. It estimates that public relations employees currently number 655,000, including staff and clerical as well as professional positions. This number is expected to rise to 1.1 million by 2005.[1]

Competition for entry-level positions will remain keen, but the rewards for those prepared to meet the challenges of a rapidly changing environment will be great. As *USA Today* points out, the practice of public relations has changed greatly to keep in step with business and society: If PR was once the haven for burned-out news reporters looking to make a better buck for coloring the truth, it is no longer. The field has evolved, says Joseph Awad, former president of the Public Relations Society of America, into "a whole management discipline, if you will, that is concerned with all the relationships of an organization and society."[2]

The Expanding Scope of Public Relations Practice

As management becomes increasingly aware of the importance of effective public relations, public relations staffs grow both in number and in influence. All but 58 of the *Fortune* 500 companies have public relations departments.[3] The 1995 International Association of Business Communicators (IABC) member profile noted that respondents were most likely to hold the title "manager" or "director."[4]

As practitioners gain middle- and upper-management status, they are being called on to solve a greater range of consumer and corporate environmental problems. A quick publicity fix will not suffice. Some CEOs spend half their time trying to manage or avert crises, so they are demanding more help from their public relations practitioners in responding to shareholder, staff, public, and media pressure for information.[5] Practitioners were on the crisis management teams in the case of Coca-Cola's switch and reversal on its sugared soft drinks and in Pepsi-Cola's classic plan to save Pepsi's market share after tampering incidents.

The involvement of public relations staffs was critical in the name and image change of International Harvester (now Navistar), in the successful introduction of Apple's MacIntosh computer, and in Union Carbide's recovery from the Bhopal, India, disaster. Practitioners must keep pace with governmental regulations and political trends as Congress and the courts are calling on companies to be more accountable to the public.

New directions for public relations careers have also been opening up outside corporate settings. The IABC's *Profile/95* member survey showed a slight decrease in the percentage of members on corporate payrolls—from 46 percent in 1989 to slightly more than 44 percent in 1995. Although public relations has long been part of the operations of not-for-profit entities like hospitals and universities, public relations practitioners now work for consumer groups, labor unions, government agencies, television stations, and numerous other types of organizations, all of which recognize the need to approach their dealings with the public in an organized and coherent fashion.

Public Relations Practitioner Profiles

Several recent surveys have detailed who practices public relations and how, although the averages included in their results may mask the profession's variety and complexity. Among the 4,679 respondents to the 1995 IABC Profile, 66 percent of the public relations specialists were college graduates, 26 percent had master's degrees, and 1 percent held doctorates.

The traditional profile of the public relations practitioner as a white, middle-aged male has been relegated to the outdated stereotype heap as women now appear to hold the majority of public relations jobs. The 1995 IABC survey reported that nearly 71 percent of the association's members were women. The typical public relations communicator was female, age 37, and a college graduate earning $49,300 as a manager or assistant manager in a corporate communication department.[6] PRSA has more men than does IABC, but the majority of its members likewise are female (58%).

Salary Trends

That same 1995 IABC survey showed the average income for respondents to be $49,300, compared with $40,300 in 1989. The *Public Relations Journal*'s 1993 salary survey reported a median salary of $46,204, with an average of $58,477 for men and $39,542 for women.[7] That survey found entry-level salaries to be $21,310. Top median salaries, at $66,707, in the *Public Relations Journal* survey went to those working in investor relations. See tables 20.1 and 20.2 for the salary distributions by area of public relations.

A public relations consultant conducts a brainstorming session designed to provide alternative solutions for a problem.

TABLE 20.1   Public Relations Journal Salary Survey

Industry	Median Salary	Percent Men	Percent Women
Industrial/manufacturing	$62,303	57	43
PR counseling firms	53,728	50	50
Utilities	52,672	49	51
Financial/insurance	49,602	43	57
Media/communications	49,473	42	58
Miscellaneous services	47,915	37	63
Scientific/technical	44,351	38	62
Government	44,019	51	49
Association/foundation	43,388	46	54
Solo practitioner	43,101	42	58
Transportation/entertainment/ hotels/resorts	41,843	31	69
Health care	41,550	30	70
Advertising	41,066	36	64
Education	41,008	42	58
Miscellaneous professional services	40,235	30	70
Retail	39,780	21	79
Religious/charitable	35,545	34	66
Miscellaneous nonprofits	32,910	10	90
Miscellaneous marketing	32,877	36	64
Other	41,618	38	62
All respondents	$46,204	43%	57%

Source: *Eighth Annual Salary Survey: Salary Growth Stalls But Women Gain* (New York: Public Relations Society of America, July 1993).

TABLE 20.2   IABC Salary Survey

Industry	Percent of Respondents	Median Income
Communication	25	$45,000
Corporate relations	22	49,120
Marketing/advertising	17	41,000
Public relations	14	41,000
Internal communication	10	47,500
Public affairs	8	50,000
Human resources	5	50,000
Community relations	4	40,000
Public information	4	42,000
Administration	3	45,000
Video/AV	2	50,000
Other	6	45,000
Refused to respond	2	42,500

Source: *Profile: A Survey of IABC Communicators' Salaries and Responsibilities* (San Francisco: IABC and IABC Research Foundation, 1995).

Preparing for a Public Relations Career

In 1994 there were 2,887 graduates with bachelor's degrees, with a total of 10,236 public relations majors enrolled in 431 journalism and mass communications programs in U.S. universities. These figures represent a slight decrease in both majors and degrees from 1992 and 1993; however, graduate enrollments have increased.[8]

Future Educational Requirements

The scope of public relations education may need to be broadened. As the profession's responsibilities increase, so will the requirements for job entry. Some organizations want their practitioners to have courses in business, finance, or specific technologies in addition to public relations. Some now prefer the master's degree. Bill Cantor, president of Cantor Concern, an executive search firm, says public relations practitioners will have to understand business, finance, economic principles, and the marketplace. "Above all, they will be required to understand more thoroughly their employer's or client's business and industry if they are to demonstrate to top management the effectiveness of their roles."[9] Pat Jackson, head of a New Hampshire public relations counseling firm, says, "It is clear to me after 46 years of practice that the only result that matters—indeed, the only outcome that can rightly be called a result—is to have motivated, reinforced or modified behavior. Nothing else counts."[10] Thus, he says, future practitioners need to add courses in behavioral science to their public relations studies. Technological expertise will also be important, Cantor notes: Professionals will need an understanding of the newer media like cable television, teleconferencing, videotape, and satellite conferencing as well as a good working familiarity with computers. In public relations spotlight 20.1, four professionals tell what they look for when they hire college graduates.

College Preparation

Public Relations Spotlight 20.1

Jane Bahls asked 10 prominent public relations professionals what they looked for when hiring graduates. The following are excerpts from four of the interviews:

1. *James E. Alderman Jr., Vice-President, Public Affairs, Energen, Birmingham, Alabama*

   "I prefer someone with a journalism degree because of the writing skills they develop. Too many public relations majors don't develop writing skills well enough, and that's a serious shortcoming. Too many people come out of school saying 'I just love working with people.' I tell them we don't work much with people; we do a lot of writing. So while I will not hire someone without a degree, neither would I hire someone out of college who hasn't worked for a college newspaper or public relations department. If you managed a baseball team, would you hire someone who had studied sports but never played?"

2. *Michael J. Rourke, Vice-President, Communication and Corporate Affairs, Great Atlantic & Pacific Tea Co., Montvale, New Jersey*

   "The only preference I would give is if the applicant had a public relations or journalism major it would be a really strong indication of a desire to work in the field. That would help in the initial interview. But I'd mainly look for writing skills, communication skills and, if they were going to work with the public, personality."

3. *Helen Frank Bensimon, APR, Director, Public Relations, American Society for Training and Development, Alexandria, Virginia*

"I would look for a liberal arts degree with strong evidence of writing ability. One of the things that's important in public relations is to be a well-educated person who knows how to think, how to inquire and how to analyze a complex subject. The technical things you can learn on the job or in night school once you have the entry-level job, but knowing how to learn is something you either get or you don't."

4. *John L. Gregory, Executive Director, Corporate Communications, Bellcore, Livingston, New Jersey*

"I would hope for someone with a degree in journalism or public relations, but what I'd really look for is a demonstrated writing ability such as working for the school paper or an internship. I think writing is terribly important in any public relations job. If they don't have the writing ability, it really limits their ability to move around in the company. Also, quite often there's a PRSSA chapter on campus where people can get some hands-on experience while they're in school."

Source: Jane Easter Bahls, "What Credentials Do You Seek When You Hire?" *Public Relations Journal* (September 1992): 22.

Written and oral communication skills, judgment, and an understanding of media functions still top the list of what public relations firm CEOs look for in new hires.[11] As Jackson observes, however, public relations seems to be moving beyond a total emphasis on journalism toward more preparation in management, sociology, and psychology, particularly as more public relations specialists join management ranks.

Recent graduates are more confident of their general business skills than were their earlier counterparts, but budgeting and computers confound them, according to a survey of former members of the Public Relations Student Society of America.[12] Despite the need for a broader range of skills, any expansion of public relations curricula must not shortchange the writing and media skills that have long been the hallmark of professionals.

The most important qualifications for a public relations career can be summed up as good judgment, creativity, good writing skills, articulateness, good organization, sensitivity to people, self-confidence, an understanding of human psychology, the enthusiasm necessary to motivate people, a highly developed sense of competitiveness, and the ability to function as part of a team.[13]

Professional Organizations

Important to any profession are the organizations that promote professional standards for its practitioners. Public relations professional organizations include the following:

Agricultural Relations Council

American Society for Hospital Public Relations Directors

Bank Marketing Association

Council for the Advancement and Support of Education (CASE)

Chemical Public Relations Association

International Association of Business Communicators (IABC)

Library Public Relations Council

National Association of Government Communicators (NAGC)

National School Public Relations Association

Public Relations Society of America (PRSA)

Railroad Public Relations Association

Religious Public Relations Council

The largest of these are the Public Relations Society of America, with more than 17,000 members, and the International Association of Business Communicators, with slightly more than 12,000 members. PRSA was founded in 1947 through the merger of the National Association of Public Relations Council and the American Council on Public Relations. In 1961, the American Public Relations Association also joined PRSA to make it one of the dominant professional organizations in the field. Most professional organizations offer their members career development training and job placement services.

Finding a Job in Public Relations

As we have already discussed, public relations practitioners are employed in a variety of organizations. Despite corporate downsizing, corporations still appear to offer the most entry-level opportunities. Cantor and another executive search consultant, Larry Marshall, note the continuing trend toward involvement of public relations specialists in upper management,[14] and *Fortune* 500 public relations executives say their CEOs are giving them more support.

An internship with an organization is becoming almost a necessity for the professional experience needed to get an entry-level job. In fact, it may be the best way of getting into a public relations agency right out of college. "Indeed, in the current buyer's market for public relations personnel, an internship may be the best stepping-stone to a permanent slot in a counseling firm,"[15] according to an article on counseling firms using internships to test entry-level job seekers. Competition is still keen for entry-level public relations jobs, and finding the one that is right for you will take some doing. While the best job sources appear to be undergraduate internships, several additional strategies can help you get not only your first job in public relations but subsequent ones as well.

Job-Hunting Strategy

Job hunting should be organized and carefully executed. If you are in a panic to apply for any available opening, you may get some kind of job. But to land the right job, you should begin by doing careful research. These are the areas you need to consider:[16]

1. Your skills and knowledge.
2. Your selected geographical area.
3. Your prospective employers.

Know Yourself   Getting a job is essentially a process of selling yourself, so get to know the product. Make a list of your qualifications. Remember that all prospective employers will be asking themselves the same question: What does this person have that my organization needs?

Gather together your documents: transcripts, awards, current and former job descriptions, old résumés, and anything else that may apply. With this information in hand, you are ready to start your self-analysis.

A helpful exercise is to write down brief descriptions of all your strengths and weaknesses. No item is too old, small, or insignificant to be included. Write everything down, and then begin to eliminate trivial items.

Next, reflect on your experiences at school, at work, or in other organizations. Look at each experience singly, recalling your accomplishments, achievements, or contributions; your specific responsibilities; and the skills or knowledge you gained that will apply to other situations. Be sure also to ask yourself what you disliked. Your list of negative factors can help identify the types of jobs you would not enjoy regardless of salary.

After you have made your two lists, examine your strengths in more detail. Look for common themes or threads. Frequently, skills and knowledge can be classified into four categories: people, ideas, data, and things. Sort out all your experiences that relate to these four and any other categories you feel are important. Once your strengths are distributed under various headings, go through each list and weigh each strength according to its importance. Some skills are more highly developed than others; some knowledge is more complete. This method will give you two bases for comparison among your categories: quantity (number of items per list) and quality (significance of items).

A final step in deciding which strengths may be attractive to a potential employer is to review your list of weaknesses. Compare your unrewarding or negative experiences to your categories of strengths. Don't be surprised if you find some similarities. We often develop skills and knowledge in areas that we do not particularly enjoy. Experience teaches whether you will enjoy a particular activity.

Select the Proper Target   Again, the key to choosing the right employer is to research the region in which you would like to work, the kinds of organizations that need your skills and knowledge, and the prospective organizations themselves. This is one of the most important and frequently skipped phases of the job search process. If you have contacts who may know of job openings, don't hesitate to ask them for help or for information about employers or areas they are familiar with. Research using library sources, computer data bases, and personal contacts (including professors involved with your communications association) is the best way to screen for and choose your new public relations career, geographical area, and employer.

Researching distant geographical areas can present an extra challenge. Chambers of commerce may have lists of area organizations that employ people in the job categories you have identified, as well as other information about climate and economic conditions. Your local library will have several sources, including the *Editor and Publisher International Year Book* on newspapers and other publications. In addition to other information, this yearbook provides profiles of major U.S. communities. If the town you are considering has a library, you can also write directly there for information.

Next, try to learn about specific organizations in the communities that interest you. You should answer the following questions: Which organizations are most likely to need my skills and knowledge? What problems do they face that my particular abilities could help solve? Who has the power to hire in my job classification at each of these organizations? Again, your local library and computer data bases are good starting points. These are some helpful sources:

O'Dwyer's Directory of Public Relations Firms, J. R. O'Dwyer Co., Inc., New York

PR Blue Book (4th ed.), PR Publishing Co., Meriden, New Hampshire

Dun & Bradstreet Million Dollar Directory

Dun & Bradstreet Middle Market Directory

Standard and Poor's Register of Corporations, Directors, and Executives

Thomas' Register of American Manufacturers

Fortune's "Directory of Largest Corporations"

Fortune's "Annual Directory Issue"

Black Enterprise's "The Top 100"

College Placement Annual

Membership directories of professional and trade organizations

Annual reports and other publications of organizations

NEXIS business publications

Internet resources (see figure 20.1; resources added every day, but a sample):
Online Job Services: http://rescomp.stanford.edu
The Monster Board: http://www.monster.com
Career Mosaic: http://www.careermosaic.com
Online Career Center: http://www.iquest.net/occ

Naturally, you can write or call the organizations and request information. Thorough research beforehand will ensure that you ask the right questions.

You should now be able to compile a list of jobs that use your skills and knowledge, geographical areas in which those jobs can be found and in which you would like to live, prospective employers who meet your criteria, and individuals within those organizations who have the authority to hire you.

Keep Records   You may want to establish a file for each prospective employer to keep track of the jobs you are applying for and the progress you are making toward each. Every piece of correspondence should be filed with basic information about the company and about those who make employment decisions.

Career opportunities are available on the Internet for interested job seekers.

Check out new career opportunities and information here at First USA within our OVERVIEW, NEWS FORUM, and EMPLOYEE OPPORTUNITIES.

Make Contacts   It is important to get acquainted with people who know where the jobs are. It helps considerably if you belong to a student professional organization like PRSSA or an IABC student chapter. Contacts you make with professionals in the local chapter and nationally are important. You should find out if there is a job placement officer in the professional chapter. PRSA has a list of chapter placement coordinators, which you can obtain from the association's national headquarters. Find out who professionals think has the best grasp on job possibilities in the city where you want to work. Ask to speak to that person simply to talk generally about jobs in the area. The national PRSA office contracts with a firm to publicize job opportunities nationally through a newsletter entitled *Career Opportunities.* Other professional associations often have similar placement possibilities.

The placement coordinator in your college, university, or department should be able to help you at least in preparing material, if not in locating potential employers and setting up interviews. Often student public relations groups or classes in public relations call on groups of local professionals to speak about career possibilities and job-hunting approaches. PRSSA, for instance, will sometimes schedule workshops with professionals to give practice in interviewing. Sometimes practice interviews are videotaped so candidates can analyze their strengths and weaknesses. If your local public relations student groups are not offering these activities, initiate them yourself.

Prepare a Résumé and a Letter of Application   Once the target organizations and provisions are identified, write a résumé and a letter of application to accompany each. This step is an initial screening to identify organizations that may have an interest in you. Early elimination of organizations that are not interested will save time, money, and frustration. We will discuss techniques for writing letters and résumés later. For now, keep in mind that they must be personalized and directed toward specific jobs. Record the dates when you send each application letter and résumé, and keep copies of them. You may wish to send follow-up letters.

Tips for the Initial Interview   In response to your letter and résumé, you may receive an invitation to be interviewed by someone in the target organization. Reply immediately by telephone to the person who issued the invitation. When setting the date for this initial interview, leave yourself time to prepare, and try not to appear too eager. Follow your telephone conversation with a letter of confirmation. This two-step approach allows you to (1) make personal contact with the interviewer before the interview and (2) remind the interviewer of your interest just before the interview. After the interview, jot down your impressions and other information you obtained for future reference. Always follow this initial interview with a letter thanking the interviewer for his or her time and consideration. The thank-you letter is a good opportunity to reinforce your expressed interest in the job.

Of course, you may receive a rejection letter instead of an invitation for an interview. If you do, it is usually best to take the organization out of your file and forget it. It is not likely that they will contact you again, even if they have promised to keep your résumé. If you receive no reply, a follow-up letter and another résumé will be in order after sufficient time has passed. Use this opportunity to restate your interest in the organization. A follow-up phone call can be substituted if you have a specific person to contact.

How to Handle Job Offers   Handling job offers is not a problem when you know you have been offered the best position of all those for which you applied. It is frequently impossible, however, to know whether a better offer may result from one of your other inquiries until everyone has had an opportunity to review your qualifications. Therefore, if you receive an early job offer that you feel may not be the best possible opportunity, it is appropriate to request a reasonable delay before accepting. You may do this by letter or telephone or both. If you do ask for more time to take care of unfinished business and consider the offer thoroughly, be certain your request is reasonable. An employer may be able to wait a few days or even a week, but a longer delay would disregard his or her need to fill the position. On the other hand, you must be careful not to accept a job you really do not want just because it is the first one offered.

When you determine which job offer you wish to accept, send a follow-up acceptance letter even if you were notified and have already accepted by telephone. If, after accepting a position, you receive other offers, promptly respond with letters of refusal thanking those making the offers for their consideration. If you have asked for time to consider other offers, respond with similar letters as soon as you have accepted a job and received written confirmation of your employment.

Now that we have outlined the basic job-seeking strategies, we will discuss three key elements in the process: letters of application, résumés, and interviews.

A letter of application is often the first step in the process of getting a job. A good letter will not usually **get** you the job; rather, you hope that it will get you an interview. At the interview, you must present yourself as qualified, energetic, reliable, and enthusiastic. Few companies hire without interviewing. Even so, the application letter is crucial. Many letters of application are **solicited,** most of them being sent in response to advertisements. The United States Congress has passed laws regulating equal employment opportunity. As part of companies' efforts to comply, they use advertisements much more frequently than they formerly did. Although some of these ads run in community newspapers and in magazines of general circulation, most appear in specialized newspapers, magazines, and publications. The latter are good sources to check when you are looking for a job.

Writing a Letter of Application

Feel free also to send **unsolicited** letters of application. Analyze your qualifications carefully, identify companies or institutions you wish to work for, and send the strongest letter you can. It is not uncommon for a graduating college student to send 20 or 25 unsolicited letters. Usually some are answered, and a chance for an interview may develop. Mass mailing of unsolicited letters, however, is expensive and takes a lot of time. It is often better to narrow your sights and write only to companies or institutions in which you have genuine interest. Follow the suggestions given earlier for selecting the right prospective employer.

In preparing a letter of application, follow these general rules:

1. Emphasize your strong points. In one sense, you are writing a sales letter. Do not exaggerate.

2. Remember that each time a company hires somebody, it takes a risk. Think about what the company wants, and take that into account in preparing your letter. If you have done your research properly, this will be easy.

3. Never say critical things about other places you have worked or other people you have worked for. Most potential employers believe that if you were unhappy elsewhere, you will be unhappy with them.

4. Do not talk about what you want in terms of salary and benefits. Normally these subjects come up in the interview.

5. See that your letter is perfectly prepared. A smudgy letter could ruin you. A typographical error or an incorrect spelling will be spotted at once. Use good-quality bond paper. Never send a carbon or photocopy of a letter.

6. Where possible, address your letter to a person, not to "Personnel Manager" or "President."

7. Remember that there is no single correct format for your letter. The letter should reflect your personality and strengths, and it should also address the particular job you are seeking.

8. Don't forget to request an interview at the end of your letter.

Developing a Résumé and Portfolio

Most job applications are in two parts—the letter itself and an attachment or enclosure. The attachment or enclosure is variously called the résumé, vita, data sheet, qualification sheet, or personal profile. Although all five titles are correct, we shall hereafter use the term **résumé.** Both letter and résumé are important; neither should be slighted.

The letter usually should be typed. You often see printed letters of application, but they suggest a mass mailing, which means they will be taken less seriously than individually typed letters.

A résumé is a kind of tabulation of a candidate's qualifications. It is an impersonal document with no room for wasted words. The contents are balanced on the page to look appealing. When a second page is necessary, a carryover heading goes at the top. Most employers prefer one-page résumés, especially for beginning workers.

Most résumés have several parts, although the order in which they come is not fixed (except for the heading), and the form in which the information is placed on the page is flexible. Résumés do not all look alike. The heading, however, always comes first. It gives your name, address, and telephone number (if appropriate). It may give the name of the company you are applying to, but that may be omitted if copies of your résumé are going to many companies. After the heading, put the strongest part of your résumé first: education, experience, personal details, activities and achievements, and (sometimes) references. As a general rule, the personal data section should be brief and not near the top of the résumé. Employers do, however, expect to read something about you as a person that will help them visualize you and give them information to draw on during the interview. Include whatever data you feel will help you the most. Activities and achievements could include participation in youth organizations and religious organizations, for example. Applicants generally name at least three references, or they simply state that references will be furnished on request.

A résumé needs constant updating, even when you are not in the job market, so that it will be ready whenever needed. Résumés are frequently used for more than just job hunting. If you are asked to speak at a meeting, the chairperson may ask for a résumé to use in preparing introductory remarks. Frequently, organizations ask that personal data in one form or another be submitted when a person is being considered for promotion. Perhaps most important, keeping an up-to-date résumé helps you maintain a healthy view of the way your career is progressing.

A **portfolio** should include a résumé at the beginning and then provide an organized sampling of your work (clippings, news releases, scripts, plans, etc.). Your portfolio helps show a potential employer that you have the skill and experience to do the job for which you are interviewing. That's why it is important to begin building your portfolio from the start of your college years, or at least from the time you begin to take public relations courses and do any work that would produce communication materials. Never throw away anything that you produce. You may need it for your portfolio years later. See public relations spotlight 20.2 for tips on portfolio preparation.

Public Relations Spotlight 20.2

- There is no one "right" way to put your portfolio together. Every portfolio is different; yours should reflect your personality.
- Your portfolio is your chance to show and tell potential employers what you are all about. When you present your portfolio, remember that you are in control, and explain how these various public relations materials relate to your overall skills and the position you are applying for.
- The most important aspect of your portfolio is the quality of the material you are displaying. Don't ever include items of your work that you wouldn't want potential employers to read or see just for the sake of having a "full" portfolio.
- Your portfolio should include samples of your best work while also showing your range of capabilities.
- Future public relations practitioners should have news clips, but the portfolio should also include items to reflect diversity in other areas such as design and layout, publicity, planning, and so on.
- Portfolio cases come in many different sizes and styles. The zippered case with handles works well. The portfolio size depends on the type of work you will include in it.
- Always put your résumé on the front page. It is a good introduction, and if you ever have to leave your portfolio behind for review, it serves as a reminder of your credentials.
- Put your best work in the front part of the portfolio case.
- Group related items together, creating an appealing layout to increase their impact.
- Tailor your portfolio for a specific job by removing items or inserting more as needed. For example, if interviewing for a sports information director position, move all sports-related items to the front, and take out some of the nonrelated items.
- You may want to affix labels near each item or group of items explaining your role in the project or the results the project produced. This is especially helpful when you know you will be leaving your portfolio behind and won't have a chance to explain personally.
- Always carry at least four or five extra résumés and references in the side pocket of the portfolio. Often there are other executives at your interview who need copies.
- Make photocopies of your best writing samples, and keep them handy in the side pocket. You'll need them to leave behind with potential employers who may not have time to read them during the interview or who may want to keep them on file with your résumé for future reference.

As we indicated earlier, the job interview is a key part of the hiring process in American industry. Even organizations that do a poor job of interviewing seem to place a great deal of emphasis on the process. When you are invited for an interview, remember that you are an active participant, just as you would be in any other person-to-person encounter. You must be prepared and willing to do your part to make the interview a success.

Communicating in the Job Interview

Planning for the Interview   Once you have been invited to an interview, refer to your files and develop a data sheet that will help you prepare. Your research should have yielded certain information about the organization, such as major products or services, names of and facts about top executives, other locations, gross sales, assets, number of employees, market share, financial position, history, closest competitors, and problems—especially those that need your public relations skills and knowledge. This data sheet should also help you identify the gaps in your knowledge about the organization. Use those gaps to prepare questions to ask during the interview. In addition, be sure you know the interviewer's name and can pronounce it. If you have any doubts, check with the secretary or receptionist before you go into the interviewer's office. (Also, get the secretary's name; it may be useful later.)

While you are preparing for the interview, refer to your original self-analysis inventory, and identify the particular strengths you think would be appropriate for this job. You will want to reflect on your educational and job experiences and single out examples of the skills and knowledge you have to offer. Organize these examples in your mind so that you can describe each and make your points quickly and effectively. Your personal success stories are ammunition to use during the interview to sell yourself.

Try to predict what questions an interviewer may ask you. Gary T. Hunt and William F. Eadie suggest several broad categories of questions that appear fairly consistently in many employment interviews (see public relations spotlight 20.3). Your answers to questions like these can appear more direct and sincere if you think them through before the interview.

Taking an Active Role in the Interview   Take an active role in directing and shaping the interview. Although the interviewer expects to control the interaction and you should not violate this expectation, you do have considerable latitude in responding to his or her questions. Make the most of opportunities to showcase your experience, education, skills, and knowledge. Most skilled interviewers will ask broad, open-ended questions that require more than brief replies. They want to find out what you think is important. Then they will follow up with more specific questions about areas that concern them. Use these questions to mention as many of your unique selling points as possible.

Good interviewers want you to talk more than they do; be sure you have something to say. You must be aware, however, that not all interviewers are good at their jobs. If an interviewer does not encourage you to talk and seems to prefer to do the talking, do not get in the way. You must be prepared to take the role of active listener. Sometimes people are hired as interviewers because they enjoy talking to others and have outgoing personalities, but if they do not understand the function of the employment interview, they may end up giving far more information than they receive.

The best way to handle such interviewers is to let them talk, even encourage them. It is not your place to teach the talkative interviewer his or her job. Even though you have prepared all your selling points in advance, do not try to force them in when they are not wanted. Instead, be attentive, and respond with positive

Public Relations Spotlight 20.3

Categories of Questions in the Job Interview

Topic: Future Orientations

1. What is your life's one-year plan? Five-year plan? Ten-year plan?
2. Where do you want to be in five years? Ten years? Twenty years?
3. What is your ultimate goal in life? Why?
4. What are your future educational goals? Training goals?

Topic: Technical Competence

1. What makes you think that you can do this job?
2. In your work experience, what have you done well? Not so well?
3. How would you hire someone? Fire someone? Discipline someone?
4. What is your greatest professional (or personal) strength? Weakness?

Topic: Personal Qualities

1. What personal assets would you bring to our organization?
2. When are you at your best? Worst?
3. What are your hobbies? Leisure-time activities? Nonjob interests?
4. Why are you a good employment risk for us?

Topic: Potential

1. How would you assess your own managerial potential?
2. In addition to a steady income, what does a position in this organization mean to you?
3. By your own assessment, how far can you go in this field? In life?

Source: "Handling Questions in the Employment Interview" from *Interviewing: A Communication Approach* by Gary T. Hunt and W. T. Eadie, copyright ©1987 by Holt, Rinehart and Winston, Inc. Reprinted by permission of the publisher.

feedback such as, "I see your point" or "Please tell me more." Remember that this person enjoys the sound of his or her own voice and will like you if you seem to enjoy it as well.

During the interview, prepare questions that are based on what you have heard. Questions indicate your interest and perceptiveness. You may want to make brief notes about some details unless it bothers your interviewer. As soon as possible after the interview, write down the facts and impressions you have gained for future reference.

Nonverbal Communication in the Interview Nonverbal cues take on great importance in an interview. Interviewers are usually very sensitive to these signals, so give them some thought. Eye contact is very important for establishing a climate of trust between you and the interviewer. Be sure to look him or her in the eye when you talk. Do not stare, but indicate that you feel comfortable looking directly at the interviewer. Do not let your facial expressions reveal thoughts you may not want known. If you are disappointed (or even if you are thrilled), it may not be to your advantage to show your feeling.

Hands and legs can betray nervousness and anxiety. Control your motions at all times to give an impression of confidence. Avoid habitual or nervous gestures such as foot swinging, toe tapping, and other possibly irritating movements. Dress is important in job interviews. No matter how strongly you feel that you should be hired for your talents rather than your clothes, you must consider the interviewer's initial impression. If you are in doubt, visit the interviewer's office unannounced ahead of time and observe the way people there dress. Personal features should not get in the way of the interviewer's perception of your ability.

Getting your first public relations job is a matter of careful planning and preparation. There are no magical tricks or easy formulas, but if you are willing to follow the suggestions presented here, you will be well on your way to finding the job that is right for you.

Summary

While communication skills and media knowledge are still the backbone of professional public relations practice, the need for new training in business, technology, and the social and behavioral sciences is evident. Perhaps the most important message of this book is that public relations is a complex and changing field. Therefore, those who earn their living through public relations must be able to apply a variety of skills to many new and unique situations. Public relations practitioners cannot be stamped out of a common mold or simply trained to perform routine functions. The field is changing so rapidly that tried-and-true methods may no longer be successful. Instead, each practitioner must approach his or her career equipped with a knowledge of the past and the skill to find new solutions for the present and the future.

Job Hunting

Case Study

Y our spouse has decided to attend medical school at the University of Tennessee, Memphis. You will finish this semester in the public relations program at your university. You have had an internship with a nonprofit organization and worked for the college newspaper as well. As a member of PRSSA, you have made contacts with a number of professionals in your community. You talk with your faculty advisor. She and two of the professionals in the local PRSA chapter suggest that you contact several places in Memphis. They also suggest you contact the job placement person in the Memphis chapter of PRSA. With his help, you learn of openings at three places in Memphis where you might be quite interested in working: The Federal Express media relations department needs a news writer, Baptist Hospital needs someone to work on its internal publications, and ALSAC (the fund-raising arm of St. Jude Children's Research Hospital) needs someone to work with community relations.

Questions

1. Research the three organizations. How many people are employed in each organization? What is each organization's purpose? Who is the person that you should contact about the job?

2. Write a letter of application to one of the three organizations.

3. Prepare your résumé for one of the three jobs.

4. Prepare your portfolio.

Notes

1. Bureau of Labor Statistics, Office of Employment, U.S. Department of Labor (November 1993).

2. Robert Garfield, "What Are the 3 Toughest PR Jobs?" *USA Today* (10 November 1982): 38.

3. J. R. O'Dwyer, *Annual Survey of the Fortune 500,* (New York: 1985).

4. *Profile/95: Special Report* (San Francisco: International Association of Business Communication, 1995).

5. Bill Cantor, "Forecast '85: The Year in Public Relations," *Public Relations Journal* (February 1985): 24.

6. *Profile: A Survey of IABC Communicators' Salaries and Responsibilities.* (San Francisco, CA: IABC and IABC Foundation, 1995), 9.

7. "Eighth Annual Salary Survey," *Public Relations Journal* (July 1993): 12.

8. Lee Becker and Gerald Kosici, "Graduate Degrees Increase 23%, but Bachelor Numbers Decline," *Journalism Educator* (Autumn 1995): 61–76.

9. Cantor, "Forecast '85," 22–25.

10. "Lessons Learned: What Winners Would Study Today," *Public Relations Journal* (October/November 1994): 40.

11. Fred D'Sousa Fenner, "How to Get the Right First Job in Public Relations," *Public Relations Journal* (April 1985): 25.

12. Frederick Teahan, "New Professionals: A Profile," *Public Relations Journal* (March 1984): 26–29.

13. U.S. Department of Labor, *Occupational Outlook Handbook* (1980), 478.

14. Larry Marshall, "The New Breed of PR Executive," *Public Relations Journal* (July 1980): 9–13.

15. Susan L. Bovet, "Firms Use Internships to Test Entry-Level Job Seekers," *Public Relations Journal* (September 1992): 26.

16. Material in this section adapted from Aronoff et al., *Getting Your Message Across* (St. Paul: West Publishing Co., 1981). Reprinted by permission.

GLOSSARY

A

action implementation
Any attempt to spread information within a target audience as part of a public relations plan.

active public
People who are aware of a problem and will organize to do something about it.

annual meeting
A yearly meeting at which a corporation's stockholders have the opportunity to meet and vote on various issues related to company management.

annual report
A yearly report to stockholders prepared by publicly-held corporations, containing required financial performance information and other material designed to promote the organization.

appropriation
Commercial use of an entity's picture, likeness, or name without permission.

ASCII
The American Standard Code for Information Exchange. It is used to transfer data to be used in any word processing program.

audience coverage
Whether and how well intended publics were reached, which messages reached them, and who else heard the messages.

audit
An evaluation and inventory of an organizational system.

aware public
People who know about a problem but don't act on it.

B

boundary spanners
Individuals within organizations assigned responsibility for communicating with other organizations.

B-roll
Extra video footage often sent along with a Video News Release (VNR) for use by TV stations to prepare their own video stories about the topic on the video.

brainstorming
A technique of group discussion used to generate large numbers of creative alternatives or new ideas.

brandstanding
Corporate sponsorship of special events as a way of getting publicity and gaining goodwill.

burnout
The idea that a message loses its punch if consumers hear it too often or too far in advance of an event.

C

censure
An official expression of disapproval broadcast to fellow members of a group and possibly to the public.

civil libel
Damaging, negligently published communication that injures an identified individual.

closed-system evaluation
A pre-/postevent assessment that considers only the controlled message elements.

code of ethics
A formal set of rules governing proper behavior for a particular profession or group.

collective bargaining
A continuing institutional relationship between an employer and a labor organization concerned with the negotiation, administration, interpretation, and enforcement of contracts covering wages, working conditions, and other issues related to employment.

commercial speech
Public communication by business organizations through advertising or public relations to achieve sales or other organizational goals.

communication climate
The degree of trust and openness that exists in the communication processes of an organization.

communication flow
The direction (upward, downward, or horizontal) messages travel through the networks in an organization.

communication load
The total amount of communication received and initiated in a given channel.

communication networks
The patterns of communication flow between individuals in organizations.

communication policies
Final statements of organizational positions related to communication

activities and behaviors and information sharing.

communication rules
Mutually accepted standards of communication behavior that provide the basis for coordinated interpersonal interaction.

community relations
A public relations function consisting of an institution's planned, active, and continuing participation with and within a community to maintain and enhance its environment to the benefit of both the institution and the community.

content analysis
Systematic coding of questionnaire responses or other written messages into categories that can be totaled.

contract
An agreement containing a legal offer, a legally effective acceptance, and an exchange of acts or promises called consideration.

controlled media
Those media that the public relations practitioner has actual control over, such as a company newsletter.

copyright
Legal protection from unauthorized use of intellectual property fixed in any tangible medium of expression.

corporate philanthropy
Recognition of corporate obligations and responsibilities to communities represented by monetary and other contributions to charitable organizations.

counseling firm
A public relations or marketing company hired by another organization to help with campaigns or run an entire public relations function.

criminal libel
Public defamatory communication causing breach of the peace or incitement to riot.

cybernetics
The study of how systems use communication for direction and control.

cyberspace
A term used to refer to the place where on-line conversations and information exchange take place.

D

defamation
Any communication that holds a person up to contempt, hatred, ridicule, or scorn.

Delphi Model
A technique for reaching consensus through mailed questionnaires.

diffusion of information
The way in which information spreads through a public.

E

econometric
Involving statistical measurement of the economy.

economic education
Widespread efforts to overcome economic illiteracy.

economic illiteracy
A lack of understanding on the part of individuals or the general public concerning economic concepts, relationships, and issues.

ecosystem
A system serving as an environment for several smaller systems.

employee benefits
Aspects of employee compensation, often including health and life insurance, vacation and sick leave, pension programs, and other valuable considerations.

environmental monitoring
Formal systems for observing trends and changes in public opinion that are used either once, periodically, or continuously.

ethics
Standards of conduct and morality.

evaluation
An examination of the effectiveness of a public relations effort.

F

fair comment
A defense against libel, the expression of opinion on matters of public interest.

Federal Trade Commission (FTC)
That federal government regulatory body charged with assuring fair dealing in relation to goods and services in terms of such things as truth in advertising.

feedback
Information received in response to actions or messages about those actions or messages.

financial analysts
Investment counselors, fund managers, and others whose function is to gather information about various companies, develop expectations of the

companies' performances, and make judgments about how securities markets will evaluate these factors.

financial budget
A detailed estimate of how much an organization expects to spend in a given period and where the money will come from.

financial press
Media outlets devoted to coverage of business and financial information.

financial public relations
The process of creating and maintaining investor confidence and building positive relationships with the financial community through the dissemination of corporate information.

First Amendment
The initial section of the United States Bill of Rights that guarantees the freedoms of press, speech, assembly, and religion.

flack (or flak)
A derogatory term sometimes applied to public relations practitioners, primarily by reporters and editors.

focus group
A group of people representative of an organization's various publics who are called together, usually only once, to give advance reaction to a plan.

Food and Drug Administration (FDA)
A federal government regulatory agency dealing with the efficacy, labeling, packaging, and sale of food, drugs, and cosmetics.

Form 10-K, Form 10-Q, and Form 8-K
Reports required by the Securities and Exchange Commission from publicly traded companies.

forum
A gathering place on an online service such as CompuServe, Prodigy, or America Online where people "meet" about a topic or theme. Messages are left, other people add to the discussion, and at times people "chat" on line.

Freedom of Information Act (FOIA)
A law passed in 1974 requiring disclosure of certain categories of government information.

ftp
File transfer protocol, the main means by which one retrieves files from the Internet.

G

Gantt chart
A graphic illustration of the time required to accomplish various jobs in a project.

gatekeeper
An individual who is positioned within a communication network so as to control the messages flowing through communication channels.

gopher
A means of finding information on the Internet.

grass-roots lobbying
Organizing local constituencies to influence government decision makers.

H

hierarchy
A proposition underlying systems theory that maintains that systems are organized in a successively more inclusive and complex pattern and that to understand systems of behavior, several appropriate levels should be examined.

home page
A site on the Internet or World Wide Web where one can place data, including words, sound, and graphics, to be retrieved by Internet users.

I

inferential data
Information that not only characterizes a particular group or situation but also allows researchers to draw conclusions about other groups or situations.

interdependence
A proposition underlying systems theory that maintains that elements of systems cannot act unilaterally and that all elements of a system influence one another. Behavior is the product of systems, not individual system elements.

Internet
A vast, interconnected computer network that allows computers anywhere in the world to communicate instantly with computers in another part of the country or the world.

interorganizational communication
Structured communication among organizations linking them with their environments.

interpersonal communication
The exchange of messages between individuals through which needs, perceptions, and values are shared and by which mutual meanings and expectations are developed.

intervening public
People who may make it more difficult for an organization to reach those it is aiming to influence or gain approval from.

intrusion
Surreptitious recording or observing of other people's private documents, possessions, activities, or communications.

invasion of privacy
Four areas in which one entity may violate the privacy of another: appropriation, publication of private information, intrusion, or publication of false information.

investment conferences
Meetings attended by investment professionals especially for the purpose of hearing company presentations.

issue advertising (advocacy advertising)
Advertising designed to communicate an organization's stand on a particular issue and seeking to generate support for that position.

issues management
The process of identifying issues that potentially impact organizations and managing organizational activities related to those issues.

K

key contacts
People who either can influence the publics an organization is trying to reach or have direct power to help the organization.

L

latent public
People who are not aware of an existing problem.

level of analysis
In the systems approach, the magnitude of the system chosen for examination.

liaisons
Individuals who serve as linking pins connecting two or more groups within organizational communication networks. Sometimes referred to as internal boundary spanners.

libel
Published defamation.

licensure
A formal certification process that indicates a person measures up to a set of professional standards and qualifications.

line organization
A method of structuring organizations as a sequence of ascending levels of responsibility for the production of goods or services.

lobbying
The practice of trying to influence governmental decisions, usually done by agents who serve interest groups.

M

malice
A requirement of libel in cases involving public figures, knowledge of the falsity of published material, or a reckless disregard for the truth.

management-by-objectives (MBO)
A process that specifies that supervisors and employees will jointly set goals for employees. Usually followed by a joint evaluation of the employee's progress after a set period of time.

mass opinion
The consensus of the public at large.

model
A way of looking at something.

moderating public
Those people who could make it easier for an organization to get its message through to the public it really wants to reach.

mutual expectations
Shared similar responses to messages and events.

N

National Labor Relations Board (NLRB)
That federal government regulatory body charged with overseeing union activities and union/management relations.

network
Two or more computers linked together.

news conferences
Structured opportunities to release news simultaneously to all media.

news release
A story prepared for the media to share information and generate publicity.

newsroom
An area set aside to provide information, services, and amenities to journalists covering a story.

not-for-profit organization
A group or company whose primary purpose is not to make a profit, regardless of whether it actually does so in a given year.

O

off-the-record
An agreement with an interviewer not to print information provided.

on line
A situation where two or more computers are "talking" to each other.

open-system evaluation
An ongoing assessment of the effectiveness of public relations actions considering the impact of uncontrolled elements.

operating budget
An estimate of the amount and costs of goods and services an organization expects to consume.

opinion leaders
People who are instrumental in influencing other people's attitudes or actions.

organizational climate
The collective subjective perceptions held by an organization's employees concerning organizational policies, structure, leadership, standards, values, and rules.

organizational communication
The exchange and interaction of informal and formal messages within networks of interdependent relationships.

P

perception
The process of making sense of incoming stimuli.

perceptual screens
Filters composed of needs, values, attitudes, expectations, and experiences, through which individuals process messages to derive meaning.

planned publicity
Publicity that is the planned result of a conscious effort to attract attention to an issue, event, or organization.

policy
A type of standing plan that serves as a guide for decision making and usually is set by top management.

political action committee (PAC)
A group of people who raise or spend at least $1,000 in connection with a federal election.

press agent
One who uses information as a manipulative tool, employing whatever means are available to achieve desired public opinion and action.

press kit
A collection of publicity releases packaged to gain media attention.

primary public
The group of people an organization ultimately hopes to influence or gain approval from.

primary research
The gathering of information that is not already available.

privilege
A defense against libel; the allowance of what might otherwise be libelous because of the circumstances under which a statement was produced.

procedure
A type of standing plan that consists of standard instructions for performing common tasks. Procedures carry out an organization's policies.

product liability
The principle that companies are responsible for any damage or disease that might be caused by the use of their products. Companies are being held to increasingly stricter standards, sometimes losing lawsuits even though the harm the product caused, or was linked to, resulted from improper use.

program evaluation and review technique (PERT)
A network representing a plan to accomplish a project showing the sequence, timing, and costs of the various tasks.

propaganda of the deed
Provocative actions designed solely to gain attention for ideas or grievances.

public
A group of individuals tied together by a sense of common characteristics or responses.

public affairs
That aspect of public relations dealing with the political environment of organizations.

public communication
A multistep, multidirectional process in which messages are disseminated to a broad, and sometimes undifferentiated, audience through complex networks of active transmitters.

public information/public affairs officers (PIOs/PAOs)
Public relations practitioners working for the U.S. government or other institutions using those titles.

public opinion
An attitudinal measure of the image a public holds concerning some person, object, or concept.

public relations
A management function that helps define an organization's philosophy and direction by maintaining communication within a firm and with outside forces and by monitoring and helping a firm adapt to significant public opinion.

public relations counselor
One who informs both publics and organizations in the effort to create relationships of mutual benefit and support.

publicity
Publication of news about an organization or person for which time or space was not purchased.

publicity agent
One who serves as a conduit of information from organizations to publics, using the information to promote understanding, sympathy, or patronage for the organization.

Q

qualitative research
A method of delving into audience opinion without relying on formal, rigorous, number-based research methods.

R

readability study
An assessment of the difficulty an audience should have reading and comprehending a passage.

readership survey
A study to determine the characteristics, preferences, and reading habits of an audience.

regulation
A proposition underlying systems theory that maintains that the behavior of systems is constrained and shaped by interaction with other systems.

sanctions
Restrictions imposed on a member of a profession by an official body.

scenario construction
A forecasting tool that explores likely consequences of alternative courses of action in a hypothetical, logical future situation.

secondary research
The gathering of available information.

Securities and Exchange Commission (SEC)
That federal government regulatory body charged with overseeing the trade of stocks and bonds and the operations of financial markets.

single-use plans
Plans developed for use in one specific situation.

slander
Oral defamation.

spontaneous publicity
Publicity accompanying unplanned events.

staff
Organizational personnel employed to provide support and advice to line management.

stakeholder analysis
A method for characterizing publics according to their interest in an issue.

standing plans
Plans for dealing with certain types of situations, particularly common situations and emergencies.

strategic plans
Long-range plans concerning a group's major goals and ways of carrying them out. These plans usually are made by top management.

subsystem
A component of a system.

synergy
A proposition underlying systems theory that maintains that the whole is greater than the sum of its parts.

system
A set of objects or events grouped together by sets of relationships.

Sunshine Act
A law requiring meetings of governmental boards, commissions, and agencies to be open to the public.

tactical plans
Short-range plans for accomplishing the steps that lead up to achievement of an organization's goals. These plans are carried out at every level of an organization and on an everyday basis.

target audience
The primary group an organization is trying to influence.

theory
An explanation or belief about how something works.

trademark
A legally protected name, logo, or design registered to restrict its use.

uncontrolled media
Those media whose actions are not under the public relations practitioner's control, such as community newspapers and radio stations.

universe
A system providing the environment for ecosystems.

V

variable
A concept, object, or event that can be measured or manipulated.

VNR
Video News Release. A video package sent as a news story for use on television news broadcasts.

W

whistle-blowing
Insiders telling the media what they know about improper practices by others, usually in the same company, with the hope of improving the situation.

World Wide Web
Another term for the Internet, or interconnected computer system.

CREDITS

INDEX